Encyclopedia of
the Vatican
and Papacy

Encyclopedia of the Vatican and Papacy

Edited by
FRANK J. COPPA

Greenwood Press
Westport, Connecticut

Library of Congress Cataloging-in-Publication Data

Encyclopedia of the Vatican and papacy / edited by Frank J. Coppa.
    p. cm.
  Includes bibliographical references and index.
  ISBN 0–313–28917–4 (alk. paper)
  1. Popes—Biography—Encyclopedias. 2. Papacy—History—
Encyclopedias. 3. Councils and synods, Ecumenical—Encyclopedias.
I. Coppa, Frank J.
BX955.2.E53 1999
262'.13'09—dc21   98–15328

British Library Cataloguing in Publication Data is available.

Library of Congress Catalog Card Number: 98–15328
ISBN: 0–313–28917–4

First published in 1999

Greenwood Press, 88 Post Road West, Westport, CT 06881
An imprint of Greenwood Publishing Group, Inc.

Printed in the United States of America

The paper used in this book complies with the
Permanent Paper Standard issued by the National
Information Standards Organization (Z39.48–1984).

10 9 8 7 6 5 4 3 2 1

Copyright Acknowledgments

The author and publisher gratefully acknowledge permission to use the following material:

The entries on *La Civiltà Cattolica* and *L'Osservatore Romano* originally appeared in *Dictionary of Modern Italian History,* edited by Frank J. Coppa, © 1985 Greenwood Press. Reprinted by permission of Greenwood Press, an imprint of Greenwood Publishing Group, Inc., Westport, CT.

Contents

Preface

This volume, which is a collaborative effort involving more than forty contributors from the United States and abroad, focuses on the historical, political, diplomatic, social, cultural, and religious role of the Vatican and the papacy in the modern world. The major emphasis is therefore on the Vatican since the time of the Renaissance, as the various entries examine developments within the broader context of European and world history. However, the editor and the contributors concurred that such a work should not, and could not, be restricted to the modern age. For one thing we agreed that there should be coverage of the entire papacy with entries on all the popes from Peter to John Paul II as well as the antipopes and even mythical ''popes'' such as Joan. The reader will find that the length of these papal entries varies and that not all the popes have been extended the same depth of treatment. In determining coverage, the editor and contributors considered a number of factors, including an evaluation of their impact upon the institution and the church, the material available, the period in which they pontificated, and, above all, space constraints.

By and large, other things being equal, we have accorded broader coverage to the more modern popes—especially those who have had to confront the intellectual revolution, the Industrial Revolution, and the age of ideologies. Although the emphasis is on the modern papacy, we found it necessary to include the twenty-one Councils from Nicaea (325) to Vatican II (1962–1965), rather than simply focusing on the three most recent: Trent in the sixteenth century, Vatican I in the nineteenth, and Vatican II in the twentieth. Furthermore, crucial pre-Renaissance conflicts, pronouncements, encyclicals, concordats, and treaties have been added. There are also entries on the structure of the Holy See and the organizational church such as the College of Cardinals, congregations, secretariates, tribunals, nuncios, internuncios, religious orders, the Index, the Inquisition, and so on and their historical development. The reader will find information and entries on the Vatican Archives and mechanisms of Vatican communication, such as *La Civiltà Cattolica* and *L'Osservatore Romano*. There are also entries on the major religious orders such as the Jesuits, Franciscans, and Vincentians.

Substantial consideration is accorded Vatican diplomacy, including the structures through which this influence is exercised as well as the mechanisms through which its aims are achieved from the more formal concordats—we have included a series of these specific accords—to the more informal modus vivendi and understandings. There are entries on Vatican relations with particular powers, including Great Britain, the United States, France, imperial, Weimar, and Nazi Germany, liberal and fascist Italy, the Soviet Union, Spain, Ireland, and Israel. Furthermore, the Vatican's position in World War I, the Ethiopian War, the Spanish civil war, and World War II is likewise included, as well as the Vatican's stance and relationship to the League of Nations and the United Nations. The reader will also find a rather extended treatment of church–state relations, including entries on integralism, Gallicanism, Josephism, placet, and so on.

The attitude and reaction of the Vatican to key historical events are considered in entries on the Reformation, the Renaissance, the Enlightenment, the French Revolution, the Congress of Vienna, imperialism, the Action Français in France, the communist revolution in Russia, liberalism, socialism, communism, fascism, Nazism, and the Holocaust. While the treatment and analysis of Vatican and papal institutions and policies with the broader world are generally historical, certain theological questions and issues are, of necessity, considered. Thus, heresies, condemnations, and the Vatican reaction to ideological movements are all included with entries on Arianism, Jansenism, gnosticism, Febronianism, liberalism, nationalism, Zionism, fascism, Nazism, racism, quietism, Marxism, indifferentism, Modernism, and Americanism, among others. Current issues such as the papal position on capital punishment, social justice, abortion, homosexuality, liberation theology, and birth control are also included.

The miniarticles and shorter entries have been drafted to provide the essential information about the person, place, movement, institution, or event with an explanation of why each is important. Capitalized terms in the text, for example, AMERICANISM, indicate that this subject is treated in a separate entry. Some terms are followed by an explanation in parentheses, so that First World War is followed by (see World War I), indicating that the subject is treated under that heading. Entries vary in length and depth depending on the topic and the consensus of editor and contributor, with each having bibliographical references. Some of the longer articles have many more. Here again, with some very important exceptions, there is broader and greater treatment provided developments in the modern age. We have included an index, a list of contributors, a list of popes, a list of the antipopes, as well as a list of the twenty-one Councils. We trust that our collaborative effort will be useful for those interested in the social, political, cultural, and religious developments affected by the impact of the Catholic Church and the papacy.

A

ABORTION AND PAPACY. The Catholic Church has often found itself in a countercultural position with societies that reject the intrinsic value of human life and therefore has found it necessary to reaffirm that abortion is a grave injustice. The *Didaché*, or Doctrine of the Twelve Apostles c. A.D. 60–90, stated, "You shall not kill the fruit of the womb and you shall not murder the infant already born." Although in the Middle Ages there was discussion of "penal sanctions" to be inflicted for the sin of abortion in the first days of a pregnancy, it was never denied that any procured abortion was objectively a grave sin. The POPES were always careful to separate the church's authentic moral message from the errors of moral theologians caught up in the philosophical and moral climate of their times. The claim that abortion is a private matter because a mother is destroying part of her body and not a new human life does not recognize that conception brings forth a unique being with its own human DNA and RNA. Thus, in electing an abortion, the mother is not destroying a part of her own body but the life of another, which is not a private matter.

The attempts to found human rights on conventional morality and legislated laws have foundered, according to the papal position. This is true for those who tried to root human rights in the conventions based on the ideologies of the nineteenth and twentieth centuries, as well as those who tried to root human rights in conventions flowing from the notions of truth put forth by Nietzsche and Sartre or the moral silence called for by analytical philosophy, phenomenology, and pragmatism. These conclude that since we cannot claim to know any genuine moral truth, we should be silent in such matters, leaving persons through their own will to create their own values and to be the source determining what is good or evil. For some the only limits on human behavior are those that do not conflict with the ever-changing conventions of society. The papacy disagreed, reminding the world at the 1994 Cairo Conference on population that the preceding notion of moral conscience is fundamentally flawed.

JOHN PAUL II warned moral theologians who accepted such a notion of conscience that they placed themselves in opposition to authentic Christian teaching.

The papacy has proclaimed the right to life as the first right, from which all others flow. To put any other right before or above the right to live is to deny all rights. To assure the right to make a choice a higher priority than the right to life of another represents a total inversion of the intelligibility of the moral order and human rights. Good and evil enter into human action in regard to the means one chooses to achieve one's ends.

Thus, the new CANON LAW states that a person who procures a successful abortion incurs an automatic excommunication. To understand this, one must distinguish a procured, direct, elective abortion from indirect abortions, where the principle of double effect applies. A procured abortion is always per se evil. This does not mean that an indirect abortion, where one chooses a good means to obtain a good end, is intrinsically evil. The principle of double effect permits the choosing of a good means to save the mother's life. Let us say that the anesthetic during brain surgery that is necessary to save a mother's life has an unintended, unavoidable consequence of provoking a spontaneous abortion. However, if the evil effect is avoidable by employing some other means, for example, a different anesthetic, then the means that would eliminate the risk to the child should be chosen.

For further reference: Joseph Califano, ''The Self Intersubjectivity and the Common Good,'' in *Freedom, Virtue and the Common Good*, ed. Curtis Hancock (Notre Dame, IN: University of Notre Dame Press, 1994), and *Veritatis Splendor*, 6 August 1993; *Quaestio de abortu*, 18 November 1974, Sacred Congregation for the Doctrine of the Faith.

Joseph J. Califano

ACACIAN SCHISM. SEE LAWRENCE; SYMMACHUS.

ACTA APOSTOLICAE SEDIS. ''Acts of the Apostolic See,'' the *Acta Apostolicae Sedis*, is the official record of the Holy See. It lists ENCYCLICAL letters, important decrees, acts of Roman CONGREGATIONS, TRIBUNALS, and COMMISSIONS, as well as ecclesiastical appointments and deaths. It occasionally registers statements made by the POPE to pilgrims and visitors to Rome. Publication in the *Acta Apostolicae Sedis* establishes the legal standing of a decree, which normally takes effect three months later. The journal was created by PIUS X's constitution, *Promulgandi*, on 29 September 1908. Its first edition, subsequently and largely on a monthly basis, appeared in January 1909. It superseded the *Acta Sanctae Sedis*, which had been founded in 1865 and had achieved official status in 1904.

For further reference: Stanislaus Woywod, *A Practical Commentary on the Code of Canon Law*, 2 vols, rev. Callistus Smith (New York: J. F. Wagner, 1962).

Roy Palmer Domenico

ACTA SANCTAE SEDIS. SEE *ACTA APOSTOLICAE SEDIS.*

ACTION FRANÇAISE AND THE VATICAN. The Action Française emerged in 1899 in opposition to Dreyfus. An agnostic and a positivist, Charles Maurras, the movement's principal leader, reasoned his way to royalism and to the Catholic Church, both of which became functions of his nationalism. Uncomfortable with the rebel "Hebrew Christ," Maurras admired the Catholic Church for its order, authority, discipline, hierarchy, and roots in classical civilization. With a daily newspaper, *L'Action Française*, and a strong-arm group, the Camelots du Roi, both founded in 1908, Maurras waged war against the Third Republic and its individualism, laicism, Freemasonry, parliamentary politics, liberalism, and socialism. He defined the French nation narrowly, attacking Jews, Protestants, and foreigners. Different religious perspectives and competition for influence over French Catholics led the Vatican to condemn the Action Française in 1926. A reconciliation of sorts followed in 1939.

The assault by PIUS X (1903–1914) on "MODERNISM" in the Catholic Church, combined with the POPE's reactions against the post–Dreyfus affair, anticlericalism, and the separation of church and state in France, laid the basis for close cooperation between the Vatican and the Action Française. As Pius X moved away from the RALLIEMENT, his "integrism" within the church and Maurras' "integral nationalism" embodied similar critiques of liberal democracy. The pope appointed sympathizers with the Action Française to leadership positions in Rome and in France. Christian democracy ranked as one of the primary targets of Maurras' wrath. In 1910, Pius X condemned the Sillon, and Marc Sangnier submitted to the pope's authority. Nevertheless, in 1914 the Congregation of the INDEX condemned seven of Maurras' works and the *Revue de l'Action Française*. Pius X accepted the decision but delayed its publication. In 1915, BENEDICT XV (1914–1922), given the exigencies of war, relegated the dossier to the archives.

The years 1914–1925 brought the influence of the Action Française in France to a climax. During the conservative Bloc National or "Blue Horizon" Parliament from 1919 to 1924, which restored French relations with the Vatican, broken in 1904, and during the Cartel des Gauches government of 1924–1925, with its renewed twinge of anticlericalism, the prestige of Maurras' organization remained high among many Catholics, ultimately provoking a conflict with the Vatican. In May 1925, in answer to a question in *Les Cahiers de la Jeunesse Catholique belge* asking which contemporary writers they regarded as their "Maîtres," or masters, Belgian Catholic University students chose Maurras ahead of others. Subsequent criticisms of the royalist leader reached Rome and, dovetailing with wider currents there and within French Catholicism, led to the condemnation of Maurras and the Action Française.

Pope PIUS XI (1922–1939) wished to engage French Catholics in Catholic Action activities under Vatican auspices and church control. As one aspect of this policy, the Vatican would reach agreements and CONCORDATS with states. Popes Benedict XV and Pius XI both rejected "integrism," and the latter sought a second *Ralliement*. During the first half of the 1920s, though, the Action Française's intransigence, its nationalism, its raucous celebrations of Joan of Arc, its antirepublicanism, and its defense of the Catholic Church attracted support among Catholic youth, intellectuals, the HIERARCHY, and other French Catholics. It is perhaps less remarkable that a divorce came in 1926 between the Vatican and an organization that trumpeted *politique d'abord* (politics first) and utilized violence, character assassination, and virulent rhetoric against minorities, than that it occurred during only the third decade of the Action Française's existence. Pius XI broke with the organization to bolster Catholic Action, eliminate the Action Française's influence over the French church, strengthen anticommunist and antisocialist conservative and moderate elements within the Third Republic, and foster international reconciliation between nations. Perhaps the pope also remembered Maurras' opposition to his elevation to the papacy.

In August 1926, under Pius XI's urging, Cardinal Paulin Andrieu, archbishop of Bordeaux, accused the Action Française of disregarding Catholic beliefs and morality. In December 1926, Pius XI put into effect the 1914 condemnation of Maurras' works and added Maurras' daily newspaper. He forbade French Catholics from belonging to the organization, asserting that the Action Française placed political party above religion. The Action Française refused to comply with the pope's interdict, claiming obedience would betray France and alleging German influence on the Vatican. Some French Catholics supported Pius XI, for example, Francisque Gay and his weekly *La Vie Catholique*. Facing resistance from numerous Catholics, the pope commanded obedience and arranged for a change in director of the mass-circulation newspaper *La Croix*. The secretary of state, Cardinal Gasparri, and NUNCIOS to France Msgr. Ceretti (1921–1926) and Msgr. Maglione (1926–1936) played significant roles in Vatican policy toward the Action Française.

After the circulation of *L'Action Française* and the Action Française's links to French Catholics had weakened, changes in France, Europe, and the Vatican contributed to a reconciliation. Although sales of *L'Action Française* rose dramatically at crisis moments in France in 1934 and 1936, the condemnation, its aftermath, and the rise of competitors for the same political clientele reduced the organization's potency. At the same time, similar responses to the Italian invasion of Ethiopia (see Ethiopian War), the SPANISH CIVIL WAR, and the Popular Front government in France brought Maurras and the Vatican closer together. On 5 July 1939, shortly after he became pontiff, PIUS XII permitted Catholics once again to belong to the Action Française and to read its newspaper.

For further reference: Oscar Arnal, *Ambivalent Alliance: The Catholic Church and the L'Action Française 1899–1939* (Pittsburgh: University of Pittsburgh Press, 1985); Harry W. Paul, *The Second Ralliement: The Rapprochement between Church and State in France in the Twentieth Century* (Washington, DC: Catholic University of America Press, 1967); Lucien Thomas, *L'Action Française devant l'église (de Pie X à Pie XII)* (Paris:

Nouvelles Editions Latines, 1965); Eugen Weber, *L'Action Française: Royalism and Reaction in Twentieth-Century France* (Stanford, CA: Stanford University Press, 1962).

Joel Blatt

ADALBERT. SEE ALBERT.

ADEOTATUS I. SEE DEUSDEDIT.

ADEODATUS II (672–676). Although obscurity surrounds the short reign of this POPE, he inaugurated the practice of dating events in terms of his own reign. A native Roman, this son of Jovinianus was an elderly monk at the time of his election to the papacy. He had spent the majority of his life as a Benedictine monk in the community of St. Erasmus on the Coelian Hill. His election received imperial approval within a few weeks. Prompt confirmation did not lessen his opposition to monothelitism, which was favored by the imperial court. Having rejected the synodical letters and the profession sent by Constantine I, patriarch of the Eastern capital, the name of Adeodatus/Deusdedit was ordered struck from the diptychs (the names of loving and departed publicly prayed for at mass) of Constantinople. Little else is known of this pope, except that he had a reputation for generosity. He also took special care to increase the position of his former community of St. Erasmus.

For further reference: J. N. D. Kelly, *The Oxford Dictionary of Popes* (Oxford: Oxford University Press, 1986); *New Catholic Encyclopedia* (1967), vol. 1, p. 128.

Patrick J. McNamara

AD LIMINA **VISITS.** *Ad limina* visits, or "visits to the threshold," consist of periodic trips to Rome, required of all residential bishops and military vicars. The threefold purpose of the *ad limina* visit is to pray at the basilicas of Sts. Peter and Paul, to deliver reports in person to the POPE, and to submit a written survey on the state of the diocese, usually to the Consistorial CONGREGATION or to the *Propaganda fide*. The written document, or *relatio de statu diocesis*, is often referred to as the "quinquennial report" since one should be delivered every five years. European bishops are required to personally undertake the *ad limina* visit every five years, while extra-Europeans, although still obligated to submit the "quinquennial report," must travel to Rome only once every ten years.

The origins of the *ad limina* visits are lost in history but reflect the primacy and the regulation of discipline surrounding the see of St. Peter from very early times. Late in the Roman empire, all Italian, Sicilian, and Sardinian bishops had regularly been summoned to papal councils. The obligation was further extended by the Council of Rome (743) under Pope ZACHARY (741–752), although it remained a vague and debated custom until it was virtually abandoned during the era of the Great Western Schism (see Schism). Pope SIXTUS V (1585–

1590) revived and codified regular consultations, with severe penalties for non-observance, in his constitution, *Romanus Pontifex*, of 1585. After modifications in the eighteenth century by Popes BENEDICT XIII (1724–1730) and BENE-DICT XIV (1740–1758), regulations for the *ad limina* visit were incorporated in the CANON LAW Code under BENEDICT XV (1914–1922) in 1917.

For further reference: James J. Carroll, *The Bishop's Quinquennial Report. A Historical Synopsis and Commentary* (Washington, DC: Catholic University of America Press, 1956); Maria Chiabo, Concetta Ranieri and Luciana Roberti, *Le diocesi suburbicarie nelle "Visitae ad limina" dell'archivio segreto vaticano* (Vatican City: Vatican Archive, 1988).

Roy Palmer Domenico

ADOPTIONISM. SEE ZEPHYRINUS.

ADRIAN I (772–795). During Adrian I's pontificate from 1 February 772 to 25 December 795, the last vestiges of papal submission to Eastern Roman imperial authority were abandoned. At the same time, papal juridical relations with the Carolingian Franks in the West were established, making it possible, five years after Adrian's death in 795, for Charles the Great, king of the Franks, to be crowned Holy Roman Emperor by Adrian's successor, Pope LEO III (795–816). Indeed, after Charlemagne's death in 814, the relations of Adrian I and Leo III with Charlemagne tended to be viewed by many as a single whole. Dante, in his *De monarchia* (c. 1312), tells us that champions of a papal hegemony in his day claimed that when the Lombards were oppressing the church, Pope Adrian implored the help of Charles the Great and that it was from him that Charles received the imperial dignity, on which account all who have become Roman emperors after him have been asked to protect the church.

Though orphaned in childhood, Adrian enjoyed the advantages of membership in Rome's powerful Colonna family. He was a career diplomat in the papal service before being elected POPE upon the death (24 January 772) of Pope STEPHEN III (767–772). His elevation coincided with the emergence of Charlemagne as sole ruler of the Franks after the death of his brother Carloman in 771. The Lombard king Desiderius had at once tried to enlist the support of dissident Franks, as well as the new pope, against Charlemagne. But, breaking with the practice of Stephen III in this regard, Adrian remained "hard as adamant" in resisting the Lombards, even when Desiderius marched against Rome. Adrian called on Charlemagne to intervene, and, by June 774, the Lombard forces in central and northern Italy were crushed. Before the final victory, Charlemagne visited Rome to assist in the Holy Week papal services. He reconfirmed the mutual security treaty that his father and STEPHEN II (752–757) had signed on Easter Sunday, 14 April 754—a date that in papal secular history ranks as the closest analogy to the American 4 July 1776. As heir to Pepin, Adrian I became secular ruler not only of the old Roman dukedom but also of the entire exarchate of Ravenna and some of its possessions in southern Italy.

In 787, Adrian I sided with Charlemagne against the Eastern emperor in upholding the second Council of Nicaea's (see Nicaea II, Council of) condemnation of iconoclasm in the church (though for a time it seemed that he was still prepared to compromise on image worship for the sake of peace with Constantinople). He was adamant, however, in condemning the view that Jesus was divine (as the Son of God) only by adoption. When Adrian I died in 795, the PAPAL STATE had attained a juridical status that qualified it to rank as sovereign in the modern sense. What it lacked, however, was confidence that it could safely maintain itself in the face of the many Germano-ethnic powers still vying for place in Italy. In that respect the break of 781, when the Eastern empire finally closed down its "Italian office" in Ravenna, proved to be very painful. Adrian I knew that Charles the Great could become another Constantine for the West only if, by "Grace of God," he could somehow be raised above all temporalities. How that might be done was left for Charlemagne and Adrian I's successor, Pope Leo III, to work out, but only after a hiatus of imperial authority in Italy that lasted nineteen years, from A.D. 781 to 800.

For further reference: E. Casper, *Das Papstums unter fränkische Herrschafft* (Darmstadt; J. Mohr, 1956), pp. 35–113; E. John, *The Popes* (New York: Hawthorn Books, 1964), pp. 129–132; H. K. Mann, *The Lives of the Popes in the Early Middle Ages* (London: K. Paul, 1902–1932); Paget Toynbee, *Concise Dante Dictionary* (Oxford: Clarendon Press, 1914).

Anne Paolucci

ADRIAN II (867–872). A Roman Cardinal (see Cardinals, College of) of the aristocratic family that produced Popes STEPHEN IV (816–817) and SERGIUS II (844–847), Adrian had twice (855, 858) declined to be a candidate for POPE. Then, at the age of 75, he was elected as a compromise candidate to succeed NICHOLAS I (858–867). Adrian attempted to follow the policies of Nicholas but was hobbled by age and personal tragedy. His actions increasingly belied his pronouncements, which stressed the authority of the pope as the supreme arbiter in Christendom.

In his first papal letter Adrian followed Nicholas I's policy of ordering King Lothair II to take back his wife, Theutberga. This letter argued that the pope is the vicar of St. Peter (see Peter, Pope and Saint), to whom Christ had given the power to loose and to bind. But Adrian may have been preparing to grant an annulment to Lothair just before the king's death (869). In admonishing Charles the Bald, Adrian argued that, as supreme moral arbiter, the pope could call kings to account for all actions involving justice. Then, in 872, as Charles advanced on Rome, Adrian sent him a flattering letter in which he promised to recognize him as the next Holy Roman Emperor.

Adrian approved the Slavonic translation of the Gospels and the liturgy by the brothers St. Cyril (827–869) and St. Methodius (826–885), despite widespread objections to using another language for the liturgy. Adrian also bestowed his approval on the actions of a council (869) held at Constantinople (see Constantinople IV), repudiating Photius, condemning iconoclasm, and affirming the unity of the soul. But the compilations of the acts, one in Latin, the other in Greek, differed. This was ranked by Latins as the Eighth Ecumenical Council, by the Greeks as the Fourth Council of Constantinople. Ignatius, the restored patriarch, then ignored Rome's claim to ecclesiastical jurisdiction in the Balkans. Before this new crisis came to a head, Adrian died sometime between mid-November and 13 December 872. His feast day is celebrated on 14 December, the anniversary of his election.

For further reference: F. Dvornik, *The Photian Schism* (Cambridge: Cambridge University Press, 1948); W. Ullmann, *The Growth of Papal Government in the Middle Ages*, 2d ed. (London: Methuen, 1965).

Frank Grande

ADRIAN III (884–885). Little is known about this brief pontificate. Adrian adopted Carloman, king of France, as his spiritual son: he prevented the bishop of Nimes from annoying the monks at the St. Giles Abbey: he used every means available to avert a famine in Rome; he was sympathetic to the policies of his predecessor, JOHN VIII (872–882); and he adopted a conciliatory attitude toward the East.

The most notable accomplishments of his reign were two decrees issued at the request of the Italian nobility. The first declared that the pontiff-elect could henceforth be consecrated without waiting for the presence of the emperor or his ambassadors. The second stipulated that if Emperor Charles died without a male heir, the kingdom of Italy with the title of emperor would be placed in the hands of the Italian princes, who could select a new emperor. Following this second decree, Adrian was summoned to an imperial diet at Worms in the summer of 885 by Emperor Charles (the Fat) (881–888) to settle the matter of his succession. Charles had no legitimate male heir and wished his bastard son, Bernard, to succeed him. Adrian died en route.

Adrian's sainthood was approved in 1891, though little is known to indicate why he is so venerated. Nevertheless, he receives continual liturgical *cultus* in the diocese of Modena. His feast day is 8 July.

For further reference: Eric John, ed., *The Popes: A Concise Biographical Dictionary* (New York: Hawthorn Books, 1964); Hans Kuhner, *Encyclopedia of the Papacy* (New York: Philosophical Library, 1958); H. K. Mann, *The Lives of the Popes in the Early Middle Ages* (London: K. Paul, 1902–1932).

John C. Horgan

ADRIAN IV (1154–1159). Born early in the twelfth century at Abbott's Langley, Hertfordshire, Nicholas Breakspear became the only English POPE as Adrian IV. In the early 1120s Nicholas left England to join the Augustinian canons of St. Rufus, near Avignon. He became abbot in 1137, and in 1149 Pope EUGENE III (1145–1153) made him cardinal-bishop of Albano. In 1152 Nicholas left Rome on a mission to settle difficulties in Norway and Sweden. In Norway he provided for the autonomy of the Norse church by erecting a metropolitan see at Trondheim. He was less successful in Sweden but laid the groundwork for later developments. Breakspear returned to Rome in the fall of 1154.

Following the death of Pope ANASTASIUS IV (1153–1154) on 4 December 1154, Breakspear was elected pope. He faced daunting challenges: the Byzantine emperor Manuel I was attempting to reassert his authority in southern Italy; the German king Frederick I was determined to assert his rights in northern Italy; the new Sicilian king, William I, was restless under papal vassalage; the city of Rome, under the inspiration of Arnold of Brescia, was in virtual rebellion; and numerous problems beset the church arising from the failure of the Second Crusade and the rise of new dialectical methods of inquiry, exemplified in the conflict between Bernard of Clairvaux and Peter Abelard.

Adrian proved himself equal to the tasks confronting him. The Roman government was brought to heel when Adrian placed the city under interdict for the first time in its history, removing the ban only in 1155, when Arnold of Brescia had been expelled. In 1154 Frederick Barbarossa entered Italy, and after receiving the Lombard Crown at Pavia in April 1155, he marched toward Rome with the intention of obtaining imperial coronation. Frederick turned Arnold of Brescia over to papal agents and agreed to support the pope, and in return Adrian agreed to having him crowned emperor on 18 June 1155. Following Frederick's retreat northward and unrest in Rome in November 1155, Adrian assumed residence at Benevento. While there he granted Henry II dominion over Ireland as a papal fief. Meanwhile, relations with Emperor Frederick deteriorated, and the stage was set for a major clash between pope and emperor when Adrian died at Anagni on 1 September 1159.

For further reference: H. K. Mann, *The Lives of the Popes in the Early Middle Ages*, (London: K. Paul, 1902–1932); Richard W. Southern, "Pope Adrian IV," in *Medieval Humanism and Other Studies* (New York: Harper and Row, 1970).

William C. Schrader

ADRIAN V (1276). Ottoboni Fieschi of Genoa, nephew of Pope INNOCENT IV (1243–1254), was papal LEGATE in several major cities before his uncle made him cardinal-deacon of S. Adriano in 1252. He was sent by Pope CLEMENT IV (1265–1268) to mediate between England's King Henry III and his barons. His success earned him esteem in Rome, culminating in his election as POPE in the Lateran palace on 11 July 1276. Like his predecessor, INNOCENT V (1276), Adrian V was the choice of Charles of Anjou, king of Sicily, who used his authority as a Roman senator to get his favorite elected. In the end, Adrian, who was not a priest, was never consecrated or crowned as pope; and his pontificate, which ended with his death at Viterbo on 18 August 1276, proved to be one of the shortest. In his one notable administrative act he annulled the "many intolerable and obscure provisions" of the enactments of GREGORY X (1271–1276) on papal conclaves. Largely because of Adrian V's ties with Charles of Anjou. Dante represents him as bound, face-down, among the avaricious being purged in Circle V of his *Purgatory*.

For further reference: E. John, *The Popes* (New York: Hawthorn Books, 1964); Paget Toynbee, *Concise Dante Dictionary* (Oxford: Clarendon Press, 1914).

Anne Paolucci

ADRIAN VI (1522–1523). He was the first pontiff selected following the outbreak of the Lutheran revolt (see Reformation). In 1515 Adrian Flornsz Dedal, a carpenter's son, was born in Utrecht. He subsequently studied at Louvain and was later dispatched on a diplomatic mission to Spain, where he befriended Cardinal Ximenez of Cisniros. Following the death of King Ferdinand of Aragon in 1516, the two assumed the regency until the accession of Charles in 1517. In 1522, while still in Spain, he was elected POPE after a tempestuous conclave, the last non-Italian pope until the election of Karol Wojtyla as JOHN PAUL II in 1978. The new pope sought to check the REFORMATION by a reform of the CURIA and rallying Christian Europe against the Ottoman Turks. His efforts were hampered by the ongoing war between Francis I of France and the emperor, the advance of the Turks, and the frustration of his reformism at the diet of Nuremberg of December 1522.

For further reference: Matthew Bunson, *The Pope Encyclopedia* (New York: Crown Trade Paperbacks, 1995); J. N. D. Kelly, *The Oxford Dictionary of Popes* (New York: Oxford University Press, 1986).

Patrick McGuire

AGAPITUS I (535–536). The short reign of Agapitus I (13 May 535–22 April 536) has been characterized as one of the few brighter intervals in the gloom of Byzantine tyranny over the church. Agapitus left his mark on the strength of legends that developed after his death, particularly about the spiritual influence he had on Justinian I—an influence that amounted to conversion of an allegedly pagan emperor to the Christian faith. In his history of the papacy, Erich Caspar quotes Dante's account of that legend in *Paradiso* where Justinian says that, before being "corrected" by the "blessed Agapitus," he had adhered to the Eutychian HERESY, which denied that the Person of Jesus was human as well as divine in nature.

Agapitus was born of a noble Roman family, reportedly the son of the martyred priest Gordianus. After becoming POPE in May 535, on the urging of his learned friend Cassiodorus, he hoped to make Rome a cultural center such as Alexandria. But he had not been pope long before he was asked by the Ostrogothic king Theodoric to go on a special mission to Constantinople. Believing Justinian planned to send his great general Belisarius into Italy to destroy the

Ostrogothic kingdom and restore Roman imperial rule, Agapitus was pressed to plead with the emperor to recognize the Ostrogoths as loyal allies.

Justinian, in the midst of his spiritual "conversion," replied that it was too late to stop the invasion of Italy. But, in every other respect, Agapitus' mission proved to be a great success. He had been warmly received, greatly honored, and heeded in his pastoral teaching. When he learned that Anthimus, the newly appointed patriarch of Constantinople and a favorite of Empress Theodora, was a Monophysite, he refused to acknowledge him and prevailed with the emperor to have him replaced.

Justinian was persuaded by Agapitus to make peace with the Ostrogoths in Italy as soon as possible. When the pope unexpectedly died in Constantinople on 22 April 536, the Eastern capital publicly celebrated him with a funeral grander than any bishop or emperor had ever enjoyed. His body was then transported to Rome for burial in St. Peter's. That seemed to promise an early and honorable "Catholic peace" after the imperial invasion. Instead, within a year, Belisarius reduced the papacy to vassalage and Agapitus' successor, SILVERIUS (536–537), was accused of conspiring with the Ostrogothic court against the Eastern empire. Silverius was deposed and banished, replaced by VIGILIUS (537–555). The legend of Agapitus' "conversion" of Justinian endured.

For further reference: E. Caspar, *Das Papstums unter fränkische Herrschafft* (Darmstadt: J. Mohr, 1956), pp. 199–229; E. John, *The Popes* (New York: Hawthorn Books, 1964); Paget Toynbee, *Concise Dante Dictionary* (Oxford: Clarendon Press, 1914).

Anne Paolucci

AGAPITUS II (946–955). Reigning from 10 May 946 to December 955, Agapitus II was the successor to MARINUS II (942–946). He owed his position to the support of Alberic II (c. 905–954), the prince of Rome and, from 932 to 954, its dominant ruler. Little is known of Agapitus' origins, early life, or career except that he was a Roman by birth. But, while earlier POPES appointed by Alberic had been largely restricted to ecclesiastical roles, he was able to exercise considerable influence in politics inside and outside Italy.

Agapitus encouraged monastic reforms, confirming the special status of the monastery of Cluny and arranging for monks to come to Rome from the diocese of Metz to restore discipline in the abbey attached to St. Paul's Outside the Walls. Furthermore, his LEGATE was sent in 948 to the court of King Otto I of Germany, who became emperor in 962, to preside with Otto and Louis IV of France (936–954) at the important synod of Ingelheim, called to settle the contested succession to the see of Rheims.

In a bull dated 2 January 948 Agapitus extended the jurisdiction of the metropolitan of Hamburg over Denmark and other northern areas. He also worked closely with Otto, whom he admired; when the king of Saxony crossed the Alps in 951 to assume the royal power at Pavia, he sent envoys to the pope at Rome rather than the prince Alberic, to negotiate for the imperial title. Had Agapitus been free to offer the Crown to him, he would have done so. However, he was obliged to refuse since Alberic, who did not want to see Rome dominated by a foreign power, opposed this move. Nonetheless, Agapitus continued to support Otto actively, granting him broad jurisdiction over important monasteries, permitting his brother Bruno, the archbishop of Cologne (953–965) to wear the pallium, and endorsing the king's plan to transform the monastery of St. Maurice, which he had founded in 937 at Magdeburg, into a metropolitan see with oversight of the mission to the Slavs, while giving the king authority to establish archbishoprics and bishoprics and to define their ecclesiastical boundaries. In these ways, Agapitus played a significant role in the eventual restoration of imperial authority in 962.

Despite his independence and determination, the vulnerability of Agapitus' position was demonstrated at the time of Alberic's death in 954. He was succeeded as prince by his son Octavian, who, with the death of Agapitus a little more than a year later, became pope as well. Agapitus was buried in the apse of St. John Lateran.

For further reference: L. Duquesne, ed., *Liber Pontificalis* (Paris: E. de Boccard, 1955); P. Hughes, *The History of the Church* (New York: Sheed and Ward, 1955); H. K. Mann, *The Lives of the Popes in the Early Middle Ages* (London: K. Paul, 1902–1932).

William Roberts

AGATHO (678–681). Agatho's pontificate was highlighted by his ability to persuade the Byzantium emperor to abandon his support of monothelitism, which recognized both a divine-human will and divine-human operation in Christ. Emperor Constantine IV (668–685) proposed a conference, to be held in Constantinople (see Constantinople III, Council of), between representatives of both Eastern and Roman churches to discuss the issue of whether Christ had two wills or one, also hoping to restore a measure of unity between the two churches. Agatho responded enthusiastically, instructing the churches in the West to deliberate on the monothelitist doctrine and provide him with their recommendations. On Easter 680, Agatho and the bishops composed a profession of faith condemning monothelitism, claiming that Rome had supremacy over the whole church, and declaring that Rome had never erred regarding matters of faith.

Constantine, at the Sixth General Council (see Constantinople III, Council of) (7 November 680–16 September 681), concurred with the Western position on the issue of the two wills of Christ, condemned the principal leaders of the HERESY, and recognized that the true faith had come from God to the Roman church. The Sixth Council (see Constantinople III, Council of) not only ended the controversy surrounding the monothelite heresy but helped to heal the SCHISM between Rome and Constantinople. Foreshadowing future events, Agatho became the first POPE to appeal to papal INFALLIBILITY as Honorius I (625–638) was condemned by the council for heresy because of his support of the monothelitist position. Agatho died before the conclusion of the council, but his participation was recognized in the final decrees. Subsequently, he was elevated to sainthood. His feast day is 10 January.

For further reference: Hans Kuhner, *Encyclopedia of the Papacy* (New York: Philosophical Library, 1958); H. K. Mann, *The Lives of the Popes in the Early Middle Ages* (London: K. Paul, 1902–1932). The best beginning primary source remains the *Liber Pontificalis* (Paris, 1886–1892).

John C. Horgan

ALBERT (ADALBERT), ANTIPOPE (1101). The turn of the twelfth century found the papacy embroiled in numerous controversies, not the least of which concerned an ongoing dispute between the papacy and the German kings over the investiture issue (see Investiture Controversy). Albert, the former cardinal-bishop of Silva Candida, was elected by supporters of an earlier ANTIPOPE, CLEMENT III (1080, 1084–1100), with the tacit consent of the German emperor, Henry V. Albert's election touched off riots throughout Rome, forcing the usurper to flee to the residence of a local sympathizer, who, upon receiving a bribe of sufficient amount, handed over Albert to Pope PASCHAL II (1099–1118). The POPE promptly stripped Albert of his pallium and, after a brief imprisonment, banned the disgraced antipope to a monastery north of Naples.

For further reference: Joseph S. Brusher, *Popes through the Ages* (Princeton: D. Van Nostrand, 1964); H. K. Mann, *The Lives of the Popes in the Early Middle Ages* (London: K. Paul, 1902–1932); Walter Ullman, *A Short History of the Papacy in the Middle Ages* (London: Methuen, 1972).

John C. Horgan

ALBIGENSES. Albigenses were members of a Christian sect centered in Albi in southern France during the twelfth and thirteenth centuries. They followed the teachings of the Catharist movement, an early form of Manichaeism, which sought purification from bodily and material things, hence, the name "Cathari," from the Greek *katharo*, or "pure." The Albigenses' religious beliefs were also similar to those of the Bogomils of the Balkan region. Possibly, these beliefs were transmitted from East to West over trade routes.

The Albigenses followed Manichaean dualism, attempting to resolve the problem between good and evil. They asserted the existence of two ultimate principles, a good deity (the God of the New Testament) who created Light and Spirit and an evil one (the God of the Old Testament) who created Matter and Darkness. Accordingly, they condemned as evil marriage and procreation. The spirits trapped inside human bodies are awaiting a return to heaven. Life on earth is itself a punishment and the only hell that exists. Like the Arians (see Arianism), they believed that Christ was merely a created being who took on a human form and, out of pity for humankind, came to earth to teach the way to heaven. He never really died on the cross, and his redemption was chiefly the example of a noble and moral life. The Albigenses also believed in perpetual chastity and abstinence from milk, meat, and animal products, accepted only the New Testament as a source of authority, and forbade oaths, war, and capital punishment.

In practice, the Albigenses distinguished between the *perfecti*, the perfect, and ordinary believers. The former were a small minority who held strictly to the observances of the early Cathari: the *consolamentum*, or spiritual baptism, the *appareillamentum*, or public confession, and the *endura*, or self-imposed starvation so as to free the spirit from the body. Most believers were affiliated with the sect only by the promise to receive the *consolamentum* before they died, and they often delayed this rite until shortly before death so as to avoid a relapse into sin. It was, in fact, the only requirement asked of believers. Other practices included study of the New Testament and a common meal, the *agape*. The Albigenses' hierarchy consisted of bishops, chosen from among the perfect, and deacons, chosen from the faithful. The simplicity and decent behavior of the believers attracted many to the sect. While exact figures are not available, it is certain that they had influence in more than 1,000 towns and cities in France during their height.

A threat to the authority and influence of the church, the movement was condemned at the Third and Fourth Lateran Councils (see Lateran Council III and Lateran Council IV) in 1179 and 1215. In fact, the legislation passed at the Third Lateran Council against the Albigenses marks the beginning of the medieval INQUISITION, in which the Dominican order, founded in 1216, would play a central role. Earlier, in 1208, Pope INNOCENT III (1198–1216) had called for a crusade against the Albigenses, which took place between 1209 and 1228, under the vassals of the king of France and especially Simon of Montfort. Both the church and state had interests in the destruction of the Albigensian, or Cathari, movement. A brutal repression was carried out throughout southern France and the Languedoc, but the movement persisted until 1245, when the remaining Albigensian leaders and faithful died in the bloody attack on their stronghold at Montségur, where great numbers were massacred or executed. Land and property of the Albigensians were confiscated by both the church and the vassals of the French king. For the French monarchy the crusade meant the annexation of the Languedoc region, achieved in the Treaty of Meaux in 1229. Whatever remained of the Albigensian movement was gradually eliminated by the end of the fourteenth century by the papal Inquisition.

For further reference: W. D'Ormesson, *The Papacy* (London: Hawthorn Books, 1959); P. Hughes, *The History of the Church* (London: Sheed and Ward, 1955); D. Waley, *The Papal State in the Thirteenth Century* (London: Macmillan, 1961).

William Roberts

ALEXANDER I (c. 109–c. 116). In the earliest succession lists of bishops of Rome he ranks fifth in the line that began with PETER. Early documents differ about the length of his reign, and the figures given, varying from seven to ten years, are essentially estimates. The *Liber Pontificalis* states that he was by background a Roman, the son of another Alexander. It attributes to him, too, perhaps somewhat anachronistically, the insertion of the narrative of the Last Supper into the mass, as well as the introduction of the custom of blessing houses with water mixed with salt. A Roman tradition claims he died a martyr, being beheaded on the Via Nomentana leading out of Rome. But this is most likely the result of confusing him with another martyr of the same name whose tomb was discovered on that road in 1855. Because of the silence of early authorities, it is improbable that he was martyred. Little else is known about him except that he held the leading position in the Roman church. His feast is celebrated on 3 May.

For further reference: L. Duchesne, ed., *Liber Pontificalis* (Paris: E. de Boccard, 1955); J. Lebreton and J. Zeiller, *The History of the Primitive Church* (New York: Burns, Oates and Washbourne, 1948); M. Winter, *St. Peter and the Popes* (London: Helicon Press, 1960).

William Roberts

ALEXANDER II (1061–1073). Anselmo da Baggio was born near Milan, ordained in 1055, and named bishop of Lucca in 1057. Under NICHOLAS II (1059–1061) he served as a LEGATE to Milan. Alexander succeeded Nicholas II, becoming the first POPE elected by the cardinals (see Cardinals, College of) according to Nicholas' decree of 1059. A month after the election of Alexander II, Cadalous, bishop of Parma, was elected as HONORIUS II (1061–1064), an ANTIPOPE. But in 1062 Archbishop Anno of Cologne replaced the empress Agnes as regent and threw his support to Alexander II. St. Peter Damien was then able to persuade a majority of the German ecclesiastics to follow.

In 1063 Alexander condemned the treatment of Jews in southern France and in Spain, where they were being pressured during the reconquest of territory held by Muslims since the ninth century. For the most part, however, Alexander had to act more politically, often looking for countervailing support to temporal rulers, rather than dictating to them. Steigand, archbishop of Canterbury, an opponent of Alexander, crowned King Harold of England. In turn, Alexander blessed William of Normandy before his invasion (1066) of England. On the accession of the Byzantine emperor Michael VII Ducas (1071–1078), Alexander sent representatives to reopen contacts with the East—the first since the split in 1054. However, nothing permanent resulted from this gesture.

In Germany, when Henry IV turned twenty-one in 1071, he tried to make up for the power lost during his minority by controlling ecclesiastical appointments, intervening in the election of the archbishop of Milan, one of the largest and richest cities in the empire. Alexander came down on the side of the reform candidate and excommunicated (see Excommunication) the advisers of Henry, but not the young king, whom he hoped to win to his view. This conflict foreshadowed the INVESTITURE CONTROVERSY between Alexander II's successor, GREGORY VII (1073–1085), and the emperor Henry IV.

For further reference: T. Schmidt, *Alexander II (1061–1073) und die romische Reformgruppe seiner Zeit* (Stuttgart: Hiersemann, 1977); B. Tierney, *The Crisis of Church and State, 1050–1300* (Englewood Cliffs, NJ: Prentice-Hall, 1964).

Frank Grande

ALEXANDER III (1159–1181). The pontificate of Alexander III is one of the longest and most important in papal and church history. As the first of the great lawyer POPES, Alexander was able to dominate the creation of significant laws, a large number of which still exist in the canon (see Canon Law). Orlando (Roland) Bandinelli, son of Ranuccio, was born in Sienna c. 1100. He was a learned man and professor of law at Bologna. Roland's election on 1 September 1159 was a tumultuous affair. Although he was supported by a majority of the cardinals (see Cardinals, College of), a small group of pro-imperial voters selected Cardinal Ottaviano, who had close ties to Emperor Frederick. The ensuing struggle forced Roland and his supporters to hide in the Castel Sant' Angelo before fleeing to Ninfa under the protection of the Frangipani. Here, the coronation was completed, and Roland assumed the name of Alexander III.

The conflict over the election resulted in a SCHISM, with Ottaviano being consecrated and assuming the name VICTOR IV. That schism was to last for eighteen years and would force Alexander to grapple with four different ANTIPOPES. The schism also proved to be the perfect instrument for Frederick to assert his dominance over the church. When both parties appealed to him for intervention, he summoned them to appear before a council, made up mostly of imperial German and Italian bishops, in Pavia in February 1160. After excommunicating (see Excommunication) Victor, Alexander refused to recognize the authority of the council and would not appear before it. The council endorsed the election of Victor and installed him as pope. In response Alexander convened an assembly of bishops from virtually every Western country at Toulouse under the auspices of Henry II of England and Louis VII of France, which declared him the legitimate pontiff.

Political conflict threatened to occupy the bulk of Alexander's attention, especially in the early years. The first significant event threatened to alienate Alexander from the Church of England. Thomas Beckett, archbishop of Canterbury, refused to endorse the Constitution of Clarendon, commonly known as the ''Norman customs'' of the Crown, because he felt that they illegally limited the powers of the church and pope. Beckett fled to France in 1164 and appealed to Louis VII for protection. Alexander was put in the difficult position of wishing to support Beckett but feared a threatened alliance between Henry and Frederick. Fortunately for Alexander, the diplomatic impasse was resolved with the murder of Beckett in 1170. Alexander returned from France in 1165, eventually settling in Benevento, in part to solidify his relationship with the Lombard

League, a coalition of northern cities created to oppose Frederick's tyrannical reign. The league supported the efforts of Alexander and named the newly formed city of Alexandria after him.

Constant conflict resulted from the schism. After the death of Victor in 1164, three other antipopes followed: PASCHAL III (1164–1168), CALLISTUS III (1168–1178), and INNOCENT III (1179–1180). While none of these antipopes proved to be as difficult to handle as Victor, each served as a distraction. In 1176, the imperial army suffered a crushing defeat at the hands of the Lombard League when Frederick attempted to invade Milan. The Peace of Venice, signed in 1177, required Frederick to make major concessions to Alexander: to recognize him as the legitimate Pope, to reject Callistus III as antipope, and to agree to armistices with the Lombards and Sicily. Although peace would not last, the Venice agreement allowed Alexander to return to Rome and to address the more spiritual matters of the church.

In March 1179, Alexander assembled the Third Lateran (see Lateran Council III) (Eleventh General) Council to deal with a broad range of issues. The sessions produced twenty-seven canons important to the development of papal legislative authority. During his pontificate, Alexander issued an enormous number of decisions that still exist today in CANON LAW. By one count, 75 percent of all judgments from popes entered into law since the twelfth century had been penned by Alexander. In 1179, another of the ongoing conflicts with the senate forced the pontiff to leave Rome. He died in Città Castellana in 1181. A hostile crowd insulted the body as it was brought for burial to the Lateran basilica, providing an ironic ending to one of the greatest pontificates in history.

For further reference: Eric John, *The Popes: A Concise Bibliographical History* (London: Burns and Oates, 1964); H. K. Mann, *The Lives of the Popes in the Early Middle Ages* (London: K. Paul, 1902–1932).

Christopher S. Myers

ALEXANDER IV (1254–1261). Born to the title of count of Segni, Rinaldo Conti was the nephew of Pope GREGORY IX (1227–1241), who had made him a cardinal-deacon in 1227 and then cardinal-bishop of Ostia in 1231. Conti became POPE as Alexander IV on 12 December 1254. His pontificate ran to 25 May 1261.

During his predecessor's pontificate, Rome had been literally torn apart by its Guelf (papal) and Ghibelline (imperial) factions. Fearful of both, the "people" of Rome had fled for safety to live among the city's ancient ruins, only to find that gangs of robbers had made those ruins focal points of attack for looting the entire city. A Bolognese nobleman, Brancaleone d'Andolo, a professional "captain of the people," or *podestà*, had been hired in 1252 to restore law and order, which he proceeded to do with virtually dictatorial power and such severity that, to most Romans, the cure seemed worse than the disease.

Alexander IV functioned as pope only briefly after 1255, when local cardinals forced Brancaleone out. The pope was determined to press his predecessor's hostile policy toward the Hohenstaufens in Sicily. In 1255 he offered the Crown of Sicily to Edmund, son of England's Henry III, and persisted in claiming it for him, despite his refusal. But such papal decisiveness ended in 1257, when the ousted Brancaleone returned with a vengeance. Alexander IV was expelled, and the Romans elected Manfred to their senate. In the spring of 1261, the imperial faction succeeded in electing Manfred senator, inflicting a final humiliation on the exiled pope, who died at Viterbo in May of that same year.

Alexander's achievements may be said to lie in his efforts to consolidate church affairs. He launched the INQUISITION in France in 1255, attempted to unite the Greek and Latin churches, canonized St. Clare of Assisi, and supported the mendicants in Paris. He may be among the simoniac popes who bought and sold sacred offices mentioned by Dante.

For further reference: E. John, *The Popes* (New York: Hawthorn Books, 1964), pp. 130–131, 245; H. K. Mann, *The Lives of the Popes in the Early Middle Ages*, (London: K. Paul, 1902–1932), pp. 131–206; Paget Toynbee, *Concise Dante Dictionary* (Oxford: Clarendon Press, 1914), p. 21.

Anne Paolucci

ALEXANDER V, ANTIPOPE (1409–1410). Alexander V was born Peter Philarghi in Crete c. 1340. He entered the FRANCISCANS and studied at Oxford and Paris, where he received his doctorate in 1381. He gained a reputation as a gifted teacher and preacher at the Universities of Paris and Pavia. He befriended the duke of Milan and was named bishop of Piacenza (1356). Vicenza (1388), and Novara (1389), finally becoming archbishop of Milan (1402). During the Great Western Schism (see Schism) Peter sided with the Roman obedience and was named cardinal by INNOCENT VII (1404–1406). When BENEDICT XIII (1394–1417) and GREGORY XII (1406–1415) failed to end the SCHISM by resignation, Peter joined the rebellious cardinals at Pisa to settle the schism through a council, preaching at the opening of the council in March 1409. After deposing the two POPES, the cardinals on 26 June 1409 elected Peter pope with the name of Alexander V.

The new pope committed himself to call a council in three years to undertake reform. Although some still supported his rivals, the majority of Christendom acclaimed Alexander. While making his way to Rome, he died at Bologna on 3 May 1410. His election, rather than ending the schism, only complicated it, for the church now had three heads. He reigned too briefly to have an impact, but his election concretized the method of ending the schism by council, which was realized at Constance (see Constance, Council of).

For further reference: F. J. Gray, "Peter of Candia," *New Catholic Encyclopedia*, vol. 11, p. 213; John H. Smith, *The Great Schism 1378: The Disintegration of the Papacy* (New York: Weybright and Talley, 1970).

Richard J. Kehoe

ALEXANDER VI (1492–1503). Rodrigo Borgia, the future Alexander VI, was born in 1431, the son of Jofre de Borja and Isabella, the sister of Pope CALLISTUS III (1455–1458). After the death of his father, Rodrigo's family moved to Valencia, where they lived in their uncle's episcopal palace. In 1455 Callistus called him to Rome and then sent him for an abbreviated course in CANON LAW at the University of Bologna. In March 1456 Rodrigo was made a cardinal. During Callistus' pontificate, Rodrigo held a variety of posts, including papal LEGATE, commander in the papal army, and vice-chancellor of the church as well as a series of benefices in both Spain and around Rome. The Italian benefices were extremely important and allowed Rodrigo a strategic grip on the lands around Rome and great influence in future conclaves.

During this time Rodrigo acquired his reputation for delight in feminine company. While a cardinal and later as POPE, Rodrigo had a long-term liaison with Vanozza Catanei, who bore him at least four of his eight children and perhaps more, although she was married to three different men during her relationship with Rodrigo. Some sources list him as having nine children, the most famous of whom were certainly Cesare and Lucrezia. Rodrigo was committed not only to his own children but to the greater Borgia clan during his career, having had help from both Popes SIXTUS IV (1471–1484) and INNOCENT VIII (1484–1492) in strengthening their dynastic ambitions.

Following the death of Innocent VIII in 1492, it was Rodrigo's turn to inherit the papal mantle. He ruled as Pope Alexander VI from 11 August 1492 until his death on 18 August 1503. Spanning the end of the fifteenth and the early sixteenth centuries, Alexander's pontificate was, as Machiavelli said, "the first who showed how much a Pope with money and forces could make his power prevail." Alexander secularized the papacy, a movement that was begun earlier by Sixtus IV and continued by JULIUS II (1503–1513) and LEO X (1513–1521). He was a hardworking, active, and sometimes unscrupulous statesman. His children, Lucrezia most of all, were pawns for the ascendancy of the Borgia family. Alexander, through the activities of Cesare, laid the foundation for a strong PAPAL STATE in central Italy. Many saw the state as being created for Cesare and the Borgia family, not for the church. This aspect of Alexander's papacy frightened Italian statesmen and led to the eventual downfall of Cesare after Alexander's death. The dynastic aspirations of Alexander VI provoked papal wars that involved the kingdoms of France, Spain, and Naples as well as various factions within Rome and many of the Italian city-states. Thus, the reputation of the papacy moved toward its nadir during Alexander's pontificate. Actually, Alexander took good care of the church's business, but the way he went about it earned him the enmity of many.

For further reference: M. Creighton, *A History of the Papacy from the Great Schism to the Sack of Rome*, vol. 5 (London: Longmans, Green, 1923); F. Gregorovius, *History of the City of Rome in the Middle Ages*, trans. A. Hamilton, vol. 7, part 2 (London: George Bell and Sons, 1900); N. Machiavelli, *The Prince in the Chief Works and Others*, trans. A. Gilbert, vol. 1 (Durham, NC: Duke University Press, 1989); M. Mallett, *The*

Borgias (London: Granada, 1981); J. McCabe, *Crises in the History of the Papacy* (New York: G. P. Putnam's Sons, 1916).

Margery A. Ganz

ALEXANDER VII (1655–1667). After studying law, theology, and philosophy in Sienna, Fabio Chigi in 1626 associated with intellectual circles of Rome. While serving the papacy in different capacities, he was ordained and returned to Rome. Chigi was named bishop of Nardo in 1635, when he assumed the responsibility of inquisitor and APOSTOLIC DELEGATE, representing the POPE at the peace talks of WESTPHALIA in 1648. He vehemently opposed any dialogue with heretics and succeeded INNOCENT X (1644–1655) after an intensive conclave debate, mainly opposed by the French minister and Cardinal Jules Mazarin. Alexander's papal and personal weakness was nepotism. Although the Protestant leader Gustavus Adolphus' daughter, Queen Christina of Sweden, abdicated and was received in the church, she proved to be a great burden to Alexander. He was, however, influential in persuading the city of Venice to have the expelled Jesuits (see Society of Jesus) return in December 1656. In a 1656 decree, he permitted the Jesuits to serve as missionaries in China.

For further reference: Matthew Bunson, *The Pope Encyclopedia* (New York: Crown Trade Paperbacks, 1995); J. N. D. Kelly, *The Oxford Dictionary of Popes* (New York: Oxford University Press, 1986).

Patrick McGuire

ALEXANDER VIII (1689–1691). Successor to INNOCENT XI (1676–1689), Pope Alexander VIII (Pietro Ottoboni) reigned from 6 October 1689 to 1 February 1691. A member of a recently ennobled family, Ottoboni was born in Venice on 22 April 1610. Educated at Padua, he received a doctorate in law at age seventeen and three years later entered the Roman CURIA. He was governor of the PAPAL STATES from 1638 to 1643, afterward becoming a judge of the Rota, where he served until 1652. Becoming cardinal in 1652, he served as bishop of Brescia, 1654–1664, then returned to Rome to become the trusted collaborator of Innocent XI, who appointed him grand inquisitor of Rome and secretary of the Holy Office.

At the conclave of 1689, where the ambassadors extraordinary of France and the empire were represented, the cardinals (see Cardinals, College of) were resolved, because of Ottoboni's knowledge, expertise, and character, to elect him without consulting the wishes of these two monarchs. Louis XIV, who had been initially hostile to Ottoboni's election, agreed to it when Ottoboni promised to pursue conciliatory policies.

The new pope, Alexander VIII, raised Louis' candidate, Bishop Toussaint de Forbin-Janson of Beauvais, to the cardinalate, overlooking his earlier Gallican (see Gallicanism) views and the opposition of Emperor Leopold I. He also accepted the French ambassador rejected by Innocent XI. However, he stood firm on the central issue of refusing to ratify the appointment of bishops nominated by the king unless they repudiated the Gallican Liberties of 1682.

Alexander VIII proved a zealous guardian of doctrine. In 1690 he condemned the two laxist propositions of the Jesuits (see Society of Jesus) which denied the necessity of an explicit act of love for God after the attainment of reason and admitted the idea of "philosophic sin" (one committed without a knowledge of the existence of God). He then condemned thirty-one Jansenist (see Jansenism) propositions regarding baptism, penance, the Virgin, and the authority of the church. He also imprisoned the followers of the Spanish quietist Miguel de Molinos.

In contrast to his austere predecessor, Alexander VIII ruled in a lavish style and revived the nepotism that Pope Innocent had suppressed. He appointed his grandnephew, Pietro, age twenty, as cardinal and his nephew Giambattista as secretary of state while enriching other relatives. Nonetheless, he was popular in the papal states, reducing taxes and lowering food prices, even though his recruitment of troops to assist Venice against the Turks was opposed. A learned individual, he moved in literate circles and enlarged the Vatican library by purchasing the valuable manuscripts of Queen Christina of Sweden, who had settled in Rome after her abdication and conversion to Catholicism.

For further reference: W. D'Ormesson, *The Papacy* (London: Hawthorn Books, 1959); P. Hughes, *The History of the Church* (New York: Sheed and Ward, 1955); L. Pastor, *A History of the Popes from the Close of the Middle Ages* (New York: Herder, 1953).

William Roberts

AMERICANISM. Americanism is the name given to several theories concerning church and state and spiritual growth rejected by Pope LEO XIII (1878–1903) in his apostolic letter *Testem Benevolentiae* of 22 January 1899. Specifically, the errors indicated in the apostolic letter were the rejection of external spiritual direction as no longer necessary; an elevation of natural virtues over the supernatural; a tendency to prefer the active virtues over the passive ones; the rejection of religious vows as incompatible with the notion of Christian liberty; and the use of a new apologetic to explain the faith and a new approach to non-Catholics.

The actual controversy that brought about the apostolic letter was the bitter discussion in France that followed the translation into French and publication (1897) in book form of the life of Father Isaac Hecker, the founder of the Paulists. Abbé Felix Klein, a young lecturer at the Institut Catholique and an admirer of Bishop John Ireland, had added to his French translation of the original American edition by Walter Elliott a Preface highly laudatory of the American Catholic way of life and of Hecker as the priest of the future. In Rome the discussion of what the French press had called "Americanism" became entangled and confused in the local issue of the temporal power of the POPE.

In response to the request that the Hecker biography be placed in the INDEX, Leo XIII declined, choosing instead to appoint a committee of cardinals to study the issue. The committee returned a report unfavorable to "Americanism." In his carefully worded *Testem Benevolentiae* (22 January 1899), Leo did not accuse anyone of holding the specific doctrines or theories. Ordinary political and social Americanism was not included in the condemnation. The basic principle of the censured Americanism was that the church should modify its doctrines to suit better the modern times, and the church ought to de-emphasize some of its doctrines that would be unattractive to current and popular theories and methods.

The Hecker biography was withdrawn, conservative Catholic bishops in the United States were grateful for the intervention of the Holy See, and Cardinal Gibbons, to whom the letter had been addressed, denied that any knowledgeable Catholic had held the positions cited.

For further reference: Roger Aubert, ed., *Progress and Decline in the History of Church Renewal* (New York: Paulist Press, 1967); Thomas S. Bokenkotter, *A Concise History of the Catholic Church* (New York: Image, Doubleday, 1990); Thomas McAvoy, *A History of the Catholic Church in the United States* (Notre Dame, IN: University of Notre Dame Press, 1969).

Loretta Devoy

ANACLETUS (c. 79–c. 91). Reigning probably from 79 to 91, Anacletus is second, following LINUS, in the succession of bishops of Rome established by Sts. PETER and Paul and is commemorated in the earliest canon of the mass. During this early period his actual role, authority, and the extent of the power of his office can only be surmised. His name, also rendered as Anencletus, represents a Greek term for "blameless." Since it was often given to former slaves, it may provide some clue to his origins. Early lists of POPES, such as the fourth-century Liberian Catalogue and the *Liber Pontificalis*, mistakenly note two popes: Cletus and Anacletus, but the former name is really only a shortened form of Anacletus. The early writer Eusebius states that he died in the twelfth year of the emperor Domitian's reign. The *Liber Pontificalis* reports that he appointed twenty-five presbyters for Rome, erected a monument over the burial place of St. Peter, and died a martyr, which had not been substantiated.

For further reference: L. Duchesne, ed., *Liber Pontificalis* (Paris: E. de Boccard, 1955); J. Lebreton and J. Zeiller, *A History of the Primitive Church* (New York: Burns, Oates, and Washbourne, 1948); M. Winter, *St. Peter and the Popes* (London: Helicon Press, 1960).

William Roberts

ANACLETUS II, ANTIPOPE (1130–1138). Born in Rome as Peter Pierleoni, the future Anacletus II was a member of the most influential family in the city, rich Jewish bankers converted to Christianity in the eleventh century. Peter Pierleoni was educated close to King Louis VI of France, taking the monastic vows at Cluny. Back in Rome he became cardinal and served as a LEGATE to England and France under CALLISTUS II (1119–1124), becoming the most prominent candidate for the papacy.

In the 1130 papal election, however, the Pierleoni's main Roman rivals, the Frangipani, favored the candidacy of Cardinal Gregory of St. Angelo. The dispute resulted in a dual election marred by irregularities. In February 1130 Haimeric, the influential French chancellor of Callistus II and HONORIUS II (1124–1130), with other cardinals, brought the dying pope Honorius to a monastery located in the territory of his allies, the Frangipani. Following his demise they hastily ordered his burial, and on 14 February they elected Cardinal Gregory as Pope INNOCENT II (1130–1143). When the majority in the College of Cardinals (see Cardinals, College of) heard of these irregularities, they elected Pierleoni as Anacletus II. Heavy fighting broke out between the two factions. Anacletus' followers prevailed and forced Innocent to flee.

The historical interpretation of the SCHISM as a division between the promoters of the renewed spirituality practiced by new orders, represented by Innocent, and the advocates of the old monasticism, supported by Anacletus, is ungrounded. Other explanations point to the feuds between the city aristocratic families and a split within the College of Cardinals precipitating the schism. Against this backdrop the key protagonist in the struggle, Haimeric, contributed to the breach. Once exiled in France, Innocent and his chancellor, Haimeric, launched a campaign to persuade King Louis VI and the religious leaders of the lawfulness of the election. When their account of the electoral procedure proved unconvincing, they resorted to virulent remarks about Anacletus' character, pointing to his Jewish ancestry, to which they ascribed his flawed personality, his promiscuous and even incestuous sexual life, and his dark complexion and physical deformities. Based on these declarations, some churchmen, including the prominent Bernard of Clairvaux, proclaimed Innocent the better man, cooperating in the vilification of Anacletus. Their opinions helped Innocent gain the recognition by the Western European kings and the Roman emperor, while Scotland and southern Italy stood on the side of Anacletus. Anacletus' sway over Rome continued uncontested until his death on 25 January 1138.

For further reference: Stanley Chodorow, *Christian Political Theory and Church Politics in the Mid-Twelfth Century: The Ecclesiology of Gratian's Decretum* (Berkeley: University of California Press, 1972); I. S. Robinson, *The Papacy 1073–1198: Continuity and Innovation* (Cambridge: Cambridge University Press, 1990); Mary Stroll, *The Jewish Pope: Ideology and Politics in the Papal Schism of 1139* (New York: E. J. Brill, 1987).

Elda G. Zappi

ANASTASIUS I (399–401). Not long after assuming the chair of PETER, Anastasius I found himself embroiled in a controversy with the third-century Greek theologian Origen. A loose translation of Origen's *First Principles* by Rufinus of Aquileia seemed to have offended not only Jerome but several of his peers in an influential clique in Rome. Seemingly unknown to Anastasius, Alexander received a letter in 400 from the powerful patriarch of Alexandria, Theophilus, informing him of the evils of Origen's thinking as well as its recent condemnation in Egypt. Anastasius responded by convening a synod anathematizing his theological errors. He sought support from the bishop of Milan, Simplician, and his brother bishops, and, remaining skeptical of Rufinus' motives for the translation, he decided to leave any type of judgment to God.

For further reference: Matthew Bunson, *The Pope Encyclopedia* (New York: Crown Trade Paperbacks, 1995); J. N. D. Kelly, *The Oxford Dictionary of Popes* (New York: Oxford University Press, 1986).

Patrick McGuire

ANASTASIUS II (496–498). As a deacon this Roman was influential in the synod of 495. After his election to the papacy in 496, he yearned to restore a unified church East and West and proved willing to make concessions for peace. In the midst of the crisis, Anastasius II died suddenly, some suggested by divine judgment. With the exception of a letter to his bishops in Gaul, little is known of Anastasius. This letter condemned the HERESY of traducianism, "the view that human souls are not created directly by God but generated by their parents in the same way as bodies." His main contribution was his effort to end the thirty-seven year SCHISM (Acacian) between the churches of the East and West. During his papacy, he welcomed the unification of the Eastern church if it would concur with the condemnation of the patriarch Acacius. This action was received well in the East; however, Adrian's clergy in the West became hostile for not consulting them. With this came a small schism in the church that lasted for the remainder of Anastasius' pontificate and well into that of his successor, Pope SYMMACHUS (498–514).

For further reference: Matthew Bunson, *The Pope Encyclopedia* (New York: Crown Trade Paperbacks, 1995); J. N. D. Kelly, *The Oxford Dictionary of Popes* (New York: Oxford University Press, 1986).

Patrick McGuire

ANASTASIUS III (911–913). Little is known of the early life or even the circumstances of the election of this Roman as POPE. During this turbulent period, Rome was ruled by the senator and consul Theophylact, who was also financial director of the Holy See, and his ambitious wife, Theodora the Elder. The papacy itself was controlled by this powerful and unscrupulous family. At the request of King Berengar I of Italy, Anastasius granted certain honors to the bishop of Pavia, an important city in Berengar's kingdom. In 912, Anastasius received a lengthy and critical letter from the newly restored patriarch of Constantinople, Nicholas I Mysticus, deploring Rome's approval of Byzantine emperor Leo VI's fourth marriage, as well as the attitude of the previous pope Sergius III's (904–911) envoys who had visited Constantinople earlier. Anastasius' reply is not known, but it must have been unfavorable because Nicholas subsequently removed the pope's name from the diptychs, widening the chasm between Constantinople and Rome.

For further reference: L. Duchesne, ed., *Liber Pontificalis* (Paris: E. de Boccard, 1955); P. Hughes, *The History of the Church* (London: Sheed and Ward, 1955); H. K. Mann, *The Lives of the Popes in the Early Middle Ages* (London: K. Paul, 1902–1932).

William Roberts

ANASTASIUS IV (1153–1154). On the day of the death of EUGENE III (1145–1153), the 80-year-old Roman Corrado was elected as his successor and installed in the Lateran on 12 July 1153 as Anastasius IV. Anastasius' brief tenure as pontiff was, on the whole, uneventful. Unlike his predecessors, Anastasius enjoyed cordial relations with the senate, as evidenced by his consecration in the Lateran and by his ability to reside in Rome. His greatest challenge was the relationship between the see and King Frederick of Germany. In 1152, Eugene III refused the translation, without his consent, of Archbishop Winchmann from Naumburg to Magdeburg, which was recommended by Frederick. Anastasius, seeking to rectify the situation through diplomatic means, sent Gerard, cardinal-deacon of St. Maria in Via Lata, to Germany in an attempt to have Frederick withdraw his support. The cardinal-deacon, however, was summarily dismissed by the king.

Frederick sent Winchmann to Rome to receive his pallium. Various theories seek to explain why Anastasius granted the pallium to the archbishop: the pope failed to examine the records of Eugene III, he was left uninformed due to Gerard's untimely death, or he gave the pallium out of deference to Frederick. Regardless of his motive, the king felt that he had won a victory over the pontiff. It was a sign of his increasing influence over the policies of the church in Germany. After a brief pontificate of one and one-half years, Anastasius died on 3 December 1154. He is buried in the Lateran basilica.

For further reference: J. N. D. Kelly, *The Oxford Dictionary of the Popes* (Oxford: Oxford University Press, 1986); H. K. Mann, *The Lives of the Popes in the Early Middle Ages* (London: K. Paul, 1902–1932).

Christopher S. Myers

ANASTASIUS BIBLIOTHECARIUS, ANTIPOPE (855). The nephew of the powerful bishop of Orte was ordained a cardinal-priest of S. Marco in 847/848, under LEO IV (847–855). A man of talents and culture, Anastasius immediately found himself at odds with the POPE, seeking refuge in the diocese of Aquileia at the residence of Emperor Louis II. Rejecting Leo's repeated attempts to summon him to Rome, Anastasius was excommunicated (see Excommunication) and humiliated at the synods of 850 and 853, removed from the Lateran, and stripped of his papal insignia. However, Pope BENEDICT III (855–858) agreed with Louis' envoys not to carry out any further reprisals. He reduced Anastasius to lay communion and had him confined to a monastery in Trastevere.

Following the death of Benedict, Anastasius regained his previous status, becoming an adviser for the next three popes: NICHOLAS I (858–867), ADRIAN II (867–872), and JOHN VIII (872–882). Nicholas utilized his talent for drafting letters, especially in Byzantine affairs. Adrian II lifted his suspension as priest, while Louis II sent him on a diplomatic mission to Constantinople, where he participated in the last session of the Eighth General Council (see Constantinople IV, Council of) (869–870). Many thought Anastasius was the compiler of the *Liber Pontificalis*, but currently it is believed he authored the notices of Nicholas I and Adrian II.

For further reference: Matthew Bunson, *The Pope Encyclopedia* (New York: Crown Trade Paperbacks, 1995); J. N. K. Kelly, *The Oxford Dictionary of Popes* (New York: Oxford University Press, 1986).

Patrick McGuire

ANGLICAN–VATICAN RELATIONS. With roughly 70 million adherents worldwide, the Anglican Communion of Churches, including the Church of England, the Episcopal Church in the United States, the Anglican Church of Canada, and so on and the recently emerged churches in Africa, Asia, and Latin America, is one of the largest international Christian communities. The distinguishing marks of churches in the Anglican Communion are their episcopal order, their theology and worship life, based on the "Lambeth Quadrilateral," which, it is claimed, is both Catholic and Reformed, and their communion with the archbishop of Canterbury, the primate of the "mother" Church of England.

According to legend, the papacy first took cognizance of England when Pope GREGORY I (590–604) allegedly said of young men in the Roman slave market, "They are not Angles but Angels." True or otherwise, Gregory dispatched Augustine to England, where he converted the Kentish people of the southeastern tip of the island and founded the primatial see of Canterbury in A.D. 600. After the Synod of Whitby had brought the English liturgical calendar and other ecclesiastical usage firmly in line with that of the Western church, England (and Wales) passed under the jurisdiction of Rome, forming two provinces, Canterbury and York.

The "Church of England" came into being in the reign of Henry VIII (1509–1547) for political and disciplinary, rather than doctrinal, reasons. The jurisdictional takeover of the church and the exappropriation of its lands were an assertion of nascent Tudor state power. They were also a result of international power politics, the refusal of Pope CLEMENT VI (1342–1352), under pressure from the emperor Charles V, to divorce the latter's aunt, Catharine of Aragon, from Henry VIII. Doctrinal and liturgical changes followed Henry's Act of Royal Supremacy of 1534, in which he declared himself "Supreme Head under

God of the Church of England.'' His son Edward VI (1547–1553) came under heavy reforming influences from the Continent. After a brief interlude under Mary I (1553–1558), who made an attempt at a full restoration of papal authority, a final settlement of religious affairs was brought about by her successor, Elizabeth I (1558–1603).

Nevertheless, at the beginning of the seventeenth century neither Rome nor some Anglican divines had given up hopes of a general reunion of Christendom. The mainstream of Anglican theology, including that of the Laudians, however, believed in the Catholic tradition, that the Church of England was a part, albeit detached, of the Catholic Apostolic Church, but antipapal.

Despite the warm reception given to French Catholic exiles (including clergy and nuns) during the French Revolution, the Church of England, especially its bishops, remained hostile to Rome and its claims, as revealed by the debates over Catholic relief bills in the House of Lords, where the bishops sat by right. That hostility continued long after the CATHOLIC EMANCIPATION of 1829, the latter considered a mortal threat to the ecclesiastical establishment. The restoration of the Catholic HIERARCHY by PIUS IX in 1850 evinced a similar reaction, the government's ''no popery'' policy taking the concrete form of the Ecclesiastical Titles Act, forbidding Catholic bishops from appropriating geographical place-names already used by their Anglican counterparts.

The emergence of the Oxford movement, with its stress on the need of the Church of England to recover its ''catholicity'' through the sacraments, had profound consequences on the development of relations between Rome and Canterbury. On one hand, it led to a steady stream of converts to Rome, including two future cardinals, Newman and Manning. On the other, it created a deep cleavage in the Church of England between the more Protestant Evangelicals and Anglo-Catholics. A longer-term consequence of the Oxford movement was the emergence of the first groups committed to reunion with Rome, the Society for the Promotion of the Unity of Christendom and the Order of Corporate Reunion. Their efforts suffered a setback with the proclamation in 1870 of the doctrine of papal INFALLIBILITY, which was later condemned by the Lambeth Conference, the convention of bishops of the emerging Anglican Communion. A more devastating blow was delivered by Rome itself. In 1896, in his statement *Apostolicae Curae*, Pope LEO XIII (1878–1903) declared Anglican orders ''absolutely null and utterly void.''

The hardening of attitudes within the Roman church was reinforced during the reign of Leo XIII's successor, Pope PIUS X (1903–1914) when the Roman church pursued a defensive, inward-looking stance. The Anglican Communion, growing in strength and prestige as new provinces and dioceses were established in the colonies and dominions of the empire, looked outward and began to establish links not only with other Protestant churches but with Orthodox, Old Catholic, and Scandinavian Lutheran churches. In these circumstances the Malines Conversations took place from 1922 to 1926 between Cardinal Mercier, archbishop of that Belgian city, and Lord Halifax, the leading lay representative of the Anglo-Catholic wing of the Church of England. These first serious discussions between Roman Catholics and Anglicans about the bases for reunion were conducted with enthusiasm and goodwill on both sides but also with an unrealistic understanding of Anglicanism by Cardinal Mercier.

After the failure of the talks, the two sides drifted apart in the 1930s. The invasion of Ethiopia (see Ethiopian War) by fascist Italy in 1935 outraged British public opinion, as did Pope PIUS XI's alleged enthusiasm for an Italian victory. The decision of the Lambeth Conference of 1948 to give qualified approval to the use of artificial contraceptives worsened matters.

The Second Vatican Council (see Vatican Council II) (1962–1965) ushered in a new era in Anglican–Roman Catholic relations. The decision to establish the Secretariat for the Promotion of Christian Unity signified a commitment to ecumenism, and the tone of future relations with Anglicans was set by Pope PAUL VI (1963–1978), who talked of the Anglican Church as a ''beloved sister'' and declared: ''Among those [churches] in which some Christian traditions and institutions continue to exist, the Anglican communion occupies a special place.'' The visits to the Vatican of a succession of archbishops of Canterbury, the establishment of the Anglican center in Rome, and, above all, the inauguration of permanent dialogue through ARCIC—the Anglican-Roman Catholic International Commission—followed.

More recently, relations between Rome and Canterbury have been dominated by the decision of the General Synod of the Church of England to ordain women priests. The flight of a number of prominent laity and clergy to Rome has raised anew the question of the validity of Anglican orders. Rome has set its face against women priests, and this has rendered Anglican–Vatican relations more difficult than they have been for over forty years.

For further reference: Anglican-Roman Catholic International Commission, *Church and Communion: An Agreed Statement* (London: Church House and C.T.S., 1991); J. H. Hughes, *Absolutely Null and Utterly Void* (London: Sheed and Ward, 1968); H. Montefiore, *So Near and Yet So Far* (London: SCM Press, 1986); B. Pawley and M. Pawley, *Rome and Canterbury through Four Centuries, 1530–1973*, 2d ed. (London: Mowbray's, 1981).

John F. Pollard

ANGLO–VATICAN RELATIONS. By ''Anglo-Vatican relations,'' we mean relations between the papacy and the English state from its Anglo-Saxon origins to the present day. From its origins until the REFORMATION, the English state's relations with the papacy were characterized by two contrasting tendencies: on one hand, the establishment and consolidation of the English church were the result of cooperation between English monarchs and Roman pontiffs; on the other hand, relations between the Anglo-Norman monarchy and the papacy were frequently characterized by conflict. Apart from the papal claims to universal lordship, there were problems connected with papal tax exactions, appeals from English church courts to Rome, and the provision to ecclesiastical benefices. During the reign of John (1199–1216) the conflict reached unprecedented heights as England was placed under an interdict. Yet at other times in the Middle Ages, English monarchs lent individual POPES support in their struggles against the Holy Roman Emperors or even general COUNCILS of the church. In the early sixteenth century, there was no expectation of a rupture with Rome.

The Henrician reformation is described elsewhere (see Anglican-Vatican Relations), but it is relevant to reiterate that this rupture was initially a function of realpolitik in both domestic and international affairs rather than the result of movements for doctrinal change. After a brief interlude in which Mary I (1553–1558) entered the Catholic camp in European affairs, in the reign of her sister Elizabeth I (1558–1603) the break with Rome became irrevocable. Rome retaliated by excommunicating (see Excommunication) the queen and releasing her subjects from their allegiance. The defiance of the papacy became a matter of national survival when Spain unleashed the Armada against England in 1588. Communication with Rome was prohibited by state law, and practice of the Catholic religion was proscribed.

The era of the Stuart monarchs witnessed a series of "flirtations" with the papacy. Charles I (1623–1649), Charles II (1649–1686), and James II (1686–1688) all married Catholic princesses, necessitating some contact between the courts of London and Rome. James II practiced his Catholicism openly, and formal diplomatic relations were reopened with Rome. The "Glorious Revolution" of 1689 swept James II away, and his exiled successors found refuge at the papal court. Yet in the last decades of the eighteenth century, the Catholic threat to the Protestant monarchy in Britain receded sufficiently for George III to seek better relations with Rome.

The French Revolution of 1789 and the revolutionary war that followed helped effect a rapprochement between Britain and the papacy. United in opposition to the "principles of 1789," the two were also drawn together on a practical level: many émigré French secular and religious clergy were given asylum in Britain. In 1793 there was an exchange of unofficial envoys between Britain and the papacy, and at the Congress of Vienna in 1814–1815 Cardinal CONSALVI achieved the restoration of the temporal power over the PAPAL STATES, with British support.

In the mid-nineteenth century, official relations were limited to the presence of British consular agents in various parts of the papal states. Unofficially, a British diplomatic presence was secured by seconding an attaché at the British legation to the grand duchy of Tuscany to reside in the Eternal City. Thus, between 1858 and 1870, Britain was represented in Rome by Odo Russell. After the proclamation of the unified Italian kingdom in 1861, Russell was attached directly to the Foreign Office "in Special Service under the immediate orders of the Secretary of State for Foreign Affairs," demonstrating the importance for the Foreign Office of relations with the Holy See. Russell's mission proved difficult, given the rising hostility in Britain to the pope's temporal power and, conversely, the strong support for the Italian nationalist movement. Britain's role in the processes that led to Italian unification between 1859 and 1861 effectively destroyed any remaining sympathy between London and Rome. The last special envoy left in 1874, when the status of the Vatican, following the Italian occupation of Rome, could not be clarified by British lawyers.

Despite some unofficial contact during the remainder of Queen Victoria's reign, Anglo–Vatican relations languished until the establishment of Sir Henry Howard's "special mission" to the Holy See shortly after the outbreak of WORLD WAR I. The mission was prompted by the absence of a British or French representative at the Vatican, which proved disadvantageous to the entente powers in comparison with their enemies, the Central Powers of Germany and Austria–Hungary.

During the course of the war, the Vatican's relations with other European powers were the primary object of British interest. The Vatican's efforts to dissuade Italy from entering the war on the side of the entente powers in 1915 drew inevitable British criticism, as did Pope BENEDICT XV's "Peace Note" of 1917. But before the end of hostilities, the dominant themes of the postwar relationship between the Holy See and Britain had emerged, and these were essentially colonial questions.

The first was Ireland (see Irish Nationalism), which occupied more of the British minister's time than any other issue. Britain was anxious to secure Vatican support for its position during the conflicts that began with the Easter Rising of 1916 in Dublin. Despite strong lobbying by the rector of the Irish College in Rome, the Vatican remained amenable to the British point of view. As Thomas E. Hachey points out, in later years, "The Holy See deferred to the British on all matters affecting Ireland despite that nation's new status as the Irish Free State."

A colonial issue that bedeviled Anglo–Vatican relations was the British colony of Malta. In the late 1920s Britain and the Vatican were drawn into a miniature church–state conflict in a battle between the progressive prime minister of Malta, Lord Strickland, and the local clergy. For a brief period the British minister was withdrawn from Rome in protest and replaced by a chargé d'affaires, this situation being resolved in March 1933. The future of Palestine (see Zionism) also remained a factor in Anglo–Vatican relations until the end of Britain's mandate there in 1948. Britain was actually the Vatican's preference as mandatory power, hence, its refusal to be drawn into MUSSOLINI's intrigues in the early 1930s to win the mandate for fascist Italy. But the Vatican had major concerns about British proposals for the partition of the Holy Land and the allocation of some of the most important Christian holy places, such as Nazareth, to a putative Jewish zone, as well as the status of Jerusalem and the position of the Christian minority. Another cause of dispute between Britain and the Vatican was the Italo–Ethiopian conflict (see Ethiopian War) of 1935–1936. The British resented the Vatican's perceived satisfaction with the Italian victory.

As the international situation became increasingly polarized between the fascist dictatorships and the Western democracies in the late 1930s, the Vatican drew closer to the latter, and relations with Britain accordingly improved, and in 1938 an APOSTOLIC DELEGATE was appointed to Britain for the first time. Relations with the Holy See became even more important to Britain after the outbreak of WORLD WAR II in 1939. German opponents of HITLER sought to use the Vatican to open channels with the British government, and, for the duration of the war, the British regarded the Vatican as a vital "listening post" in occupied Europe. During the ensuing COLD WAR, links between Britain and the Holy See remained close. Despite differences over both the Falkands and Gulf Wars, formal relations have actually been strengthened by the transformation of the British legation of the Holy See into a full embassy and the elevation of the apostolic delegate to the rank of pronuncio.

For further reference: Owen Chadwick, *Britain and the Vatican during the Second World War* (Cambridge: Cambridge University Press,1986); Thomas E. Hachey, ed., *Anglo-Vatican Relations, 1914–1939: Confidential Annual Reports of the British Ministers to the Holy See* (Boston: G. K. Hall, 1972); C. H. Lawrence, ed., *The English Church and the Papacy in the Middle Ages* (London: Burns and Oates, 1965); C. T. McIntire, *England against the Papacy, 1858–1861: Tories, Liberals and the Overthrow of the Papal Temporal Power during the Italian Risorgimento* (Cambridge: Cambridge University Press, 1983); Thomas Moloney, *Westminster, Whitehall and the Vatican: The Role of Cardinal Hinsley, 1935–43* (Tunbridge Wells: Burns and Oates, 1985); B. Pawley and M. Pawley, *Rome and Canterbury through Four Centuries: 1530–1973* (New York: Seabury Press, 1975).

John F. Pollard

ANICETUS (c. 155–c. 166). Anicetus is the tenth successor in the papacy to ST. PETER. The *Liber Pontificalis* presents him as a Syrian from Emesa, and the third-century writer Eusebius notes he reigned for eleven years. Soon after his accession he received a visit from Polycarp, the octogenarian bishop of Smyrna and disciple of St. John, who, after they had reached agreement on other issues, tried to persuade him to adopt the practice of the churches in Asia Minor of observing Easter on the fourteenth day of the Jewish month of Nisan, the date of the Passover, regardless of the day of the week that date fell on. The Roman church and probably most other churches observed Easter on Sunday. They failed to reach an agreement, Anicetus pleading that he felt obliged to keep his predecessor's custom of celebrating the Resurrection on a Sunday. Although little else is known of Anicetus, it was probably he who erected the memorial shrine to St. Peter on Vatican Hill that was to become so familiar to visitors as early as 200 and was revealed in the 1939–1949 excavations on the site. St. Anicetus' feast is 17 April.

For further reference: L. Duchesne, ed., *Liber Pontificalis* (Paris: E. de Boccard, 1955); J. Lebreton and J. Zeiller, *The History of the Primitive Church* (London: Burnes, Oates, and Washbourne, 1948); M. Winter, *St. Peter and the Popes* (London: Helicon Press, 1960).

William Roberts

ANNUARIO PONTIFICIO. The *Annuario Pontificio* is one of several publications produced each year by the Holy See. Although currently compiled and distributed by the Vatican Polyglot Press, the official printing press of the Vatican, this annual volume was initially a privately published edition that has undergone several changes in title since its first appearance as the *Annuario Pontificio* in 1860. It contains statistical information pertaining to the organization and administration of the Roman Catholic Church worldwide.

Among the most significant data provided within this volume, the following are included: the dicasteries and offices of the Holy See and the names of all church officials serving in their administration; a list of the names of all the members of the church HIERARCHY and monsignori as well as their places of residence; a list of administrative, educational, charitable, and apostolic organizations officially sponsored or administered by the church; other information relevant to male and female institutes and societies of religious apostolic life, to secular institutes, to local (diocesan) churches, and to other ecclesial bodies throughout the world.

The *Annuario Pontificio* is published in Italian, although some portions of the volume appear in other languages. It represents a tremendous effort by the Holy See to locate in only one place the most important ecclesiastical statistics and to make this information universally available.

For further reference: *Annuario Pontificio Per l'anno* (Vatican City: Tipografia Poliglotta Vaticana, 1912–); P. J. Kenedy and Sons, *The Official Catholic Directory 1993* (New York: P. J. Kenedy and Sons, 1993).

David M. O'Connell

ANTERUS (235–236). The Liberian Catalogue fixed the date of the ordination of Anterus as bishop of Rome at 21 November 235. The brief entry continues with the note that he "fell asleep" only six weeks later (3 January 236). Although he was generally regarded as a martyr, the entry is usually employed for those who were not martyrs, and we may be reasonably certain that Anterus died a natural death since his name does not appear in the early lists of martyrs. He was the first POPE to be buried in the new papal crypt in the Cemetery of Callistus. The church celebrates his feast on 3 January.

For further reference: J. N. D. Kelly, *The Oxford Dictionary of Popes* (New York: Oxford University Press, 1986); J. Lebreton and J. Zeiller, *The History of the Primitive Church*, vol. 4 (London: Burns, Oates, and Washbourne, 1948).

Bernard J. Cassidy

ANTIPOPE. The term "antipope" attaches to anyone who assumes the title of POPE in opposition to a legitimate pontiff. The phenomenon has occurred in varied historical circumstances. Judgment concerning the legitimacy of the claimants must be left to history. A dispute over church practice caused the first SCHISM involving an antipope. In Rome HIPPOLYTUS (217–235) gathered followers who sided with his opposition to the decisions of CALLISTUS I (217–222) to admit repentant adulterers and murderers to the church and to recognize marriages between freewomen and slaves.

During the Middle Ages the titles of some claimants to the papacy were not clear because of the uncertainties surrounding their accession. This occurred frequently during the ninth and tenth centuries. Political motives raised antipopes to their posts during the conflicts between the empire and the papacy. Uncertain elections gave birth to antipopes in 1130 and during the Western Schism (see Schism). The judgment concerning the validity of claimants is sometimes not too complicated, as in the case of the creations of Emperor Henry IV. But great obscurity surrounds the claims of some candidates, especially during the Western Schism. Because of the historical problems surrounding some disputed elections, composing a list of antipopes remains problematic.

For further reference: H. G. Beck, "Antipope," *New Catholic Encyclopedia*, vol. 1, 632–633.

Richard J. Kehoe

ANTONELLI, CARDINAL GIACOMO. This last of the "lay cardinals" is associated with Pope PIUS IX's (1846–1878) reformism, the revolutionary upheaval of 1848, and the papal reaction that followed the restoration of the temporal power in 1849. Secretary of state for some three decades (1848–1876) and effective head of the papal state until its total collapse in 1870, he played a key role in the counterrisorgimento that opposed Italian unification and influenced Italian and European affairs in the process.

Born on the southern tier of the PAPAL STATES on 2 April 1806, Giacomo was earmarked by his wealthy father for a career in the pontifical administration. In 1834 he secured admission to the Civil Tribunal in Rome, and in 1835 he was appointed APOSTOLIC DELEGATE to the province of Orvieto. GREGORY XVI (1831–1846) named him Apostolic Delegate to Viterbo (1836) and Macerata (1839). In 1841 Antonelli became Gregory's undersecretary of state for the interior and received sacred orders up to the deaconate—resisting parental pressure to become a priest. Subsequently, he served as deputy treasurer (1844) and minister of finance (1845).

In 1847 Pius IX named him cardinal-deacon. Supporting the reformist course of the pontiff, he was appointed president of the consultative chamber created by the POPE. In 1848 Antonelli helped to draft the Constitution of the papal states, and Pius IX made him effective head of his constitutional ministry. Constrained to resign when his cabinet called for war against Austria, which the pope opposed, the cardinal remained the pope's trusted adviser, and who arranged the pope's flight from Rome to the kingdom of Naples at the end of 1848.

Antonelli orchestrated the intervention of France, Austria, Spain, and the kingdom of the Two Sicilies, which overturned Mazzini's Roman Republic and restored papal power. The pope relied on Antonelli to resist Louis Napoleon's pressure for liberal institutions. Pursuing his sovereign's instructions, Antonelli drafted the decree of 12 September 1849 that promised administrative concessions to the people of the papal states, assuring that political power would remain in the pope's hands. During the decades from 1850 to 1870 Antonelli assumed many of the burdens of state, while Pius IX dealt with religious issues and the affairs of the universal church. Unable to prevent Italian unification in 1859–1861, Antonelli did constrain Napoleon to retain French troops in Rome, preserving it for the papacy until the Franco–Prussian War (1870).

Antonelli continued to serve Pius IX. During the Vatican Council (see Vatican Council I) he downplayed the political impact of papal INFALLIBILITY, assuring the powers they had no reason for concern. After 1872 he proved helpful in resisting the KULTURKAMPF in Bismarck's Germany and in protesting the anticlerical policies of the French Republic and the kingdom of Italy. Antonelli also offered the pope his economic experience, revising the collection and investment of Peter's Pence and converting it into the primary source of papal income. Despite, and perhaps because of, his loyal service to Pius IX, Antonelli has long been maligned. Liberals disliked the cardinal for making papal absolutism viable after 1850, nationalists for his attempt to block Italian unification, and some conservative Catholics for his failure to do so.

For further reference: Frank J. Coppa, *Cardinal Giacomo Antonelli and Papal Politics in European Affairs* (Albany: State University of New York Press, 1989); Frank J. Coppa, "Cardinal Giacomo Antonelli: An Accommodating Personality in the Politics of Confrontation," *Biography* 2 (Fall 1979): 283–302; Carlo Falconi, *Il Cardinale Antonelli. Vita e carriera del Richelieu italiano nella chiesa di Pio IX* (Milan: Mondadori, 1983).

Frank J. Coppa

APOSTOLIC DELEGATE. The apostolic delegate is a prelate within the church, usually an archbishop, who has been appointed by the POPE to be his personal representative to the faithful, clergy and laity alike, of a local church. Unlike an apostolic NUNCIO, he has no responsibilities before civil or national governments, nor does he possess any rank or status within the diplomatic corps assigned to a country. His is purely an internal, religious role to the Catholic people of a region exercised on behalf of the Apostolic See (see Legates).

For further reference: *The HarperCollins Encyclopedia of Catholicism*, ed. Richard P. McBrien (San Francisco: HarperCollins, 1995), p. 76.

David M. O'Connell

ARCHIVIO SEGRETO VATICANO. SEE SECRET VATICAN ARCHIVES.

ARIANISM. Arianism is the term for the anti-Trinitarian teachings of Arius, a priest of Alexandria (c. 265–356), and his followers, which denied the divinity of Christ. Rooted in GNOSTICISM and early Greek theological speculations, Arianism was an attempt to define the relationship of Christ to God according to natural reason. Arius himself was influenced by the teachings of the bishop of Antioch, Paul of Samosata, who denied the Trinity and stated that, although Christ embodied divine wisdom, he was not the incarnate Son of God. Arianism's centers were Antioch and Alexandria, and it quickly proved to be one of the most formidable challenges to orthodox teaching. During most of the fourth century it had the enthusiastic support of the Roman emperors and government and appealed to various social classes and intellectual groups.

Arius taught that while God is unique and unbegotten, the Word or Logos, Christ, while existing before time, was not eternal. There was a period when the Word did not exist; therefore it was created. Christ's relationship to God is, in fact, adoptive. The incarnate Word, Christ, is consequently inferior to God but is to be worshiped since he is above all creatures and is both Redeemer and Ruler. From its beginnings Arianism was a fully developed doctrine. In 325, bishops at the Council of Nicaea (see Nicaea I, Council of), representing the churches of both the West and the East, condemned and exiled Arius and then declared that the Son was of the same substance, *homoousios*, with the Father. But the theologian Eusebius of Nicomedia, although he had agreed to this formula at the council, soon repudiated it. His influence at the imperial court of Constantine allowed him to gain Arius' return from exile and the removal of Athanasius of Alexandria, the leading proponent of the orthodox position as stated at Nicaea. Eusebius himself represented an especially rigid form of Arianism, but, in fact, by the mid-fourth century there were actually three groups of Arians, all of whom sought imperial support. The first group consisted of the strict Arians, called Anomoeans, who maintained that the Son was unlike the Father. The second group, formed at the Synod of Ancyra and known as Semi-Arians, or Homoeousians, stated that Christ is similar in substance to the Father, and the third group rejected earlier distinctions and maintained that the Son was like the Father and, in fact, differed but little from the position of the second group.

The Semi-Arian, or Homoeousina, faction was considered close to the orthodox position and was favorably regarded by Athanasius and the leaders of the Council of Alexandria in 362. Moreover, the teaching of the Cappadocian fathers of the church further resolved the issue by demonstrating that the essential doctrinal problem could be resolved by the recognition of one nature and three persons. Over the extreme opposition of the emperor Valens, the orthodox Nicaean position eventually prevailed in the West and in time also triumphed in the East. The entire Eastern church subscribed to these doctrines proclaimed at Rome in 378 and 379, and the emperor Theodosius became a fervent supporter

of the orthodox formula of the Nicaean Creed. Later, the Synod of Constantinople, eventually recognized as the second Ecumenical Council, would reaffirm
the Nicaean Creed with only minor changes. The Arian movement was subsequently suppressed in the empire but would prevail among the various Germanic
tribes, especially through the missionary work of Ulfias, who had been consecrated as a bishop by Eusebius, and became the official religion of the Ostrogoths, Visigoths, Suevi, Burgundians, Lombards, and Vandals. Only with the
conversion of the Frankish king Clovis in 496 did the movement decline, although it flourished in the Visigothic kingdom of Spain until the Council of
Toledo in 589.

For further reference: F. Dvornik, *The Ecumenical Councils* (New York: Hawthorn
Books, 1961); P. Hughes, *The History of the Church* (London: Sheed and Ward, 1955);
J. Palanque, *The Church in the Christian Roman Empire* (New York: Macmillan, 1953).
William Roberts

ARNOLD OF BRESCIA. SEE ADRIAN IV.

AVENIR, L'. In July 1830, Félicité de Lamennais with others, including Gerbet,
Lacordaire, and Montalembert, published a newspaper called *L'Avenir*. After
1831, when the newspaper ceased printing, the persons who held the ideas it
had championed became known as the L'Avenir movement. Although Lamennais was a type of ultramontanist, that is, one who favored the primacy of the
position of the POPE, his position was different from that of the most famous
French ultramontanist, Joseph de Maistre. Lamennais and his collaborators,
through the newspaper, called for the separation of church and state, freedom
of professional association and freedom to join associations, freedom of the
press, decentralization, liberty of conscience, which included freedom to choose
one's religion, a limitation on the hours of work, and universal suffrage for all
communal elections. Lamennais saw that the way to social improvement was
through education for all and contended that the church was best able to facilitate
the new social order, ''the Christian emancipation of the people.''

Both bishops and theologians expressed difficulties with some of Lamennais'
tenets, causing some dioceses in France to prohibit *L'Avenir* within their bounds.
The last issue appeared 15 November 1831. Lamennais, Lacordaire, and Montalembert appealed to Rome on behalf of their cause. The new pope, GREGORY
XVI (1831–1846), had no sympathy with Lamennais' program of ''liberal Catholicism'' and responded with the encyclical *Mirari Vos* (1832). The encyclical
repudiated the doctrinal positions that had been found in *L'Avenir* on separation
of church and state, church alliance with liberal revolutionary movements, and
imprudent or immoderate freedom of the press and of opinion, as well as other
elements of the liberal program.

For further reference: Roger Aubert, *The Church in the Age of Liberalism* (New York: Crossroad, 1981); James C. Livingston, *Modern Christian Thought: From the Enlightenment to Vatican II* (New York: Macmillan, 1971).

Loretta Devoy

B

BABYLONIAN CAPTIVITY AND THE PAPACY (1308–1377). This was the period when the Holy See was relocated from its traditional seat in Rome to Avignon, France, comparing it to the 70 years when the Hebrews were exiled from Israel to Babylon. Philip IX (the Fair) defied POPE BONIFACE VIII (1294–1303) by abridging the power of ecclesiastical courts to exempt clergy who violated civil law from prosecution, while controlling the forwarding of moneys collected in French churches to Rome. This French ruler also established the legitimacy of royal taxation of clergy and clerical institutions during national emergencies and eventually persuaded Pope CLEMENT XI (1305–1314), himself French, to transfer the papacy from Rome to Avignon, an archdiocese on the left bank of the Rhone River in southwest France. This was effectuated in 1308.

French Catholics were pleased to have the capital of the church shifted from a turbulent Rome to Avignon, a thriving center of Latin Christendom. Under French pressure, Clement appointed nine French cardinals and backed away from the overriding claims and exclusive prerogatives Boniface had reserved for the church and the papacy in his bull *Unam Sanctam*, 1302. Nostalgia for the Eternal City and the apparent subordination of the pope to French authority left most segments of Roman Catholicism disturbed. Special appeals were directed to the Avignon popes for the return of St. Peter's throne to Rome. St. Catherine of Siena and St. Bridget of Stockholm, two champions of church reform and spiritual renewal, undertook personal pleas to Pope GREGORY XI (1370–1378). Whatever may have been his ultimate intentions, Gregory's visit to Rome in 1377 and his death there a year later are accepted as the end of the papal–church captivity. The Avignonese episode, however, provoked the Great Western Schism (see Schism) (1378–1417).

For further reference: Guillaume Mollat, *The Popes at Avignon, 1305–1378*, trans. from the French by Janet Love (London: Nelson, 1963); Ludwig Pastor, *The History of the*

Popes from the Close of the Middle Ages, Drawn from the Secret Archives of the Vatican and Other Original Sources, trans. from the German, 40 vols. (St. Louis: Herder, 1923–1969); Yves Renouard, *The Avignon Papacy, 1305–1403,* trans. from the French by Denis Behtell (London: Faber and Faber, 1970).

Ronald S. Cunsolo

BASEL (FERRARA-FLORENCE), COUNCIL OF (1431–1449). Intent on the reform of the church but exhausted by the task of restoring a unified papacy, the Council of Constance (see Constance, Council of) (1414–1418) passed the decree *Frequens,* mandating periodic councils. MARTIN V (1417–1431) convoked the Council of Basel in 1431, and named Cardinal Julian Cesarini LEGATE. When Martin died, EUGENE IV (1431–1447), his successor, confirmed this convocation. The council opened on 23 July 1431, presided over by deputies appointed by Eugene. Attendance was feeble, leading Cesarini to attempt to recruit greater numbers for the council. Informed of the poor attendance and the invitation sent to the Hussites, Eugene directed Cesarini to dissolve the council and convoke another in Bologna.

Cesarini, fearing the consequences, urged the POPE to reconsider. The fathers at Basel refused to disperse and reaffirmed the decrees of Constance that asserted the superiority of the council over the pope. They demanded the pope and cardinals attend the council or risk condemnation. For some two years the council and the papacy dueled. The council received increasing support from the princes. It brought the Hussites to Basel and reincorporated them into the Catholic world by the signing of the *Compactata,* which granted some of their demands. Eventually, worn out by the contest and driven from Rome by insurgents, Eugene withdrew his dissolution of the council on 15 December 1433.

Flush from its victory over the pope, the council tackled reform by questioning curial privileges. It struck down papal rights to grant benefices by demanding local elections. It forbade annates being paid to Rome and restricted appeals to Roman courts. High on both the papal and conciliar agendas was the Greek SCHISM. Desperate for aid against the Turks, the Byzantine emperor sought to end the schism to secure Latin military aid. Both the pope and the council courted the Greeks, who accepted the papal invitation to a council to be held in an Italian city. Eugene moved to transfer the council to Ferrara to meet with the Greeks. But Basel insisted that the Greeks come there or to some non-Italian city. A minority at Basel sided with Eugene and voted to move to Ferrara. A majority remained at Basel, deposed Eugene, and elected Duke Amadeus VIII of Savoy as Pope FELIX V (1439–1449). The civil authorities remained neutral, supporting the reforms of Basel but recognizing Eugene as pope. Basel gradually lost support. In 1449, after the resignation of Felix V, it elected NICHOLAS V (1447–1455), who dissolved the council on 25 April 1449.

The Greeks gathered at Ferrara and then at Florence to discuss reunion with the Latins. Discussions centered on the addition of the *filioque* to the creed, purgatory, the Eucharist, and the primacy. The exchanges were frequent and lively. Agreement was reached on these issues, and the union of the churches was promulgated on 6 July 1439. It was approved by all but one of the Greek prelates. The impulse for unity carried over to effect reunions with the Armenians (1439), the Copts (1442), and the Chaldeans and Maronites of Cyprus (1445). Unfortunately, the reunion with the Greeks proved short-lived. Popular reaction in Constantinople forced the Greek prelates to repudiate it. Constantinople fell in 1453, due, in part, to the lack of Western military support.

For further reference: Anthony Black, *Council and Commune. The Conciliar Movement and the Fifteenth Century Heritage* (Shepherdstown, WV: Patmos Press, 1979); D. J. Geanakoplos, *The Council of Florence (1438–39) and the Problem of Union between the Byzantine and Latin West* (Oxford: Basil Blackwell, 1966); J. M. Hussey, *The Orthodox Church in the Byzantine Empire* (Oxford: Clarendon Press, 1986); Joachim W. Stieber, *Pope Eugenius IV, The Council of Basel and the Secular and Ecclesiastical Authorities in the Empire* (Leiden: E. J. Brill, 1978).

Richard J. Kehoe

BAVARIA, CONCORDAT OF 1924 WITH VATICAN. The Weimer Constitution left to the Reich the prerogative of establishing principles for the regulation of church organizations, education, and state financial support of the churches. On the other hand, it gave the states legal competence in church–state affairs and in the administration of education and allowed each the right to maintain relations with the Holy See. When the Reich government informed the states during January 1921 of its intention to negotiate a Reich CONCORDAT, Bavaria and most of the other states announced their opposition to a general Reich treaty.

A renegotiation of Bavaria's Concordat of 1817 had already begun in 1919. It appears that the Vatican favored the conclusion of a Bavarian treaty prior to one with the Reich because of Bavaria's long-standing diplomatic relations with the Vatican, its strong Catholicity, and the Vatican's reluctance to offend Bavaria's particularism. A Bavarian concordat generous to the church might also serve as a precedent for treaties the Vatican expected to sign with the other states and the Reich. The papal NUNCIO, Eugenio Pacelli, who negotiated the treaty, attempted to maximize the rights of the church. The concordat was very important to PIUS XI (1922–1939), who supervised and approved all of its provisions.

Concluded on 29 March 1924, it was ratified by the Bavarian Parliament in January 1925. The concordat did not meet with the unanimous approval of Catholics and some of the bishops. There was considerable protest over the education clauses, which were opposed by the Bavarian Teacher's Association and the Evangelical League. Its provisions were formulated in fourteen articles. Most explicated the responsibilities of the state to the church (art. 1–11), with two (art. 12–13) listing the responsibilities of the church to the state. Catholics were guaranteed religious freedom. The church was granted the right to legislate for its members. No restrictions were to be placed on the establishment of religious orders. As under the Concordat of 1817, the church was to receive financial support from the state, which was extended to include seminaries for minors. Although the Bavarian state had desired to maintain some involvement in the selection of ecclesiastical authorities, the church was granted complete freedom (art. 14). All bishops and chief administrators of religious orders had to be German citizens. Diocesan borders were not be altered without state consent (art. 12), which it was hoped would prevent a separation of the Saar from the dioceses of Speyer and Trier. In fact, the Bavarian concordat was suspended there until the Saar was returned to Germany.

The educational provisions were the most important. Church schools were protected. Religious instruction was to be continued in state middle and higher schools. Religious instructors had to have the approval of the diocesan bishops. The church was guaranteed control over the education of the clergy and had to be consulted on appointments to Catholic theological faculties at state institutions. The state was obligated to dismiss those professors whose teaching or conduct the church found objectionable.

The church had succeeded in extending its rights and privileges over those that had been granted in 1817. A strong precedent for future concordats in Germany had been established. With the treaty, Bavaria acquired diplomatic support for its efforts to protect its rights against the claims of the Weimar Republic. The agreement was perhaps the last symbol of Bavarian sovereignty and historic identity. It also represented a victory for conservative Catholic forces in their long struggle against liberalism and secularism.

For further reference: Ernst C. Helmreich, *The German Churches under Hitler* (Detroit: Wayne State University Press, 1979); Lothar Schoppe, *Kondordate seit 1800* (Frankfurt am Main: Verlag, 1964); Stuart Stehlin, *Weimar and the Vatican, 1919–1933* (Princeton, NJ: Princeton University Press, 1983).

Joseph A. Biesinger

BENEDICT I (575–579). A native Roman, Benedict I was elected POPE shortly after the death of JOHN III (561–574) in 574. Like his predecessor, he had to wait for imperial confirmation of his election, in his case almost seven months. Little is known about the particulars of his reign aside from the fact that he took active steps to strengthen his administrative staff and strove to promote good relations with the imperial government. During Benedict's reign the Lombards pushed more aggressively into southern Italy, in 579 laying siege to Rome. Imperial troops sent by Justin II proved unable to lift the siege, and grain ships sent from Egypt provided only temporary relief for the city's inhabitants. Benedict I died during the siege and was buried in the sacristy of St. Peter's.

For further reference: J. N. D. Kelly, *The Oxford Dictionary of Popes* (New York: Oxford University Press, 1986); *New Catholic Encyclopedia* (1967), vol. 2, p. 271.

Patrick J. McNamara

BENEDICT II (684–685). Having served POPES AGATHO (678–681) and LEO II (682–683), Benedict, a Roman, was consecrated in June 684 after the chair of St. Peter sat vacant for nearly a year due to lack of approval from the emperor. Benedict convinced Constantine IV (668–685) that to minimize the delay between the selection of a new pontiff and his consecration, the approval of the clergy, people of Rome, and the exarch in Italy was sufficient. He continued Leo II's policy of persuading Western churches to agree to the condemnation of monothelitism agreed to at the Sixth Council, that of CONSTANTINOPLE III, (680–681). Another notable achievement involved the restoration of churches, including St. Peter's. Proclaimed a saint in 1964, Benedict was named patron of Europe by Pope PAUL VI. His feast day is celebrated on 8 May.

For further reference: Joseph S. Brusher, *Popes through the Ages* (Princeton: D. Van Nostrand, 1964); H. K. Mann, *The Lives of the Popes in the Early Middle Ages* (London: K. Paul, 1902–1932). The best beginning primary source remains the *Liber Pontificalis* (Paris, 1886–1892).

John C. Horgan

BENEDICT III (855–858). Benedict's ascendancy to the papacy, in contrast to his uneventful reign, occurred amid intense struggles between pro- and anti-Carolingian factions within Rome. The anti-Carolingian party insisted that the chair of St. Peter should be reserved for candidates from noble, Roman families. Nominated to succeed LEO IV (847–855), Benedict's consecration was postponed when pro-Carolingian forces, led by their candidate Anastasius, secured the Lateran palace by force and imprisoned Benedict. Word of the usurpation provoked a hostile public reaction against Anastasius, thereby forcing Emperor Louis II to withdraw support for his nomination. Benedict successfully struck a deal with Louis, details of which remain unknown, removed Anastasius from the Lateran, and confined him to a monastery for the remainder of his life.

For further reference: Eric John, ed., *The Popes: A Concise Biographical Dictionary* (New York: Hawthorn Books, 1964); H. K. Mann, *The Lives of the Popes in the Early Middle Ages* (London: K. Paul, 1902–1932). The best beginning primary source remains the *Liber Pontificalis* (Paris, 1886–1892).

John C. Horgan

BENEDICT IV (900–903). This upper-class Roman cleric, who succeeded JOHN IX (898–900), saw his election to the chair of St. Peter marred by violent struggles within Rome and the church between supporters and opponents of his predecessor, FORMOSUS (891–896). The few details of his reign highlight continued involvement in political, rather than ecclesiastical, issues. Benedict supported King Louis ("the Blind") of Provence (887–928) against Berenger I of Friuli (850–924), king of Italy, in their struggles for control of Italy and the empire. Louis gained the upper hand momentarily when Berenger's forces suffered a humiliating defeat by the Magyars in 899, thus providing the opportunity for Benedict to crown Louis emperor in 901. In time, Berenger regrouped, defeating Louis' forces in 902 thus leaving Rome without a secular protector. An unrelated incident in Germany, again originating from a political dispute, caused Benedict to excommunicate (see Excommunication) a group who had murdered the archbishop of Rheims.

For further reference: Eric John, ed., *The Popes: A Concise Biographical Dictionary* (New York: Hawthorn Books, 1964); H. K. Mann, *The Lives of the Popes in the Early Middle Ages* (London: K. Paul, 1902–1932). The best beginning primary source remains the *Liber Pontificalis* (Paris, 1886–1892).

John C. Horgan

BENEDICT V (964). Benedict, of Roman origin, favored reform in the church and was described by contemporaries as moral, devout, and learned. Although he apparently took part in the election of Pope LEO VIII (963–965) in 963, after the temporary deposition of JOHN XII (955–964), Benedict did not play a part in the factional strife of the period or John's deposition of Leo. On John's death, the Romans sent envoys to Emperor Otto I, asking his support in the election of the reformer Benedict. Although Otto refused, Benedict was elected and enthroned on 22 May 964. The Romans swore to defend him at all costs, while Benedict hurled anathemas at Otto's army, which besieged the city. Starved into submission, the Romans were forced to surrender Benedict. A synod was immediately held in the Lateran, presided over by Leo and Otto, which condemned Benedict as a usurper. Refusing to defend himself, he was deposed on 23 June 964 and divested of his pontifical robes and insignia, while his pastoral staff (the first mention of such a papal emblem) was broken over his head by Leo. On Otto's intervention he was allowed to retain the rank of deacon and exiled to Hamburg. He died there in 966, deeply revered for his saintly life. In 988 his remains were returned to Rome.

For further reference: L. Duchesne, ed., *Liber Pontificalis* (Paris: E. de Boccard, 1955); H. K. Mann, *The Lives of the Popes in the Early Middle Ages* (London: K. Paul, 1902–1932).

William Roberts

BENEDICT VI (973–974). Benedict reigned from 19 January 973 to July 974, but little is known of his background except that he was Roman and had became a monk. The circumstances of his election remain obscure. The rising Roman family of Crescentii had backed their own candidate, the deacon Franco, but Benedict had the support of the imperial party and reformists opposed to a purely political candidate. Most likely elected in September or October 972, the delay in his consecration was caused by the necessity of obtaining the authorization of the emperor Otto I.

At this point the Crescentii had to accept the election and consecration of Benedict. He embarked on policies characteristic of the Ottonian popes, confirming the precedence of Trier as the oldest see in Germany, favoring reforming monasteries, and forbidding bishops to charge fees for ordinations and consecrations. The death of Otto in May 973 undermined his position, and a year later, at a time when the new emperor, the nineteen-year-old Otto II (973–983) was preoccupied with troubles in Germany, a Roman party rose against him. Very likely the Byzantines, eager to exploit the crisis in the empire and overthrow German rule in Italy, played a part in the revolt. In June 974, Benedict was seized by the rebels and imprisoned in Castel Sant'Angelo to await trial. The deacon Franco was hastily elected and consecrated as pope with the name BONIFACE VII. The imperial representative demanded Benedict's release, but in vain. Boniface had him strangled. Shortly afterward in that same year, Otto forced the deacon Franco to flee and take refuge in Constantinople.

For further reference: L. Duchesne, ed., *Liber Pontificalis* (Paris: E. de Boccard, 1955); H. K. Mann, *The Lives of the Popes in the Early Middle Ages* (London: K. Paul, 1902–1932).

William Roberts

BENEDICT VII (974–983). A Roman aristocrat, the son of a kinsman of Prince Alberic II who had earlier ruled Rome, Benedict VII reigned as POPE from October 974 to 10 July 983. Connected to the powerful Crescentii family, he had the approval of the emperor's representative, who refused to accept the antipope BONIFACE VII (974, 984–985). In 974 a new election was held. Benedict emerged as a sensible compromise: he was the candidate of the imperial party but was acceptable to the noble families of Rome. Boniface was excommunicated (see Excommunication) but from southern Italy he carried out a coup in the summer of 980, forcing the pope to leave Rome. Benedict was able to return only in March 981, when Otto reestablished himself in Italy.

Benedict VII was deeply religious, promoting monastic reforms while collaborating with the emperor. Many of his early decisions settled the status of the major German sees. In 975, for instance, he granted the bishop of Mainz the right to crown the German kings and also confirmed his primacy as apostolic vicar. Upon the emperor Otto's return to Rome in 981 there were even closer relations with the empire. The emperor was present with Benedict at an important synod in March of that year that issued a prohibition of simony. At the Lateran synod of 9–10 September 981 the pope, in agreement with the emperor's wishes, suppressed the diocese of Merseburg. Benedict also supported Otto's policies in southern Italy, making Salerno an archepiscopal see and establishing a Latin diocese at Trani, independent of Byzantine-controlled Bari.

Despite his compliance with the emperor's wishes, the reign of Benedict VII witnessed an enhancement of the Holy See in the eyes of the Christian West.

Visits by leading clerics and laity (the AD LIMINA VISITS "to the threshold" of the apostles Peter and Paul: technically an official visit to the Holy See) became more frequent, and the practice of referring issues directly to the pope increased. Not only did patriarch Sergius seek refuge in Rome, but James, the elected bishop of Carthage, came to Rome to be consecrated because of difficult conditions at home. Benedict was buried in S. Croce in Gerusalemme.

For further reference: L. Duchesne, ed., *Liber Pontificalis* (Paris: E. de Boccard, 1955); H. K. Mann, *The Lives of the Popes in the Early Middle Ages* (London: K. Paul, 1902–1932).

William Roberts

BENEDICT VIII (1012–1024). His pontificate ran from 17 May 1012 to 9 April 1024. Following political upheaval and rivalry in Rome, the second son of Count Gregory of Tusculum crushed the Crescentians and assumed the papacy under the name of Benedict, while his brother, later JOHN XIX (1024–1032), seized the Roman civil government. Following his coronation, a synod was called wherein Benedict consecrated his half brother Arnold and yielded to the request of Henry to subscribe to the northern practice of singing the creed at mass. Subsequently, Benedict and Henry relocated to Ravenna. Another synod was convoked calling for a minimum age for ordination and legislating against simony and other abuses. Benedict's achievements include the restoration of relations with the royal house of Germany. He also suggested that Henry visit Rome, which he did in February 1014, where he was crowned emperor in St. Peter's.

An effective soldier and administrator, Benedict campaigned to make Rome the center of Italy. By force of arms, Benedict restored papal authority in Roman Tuscany and Campagna. In a sea battle, he liberated Sardinia in 1016 and, in alliance with Pisa and Genoa, defeated the Arab invaders in north Italy. In 1019, the Byzantines crushed the insurgents at Cannae. This led Benedict to Germany to seek Henry's assistance. Henry and Benedict convened at Bamberg in 1020, where Henry bestowed on Benedict an imperial privilege reflecting that of Otto I. Henry also promised Benedict military aid. In 1022 his promise was fulfilled, as Henry, accompanied by Benedict, led a powerful army into southern Italy, halting the Byzantine advances. Although not a spiritual man, Benedict was a man of action who enhanced the prestige of the papacy.

For further reference: Matthew Bunson, *The Pope Encyclopedia* (New York: Crown Trade Paperbacks, 1995); J. N. D., Kelly, *The Oxford History of Popes* (New York: Oxford University Press, 1986).

Patrick McGuire

BENEDICT IX (1032–1044, 1045, 1047–1048). After the death of his two brothers, BENEDICT VIII (1012–1024) and JOHN XIX (1024–1032), Alberic III, count of Tusculan, procured the election for one of his sons, Theophylact, who ruled as Benedict IX. He was the only POPE to occupy the throne for three separate periods: 1032–1044, when he was driven out of Rome by a revolt; 1045, when he abdicated after two months, apparently selling the office; and 1047–1048, when he was finally deposed by the Holy Roman Emperor Henry III. During the years he occupied the papacy he was dissolute and duplicitous— one of the worst popes prior to the Gregorian reforms of the late eleventh century.

Benedict was not an ordained priest when elected pope. In 1036 he was driven out of Rome, but he regained his throne the following year with the help of the Holy Roman Emperor Conrad II (1024–1039). In September 1044 Benedict was driven out again. By 20 January 1045 the rival Crescentian family, hoping to regain control of the city they had lost to the Tusculans in 1012, obtained the election of Bishop John of Sabina, who took the title of SYLVESTER III (1045). He reigned less than two months and is considered an ANTIPOPE by some.

Benedict, never formally deposed, excommunicated (see Excommunication) Sylvester and returned to Rome on 10 March 1045, with help from his brothers. But then, desiring to marry a cousin, he apparently sold Tusculan influence for the election of his godfather, John Gratian, and resigned on 1 May. Gratian, who took the title of GREGORY VI (1045), apparently wanted to reform the papacy but had to contend with both Sylvester III and Benedict, who quickly had a change of heart and decided to reclaim his office. Hildebrand, the Cluniac monk who later became Pope GREGORY VII (1073–1085), appealed to Gratian's conscience and persuaded him to resign because he had committed simony. The Holy Roman Emperor Henry III (1039–1056), successor to Conrad II, came down to Italy with his troops (1046) and called a series of synods, which confirmed the resignations of Benedict IX and Gregory VI and deposed Sylvester III. The emperor then nominated as their replacement Suidger, bishop of Bamberg. He was installed on 25 December 1046 but died on 9 October 1047. Benedict returned with an army, retook the city and the papacy on 8 November, and ruled until 16 July 1048, when the count Boniface of Tuscany forced him out on orders from the emperor.

Another imperial candidate, Poppo von Beyern, bishop of Brixon, was installed as DAMASUS II (1048) on 17 July but died on 9 August. In 1049 St. Bruno of Egisheim, a cousin of the emperor, made a barefoot pilgrimage to Rome, hoping to inspire a proper canonical election. He was elected Pope LEO IX (1049–1054), introducing in Rome ecclesiastical reforms that had already been effected in the Germanic lands. Benedict IX died at a monastery in Grottaferrata in the Alban hills in 1055, after failing in several more attempts to retake the papacy.

For further reference: Matthew Bunson, *The Pope Encyclopedia* (New York: Crown Trade Paperbacks, 1995); J. N. D. Kelly, *The Oxford Dictionary of Popes* (New York: Oxford University Press, 1986).

Frank Grande

BENEDICT X, ANTIPOPE (1058–1059). The mid-eleventh century was fraught with turmoil for the papacy: the final division between the Eastern and

Western churches occurred in 1054; the German court's authority and interference in papal politics ceased with the election of STEPHEN X in 1057; and the reformers in the church set their sights on ending the intrusion of the Roman nobility in papal affairs. Benedict's "pontificate" represented a final attempt by the Roman aristocracy to control the papacy. The Roman clergy, desirous of fulfilling Stephen's dying wish, postponed the papal election until the return of Hildebrand, a leading church reformer and later GREGORY VII (1073–1085), from Germany. The nobles, pressing their advantage, chased the cardinals from Rome and, in an irregular consecration, elevated Benedict to the papacy. Benedict performed one official act: extending the pallium to Archbishop Stigand of Canterbury.

While in exile, the cardinals elected NICHOLAS II (1058–1061) in December 1058 as successor to Stephen. Nicholas convened a synod, which promptly excommunicated (see Excommunication) Benedict. In January 1059, he retook Rome, causing Benedict to flee. Later that autumn, Benedict renounced his title and authority and was subsequently imprisoned. In 1060, Benedict, as a result of a public trial conducted by Hildebrand, was sentenced to confinement in the hospice at St. Agnes, where he died and was buried in 1073.

For further reference: H. K. Mann, *The Lives of the Popes in the Early Middle Ages* (London: K. Paul, 1902–1932); Walter Ullman, *A Short History of the Papacy in the Middle Ages* (London: Methuen, 1972). The best beginning primary source remains the *Liber Pontificalis* (Paris, 1886–1892).

John C. Horgan

BENEDICT XI (1303–1304). Benedict's nine-month papacy was devoted to restoring order after the seizure and death of his predecessor, BONIFACE VIII (1294–1303). Nicholas Boccasino was born in Treviso in 1240. He joined the Dominican order at fourteen, became a friar, and was elected Dominican provincial for Lombardy in 1286. He became master-general in 1296 and was created cardinal by Boniface in 1298. Boccasino, a staunch defender of Boniface, was elected POPE ten days after his death, assuming the name Benedict XI, after Boniface's original name, Benedetto. He was 63 at the time of his ascent. In his short reign, Benedict spent much of his time meting out punishment for the outrages committed against Boniface VIII.

The two Colonna cardinals, Giacomo and Pietro, who had been excluded from the papal election, protested the election as invalid. In an effort to promote unity, Benedict forgave them and withdrew their sentence of EXCOMMUNICATION. His leniency was seen by some as weakness, and, given the hostile climate, he was forced to move to Perugia in April 1304. After resolving the split between the CURIA and Colonna cardinals, the larger problem of Philip IV of France required his attention. Considered excommunicated, Philip had not been notified of Benedict's election. In a conciliatory gesture, Philip sent an embassy to Rome in the spring of 1304 to congratulate the new pontiff on his election. Benedict responded by absolving Philip and his family of any guilt and rescinding the order of excommunication that had been established by Boniface. Benedict went so far as to publish a bull overriding Boniface's writ that prohibited princes from taxing their clergy without the consent of Rome.

Establishing firm ties with the French monarchy enabled Benedict to take a firm stand against the major figures behind the uprising against Boniface. On 8 June 1304, Benedict issued the bull *Flagitiosum scelus*, in which he accused Nogaret and sixteen others of criminal acts against Boniface. He ordered all named to appear before him by 29 June or face excommunication. All ignored his command, but, on 7 July, before any further steps could be taken, he died in Perugia of dysentery. Benedict was interred in St. Domenico, and miraculous cures were soon reported at his tomb. He was beatified by CLEMENT XII in 1736.

For further reference: Eric John, *The Popes: A Concise Bibliographical History* (London: Burns and Oates, 1964); H. K. Mann, *The Lives of the Popes in the Early Middle Ages* (London: K. Paul, 1902–1932).

Christopher S. Myers

BENEDICT XII (1334–1342). As a young boy, Jacques Fournier joined the Cistercian house at Boulbonne. After completing his studies in theology, he succeeded his uncle as abbot at Fontfroide. A well-learned theologian, as bishop of Pamiers and later Mirepoix, he cultivated the art of extracting confessions from suspected heretics and is alleged to have sent a few to the stake. In 1327 he was promoted to cardinal-priest of Sta Prisca by JOHN XXII (1316–1334). His main interest as POPE rested in reforming abuses rather than in politics, attempting to restore religious communities to a simple life.

He responded to the controversial theological discussion of beatific vision, which plagued John XXII's papacy (1316–1334), by issuing *Benedictus deus*, which stated that after death, souls would enjoy a face-to-face vision with the Divine. He tried unsuccessfully to prevent the eruption of the Hundred Years' War between England and France and failed to maintain John XXII's efforts to secure the papacy's independence. At the beginning of his papacy, Benedict called for a resolution of the ecclesiastical sanctions imposed by John XXII on Emperor Louis IV the Bavarian. Louis IV seemed receptive until the leaders of France, Naples, and Germany opposed the reconciliation. As a result, the first diet of Frankfurt promulgated the *Fidem Catholicam*, which proclaimed that imperial authority comes from God and not from the chair. At the second diet of Frankfurt, Louis, in 1338, published the imperial law *Licet iuris*, which declared that power, although dependent on God, belonged to him, and the consent of the Holy See was not mandated. Accused of being too legalistic and unimaginative, Benedict has been described as an "unfit and drunken helmsman of the church" by critics dissatisfied with his reforms and the personal grudges of Petrarch. Despite such criticism, Benedict did not succumb to nepotism.

For further reference: Matthew Bunson, *The Pope Encyclopedia* (New York: Crown Trade Paperbacks, 1995); J. N. D. Kelly, *The Oxford Dictionary of Popes* (New York: Oxford University Press, 1985).

Patrick McGuire

BENEDICT XIII (1724–1730). Benedict XIII was born Pietro Francesco Orsini on 2 February 1649 near Bari in southern Italy. Orsini's aristocratic family had already contributed two POPES as well as numerous cardinals to the church. In 1667, at the age of eighteen, the future pope decided to become a Dominican. Only five years later, in 1672, he was appointed a cardinal by CLEMENT X (1670–1676). In 1686 he was sent to Benevento as archbishop, where he would remain for the next thirty-eight years. Orsini's ascetic lifestyle and deep spirituality contributed to his popularity in Benevento. His great display of charity after the earthquakes of 1688 and 1702 increased his esteem among the general public.

Orsini was elected pope on 29 May 1724. The conclave chose Orsini as a compromise candidate. In spite of his unwillingness to accept the position, he was convinced by the general of the Dominican order to do so. Thus, Orsini, now named Benedict XIII, assumed his responsibilities with a reputation for doctrinal strictness and personal asceticism that made many within the church hierarchy uncomfortable. His immediate efforts were directed at a reform of clerical morals and imposing greater discipline upon the church. Benedict was spared the tumultuous times that befell those who followed him during the eighteenth century.

Few question Benedict's sincere spirituality, but his complete dedication to the religious aspects of the papacy was to cause serious damage to the finances and credibility of the Holy See. Throughout the years of his rule, Benedict XIII worked to assure church discipline. Benedict confirmed the bull *Unigenitus* of 1713, which sought to suppress the Jansenists (see Jansenism), and to that end proscribed all of their writings. Within the PAPAL STATES, Benedict XIII sought to lower taxation, promote agriculture, increase commerce, and build hospitals that would aid the needy. Church restorations were ordered, and the facade of St. John Lateran was completed. He wrote three volumes of theological works, which were published at Ravenna in 1728. Benedict XIII died on 21 February 1730 in Rome and is buried in Santa Maria sopra Minerva.

For further reference: F. Gontard, *The Chair of Peter* (New York: Holt, Rinehart, and Winston, 1964); L. Pastor, *The History of the Popes, from the Close of the Middle Ages* (St. Louis: B. Herder, 1923); J. T. Shotwell, *The See of Peter* (New York: Columbia University Press, 1927).

John J. Tinghino

BENEDICT XIII, ANTIPOPE (1394–1417). Pedro de Luna was born in Spain of noble parents in 1342. He joined the CURIA at Avignon, where he was created cardinal in 1375. He accompanied GREGORY XI (1370–1378) to Rome in 1377 and participated in the elections of *Urban VI* (1378–1389) and the antipope CLEMENT VII (1378–1394). A staunch defender of the Avignon papacy, he won the recognition of the kingdoms of the Iberian Peninsula for Clement VII and served as LEGATE to France, Flanders, and Scotland.

Peter was elected to succeed Clement on 28 September 1394 as Benedict XIII. Although he had sworn to resign to end the *Western Schism* (see Schism), he resisted the demands of the French king and the University of Paris to abdicate. France attempted to force his resignation by besieging Avignon for four and a half years. Benedict escaped on 12 March 1403. France again recognized him, and he negotiated with the Roman claimants for their mutual resignations. When this failed, the cardinals of both sides deposed Benedict and his rival at the Council of Pisa and elected ALEXANDER V (1409–1410), who gained the allegiance of most of Europe. Benedict withdrew to Perpignan, Aragon. When he refused to abdicate, the Council of CONSTANCE deposed him on 26 July 1417. He continued to conduct himself as pope until he died on 23 May 1423. His successor, CLEMENT VIII (1423–1429), made his peace with Rome in 1429.

For further reference: M. Creichton, *A History of the Papacy* (New York: AMS Press, 1969); A. Glasfurd, *The Antipope (Peter de Luna. 1342–1423)* (New York: Roy, 1965); G. Pillement, *Pedro de Luna dèrnier Pape d'Avignon* (Paris: Grasset, 1955).

Richard J. Kehoe

BENEDICT XIV (1740–1758). Born Prospero Lorenzo Lambertini on 31 March 1675 in Bologna, this brilliant youngster was sent to Rome to continue his education. By 1694, he had received his doctorate in law and theology at the University of Rome. His ascent through the church hierarchy came quickly, the result of his strict work ethic and a highly pleasing personality. In 1727 he was appointed archbishop of Ancona. In May 1731 CLEMENT XII (1730–1740) transferred Lambertini to Bologna, where he served as archbishop, overseeing the restoration of several churches and the seminary of Bologna. In addition to his temporal concerns, the future POPE published a series of theological works, which were well received.

The conclave that elected Lambertini Pope Benedict XIV lasted approximately six months. Within the PAPAL STATES, Benedict was almost constantly troubled by financial problems, which were becoming endemic. He made a series of attempts to improve the financial health of the Roman Court and his domain. Reductions were made in the size of the militia in Rome, and the army was cut in size. In order to raise revenues, Benedict imposed a special tax, which remained in effect for one year. This tax was applied to a wide array of items, including property and the sale of salt and lime. Benedict also took a serious interest in the missionary work pursued overseas. In 1711 he issued the bull *Immensa pastorum principis*, in which he insisted that the Indians of Brazil and Paraguay receive more humane treatment. In his conduct of foreign affairs, Benedict tried to maintain good relations with the European powers. However, he was no less committed than his predecessors had been in demanding the submission of the Jansenists (see Jansenism) to *Unigenitus*. At the same time he reiterated Clement XII's prohibition against FREEMASONRY.

Benedict XIV initiated a large-scale program of public works. Hospitals were constructed, churches were either built or renovated, the restoration of the Colosseum was commenced, and the Vatican Library was expanded. His dedication to art and learning was made apparent by his brilliant scholarship. He fostered the growth of the University of Rome and improved its faculty. At Bologna a scientific institute was created. Finally, he instructed the congregation of the INDEX to be less zealous in banning works. Benedict XIV was highly regarded throughout Europe during his reign. His intellect, dedication, good nature, and spirituality are cited often in characterizing his papacy. He died on 3 May 1758 in Rome. He is buried in St. Peter's Basilica.

For further reference: Artaud de Montor, *The Lives and Times of the Popes*, trans. from *Les Vies des Papes* (New York: Catholic Publication Society of America, 1911); C. Hollis, *The Papacy* (New York: Macmillan, 1964); F. X. Seppelt and C. Loffler, *A Short History of the Popes* (St. Louis: B. Herder, 1932).

John J. Tinghino

BENEDICT XIV, ANTIPOPE (1425). Even in the aftermath of the Great SCHISM of the Avignon POPES (1378–1417), tensions had not died down. Bernard Garnier, a sacrist of Rodez, was nominated and elected pope by Jean Carrier in a one-man conclave. Carrier had served as vicar-general of the county of Armagnae and cardinal to antipope BENEDICT XIII (1394–1417) of the Avignon obedience. Upon the death of Benedict XIII, three of his cardinals convoked a conclave and elected antipope CLEMENT VIII (1423–1429). Carrier, upon receipt of the news, declared the election invalid, accusing the three cardinals of simony, concealing the death of Benedict, theft from the treasury, and bowing to undue pressure. Carrier also alleged that the new usurper, Clement, was a sinner. No known reason exists for why Carrier waited two years until electing Benedict. The only known act of Benedict's "reign" was to appoint one Jean Farald as a cardinal. Upon Benedict's death, probably in 1433, Farald elected Carrier as pope, who reigned as antipope Benedict XIV the second until his own death.

For further reference: Joseph S. Brusher, *Popes through the Ages* (Princeton: D. Van Nostrand, 1964); J. N. D. Kelly, *The Oxford Dictionary of Popes* (Oxford: Oxford University Press, 1986); Hans Kuhner, *Encyclopedia of the Papacy* (New York: Philosophical Library, 1958).

John C. Horgan

BENEDICT XV (1914–1922). Giacomo Della Chiesa, born 21 November 1854 of an aristocratic Genoese family, was elected Pope Benedict XV on 3 September 1914. After ordination in 1878, he received doctorates in theology (1879) and CANON LAW (1880) and attended the College for Noble Ecclesiastics in Rome. As personal secretary to Cardinal Rampolla del Tindaro, LEO XIII's secretary of state, Della Chiesa developed admirable diplomatic talents. In appearance diminutive and frail and known as "the little one," the POPE's bearing and presence were dignified. Della Chiesa became archbishop of Bologna in 1907 and was elevated to cardinal three months before becoming pope. Elected for his diplomatic skills to guide the church in time of war, he manifested other characteristics befitting an apostle of peace to a war-torn world.

A strong opponent of MODERNISM under PIUS X, Benedict continued this policy with its condemnation in *Ad Beatissimi*, his first encyclical. He was not, however, an integralist, whose restrictiveness he deplored. In this first of twelve encyclicals Benedict expressed his goals, principal among them the establishment of peace between nations and social classes and within the church. In *Humani generis* he emphasized the importance of utilizing Holy Scripture in preaching. In fact, Benedict can be credited for the church's emphasis on the Bible in the twentieth century. Most of his other ENCYCLICALS published between 1919 to 1921 included appeals for the children of Europe and prayers for the peace conference and for Christian principles of peace.

A comprehensive codification of canon law, initiated by Pius X, was published on 28 June 1917. It was an unprecedented accomplishment. Benedict himself established rules for the teaching of the code and founded the commission for its interpretation. Extensive charitable work was characteristic of Benedict's pontificate and extended from the hospitalization of sick prisoners of war to large gifts of money, food, and medicine. Gifts were distributed throughout Europe from France to Lithuania. Relief efforts were made in Russia during the civil war and famine. Church–state relations between Italy and the Vatican improved during Benedict's pontificate. Reversing his predecessor's distrust of Catholic political parties independent of ecclesiastical control, Benedict permitted Don Luigi Sturzo to establish the POPULAR PARTY in December 1918. Just prior to the 1919 Italian elections, the pope removed the restrictions on Catholic political participation imposed by the *non expedit*.

Benedict was radical, perhaps revolutionary, in reorganizing the church's missionary activity. In his encyclical *Maximum Illud* (30 November 1919), he insisted on the establishment of native clergies and hierarchies. Breaking the church's connection with imperialism, Benedict condemned nationalism among missionaries and insisted that they respect native cultures. To establish native clergies and episcopates, he reorganized the Society for the Propagation of the Faith and organized the Missionary Union of the Clergy. WORLD WAR I had calamitous consequences on orthodox Christians in the East. Benedict reversed the policies of Pius X that had sought to Romanize the Eastern Uniate Churches. He created the Sacred CONGREGATION of the Eastern Church in order to protect the interests of Eastern Catholics, while opening the newly formed Pontifical Institute to orthodox students.

Benedict was a pope of peace and bridge builder between nations. He made numerous attempts to end the war, but his efforts were misunderstood and rejected. Yet, by the end of World War I, the prestige of the Holy See had improved worldwide.

For further reference: M. C. Carlen, *Dictionary of Papal Pronouncements: Leo XIII to Pius XII, 1878–1957* (New York, 1958); Carlo Falconi, *The Popes of the Twentieth Century* (London: Weidenfeld and Nicolson, 1967); Walter H. Peters, *The Life of Benedict XV* (Milwaukee: Bruce, 1959).

Joseph A. Biesinger

BERNETTI, CARDINAL TOMMASO. Born at Fermo on 29 December 1779, Bernetti entered the papal administration in 1802 and rose rapidly in it, though he never took holy orders and remained a deacon. After serving as delegate of Ferrara from 1816 to 1820, he was appointed governor of Rome and head of the papal police. Pope LEO XII (1823–1829) named him a cardinal in 1827 and appointed him secretary of state in 1828–1829. At the conclave of 1830–1831, he secured the election of Pope GREGORY XVI (1831–1846), who appointed him secretary of state (1831–1836). He was at once faced with the revolution of 1831, which he repressed with the aid of Austrian troops. Thereafter, he sought to follow a neutral policy, but the continued threat of revolution made the papacy dependent on Austrian protection.

Conservative at heart, under Austrian pressure he introduced some reforms into the papal government, though they proved inadequate to win popular support for his regime. Hoping to create a military basis for papal authority, thus escaping from dependence on Austria, in 1832 he organized a paramilitary force, the Centurions. However, their extralegal violence aroused more opposition than it quelled and alarmed conservatives. Their influence persuaded the POPE in 1836 to dismiss Bernetti, whose health had by this time suffered under the pressure of his office. He remained an influential figure at Rome until his death at Ferno on 21 March 1852.

For further reference: Emilia Morelli, *La politica estera di Tommaso Bernetti* (Rome: Edizioni di Storia e Letteratura, 1953); Alan J. Reinerman, *Austria and the Papacy in the Age of Metternich*, vol. 2, *Revolution and Reaction, 1830–1838* (Washington, DC: Catholic University Press, 1989).

Alan J. Reinerman

BIRTH CONTROL AND PAPACY. The nineteenth and twentieth centuries' secular views on human sexuality, marriage, and artificial contraception have challenged the relevance of traditional religious authority in moral life. Marriage is seen as an institution invented by human convention, reduced to a civil contract. Likewise, sexuality has increasingly been viewed as a matter of style, with the purpose of sexual acts determined solely by the individuals performing them.

Thus, an ethics of the absolute autonomy of the human will has emerged with the notion that evaluating sexual activity is purely subjective.

In this context, artificial contraception moved from its original use, as a means of preventing the spread of venereal diseases and conception in brothels and other sexual activities outside marriage, to use within marriage. In the past century, the papacy has explored the church's understanding of the nature of marriage, conjugal love, and sexuality in the light of Scripture and the natural moral law. In a series of ENCYCLICALS, including LEO XIII's *Arcanum Divinae Sapientiae* (10 February 1880), PIUS XI's *Casti Connubii* (31 December 1930), and PAUL VI's *Humanae Vitae* (25 July 1968), among others, the POPES have posited that the only proper place for sexual activity is a heterosexual marriage. The core of the papal responses to the secular view of sexuality is that marriage is a holy institution, a sacrament created by God for the good of individuals and members of the community. Marriage is a vocation and a holy covenant where husband and wife are collaborators with God in the transmission of human life.

The papacy has stressed that God as the creator of life has the right to direct what men and women do with the means of procreation. Sex is good in its marital context but out of that context can become destructive of the self and one's relationship to others. Marriage, with its manifold forms of love, has both a unitive and procreative element essential in it. The POPES have stressed that because sex, by its very nature, is intrinsically related to procreation, it finds its proper place only within a monogamous marriage that does not use artificial means to limit the number of children in a family. The reduction of one's partner to a sexual object is not conducive to the development of virtues of enduring charity and benevolent and preferential love at the foundation of successful marriages.

The popes have affirmed there are moral means of controlling the number of children in a marriage that cooperate with the natural periods of infertility in a woman's monthly cycle, in union with the development and practice of Christian virtues of charity and chastity. The popes have also made it clear that there are moral treatments of certain pathological conditions that might, as an unintended, unavoidable side effect, produce either temporary or permanent sterility. However, violent means (artificial contraception) that have as their sole purpose the direct rendering of procreation impossible, are not morally permissible.

Paul VI reaffirmed the preceding in his *Humanae Vitae*, even though a majority of theologians on a commission appointed by John XXIII disagreed. However, subsequent documents, including the new *Catechism of the Catholic Church*, approved by the bishops, confirmed the view of *Humanae Vitae*.

For further reference: Joseph Califano, ''Technology and Violence,'' *Divus Thomas* (Piacenza, 1975); *Catechism of the Catholic Church* (New York: Image Books, 1994); *Humanae Vitae of 25 July 1968 and Evanglium Vitae of 25 March 1995.*

Joseph J. Califano

BONIFACE I (418–422). When POPE ZOSIMUS (417–418) died on 26 December 418, two rival candidates succeeded him in a matter of days: EULAL-

IUS, a deacon, and Jucundus, a priest. Eulalius enlisted the support of the emperor Honorius in Ravenna, but Honorius' imperial sister, Galla Placidia, backed Jocundus, who, as pope, took the name of Boniface I. To settle the dispute, Honorius ordered both contenders to leave Rome, and both initially complied; but then Eulalius marched on Rome with his supporters, provoking a riot and his expulsion. Boniface was declared pope. The appeals of the rival candidates to the imperial court gave it its first opportunity for intervention, thereby establishing a precedent.

In the East, Boniface reaffirmed the authority of the bishop of Thessalonica to act as Rome's vicar among the bishops of Illyricum. Backed by Honorius, he prevailed on Theodosius II to say he would rescind his earlier call for the bishop of Constantinople to exercise in the Eastern empire what had been the "privileges of ancient Rome," but, in fact, the practice became part of the Theodosiasian code and thus a "most fertile seed of future SCHISM."

Of abiding influence was Boniface I's intervention in the struggle against Pelagianism. He called on St. Augustine to answer letters sent to ZOSIMUS by Julian of Eclanum and eighteen other Pelagian bishops. In his replies to Boniface, Augustine worked out his "doctrine of predestinating grace." Later, in a letter to the Synod of Corinth (11 March 422), Boniface insisted that it has "never been lawful for what has once been decided by the apostolic see to be reconsidered." Those words have earned him a place in the *Enchiridion Symbolorum* on "matters of faith and morals." Boniface, a staunch Augustinian in spirit, died on 4 September 422 and was buried in Rome. Subsequently, he was named a saint.

For further reference: E. Caspar, *Geschichte des Papstums von den Anfängen bis zur Höhe der Weltherrschaf*, vol. 1 (Tübingen: Verlag von J. C. B. Mohr [Paul Siebeck], pp. 359–364; J. N. D. Kelly, *The Oxford Dictionary of Popes* (Oxford: Oxford University Press, 1986).

Henry Paolucci

BONIFACE II (530–532). Born in Rome, Boniface was the first POPE of German lineage. He served as an archdeacon under Pope FELIX IV (526–530), who, upon his deathbed, formally named Boniface as his successor. Felix desired to secure a pontiff favorable to the imperial court in Ravenna. At the time of Felix's death, however, the bulk of the Roman clergy refused to accept Boniface, electing the deacon Dioscorus of Alexandria. DIOSCORUS died on 14 October 526, after a reign of only twenty-two days, and with his passing the recalcitrant Roman clergy finally accepted Boniface.

At a synod held in St. Peter's in 531, Boniface proposed a constitution granting him the right to appoint his own successor, and he forced the clergy to take an oath subscribing to the legitimacy of this action. In the face of imperial protest, however, he was forced to revoke the document at a subsequent synod. During the year 531 Boniface confirmed the Acts of the Second Council of Orange (529), which ended the controversy over semi-Pelagianism. After the patriarch of Constantinople had deposed and excommunicated (see Excommunication) the bishop of Larissa (Greece), Boniface held a synod in 532, declaring this action invalid, since Larissa came under Roman jurisdiction. Boniface II is buried in St. Peter's.

For further reference: J. N. D. Kelly, *The Oxford Dictionary of Popes* (New York: Oxford University Press, 1986); *New Catholic Encyclopedia* (1967), vol. 2, pp. 669–670.

Patrick J. McNamara

BONIFACE III (607). Born in Rome of a Greek family, Boniface first came to notice in 603, when GREGORY I (590–604) appointed him NUNCIO to Constantinople. It is generally assumed that he was still in Constantinople when his predecessor, SABINIAN (604–606), died in February 606, because Boniface was not elected until February 607. He reigned less than ten months, during which he continued to defend the independence of the papacy. The emperor Phocas (603–610), who had usurped the throne, sought to regularize relations with Rome and therefore asked Gregory to appoint a nuncio. As part of his mission, Boniface was able to secure from Phocas a declaration that the See of Rome was head of all the churches, thereby opposing the claims to worldwide jurisdiction that many considered to be implicit in the title of "ecumenical patriarch."

After his election, Boniface summoned a council, which decreed that at least three days must pass between the death of one POPE and the election of his successor. Any discussion of the election in the interim was ruled anathema. Boniface died 12 November 607 and was buried in St. Peter's. He was succeeded by BONIFACE IV (608–615).

For further reference: Matthew Bunson, *The Pope Encyclopedia* (New York: Crown Trade Paperbacks, 1995); J. N. D. Kelly, *The Oxford Dictionary of the Popes* (New York: Oxford University Press, 1986).

Frank Grande

BONIFACE IV (608–615). Dedicated to GREGORY I (492–496), Boniface IV sought to imitate this saintly predecessor. His consecration was delayed for ten months after the election, until official approval was received from Constantinople. As POPE he continued in his monastic lifestyle, converting the papal residence into a monastery. In 609 the emperor Phocas allowed Boniface to convert the Roman Pantheon into a Christian church, the basilica of Sancta Maria ad Martyres. This was the first time a pagan temple had been turned into a church. In 610 Boniface held a synod in Rome dedicated to the renewal of the monastic life. At that time the pope conferred with Mellitus, the first bishop of London. He presented Mellitus a copy of the decrees of the synod, along with papal letters addressed to the archbishop of Canterbury, the king of Kent, and the English people. During Boniface's reign, several Lombard bishops in northern Italy continued to reject the Second Council of Constantinople's (see Constantinople II, Council of) condemnation of the Three Chapters. Boniface IV died in 615 and was later declared a saint. He is buried in St. Peter's.

For further reference: J. N. D. Kelly, *The Oxford Dictionary of Popes* (New York: Oxford University Press, 1986); *New Catholic Encyclopedia* (1967), vol. 2, p. 670.

Patrick J. McNamara

BONIFACE V (619–625). A native of Naples, little is known about Boniface's early life. Like many of the POPES of the early church, Boniface waited thirteen months between his election and consecration for the emperor's approval. Once in office, Boniface favored the secular clergy over monastics, a reaction against GREGORY I (590–604), who, as the first monk to become pope, promoted monasticism by granting monks special privileges and admitting them into his immediate circle of advisers. Boniface enacted legislation preserving the rights of priests to transfer the relics of martyrs and disallowing monks from acting as substitutes at baptisms. Boniface also renewed Gregory's decree establishing Canterbury as the metropolitan of all Britain; commanded that the sanctity of wills drawn up by the clergy or ecclesiastical notaries be maintained; and confirmed the right of asylum in the churches as a means of protection for those fleeing persecution.

For further reference: Eric John, ed., *The Popes: A Concise Biographical Dictionary* (New York: Hawthorn Books, 1964); H. K. Mann, *The Lives of the Popes in the Early Middle Ages* (London: K. Paul, 1902–1932). The best beginning primary source remains the *Liber Pontificalis* (Paris, 1886–1892).

John C. Horgan

BONIFACE VI (896). The late ninth century was a period of turmoil in the West with the disintegration of the Carolingian empire. Anti-German riots had broken out in Rome against the German emperor Arnulf (896–899), whom Pope FORMOSUS (891–896) had crowned Holy Roman Emperor over the objections of native Italians who supported Duke Guido III of Spoleto. Guido, crowned emperor by Pope STEPHEN V (885–891), threatened the papacy, causing Formosus to summon Arnulf to defend Rome. A mob forced the election of Boniface upon Formosus' death in reaction to the latter's actions. A Roman by birth, Boniface was the son of the bishop Hadrian. His early career in the church was tinged with scandal and immorality, which led to his being degraded (reduced to lay state) twice by JOHN VIII (872–882). Boniface died from gout after a pontificate of only fifteen days (there is some speculation that he may have been removed to provide for the accession of STEPHEN VI). He was condemned by JOHN IX (898–900) in 898 as an intruder, and his election was declared null.

For further reference: Joseph S. Brusher, *Popes through the Ages* (Princeton: D. Van Nostrand, 1964); H. K. Mann, *The Lives of the Popes in the Early Middle Ages* (London:

K. Paul, 1902–1932). The best beginning primary source remains the *Liber Pontificalis* (Paris, 1886–1892).

John C. Horgan

BONIFACE VII, ANTIPOPE (974, 984–985). As the tenth century drew to a close, struggles over secular power in Rome, particularly among the aristocratic families, affected papal integrity. In a struggle over the succession to JOHN XIII (965–972), Boniface's candidacy, supported by the Crescentii, Rome's most powerful family, clashed with Emperor Otto I's (962–973) choice. Upon the death of Otto I and while his successor, Otto II (973–984) was preoccupied with German matters, the Crescentii engineered a successful uprising in June 974 against Benedict, cast him into prison, and consecrated Boniface. However, the Roman people revolted against Boniface, forcing him to flee. Once order was restored, BENEDICT VII (974–983) convened a synod, which promptly excommunicated (see Excommunication) Boniface.

In 980, during Benedict's absence from Rome, Boniface attempted an unsuccessful coup and fled again, this time to Constantinople. Returning to Rome in 984 upon the death of Otto II, Boniface, supported by his allies and Byzantine funding, overthrew Benedict's successor, JOHN XIV (983–984) and reassumed the papal chair. John was first imprisoned and subsequently killed. Within a year, Boniface was dead, possibly the result of an assassination. Despised by the people of Rome, his body was stripped naked, dragged through the streets, and mutilated. Two known acts of Boniface's papacy were the consecration of a church honoring St. Benedict and the coining of money bearing both his and the emperor's name. Although Boniface is generally classified as an ANTIPOPE, he was regarded by tenth-century contemporaries as a bona fide POPE.

For further reference: Eric John, ed., *The Popes: A Concise Biographical Dictionary* (New York: Hawthorn Books, 1964); Walter Ullman, *A Short History of the Papacy in the Middle Ages* (London: Methuen, 1972). The best beginning primary source remains the *Liber Pontificalis* (Paris, 1886–1892).

John C. Horgan

BONIFACE VIII (1294–1303). Born Benedict Gaetani at Anagni around 1235, this aristocratic POPE was the last significant upholder of the concept of Christendom under a papal monarchy, in the tradition of GREGORY VII (1073–1085), INNOCENT III (1198–1216), and INNOCENT IV (1243–1254). After studies in Roman and CANON LAW at Bologna, Gaetani entered the papal service, earning a reputation as an upholder of the more authoritarian claims of the papacy. At the end of 1294, he helped obtain the abdication of the holy, but incompetent, Pope CELESTINE V (1294). Shortly thereafter, on 24 December, he was elected to the papal throne.

Boniface's pontificate was beset by numerous enemies, including the Franciscan Spirituals (see Franciscans), who had been favored by Celestine and who regarded his abdication as invalid. Another significant force was the noble house of Colonna, feudal rivals to the pope's family and patrons of Celestine. Boniface made the situation worse by his nepotism. He was confronted with problems in the kingdom of Sicily and the empire, but the greatest of Boniface's difficulties was with Philip IV of France. Philip IV was determined to assert his sovereignty, while Boniface proved equally determined to preserve the papal rights propounded by his recent predecessors. The first phase of the struggle arose over the demands of Philip and his rival, Edward I of England, to tax church property to finance their mutual struggle. Boniface issued his bull *Clericis laicos* in 1296, prohibiting taxing the clergy without papal approval and stopping the clergy from paying new imposts. The bull was aimed equally at England and France and in both countries created difficulties. In England, Robert Winchelsey, archbishop of Canterbury, refused further taxation of the clergy, while in France, King Philip prohibited the export of wealth to Rome.

In 1300, Boniface presided over the first Jubilee Year in the history of the church, but his role as visible head of Christendom, exemplified in that celebration, was soon undermined. In 1301 King Philip arrested Bernard Saisset, bishop of Pamiers, on a charge of treason and tried him in a royal court, in defiance of clerical rights of immunity and papal claims to jurisdiction. In the bulls *Ausculta fili* of 1301 and *Unam Sanctam* of 1302, the pope responded with an explicit claim to authority over kings in secular as well as spiritual matters. While Boniface was primarily concerned with the unity of the church and Christendom, his use of intemperate language lost him needed support. At a meeting of the French Estates Général in March 1303, the king's minister, Guillaume de Nogaret, demanded that Boniface be tried before a general council of the church. Departing for Italy, Nogaret made common cause with the Colonnas and on 7 September 1303 seized the person of the pope in what is known as "the terrible day of Anagni." Boniface was released three days later but died in Rome 11 October 1303. Although Boniface VIII championed the independence of the church and the unity of Christendom, his personal flaws and excessive devotion to his family mar his memory.

For further reference: Robert Fawtier, *The Capetian Kings of France* (New York: St. Martin's Press, 1968); H. K. Mann, *The Lives of the Popes in the Early Middle Ages* (London: K. Paul, 1902–1932); Brian Tierney, "Boniface VIII, Pope," *New Catholic Encyclopedia* (1967), vol. 2, pp. 671–673.

William C. Schrader

BONIFACE IX (1389–1404). Boniface IX was born Pietro Tomacelli in Naples c. 1355. He succeeded URBAN VI (1378–1389), thus continuing the Roman obedience and the Western Schism (see Schism). Boniface faced the task of repairing the losses inherited from his predecessor. To assure the support of Naples, Boniface crowned the young Ladislas Durazzo king and supported him with money and troops in his ten-year struggle against Louis of Anjou. He

courted Wenceslas of Bohemia, only to be deceived when the emperor designated Gian Galeazzo Visconti duke of Milan. To pacify the PAPAL STATES,
the POPE turned to the support of condottieri and has been implicated in the
rapacity of these soldiers of fortune. The factious Roman nobility forced him
into long exiles, for example, 1494–1498.

Always in need of money, Boniface extended the fiscal irregularities that
plagued the RENAISSANCE PAPACY. The indulgences he sanctioned for crusades and jubilees were tainted with simony. When challenged, Boniface appealed to the "plenitude of papal power." Boniface's faults prolonged the
Western Schism, but he never wavered in his conviction of the legitimacy of
his claim to the papacy. He renewed the EXCOMMUNICATION of his rival
in Avignon and refused to consider any solution short of the resignation of the
Avignon claimant. When BENEDICT XIII, forced by the French king, offered
to meet Boniface in Italy to end the schism, Boniface raged at the negotiators
and forbade his cardinals to deal with them. He died shortly after in the fall of
1404.

For further reference: John H. Smith, *The Great Schism 1378: The Disintegration of
the Papacy* (New York: Weybright and Talley, 1970); E. Vansteenberghe, "Boniface
IX," *Dictionnaire d'histoire et de géographie ecclésiastiques*, vol. 9 (Paris, 1912),
pp. 909–922.

Richard J. Kehoe

C

CALLISTUS I (217–222). The reign of Callistus is known primarily from the biased account of his critic, the antipope HIPPOLYTUS (217–235). In his youth Callistus had been the slave of a Christian freedman who made him his banker. According to Hippolytus, Callistus was arrested for brawling in a synagogue on the sabbath and was sentenced to labor in the mines of Sardinia. Only when Marcia, the Christian mistress of Emperor Commodus (180–192) asked the POPE, VICTOR I (189–198), for the names of Christians in the mines to obtain their release, was Callistus freed. Then, Victor's successor, ZEPHYRINUS (198–217), made him his principal deacon and adviser. Callistus became the real power in the Roman church and, on that pope's death, was elected pontiff. However, Hippolytus refused to accept his election and got himself elected bishop of a schismatic group.

Callistus' reign was marred by the conflict with this aggressive antipope, who accused him of modalism and laxity of discipline. The charge of modalism can be disregarded since Callistus excommunicated (see Excommunication) Sabellius, the leader of the movement that maintained that the three persons of the Trinity do not represent distinct realities but reflect successive modes of its self-revelation. Hippolytus also complained that Callistus allowed a bishop guilty of grave offenses to remain in office, ordained married men, and did not condemn clergy who had married, readmitting heretics and schismatics to the church without a preliminary penance.

Although Callistus is listed in a fourth-century calendar of martyrs, this is unlikely, in view of the absence of persecution during the reign of Emperor Alexander Severus (222–235). One source describes a violent death, possibly in a riot, indicating that he was buried in Trastevere, on the Via Aurelia, rather than in the cemetery that bears his name. In 1960, his tomb was discovered in the Cemetery of Calepodius on the Via Aurelia, and the crypt was decorated with frescoes depicting his alleged martyrdom. His feast day is 14 October.

For further reference: L. Duchesne, ed., *Liber Pontificalis* (Paris: E. de Boccard, 1955); J. Lebreton and J. Zeiler, *The History of the Primitive Church* (New York: Macmillan, 1948).

William Roberts

CALLISTUS II (1119–1124). Guy, son of Count William of Burgundy, born in 1050, became archbishop of Vienne in 1088. As archbishop he was an indefatigable champion of reform, leading the attack on Pope PASCHAL II's enforced capitulation on investiture to Emperor Henry V (1106–1125), and in September 1112 he presided over a synod at Vienne that denounced lay investiture as a HERESY and excommunicated (see Excommunication) the emperor. On the death of Pope GELASIUS II (1118–1119) at Cluny in January 1119, the small group of cardinals with him elected Guy, who was crowned as Callistus II at Vienne on 9 February.

The new POPE and the emperor both recognized that some settlement had to be made over the INVESTITURE CONTROVERSY, the chief issue between the church and the empire. For this reason, Callistus sent envoys to deal with Henry at Strasbourg. Both sides agreed to a tentative agreement, but, through mutual mistrust, this first attempt failed. Discouraged, Callistus reissued the prohibition of investiture and the anathema on Henry on 29–30 October 1119 at Rhiems. He then proceeded to make a triumphal progress through Lombardy and Tuscany and was received at Rome on 3 June 1120 with great enthusiasm. The antipope GREGORY VIII (1118–1121), whom Henry had initially supported, fled to Sutri, but after a siege its citizens surrendered him to Callistus, who had him shut up in the monastery of La Cava.

When Callistus reopened negotiations with the emperor in 1121, the German princes urged Henry to recognize the pope. Representatives were sent to Rome early in 1121, whom Callistus favorably received, and he dispatched Lamberto of Ostia (later HONORIUS II) and two other cardinals as plenipotentiaries to Germany. After three weeks of arduous negotiations the famous Concordat of Worms was concluded on 23 September 1122. Under this agreement the emperor renounced the right to invest with ring and crozier, symbols of spiritual authority, and guaranteed canonical election and free consecration. For his part, Callistus conceded that elections to bishoprics and abbacies should be held in the emperor's presence and that the emperor should invest the person elected with the temporalities by means of the scepter, the symbol of temporal authority. Meanwhile, outside Germany, the emperor's presence at elections would not be required, but investiture with the temporalities was to follow within six months after consecration. The Concordat of Worms ended the long struggle between church and empire over investiture. In March 1123, the pope convened the First Lateran Council (see Lateran Council I), which ratified the concordat. The council also declared the antipope Gregory VIII's ordinations void.

For further reference: P. Hughes, *The History of the Church* (London: Sheed and Ward, 1955); L. Duchesne, ed., *Liber Pontificalis* (Paris: E. de Boccard, 1955).

William Roberts

CALLISTUS III, ANTIPOPE (1168–1178). At the death of antipope PAS-
CHAL III (1164–1168) on 20 September 1168, a small number of schismatic
cardinals elected John, abbot of Struma, as his successor, with the name of
Callistus III. He remained in a weak position. Emperor Frederick I had not
participated in his election but nevertheless gave him his support and thus extended the life of the breach initiated in 1159 with the dual election of pope
ALEXANDER III (1159–1181) and antipope VICTOR IV (1159–1164). The
schismatic popes were the emperor's allies in his aspiration to keep the church
and the Italian peninsula under his power. Frederick, however, could neither
bring Alexander to his side nor break the resistance of the northern Italian cities.
These cities, banded together in the Lombard League since 1167, and the Alexandrian curia constituted a powerful, united front against Barbarossa and Callistus.

In 1174, Frederick made his fifth expedition to Italy and attempted to reach
a negotiated settlement with the Lombard League. Since it refused to forsake
Alexander, the hostilities continued. Only after his defeat at Legnano in May
1176 did the emperor decide to drop his ANTIPOPE. Frederick's reconciliation
with Alexander concluded long negotiations, beginning with the agreement of
Anagni of November 1176 and culminating with the Peace of Venice of July
1177, when Alexander raised the EXCOMMUNICATION that he had decreed
against Frederick in 1160. Callistus, who was at Viterbo, was not ready to
capitulate. Finally, he decided to meet Alexander at Tusculum and surrender to
him on 29 August 1178. The 1159–1178 SCHISM came to an end. It had been
stipulated at Anagni that Callistus would enter a monastery; however, it seems
that Alexander, who granted him pardon, provided a clerical position and later
made him governor of the papal lands at Benevento.

For further reference: Marshall W. Baldwin, *Alexander III and the Twelfth Century*
(Glen Rock, NJ: Newman Press, 1968); Walter Ullmann, *A Short History of the Papacy
in the Middle Ages* (London: Methuen, 1972).

Elda G. Zappi

CALLISTUS III (1455–1458). Born on the last day of 1378 near Valencia,
Alfonso de Borgia was 77 years old when elected POPE as a compromise candidate in April 1455. A Catalan of an old noble family, Borgia studied and
taught CANON LAW at Lerida. After service to King Alfonso V of Aragon,
he was rewarded by MARTIN V (1417–1431) with the bishopric of Valencia
in 1429 for obtaining the abdication of the antipope CLEMENT VIII (1423–
1429). Entering Naples with the victorious Catalans, Borgia negotiated a reconciliation between King Alfonso and Pope EUGENE IV (1431–1447) and was
made a cardinal in 1444. The cardinal of Valencia was known as a man of
irreproachable morals and administrative ability, a medieval canonist in outlook,
indifferent to the humanism of the Renaissance.

Elected to succeed Pope NICHOLAS V (1447–1455) in 1455, Callistus sought
to stem the rising tide of Islam in the form of the Ottoman empire. Through the

efforts of Cardinal Juan de Carvajal and St. John Capistran, Callistus encouraged the regent of Hungary, John Hunyadi, to go to the relief of Belgrade in 1456. In 1457 he appointed the Albanian hero George Castriotis (Skanderbeg) as captain general of the church for the crusade. However, the pope was unable to obtain the commitment from the West needed to reverse the tide of Turkish conquest. Despite his personal virtues and austerity, Callistus was guilty of one overriding fault, the uncritical favor that he bestowed upon his fellow Catalans and especially the nepotism that led to the appointment of his many kinsmen to high office. Among these, by far the most significant was his nephew Rodrigo Borgia, the future Pope ALEXANDER VI (1492–1503), under whom the RENAISSANCE PAPACY reached its nadir. Pope Callistus died in Rome on 6 August 1458.

For further reference: Miguel Batllori, "Callistus III, Pope," *New Catholic Encyclopedia* (1967), vol. 2, pp. 1081–1082; Clemente Fusero, *The Borgias*, trans. Peter Green (New York: Praeger, 1972); Ludwig Pastor, *The History of the Popes*, vol. 2, 7th ed., Frederick Ignatius Antrobus (St. Louis: B. Herder, 1949).

William C. Schrader

CANON LAW. The expression "canon law" as used within the contemporary church refers to a complex system of rules, regulations, and procedures governing the public order, discipline, and life of the Catholic community. Derived from the Greek word *kanon*, which means "rod" or "rule," the "canons" that constitute this body of law have come to mean normative standards for living in the church. The purpose of canon law is not to express Christian dogma or beliefs but, rather, to provide normative and binding guidelines for external actions within the Catholic community. As a legal system, it represents a highly developed approach to membership, rights, and responsibilities within the church that is the result of centuries of tradition. As a human society established with hierarchical character, the church experiences the same needs for order, preservation of the common good, and protection of individual and corporate rights balanced with the fulfillment of individual and corporate responsibilities as any other human community. Canon law is one dimension of the church's efforts to bring a spiritual purpose to the surface while meeting society's needs within the framework of a supportive community of faith.

When the expression "canon law" is popularly used, most people ordinarily think of the "Code of Canon Law," a special set of laws promulgated by the Roman pontiff binding the baptized members of the church. That is not completely correct. In the broadest sense, canon law includes the "Code of Canon Law." In fact, there are two such "codes" in effect: one for the Latin church and one for the Oriental churches, along with every other type of legislation promulgated by the church for its members: liturgical laws not contained in these codes as well as ecclesiastical laws and procedures found in other official church documents and directives.

The "Code of Canon Law" is a more specific designation for certain laws or "canons" governing the daily life and activity of the church that have been "codified" or ordered within a single volume. It should be noted that the legal tradition of the church has been the fruit of the Christian community's constant efforts to reform, renew, and adapt itself to successive periods in the church's long history. The development of the church's system of laws and structures will necessarily reflect the reality of secular laws and institutions of any given period of history. The tremendous influence of Roman and, later, of Germanic law, the organizing principles of Scholastic philosophy, and the impact of CON-CORDATS and other civil law structures all blended together with the direction provided by ecclesiastical doctrines and decrees to produce a legal system by which the church could govern itself.

Within the early church, written documents such as the *Didache* (100), the *Traditio Apostolica* (218), the *Didascalia* (259), and the *Canones Apostolorum* (300) were circulated among Christian communities as a means of acquainting their members with the prevailing customs influencing church life. These "customs," combined with the decrees and "canons" of early church councils, became important sources of law within the early church.

During the twelfth century, a Camaldese monk named John Gratian compiled a collection of canons popularly referred to as "Gratian's *Decretum.*" Completed around 1140, this massive compilation organized in one place all of the canonical literature and their sources available at that time. By the beginning of the sixteenth century, Gratian's collection was revised and expanded in the form of the *Corpus Iuris Canonici* or "body of canon law." This corpus, containing Gratian's *Decretum* and five subsequent collections, became the main source for canonical legislation prior to the Council of Trent (see Trent, Council of), (1545–1563) and, afterward, along with Trent's decrees, served as the church's principal book of laws until the first "code" appeared in 1917. By the beginning of the twentieth century, Pope PIUS X (1903–1914) ordered a new publication of the laws of the Catholic Church. It had become clear that the sheer number of individual "laws," the lack of order among them, and the presence of legislation that was no longer useful, pertinent, or, in some cases, inherently contradictory required a comprehensive revision.

On 19 March 1904, in his *motu proprio, Arduum sane munus*, Pope Pius X declared that the laws of the church should be brought together and arranged in lucid order. To that end, he appointed a pontifical commission headed by Pietro Gasparri (1852–1934), later promoted to the rank of cardinal. Gasparri initiated an unprecedented consultation of the HIERARCHY and Catholic universities throughout the world. The COMMISSION made a critical decision, approved by the POPE, to issue a "code" of laws rather than merely a revised collection or compilation. Gasparri's influence and expertise as a canonist, perhaps the greatest legal mind in the church of his day, resulted in his bearing the brunt of the extensive labor involved.

This task took thirteen years to complete. Following the death of Pope Pius X in 1914, his successor, Pope BENEDICT XV (1914–1922) vigorously supported Gasparri's efforts. On 27 May 1917, he issued an apostolic constitution, *Providentissima mater ecclesia*, in which the church's Code of Canon Law was promulgated, made effective for the universal church on 19 May 1918. Containing 2,414 canons in five books categorized according to the ancient Roman civil law classification of the *Institutiones* of Justinian, the "Pio-Benedictine" Code of Canon Law was hailed at the time as "the greatest ecclesiastical event of the twentieth century. Canonists cautioned, however, that the code was not to be considered a book of case law but, rather, a practical, normative edition of the church's binding laws.

The 1917 Code of Canon Law's five books dealt with the following general topics: Book I presents general norms of the law; Book II provides canons "on persons" in the church, especially clergy and religious; Book III treats "things" within the church, among them sacraments, sacred places, times, and divine worship; the ecclesiastical magisterium; church benefices; and temporal goods; Book IV gives legislation on church procedures, especially judgments and canonizations; Book V presents the church's system of penalties. This first code governed life and ministry in the Latin church for some 70 years.

While much of the church's attention with regard to canon law and its application seemed focused upon the Latin church, there was a realization that the rich traditions, canonical and otherwise, of the Eastern or Oriental Catholic churches should not be ignored. Despite their differences, the respective hierarchies initiated efforts to produce a common body of laws affecting all Oriental churches in the years following the promulgation of the Latin church's code in 1917.

In 1929, Pope PIUS XI (1922–1939) began a consultation with these hierarchs to determine the extent to which an "Oriental code" was desired and necessary. The result was a nearly unanimous affirmation of both the desire and need. A papal commission was established in November of that year to recommend a course of action to be followed. For almost two decades and with strong papal support, this commission and a new commission assisted by canonical experts, created in 1935, pursued the work of producing a common law for the Oriental churches. In 1948, a draft of legislation was presented to Pope PIUS XII (1939–1958), who decided to promulgate it in stages, prior to the publication of any comprehensive "Oriental code."

On 22 February 1949, Pope Pius XII published a *motu proprio* concerning the Oriental discipline for sacramental marriage entitled *Crebrae allatae sunt*, effective 2 May 1949. This legislation was followed by three apostolic letters given *motu proprio*, promulgating other important areas of canon law: on 6 January 1950, *Sollicitudinem Nostram*, concerning ecclesiastical trials, effective on 6 January of the following year; on 9 February 1952, *Postquam Apostolicis*, dealing with religious life, temporal goods, and the interpretation of law, effective 21 November of that year; and, finally, on 2 June 1957, *Cleri sanctitati*, on Eastern rites and the status of persons, effective 25 March 1958.

On 25 January 1959, the newly elected Pope JOHN XXIII (1958–1963) surprised the Catholic world by announcing both a general ecumenical council and a revision of the 1917 code, which by that time had become outdated. He created a pontifical commission to begin the process of canonical reform, the work of which was temporarily suspended while the Second Vatican Council (see Vatican II, Council of) (1962–1965) was in session. After Pope John's death in 1963, Pope PAUL VI (1963–1978) continued the momentum initiated by his predecessor. Not only did Pope Paul VI resume the pontifical commission's efforts to revise the code following Vatican II, but he also charged the group with the task of presenting a new approach to canon law and its implementation according to the mind and spirit of the Second Vatican Council.

In 1967, Pope Paul VI and the Synod of Bishops approved a framework of principles by which canon law was to be revised. Among the principles recommended were the preservation of the juridic character of the code, with particular concern for the rights and responsibilities of all the faithful; protection against conflict between the external life of the church and the forum of conscience; the pastoral care of souls incorporating essential elements of justice and charity; application of the conciliar principles of subsidiarity and fundamental equality among all the baptized; and the reduction of unduly harsh or rigid norms and canonical penalties.

In 1968, over 200 members of the church's hierarchy, clergy, and laity began the task of canonical reform, in light of these principles. The next fifteen years witnessed an effort on the part of the commission to produce schemas and drafts of law for papal consideration, the result of which would be the "final document" of Vatican II, a revised Code of Canon Law for the Latin Catholic Church.

Pope Paul VI, well aware of previous attempts to codify the canonical discipline of the Oriental churches, had also established a pontifical commission for this purpose in 1972. Its labors were to be carried out according to the innovations introduced by Vatican II as well as the "principles" approved by the 1967 Synod of Bishops, with due regard for all Eastern church traditions. On 25 January 1983, Pope JOHN PAUL II (1978–   ) promulgated a revised code for the church with his apostolic constitution *Sacrae disciplinae leges*. Binding baptized members of the Latin church, this code replaced its predecessor and became effective on 27 November 1983. Containing 1,752 canons, significantly reduced from the 1917 Code's 2,414 canons, the 1983 Code of Canon Law was divided into seven books: Book I provided "general norms" regulating the interpretation of promulgation of law in the church; Book II legislated on those matters affecting the Christian faithful as a whole and the rights and responsibilities of the laity, the clergy, and the hierarchy; Book III presented canons on the preaching and teaching mission of the church; Book IV handled ecclesiastical legislation concerning the sacraments, divine worship, and sacred times and places; Book V dealt with the temporal goods of the Church; Book

VI, "Sanctions in the Church," considered ecclesiastical penalties and their application; Book VII provided canonical provisions for adjudication of rights and responsibilities within the church.

On 18 October, 1990, Pope John Paul II issued his apostolic constitution *Sacri canones*, promulgating the "Code of Canons of the Eastern Churches," effective 1 October 1991, the fruit of almost twenty years of labor by the pontifical commission charged with its production. Another pontifical commission was established to handle questions concerning the meaning and implementation of the 1983 Code. Its modified title was the Pontifical Council for the Interpretation of Legislative Texts, and its competence was enlarged to include the publication of authentic interpretations of the universal laws of the church. It was confirmed by papal authority with the promulgation of the apostolic constitution *Pastor Bonus* on 28 June 1988 by Pope John Paul II. The Code of Canons of the Eastern Churches would also be subject to their interpretation.

For further reference: Harold J. Berman, *Law and Revolution: The Formation of the Western Legal Tradition* (Cambridge: Harvard University Press, 1983); T. Lincoln Bouscaren and Adam C. Ellis, *Canon Law: A Text and Commentary* (Milwaukee: Bruce, 1957); Amleto G. Cicognani, *Canon Law* (Philadelphia: Dolphin Press, 1934); *The Code of Canons of the Eastern Churches: Latin-English Edition*, trans. prepared under the auspices of the Canon Law Society of America (CSU) (Washington, DC: CLSA, 1992); Eugenio Corecco, *The Theology of Canon Law: A Methodological Question* (Pittsburgh: Duquesne University Press, 1992); James A. Coriden, *An Introduction to Canon Law* (New York: Paulist Press, 1991); James A. Coriden et al., eds., *The Code of Canon Law: A Text and Commentary* (New York and Mahwah, NJ: Paulist Press, 1985); James H. Provost and Knut Walf, *Canon Law/Church Reality* (Edinburgh: T. and T. Clark, 1986); James R. Sweeney and Stanley Chodorow, eds., *Popes, Teachers and Canon Law in the Middle Ages* (Ithaca, NY: Cornell University Press, 1989); Condtant van de Wiel, *History of Canon Law* (Leuven: Peeters Press, 1991).

David M. O'Connell

CAPITAL PUNISHMENT AND THE PAPACY. The issue of the death penalty has been debated throughout the history of the church, with sacred Scripture containing arguments both for and against it. The fourth century saw the first recorded occasion of Christians killing Christians because of doctrinal disagreements, or death as a punishment for HERESY. Many Christian leaders vehemently condemned this action, including Pope SIRICIUS (384–399). St. Augustine's thought contributed to the subsequent policy decisions to use force against heretics. In dealing with the early Pelagian crisis, his view was to punish but not kill, while in dealing with the later Donatist crisis, that changed to an attitude of kill them if they will not recant.

In the fifth and sixth centuries death was the penalty prescribed for numerous crimes. Pope NICHOLAS I (858–867), in a letter to the newly converted Bulgars in 866, recommended abolition of the death penalty: "You should save from death not only the innocent but also criminals, because Christ has saved you from the death of the soul." This attitude was not to prevail because of the dilemma of dealing with heretics. In the mid-twelfth century, Hugh of St. Victor described the church's position toward the killing of thieves: "This is by no means the justice of the gospel, that a man be killed for stealing a horse, or an ox, nor is such a precept to be found anywhere in the entire gospel. Nor does the church do it, but only permits it."

In coping with the Waldensian challenge, Pope INNOCENT III (1198–1216) in 1208 made, apparently, the only known medieval papal statement directly concerning the death penalty, which became a standard text thereafter: "With regard to the civil power, we affirm that it is permissible to exercise the law of capital punishment, but with the provision that reprisals should not be taken out of hatred but in a spirit of wisdom, not inconsiderately but after mature reflection." Sixty years later Thomas Aquinas gave it prominence in the *Summa* (I–II, q. 64, art. 2), and church tradition has emphasized it to modern times.

In 1976, the Pontifical Council for Justice and Peace prepared a study paper on capital punishment, at the request of the U.S. bishops. This noted that while the church recognizes the right of states to impose the death penalty, it has never supported or prohibited the exercise of that right. It continued that there is no convincing evidence that the death penalty is a deterrent, lamenting the fact that it obviously negates the possibility of the criminal's rehabilitation. It favored the abolition of capital punishment because of the ethical values involved and because it did not perceive conclusive arguments indicating its benefit.

In April 1992, Cardinal Fiorenzo Angelini, president of the Pontifical Council for Pastoral Assistance to Health Care Workers, said: "Among the individuals and groups against legalized abortion in the United States, there are some who support the continuation of capital punishment. This is an inconsistency and an unacceptable contradiction." Cardinal Angelini reflected the current trend among Catholic HIERARCHY with his further comment that "in other times Catholic theologians accepted the death penalty. But today it is no longer admissible." In his encyclical letter *Evangelium Vitae* (The Gospel of Life) of 30 March 1995, Pope JOHN PAUL II (1978–) issued a strong condemnation of capital punishment.

While there has been no Vatican prohibition against all capital executions, popes and Vatican officials on various forums over the past twenty years have indicated that the Catholic Church condemns the use of the death penalty as a punishment for crime. The *Catechism of the Catholic Church* reaffirms the traditional teaching of the church in that it has acknowledged as well founded the right and duty of legitimate public authority to punish malefactors by means of penalties commensurate with the gravity of the crime, not excluding, in cases of extreme gravity, the death penalty. It states, however, "If bloodless means are sufficient to defend human lives against an aggressor and to protect public order and the safety of persons, public authority should limit itself to such means, because they better correspond to the concrete conditions of the common good and are more in conformity to the dignity of the human person."

For further reference: Peter Brown, "St. Augustine's Attitude to Religious Coercion," *The Journal of Roman Studies* 54 (1964): 107–116; *Catechism of the Catholic Church* (New York: Doubleday, 1995); M. B. Crowe, "Theology and Capital Punishment," *Irish Theological Quarterly* 31 (1964): 24–61, 99–131; J. Megivern, *The Death Penalty Repudiated: A Tale of Two Catechisms* (Mahwah, NJ: Paulist Press, 1995); Pope Innocent I, *Epistola VI*, Chapter 3, n. 7, as cited in Francesco Compagnoni, "Capital Punishment and Torture in the Tradition of the Catholic Church," in *The Death Penalty and Torture*, ed. Franz Bockle and Jacques Pohier, *Concilium*, No. 120 (October 1978), p. 41; Pope Nicholas I, *Epistola 97*, Chapter 25, as cited in Francesco Compagnoni, pp. 47, 48.

Tom Scheuring

CANOSSA. SEE INVESTITURE CONTROVERSY.

CARDINALS, COLLEGE OF. The title "cardinal" is used to describe those individuals so designated by the Roman pontiff to assist him in the administration of the church at the highest level. They are traditionally referred to as "princes of the church." Although this honor had been conferred historically on members of the clergy and laity alike, the 1917 Code of CANON LAW required that men promoted to the rank of cardinal must be, at least, ordained priests. In more recent times, Pope JOHN XXIII (1959–1963) declared that men receiving cardinalatial honors must be ordained bishops.

Additional criteria for such appointments, as prescribed in canon law, include candidates' being outstanding for their doctrine, morals, piety, and prudence. If a priest selected by the Roman pontiff to be a cardinal is not also at the same time a bishop, he must receive episcopal ordination before his inclusion in the College of Cardinals. The POPE himself selects the men to be raised to the rank of cardinal, investing them during special papal ceremonies. Occasionally, a man is named a cardinal by the pope, but that dignity is kept secret.

Until some disclosure is made of his rank, this "cardinal in pectore (in petto)" enjoys no title, rights, or obligations.

The College of Cardinals, established during the twelfth century by Pope ALEXANDER III (1159–1181), is made up of the cardinals of the Catholic Church, who advise the pope, assist in the central administration of the church, head the various curial offices and congregations, administer the Apostolic See during a vacancy, and elect a new pope. Although cardinals who head departments of the Roman CURIA are asked to submit their resignations at the age of 75, they automatically cease to function in these capacities at the age of 80, when they also lose the right to participate in papal elections. These limitations were placed upon members of the College of Cardinals by Pope PAUL VI (1963–1978) in 1970.

There are three ranks in the College of Cardinals, corresponding to the historical origins of cardinals in the Roman Catholic Church. Although all cardinals within the college are bishops, their rank within the College of Cardinals is characterized by one of the hierarchical ranks of bishop, priest, or deacon.

Cardinals are given honorary title to churches in the city of Rome. Cardinal-bishops include those appointed by the pope as titular bishops to one of the six suburban dioceses of Rome and those Eastern-rite patriarchs who are heads of sees with apostolic origins assigned to the College of Cardinals. Cardinal-priests are bishops whose dioceses are outside Rome and are assigned a purely honorary "titular church," one of the churches in Rome. They have no pastoral authority over their titular church. Cardinal-deacons are titular bishops assigned to full-time service in the Roman Curia. The canonical provisions concerning the selection, rank, obligations, rights, and privileges of cardinals in the church can be found in canons 349–359 of the 1983 Code of Canon Law.

For further reference: James A. Coriden et al., eds., *The Code of Canon Law: A Text and Commentary* (New York and Mahwah, NJ: Paulist Press, 1985); Petrus Van Lierde and A. Giraud, *What Is a Cardinal?* (New York: Hawthorn, 1964); Carlo Prati, *Popes and Cardinals in Modern Rome* (New York: Dial Press, 1927).

David M. O'Connell

CARLISM. Carlism is a Spanish conservative and ultra-Catholic political movement that originated in the early nineteenth century and derives its name from Don Carlos (1788–1855), a younger son of King Carlos IV. This movement arose in 1812 among deputies of the Cortes of Cadiz, who opposed the liberal tendencies of the majority. These "traditionalists" wished to preserve the characteristics of the old monarchy and the authority of the INQUISITION. These ultraconservatives dominated the restoration regime until the succession crisis of 1830, when the king's maneuvers to set aside the Salic Law and make his daughter Isabel heir to the throne estranged them from him. The king's brother, Don Carlos, emerged as their candidate for the Crown. Upon the death of Ferdinand VII in 1833, the traditionalists, now generally known as Carlists, precipitated a civil war. The child-monarch Isabel II and her regent Queen Mother, Maria Cristina, were supported by Spanish liberals and by Britain and France.

The Carlists drew their strength from conservative and ultra-Catholic elements, particularly from the northern regions (the Basque provinces, Catalonia, and Aragon), which had a long history of autonomist ambition. The conservative powers of Europe, led by Austria, sympathized with the Carlists. The papacy, fearing the anticlerical tendencies of the regent's advisers, likewise favored the Carlist cause. The First Carlist War (1833–1839) was both an internal dynastic conflict and a battleground in the general European conflict between liberalism and conservatism. France dispatched its new Foreign Legion to aid the regent, and Britain permitted the raising of a British Legion of volunteers to serve the same cause. Several Carlist bishops who traveled to Ireland to enlist "good Catholics" to fight for a cause that they declared to be close to the POPE's heart were undercut by the liberal Catholic leader, Daniel O'Connell (see Irish Nationalism; Catholic Emancipation in Great Britain and Ireland), who encouraged his countrymen to join the British Legion and fight against the Carlists. In the end the Carlist generals made peace with the government.

Carlism retained an emotional hold in the northern regions during the decades that followed the end of the war, and loyalties were transferred to the pretender's successors, living in exile. The disturbed politics of Isabel II's reign culminated in her deposition in 1868. There followed, in rapid succession, the brief reign of an Italian duke, who fled in disgust, and the proclamation of a republic inspired by anarchist principles. The time seemed ripe for the launching of the Second Carlist War (1873–1876). The latest in the dissident dynasty, calling himself Carlos VII, was recognized as the rightful king of Spain by Pope PIUS IX (1846–1878). The Carlists again raised the banner of decentralized government, with freedom for provinces and municipalities. The Catholic religion was to be supreme. The king was to reign by divine right, limited only by the "justice of God" and the traditional rights and privileges of the regions. The struggle that the Carlists waged against a series of opposing armies was bitter and often brutal. The balance began to tip against them in 1875, when the Spanish military restored the Bourbons in the person of Alfonso XII. Following the pretender's flight into exile in February 1876, the pope was persuaded to reconcile with the Madrid government by a number of concessions ranging from an increase in ecclesiastical allowances to the elimination of civil marriage and the closing of Protestant institutions.

The last years of Carlos VII (who died in 1909) were marked by divergences within the Carlist movement. The partisans of *Integrismo* accused him of liberal tendencies, suggesting that he was not true to the integral Catholic tradition of Spain. His son and successor, Don Jaime, provoked further tumult within Carlist ranks by expressing his sympathy for Britain and France during WORLD WAR I (in which Spain remained neutral). Juan Vazquez de Mella, a Carlist intellectual, established a traditionalist party that ignored the pretender and concentrated on the "original and fundamental values" of Spanish Catholic traditions. The competition between his movement and *Jaimisno* continued even after the death of Vazquez de Mella in 1928 and that of Don Jaime in 1931. The new Carlist pretender was Don Alfonso Carlos, the elderly uncle of Don Jaime, who led the Carlists as a separate political and military faction into the nationalist insurrection that began in July 1936.

During the SPANISH CIVIL WAR of 1936–1939, Carlist activity was largely confined to what had now become the heartland of the movement. Aragon, Catalonia, and the western Basque provinces had moved into the mainstream of modernization. Navarre, however, remained a stronghold of the "old ways," exhibiting in its villages an almost medieval relationship between priests and peasants.

Although the cause to which they were allied won the civil war, and Catholicism was restored, the Carlists received little else from the regime of General Francisco Franco (1939–1975). Political life in Franco's Spain was subordinated to the structure of the Falangist Party (see Spain and the Vatican). Carlist genealogists had assigned the rightful succession (after the death of Don Alfonso Carlos in 1936) to the Bourbon–Parma line, but their claims received no official recognition. Instead, Franco groomed Prince Juan Carlos, the grandson of Alfonso XIII, to be his successor, and in 1975 this descendant of Isabel II became king of Spain. While the Carlists have preserved a certain influence among conservative Catholics, they have remained essentially marginalized as a political force in the post-Franco era.

For further reference: J. F. Clements, *The Traditionalist Movement in Spain* (London: Vincey, 1990); Edgar Holt, *The Carlist Wars* (London: Methuen, 1980).

Julia L. Ortiz-Griffin

CATHOLIC EMANCIPATION IN GREAT BRITAIN AND IRELAND. By the end of the seventeenth century, Catholics constituted only a tiny minority in Great Britain. In Ireland, however, they made up some 85 percent of the population and were considered a threat to Protestant domination. As a punishment for past rebellion and a restraint of future disruption, the so-called penal laws were passed between 1692 and 1710. These statutes deprived Catholics of virtually all political, economic, and social rights. By the late 1760s, a process of accommodation between the British government and the papacy had begun that led to the repeal of certain penal laws (chiefly related to property ownership) during the 1770s.

Further concessions followed, including grant of the franchise and access to lower-level public offices in 1793 and the establishment of a Catholic seminary under royal patronage in 1795. These latter measures were facilitated by a closing of ranks between the papacy and conservative forces in Europe, both Catholic and Protestant, in the face of the French Revolution. Full Catholic emancipation was, in fact, promised by Prime Minister William Pitt in connection with the Act of Union between Britain and Ireland in 1800. This final conclusion to the penal era was prevented by the refusal of George III to countenance what he regarded as a violation of his coronation oath to uphold Protestant supremacy.

During the period 1801–1820, further efforts to secure Catholic emancipation were made sporadically in the Parliament of the new United Kingdom of Great Britain and Ireland by liberal-minded Protestants. Hopes were raised when George IV succeeded his father in 1820, but the new monarch failed to live up to his earlier reputation for tolerance and succumbed to the pressure of the Loyal Orange Order and other ultra-Protestant organizations to stand firm against "popery."

The initiative now passed to rank-and-file Irish Catholics, organized and led by the charismatic Daniel O'Connell (1775–1847). This prominent lawyer and orator, with a few colleagues, founded the Catholic Association in Dublin in 1823. Based on the principle of mobilizing popular support through individual financial contributions to the cause (a penny-a-month membership fee), the association was the first truly democratic political organization in Europe. O'Connell worked in conjunction with the Catholic bishops, who allowed him to use the parish structure in Ireland as a framework for collecting the "Catholic rent" and maintaining the organization throughout the country. Within a year, the association had hundreds of thousands of members and was carrying on vigorous propaganda and agitation.

The restored papacy, eager to promote further good relations with the conservative British regime but also anxious to attain Catholic emancipation, had dispatched Patrick Curtis (1740–1832) to serve as archbishop of Armagh and primate of Ireland in 1819. Thoroughly familiar with the current of events in Catholic Europe, Curtis (who had lived in Spain for some 60 years) was an important link between papal policy and Irish enthusiasm. While O'Connell's association mobilized massive support for pro-emancipation candidates in parliamentary elections between 1826 and 1828, Curtis carried on persuasive diplomacy with Britain's political leaders. His correspondence with the duke of Wellington, now prime minister but an old friend from the days of his Spanish campaigns, was important.

The crisis of Catholic emancipation was precipitated by Daniel O'Connell's election in 1828 to a parliamentary seat for County Clare. Although legally entitled to stand for the election, he was rebuffed when he tried to take his seat at Westminister because, as a Catholic, he could not endorse the Oath of Protestant supremacy. In February 1829 Wellington recognized that repetition of this process might leave virtually all of Ireland's parliamentary seats vacant, thus rendering Britain's vaunted representative system a mockery. Despite resistance from his own Tory Party and the king, Wellington secured enactment of a Catholic Emancipation Bill in April 1829. By its provisions, all the remaining discriminatory restrictions were abolished, and Catholics (British as well as Irish) were given full access to membership in Parliament and other offices (except that of sovereign). O'Connell, known thereafter as "the Liberator," became a figure of worldwide renown. Despite his role in the "freeing" of his coreligionists, however, his growing identification with liberal Catholicism would make him an object of suspicion within conservative circles and the papal Rome of GREGORY XVI (1831–1846).

For further reference: Maurice R. O'Connell, ed., *Daniel O'Connell: Political Pioneer* (Dublin: Institute of Public Administration, 1991); Fergus O'Ferall, *Catholic Emancipation* (Dublin: Gill-Macmillan, 1985).

William D. Griffin

CELESTINE I (422–432). Celestine was born in Italy and was a deacon under Pope INNOCENT I (401–417). He became bishop of Rome in 422 and actively opposed heretical movements, extending the papal powers of intervention East and West. He crushed Novatianism in Rome, reputedly sent Germanus of Auxerre in 429 to fight Pelagianism in Britain, wrote against the semi-Pelagianism of John Cassian, and urged the bishops of Gaul to remain faithful to Augustine. He became embroiled in ecclesiastical problems in Illyria, and his intervention in an episcopal dispute in North Africa led the bishops of that area, in a synod held at Carthage in 424 or 426, to protest his infringement of their autonomy.

When Cyril of Alexandria appealed to Celestine during his confrontation with Nestorius, bishop of Constantinople, he reviewed the matter and condemned Nestorius in a synod held at Rome in August 430. He delegated to Cyril the responsibility of conveying this condemnation to Nestorius with a view to eliciting repentance. Cyril exceeded his authority, however, and presented Nestorius not only with the papal condemnation but also with a list of ten anathemas to which he demanded that Nestorius subscribe. This conflict led to the convocation by the emperor Theodosius II of a universal church council (the Third Ecumenical Council) at EPHESUS in 431.

Cyril opened the council before the arrival of the defenders of Nestorius. Celestine did not attend the council himself but sent delegates, who also arrived after Cyril's proceedings were finished, and Nestorius had been condemned. They endorsed the actions taken, and Celestine expressed his personal approval in letters written in March 432. Celestine strongly affirmed the papal right, based on the pope's role as successor of PETER, to direction over the whole church, both East and West. He died in 432 and was subsequently proclaimed a saint of the church.

For further reference: F. L. Cross and E. A. Livingstone, eds., *The Oxford Dictionary of the Christian Church*, 2d ed. (London: Oxford University Press, 1974); J. N. D. Kelly, *The Oxford Dictionary of Popes* (Oxford and New York: Oxford University Press, 1986); J. P. Migne, *Patrologia Latina* vol. 50 (Paris, 1844–64), pp. 417–558.

Gerard H. Ettlinger

CELESTINE II, ANTIPOPE (1124). This Roman-born cardinal-priest of S. Anastaio was unanimously elected POPE after the candidacy of Cardinal Saxo of S. Stefano failed to garner a majority. Divisions existed with the College of Cardinals (see Cardinals, College of) between the Gregorian faction and the younger reformers, primarily of Italian and French origin, who sought a renewal of the church. The latter group was led by the chancellor of the Roman church, Aimeric. Simultaneously, tensions between Roman aristocratic families, which spilled over into the College of Cardinals, continued to mar papal elections throughout much of the twelfth century. Celestine received significant backing from the Pierloni family, bitter rivals of the Frangipani. Robert, a leading member of the Frangipani, interrupted the ceremonial proceedings right after the election. Escorted by troops and with the tacit support of Aimeric, who desired a pope favoring his policies, Robert proclaimed Cardinal Lamberto of Ostia (later, HONORIUS II, 1124–1130) as the new pontiff. In the ensuing melee, Celestine was beaten and forced to resign. Since his election had not been consecrated, he is regarded as an ANTIPOPE.

For further reference: Matthew Bunson, *The Pope Encyclopedia* (New York: Crown Trade Paperbacks, 1995); Eric John, ed., *The Popes: A Concise Biographical Dictionary*

(New York: Hawthorn Books, 1964); J. N. D. Kelly, *The Oxford Dictionary of Popes* (New York: Oxford University Press, 1986).

                                                                            John C. Horgan

CELESTINE II (1143–1144). The history of the papacy of Celestine II is brief and relatively uneventful. He died within six months of his ascent, and his time as POPE left no major marks on history. Born into an aristocratic family in Città di Castello in Umbria, Guido was an intellectual whose early mentor was the philosopher and theologian Peter Abelard (1079–1142). Appointed a cardinal by HONORIUS II (1124–1130) in 1127, he served as papal LEGATE in Cologne, Aachen, and France, as well as governor of Benevento. His election to the papacy was the first undisturbed papal vote in Rome in 82 years. He was unanimously selected on 26 September 1143. The election of this elderly prelate was well received within the church and was supported by the widow of Henry V, Empress Matilda.

   Two major events marked his time as POPE, and both actions involved changes in the policies established by INNOCENT II (1130–1143). At the time of Celestine's election, France was under an interdict, decreed by Innocent II in 1141. The interdict was proclaimed when Louis VII, on the death of Alberic, archbishop of Bourges, campaigned to have one of his courtiers elected to the post. He opposed Pierre de la Châtre, and the matter was brought to Innocent II, who ruled in favor of Châtre. Louis refused to accept the decree, incurring the wrath of the papacy. When Louis finally agreed to accept the decision, after the death of Innocent, Celestine, at the request of Abbot Suger of St. Denis and Bernard of Clairvaux, rescinded the interdict. Celestine II also refused to ratify the Treaty of Migniano, drafted in 1139, in which Innocent, taken prisoner in battle, had been forced to recognize Roger II of Sicily's sovereignty over southern Italy. No other action was taken against the powerful Sicilian monarch.

   Celestine died on 8 March 1144 at the monastery of St. Sebastian on the Palatine. He was buried in the Lateran basilica. In recognition of his birthplace, Celestine left 56 volumes from his personal library to the church of S. Florido, Città di Castello, as well as a well-preserved silver altar.

For further reference: Eric John, *The Popes: A Concise Bibliographical History* (London: Burns and Oates, 1964); H. K. Mann, *The Lives of the Popes in the Early Middle Ages* (London: K. Paul, 1902–1932).

                                                                    Christopher S. Myers

CELESTINE III (1191–1198). A noble Roman born in 1105, Hyacinth Bobo was created a cardinal by CELESTINE II (1143–1144) in 1144 and in 1191 reluctantly accepted the papal office. As with many of his twelfth-century predecessors, Celestine III was forced to devote much of his attention to the conflict between church and empire. Eighty-five at the time of his election, he proved a worthy adversary to the emperor and, at the time of his death in 1198, left the church positioned to assume unprecedented authority over the Christian world.

Celestine's success was inextricably linked to Henry, the new king of the empire after his father, Frederick's, death in 1190. The pontiff's first act was to consecrate him on 15 April 1191. After the crowning, Henry pushed south to claim the kingdom of Sicily but failed to subdue Naples. This, along with unrest among the German population, forced Henry to return to Germany. Once there, he assumed a belligerent attitude toward the church, in retribution for Celestine's act of consecrating Tancred Lecce as king of Sicily in January 1192. Henry severed the church in Germany from the papacy and nominated his own bishops.

In 1194 Tancred died, and Henry conducted a second campaign, conquering the Norman kingdom. On 25 December, he was crowned king of Sicily, and, on the following day, his wife gave birth to a son, destined to become Emperor Frederick II. Henry immediately took steps to curtail the papal influence on the Sicilian church, but a combination of events turned his attention to other matters. In 1193, Saladin died. Because he wished for young Frederick to be baptized by the pontiff, he made conciliatory gestures toward Celestine, proposing a new crusade to a reluctant POPE. He traveled to Italy in 1196 to appeal directly to him, but the pontiff responded by delaying tactics. In an attempt to hold his kingdom together, Henry returned all of the territories he had conquered to papal control. He requested that Celestine consecrate his son in Sicily, and, should Frederick II die without heir, the kingdom would be returned to the papacy. The death of Henry in 1197 marked the end of a half century of aggression against the Roman church. In December 1197, at the age of 92, Celestine requested that the cardinals allow him to abdicate. They refused his request, but he died eight weeks later on 8 January 1198. His remains were interred in the Lateran basilica.

For further reference: Eric John, *The Popes: A Concise Bibliographical History* (London: Burns and Oates, 1964); H. K. Mann, *The Lives of the Popes in the Early Middle Ages* (London: K. Paul, 1902–1932).

Christopher S. Myers

CELESTINE IV (1241). Reigning from 25 October to 10 November 1241, Goffredo da Castiglione was of an aristocratic Milanese family. A competent theologian, he was created cardinal-priest of San Marco in September 1227 by GREGORY IX (1227–1241), who entrusted him with missions in Tuscany and Lombardy in 1228–1229. His lack of success there confined him to the CURIA, performing routine duties until 1238, when he was made cardinal-bishop of Sabina. At the time of Gregory's death in 1241 the cardinals numbered only twelve, two of whom were kept prisoner by Emperor Frederick II (1220–1250). The remaining ten were deeply divided, some supporting, others opposing the late POPE's implacable hostility to the emperor.

To force the cardinals to reach a decision, the senator Matteo Rosso Orsini, the real ruler of Rome, had them shut up, in deliberately uncomfortable conditions in the crumbling palace of the Septizonium, which was part-fortress. There, at the first ballot, Goffredo, the candidate of the emperor's ally Cardinal John Colonna, obtained more votes than the anti-imperial candidate but not the two-thirds majority required by the Third Lateran Council (see Lateran Council III) of 1179. The cardinals then considered electing someone from outside their ranks, but Orsini warned them against it. Finally worn out by the harsh treatment and the death of one of their number, the cardinals on 25 October 1241, after 60 days of brutal confinement, elected Goffredo, who took the name of Celestine IV. Probably his age and ill health were a consideration, expecting his reign would be short, and afterward the cardinals could hold a free election under less restrictive conditions. He died on 10 November, after being consecrated pope.

For further reference: L. Duchesne, ed., *Liber Pontificalis* (Paris: E. de Boccard, 1955); H. K. Mann, *The Lives of the Popes in the Early Middle Ages* (London: K. Paul, 1902–1932).

William Roberts

CELESTINE V (1294). After a long vacancy following the death of NICHO-LAS IV (1288–1292), a bitterly divided CURIA elected the Benedictine monk and saintly hermit Pietro de Morrone, in his late 80s, as POPE, on 5 July 1294. Having spent most of his long life in prayer, Pietro had attracted a large personal following within the Benedictine order (the group later to be known as "Celestines") and, with the backing of Charles I of Anjou, had established a monastery on the lonely heights of the Maiella, among the peaks of the Gran Sasso d'Italia in the Abruzzi.

Pietro reluctantly left his secluded life. In the end, he let himself be persuaded to enter his new life like another Christ, astride a donkey, escorted by Charles II and his young son Charles Martel, already crowned king of Hungary, whose royal promise is so movingly celebrated by Dante in *Paradiso* viii. It soon became clear that the venerable monk was not up to the job. Instead of the church's supreme pastor, he showed himself to be a mere lackey of the Anjous. Five months after his consecration, Celestine abdicated—encouraged to do so, no doubt, by the ambitious Benedetto Gaetani, who a few days later actually succeeded him as Pope BONIFACE VIII (1294–1303). Boniface kept the ex-pope under strict surveillance, and after a failed attempt at escape, Pietro was imprisoned in the tower of Castel Fumone, near Ferentino. He died there on 19 May 1296. In 1313 he was canonized by CLEMENT V (1305–1314).

Celestine V was the idol of apocalyptic visionaries. Like Joachim of Floris, he looked to a renewed monasticism for deliverance. He believed that, as pope, he could bring this about. When he failed, he ascribed this to his own inability. Humble in the face of vicious attacks by the Roman elite, who scorned his monkish austerity, and realizing he could not lead the church as he had hoped, he abdicated, in the same spirit of humility he had displayed throughout his life. Ironically, Celestine's abdication was registered in Dante's great poem as a cowardly act. Boniface VIII (1294–1303) fares much worse in Dante's work, as the epitome of a demonic ambition that tore the church apart and destroyed the dream of universal imperial rule in the process.

For further reference: E. John, *The Popes* (New York: Hawthorn Books, 1964); H. K. Mann, *The Lives of the Popes in the Early Middle Ages* (London: K. Paul, 1902–1932); Paget Toynbee, *Concise Dante Dictionary* (Oxford: Clarendon Press, 1914).

Anne Paolucci

CENTER PARTY AND THE VATICAN. Most German Catholics were ultramontane in their sympathies before the Catholic Center Party's creation in early 1871, reflecting their concerns over the minority status of Catholics in this Protestant country. The initial response of Cardinal Giacomo ANTONELLI, the papal secretary of state, eager to win the Great Powers' aid in recovering the city of Rome for the papacy, proved sympathetic to the difficulties of the German chancellor vis-à-vis the Center Party. However, in 1872, Bismarck offended Pope PIUS IX (1846–1878) by proposing to send Cardinal Gustave von Hohenlohe, the brother of a close political ally, as the Prussian envoy to the Holy See. Three years later, the POPE decreed that any Catholic churchman who obeyed any of the May laws of 1873–1874 would be automatically excommunicated (see Excommunication). The German chancellor, now skeptical of the *KULTURKAMPF*'s value, sought a more diplomatic pope.

LEO XIII (1878–1903) proved to be such a pontiff, though he would make Bismarck wait for eight years before he would agree to a compromise settlement of the *Kulturkampf* with Prussia. Still, it is a moot question just when Leo XIII would have accepted a compromise settlement with Prussia if he had not mistakenly assumed that the German chancellor would help the papacy recover the city of Rome. That belief led him, at the chancellor's repeated urging, to ask Windthorst to throw his party's support behind the imperial government's army bill of 1886–1887, but the Center's leader ignored the pope's requests. Some months later, the CURIA learned that Germany had renewed its alliance with Austria-Hungary and Italy. Leo XIII then began to cultivate the goodwill of France and tsarist Russia.

The Holy See's new activist diplomacy proved embarrassing to the Center Party. Its leaders had sought since early 1890 to enter into a working relationship with Chancellor Leo von Caprivi, Bismarck's successor, who was, in turn, eager for their support. Caprivi and William II, the young emperor, were nervous over the rapprochement between France and Russia. Bismarck had long charged that the Center was not a patriotic party, so it was painful for that party when the Vatican press began to attack the Triple Alliance on the grounds that it did not respect the rights of the Holy See. To the Center's relief the relations between Germany and Russia and those with France, to some extent, began to improve after 1895, when all three powers focused their attention on their overseas rivalries with Great Britain. Meanwhile, Leo XIII was unable to prevent the deterioration in the relations between the French Catholic Church and the republican government.

PIUS X (1903–1914) eschewed an activist foreign policy and concentrated his attention on the Catholic Church's spiritual renewal and social issues. Nevertheless, his pontificate caused some problems for the Center. The pope and Cardinal Rafael Merry del Val, his secretary of state, accepted the political coalition between the Center and the Protestant conservatives in hegemonical Prussia because it upheld the dominant position of the two Christian churches in the Prussian school system. They did not approve, however, of interconfessional activities in any form and were displeased when the Center promoted the cause of the new interdominational trade union movement to counterbalance the rapidly growing Social Democratic labor movement. Only with reluctance did Pius X give formal tolerance to the Christian trade union organization in 1912.

There appeared to be considerably less strain in the relations between the Center and the Holy See in the pontificate of BENEDICT XV (1914–1922) than in those of his two predecessors, even though the party and the papacy assumed sharply different positions on the peace question in WORLD WAR I. The pontiff, a diplomat by training, strongly favored a compromise peace based on the status quo of 1914, at least in the West, while the Center had firmly locked itself into an annexationist coalition at an early date. Its course reflected the widespread German Catholic belief that an expansionist peace would bring many more Catholics into the German empire. It was also based on the Center's desire to maintain its prewar alliance with the Prussian Protestant conservatives who were radical annexationists.

In 1916, Matthias Erzberger, a dynamic Center deputy, surmised that the Holy See thought that the Allies would win the war. After the United States entered the conflict in April 1917, Erzberger overthrew his party's senior leadership in early July, and about two weeks later the Center and the Social Democrats collaborated in sponsoring a Reichstag resolution calling for a "peace of compromise and reconciliation." On 1 August 1917 Benedict XV, issued his peace plan, which, among other things, called for a return to the status quo of 1914 in the West and the restoration of Belgium's independence and prewar boundaries. The papal initiative failed to elicit any serious response from the belligerents.

Before Benedict XV's death in January 1922, the Holy See had come to believe that it could negotiate a CONCORDAT with the new Weimar Republic. Under his successor, PIUS XI (1922–1939), Cardinal Pietro Gasparri, the secretary of state, and Archbishop Eugenio Pacelli, the papal NUNCIO to Munich and Berlin, were the prime promoters of that undertaking. However, it became clear by the mid-1920s that there was no parliamentary majority for acceptance of a concordat that guaranteed the existence and expansion of church schools. Eugenio Pacelli, now a cardinal and the papal secretary of state, recognized that HITLER's Nazi Party clearly sought a positive relationship with the Holy See. Some believe that Pacelli preferred to sacrifice the Center Party rather than to let the negotiations for a concordat (see Germany, Concordat of 1933) fail, and he did so in agreeing that German priests could no longer be politically active, a concession that withdrew church sanction of the Center. A few days later, on 5 July 1933, Heinrich Brüning, the Center's last leader, and his colleagues formally dissolved their old party.

For further reference: Margaret L. Anderson, *Windthorst, a Political Biography* (Oxford: Oxford University Press, 1982); Klaus Epstein, *Mattias Erzberger and the Dilemma of German Democracy* (Princeton: Princeton University Press, 1959); John Zeender, "The Genesis of the Concordat of 1933," in *Studies in Catholic History in Honor of John Tracy Ellis*, ed. Nelson H. Minnach, Robert B. Eno, and Robert F. Trisco (Wilmington, DE: Michael Glazier, 1985).

John K. Zeender

CHALCEDON, COUNCIL OF (451). As the Council of Constantinople in 381 (see Constantinople I, Council of) closed an era that began at the Council of NICAEA (325), so the Council of Chalcedon in 451 was intended to put an end to controversies that stemmed from the Council of EPHESUS (431). Although Cyril of Alexandria and John of Antioch came to a formal agreement of reconciliation in 433, adherents of both remained dissatisfied. Many of Cyril's followers felt that compromise with the Antiochene position diluted and ultimately denied the true teaching of Cyril, while their opponents believed that the supporters of Nestorius and perhaps even Nestorius himself had been treated unjustly. John died in 441, Cyril in 444, and the conflict then flared up again, with Theodoret of Cyrus and Flavian of Constantinople representing the Eastern side against Dioscorus, bishop of Alexandria.

Eutyches, a monk of Constantinople and an opponent of Nestorius, had been accused of teaching a doctrine that blended the two natures of Christ into one. He was deposed, after a synod, by Flavian of Constantinople but appealed to LEO I (440–461), the bishop of Rome. In June 449 Leo sent Flavian a document (the *Tome*) that condemned Eutyches and detailed Leo's understanding of Christ's two natures. In August 449 Emperor Theodosius II called a council at Ephesus, under the leadership of DIOSCORUS. This meeting, which Leo labeled an outrageous robbery (*latrocinium*), acquitted and rehabilitated Eutyches, while condemning and deposing Flavian and other bishops, including Theodoret. After the death of Theodosius the new emperor Marcian called a council at Chalcedon to settle the matter.

The reported number of bishops at Chalcedon varies from 500 to 600. Both sides were represented, and delegates from Rome not only attended but also presided at the sessions. The council rejected the decisions of the *latrocinium*, condemned Eutyches, and rehabilitated Theodoret and those who had been deposed in 449. After reaffirming the Nicene Creed and the creed that it attributed to the council of 381 in Constantinople, this council formulated a new statement of faith that it said was in accord with those earlier creeds. It maintained there were two real natures of Christ united in one person of the divine Word. The language of the document contains elements from the traditions of both Cyril of Alexandria and John of Antioch, especially from *The Formula of Union*, and is also dependent on Leo's *Tome* to Flavian. The council mentioned Leo explicitly and praised him, saying that in his words they heard the voice of PETER. The council enacted thirty canons, twenty-seven of which are disciplinary. The most controversial was canon 28, which refers to canon 3 of CONSTANTINOPLE I and restates, in lavish terms, the prerogatives of the See of Constantinople. The Roman delegates rejected this canon, and for that reason Leo I did not ratify the council immediately. To avoid misuse of his hesitation by heretics, Leo, while continuing to reject canon 28, officially approved the council's actions on 21 March 453.

The Western church and much of the Eastern church accepted the decision of this council to condemn the HERESY called Monophysitism, but significant portions of the Eastern church rejected it on the grounds that it had not been faithful to the teaching of Cyril of Alexandria. This split gave rise to new controversy that would eventually result in the Fifth and Sixth Ecumenical Councils, both held at Constantinople in 553 and 680 (see Constantinople II and Constantinople III).

For further reference: P.-T. Camelot, *Ephèse et Chalcédoine, Histoire des Conciles* (Paris: Editions de l'Orante, 1961); L. D. Davis, *The First Seven Ecumenical Councils (325–787): Their History and Theology* (Wilmington, DE: Michael Glazier, 1987); A. Grillmeier and H. Bacht, *Das Konzil von Chalkedon*, 3 vols. (Würzburg: Echter-Verlag, 1951–1954); R. V. Sellers, *The Council of Chalcedon. A Historical and Doctrinal Survey* (London: SPCK, 1961); N. P. Tanner, ed., *Decrees of the Ecumenical Councils* (London: Sheed and Ward; Washington, DC: Georgetown University Press, 1990).

Gerard H. Ettlinger

CHRISTIAN DEMOCRACY IN ITALY. This was the Catholic ideological movement that began in the late nineteenth century in northern and central Italy as both a concomitant and consequence of the church–state quarrel that resulted from the unification of Italy. In inspiration and/or organization, the movement owed much to Pope LEO XIII (1878–1903) (especially his *Rerum novarum*), Giuseppe Toniolo, ROMOLO MURRI, and Luigi Sturzo. Christian democracy stood for political decentralization, pluralism, woman suffrage, freedom for the church, and far-reaching socioeconomic reforms. As a political party, Christian democracy first found expression in the POPULAR PARTY (Partito Popolare) from 1918 to 1926 and then in the Christian Democratic Party (Democrazia Cristiana) from 1943 to 1994. In 1994 the Christian Democratic Party reverted to the original name of Popular Party, but by this time Christian democrats bore little ideological resemblance to the original Popularists.

The Christian democratic movement, an offshoot of Italian social Catholicism and the Congress movement, was originally proclaimed in 1899, and the militant Catholics who called themselves Christian democrats were led by Don Romolo

Murri, a priest from the Marches. Murri subsequently incurred the wrath of Pope PIUS X (1903–1914) and was excommunicated (see Excommunication). In the period between 1918 and 1924 the Christian democratic movement was associated primarily with the name of Don Luigi Sturzo, the principal founder of the Popular Party. In the period after WORLD WAR II and until his death in 1954, ALCIDE DE GASPERI was the major spokesperson for the Christian Democratic Party.

In the post–World War II period, some of the planks of the Christian Democratic Party platforms, such as structural changes and regionalism, were slow in being implemented or were only partially implemented. Failure to carry out previous pledges was due to factors such as the strength of the conservative wing of the party, the ongoing COLD WAR, and the rivalry with the Italian Communist Party. Nevertheless, under the leadership of the Christian democrats and their parliamentary allies, Italy enjoyed almost a half century of political stability (despite frequent ministerial reorganizations) and an unprecedented prosperity.

As the decade of the 1990s unfolded, the revelation of widespread corruption in the Christian Democratic Party, as well as in that of its allies, produced popular resentment, resulting in a resounding defeat for the Christian democrats in the 1994 parliamentary elections. Because Italy had become more secular, and the cold war had ended, Christian democracy as an ideology also suffered a precipitous, if not fatal, fall.

For further reference: Elisa Carrillo, "Christian Democracy," in *Modern Italy*, ed. Edward R. Tannenbaum and Emiliana P. Noether (New York: New York University Press, 1974); Gabriele De Rosa, *Da Luigi Sturzo ad Aldo Moro* (Brescia: Morcelliana, 1988); Mario Einaudi and Francois Goguel, *Christian Democracy in Italy and France* (Notre Dame, IN: University of Notre Dame Press, 1952).

Elisa A. Carrillo

CHRISTOPHER, ANTIPOPE (903–904). At the opening of the tenth century the papacy appeared to be in decline. Weak Frankish emperors, Byzantium's reassertion of control in southern Italy and its patriarchs' attempts to wrestle control of the papacy from Romans, and the papacy's ongoing struggles to maintain its independence from the dukedoms that surrounded the city permitted a succession of POPES whose reigns were often measured in days and weeks. Christopher, a Roman priest, apparently led a coup against LEO V (903), who was resented for being an outsider and not a member of the Roman clergy. Within months Christopher was assassinated by SERGIUS III (904–911) and his followers.

For further reference: Hans Kuhner, *Encyclopedia of the Papacy* (New York: Philosophical Library, 1958); H. K. Mann, *The Lives of the Popes in the Early Middle Ages* (London: K. Paul, 1902–1932); Walter Ullman, *A Short History of the Papacy in the Middle Ages* (London: Methuen, 1972).

John C. Horgan

CISALPINE REPUBLIC AND THE PAPACY. The Cisalpine Republic was created by Napoleon in 1797 as a satellite state through which he could dominate northern Italy. To its original nucleus of Lombardy he added the LEGATIONS that he had conquered from the PAPAL STATE. Its Constitution, modeled on the French of 1795, set up a plural executive, the Directory, made up of Italians sympathetic to revolutionary France. Napoleon remained the paramount authority. Relations between the new republic and the papacy were strained, partly by papal resentment at the annexation of its legations but primarily because of the anticlerical policies of its Directory. Bishops were to be nominated by the Directory, priests were to be elected, the clergy had to take an oath of fidelity to the government, and papal bulls and other documents could be published only with prior governmental approval. Moreover, as in France, church property was confiscated, many religious orders suppressed, and monastic vows abolished. These measures aroused Rome's opposition.

Napoleon, seeking good relations with the Catholic Church, which he hoped to use as an instrument to strengthen his power, was inclined to be conciliatory, but after his departure for Egypt in 1798 anticlericals in Italy took a more intransigent line. The arrest and death in captivity of Pope PIUS VI (1775–1799) and the overthrow of the republic by the Austrians in 1799 brought a temporary lull, but in 1801 Napoleon's victories led to the re-creation of the Cisalpine state. In 1802, a congress of lay and clerical Italian notables at Lyons, summoned by Napoleon, converted it into the Italian Republic, equally under French control; the papacy eventually signed a CONCORDAT with it in 1803, modeled on that signed with France in 1801 (see Concordat of 1801 with Napoleon).

For further reference: E. E. Y. Hales, *Revolution and Papacy* (New York: Hanover House, 1960); Margaret M. O'Dwyer, *The Papacy in the Age of Napoleon and the Restoration; Pius VII* (Lanham, MD: University Press of America, 1985).

Alan J. Reinerman

CIVILTÀ CATTOLICA, LA. A semi-official journal of the Vatican under the direction of the SOCIETY OF JESUS, *La Civiltà Cattolica* was founded by Carlo M. Curci in April 1850. Its original spirit was legitimist and anti-*Risorgimento*, and it was no accident that it was first established in Naples, the capital city of the Bourbon Kingdom of the Two Sicilies. Continuing uninterrupted publication from 1850 to 1870, the Jesuit Fathers suspended *La Civiltà*, then headquartered in Rome, in 1870 to protest the seizure of Rome by Italian troops. Later that year the editors moved its offices to Florence, refusing to remain in a nonpapal Rome. Only in 1888 did *La Civiltà* return to the Eternal City, taking offices in the Via di Ripetta, where it remains to this day. Many of the most famous Italian Jesuits have written for and edited *La Civiltà*, including Luigi Taparelli D'Azeglio, Antonio Bresciani, and Enrico Rossi. *La Civiltà* has always exhibited intense loyalty to the Vatican, thus earning the right to be considered a mouthpiece for the POPES.

For further reference: Richard P. McBrien, ed., *The HarperCollins Encyclopedia of Catholicism* (San Francisco: Harper, 1995).

Richard J. Wolff

CLEMENT I (c. 91–c. 101). While his tenure as bishop of Rome has been dated anywhere from A.D. 88 to 101, most agree that he flourished in the last decade of the first century. According to Irenaeus, Clement was the third bishop of Rome after PETER, following LINUS and ANACLETUS; Tertullian, however, claims he was consecrated by Peter himself and succeeded him. In the First Letter of Clement, the author's name is never mentioned. The occasion of the letter was a factional dispute among the Christians of Corinth, and the Roman bishop politely, but firmly, admonishes the Corinthians to change their ways and follow correct ecclesiastical procedure. The letter presumes no juridical power but speaks in the name of true Christian tradition. It urges the Corinthians to strive for harmony and unity, criticizing them for deposing legitimate leaders who had been appointed by the apostles and their successors. The letter clearly depicts a church order. But it does not reflect the kind of monarchical episcopate that developed in the third and fourth centuries.

The author is clearly writing in the context of what can be called Jewish Christianity; he alludes to New Testament texts, but most of his scriptural material is drawn directly from the Jewish Bible. His concentration on the one God as the goal of Christian activity is the mark of a faith formed in a Jewish ambience; Jesus is the savior, the mediator who shed his blood for the salvation of believers, and through him they will come to the one God. One prays, therefore, not to Jesus but through Jesus, to God.

This Clement was not the author of the so-called Second Letter of Clement, which is, in fact, a homily. It is perhaps the earliest extant example of a full Christian homily, whose date, author, and place of composition remain disputed. It was attributed to Clement early on, which may argue for a Roman origin, but its tone is quite different from that of the authentic letter. The Jewish atmosphere is absent; the homilist exhorts his audience to repentance and good works, and there is more focus on typical Christian themes such as the church, although there is a tendency to speak of preexistence and spiritual existence in a way that suggests a gnostic (see Gnosticism) background. The attribution of this work to Clement shows that the boundaries of orthodoxy were quite expansive in the early church, even in connection with the bishop of Rome. Clement was a highly respected figure, and many later works, including the *Pseudo-Clementines* (*Homilies* and *Recognitions*) of the third century and the fourth-century *Apostolic Constitutions*, were wrongly ascribed to him.

For further reference: B. Bowe, *A Church in Crisis: Ecclesiology and Paraenesis in Clement of Rome* (Philadelphia: Fortress Press, 1988); K. P. Donfried, *The Setting of Second Clement in Early Christianity* (Leiden: Brill, 1974); J. Fuellenbach, *Ecclesiastical Office and the Primacy of Rome: An Evaluation of Recent Theological Discussion of First Clement* (Washington, DC: Catholic University Press, 1980); R. M. Grant and H. H. Graham, *The Apostolic Fathers*, vol. 2, *First and Second Clement* (New York and Toronto: Thomas Nelson and Sons, 1965); D. A. Hagner, *The Use of the Old and New Testaments in Clement of Rome* (Leiden: Brill, 1973); Hermas, *Shepherd*, Visions 2, 4; Irenaeus, *Against Heresies*, 3, 3, 3; Jerome, *Lives of Illustrious Men*, 15; Tertullian, *Prescription against Heretics* 32; Eusebius of Caesarea, *Church History*.

Gerard H. Ettlinger

CLEMENT II (1046–1047). The son of a Saxon noble, Suidger, count of Morsleben, rose quickly in the German episcopacy and came to the attention of the emperor Henry III (1039–1056). As bishop of Bamberg in Bavaria, Suidger was in the entourage of Henry III when he went to Italy in 1046. Henry called a series of councils that put aside the conflicting claims of BENEDICT IX (1032–1044, 1045), SYLVESTER III (1045), and GREGORY VI (1045–1046). Henry then nominated Suidger, who was elected on 24 December and consecrated as Clement II on 25 December 1046. Clement's first official act on the day of his consecration was to crown Henry as Holy Roman Emperor and invest him with the title of ''patrician,'' which conferred the right (formerly exercised by the Tusculan family) to nominate candidates for the papacy. The following month Clement presided over a synod in Rome that condemned simony. But he did not live to accomplish much else. On a journey to the north he became ill and died on 9 October 1047 at the monastery of S. Tommaso, near Pesaro. His body was taken to Bamberg, where he was buried in the cathedral—the only pope buried in Germany.

Rumors spread that Clement II had been poisoned by agents of Benedict IX, once more anxious to reclaim the papacy. These rumors are considered groundless, even though investigators who examined the remains of Clement II in 1942 concluded that he may have died of lead poisoning. Benedict IX reclaimed the pontificate for the third time in 1047 but was ousted the following year on orders from the emperor Henry IV.

For further reference: Matthew Bunson, *The Pope Encyclopedia* (New York: Crown Trade Paperbacks, 1995); J. N. D. Kelly, *The Oxford Dictionary of Popes* (New York: Oxford University Press, 1986).

Frank Grande

CLEMENT III, ANTIPOPE (1080, 1084–1100). Prior to his elevation to the papacy as an ANTIPOPE, Clement supported the antipope HONORIUS II (1061–1064). In 1072 he was appointed archbishop of Ravenna by Henry IV but in the following year was suspended by Pope GREGORY VII (1073–1085) for his failure to attend a Lenten synod. Three years later, in 1076, he was excommunicated (see Excommunication) by Gregory for conspiring with a group of Lombard bishops to overthrow him. These were years of bitter hostility between Henry IV and Gregory, centered on the investiture issue (see Investiture Controversy). Gregory had reaffirmed, in *Dictatus papae* (1075), papal supremacy over all secular princes as well as judicial and legislative authority over all Christians. In subsequent synods (1074–1075), Gregory further prohibited clerical marriage, simony, and lay investiture. In response, Henry convened a group of German bishops at Worms (1076) and deposed Gregory. The POPE promptly excommunicated Henry for his action, while releasing Henry's subjects from their oaths of loyalty to the king and favoring Henry's rival, Rudolf of Swabia, as the new monarch. Henry retaliated by assembling a group of imperial bishops at Brixen, who deposed Gregory and elected Archbishop Guibert of Ravenna as Clement III.

Henry's invasion of Rome in 1084 prompted Gregory to flee to Salerno, where he would die the following year. Henry demanded that the Roman people and clergy recognize Clement III. This antipope's first official act was to crown Henry IV emperor. A Norman army, loyal to Gregory, forced Henry's retreat to Germany and Clement's return to Ravenna. Clement's exile was short-lived. With the assistance of thirteen cardinals and a well-organized anti-Gregorian propaganda campaign, Clement returned to Rome, where he continued to function as the pretender to the chair of St. Peter during the reigns of VICTOR III (1086–1087) and URBAN II (1088–1099).

Supporting the reform impulse within the church, Clement spoke out forcibly against clerical marriage and simony. Clement can also be indirectly credited with establishing the College of Cardinals (see Cardinals, College of), as his support among the church's HIERARCHY was so strong that Urban was forced to treat Clement's backers with equal respect. In 1098, he was once again driven from Rome, this time by the forces allied with the aristocratic Pierleoni family. Clement made one last feeble attempt to reclaim his position at the time of PASCHAL II's election to the papacy in 1099 but failed. He died shortly thereafter.

For further reference: Matthew Bunson, *The Pope Encyclopedia* (New York: Crown Trade Paperbacks, 1995); Eric John, ed., *The Popes: A Concise Biographical Dictionary* (New York: Hawthorn Books, 1964).

John C. Horgan

CLEMENT III (1187–1191). Clement III is perhaps best known for the completion of the work started by GREGORY VIII (1187) of organizing the ill-fated Third Crusade (1189–1191). He also settled a long-running dispute with the commune in Rome and, as a result, was able to live peacefully in the Lateran for the duration of his pontificate. The date of Paul Scolari's birth is unknown. Born in Rome, he became cardinal-bishop of Palestrina in 1180. On 19 December 1187, two days after the death of Gregory VIII, the cardinals at Pisa elected Cluniac Theobald of Ostia as the new pontiff. Theobald declined, so they turned to their second choice, Scolari. He took the name Clement III.

Clement's most important tasks were improving relations with Frederick I (Barbarossa) and the ongoing organization of the new crusade to wrest the Holy Land from the grip of Saladin, who had conquered Jerusalem that year. Clement was considered weak, physically and administratively, although the latter might be attributed to a lack of experience in the Roman church. By negotiating away much of his control, he was able to make peace with the commune in Rome and, in February 1188, install the papacy in the Lateran for the first time in six years.

Clement also sought to mollify Frederick. The SCHISM caused by the split election for the See of Trier was resolved when the pontiff agreed to Frederick's proposal to nullify the first vote and hold a new election. In return, Frederick agreed to return the state, which had been occupied by his son Henry since 1186, to papal control. To increase the Holy See's wealth and to finance the coming crusade, Clement established a new treasury, to be administrated by Cencio Savelli, who would later become HONORIUS III (1216–1227).

Clement devoted most of his attention to the organization of the Third Crusade, begun by Gregory VIII. He resolved the differences between Pisa and Genoa, thus assuring a powerful naval force. He continued to exhort Christian countries throughout Europe to make peace among themselves and to support the crusade. In May 1189, Frederick set out for the Holy Land. In 1190, both King Richard of England and King Philip of France began their trips east. The death of William II in 1189 brought new turmoil for Clement. Because he died childless, Constance was next in line for the throne, and Roger pressed for the Crown. The Sicilians, however, opposed a foreign ruler and supported Count Tancred of Lecce, an illegitimate grandson of Roger II. A coronation was set for January 1190, and the pontiff agreed to the proceedings, although he refused to invest Tancred. In June 1190, Frederick died in Anatolia. As heir and claimant of Sicily, Henry set out for Italy to claim his Crown. Before he reached Rome, however, Clement died in late March 1191. He was buried in the Lateran basilica.

For further reference: J. N. D. Kelly, *The Oxford Dictionary of the Popes* (Oxford: Oxford University Press, 1986); H. K. Mann, *The Lives of the Popes in the Early Middle Ages* (London: K. Paul, 1902–1932).

Christopher S. Myers

CLEMENT IV (1265–1268). The pontificate of URBAN IV (1261–1264) was followed by a papal vacancy of four months, caused by an impasse in deciding upon a successor. Finally, Guy Foulques, a Frenchman, native of Languedoc, was chosen. Son of a judge, himself a student of law, married and with two children, Guy Foulques became a high-ranking official under King Louis IX. After his wife's death, he entered the church and quickly rose to become bishop of Puy in 1256, archbishop of Narbonne in 1259, and then, at the hands of Urban IV in December 1261, cardinal-bishop of Sabina. He also served as LEGATE to England, backing Henry III against the barons, and was on his way home from England when he was elected to the Holy See on 5 February 1265.

Like ALEXANDER IV (1254–1261) and Urban IV, this POPE sided with Charles of Anjou, brother of King Louis IX of France, against the Hohenstaufens. He conferred upon Charles the kingdom of Naples, in order to end Manfred's dominance in the peninsula. Later he tacitly supported the execution of Manfred's nephew, the young Conradin, last of the Hohenstaufens. Dante, with his keen sense of the dramatic irony of history, immortalized this moment in his glorification of Manfred in the *Commedia*. Absolved by Dante of any political wrongdoing, Manfred is eternally "saved" by being assigned to Purgatory, while the popes who destroyed the Hohenstaufens are destined to rot in Hell. In retrospect, the events orchestrated by Clement IV clearly mark the end of the universal empire and the breakup of the universal church: the beginning of the nation-state system in the modern world and the end of the religious hegemony of the church in the West.

For further reference: E. John, *The Popes* (New York: Hawthorn Books, 1964); H. K. Mann, *The Lives of the Popes in the Early Middle Ages* (London: K. Paul, 1902–1932); Paget Toynbee, *Concise Dante Dictionary* (Oxford: Clarendon Press, 1914).

Anne Paolucci

CLEMENT V (1305–1314). Clement, who chose to live in France from 1307 to 1308, was addicted to nepotism. In 1305 he appointed ten new cardinals, four of whom were his nephews. Plagued with cancer, Clement, though intelligent, proved weak and indecisive. He seemed to be in constant fear of France's king Philip IV. Yielding to the request of Philip, Clement established the CURIA in Avignon, initiating the BABYLONIAN CAPTIVITY of the papacy for 70 years. For 6 years Philip called for a general council to condemn BONIFACE VIII (1293–1303), charging him with HERESY and other crimes. In 1309 at Candlemas, Clement hesitantly opened proceedings. In April 1311, Philip suspended the proceedings due to political events.

Clement suffered significant humiliation in executing the following: the annulment of Boniface's activities that were prejudicial to French interests, the absolution of Philip's minister, who was the ringleader of the assault on Boniface, and his bull *Rex gloriae* (27 April 1311), commending Philip's zeal in his attack on the deceased pope. Clement experienced further humiliation in his suppression of the Knights Templars, who were affluent bankers and property owners. In 1307 Philip had the Templars arrested. Besieged with threats to reopen the charges against Boniface, Clement dissolved the order in 1312 in an administrative ordinance, *Vox clamantis*. In the theocratic tradition, Clement wrote his famous bull, *Pastoralis cura*, proclaiming the superiority of the Holy See over the Roman empire.

For further reference: Matthew Bunson, *The Pope Encyclopedia* (New York: Crown Trade Paperbacks, 1995); J. N. D. Kelly, *The Oxford Dictionary of Popes* (New York: Oxford University Press, 1986).

Patrick McGuire

CLEMENT VI (1342–1352). Clement entered the Benedictine house of La Chaise-Dieu at the age of ten. A monk since 1301, Clement held a doctorate in theology, granted by JOHN XXII (1316–1334). An orator and diplomat, King Philip VI of France and John XXII were impressed with Clement's learning, mannerisms, and diplomatic skills, which helped him secure election in the conclave of 1342. Despite his abilities and influence, Clement was unable to end the Hundred Years' War but played a pivotal role in establishing the Truce of Malestroit in 1343. An avid opponent of Emperor Louis IV, the Bavarian,

Clement wished to end the struggle that continued from the papacy of John XXII. He reinstated John's anathemas and called for Louis to abandon his imperial office as he sought to secure the election of Charles as the king of Bohemia. Although Louis made some effort to submit to Clement's request, Clement excommunicated (see Excommunication) him in 1346.

Clement has been judged inconsistent in the execution of his papal office, delighting in banquets and festivities yet generous to all those in need. A protector of the poor, Clement exhibited charity to those suffering from the Black Death and defended the Jews, who were blamed for it. Although vehemently opposed by the bishops, Clement decreed that all churches, offices, and dignities were subject to the provision of the papal office. He was buried in La Chaise-Dieu after a brief illness. In 1562, the Huguenots burned Clement's remains.

For further reference: Matthew Bunson, *The Pope Encyclopedia* (New York: Crown Trade Paperbacks, 1995); J. N. D. Kelly, *The Oxford Dictionary of Popes* (Oxford: Oxford University Press, 1986).

Patrick McGuire

CLEMENT VII (1523–1534). Giulio dei Medici was born in Florence on 26 May 1478, the posthumous son of Giuliano (the brother of Lorenzo the Magnificent) and of Fioretta d'Antonio, a woman of humble origins. He was subsequently declared to be the offspring of a clandestine, but valid, marriage, on the findings of an inquest ordered by his first cousin LEO X (1513–1521) in 1513. Giulio's uncle Lorenzo raised him as a son, providing him the same humanistic education given to his son Giovanni, Giulio's senior by two and a half years. Giulio even studied CANON LAW with him at the University of Pisa (1489–1491). Giulio was very close to his cousin, often living in his household and sharing his teachers, exile from Florence (1494–1512), residence in Rome, trip through the empire and France (1499–1500), and choice of a clerical career. He participated in two failed military attempts to restore the Medici to power in Florence and accompanied his cousin Giovanni, cardinal LEGATE, to the army of the Holy League, at the Battle of Ravenna (1512), escaping capture.

Giulio's ecclesiastical career advanced rapidly with the help of Giovanni dei Medici, who was elected Pope Leo X. Of the numerous episcopal sees bestowed on him, the most important was that of the archbishopric of Florence in May 1513. Appointed a cardinal-deacon on 23 September 1513 and cardinal-priest on 26 June 1517, he received the episcopate on 21 December 1517. As cardinal he held various legations and was cardinal-protector of England (1514–1523) and vice-chancellor of the church (1517–1523). He was among Leo X's most influential advisers. While residing in Rome, he maintained close ties to Florence, advising his cousins on the city's civil administration and eventually assuming direct control on their deaths and instructing his spiritual vicar in the diocese to implement through a provincial council (April 1517) the reform decrees of the Fifth Lateran Council (see Lateran Council V) (1512–1517). When the case of Luther (see Reformation) was referred to Rome, he actively worked to secure his condemnation with the bull *Exsurge Domine*.

A patron of the arts, he commissioned from Raphael the *Transfiguration* and the design for the Villa Madama on Monte Mario outside the Roman walls; from Michelangelo he requested work at the complex of St. Lorenzo in Florence: on the church's facade, on a funeral chapel of the Medici in the church's New Sacristy, and on the Laurentian Library next to the church. On the death of Leo X, he became the pope's legal heir, but, unable to secure his own election, he supported the successful candidate of the imperial party, Adrian of Utrecht. Initially out of favor with the new, austere POPE, Giulio retired to Florence, where he managed the affairs of the city. Toward the end of ADRIAN VI's pontificate (1522–1523), Giulio was called to Rome, becoming one of the pope's principal advisers. At the next conclave (1 October–19 November 1523) after negotiations with the suspicion of simoniac promises, Giulio was elected pope on 19 November 1523 and took the name Clement.

Clement began his pontificate with attempts at church reform. In Rome he implemented (1524) some of the reform decrees of the recent Fifth Lateran Council, prepared the city for the Jubilee of 1525, and worked to convoke (1524–1525) an international conference in Rome to deal with questions of church reform but met opposition from Christian princes, and not a single bishop accepted his invitation. To resolve the complaints of the German nation against the church, Clement sent Cardinal Lorenzo Campeggio as legate to Germany, where he held a conference at Regensburg (1524) that issued 38 reform decrees that were implemented by the Catholic states of southern Germany. Fearing a radical reform would weaken papal power and give the princes greater control of the church, he opposed a German national council. He resisted pressures to call a general council for similar reasons, fearing a revived conciliarism (see Conciliar Movement) and a council's deposition of him on ground of his illegitimate birth and simoniac election. Clement VII misjudged the seriousness of the theological division between Lutherans and Catholics, indirectly supported the Lutherans by his opposition to Hapsburg hegemony, and thought reconciliation could be achieved by political means. He was willing to make many concessions, such as the chalice to the laity and a married clergy. His conciliatory stance allowed Prussia, Denmark, and Sweden to go Lutheran, and he failed to support the Catholic cause militarily in Switzerland and Württemberg. His procrastination from 1527 to 1534 in affirming the validity of the marriage of Henry VIII to Catherine of Aragon gave the king, married in 1533 to Anne Boleyn, ample time to lead England into SCHISM in 1534. Some of Clement's actions that successfully promoted church interests include his approbation of new religious orders: the Theatines (1524), Capuchins (1528), Franciscan Reformati (1532), and Barnabites (1533). He also helped to organize the church in mission lands by erecting bishoprics in Spanish Central and South America and in Portuguese Africa and India.

Clement VII's foreign policy aimed at preventing Hapsburg hegemony in

Italy, securing Medici interest in Florence, and defending Christendom from the Turks. Although considered an imperialist, as pope he tried to balance Hapsburg power by supporting France until circumstances forced him to ally with Charles V. Thus, he allied with Francis I (1524) until the king's capture at the Battle of Pavia (1525) led the pope briefly to ally with the emperor. To weaken Hapsburg power, he joined the League of Cognac (1526) and was punished by the imperial forces with the Sack of Rome (1527). Thereafter he was a formal, if unenthusiastic, ally of Charles V, who helped to restore the Medici to power in Florence, had his illegitimate seven-year-old daughter Margaret betrothed (1529) to the pope's cousin Alessandro (who became duke of Florence in 1531), and became the last emperor to be crowned by a pope (1530). Clement VII tried to keep his ties with Francis I, marrying (1533) his youthful cousin Caterina to the king's second son, Henry. In the hope of preserving Medici influence in Rome, he raised his cousin Ippolito to the cardinalate (1529) and to the vice-chancellorship of the church (1532). Clement VII also provided for the needs of his fellow Knights of St. John by offering them temporary refuge at Viterbo after their expulsion from Rhodes and securing from the emperor (1530) their investiture with the islands of Malta. The pope also labored to rally Christian forces to oppose the Turks, especially after the defeat at Mohacs (1526) and siege of Vienna (1529).

Clement was a man of culture who employed the humanist Jacopo Sadoleto as his secretary. The contemporary history writers Paolo Giovio and Francesco Guicciardini were entrusted with diplomatic and administrative posts. With Erasmus he maintained friendly relations and intervened to silence some of his critics. Financial problems so limited his patronage of letters that he even closed the Sapienza University in Rome (1531) to save money. He built the Zecca (mint) and continued work on St. Peter's Basilica and on the three roads that fan out from the Piazza del Popolo. He completed the *Stanze* by having Giulio Romano and Francesco Penni fresco the Sala di Costantino. Under his pontificate the Clementine mannerist style developed in Rome. His last major commission was to Michelangelo to fresco the front and rear walls of the Sistine Chapel with the *Last Judgment* and *Fall of the Angels*.

Death ended his unhappy pontificate in Rome on 25 September 1534. To Alessando he bequeathed Florence and to Cardinal Ippolito, the rest of his estate. He was buried at first in St. Peter's and then moved to a tomb in S. Maria sopra Minerva that faced that of his cousin Leo X.

For further reference: Andre Chastel, *The Sack of Rome, 1527*, trans. Beth Archer [Bollingen Series 35, 26] (Princeton: Princeton University Press, 1983); Roger Mols, *Clement VII, Dictionnaire d'histoire et de géographie écclésiastiques XII* (Paris: Librairie Letouzey St. Ane, 1953), cols. 1175–1244; Gerhard Muller, *Die romische Kurie und die Reformation 1523–1534: Kirche und Politik wahrend des Pontificates Clemens' VII.* [Quellen und Forschungen zur Reformationsgeschichte, 38] (Gutersloh: Gerd Mohn, 1969); Ludwig Pastor, *History of the Popes from the Close of the Middle Ages*, 3d ed., vols. 9, 10, trans. Ralph Francis Kerr (St. Louis: B. Herder Books, 1923).

Nelson H. Minnich

CLEMENT VII, ANTIPOPE (1378–1394). Robert of Geneva was born in 1342, becoming bishop of Therouanne in 1361, archbishop of Cambrai in 1368, and cardinal in 1371. As papal LEGATE he commanded the military forces in the PAPAL STATES. In this office he earned the title of the "Butcher of Cesena" for ordering the massacre in that city in 1377. Robert supported the election of URBAN VI (1378–1389) at the conclave of April 1378 but then joined the rebellious cardinals, who declared this election null and elected Robert POPE as Clement VII on 20 September 1378, giving birth to the Western Schism (see Schism). When the Italian states rejected him, Clement returned to Avignon in June 1379. France and the Iberian kingdoms recognized him. England and most of the empire spurned his claims. Clement multiplied financial exactions on the clergy to support his military and diplomatic ventures and the splendid court at Avignon. This arrogant aristocrat devoted his energies to solidifying his position and made no attempt to solve the dilemma of the two popes other than by force. He thwarted initiatives by courts and universities to end the schism by other means, an effort in which he was embroiled when he died on 16 September 1394.

For further reference: John H. Smith, *The Great Schism 1378: The Disintegration of the Papacy* (New York: Weybright and Talley, 1970); R. N. Swanson, *Universities, Academics and the Great Schism* (Cambridge: Cambridge University Press, 1979); Walter Ullmann, *The Origins of the Great Schism* (London: Burns, Oates, and Washbourne, 1948).

Richard J. Kehoe

CLEMENT VIII, ANTIPOPE (1423–1429). Gil Sanchez Munoz, archpriest of Tervel and provost of Valencia, became the last ANTIPOPE in the final years of the Great Western Schism (see Schism). Successor to BENEDICT XIII (1394–1417), the last Avignon POPE, Munoz chose his name in honor of CLEMENT VII (1378–1394), the first antipope of the schism. Benedict had secured from his four cardinals a promise to choose a successor, but only three participated in Clement's election in Spain. The fourth cardinal, Jean Carrier, was excommunicated (see Excommunication) by Clement for his failure to attend. Carrier accused the three cardinals of a range of improprieties and declared Clement's election invalid. Carrier proceeded to nominate and elect his own pope, antipope BENEDICT XIV (1425), and later was himself elected pope, reigning as antipope Benedict XIV the second until his death.

Clement's reign coincided with that of Pope MARTIN V (1417–1431) and initially received tacit support from King Alfonso V of Aragon (1416–1458). Naturally, suspicion and hostility grew between Martin and Alfonso due to the king's failure to denounce Clement's election. However, Alfonso appointed a delegation, headed by the later Pope CALLISTUS III (1455–1458), to urge Clement's abdication, an action the king undertook prompted by a bribe from Martin to forswear the pretender. Without any support, Clement stepped down and publicly recognized Martin's legitimacy. In a show of magnanimous generosity, Martin appointed the ex-antipope bishop of Majorca; a post that he held until his death in 1446.

For further reference: J. N. D. Kelly, *The Oxford Dictionary of Popes* (Oxford: Oxford University Press, 1986); Hans Kuhner, *Encyclopedia of the Papacy* (New York: Philosophical Library, 1958).

John C. Horgan

CLEMENT VIII (1592–1605). Ippolito Aldobrandini was born at Fano, 24 February 1536, the son of a noted Florentine lawyer driven from Florence by the Medici. The support of Cardinal Alessandro Farnese allowed him to study law, and in 1569 he was named to the Rota by Pius V (1566–1572), the protector of his family. In 1571–1572 that POPE sent him on diplomatic missions to Spain and France. In 1580 he was ordained a priest. Under SIXTUS V (1585–1590), he was made a datary, the head of the department responsible for appointments to the Holy See, and by 1586 was a cardinal-priest. In 1558–1589 he had diplomatic success as LEGATE to Poland.

He had been a serious contender at the three conclaves held in 1590–1591 and at the last was elected pope, succeeding INNOCENT IX (1591). The new pontiff, Clement VIII, was a strong supporter of Catholic reform. A conscientious and tireless administrator, he was admired for his piety and austerity. Philip Neri, who predicted his election, was his confidant, and Cesare Baronius, the noted church historian and Oratorian, was his confessor. Among those he advanced was the saintly Jesuit theologian Robert Bellarmine. Although as a cardinal he had criticized nepotism, he promoted his own nephews to the cardinalate.

Nonetheless, Clement sought to implement the decrees of the Council of Trent (see Trent, Council of). He promoted the reform of religious houses and in 1592 published a corrected version of the Vulgate that remained authoritative until the twentieth century. Clement enlarged the INDEX in 1596 to include a ban on Jewish books and intensified the INQUISITION, which during his reign sent more than 30 heretics, including the ex-Dominican philosopher Giordano Bruno, to the stake. His concern for orthodoxy and his indecisive nature were demonstrated during the dispute that took place from 1595 to 1605 between the Jesuits (see Society of Jesus) and Dominicans over the teachings of Luis de Molina concerning grace and free will.

His major political decision was the recognition of Henry IV as king of France in 1595. This entailed the reluctant acceptance by Clement of the Edict of Nantes, which allowed the Huguenots religious freedom. In that same year he endorsed the proposals that were subsequently accepted at the synod of Brest-Litovsk, under which the Orthodox Christians in Poland joined the Roman church while retaining their rites and liturgy. Since the papacy was now free from Spanish domination, Clement was able to negotiate the Peace of Vervins in 1598 between Spain and France. In 1599 he appointed Francis de Sales as coadjutor bishop of Geneva, thus strengthening the efforts of the COUNTER-REFORMATION in Switzerland.

There were several diplomatic failures during his reign, most notably, his inability to forge a Christian coalition against the Turkish threat to Austria and Hungary and the controversies surrounding his unsuccessful efforts to restore Britain to the Catholic fold. In Sweden his dreams of a Catholic restoration collapsed when the Catholic king there, Sigismund III of Poland, was defeated and deposed that same year by his Protestant uncle Charles IX. In 1600 Clement proclaimed a Jubilee Year, which brought millions of pilgrims to the Eternal City.

For further reference: T. Jalland, *Church and Papacy* (London: SPCK, 1944); J. N. D. Kelly, *The Oxford Dictionary of Popes* (Oxford: Oxford University Press, 1986).

William Roberts

CLEMENT IX (1667–1669). Reigning from 20 June 1667 to a December 1669, Giulio Rospigliosi was born at Pistoia on 27 January 1600 to a noble family of the region. He began his studies with the Jesuits (see Society of Jesus) in Rome and later studied theology and law at Pisa. With the patronage of the Barberini and Urban VIII (1623–1644) he rose steadily in the CURIA and in 1644 was made an archbishop and sent as NUNCIO to Spain. In 1653 he left Spain to become governor of Rome and in 1657 was named a cardinal and secretary of state to Pope ALEXANDER VII (1655–1667). On Alexander's death, with the strong backing of France, he was elected POPE. He assumed a name that re-called policies of conciliation and immediately broke with the traditions of papal nepotism, giving his family only modest assignments and incomes. Known for his personal piety and charity, he often helped the poor and frequently heard confessions in St. Peter's.

Clement's short reign was devoted to resolving the existing tensions between the major powers and the papacy. He allowed Louis XIV a freer hand in church appointments in his kingdom and was negotiator in the Peace of Aix-la-Chapelle, which ended the War of Devolution (1667–1668) between France and Spain. France's brilliant foreign minister, Hugues de Lionne, was the real architect of the noted ''Clementine Peace'' (1669) that brought a temporary respite over the Jansenist controversy (see Jansenism) then raging in France. Clement accepted the subscription by Jansenist bishops to the formulary, which condemned the theologian Cornelius Jansen's original propositions, but the peace was actually a victory for Louis XIV, who considered the Jansenists a threat to his country's unity.

Clement planned to assist Venice in the recovery of Crete, occupied for some time by the Turks. In 1668–1669 the pope was able, with the help of France, Spain, and the empire, to organize two expeditions. Despite its naval superiority, the Christian coalition collapsed due to internal disputes. In 1669 the Venetians were forced to surrender their last stronghold on the island, leaving the Holy See with the large debts incurred by the expedition. News of the loss of Crete hastened his death in 1669. Clement was also a man of letters and had the distinction of creating the comic opera as a dramatic form, with his *Chi soffre speri* being premiered in Rome in 1639. As pope, Clement canonized the first saint from the New World, St. Rose of Lima.

For further reference: N. J. Abercrombie, *The Origins of Jansenism* (Oxford: Clarendon Press, 1936); Pierre Blet, *Le clergé de France, Louis XIV et le Saint Siège de 1695 à 1715* (Vatican City: Archivio vaticano, 1989).

William Roberts

CLEMENT X (1670–1676). Reigning from 29 April 1670 to 22 July 1676, Emilio Altieri was born to a distinguished Roman family on 12 July 1590. He studied at the Roman College, becoming doctor in laws in 1611, served as a lawyer and judge of the Rota, and was ordained in 1624. He was an auditor in the Polish nunciature, after which he returned to Italy and served as bishop of Camerino (1627–1654) and in 1644 was named NUNCIO to Naples. In this last capacity, he did not satisfy INNOCENT X (1644–1655) and was recalled in 1652. However, under ALEXANDER VII (1655–1667), he was appointed consultor to the Holy Office. In 1669 CLEMENT IX (1667–1669) named him cardinal, and as POPE he would take his patron's name. Altieri was elected pope at age 79 after a five-month conclave during which France and Spain had vetoed various candidates.

Because of his age, the new pontiff needed assistance and appointed Cardinal Paoluzzi degli Albertoni as cardinal nephew. Paoluzzi had married a niece of Clement's and added the name Altieri to his own. In his new position, the cardinal nephew assumed control of affairs of state and used his post to enrich and aggrandize his family. Huge sums were spent on his Palazzo Altieri, outraging public opinion so that Clement deemed it prudent never to visit it. Paluzzi also alienated the diplomatic corps by commuting their tax immunities.

A major issue of Clement's reign that reached a crisis in the next pontificate was the issue over the right of regalia, or *régale*, claimed by the kings of France. The *régale* conferred on the king the temporalities of vacant sees and abbeys until the new bishop or abbot had been consecrated and taken the oath of fealty. Traditionally, this right extended only to those benefices founded by the kings of France. In 1673 Louis XIV issued a decree by which all sees were made subject to the same ruling. The pope protested to the French ambassador, and his nephew, Paoluzzi, at the same time, ill advisedly imposed customs duties on the French Embassy in Rome. This was a violation of diplomatic privilege, leading to a deterioration in church–state relations.

For further reference: W. D'Ormesson, *The Papacy* (London: Hawthorn Books, 1959); P. Hughes, *The History of the Church* (London: Sheed and Ward, 1955).

William Roberts

CLEMENT XI (1700–1721). Giovanni Francesco Albani was born at Urbino on 23 July 1649 to a noble Umbrian family. One of his uncles served as the archbishop of Urbino. Albani, who received a doctorate in canon and civil law, became an official of the PAPAL STATE, holding successively the governorships of Rieti, Sabina, and Orvieto and in 1687 became the secretary of papal briefs. In 1690 Albani was elevated to cardinal. He wielded great influence under ALEXANDER VIII (1689–1691) and INNOCENT XII (1691–1700), drafting the latter's bull banning nepotism. In 1700 he was elected POPE following a 46-day conclave divided by French and imperial factions. He was the nominee of the *ZELANTI*, a third party, which insisted that the pope should remain neutral and defend the interests of the church.

Despite the efforts of Clement XI to preserve the authority of the church, his reign witnessed a major decline in papal power vis-à-vis the absolutist monarchies. The crisis of the Spanish succession, pitting the Bourbon and the Hapsburg dynasties against each other, was brewing, leading to the War of Spanish Succession (1701–1713). Clement XI chose to stay neutral, trying unsuccessfully to mediate between the two Catholic powers. Papal neutrality in the conflict proved impossible. When Philip of Anjou was crowned in Madrid as Philip V, Clement XI recognized the new Spanish monarch. This caused a major strain in his relations with Emperor Leopold I, who supported the Hapsburg archduke Charles for the Spanish throne. Prince Eugene's triumphant campaign in northern Italy and his victory at the Battle of Turin (1706) placed Italy at the mercy of the Hapsburgs, whose forces conquered Naples in 1707 and in May 1708 seized the papal town of Comacchio.

During the peace negotiations at Utrecht (1713) and Rastadt (1714), Clement XI's representative was unable to take part in the deliberations. Moreover, his investiture rights in Sicily, Parma, and Piacenza were ignored. Clement suffered a further setback when the Savoyard ruler, Victor Amadeus II, who ruled over Sicily, rejected the pope's demand that he recognize that island as a papal fief. Victor Amadeus also prohibited the collection of the *crociata*, the tax paid by the Sicilian clergy. The pope's support of the Stuarts' return to England in the hope of restoring Catholicism also failed, and the Hannoverian dynasty became Britain's rulers. The recognition of the Protestant elector of Brandenburg as king of Prussia also went against the pope's wishes. In an effort to reclaim the Balkans from the Turks for Christianity, Clement helped Venice in its war against the Turks in 1714. To his dismay, however, Cardinal Alberoni, the Spanish prime minister, diverted the Spanish fleet, which the pope had helped to equip, from fighting the Turks to conquering Sardinia from the empire.

Clement XI played an important role in combating the Jansenists (see Jansenism) in France. Most important was his famous bull *Unigenitus Dei Filius*, issued on 8 September 1713 at the insistence of Louis XIV, which condemned 101 Jansenist propositions included in the *Réflexions morales sur le Nouveau Testament* (1693), written by the Jansenist leader, Quesnel. Despite considerable opposition, Clement XI refused to modify it, and in 1720 the French government forced the *parlement* to register the bull. Clement XI also promoted missionary activity in India, the Philippines, and China. In 1708 he announced the feast of the Immaculate Conception of the Blessed Virgin Mary as an obligatory holy day.

Regarding internal affairs, Clement XI established new institutions designed to propose reform projects to improve economic conditions. Programs aimed at enhancing agriculture and reforming the tax system were developed but remained unrealized. Artistic and literary activities, on the other hand, flourished. The pope was a generous patron of art, architecture, and scholarship, turning Rome into one of the most beautiful cities in Europe in the early eighteenth century. Clement XI died in Rome on 19 March 1721.

For further reference: Matthew Bunson, *The Pope Encyclopedia* (New York: Crown Trade Paperbacks, 1995); Christopher M. S. Johns, *Papal Art and Cultural Politics in the Age of Clement XI* (Cambridge: Cambridge University Press, 1969).

Alexander Grab

CLEMENT XII (1730–1740). Clement XII was born Lorenzo Corsini on 7 April 1652 in Florence. The scion of an aristocratic family, Corsini did not pursue a church career until a relatively late age. After earning a doctor of laws degree at the University of Pisa, Corsini renounced his rights of primogeniture and, in 1685, began his ecclesiastical career. He was to hold several positions, including NUNCIO to Vienna, treasurer general, and governor of Castel Sant' Angelo in Rome. He also served as cardinal-bishop of Frascati in 1706. Corsini's election as POPE followed a conclave that lasted several months and was dominated by bickering among the factions. Corsini chose the name Clement as a sign of gratitude to his mentor, CLEMENT XI (1700–1721). Elected pope in his late 70s, Clement was both old and in feeble health. He would be totally blind in two years and was confined to bed throughout the remainder of his life.

In his efforts to increase revenues, Clement reinstated a public lottery in the PAPAL STATES. In 1738 Clement issued a bull that condemned FREEMASONRY. He believed that Masonic lodges were dangerous centers of anti-Christian thought and practices. His reign was also marked by advances in missionary activity abroad and attempts to bring various Christian denominations back into the church fold. Nearly 10,000 Copts returned to the church under Clement's guidance, while he pursued efforts to regain the allegiance of the Greek Orthodox. In order to help achieve this goal, Clement founded the Collegio Corsini in Calabria for Greek students. In Naples, an institute was founded for the education of Chinese converts.

Foreign affairs brought the papacy into conflict with various powers in Europe. Ecclesiastical jurisdiction was challenged in Sardinia and Naples, while the pope's rights and privileges in Parma were ignored. Always fearful of the Ottoman threat to Europe, Clement financed the Venetians and Poles in their ongoing conflict with the Turks. Finally, Clement was quick to renounce Cardinal Alberoni's annexation of San Marino to the papal states.

Clement XII was active in promoting the beautification of Rome and other public works. He ordered the reconstruction of churches, began the restoration of the Arch of Constantine, initiated work on the Trevi Fountain, and sought to have the streets of Rome paved. The Capitoline Museum was opened to the public, and Clement enriched its holdings with many ancient marbles and manuscripts. He also donated a large collection of Oriental manuscripts to the Vatican Library. Within the papal states, Clement undertook land reclamation projects around Lake Trasimeno and built a port at Ancona, as well as a road that was intended to improve commerce from that city into the interior. Clement XII died on 6 February 1740 at the Quirinal in Rome. In 1742 his remains were transferred to the Lateran.

For further reference: M. Caporilli, *Tutti i Papi* (Rome: Nuova Spada, 1982); L. Pastor, *The History of the Popes, from the Close of the Middle Ages* (St. Louis: B. Herder, 1923).

John J. Tinghino

CLEMENT XIII (1758–1769). Clement XIII was born Carlo della Torre Rezzonico on 7 March 1693 in Venice. His wealthy and noble family sent him to Bologna to be educated by the Jesuits (see Society of Jesus). He graduated from the University of Padua with degrees in theology and law. Prior to his elevation to the papacy, Rezzonico held a succession of positions within the church HIERARCHY. On 15 May 1758 a conclave met to select a successor to BENEDICT XIV (1740–1758). Rezzonico was elected POPE on 6 July 1758, assuming the name Clement XIII. The fate of the Jesuits dominated his reign. During the 1750s, the Jesuits were vilified by the state authorities of Catholic Europe, while governments desired further centralization of power within the state, and the rationalists, Jansenists, and other ideologues were united in their contempt for this common enemy. In 1759 the Jesuits were suppressed in Portugal. Anti-Jesuit measures were passed in France, and, in 1767, they were expelled from Spain. Both Parma and Naples followed the Spanish lead shortly after (see Society of Jesus, Abolition of).

France seized Avignon, while Naples took Benevento and Ponte Corvo. Clement's issuance of bulls supporting the Jesuits was without effect abroad. His most forceful one, *Apostolicum pascendi munus*, fell on deaf ears. Unable to deter the expulsions of the Jesuits and their suppression elsewhere, Clement compounded his problems by poorly handling their arrival from Spain. He refused them the privilege of landing at Civitavecchia, sidetracking the expropriated and expelled Jesuits to Corsica.

With his freedom to conduct foreign policy severely limited, Clement faced still another humiliation. In January 1769, the ambassadors of France, Naples, and Spain presented identical notes to the papacy, demanding the complete suppression of the Jesuits worldwide. Clement agreed to convene a consistory to review this question. At the same time Clement had to deal with the attacks against the church launched by the *philosophes*, condemning many of their works, including the *Esprit* of Helvetius and the *Encyclopédie* of D'Alembert and Diderot.

At home, Clement XIII began attempts to drain the Pontine Marshes while completing work on the Trevi Fountain. He died of a stroke in Rome on 2 February 1769, only two weeks after the demands for the worldwide suppression of the Jesuits had been handed to him. He was interred at St. Peter's basilica. Clement is often viewed as a well-meaning individual, deeply religious and resolute in his defense of church interests but undermined by a certain timidity that led his enemies to question the ultimate resolve of his policies in unsettled times.

For further reference: Artaud de Monton, *The Lives and Times of the Popes*, trans. from *Les Vies des Papes* (New York: Catholic Publication Society of America, 1911); G. F. X. Ravignan, *Clément XIII et Clément XIV. Volume Suppleméntaire* (Paris: Julien, Lanier Editeurs, 1854).

John J. Tinghino

CLEMENT XIV (1769–1774). Clement XIV was born Giovanni Vincenzo Antonio Ganganelli on 31 October 1705 at Sant' Arcangelo on the outskirts of Rimini. His father, a local doctor, sent his son to Rimini, where he was educated by the Jesuits (see Society of Jesus). By 1759 he had been appointed a cardinal by CLEMENT XIII (1758–1769). With the death of Clement, the sacred college assembled in conclave on 15 February 1769 to elect his successor. The conclave found itself split between pro-power "court cardinals" and the pro-Jesuit "zealots" (see Zelanti). Although the zealots, who opposed secular considerations in the election of the next POPE, were in the majority, their opponents were able to use threats to influence the voting. For example, Cardinal de Bernes of France spoke of a possible blockade of Rome, while the Spanish delegation demanded a written statement that the person elected would agree to disband the Jesuits. At this point, Ganganelli showed himself to be an astute politician. He was able to appease both sides while successfully avoiding definite commitments to either. Under these conditions, Ganganelli was elected pope on 18 May 1769, gaining 46 of the 47 votes cast. All eagerly awaited to see how Clement XIV would resolve the problems inherited from his predecessor.

It was evident that Clement XIII's policy, based on moral and spiritual considerations, had failed. By insisting on supporting the Jesuits, his predecessor had brought the Vatican into open conflict with a large part of Catholic Europe. Relations with Portugal, France, Naples, Spain, and Parma were seriously impaired. The papacy had even seen its territory violated in Avignon, Ponte Corvo, and Benevento. Church rights and privileges had been attacked as well. Clement XIV now embarked upon a policy of reconciliation with the European powers. As early as July 1769 the Bourbon monarchs made approaches to the new pope to remind him of their determination to see the destruction of the Jesuits. Finally, in July 1773 Clement issued *Dominus ac Redemptor*, which officially sanctioned the suppression of the Jesuits (see Society of Jesus, Abolition of). Once the Catholic powers had achieved their goal, Avignon, Benevento, and Ponte Corvo were returned to the papacy. Clement was confident that the Bourbon monarchs now would be more amenable to his campaign against the *philosophes*.

Undeniably, the controversy surrounding the fate of the Jesuits dominated Clement's reign, but he interested himself in other aspects of papal policy as well. Missions in Asia, Africa, and America were encouraged. Inside the PAPAL STATES, Clement encouraged advances in the arts and learning, made attempts to reduce expenditures, and tried to overhaul the financial administration in general. He continued earlier efforts to drain the Pontine Marshes, founded the town of Fiumicino, and established the Clementine Museum in Rome. He died on 22 September 1774 and was buried in the Church of the Twelve Apostles where his body had been moved from the Vatican grottoes.

For further reference: C. Castiglione, *Storia dei Papi* (Turin: Unione Tipografico, 1957); G. Cretineau-Joly, *Clemente XIV E I Gesuiti* (Parma: Pietro Fiaccadori, 1848).

John J. Tinghino

COLD WAR AND PAPACY. PIUS XII (1939–1958), who considered Stalin's communism more dangerous than HITLER's national socialism (see Nazi Germany and Vatican), was unhappy with Roosevelt's unconditional surrender policy vis-à-vis Germany. At the war's end the POPE's fears materialized when communist regimes emerged in Eastern Europe and China, while powerful communist parties appeared in France and Italy. Pius was scandalized by the communist relentless campaign against the Roman Catholic Church in Eastern Europe. In 1945 a consistory urged the faithful to vote only for those candidates who were dependable in their attitude toward Catholicism, and in March 1948 the pope personally conveyed this message during the Italian Republic's first parliamentary elections.

On 1 July 1949 the Holy Office condemned COMMUNISM and called for EXCOMMUNICATION for those who assumed membership in that party. This was followed on 28 July 1950 by an admonition against joining communist youth organizations. To make its position clear, the Vatican dispatched numerous letters of instruction to church authorities in Poland (September 1949 and September 1951), in Czechoslovakia (28 October 1951), and in China (18 January 1952). In Western Europe Pius was delighted to see the communists dropped from the councils of ministers in France and Italy in May 1947 and by the victory of the Christian democrats in Italy's parliamentary elections of 18 April 1948. At the same time he gave tacit support to the formation of the Western European Union alliance (1948) and in April 1949 nudged DE GASPERI's Christian Democratic Party to adhere to the North Atlantic Treaty Organization (see NATO and the Papacy).

A reduction in Cold War tensions began slowly to take place after the death of Stalin in 1953, the end of the Korean War (1950–1953), and the rise to power of Khrushchev in the Soviet Union. This transition toward possible "coexistence" between East and West accelerated when JOHN XXIII (1958–1963) succeeded PIUS XII as pope in October 1958. His decision to promote a renewal of the church by means of VATICAN II and issuance of the encyclical *Pacem in terris* (April 1963), which called for peace based on truth, justice, and liberty for all, were milestones on this new course. In 1963, Pope John was able to obtain the release of the Ukrainian metropolitan of Lvov, Josyf Slipyi, and during the Cuban missile crisis of 1962 appealed to Kennedy and Khrushchev to negotiate a solution. For his efforts he was awarded the International Balzan Peace Prize for 1962.

John's successor, Giovanni Montini, who became PAUL VI (1963–1978) in 1963, continued the pacific policies of his predecessor. In March 1964, he established the office of a permanent observer to the UNITED NATIONS and on 4 October 1965 addressed the General Assembly in New York, where he met with Soviet foreign minister Andrei Gromyko. An agreement with the Hungarian government in 1964 allowed the Vatican to fill a number of empty sees, and in 1965 an accord with the Czech government permitted the release of Archbishop Josef Beran of Prague. In January 1967, Soviet president Nikolai Podgorny paid a formal visit to Paul VI in the Vatican, and in March 1971 there was a state visit by President Tito of Yugoslavia.

The accession of the anticommunist Pole Karol Wojtyla to the papal throne as JOHN PAUL II (1978–) on 14 October 1978 marked the start of the final phase of the Cold War. The new pontiff traveled extensively and made several trips to Poland, where he attracted adoring crowds, which looked to the church as an alternative to their communist regime. John Paul's first trip in June 1979 influenced Lech Walesa, who in 1980 organized the "Solidarity" labor movement in the shipyards of Gdansk. Alarmed by this development, the government of General Wojciech Jaruzelski imposed martial law in December 1981 and arrested Walesa. However, Jaruzelski was compelled to release Walesa prior to the pope's next visit to Poland in the summer of 1983. Meanwhile, Mikhail Gorbachev's advent to power in Moscow in May 1985 ushered in an enduring thaw in East–West relations as this communist reformer pushed his program of perestroika (political restructuring) and glasnost (openness). In Poland General Jaruzelski was forced to legalize Solidarity and permit free elections for a new Polish Parliament.

In the ensuing months, while Gorbachev adopted a "hands-off" policy, other communist regimes throughout Eastern Europe collapsed like falling dominoes. By 9 November 1989, the Berlin Wall was opened without a shot being fired. On 1 December 1989, John Paul II received Soviet president Gorbachev in a friendly visit, and later that month Walesa was elected president of the new democratic Poland. Within the next years, Gorbachev was superseded by Boris Yeltsin, by this time a critic of communism, and the Soviet Union collapsed. The Cold War had come to an end. One of the many factors that helped bring this about was the Vatican's adamant opposition to communism as an ideology, but an opposition that had been tempered after the mid-1950s by a number of pragmatic accommodations with specific communist regimes.

For further reference: Eric O. Hanson, *The Catholic Church in World Politics* (Princeton: Princeton University Press, 1987); Ennio Di Nolfo, ed., *Vaticano e Stati Uniti 1939–1952 (dalle carte di Myron C. Taylor)* (Milan: Franco Angeli, 1978); Hansjakob Stehle, *Eastern Politics of the Vatican, 1917–1979*, trans. S. Smith (Athens: Ohio University Press, 1981).

Charles F. Delzell

COLLEGES OF ROME. The first school at Rome for Christian indoctrination was opened by Justin Martyr (c. 100–c. 165) toward the middle of the second century as a private enterprise of this convert-layman, without any explicit mandate from the ecclesial authorities. The direction of clerical formation soon passed to the exclusive care of the HIERARCHY, and before the end of the sixth century a school was functioning at the Lateran, which became the focal point for almost 1,000 years and attracted students from even the most remote parts of Western and Central Europe, extending its influence to the entire Latin church.

Pope INNOCENT IV (1243–1254) founded the *studium* of the Roman CURIA, around 1244–1245, while in residence at Lyon. This school for the teaching of theology and canon and civil law (see Canon Law) to aspirant clerics remained directly dependent on the POPES and followed the papal court wherever it went. Subsequently, its status was raised to that of a university on a par with Bologna, Oxford, Paris, and Salamanca. It continued to function until the sixteenth century, then became superfluous and ceased to exist. Pope BONIFACE VIII (1294–1303) founded the true university of Rome, the *Sapienza*, in 1303, which flourishes to the present day. Theology and canon and civil law were among disciplines taught there.

Throughout the Middle Ages the Roman monastic communities fostered intellectual formation for the religious, while the thirteenth century witnessed the foundation of new scholastic centers for the FRANCISCAN, Dominican, Augustinian, and Carmelite friars. In 1457 Cardinal Domenico Capranica founded a college for young clerics, which was to be the precursor of the renewal of the church. The upheaval caused by the REFORMATION and the challenge presented by the evangelization of the New World created a pressing need for a more adequately trained clergy. To meet this urgency, Ignatius Loyola founded the Roman College in 1551, and it soon became the fulcrum of religious studies of the COUNTER-REFORMATION church. The following year the Jesuits (see Society of Jesus) opened a college for German seminarians (1552), and similar establishments were founded, in rapid succession, for neophytes (1577), Greeks (1577), English (1579), Hungarians (1579), Poles (1583–1584), Maronites (1584), and Scots (1600). Two other foundations were made under Pope UR-

BAN VIII (1623–1644): the college "de Propaganda Fide" (1627) and the Irish college (1628). As part of this ferment to implement the conciliar decree of TRENT on seminaries, the Roman Seminary was erected (1565) at the express wish of Cardinal Charles Borromeo.

The religious orders, too, played an important role in the reawakening of intellectual and moral training: new foundations were made for the Dominicans (1577), Conventuals (1587), Irish Franciscans (1625), Premonstratensians (1626), Irish Augustinians (1656), Irish Dominicans (1667), Servites (1669), and Benedictines (1687).

The nineteenth century witnessed a notable increase in the Roman colleges, a trend that continued into the present century, with new foundations before and after the Second Vatican Council (see Vatican Council II). Equally proliferative have been the houses opened in Rome to meet the needs of the religious orders and congregations. A sign of vitality and an aspect of particular significance for the formation of the clergy, both secular and religious, have been the transformation of various Roman foundations into pontifical universities, with the affiliation of institutes and faculties of higher studies offering a vast range of disciplines and specialization for undergraduate and postgraduate students, like the Lateran University (1959), the Urban University (1962), the University of St. Thomas Aquinas (1963), and the Salesian University (1973), which with the Gregorian University (1551), offer golden opportunities for an adequate academic formation.

For further reference: "Collegi Ecclesiastici," in *Enciclopedia Cattolica* 3 (1949) (1952–1963); (Various authors), *Seminaria Ecclesiae Catholicae* (Vatican City, 1963).

Charles Burns

COMMISSIONS. In addition to the other departments of the Roman CURIA, ten papal or pontifical commissions have been established to serve the special needs of the church and the Apostolic See. Membership on these commissions varies in number at any given point, although the commission itself is considered a permanent body within the Roman Curia.

For further reference: Peter A. Baart, *The Roman Court* (New York: Fr. Putet, 1895); Edward L. Heston, *The Holy See at Work* (Milwaukee: Bruce, 1950).

David M. O'Connell

COMMUNISM AND PAPACY. Modern communism represents an attempt to impose an ancient system of organizing society on people in the nineteenth and twentieth centuries as a solution to social, political, and economic injustices of the Industrial Revolution. It advocates the involuntary imposition of collectivism by negating the right to property, providing an atheistic, deterministic, materialistic view of history and social relations. Communism claimed to be the only scientific form of SOCIALISM, calling for a solution to the problems of modernity by a transformation of the world by means of violent revolution and class warfare. Communists deride as utopian all socialisms that sought justice by peaceful means.

The church in eighteenth, nineteenth, and twentieth centuries was confronted with two unacceptable socioeconomic ideologies: laissez-faire capitalism and communism. In the church's view both were devoid of the moral content required to bring about SOCIAL JUSTICE. Capitalism and communism espoused views contrary to the church's tradition on the nature of humans, their labor, and their relationship to God and neighbor; neither reflected a Christian perspective on the accumulation of material wealth and its responsible use. Both were devoid of an understanding of human rights, their equitable concretization in justice, and, therefore, the nature of the limited right to own property. Each failed to comprehend the proper use of property and the notions of a just price and a just wage central to the Catholic understanding of economic activity, labor, and distributive social justice. Capitalism and communism, the papacy charged, displayed a disregard for the good of the family and the rights of women and children. Both required people to abdicate their moral responsibility and to concretize justice to either the god of the invisible hand of competition or the invisible god of material dialectics.

Gracchus Babeuf advocated in his *Manifesto of Equals* (1796) a revolution that would take possession of all property and create a central committee to institute a common life and administer an egalitarian communist state. Later, in 1797, Babeuf declared class struggle a historical necessity. In Germany in 1801, Hegel noted the primacy of reason over faith, proclaiming philosophical knowledge as absolute knowledge. In his *The Phenomenology of Spirit* (1807), he supposedly reduced God to a mere idea of human self-consciousness, identifying the real with the rational and rejecting the transcendent God of Christianity. This was the interpretation given to Hegel's notion of God by Bruno Bauer and the circle of young Hegelians who followed Bauer's lead, such as Ludwig Feuerbach and Karl Marx.

Ludwig Feuerbach put forth a material, dialectical interpretation of human nature and history. In thought, people are said to distinguish themselves from nature through a process of objectifying nature and becoming alienated from it. Nature, in a material sense, is the ground of people's being, and the notion of God is merely their attempt to conceptualize human nature and its attributes, without its material limitations. Thus, he replaced theology with a materialistic anthropology, and religions with God as a transcendent, existential being were perceived as a stage in human development that must be transcended. Politics, for Feuerbach, becomes the expression of the new religion to which people must devote themselves. The state is the ultimate unity and community of humankind to which we must devote our life.

The Hegelians absolutized the view that one's fundamental interaction is aggression, following Thomas Hobbes' view that humans were only material beings like atoms that crash into one another. People are compelled by their instincts to be aggressive, manifesting a desire to possess all things and dominate all. The absence of war can be achieved only by having people live in terror of punishment by death. A war of all, against all, can be averted only by giving absolute power to a ruler, a leviathan, who employs capital punishment to keep the people from killing one another. This would be absolutized and transformed by the radical Hegelians into a principle of dialectical materialism, a term that is not part of their vocabulary per se but can be said to describe their thought.

Friedrich Engels became a member of the young Hegelians in 1841, and in 1842, Moses Hess converted Engels to communism. Engels later converted Marx to communism while Marx was staying in Paris, sometime between October 1843 and the writing of the *Communist Manifesto*. Engels insisted that what was necessary was a systematic reinterpretation of history and thought from a materialistic perspective. He also advocated in the *Communist Manifesto* that they had to attain their goal through violent revolution.

Marx and Engels did not originate most of the basic ideas in their theories. They saw themselves as synthesizers of previous viewpoints. They believed that prior thinkers had established the following: the materialistic, dialectical view of history; the value theory of labor; the notions of the proletariat and the inevitability of class conflict; and the ultimate demise of capitalism from its intrinsic contradictions. They synthesized these thoughts into a political program and rationale for violent revolution as the sole solution for the terrible conditions of the working class.

The capitalists' desire to increase their profit leads to decrease utilization of labor or the wages paid to labor. This for Marx creates the fatal dialectic in capitalism, namely, that the accumulation of capital can be accomplished only if it is accompanied by an increase in poverty worldwide. However, as the capitalists succeed in their endeavors, they eventually run out of global markets to exploit. Thus, capitalists will find that as they increase the poverty in the world, there will be insufficient consumers for their products, and, in true dialectical fashion, this will lead to a collapse of their system, or it will be torn down by a proletarian revolution.

As early as the 1890s there was a broad recognition that the predictions about progress made by the proponents of capitalism and communism were questionable. Their conviction that economic justice would necessarily flow from the invisible hand of competition or the invisible hand of dialectical forces did not occur. Thus, a process of trying to revise the theories or an attempt to explain away the facts commenced within both schools. They still defended an amoral, mechanistic naturalism in which the necessary forces of history or nature would operate and bring social justice. Whether one assumed that private vice would produce the public good, or whether the collapse of capitalism would come about by violent revolution, the moral use of our freedom to bring about the common good was excluded by both.

According to the communists, the family, the state, and religion are the source of one's problems and the cause of one's alienation from nature and other people. Therefore, wherever the communists gained power, they tried to eliminate the family and religion or render them ineffectual. The education of children, according to the communists, must be taken out of the hands of parents and religious leaders, so that communism can properly indoctrinate children to the new order. The suppression of the Catholic Church in communist countries proved constant. Countries under the influence of the Soviet Union, after WORLD WAR II and communist China, beginning in 1949, made an all-out effort to stamp out all religion.

In the latter part of the nineteenth and twentieth centuries, the church sought to proclaim its own solutions to social questions, safeguarding the faithful from the extremes of capitalism and communism. In the Vatican's view of social justice, any system that denies the rights of human beings in order to obtain a supposedly good end fails to understand the relationship of means to ends in regard to concretization of the common good. Further, history cannot be made subject to laws that are similar to the deterministic laws of physics, for human beings are capable of deliberation in regard to the means they choose to obtain their end. The POPES proposed that to concretize the good in meaningful ways, one must choose a good means to a good end. From the papal perspective the two ideologies of modernity did not deliver what they promised. The Catholic principle of a just wage is rooted not in some abstract notion of how a laborer's labor creates an exchange value but in the concrete reality of the dignity of the laborer's person and what the laborer has a right to simply because of being a person.

The most important related Vatican documents on communism in their historical order are as follows: (1) *Qui Pluribus*, PIUS IX 11/9/1846; (2) *Quibus Quantisque*, Pius IX 4/20/1849; (3) *Noscitis et Nobiscum*, Pius IX 12/8/1849; (4) *Singulari Quadam*, Pius IX 12/9/1854; (5) *Quanto Conficiamur Moerore*, Pius IX 8/10/1863; (6) *Quanta Cura* (Syllabus), Pius IX 12/8/1864; (7) Documents of Vatican I, 1870; (8) *Inscrutabili*, LEO XIII 1878; (9) *Quod Apostolici Muneris*, Leo XIII 12/28/1878; (10) *Diuturnum*, Leo XIII 6/29/1881; (11) *Immortale Dei*, Leo XIII 11/1/1885; (12) *Libertas Praestantissimum*, Leo XIII 6/20/1888; (13) *Sapientiae Christianae*, Leo XIII 1/10/1890; (14) *Rerum Novarum*, Leo XIII 5/15/1891; (15) *Graves de Communi*, Leo XIII 1/18/1901; (16) Decree *Lamentabili sane*, PIUS X 7/3/1907; (17) *Pascendi*, Pius X 9/8/1907; (18) *Miserentissimus Redemptor*, PIUS XI 5/8/1928; (19) *Quadragesimo Anno*, Pius XI 5/15/1931; (20) *Caritate Christi Compulsi*, Pius XI 5/3/1932; (21) *Acerba Animi*, Pius XI 9/29/1932; (22) *Dilectissima Nobis*, Pius XI 9/3/1933; (23) *Summi Pontificatus*, 7/20/1939; (24) *Mater et Magistra*, JOHN XXIII 5/15/1961; (25) *Pacem in Terris*, John XXIII 4/11/1963; (26) *Ecclesiam Suam*, PAUL VI 8/6/1964; (27) *Gaudium et spes*, Vatican II 1966; (28) *Dignitatis Humanae*, Vatican II 1966; (29) *Populorum Progressio*, 3/26/1967; (30) *Evangelica Testificato*, 6/29/1971; (31) *Convenientes ex Universo*, 11/30/1971; (32) *Redemptor Hominis*, 3/4/1979; (33) *Laborem Exercens*, JOHN PAUL II 9/14/1981; (34)

Sollicitudo Rei Socialis, John Paul II 12/30/1987; (35) *Centesimus Annus*, John Paul II 5/1/1991; (36) *Veritatis Splendor*, John Paul II 8/6/1993; (37) *Catéchisme de l'Église Catholique Libreria Editrice*, Vaticana 1993.

For further reference: Camille Cianfarra, *The Vatican and the Kremlin* (New York: Dutton, 1950); Jean Charles-Leonard Sismondi, *Political Economy* (Fairfield, NJ: A. M. Kelley, 1991).

Joseph J. Califano

CONCILIAR MOVEMENT. Conciliarism was the theory that power is located in the church as represented by a general council, not in the POPE as a type of papal monarch. Within this theory the pope is merely a representative of the general council and the church, from which he received his power and to which he is accountable. This theory has been termed a "movement," which lasted from about the thirteenth century to the nineteenth century. The conciliarist theory existed in several degrees and forms during the Middle Ages, held by some universities and some rulers. A form of conciliarism is credited with forcing an end to the Great Western Schism (see Schism, Great Western) and its scandal of three popes with its attendant reestablishment of one pope, located in Rome. The notion of the power of council over pope continued as a tension until the Council of CONSTANCE (1439), where Pope EUGENE IV (1431–1447) appeared to conclude a reunion with the Eastern church. The tension abated but resurfaced again in the nineteenth century. The focus on papal INFALLIBILITY in VATICAN I eclipsed the notion of an independent conciliar jurisdictional power.

For further reference: Brian Tierney, *The Crisis of Church and State 1050–1300* (Englewood Cliffs, NJ: Prentice-Hall, 1980); Brian Tierney, *Foundations of the Conciliar Theory: The Contribution of the Medieval Canonists from Gratian to the Great Schism* (London: Cambridge University Press, 1968); Walter Ullmann, *A Short History of the Papacy in the Middle Ages* (London: Methuen, 1977).

Loretta Devoy

CONCORDAT OF 1801. The concordat signed between Napoleon Bonaparte and Pope PIUS VII (1800–1823) was inspired, on the part of Napoleon, by political motives and, on the part of the POPE, by religious ones. After his victory at Marengo, Bonaparte sought to further legitimate his regime by making peace with the church, from which the French government had been alienated since the Revolution. The pope sent Giuseppe Spina to meet with the French representative, Bishop Bernier. After several French drafts were reviewed and rejected by the papal secretary of state, Cardinal CONSALVI, a final version was agreed upon by both sides in the summer of 1801. The French legislature added amendments known as the Organic Articles, and the concordat was celebrated with a solemn *Te Deum* in Notre Dame Cathedral in April 1802.

The seventeen articles of the document dealt with matters of public worship,

French ecclesiastical administration, and government support of the church. Catholicism was recognized as the religion of the majority of the French, that is, the de facto, but not de jure, religion of the nation. The various articles dealt with the following: Article 1: permitted freedom of worship, to be conducted in conformity with police regulations deemed necessary for public tranquillity; Article 2: new boundaries established for dioceses and (Article 9) for parishes in collaboration with the government; Article 3: all titulars must resign or be replaced by the pope; Article 4: bishops were to be nominated first by the first consul and then (Article 5) receive canonical installation from the pope; Articles 6 and 7: bishops and priests were required to take an oath of obedience and loyalty to the government; Article 8: the prayer ''Lord, save the Republic and our Consuls'' was to be recited in all churches at the end of the Divine Office; Article 10: pastors were to be named by their bishops in agreement with the government; Article 11: each diocese was to have a seminary and a chapter, but the government was not obliged to endow them; Article 12: all churches that had not been confiscated during the Revolution were to be placed at the disposal of bishops; Article 13: the pope was to promise not to disturb those who had acquired confiscated ecclesiastical goods; Articles 14 and 15: the government would assure a suitable income to bishops and pastors; Article 16: Catholics could privately endow ecclesiastical foundations but only in the form of government bonds; Article 17: the first consul and the republic were given the same rights and privileges as former governments, but provision was made for a new agreement in case Napoleon should have a non-Catholic successor. The attached Organic Articles numbered 77 and dealt with governmental authorization for national and diocesan synods, bishops' establishment of cathedral chapters and seminaries (but they were forbidden to leave their diocese, even to go to Rome, without the permission of the first consul), a uniform national catechism and the requirement of governmental permission for religious feasts and nuptial blessings, and the regulation of the number and size of dioceses and parishes. Pius protested against these unilateral regulations in 1802 and again on his visit to Paris for Napoleon's coronation in 1804.

The church finally gained recognition from the revolutionary government, which had disestablished it twelve years earlier and ended the potential schism caused by the presence of the French constitutional church and clergy. Since the concordat did not provide for state control of the religious orders, this proved to be an area for potential growth and independence of the church in France during the nineteenth century. The concordat remained in effect until 1905.

For further reference: E. E. Y. Hales, *Napoleon and the Pope* (London: Eyre and Spottiswoode, 1961); M. O'Dwyer, *The Papacy in the Age of Restoration* (New York: University Press of America, 1961); Michel Bazoche, *Le régime legal des cultes en France* (Paris: Pub. administratives, 1953).

William Roberts

CONCORDAT OF WORMS (1122). SEE CONCORDATS.

CONCORDATS. Concordats are bilateral agreements between ecclesiastical and civil authorities that regulate matters of common interest. In concordats the Catholic Church, represented by the Holy See, and the chief executive of a state or that person's representative as mutually independent powers bind their respective sovereignties by treaties of international law to act in specific ways in matters of vital concern to both parties. In recent centuries the Holy See in its role as supreme head of the church and in the exercise of its universal jurisdiction has assumed this right. The practice arose in the early Middle Ages to end disputes between the church and civil authorities, to confirm acceptable practices, and to anticipate problems. Thus, Pope CALLISTUS II (1119–1124) and Emperor Henry V concluded the INVESTITURE CONTROVERSY with the Concordat of Worms (1122).

Concordats treat religious, civil, and mixed matters. They may provide for the appointment of bishops and priests to dioceses and parishes, regulate the creation, suppression, and divisions of dioceses, and fix norms for marriage, education, clerical salaries, and the ownership of church properties. Since the nineteenth century the number of concordats has multiplied. The modern state created the need for the church to define its status and role in an increasingly secularist society. Concordats frequently terminated dissension between the church and state, as occurred with the concordat with Napoleon (see Concordat of 1801) and the LATERAN ACCORDS (1929). These negotiations gave rise to the adage that "the history of concordats is the history of the sorrows of the church."

By concordats the church seeks the juridical guarantee and the independence required for the fulfillment of its mission. The concept of religious freedom developed since VATICAN II has called for the revision of some concordats. Some question the need for concordats to guarantee the freedom and mission of the church and assert that local episcopal conferences should settle religious matters with their governments.

For further reference: Adrianus de Jong, "Concordats and International Law," *Concilium* 58 (1970): 104–112; Robert A. Graham, *Vatican Diplomacy* (Princeton: Princeton University Press, 1959); H. Wagnon, *Concordats et droit international* (Gembloux: J. Duclot, 1935).

Richard J. Kehoe

CONGREGATION OF THE MISSION. The Congregation of the Mission, popularly known as "Vincentians" or "Lazarists" in English-speaking countries, is a global society of apostolic life founded by St. Vincent de Paul (1580–1660) in France in the seventeenth century. Although predominantly clerical, its membership also includes brothers and seminarians and numbers well over 3,500 in more than 60 countries on every continent. Along with the Daughters of Charity, also founded by St. Vincent de Paul, the universal patron of all works of charity, the Congregation of the Mission has served the poor and needy worldwide.

Born into a family of modest means in the small village of Pouy near Dax in southwest France, Vincent de Paul was acquainted with the needs of the poor. Like many young men of his day, Vincent initially saw the priesthood as an opportunity to escape from the claims that poverty made upon his neighbors. Following ordination at the age of nineteen, he searched for a parish or benefice that would provide him and his family a good income. A series of events effected a conversion in his life and thrust him into the midst of the most abandoned. Later in his life Vincent spoke of the foundation of the Congregation of the Mission as having occurred on 25 January 1617, when he preached a "mission" in Folleville, France. Over the next several years, this zealous priest assembled a small company of clerics to assist him in preaching to the rural poor of France. This traveling band of preachers called themselves "the priests of the mission," hence, the official name given to his community in 1655, the Congregation of the Mission, when its rules and constitutions were first approved by Rome.

Initially, "the priests of the mission" were not considered a religious community but, rather, a group of secular clergy who worked under the authority of the bishops in whose diocese they resided. They were, however, bound to their duties, to one another, and to their superior, Vincent de Paul. In addition to the inspiration he provided to the project of evangelizing the rural poor in France, Vincent recognized the spiritual poverty that existed among the clergy of his day. The Council of TRENT (1545–1563) had established regulations for the training of the clergy that, for various political reasons, were never put into practice in France. With the approval of the bishop of Beauvais, Vincent began to conduct retreats for ecclesiastics about to be ordained priests. These ordinands were welcomed, fed, and lodged by Vincent and his companions for approximately twenty days, during which time they received training in theology and priestly duties. Eventually, the content of these retreats was expanded and continued after ordination into a series of "Tuesday conferences." Several prominent clerics and bishops regularly joined Vincent for these sessions, which, joined to the ordination retreats he sponsored, resulted in the establishment of seminaries in France.

From its foundation, the Congregation of the Mission has had as its special apostolic purpose the preaching of the gospel to the poor and the formation of the clergy. The foundation of the Daughters of Charity with St. Louise de Marillac (1591–1660), the establishment of innumerable charitable organizations involving the laity, the sponsorship of many catechetical and educational institutions, the extension of evangelization to foreign countries, and countless other church initiatives have claimed Vincentian origins, all with a particular view toward effective apostolic service of the poor and needy. In this spirit St. Vincent de Paul and his followers have identified as their motto the words of Christ in Luke's gospel, "He has sent me to preach the Gospel to the poor."

For further reference: Emile Bougard, *History of St. Vincent de Paul, Founder of the Congregation of the Mission (Vincentians) and of the Sisters of Charity* (London: Longmans, Green, 1899); Pierre Coste, *The Life and Works of Saint Vincent de Paul*, 3 vols. (London: Burns and Oates, 1934); Stephen Vincent Ryan, *Early Lazarist Missions and Missionaries* (Philadelphia: privately published, n.d.); James E. Smith, *The Vincentians and the Re-Evangelization of France in the Seventeenth Century* (Louvain: Université Catholique de Louvain, 1965).

David M. O'Connell

CONGREGATIONS. Within the Apostolic See there are nine agencies known as "congregations," whose primary responsibility is to assist the Roman pontiff in the administration of the universal church. They are an important part of the church's Roman CURIA. Each having different specific competencies, all congregations possess the same juridical status within the organizational structure of the church. Each congregation has a cardinal as its head or "perfect" and a bishop appointed to serve as congregational secretary. Both of these officials serve at the nomination and pleasure of the Roman pontiff.

For further reference: P. J. Kenedy and Sons, *The Official Catholic Directory 1993* (New York: P. J. Kenedy and Sons, 1993); James H. Provost, "Pastor Bonus: Reflections on the Reorganization of the Roman Curia," *The Jurist* 48:2 (1988): 499–535.

David M. O'Connell

CONON (686–687). The son of a general stationed in Thrace, Conon was educated in Sicily. His election to the papacy was marked by controversy. During this period, papal succession underwent a process whereby the clergy elected the new POPE, judges and the nobility endorsed the selection, the army consented to the candidate, and the emperor confirmed the new pontiff. The death of JOHN V (685–686) caused a dispute between the clergy and the army regarding his successor. The relaxation of imperial control over papal elections, granted by Constantine IV (668–685) to BENEDICT II (684–685), provided the atmosphere for a clash between competing interests to occur. Conon emerged as a compromise candidate because of his father's military background.

Conon made no significant contributions to the church during his tenure. He was censured for appointing a deacon named Constantine as rector in Sicily, a post generally reserved for a Roman cleric. In the wake of a series of riots, Constantine was arrested and later deported. This episode highlighted the growing rivalry in Rome over the temporal power of the papacy. Another appointment by Conon proved more successful. He ordained an Irish missionary, Kilian, as a bishop without a specific see and allowed him to preach and teach among the pagans in northern Germany. In the process he succeeded in baptizing the duke of Franconia, Gosbert.

For further reference: Eric John, ed., *The Popes: A Concise Biographical Dictionary* (New York: Hawthorn Books, 1964); H. K. Mann, *The Lives of the Popes in the Early*

Middle Ages (London: K. Paul, 1902–1932). The best beginning primary source remains the *Liber Pontificalis* (Paris, 1886–1892).

John C. Horgan

CONSALVI, CARDINAL ERCOLE. Born in Rome in 1757, Consalvi entered papal service in 1776 and rose rapidly, though he never took holy orders and remained a deacon. As secretary of the conclave of 1799–1800, he promoted the compromise that broke a long deadlock with the election of PIUS VII (1800–1823). The new POPE named him a cardinal and appointed him secretary of state; the two worked closely for the rest of the reign. An open-minded realist, Consalvi saw that the French Revolution had drastically transformed European society and that only if the papacy adapted to the postrevolutionary world could it hope to survive.

In the religious field, his greatest achievement was the CONCORDAT OF 1801 with Napoleon, by which Rome abandoned its sterile support for the French monarchy and came to terms with the new regime sprung from the Revolution; it made possible the revival of Catholicism in France and also marked a notable advance in effective papal authority. After 1801, Consalvi was preoccupied with resisting Napoleon's efforts to increase his control over the church and his demand that the papacy side with him in his war with England. Furious at Consalvi's resistance, Napoleon forced his resignation in 1806 and then imprisoned both him and Pius VII in 1809.

Released in 1814 at Napoleon's fall, Consalvi was sent to the Congress of VIENNA to secure the restoration of the PAPAL STATES, a task he successfully accomplished. Later, this came to seem a doubtful success, for the restored papal states became a source of weakness for Rome: papal rule, backward and inefficient, became bitterly unpopular, undermining Rome's reputation in the eyes of world opinion. Consalvi, however, was not to blame for this. He realized that the Napoleonic years had accustomed the people to efficient secular government and that only if the papacy won popular support by thorough reform could it hope to survive. In 1816 he drew up a reform plan to modernize the administration and admit laymen in large numbers. Unfortunately, the reactionary party (see *Zelanti*) among the cardinals prevented the implementation of many of his reforms and revoked others after his fall. Their victory alienated public opinion and paved the way for the downfall of the temporal power.

Consalvi had greater success in other fields during 1815–1823. In religious affairs, he worked out CONCORDATS with Bavaria (1817) and Naples (1818) and less formal agreements with several other states that continued his adaption of Catholicism to the postrevolutionary world and encouraged its revival after a century of decline. In international policy, he saw cooperation with Austria as the best hope for protection for the Papal States against revolution or invasion. However, after 1820, METTERNICH sought to increase Austrian control over Italy; Consalvi could not tolerate a policy that threatened papal freedom of action and took the lead in defeating his plans. The death of Pius VII in 1823 and the election of the reactionary Pope LEO XII (1823–1829) led to Consalvi's fall from power. He died at Anzio on 25 January 1824.

For further reference: Ercole Consalvi, *Memorie*, ed. Mario Naselli Rocca di Corneliano (Rome, 1950); Alan J. Reinerman, *Austria and the Papacy in the Age of Metternich*, vol. 1, *Between Conflict and Cooperation, 1809–1830* (Washington, DC: Catholic University Press, 1979); John Martin Robinson, *Cardinal Consalvi, 1757–1824* (London: Bodley Head, 1987).

Alan J. Reinerman

CONSTANCE, COUNCIL OF (1414–1418). This council resolved the Great Western Schism (see Schism, Great Western), condemned the Hussite HERESY, and considered preliminary proposals for fundamental reconstruction and spiritual renewal of the church. Constance was in session in Germany from 5 November 1414 to 22 April 1418 and was the most representative and significant general council of medieval Western Christianity. The chronicler Ulrich Richental recorded the presence of 72,460 individuals, including POPES, other churchmen, kings, and ambassadors from throughout Europe, Africa, and Asia, with their retinue of officials, notables, and personal guards.

Under extreme pressure from Sigismund, emperor-elect of the Holy Roman Empire, JOHN XXIII (1410–1415), an ANTIPOPE of the Pisan line, issued the call. GREGORY XII (1406–1415), the reigning Roman pontiff, endorsed the move, as did the Avignonese antipope BENEDICT XIII (1394–1417), however hesitatingly. To meet the objections of the three contending popes and their followers, those in attendance known as the conciliarists (see Conciliar Movement) urged by Emperor Sigismund, succeeded in having the resolution *Sacrosancta* adopted on 26 April 1415. It declared that the council was demanded by wide cross-sections of the Catholic community, that its authority to act for the church was received directly from Christ, and that it was the duty of every committed Christian, including the popes, to obey the council's decisions. Although the Italian delegation supporting John XXIII was the most numerous, its prominence was severely circumscribed by the insistence of the English and German participants for a voting system by nations and not by head, with each national group having one vote in the decisive, plenary sessions.

Commissions were established to examine the merits of each of the three popes to occupy St. Peter's throne. Arrested by order of Sigismund, John was found illegitimate and guilty of gross misconduct, tried, and deposed on 29 May 1415. Having first balked at the suggestion of retirement, Gregory XII indicated he was willing to resign provided the council accepted the legitimacy of his Roman branch of descent. When this was granted, Gregory abdicated on 14 July 1415. Through his voluntary act, Gregory publicly acknowledged the council's superior power, while sparing himself undue embarrassment. Like John XXIII, Benedict XIII dismissed all entreaties, even from Emperor Sigismund, for his withdrawal. Nevertheless, in December 1414, he joined the conclave to assume personal command of his cause, believing that the French and Spanish contingents would rally to his defense. His arrogant stance gradually lost him support and eventually isolated him. Based on the commission's findings, the council on 26 July 1415 denounced Benedict for perjury, heresy, and sedition. Remaining intractable, Benedict abandoned the council. All appeals for his return failed, and he was removed from the chair of Peter on 26 April 1417.

To prepare for the election of a new pope, it was agreed, following intense debate between the conciliarists and spokesmen of papal primacy, that the search committee was to be composed of six deputies from each nation represented at the council and the cardinals of the three obediences. Requirement for election was the endorsement by two-thirds of the national delegations and two-thirds of the cardinals. On 11 November 1417, within three days of initiating the selection process, the search committee settled on Cardinal Odo Colonna, scion of a Roman aristocratic family, who chose the name MARTIN (1417–1431). Since Christendom ignored Benedict, the Great Schism was over.

John XXIII, in an obvious attempt to divide the council and the emperor, had ordered Huss' imprisonment in violation of the safe passage extended by Sigismund. In five weeks of exhaustive interrogation, the Bohemian reformer and rector of the University of Prague refused to disown the beliefs of the Englishman John Wycliffe (1324–1384). His detractors induced him to incorporate in his protestations the idea that sin polluted a civil as well as a clerical office, losing him Sigismund's goodwill. Moreover, Huss advocated full communion for the laity with both the bread and wine and denied the dogma of transubstantiation. On 26 July 1415, Huss, by a single vote, was branded a heretic and, on the same day, was burned at the stake, as was his companion Jerome of Prague. By decrees issued by plenary sessions, Wycliffe's teachings and their religious-political offspring. Lollardism, were also rejected.

Unquestionably, Huss' execution undermined the interest in institutional change. Plans for the election of a pope by two-thirds vote of the sacred college and each of five representative groups at large, specifically created for the occasion, designed to prevent a recurrence of the Great Schism, with the pontiff answerable to a general council, were tabled for future action, as was the possible replacement of the church's monarchical bureaucratic administration by a parliamentary democracy. Reform agreements concluded were loosely worded and susceptible to diverse interpretations. Having secured prior council endorsement, Martin V (1417–1431) announced a number of measures on 20 March 1418 that restricted papal control over church taxation and established criteria for papal appointments to benefices. Any pope, cardinal, or priest involved in the sale or purchase of an office was to be immediately discharged. No monitoring or enforcement machinery, however, was set in place.

Efforts of the conciliarists to have the predominance of a general council accepted as standard operating procedure provoked a backlash. Martin and his backers subordinated their public yearning for reform to the exigencies of fully reinstituting the Holy See in Rome in all its power. When Martin concluded that Constance had fulfilled its mission, he simply dissolved the council. He countered the prospect of an alliance between ardent conciliarists and influential monarchs by codifying church–state relations in CONCORDATS negotiated by pope and king. What the conciliarists had to show for their zeal was the decree *Frequens*, promulgated by the council on 5 October 1417, five weeks before the elevation of Martin V. It obligated future popes to summon a council meeting according to the schedule drawn and mandated by Constance. In retrospect the Council of Constance delivered far less than expected. It did not go much beyond settling the threefold papal division. Reform enactments were more illusory than real. It did not deal effectively with the spiritual crisis of the times, of which the Hussite episode was a dramatic symptom. Even the legality of the council has been held in doubt, especially by exponents of papal supremacy and INFALLIBITY.

For further reference: Louise Ropes Loomis, *The Council of Constance*, ed. and ann. John Hine Mundy and Kennerly M. Woody (New York: Columbia University Press, 1961); George Cornelius Powers, *Nationalism at the Council of Constance (1414–1418)* (Washington, DC: Catholic University of American Press, 1927); Phillip H. Stump, *The Reforms of the Council of Constance (1414–1418)* (Leiden and New York: E. J. Brill, 1993).

                                                                              Ronald S. Cunsolo

CONSTANTINE (708–715). A Syrian, Constantine ascended to the papacy during a period of pervasive Greek influence within the church's clergy, administration, and culture, an influence that proved valuable in dealing with the Eastern church. Constantine's reign was highlighted by a meeting with Emperor Justinian II (685–695, 705–711) to reach a compromise agreement on the acts of the Quinisext Council (692), convened by Justinian, without the participation of the West, to complete the unfinished work of the Fifth (CONSTANTINOPLE II) (553) and Sixth (CONSTANTINOPLE III) (680–681) General Councils. The final acts, anti-Western in nature, imposed new regulations on the clergy regarding discipline and morals. The agreements banned certain practices (e.g., clerical celibacy), ended the traditional Saturday fast day during Lent, granted permission for priests to marry, and renewed the twenty-eighth canon of CHALCEDON (451), which granted Constantinople equal patriarchical status to Rome. Like his predecessor, SERGIUS I (687–701), Constantine refused to endorse Quinisext in its entirety, approving only those acts without a Western bias. Justinian subsequently published a decree confirming the rights and privileges of Rome while endorsing Rome's jurisdiction over the exarch at Ravenna.

After a successful coup d'état against Justinian, the new emperor, Philippicus Bardanes (711–713), attempted to revive the monothelite HERESY (the belief of one will in Christ). Repudiating the Sixth General Council (see Constantinople III, Council of), Philippicus demanded Constantine's cooperation. The pontiff refused, decreeing that the name of Philippicus not appear in any charters, be excluded from prayers at mass, and not be stamped on any money and prohibited his image from being placed in any churches. In effect, Constantine had declared the church independent of Constantinople. The controversy ended peacefully when Philippicus was overthrown. His successor, Anastasius II (713–715), assured Constantine of his orthodoxy and agreed to abide by the decrees of the Sixth Council.

For further reference: Eric John, ed., *The Popes: A Concise Biographical Dictionary* (New York: Hawthorn Books, 1964); H. K. Mann, *The Lives of the Popes in the Early Middle Ages* (London: K. Paul, 1902–1932). The best beginning primary source remains the *Liber Pontificalis* (Paris, 1886–1892).

John C. Horgan

CONSTANTINE II, ANTIPOPE (767–768). This layman's election resulted from an internal struggle between the ecclesiastical and secular nobility of the new PAPAL STATE, a state that had been established a decade earlier by the Frankish king Pepin. Constantine's support included the Roman aristocracy, his brother, Duke Toto of Nepi, and a mob of soldiers. The clergy of Rome, led by an archdeacon, Christopher, received military assistance from the duke of Spoleto and the Lombard king, Desiderius (757–774). In the resulting coup of 30 July 768, Toto was killed, and Constantine was forcibly removed from the Lateran and imprisoned. Ironically, Constantine had become the agent of his own demise when, at the beginning of his "reign," he granted permission to Christopher to depart Rome under the false assumption that the archdeacon was retiring to a monastery.

When order was restored, and a new POPE was elected, STEPHEN III (768–772), Constantine was forced to appear before a synod, where he admitted his guilt in conspiring with his brother to have himself elected pope. In addition to sentencing Constantine to a monastery, the synod declared all acts of his papacy invalid. In 769, Pope Stephen changed the election laws to assure that no layman was permitted participation in papal elections and that only cardinals could be elevated to the position of bishop of Rome.

For further reference: J. N. D. Kelly, *The Oxford Dictionary of Popes* (Oxford: Oxford University Press, 1986); Walter Ullman, *A Short History of the Papacy in the Middle Ages* (London: Methuen, 1972). The best beginning primary source remains the *Liber Pontificalis* (Paris, 1886–1892).

John C. Horgan

CONSTANTINE, DONATION OF. SEE DONATION OF CONSTANTINE.

CONSTANTINOPLE I, COUNCIL OF (381). The condemnation of ARIANISM at NICAEA I in 325 did not bring the conflict surrounding its teachings to an immediate halt. The ensuing decades were filled with theological argumentation and political intrigue as the supporters of the Nicene faith and Arianism struggled for supremacy. A series of local councils eventually succeeded in quieting the discussion about the divinity of the second person of the Trinity, but questions about the divinity of the Holy Spirit were widely debated as the century progressed. Macedonius, bishop of Constantinople from about 342 to 360, and a group loosely called the "Pneumatomachi" (Spirit-Fighters) were considered to be the leading opponents of the Spirit's divinity. At the same time Apollinarius, bishop of Laodicaea from about 360 until his departure from the church in 375, taught Christological doctrines that were condemned by a series of Roman synods between 374 and 380.

In this context Emperor Theodosius I called a council to the Imperial City in 381. The number of bishops who attended is traditionally set at 150, plus some three dozen bishops who were followers of Macedonius but who left the council at its outset. Melitius of Antioch presided over the council until his death, when he was replaced by Gregory of Nazianzus, who had been made bishop of Constantinople after the deposition of Macarius. Gregory's appointment was contested, and he resigned his position within the year, overwhelmed by the bitterness of the political situation and desirous of seeking the peace of retirement. Nectarius, a government official in Constantinople, was then baptized and consecrated bishop of the city.

There are no extant records of the council's actions, and the creed attributed to it, the so-called Nicaeo-Constantinopolitan Creed, did not appear until the Council of CHALCEDON in 451, where it was read into the record as the creed of the 150 present at Constantinople. All agree that this creed was not actually composed by the council, but it contains additions to the Nicene Creed concerning the divinity of the Spirit that are in keeping with the council's purpose. The most recent collection of council documents (Tanner) presents an exposition of the council's actions in a letter from a synod held at Constantinople in 382 to Pope DAMASUS I (366–384) and the bishops of the West. Damasus appears to have accepted the council's doctrinal teaching, which was in general accord with his *Tome*.

The seven canons associated with the council are found in later documents; canons 5 and 6 probably come from the Synod of 382, while canon 7 has an even later origin. The first four canons seem to be authentic and are disciplinary. Canon 1 deals with the condemnation of heresies, including every form of Arianism, the Pneumatomachi, and Apollinarianism. The second imposes geographical limitations on bishops' activities, and the fourth concerns the deposition of Maximus, bishop of Constantinople. Canon 3 aroused controversy in according the bishop of Constantinople privileges of honor after the bishop of Rome; this represented a demotion for the bishops of Alexandria and Antioch, who drop to third and fourth place, respectively. The reason given for the action, that Constantinople was the new Rome, was not acceptable to the bishop of Rome, who based the claims of his see on Christ's promises to PETER and on the deaths in Rome of Peter and Paul, not on political considerations. According to the claims of later POPES, Rome did not approve of the council's canons because they were never brought to Rome's attention.

For further reference: L. D. Davis, *The First Seven Ecumenical Councils (325–787): Their History and Theology* (Wilmington, DE: Michael Glazier, 1987); G. H. Ettlinger. "The Holy Spirit in the Theology of the Second Ecumenical Synod and in the Undivided Church," *Greek Orthodox Theological Review* 27 (1982): 431–440; N. P. Tanner, ed., *Decrees of the Ecumenical Councils*, vol. 1 (London: Sheed and Ward; Washington, DC: Georgetown University Press, 1990), pp. 21–35; l; Ortiz de Urbina, *Nicée et Constantinople, Historie des Conciles*, vol. 1 (Paris: Editions de l'Orante, 1963).

Gerard H. Ettlinger

CONSTANTINOPLE II, COUNCIL OF (553). The Fifth Ecumenical Council, the second held in Constantinople, was called in 553 by the emperor Justinian in connection with the controversy over the "Three Chapters," which supporters of Monophysitism, with whom the emperor wished to make peace, were anxious to have condemned. In an edict of 543–544 he had condemned the person and writings of Theodore of Mopsuestia, the writings of Theodore of Cyrus against Cyril of Alexandria, and the letter of Ibas of Edessa to Mari, a Persian bishop. Justinian was able to secure the approval of the Eastern bishops, but in the West the bishop of Rome, VIGILIUS (537–555), rejected the condemnation because it seemed to question the Council of CHALCEDON.

In about 547 Justinian had Vigilius brought to Constantinople, and in 548, in a document called the *Judgment*, the POPE reluctantly condemned the Three Chapters, while continuing to support the decisions of Chalcedon. His action was attacked in the West, and after he was excommunicated (see Excommunication) by a synod held at Carthage, he repudiated the *Judgment*. Since Vigilius refused to attend the council, Eutychius, the patriarch of Constantinople, presided, and the majority of the 160–165 bishops who participated in the council were eastern. Shortly after the council opened, Vigilius issued a document called the *Constitution*, in which he condemned 60 propositions of Theodore. He refused, however, to condemn Theodore himself, because, he said, the church did not ordinarily anathematize the dead; he also would not condemn Theodoret and Ibas, because they had been accepted at Chalcedon. The council, nevertheless, condemned the Three Chapters and issued anathemas against the three persons involved. After some months Vigilius agreed to approve the decrees of the council and later issued another *Constitution*, in which he attempted to reconcile this council's actions with those of Chalcedon. In 555 he was allowed to return to Rome but died during the journey. Unlike its predecessors, this council did not proclaim any disciplinary canons.

For further reference: L. D. Davis, *The First Seven Ecumenical Councils (325–787): Their History and Theology* (Wilmington, DE: Michael Glazier, 1987); R. Devreesse, "Le début de la quérelle des Trois-Chapîtres," *Revue des Sciences Religieuses* 11 (1931):

543–565; W. de Vries, "Das zweite Konzil von Konstantinopel (553) und das Lehramt von Papst und Kirche," *Orientalia Christiana Periodica* 38 (1972): 331–366; F. X. Murphy and P. Sherwood, *Constantinople II et Constantinople III, Histoire des Conciles,* vol. 3 (Paris: Editions de l'Orante, 1974); N. P. Tanner, ed., *Decrees of the Ecumenical Councils,* vol. 1 (London: Sheed and Ward; Washington, DC: Georgetown University Press, 1990), pp. 105–122.

Gerard H. Ettlinger

CONSTANTINOPLE III, COUNCIL OF (680–681). The Sixth Ecumenical Council, the third held at Constantinople, was called by the emperor Constantine IV to put an end to the monothelite controversy. Monothelitism emerged in the early seventh century as a political expedient used to unite Monophysites and orthodox in the face of a common invader. Both sides accepted a formula that declared that there were two natures in Christ but only one mode of activity. Through this formula many Monophysites were reconciled to the church, but it was soon opposed by numerous bishops. In about 634 the matter was referred to Pope HONORIUS I (625–638), who apparently approved the formula but substituted the term "one will" for "one energy." This phrase became the key term for its adherents, and the dispute over it renewed the Monophysite controversy in a new form. After extensive consultation, a synod held at Rome in early 680 under Pope AGATHO (678–681) affirmed the doctrine of two wills in Christ and condemned monothelitism. A document explaining this teaching was sent to the emperor, and in late 680 a council was convened at Constantinople.

The council did not deal with any disciplinary issues; it reaffirmed the faith of the five earlier ecumenical councils, citing in particular the declaration of faith issued at CHALCEDON. It stated that, just as there were two natures in Christ, there were also two wills and two operations. While admitting a moral unity of the two wills and operations based on the unity of divine and human in the one person of the Word made flesh, the council rejected any natural union or confusion of them. Macarius, the bishop of Antioch, who rejected this teaching, was anathematized, as were other leaders of the movement, including Pope Honorius I. The council's decrees were accepted by Pope Agatho's successor, LEO II (682–683), who transmitted them to the Western bishops. The emperor's promulgation completed the dissemination of the council's teaching.

For further reference: P. Conte, "Il significato del primato papale nei padri del VI concilio ecumenico," *Archivum Historiae Pontificiae* 15 (1977): 7–111; L. D. Davis, *The First Seven Ecumenical Councils (325–787): Their History and Theology* (Wilmington, DE: Michael Glazier, 1987); F. X. Murphy and P. Sherwood, *Constantinople II et Constantinople III, Histoire des Conciles,* vol. 3 (Paris: Editions de l'Orante, 1974); N. P. Tanner, ed., *Decrees of the Ecumenical Councils* (London: Sheed and Ward; Washington, DC: Georgetown University Press, 1990).

Gerard H. Ettlinger

CONSTANTINOPLE IV, COUNCIL OF (869–870). After a disputed election to the See of Constantinople in 859, both claimants, Ignatius and Photius, appealed to Rome. A synod in Constantinople (861) with papal LEGATES present recognized Photius. A Roman synod under Pope NICHOLAS I (858–867) reversed this decision, deposed Photius, and reinstated Ignatius. With imperial support Photius continued to rule and retaliated by deposing Nicholas and attacking the addition of the *filioque* to the creed, thus creating a SCHISM. Emperor Basil's coup in 867 swept Photius from office and restored Ignatius. To heal the schism Pope ADRIAN II (867–872) sent delegates to Constantinople to attend a council, which confirmed the restoration of Ignatius and the condemnation of Photius. This sparsely attended council, listed in the West as the Fourth Council of Constantinople, also contained an affirmation of papal primacy.

As Basil I consolidated his regime, he ended Photius' exile and made him the tutor of his sons. When Ignatius died (877), Photius ascended the patriarchal throne a second time. Pope JOHN VIII (872–882) sent legates to attend a synod in Constantinople (879–880), which reinstated Photius and rescinded all judgments against him. The POPE approved of the acts of this synod. In the eyes of the orthodox this synod annulled the acts of the council of 869–870. The Eastern church counts only the first seven councils as ecumenical.

Photius lost his see again when Emperor Leo IV deposed him in 886. He died c. 895. He enjoys a justifiable reputation as one of the foremost scholars of the Byzantine Middle Ages. His controversy with Rome was complicated by a volatile political climate, lingering disputes concerning iconoclasm, and the dispute over the mission to the Bulgarians, which Rome wished to reserve for itself but which all the orthodox viewed as falling within the orbit of Constantinople. Photius is venerated as a saint by the orthodox.

For further reference: H. G. Beck, "The Byzantine Church in the Age of Photius," *History of the Church*, ed. H. Jedin, vol. 3 (New York: Crossroads, 1987); F. Dvornik, *The Photian Schism: History and Legend* (Cambridge: Cambridge University Press, 1948); J. M. Hussey, *The Orthodox Church in the Byzantine Empire* (Oxford: Clarendon Press, 1986).

Richard J. Kehoe

CORNELIUS (251–253). Cornelius was bishop of Rome from his election in early March 251 until his death in June 253. Cyprian of Carthage offers contemporary testimony concerning Cornelius and his election in letter 55, where he rejects NOVATIAN's claims to the position. Cyprian says that Cornelius was not suddenly elevated to the episcopate but served in all the stages of ecclesiastical office and reached the pinnacle "by climbing up through every grade in the Church's ministry" (55.8.2). Furthermore, Cornelius never sought the office for himself and "had to be coerced into accepting that office of bishop" (55.8.3). Cyprian's description of his election provides an insight into the practice of that time: "Moreover, Cornelius was made bishop by the choice of God and his Christ, by the favourable witness of almost all of the clergy, by the votes of the laity then present, and by the assembly of bishops, some sixteen in number.''

Cornelius was opposed by the antipope Novatian (251–258), who had himself anointed bishop of Rome not long after the former's election. The crucial issue that divided them was the penitential practice imposed on those who had fallen from the faith during the recent persecution. Novatian adopted an extremely rigorous approach that denied forgiveness to such people and called for their complete exclusion from the church; Cornelius followed the more lenient attitude espoused by Cyprian and others that readmitted them to communion after the performance of an appropriate penance. In 252, when persecution resumed under the emperor Gallus, Cornelius was exiled to Centumcellae, on the coast northwest of Rome. In the same year Cyprian addressed letter 59 to Cornelius and praised him for defending the true faith. Cyprian's letter 60 was probably written in late May 253 and praised Cornelius, who was now obviously in a more difficult situation for his witness and for the example he gave his congregation. Not long after this, in June, Cornelius died, apparently of natural causes. Although he did not suffer martyrdom, Cyprian termed him a martyr and often referred to his witness and his confession of the faith. He has been proclaimed a saint of the church.

For further reference: M. Bévenot, ''Cyprian and His Recognition of Cornelius,'' *Journal of Theological Studies* 28 (1977): 346–359; Cyprian of Carthage, *Letters* 44–60; Eusebius of Caesarea, *Church History* 6, 39, 43, 46; Jerome, *Lives of Illustrious Men* 66; J. N. D. Kelly, *The Oxford Dictionary of Popes* (New York: Oxford University Press, 1986).

Gerard H. Ettlinger

CORPORATIVISM. Corporativism is a sociopolitical and economic doctrine that, in the modern era, gained prominence during the second half of the nineteenth century. The corporativists hoped to bring capital and labor together under the umbrella of the church's tutelage to achieve a more humane, Christian social order. All social categories were to be united within mutually beneficial organizations, which were termed corporations. At a time when capitalism was the predominant economic doctrine in Europe, and SOCIALISM was gathering more workers within its ranks, corporativism was viewed as a viable alternative. On one hand, capitalism was criticized for its excessive individualism, which resulted in the degradation of the working class; socialism was condemned for its collectivist precepts and rejection of Christian influences. Under these conditions, some Catholic theoreticians sought to devise a system whereby the working class could be better integrated into society. These proponents of social Christianity believed that social peace and progress, grounded in the mutual best interests of capital and labor, would be attained through a corporativist order.

While the various corporativists often put forth proposals that differed in their specifics, all were united in a basic determination to engineer a Christian-based society. They were agreed, as well, on the need to build intermediate bodies or corporations that joined together both workers and employers. The constituencies would be united into one grand organization or organized separately and then joined into one corporation composed of the opposing forces. Thus constituted, Catholic social thought was to be used to guide the resolution of differences between competing sides. Social Christians advocated an active role for the church within society. While church officials did not, by necessity, have to predominate in the everyday functioning of the corporations, church influence was to be present via its doctrine, which was to imbue society.

The earliest corporativists were found in Central Europe. Among the most prominent in Germany were Ketteler and Hitze, while in Austria, Meyer, Lichtenstein, and Vogelsang were active. In France, La Tour du Pin, Albert de Mun, and Leon Harmel were leading exponents. Other Catholic countries, including Belgium and Italy, would produce corporativist thinkers as well. The most authoritative statement on Catholic social thought in an era of increased struggle between capital and labor would come on 15 May 1891, when Pope LEO XIII (1878–1903) issued his influential encyclical *Rerum Novarum*. Leo undertook to clarify the position of the church in attempting to create a more just social order. Clearly alarmed by socialist advances among Catholic workers, Leo encouraged them to join together in associations. Leo wrote of the ability of the church to bring all classes together and urged that organizations that joined together both employers and workers be fostered.

Leo stressed the role that the bishops were to play in these worker assemblies, while the ''most capable'' were to be entrusted with the task of arbitrating grievances, ''conforming to the rule of the association.'' Clearly, Leo had adopted many of the corporativist tenets of the social Christians. In practice, during the early twentieth century, Catholic working-class unions were to be less corporativist-inspired than Leo had hoped. On the 40th anniversary of *Rerum Novarum*, Pope PIUS XI issued the encyclical *Quadragesimo Anno* (On Reconstructing the Social Order). Pius reaffirmed the position of the church in support of Leo XIII's approach to the ''social question'' along corporativist lines. Workers and employers in the same industry or profession were urged to ''form guilds or associations, so that many are wont to consider these self-governing organizations, if not essential, at least natural to cure society.'' Rather than the free competition of economic forces, ''[l]oftier and nobler principles—social justice and social charity''—were to inspire the goals of church-directed corporativism. Such corporations, freely joined by both parties and entrusted with the upholding of labor's and capital's rights, were to have jurisdiction in labor disputes.

Within the system of Christian corporativism the church was to play as important a role as that of labor, capital, and the state. Its emphasis on reform, justice, and charity was intended to improve the lot of the worker in modern society. Various regimes have claimed to have drawn inspiration from corporativist doctrine. Perhaps the most notable, fascist Italy, often described as a corporate state, sought to govern economic relations on the basis of class collaboration. However, in fascism's corporativism, church influence was minimal, overshadowed by the ethical state.

For further reference: A. Fremantle, *The Papal Encyclicals in Their Historical Context* (New York: Putnam, 1956); A. C. Jemolo, *Church and State in Italy, 1850–1950* (Oxford: Basil Blackwell, 1960). On fascist corporativism see J. J. Tinghino, *Edmondo Rossoni: From Revolutionary Syndicalism to Fascism* (New York: Peter Lang, 1991).

John J. Tinghino

COUNCILS. Councils are assemblies or meetings of bishops and other authorized members that deliberate on questions of importance to the faith. There are several types of councils in the church. The ecumenical council is notable for its importance to the universal church and is an assembly to which all bishops and others are invited by the POPE. Ordinarily, the pope convokes this council, presides over it either personally or through a LEGATE, and is the president of the assembly. The council takes its name from the city in which it is held. There have been two ecumenical councils in the Vatican: VATICAN I (1869–1870) and VATICAN II (1962–1965). Both councils had the church for their main focus. Upon the ratification and promulgation of conciliar decrees by the pope, the ecumenical council has great influence on the church. The Roman Catholic Church accepts 21 councils as ecumenical. Provincial councils are assemblies of bishops of a particular ecclesiastical province, presided over by their metropolitan. Plenary councils, presided over by a papal legate, embrace more than one ecclesiastical province.

For further reference: Hubert Jedin, *Ecumenical Councils in the Catholic Church: An Historical Survey*, trans. E. Graf (New York: Herder and Herder, 1960); Brian Tierney, *Foundations of the Conciliar Theory* (London: Cambridge University Press, 1968).

Loretta Devoy

COUNTER-REFORMATION. Protestant historians coined this term in the nineteenth century to describe Catholic attempts in the sixteenth century to reconvert areas of Germany from Lutheranism to Catholicism. Subsequently, it achieved a broader usage, describing Catholic action and institutions from the emergence of Martin Luther until VATICAN COUNCIL II. Initially, it possessed a pejorative connotation, describing papal-controlled Catholicism in this era as conservative and repressive.

Strictly speaking, "Counter-Reformation" refers only to the efforts of Catholic princes and missionaries to reconvert Lutheran territories, but since many describe it as a larger movement, it is important to understand that broader context. A diverse spiritual and institutional revival or "reform" was created by those remaining loyal to the Roman church. This movement pre- and postdated the Protestant REFORMATION, and its capstone was the Council of TRENT, which unleashed far-reaching religious zeal identifiable in missionary activity in the Old and New Worlds. It also saw the formation of new religious orders, the reform of old ones, and the revival of a pastoral focus among diocesan clergy and even in artistic production.

The movement's proponents looked for what was useful in medieval conciliarism and devotional innovations that led to, and encouraged, reform, like the Gregorian reform and the Cistercian, FRANCISCAN, and Dominican movements, as well as to lay confraternities that pursued charitable activities. Hence, when persons as diverse as Ettore Vernazza, members of the Oratory of Divine Love, Ignatius of Loyola, and the early Jesuits (see Society of Jesus), Angela Merici and her Ursulines, Carlo Borromeo and other curialists-turned-pastors, and the lay members of Marian congregations sought to identify some unfilled need for the improvement of religious practice and social welfare, they did so with a normative model in mind: the ancient church.

Papal patronage of these efforts came in fits and starts from pontiffs like CLEMENT VII, PAUL III, PIUS IV, GREGORY XIII, SIXTUS V, and others. Clement and Paul deserve credit for the establishment of new orders such as the Theatines, Ursulines, and Jesuits. They also brought humanists like Jacopo Sadoleto, Reginald Pole, and Giovanni Morone into the Roman CURIA. Paul III, although fearful of a general council, finally initiated the Council of Trent in 1545. Its work of doctrinal clarification and reform of clerical practice was completed during the pontificate of Pius IV. A series of POPES sought to implement the Tridentine legislation that worked to empower bishops, to establish seminaries, and to bring together curial congregations that would oversee administration in the future.

The actions of these popes must be balanced with the anti-Protestant and repressive behavior of others. Paul IV and Pius V used new and revived institutions, like the INDEX of prohibited books and the Holy Office of the INQUISITION, to pursue a personalized, un-Tridentine definition of orthodoxy and in the process fought their enemies inside and outside the Roman church. Paul IV's unwarranted prosecution of Cardinal Giovanni Morone contributed to the pope's image as an intransigent, unbalanced person out of touch with the larger Tridentine movement. Personal and political considerations moved URBAN VIII to submit the Galileo controversy to Roman curial bureaucrats, whose actions contributed to the popular image of the Vatican as thwarting the pursuit of knowledge.

Noncurial devotional leaders and the literature of spirituality they created in this period should not be neglected. Individuals such as Gaetano da Thiene, Teresa of Avila, John of the Cross, and Philip Neri provide heroic examples of personal spiritual revival and commitment. Their teachings reinforced the trend toward charitable activity and individual sanctity. The mystical and devotional writings inspired the creation of other new orders and motivated the activity of artists, bishops, clerics, and lay reformers throughout the early modern world.

For further reference: Eric Cochrane, "Tridentine Reform," in *Italy 1530–1630*, ed. Julius Kirsner (New York: Longman, 1988); Erwin Iserloh, *Reformation and Counter-*

Reformation, vol. 5, in *History of the Church*, ed. Hubert Jedin and John Dolan (New York: Seaburg, 1980); John C. Olin, ed., *The Catholic Reformation: Savonarola to Ignatius Loyola* (Westminster, MD: Christian Classics, 1978); A. D. Wright, *The Counter-Reformation: Catholic Europe and the Non-Christian World* (New York: St. Martin's Press, 1982).

William V. Hudon

CURIA, ROMAN. As head of the universal church, the Roman pontiff exercises supreme executive, judicial, and legislative power within the church. Given the scope of his authority, there exists in the church an intricate and complex structure of official agencies established to administer that power within carefully defined categories. This structure is commonly known as the Roman CURIA, and its members are appointed and granted authority by the POPE. It has a history that dates back to the sixteenth century, when Pope SIXTUS V (1585–1590) issued the papal bull *Immensa* (22 January 1588), creating its fifteen CONGREGATIONS and regulating their powers. He is considered the author of the congregational system of procedure in the Roman Curia. Prior to that time, the government of the church was administered by the Roman pontiff together with synods composed of members of the Roman clergy.

In 1908 Pope PIUS X (1903–1914) introduced a series of reforms of the Roman Curia in his apostolic constitution *Sapienti consilio* (29 June 1908), which, with some revisions, were then incorporated into the 1917 Code of CANON LAW, canons 242 through 264 inclusive. As the Second Vatican Council (see Vatican II, Council of) (1962–1965) drew to a close, the organization and scope of authority of the Roman Curia once again became the subject of papal concern. Pope PAUL VI (1963–1978) published an apostolic constitution, *Regimini Ecclesiae universae*, on 15 August 1967, which attempted to bring the work of the Roman Curia into conformity with the changes in the church effected by Vatican II. Seven years later Pope Paul VI established a commission to review the implementation of his 1967 reforms that, following his death in 1978, was replaced by a new commission created by his successor, JOHN PAUL II (1978–).

The work of this commission continued through the final period of revision of the church's canon law, eventually promulgated in 1983. The recommendations of this latter commission, however, were not accepted by the 1985 Synod of Bishops, and a third commission was appointed to assist the pope with this initiative. His 1988 apostolic constitution, *Pastor Bonus* (28 June 1988), represented the fruits of their labors and established the most recent reforms affecting the organization and activities of the Roman Curia.

The agencies of the Roman curia can be divided into the following departments or dicasteries: the Papal Secretariat and the Council for the Public Affairs of the Church; nine congregations; three TRIBUNALS; twelve pontifical COUNCILS; seven OFFICES; and ten COMMISSIONS. Each of these departments will now be considered under its specific title.

I. The Papal Secretariat or secretariat of state provides immediate assistance to the Roman pontiff in the administration of the universal church and with the internal workings of all the agencies of the Roman Curia. It is divided into two sections: the first section, "for general affairs," in addition to the administration of day-to-day operations that are not part of the competence of other departments, handles all special concerns entrusted to it by the pope; this section also serves as a liaison between the pope and other curial divisions, individual bishops, and the diplomatic missions of the Apostolic See; the second section, "for relations with states," exercises jurisdiction over those matters that pertain to civil governments and individual nations.

II. Congregations. These nine organizations exercise administrative power in the government of the church, and all possess the same juridic status. Each has a cardinal and a bishop appointed by the pope as prefect and secretary, respectively, and is composed of bishops similarly appointed, assisted by an administrative and clerical staff composed of clergy and laity alike. Historically, their competencies have been altered during various pontificates. At the present time, these congregations and their competencies include the following:

1. The Congregation for the Doctrine of the Faith. Its responsibility is primarily the clarification and protection of church doctrine on matters of faith and morals as well as the correction of errors proposed by members of the church in this regard. Depending on the issue at hand, the congregation proceeds administratively or juridically.

2. The Congregation for the Causes of Saints. This handles all matters pertaining to the beatification and canonization of saints and the preservation of their relics.

3. The Congregation for the Oriental Churches. This treats those matters relevant to persons, disciplines, and liturgical ceremonies within Oriental churches.

4. The Congregation for Bishops. This provides for the naming of bishops of every rank and status as well as those who act with episcopal authority. It has responsibility for the establishment of new dioceses or provinces, for dividing or uniting them following consultation with the appropriate conferences of bishops, and for all matters concerning bishops.

5. The Congregation for Divine Worship and the Discipline of the Sacraments. Unless reserved to another congregation, all matters pertaining to the discipline of the seven sacraments are handled by this congregation, including special questions regarding the nonconsummation of marriage, dispensations, and the validity of ordination.

6. The Congregation for the Evangelization of Peoples (or for the Propagation of the Faith). It has competence for those things connected with the missionary activities of the church, including the establishment of, and support for, the missions.

7. The Congregation for Institutes of Consecrated Life and for Societies of Apostolic Life. The Apostolic See's responsibilities toward religious communities, secular institutes, societies of apostolic life, and all such varieties of evangelical or apostolic lifestyles are mediated through this congregation. It approves the establishment or, if necessary, the dissolution of such entities as well as approves their governing documents and structures in accord with canon law.

8. The Congregation for the Clergy. The rights and obligations of ordained deacons

and priests and all things personal and apostolic that pertain to the clerical state are administered by this congregation. It also promotes preaching and catechetics and has competence over the administration of temporal goods in the church not specifically committed to the vigilance of another congregation.

9. The Congregation for Catholic Education. All matters relating to seminaries as well as to all levels of the Catholic education of the laity rest within its competence. It also coordinates and promotes the church's efforts to foster ecclesiastical vocations.

III. Tribunals (see also Tribunal). Three "courts" established within the Apostolic See have responsibility for the exercise of judicial power in the church and the resolution of legal controversies.

1. The Apostolic Penitentiary. It handles only matters of conscience known as the "internal forum," whether sacramental or nonsacramental. It grants absolutions, issues dispensations, enforces or commutes ecclesiastical penalties, and so on.

2. The Supreme Tribunal of the Apostolic Signatura. This is the supreme court of the church and administers the church's judicial power and procedures at the highest level, including appeals of decisions made by, and complaints regarding, personnel within the Roman Rota.

3. The Roman Rota. This is the ordinary court of appeal for controversies decided at lower-level tribunals, especially cases alleging the nullity of marriage.

IV. Pontifical Councils. Twelve pontifical councils exist to serve the Apostolic See with regard to issues of special importance within the church. They are the Pontifical Councils for the Laity: for Promoting Christian Unity; for the Family; for Justice and Peace; *Cor Unum*; for the Pastoral Care of Migrants and Itinerants; for the Pastoral Care of the Health Care Apostolate; for the Interpretation of Legal Texts; for Inter-Religious Dialogue; for Dialogue with Non-Believers; of Culture; for Social Communications. Each of these councils is administered by, at least, an archbishop as president and has competence for promoting those aspects of the Christian life that fall within its particular embrace.

V. Offices. The seven "offices" of the Roman Curia are smaller administrative departments that exercise a special responsibility to the papacy in general or to the person of the Roman pontiff. The Apostolic Camera protects the goods and rights of the Apostolic See during a vacancy. The Prefecture of the Papal Household administers the Apostolic Palace, the papal schedules, and nonliturgical papal ceremonies. The Administration of the Patrimony of the Apostolic See handles the property of the Apostolic See, while the Prefecture of the Economic Affairs of the Apostolic See serves as the papal financial office. The Office of Pontifical Ceremonies assists in the celebration of all liturgical ceremonies involving the pope. The Central Office of Statistics gathers information and data for the church. Finally, the Archives of the Second Vatican Council preserves the acts and other documents of Vatican II.

VI. Commissions. The work of the Roman Curia is also accomplished through papal commissions created to meet some specific need. Although their membership varies in number, they are permanent or standing committees of the Apostolic See. At the present time, there are ten such organizations.

For further reference: Peter A. Baart, *The Roman Court* (New York: Fr. Putet, 1895); Edward L. Heston, *The Holy See at Work* (Milwaukee: Bruce, 1950); Peter Huizing and

Knut Walf, eds., *The Roman Curia and the Communion of Churches* (New York: Seabury Press, 1979); P. J. Kenedy and Sons, *The Official Catholic Directory 1993* (New York: P. J. Kenedy and Sons, 1993; John Paul II, apostolic constitution *Pastor Bonus* 28 (June 1988); John Paul II, *Acta Apostolicae Sedis* 80 (1988): 841–924; James H. Provost, "Pastor Bonus: Reflections on the Reorganization of the Roman Curia," *The Jurist* 48:2 (1988): 499–535; P. C. Van Lierde and A. Giraud, "The Administration in the Roman Curia," in *What Is a Cardinal?* (New York: Hawthorn Books, 1964); Kevin Smyth, "Curia," in Karl Rahner, ed., *Sacramentum Mundi*, vol. 2 (New York: Herder and Herder, 1968), pp. 49–55.

David M. O'Connell

D

DAMASUS I (366–384). Damasus was born in about 305 and died in 384. His father may have been a Spaniard, but he himself was apparently born in Rome. A deacon under Pope LIBERIUS (352–366), he went into exile with him. He returned to Rome and was allied for a time with the antipope FELIX II (355–365) but later reconciled with Liberius and in 366 was chosen to succeed him as bishop of Rome. A splinter group of loyal supporters of Liberius rejected Damasus, however, and elected URSINUS (366–367) and had him consecrated illegitimately. From 366 to 370 Ursinus was twice exiled. In 370 Ursinus was allowed to return to Italy but was banned from Rome; his followers, however, continued to attack Damasus and brought false charges of adultery against him. Damasus was declared innocent by the civil authority, which then banished Ursinus to Cologne.

Damasus was pope when the emperor Theodosius I, in 380, made Christianity the official religion of the empire. Throughout his reign he strongly emphasized the primacy of the Roman See, which he called ''apostolic,'' believing that it was based on the words of Christ himself and that he was the successor of PETER. In a period of doctrinal and disciplinary controversy, Damasus defended the apostolic faith, opposing many forms of HERESY and SCHISM. He sent representatives to the second ecumenical council at Constantinople (see Constantinople I) in 381, which not only declared the divinity of the Holy Spirit but also condemned the Trinitarian heresy of Macedonius and the Christological heresy of Apollinarius, both of which had been condemned by Roman synods under Damasus (in 368 and 369). Damasus rejected the appeal of a Spanish heretic, Priscillian, who had been condemned by a council in Saragossa in 380. In the East he cooperated with Basil of Caesarea against ARIANISM but came into conflict with him over the so-called Melitian schism in Antioch, in which he supported Paulinus rather than Flavian to replace the deceased Melitius.

He was active in Roman politics and intervened when the altar of the goddess

Victory was removed from the Roman Senate house. Pagan lawmakers, in one of the last attempts to prolong the life of traditional Roman religion, begged the emperor to overturn this action, but Damasus supported the successful appeal of the Christians to let it stand. Damasus commissioned his secretary Jerome to revise the Old Latin versions of the Bible in the light of the original languages and was thus the ultimate inspiration for a translation that became the Bible of the Western church. Although his episcopacy had a shaky beginning, his achievements make him a significant figure in the development of the papacy. He was proclaimed a saint.

For further reference: Ambrose, *Letters* 11, 17; Jerome, *Letters* 15–16, 18–22, 35–36, 45, 123; Jerome, *Lives of Illustrious Men* 103; T. C. Lawler, "Jerome's First Letter to Damasus," *Kyriakon: Festschrift Johannes Quasten*, vol. 2, ed. P. Granfield and J. A. Jungmann (Münster: Aschendorff, 1970), pp. 548–552; A. Lippold, "Ursinus und Damasus," *Historia* 14 (1965): 105–128; M. H. Shepherd, "The Liturgical Reform of Damasus I," *Kyriakon: Festschrift Johannes Quasten*, vol. 2, ed. P. Granfield and J. A. Jungmann (Münster: Aschendorff, 1970), pp. 847–863; Socrates, *Ecclesiastical History*, vol. 5, 15.

Gerard H. Ettlinger

DAMASUS II (1048). Reigning from 17 July to 9 August 1048, Damusus II was originally known as Count Poppo or Boppo. This Bavarian bishop was the second German POPE to be nominated by Emperor Henry III. Documents of 1046 mention that he was already in the king's favor and was part of Henry's entourage when he traveled to Italy in the fall of 1046, playing a prominent part in the Roman Synod of January 1047. In October, upon the death of CLEMENT II (1046–1047), the people and clergy of Rome sent a request to Henry to name a successor. Bishop Wazo of Liège argued that GREGORY VI (1045–1046), who was in exile in Cologne and whom he considered wrongly deposed, should be restored, but on Christmas Day that year the emperor nominated Poppo.

At the same time, however, BENEDICT IX (1032–1044, 1045) had returned from his retreat in Tusculan and seized the papal office with the support of the powerful Count Boniface of Tuscany. Poppo set out for Rome but was prevented from getting there by Boniface, who argued that Benedict had successfully re-established himself as pope. When Henry threatened to venture to Rome to install the new pope, Boniface thought it prudent to obey. On 17 July Poppo was consecrated and enthroned, selecting the ancient name of Damasus. He reigned for just 23 days, dying at Palestrina, where he had gone to escape the heat. While there was a suspicion of poisoning, the most likely cause of his death was malaria.

For further reference: L. Duchesne, ed., *Liber Pontificalis* (Paris: E. de Boccard, 1955); P. Hughes, *The History of the Church* (London: Sheed and Ward, 1955).

William Roberts

DE GASPERI, ALCIDE. Christian democratic premier of Italy from December 1945 to July 1953, De Gasperi played a major role in the postwar reconstruction of Italy. Born 3 April 1881 in Pieve Tesino (Trentino), Austria-Hungary, he died in Sella Valsugana (Trentino-Alto Adige), Italy, on 19 August 1954. In 1905 De Gasperi earned a degree in philology from the University of Vienna. A devout Catholic, he became active in the movement of social Catholicism and its political counterpart, the Trentine POPULAR PARTY. He was acquainted with the Italian Catholic social movement and corresponded with its leading exponents. In 1911 he was elected to the Austrian Parliament, where he supported autonomy for the predominantly Italian-speaking Trentino.

During WORLD WAR I he worked to alleviate the hardships of Italians interned by the Hapsburg government. When the Treaty of St. Germain transferred the Trentino to Italy, De Gasperi became an Italian citizen. Entering the Popular Party, he became active in Italian politics and in 1921 was elected to the Chamber of Deputies. He agreed to Popularist participation in the ministry formed by MUSSOLINI in October 1922, but by 1923 De Gaspari was denouncing FASCISM, both in Parliament and through his paper, *Il Nuovo Trentino*. To halt the consolidation of the fascist regime, he favored collaboration with Turati's right-wing socialists, but Pope PIUS XI interjected a virtual veto.

After the murder of Matteotti, De Gasperi supported the Aventine Secession, and when it failed to topple Mussolini's government, he was among the deputies deprived of their parliamentary seats. In 1927 he was arrested by the fascist police; in 1929, after his release from prison, he was hired by the Vatican Library.

During these years De Gasperi wrote for the Vatican bimonthly *L'Illustrazione Vaticana* under the pen name of "Spectator." He remained unreconciled with fascism, even though the Popular Party had been dissolved, and many of his former colleagues made their peace with the regime. The growing SCHISM between church and state (especially after the papal denunciation of racism) as well as the decisive defeats inflicted on Italy in WORLD WAR II paved the way for the rebirth of the Christian democratic movement. De Gasperi, the last head of the Popular Party, emerged as the leader of its successor, the Christian Democratic Party (Democrazia Cristiana), founded in July 1943 through a fusion of various pre–World War II groups and associations, such as the Popular Party, the La Pira Circle of Catholic Action, the Lombard Guelf movement, and the *FUCI-movimento laureati* (university students and graduates active in Catholic Action).

Becoming premier on 10 December 1945, De Gasperi presided over eight consecutive ministries, lasting eight and a half years and shaping Italy's postwar development. Until May 1947 Palmiro Togiatti's communists were members of De Gasperi's government, as were Nenni's socialists. De Gasperi expelled them, claiming they fomented disturbances in the nation. In April 1948, in the first parliamentary elections under the new Constitution, De Gasperi led his party to an impressive victory (48 percent of the vote) over the leftist coalition of communists and left-wing socialists. Despite papal disapproval, De Gasperi's governments were coalitions, with the majority of ministerial posts going to Christian democrats and the balance to Social Democrats (right-wing socialists), liberals, and republicans. The Christian Democratic Party was divided into left, center, and right factions, and De Gasperi, temperamentally and ideologically a man of the Center, expended considerable energy holding together the various factions. While De Gasperi accepted the assistance of the church in electoral contests, he opposed efforts to form a ''Catholic Party'' and shunned alliances with neofascists even when such alliances were designed to forestall communist electoral victories.

In foreign affairs De Gasperi aligned Italy with the West, especially after the intensification of the COLD WAR. A fervent believer in European unity, De Gasperi supported European integration and brought Italy into the European Coal and Steel Community. His domestic policies included a mixed economy of private and state enterprises, conservative fiscal practices, and agrarian reform. The most controversial piece of domestic legislation was agrarian reform (1950), which angered many members of the conservative faction in his party and which cost him the support of the Liberal Party. In the June 1953 parliamentary elections De Gasperi and his allies failed to obtain the majority required by a new electoral law. He then considered a center-left government with the Nenni socialists, but the refusal of the latter to give up the Pact of Unity with the Communist Party aborted the project. In July 1953 De Gasperi resigned as premier. His last political post was as secretary of the party (October 1953– August 1954). He is buried in Rome in the Church of San Lorenzo fuori le mure.

For further reference: Elisabeth Arnoulx de Pirey, *De Gasperi, le pere italien de l'Europe* (Paris: Pierre Tequi, 1991); Elisa Carrillo, *De Gasperi, the Long Apprenticeship* (Notre Dame, IN: University of Notre Dame Press, 1965); Maria Romana Catti, *De Gasperi, uomo solo* (Milan: Mondadori, 1964); Pietro Scoppola, *La proposta politica di De Gasperi* (Bologna: Il Mulino, 1977).

Elisa A. Carrillo

DEUSDEDIT (615–618). Roman by birth and the son of a subdeacon, little is known of Deusdedit's early career. Chosen by antimonastic forces within the church, he was the first priest consecrated POPE since JOHN II (533–535). Consequently, he favored the secular clergy by reinstating them in their former positions. At the time of his pontificate, Italy was ravaged by wars, epidemics, and earthquakes. Byzantine soldiers stationed in Italy revolted, due to lack of pay, resulting in the murder of the emperor's exarch at Ravenna. Despite the tumult, Deusdedit remained loyal to Emperor Heraclius (610–641). Deusdedit aided victims of the plague in Rome and, reportedly, upon meeting one of the afflicted, out of compassion kissed him, instantly restoring his health. According to tradition, Deusdedit was the first pope to use lead seals (*bullae*) on papal documents, which subsequently became known as bulls. The feast day of this saint is celebrated on 8 November.

For further reference: Joseph S. Brusher, *Popes through the Ages* (Princeton: D. Van Nostrand, 1964); Hans Kuhner, *Encyclopedia of the Papacy* (New York: Philosophical Library, 1958).

John C. Horgan

DIONYSIUS (260–268). Because of the severity of the persecution under Valerian, the papacy remained vacant for two years. Finally, in July 260, Dionysius was elected. He seems to have shared the strict position of STEPHEN I (254–257) regarding the validity of baptism administered by heretics but had adopted a more compromising attitude by the reign of SIXTUS II (257–258). Shortly after Dionysius assumed the papacy, Dionysius of Alexandria, in his zeal to condemn the Sabellian HERESY, wrote a letter that seemed to some Alexandrians to deny the eternity and consubstantiality of God the Son with God the Father and even to represent the Son as a creature. These Alexandrians condemned their bishop to Dionysius of Rome, who called a synod, which clearly presented the Roman position on the question.

This case presents an early indication of the teaching authority enjoyed by the bishop of Rome, who was called upon to review the statements of one of the world's most important bishops and censured the doctrine contained in Dionysius' letter without an appeal regarding his right to do so. Pope Dionysius reorganized the allocation of parishes and cemeteries in Rome and was praised in a letter of St. Basil almost a century later for having sent letters of encouragement to the afflicted church of Caesarea and his ransom of captives. However, Dionysius was not a martyr, as the *Liber Pontificalis* claims. He is buried in the Cemetery of Callistus. His feast is celebrated on 26 December.

For further reference: J. N. D. Kelly, *The Oxford Dictionary of Popes* (New York: Oxford University Press, 1986); J. Lebreton and J. Zeiller, *The History of the Primitive Church*, vol. 4 (London: H. Prim, 1948).

Bernard J. Cassidy

DIOSCORUS, ANTIPOPE (530). During a period that witnessed continuous warfare between imperial and Gothic armies for control of Italy, Dioscorus, a deacon from Alexandria, was elected by a majority of the clergy, who favored a pro-Byzantine pontiff. Pope FELIX IV (526–530), by naming BONIFACE II (530–532), selected by a minority as his successor, was in violation of laws that had been agreed to under the pontificate of SYMMACHUS (498–514) regulating the elections of future POPES. Although Dioscorus died within three weeks of his election, in his earlier career he had supported the findings of the Council of CHALCEDON (451), sided with Symmachus during the Laurentian SCHISM (498–499, 501–506), and assisted in resolving the Acacian schism (484–519).

For further reference: H. K. Mann, *The Lives of the Popes in the Early Middle Ages* (London: K. Paul, 1902–1932); Walter Ullman, *A Short History of the Papacy in the Middle Ages* (London: Methuen, 1972). The best beginning primary source remains the *Liber Pontificalis* (Paris, 1886–1892).

John C. Horgan

DIVINI ILLIUS MAGISTRI **(1929).** In December 1929, Pope PIUS XI (1922–1939) issued this ENCYCLICAL on the education and training of youth in the midst of a struggle between Italian FASCISM and Catholicism over the prerogatives of each in the schooling of young Italians. The letter served as a rallying cry for Catholics who were inclined to resist attempts by MUSSOLINI's state to monopolize the educational system.

In it, Pius claimed that the family and the church have the major roles to play in education, with the family exercising "priority rights" and the church "preeminent rights." The pope limited the role of the state to "complementing" the work of the family and the church. The state should not attempt to encroach upon the rights of either the family or the church in the educating and training of youth. In a direct challenge to Mussolini's educational policies, Pius claimed that the church had an absolute right to pass judgment on any educational system in terms of its effect on Christian education of youth. Specifically, the encyclical challenged the right of the fascist state to compel attendance in state schools or any attempt to effect a monopoly on education.

For further reference: *Papal Teachings* [on] *Education: Selected and Arranged by the Benedictine Monks of Solesmes* (Boston: Daughters of St. Paul, 1960).

Richard J. Wolff

DIVINI REDEMPTORIS. SEE TOTALITARIANISM.

DONATION OF CONSTANTINE. This false document was used extensively during the conflict between the papacy and the empire during the Middle Ages. Its text purports to transfer the imperial dignity, symbols, and authority of the Western Roman empire, along with the Lateran palace, from the first Christian emperor, Constantine I, to Pope SYLVESTER I (314–335), supposedly in gratitude for the gift of baptism and a miraculous cure from leprosy. Thereupon, the emperor removed his residence from Rome to Constantinople. The Donation depends heavily on the late fifth-century *Legenda S. Sylvestri* but also contains much that is new. Although there is some disagreement concerning the time of its composition, most scholars attribute it to the mid-eighth century, when it is believed someone at the Roman court assembled the rights and privileges that the papacy allegedly enjoyed. Perhaps Pope STEPHEN II (752–757) carried the Donation with him on his journey to the Frankish court in 753–754 as an added inducement to King Pepin to aid Rome against the Lombards.

Possibly the original intent of the Donation was a defense of the papal position against the claims of the Byzantine court. In the mid-eighth century relations were strained because of the Iconoclastic Controversy and conflicts over ecclesiastical jurisdictions and control over papal properties in southern Italy. As early as the tenth century Emperor Otto III claimed the Donation of Constantine was a forgery, but most medieval critics accepted its authenticity but questioned its validity, maintaining that Constantine had exceeded his authority in alienating such vast portions of his realm. In the fifteenth century the Donation was proven to be a forgery. In his *De Concordantia Catholica* of 1433 Nicholas of Cusa demonstrated the falsity of the Donation. Better known is the 1440 work of Lorenzo Valla, *De Falso credita et ementita Constantini donatione*, which relied on the philological skills honed by the Renaissance to demonstrate its falsity. Independently, the English bishop of Chichester Reginald Peacock, toward the end of his life (c. 1460), made the same points.

For further reference: Donald Bullough, *The Age of Charlemagne* (New York: G. P. Putnam's Sons, 1966); Denys Hay, *Europe in the Fourteenth and Fifteenth Centuries* (New York: Holt, Rinehart, and Winston, 1966); John Addington Symonds, *The Revival of Learning: The Renaissance in Italy* (New York: G. P. Putnam's Sons, 1960); Walter Ullman, "Donation of Constantine," *The New Catholic Encyclopedia*, vol. 4, 1000–1001.

William C. Schrader

DONATION OF PEPIN. For two centuries, the Lombards threatened to conquer Rome, and after 663, the emperors in Constantinople displayed diminished interest in defending fragments of their power in Italy. The emperor's representative, the exarch, was increasingly isolated in Ravenna, losing most of central Italy to the Lombards. By default, power in Rome fell to the POPES. In 751 the Lombard king captured Ravenna, bringing imperial power north of Naples to an end. To the north, the Merovingian monarchy among the Franks was likewise coming to an end. For the last century of their existence, the descendants of Clovis were protected only by their royal blood, while real power rested in the hands of the great nobles, led by the mayors of the palace. The great Charles Martel, champion of Christendom against the Muslims at the Battle of Tours in 732, secured this power in his family. With the death of Charles (741) and the retirement of his son Carloman to the monastery of Monte Cassino (747), Charles' young son, Pepin the Short (c. 715–768), became the real ruler of the Franks. Pepin looked to the church to legitimate his position.

In 750 a Frankish delegation set out for Rome with the question for Pope ZACHARY (741–751) "whether it was good or not that those called kings in Francia should not have the power of ruling." Zachary's answer, that it was better that power and title be combined, provided Pepin his justification for deposing the last of the Merovingians. With the support of Rome, Pepin was crowned as the new king by St. Boniface in November 751, utilizing a ceremony of anointing inspired by the biblical precedent of Samuel's displacing Saul by anointing David as king. The friendship of the Franks was very important to Rome, which was again threatened by the Lombards. On 14 October 753, Pope STEPHEN II (752–757) negotiated with the Lombards, to no avail. This pope left Pavia for the Frankish realm and in January 754 met Pepin in northeastern France. Stephen anointed Pepin and his sons, recognizing them as kings, and requested aid against the Lombards.

Pepin undertook two expeditions against the Lombards in 755 and 756, compelling them to give up the conquered lands in central Italy, which were then given not to the agents of the Byzantine emperor but to Pope Stephen II, in what is called the Donation of Pepin. This swath of land, stretching from Ravenna to south of Rome, thus formed the basis for the states of the church, which remained until 1870.

For further reference: Donald Bullough, *The Age of Charlemagne* (New York: G. P. Putnam's Sons, 1966); Ferdinand Lot, *The End of the Ancient World and the Beginnings of the Middle Ages* (New York: Harper and Row, 1931); John Michael Wallace-Hadrill, *The Barbarian West: The Early Middle Ages,* A.D. *400–1000* (New York: Hutchinson Universal Library, 1952).

William C. Schrader

DONUS (676–678). A Roman by birth, little is known of his early life or career. Upon assuming the chair of St. Peter, Donus reached agreement with the archbishop of Ravenna ending all claims of self-governance and independence from Rome. Emperor Constantine IV (668–685) began negotiations to restore a sense of unity between Constantinople and the Holy See, a relationship strained by the monothelite HERESY. Constantine, without the acquiescence of his patriarch Theodore I (677–679), himself a monothelite, suggested the creation of a council to arbitrate the theological differences. Donus died before receiving the emperor's letter of conciliation.

For further reference: Joseph S. Brusher, *Popes through the Ages* (Princeton: D. Van Nostrand, 1964); H. K. Mann, *The Lives of the Popes in the Early Middle Ages* (London: K. Paul, 1902–1932). The best beginning primary source remains the *Liber Pontificalis* (Paris, 1886–1892).

John C. Horgan

E

EAST ASIA, VATICAN AND. Although Nestorians had secured a presence in China in the seventh century, Rome's first envoys did not arrive in East Asia until the Middle Ages. The rise of Mongol power in the thirteenth century facilitated Euro-Asian contacts and prompted Pope INNOCENT IV (1243–1254) to dispatch Giovanni da Piano del Carpine as the first ambassador to the Great Khan. In 1245, Piano del Carpine reached Karakorum, the Mongol capital in central Asia, but traveled no farther. In 1294, however, another FRANCISCAN, Giovanni di Montecorvino, reached Beijing (Cambaluc) and established a successful LEGATION there. His status was enhanced in 1318, when Pope JOHN XXII (1316–1334) divided Asia into two missionary districts: Persia, entrusted to the Dominicans, and China, to the Franciscans under Archbishop Montecorvino. After Montecorvino's death in 1333 and despite the appointment of another papal legate nine years later, the Mongol collapse and the rise of China's Ming dynasty signaled an era of anti-Christian persecution, ending for two centuries effective relations between Rome and China.

The expansion of Spanish and Portuguese economic and military power revived Rome's presence in East Asia in the sixteenth century. Often from Portuguese bases at Goa (1510) and Macao (1557), Augustinians and Jesuits (see Society of Jesus) joined Franciscans and Dominicans in new endeavors to contact and evangelize. Most notable was the Basque Jesuit Francis Xavier, who reached Goa in 1542 as NUNCIO with the task of establishing Eastern missions. Furthermore, in 1573 Jesuits established a permanent mission in China under Alessandro Valignani and, after 1582, his assistant, Matteo Ricci.

After 1508, the Spanish and Portuguese Crowns managed a Catholic presence in their respective empires according to the papal grants of *patronato real* and *padroado*. Missions and papal legations to independent East Asian peoples, however, emanated from Roman authority. In 1622, partly to coordinate missionary activity and to lessen Iberian interference, Pope GREGORY XV (1621–

1623) created the Sacred Congregation for the Propagation of the Faith. The CONGREGATION designated vicars apostolic, who answered only to the POPE, for Tongking and Cochin-China (both in 1659) and China (Nanjing in 1660). It also promoted a Paris-based Foreign Missionary Society (1664) for secular priests and for the cultivation of native clergy. The naming of Lo Wen-Tsao (also known as Gregory Lo or Gregorio Lopez) as titular bishop of Basilinopolous and vicar apostolic for north China in 1674 was among the first fruits of this plan. East Asia's first seminaries were founded in Siam and Cochin-China in 1665. Others were launched in Tongkin in 1666 and in China in 1703. By 1600 East Asia claimed five episcopal sees: Macao, Funai in Japan, and Cebu, Vigan, and Manila in the Philippines. During the seventeenth century, the dioceses of Beijing and Nanjing were created or revived.

After a Japanese persecution of Christians in the mid-seventeenth century and another in China through most of the eighteenth century, Rome renewed its focus on East Asia in the nineteenth and twentieth centuries. As in the 1500s, success often depended on Europe's military power. The first missionary to Japan arrived in 1859, and Catholicism was legalized there in 1873. Following anti-Christian massacres in 1801, 1839–1846, and 1866–1869, Korea formally opened itself to missions in 1883. In Indochina, after midcentury persecutions, Catholicism benefited from French military and colonial penetration. Although the Foreign Mission Society established operations in Manchuria in 1838, Tibet in 1846, and much of southern China in 1848, Catholic activity accelerated in China mainly after 1860. In that year a treaty between Paris and Beijing sanctioned a status quo under which France assumed the protection of all Catholic missionaries in China and issued them passports. By the 1880s, however, Germany and Italy also assumed responsibility for the defense of their own national clergy. Throughout this revival, furthermore, the Holy See continued to cultivate the growth of native clergies. Rome's intentions here were evidenced in LEO XIII's (1878–1903) apostolic letter *Qae mari sinico* (1902), BENEDICT XV's (1914–1922) encyclical *Maximum Illud* (1919), the establishment of apostolic delegations to Japan in 1916 and to China in 1922, the beatification of the Korean martyrs in 1925, and PIUS XI's (1922–1939) consecration of six Chinese bishops in 1926. After WORLD WAR II, PIUS XII (1939–1958) continued this trend by naming China's first cardinal, Thomas Tien Ken-sin (1946), establishing internunciatures in Beijing (1946) and Tokyo (1952), and elevating the Chinese hierarchy. In 1948 the pontiff also inaugurated St. Peter's College for indigenous clergy in mission lands.

Nevertheless, weakened by further persecutions under Japanese military occupation, the church in postwar East Asia was battered even more severely by anticolonialist and/or Marxist regimes in the People's Republic of China, North Korea, North Vietnam, and, later, Kampuchea, where Pol Pot's regime eradicated Catholicism. Rome's contacts with hierarchies in those states were severed. Those clergy and lay leaders who resisted the new orders usually emigrated or were exiled, imprisoned, or killed. The new regimes replaced the church with puppet societies, such as the Chinese Catholic Patriotic Association (1957) and Vietnam's Liaison Committee of Patriotic and Peace-Loving Catholics (1955, superseded by the Committee for Solidarity of Patriotic Vietnamese Catholics in 1984). Regarding China, Pius XII deplored the Maoist regime's treatment of the church in his 1952 apostolic letter to the Chinese bishops and in his 1954 encyclical *Ad sinarum gentem.*

In noncommunist states, specifically, the Philippines, South Korea, South Vietnam, and Japan, the church fared better, although at the occasional cost of accommodation with authoritarian governments. Pope PAUL VI's (1963–1978) *Populorum progressio* and his 1971 visit to East Asia, however, emphasized Rome's commitment to the people of the area, a mission that had been rejuvenated by the Second Vatican Council (see Vatican Council II). Pope JOHN PAUL II (1978–) continued to develop this theme in his 1981 tour of East Asia, his criticisms of the Marcos' regime in Manila, and his support for the work of Cardinal Jaime Sin and the Philippine church to free their country from dictatorship.

For further reference: Eric O. Hanson, *Catholic Politics in China and Korea* (Maryknoll, NY: Orbis Books, 1980); Kenneth Scott Latourette, *A History of Christian Missions in China* (New York: Macmillan, 1929).

Roy Palmer Domenico

ECCLESIASTICAL PRINCIPALITIES. In Germany, the existence of secular lordships ruled by prelates, known as ecclesiastical principalities, dominated church–state relations from the tenth to the early nineteenth centuries. During most of this period, the ecclesiastical principalities encompassed roughly one-fifth of the land area of Germany and commanded about one-fourth of the wealth. This may be traced back to the concept of the proprietary church, dating from late antiquity, whereby the patron who donated the land and financed the construction of a church building acquired certain proprietary rights, frequently including the right of nomination to the benefice and a portion of the tithes. Found throughout Western Europe during the medieval period, this practice was especially significant in Germany. During the reign of Otto the Great (936–973), in an effort to limit the alienation of authority to hereditary feudal lords, the monarch intensified the granting of whole districts to such ecclesiastical figures as archbishops, bishops, abbots, and abbesses. In return for this largesse, the Crown expected to exercise the right of nomination (in practice, usually appointment) to these prelacies. The practice became common of having the prelate receive the symbols of his authority (ecclesiastical as well as feudal) from the king or emperor, leading to the INVESTITURE CONTROVERSY in the late eleventh century.

While all the feudal monarchies granted the high dignitaries of the church a special place in society, such as inclusion among the peers of France and England and eventual recognition as a constituent part of the representative bodies of the realm, this situation was exaggerated in Germany. By the Concordat of Worms (1122) and the *Confoederatio cum principibus ecclesiasticis* (1220), the German ecclesiastical princes acquired not only vast political powers but also virtual independence from the monarchy.

During the later Middle Ages, the powers of these magnates, like those of their secular confreres, developed at the expense of the central government. Among the seven princes with the right to elect the monarch, recognized in the Golden Bull of 1356, were the archbishops of Mainz, Cologne, and Trier. By the time of the Diet of WORMS (1521), the ecclesiastical princes and prelates included these three electors, four other archbishops, 45 bishops, 63 abbots and provosts, fourteen abbesses, the grand master and four provincial commanders of the Teutonic order, and the German prior of the Knights of St. John. Virtually every significant ecclesiastical dignitary in Germany was also a territorial lord, essentially independent in his own lands. During this same period, these dignitaries came increasingly to be regarded as the preserve of the aristocracy. In the cathedral chapter of Münster, for example, no nonnoble was admitted to membership after 1392.

The late medieval and early modern period saw the practice of pluralism, relatively rare in earlier days, become widespread. Luther's adversary at the time of the Diet of Worms, Albert of Brandenburg, was archbishop of Mainz, archbishop of Magdeburg, and bishop of Halberstadt. Despite the prohibitions of the Council of TRENT, the practice of pluralism continued. The chief offenders were also the chief secular supporters of the militant COUNTER-REFORMATION, namely, the houses of Austria and Bavaria. Archduke Leopold William of Austria claimed the archbishoprics of Magdeburg and Bremen, the bishoprics of Passau, Strassburg, and Halberstadt, and the abbeys of Murbach and Hersfeld in 1630. Clement Augustus of Bavaria actually possessed the archbishopric of Cologne, the bishoprics of Münster, Paderborn, Hildesheim, and Osnabrück, the grand mastership of the Teutonic order, and the provostry of Berchtesgaden at the time of his death in 1761. H. E. Feine lists 74 pluralists among the bishops of Germany during the period between 1500 and 1803.

The German REFORMATION significantly altered the number and condition of the ecclesiastical principalities. The *Reservatio Ferdinandea*, incorporated into the Peace of Augsburg (1555), required that ecclesiastical princes be Catholic, but it could not enforce religious uniformity in their territories at the expense of already existing Lutherans. Impossible to enforce, most of the ecclesiastical principalities of northeastern Germany passed into Protestant hands by the end of the century. The Peace of WESTPHALIA (1648) secularized two archbishoprics, fourteen bishoprics, and at least eleven abbeys found on the 1521 list, while others had fallen into the hands of secular authorities previously.

During the century and a half remaining to the ecclesiastical principalities, their status was never entirely secure. Ernest Augustus of Hannover attempted to secularize the bishopric of Osnabrück in the later seventeenth century, and Louis XIV reduced the sovereignty of the bishop of Strassburg in Alsace to nothing. At the conclusion of the War of the Spanish Succession, the Catholic powers were among the foremost advocates of secularization. In 1786, an essay competition was held on how to improve the condition of the ecclesiastical principalities. The most influential entry, although not the winning one, was by Friedrich Carl von Moser, who concluded in the spirit of the Enlightenment that the fundamental problem of the ecclesiastical principalities was that they were ecclesiastical principalities.

The last generation of ecclesiastical principalities, nonetheless, saw extensive efforts by their princes to enact reforms in harmony with the Catholic Enlightenment. In Mainz, Cologne, Münster, Hildesheim, Würzburg, and elsewhere extensive reforms were carried out. Nonetheless, the days of the ecclesiastical principalities were numbered. The victorious armies of the French Revolution sealed their fate when, in the Treaties of Campo Formio (1797) and Lunéville (1801), Bonaparte demanded the left bank of the Rhine for France and provided that Germany's secular princes be compensated from ecclesiastical resources. In the settlement at Rastadt (1803), the ecclesiastical principalities were sacrificed to the demands of modernity in the guise of the first consul. The sacrifice was not widely lamented, even in ecclesiastical circles. The papal NUNCIO at Cologne, Bartolomeo Pacca, wrote: ''Now one might hope in the future to have a less wealthy, to be sure, but more enlightened and more pious clergy.''

For further reference: Geoffrey Barraclough, *The Origins of Modern Germany* (New York: Capricorn Books Edition, 1963); Hans Erich Feine, *Die Besetzung der Reichsbistümer vom Westfälischen Frieden bis zum Säkularisation, 1648–1803* (Stuttgart: Kohlhammer, 1921); Erwin Gatz, ed., *Die Bischöfe des Heiligen Römischen Reiches, 1648 bis 1803: Ein biographisches Lexikon* (Berlin: Duncker and Humblot, 1990); Hajo Holborn, *A History of Modern Germany*, 3 vols. (New York: Alfred A. Knopf, 1964); Rudolfine Freiin von Oer, *Die Säkularisation 1803: Vorbereitung-Diskussion-Durchführung* (Göttingen: Vandenhoeck and Ruprecht, 1970).

William C. Schrader

EDUCATION AND PAPACY. Following Christ's commandment to teach all nations, the papacy has seen this as part of its world mission. The church has long held that we cannot be properly educated without knowing who and what we are, why we came into existence, where we are supposed to be going, and the nature of our relationship to God. Thus, the early fathers saw the church as mother and teacher. When the POPES and bishops in the patristic period recognized the limitations of teaching Christians in small groups and the need to have priests and Christian professionals educated in a Christian environment, catechetical schools emerged. The instructors in these schools, under the direction of popes and bishops, were versed in the classics of the Greek and Roman culture but understood that the truths contained in the classics had to be realized in light of God's revelation. It was believed that a Christian education had to unite all truths in authentic religious knowledge and Christian moral discipline.

With this purpose in mind, catechetical schools such as the Lateran in Rome and the one in Alexandria came into existence.

St. Augustine (354–430) recognized that not all professed Christians were so. Thus, the two cities with their different loves continued to exist, the city of God and the earthly city of human origin, and it was not easy to determine who belonged to which city. The old city was seen to be composed of people moved by the love of the goods of the earthly city. In contrast, the residents of the city of God had put temporal things in proper perspective, seeing them as means rather than ends. Thus, St. Augustine was aware of the conflicts that could exist between the family, the church, and the state in education, which would become critical in modern times. Unity, real peace, and justice could be accomplished only if all seek to serve God and live by eternal, natural, moral law and the laws of God's revelation.

From the time of Pope GREGORY I, the Great (590–604) to modern times, various educational systems developed under the auspices of the church, including monasteries and the first universities in the Western world at Paris and Bologna. The truths discoverable from the natural world and revealed by God were to be united in the education of the human person because both nature and revelation have their common origin in God. It was postulated that any discovery in the natural order and any genuine understanding of the faith could never be in real conflict. Conflict arose only when there was a misunderstanding of one or the other. This unity of both kinds of knowledge, in the speculative order and the practical order, is the goal of Catholic education.

During the RENAISSANCE, a process began and reached its culmination in modernity, which made the Greco-Roman classics the core of education, independent of faith. The unity of faith and reason was no longer conceived as attainable. Therefore, religion was viewed as a private matter or a matter chosen and politically determined by the heads of state. The goal of education and the unity of education reverted to the Greco-Roman view of preparing the individual to be of use to the state. Hegel explicitly stated the principle of the relationship of faith and reason, which had been often implied or employed as a principle of operation in modern education, when he declared the primacy of reason over faith as the hallmark of modernity. As a result, naturalism, realism, and scientism inspired much of modern education.

Throughout this period, the papacy found it necessary to reaffirm the unity of truth in education, stressing that advances in the natural and social sciences were not in conflict with authentic faith. The church also encouraged religious orders (and the formation of new religious communities) to create and sustain Catholic educational institutions that would teach the whole person. In the nineteenth and twentieth centuries religiously neutral schools were often proposed, with some suggesting that the religious and moral needs of students might be satisfied by requiring a few theology courses. Such schools were seen by the papacy as producing an atheistic perspective. On this position, see DIVINI IL-

LIUS MAGISTRI of PIUS XI, 31 December 1929; *Summi Pontificatus* of PIUS XII, 20 October 1939; and *Mater et Magistra* of JOHN XXIII, 15 May 1961.

The Vatican maintained that the exclusion from education of a proper understanding of religion provokes a distorted view of religion. Furthermore, the notion that requiring a few theology courses in the curriculum suffices to make an education Catholic ran the risk of preserving a secular model of education, with religious and moral education becoming something tacked on as an afterthought. In recent times, the popes have stressed the need for the continued resolve of families and local churches to provide children with a genuine Catholic education. In this regard see VATICAN II's *Gravissimum educationis* of 28 October 1965 and JOHN PAUL II's *Veritatis Splendor* of 6 August 1993. The new CANON LAW 16 declares the primacy of the responsibilities of the families, the pastors, and the church, at all levels, to fulfill this goal.

The pope, as late as March 1993, expressed the need for accurate and unambiguous teaching of the faith and the harm done to the faithful when some teachers ''assume the right to decide for themselves which teachings to accept'' and which to reject. Such selectivity is unacceptable, according to *Veritatis Splendor* and the new catechism. Furthermore, since secular education has often identified itself with job training and service to the state, the broader religious goals of life have been neglected. The church has consistently refused to accept this partial training as real education, the purpose of which is to lead people to the truth; nor can the church accept the state as the ultimate judge of the content and purpose of education threatening to make the state, rather than God, the end of human life.

For further reference: *Catachisme de l'église Catholique* (Rome: Libreria Editrice Vaticana, 1993); *Codex Iures Canonici* (Rome: Libreria Editrice Vaticana, 1983); *Papal Teachings on Education*, ed. the Benedictine Monks of Solemes, trans. Fr. Rebeschini Aldo (Boston: Daughters of St. Paul, 1960) (contains almost all the important papal documents, beginning with Pius VII, 15 May 1800, to John XXII, 30 December 1959).

Joseph J. Califano

ELEUTHERIUS (c. 174–189). Reigning from 174 to 189, Eleutherius is the last in the succession list of bishops of Rome recorded by Irenaeus (c. 180); that is, he is the thirteenth POPE in the line begun by St. PETER. The *Liber Pontificalis* describes him as a Greek from Nicoplis, in Epirus. A contemporary records that he was a deacon to Pope ANICETUS (c. 155–c. 166). As his Greek name means ''freeman,'' he may have been a freed slave. The *Liber Pontificalis* also gives the unusual account that a British king, Lucius, wrote to him asking to be baptized a Christian. This story, which is recorded also by Bede and later chroniclers, probably originated because of a confusion with the king Agbar IX of Edessa, who was also known as Lucius and who was later converted and perhaps had sent inquiries to the pope.

In 177 Eleutherius, as pope, was visited by Irenaeus of Lyons, who brought

him a letter from the church there, which was then undergoing severe persecution, presenting its views on Montanism, the new apocalyptic and prophetic
movement that was founded by the ascetic Montanus in Phrygia and that was
currently being intensely debated in the church. Eleutherius apparently did not
regard it as a danger, as he passed no judgments against its prophetic claims.
Otherwise, Eleutherius' reign was peaceful, and while the sources differ about
the date of his death, it seems that he died in the tenth year of the emperor
Commodus (180–192), in 189. He is first mentioned as a martyr in the *Martyrology of Ado of Vienne* compiled in 858, and his feast day is 26 May.

For further reference: L. Duchesne, ed., *Liber Pontificalis* (Paris: E. de Boccard, 1955);
Eusebius, *The History of the Church*, trans. G. A. Williamson (New York: Penguin
Books, 1989).

William Roberts

ENCYCLICALS, PAPAL. Encyclicals are formal letters written by the POPE
for the church. Pope BENEDICT XIV (1740–1758) is considered to be the
father of the modern usage of the papal encyclical. Since the beginning of his
pontificate in 1740, over 283 papal encyclicals have been written. Their "papal"
authorship as well as their content distinguish them from other types of ecclesiastical writing. Largely pastoral in tone and intention, encyclical letters have
become a common means through which the pope communicates to, or clarifies
for, the universal church or some part of it particular aspects of church discipline, doctrine, or morality. Papal encyclicals can be issued in a more solemn
form addressed only to a part or parts of the universal church or in the more
common, less solemn category addressed to the entire church or to all people
of goodwill. Usually written in Latin, encyclical letters are identified by the first
few words that appear within the texts.

Although papal letters have been written since the earliest days of the church,
recent popes have given a greater significance to their encyclical letters. In his
encyclical letter *Humani Generis* (12 August 1950), Pope PIUS XII (1939–
1958) wrote that, unless stated otherwise, the contents of papal encyclicals "belong to the ordinary magisterium" or teaching authority of the pope, therefore
requiring the intellectual assent of the faithful to the doctrines proposed, communicated, or considered therein.

For the most part, too, what is expounded and inculcated in encyclical letters
already pertains to Catholic doctrine. That is not to say that these judgments are
considered "infallible" declarations or pronouncements incapable of change at
some future date. It is, rather, an assertion that the contents of papal encyclicals
are to be considered official church teaching until, as Pope PAUL VI (1963–
1973) noted in 1964, "we [the pope] may feel obliged in conscience to modify
them."

The most controversial papal encyclical of modern times was written by Pope
Paul VI in 1968 concerning the issue of artificial birth control. Although the

intention of this letter, *Humanae Vitae* (25 July 1968), was to present a clear papal statement demanding the assent of the faithful, its publication occasioned a debate among members of the HIERARCHY, theologians and laity alike, regarding the authority of, and assent owed to, papal teaching presented in such a forum. The effects of this debate continue to be felt to the present day. For this reason, papal encyclicals require careful study and scrutiny by all concerned. Controversy itself, however, has not changed the church's official understanding of the way in which papal encyclicals are to be received by the church.

For further reference: Claudia Carlen, *The Papal Encyclicals* (Wilmington, NC: McGrath, 1981); Francis G. Morrisey, *The Canonical Significance of Papal and Curial Pronouncements* (Washington, DC: Canon Law Society of America, 1978).

David M. O'Connell

EPHESUS, COUNCIL OF (431). The Third Ecumenical Council was called by Emperor Theodosius II because of the controversy that had arisen between Cyril of Alexandria and Nestorius, who became bishop of Constantinople in 428. The latter began to preach against the popular practice of referring in prayer to Mary the mother of Jesus as "Theotokos" (Mother of God). Cyril responded by writing a letter of correction to Nestorius; an unpleasant correspondence ensued, and Cyril finally appealed to CELESTINE I (422–432), the bishop of Rome. The POPE condemned Nestorius at a synod held in Rome in 430 and delegated Cyril to communicate this action to Nestorius, with a view to enticing him to repent. Cyril sent this decision to Nestorius together with harsh anathemas to which he insisted Nestorius subscribe, but he refused to do so.

Both sides appealed to the emperor, who called a council at Ephesus in 431. Nestorius refused to attend, but a group of Eastern bishops who supported him set out for the council. On 22 June 431, however, Cyril began the council before the arrival of both Nestorius' supporters and the representatives of the bishop of Rome. The participants affirmed the faith of the Nicene Creed and declared that Cyril's second letter to Nestorius was in accord with this faith, while Nestorius' second letter to Cyril was not. They also heard Cyril's letter to Nestorius with the anathemas and then condemned and deposed Nestorius. They went on to condemn and depose John, bishop of Antioch and leader of the Eastern bishops, and a number of his colleagues.

When the Eastern bishops arrived and heard of these actions, they, in turn, condemned and deposed Cyril and his supporters. Both groups sent a report to the emperor, and although he initially accepted neither one, Nestorius was deposed and allowed to return to his monastery, and Maximianus was consecrated bishop of Constantinople. A new bishop of Rome accepted the findings of Cyril's council on 31 July 432. A reconciliation was effected between Cyril and John of Antioch in 433 and was expressed in the statement called the "Formula of Union." Nestorius was sent into exile officially in 436.

For further reference: P. T. Camelot, *Ephèse et Chalcédoine, Histoire des Conciles,* vol. 2 (Paris: Editions de l'Orante, 1962); A. D'Alès, *Le dogme d'Ephèse,* 2d ed. (Paris: Beauchesne, 1931); L. D. Davis, *The First Seven Ecumenical Councils (325–787): Their History and Theology* (Wilmington, DE: Michael Glazier, 1987); A. Grillmeier, *Christ in Christian Tradition,* vol. 1, rev. ed. (London and Oxford: Mowbray, 1975); N. P. Tanner, ed., *Decrees of the Ecumenical Councils,* vol. 1 (London: Sheed and Ward; Washington, DC: Georgetown University Press, 1990), pp. 37–74.

Gerard H. Ettlinger

ETHIOPIAN WAR AND VATICAN. A border dispute in the Horn of Africa between Italians and Ethiopians in December 1934 had been followed by a League of Nations attempt to resolve the crisis. In January 1935, MUSSOLINI concluded an agreement with French premier Pierre Laval by which Italy agreed to cooperate with France against Germany in return for a free hand in Ethiopia. While the league deliberated, Mussolini sent troops to East Africa in the summer of 1935 and, when league conciliation appeared to have failed in October, invaded Ethiopia. Mussolini's aggression was condemned by the League of Nations, which applied economic sanctions to Italy. A major attempt at mediation by Britain and France, the Hoare–Laval Plan, was leaked to the press and discredited in December 1935. The war ended with the Italian capture of Addis Ababa, the Ethiopian capital, and Mussolini's proclamation of the Italian empire in May 1936.

The war created a dilemma for the Holy See. In 1929, issues between church and state in Italy had been resolved by the LATERAN ACCORDS. As a result of these agreements, the church for the first time recognized the kingdom of Italy, which, in turn, acknowledged the temporal power of the papacy by creating VATICAN CITY as an independent state. By 1935, Mussolini's regime was popular, and the invasion of Ethiopia, with its prospects of avenging past defeats and leading Italy into the ranks of the Great Powers, received wide support from the Italian people. Italian bishops and clergy were not immune to this nationalism and, since the church was now recognized as an important Italian institution, gave enthusiastic support to the venture. The Vatican was reluctant either to disavow the Italian church or to criticize Mussolini's foreign policy.

Nonetheless, the Vatican deplored the war, both on principle and out of fear that, by destabilizing European society, it could provide opportunities for the expansion of COMMUNISM. Protestant churches supported the League of Nations and, led by the archbishop of Canterbury, asked why the POPE was not also supporting that institution. The Church of England had taken the moral high ground in support of the league and against appeasing an aggressor, while the Italian church had blessed and contributed to the Italian war effort. The national branches of the Catholic Church divided over the war: the British and Canadians were neutral, the Americans and French were against the league, and the Belgians were its strong supporters. The pope's silence worried Roman Catholics in Great Britain, who felt that the head of their church was creating the impression that all Catholics supported Mussolini. The Vatican was thus under pressure to take a stand against the Italian war in Ethiopia.

Prior to the October invasion, the pope had attempted to find some basis for compromise by transmitting a statement of Mussolini's goals in Ethiopia to the French. The Vatican did not disapprove of Italy's expansionist goals; it disapproved of Mussolini's resort to war to achieve them. The Vatican continued its search for a compromise solution. It later passed a statement of Mussolini's aims to Britain and France that became the basis for the later Hoare–Laval Plan. The Vatican was suspicious of the League of Nations, of which it was not a member, believing that the Soviet Union was using the league to provoke a full-scale European war.

In Africa, the war had a deplorable effect on Catholic missionary endeavor. Italian missionaries had been expelled by Ethiopian authorities, while the Italians expelled non-Italians from missions in areas that they controlled. The pope was disappointed when the Hoare–Laval Plan failed in December 1935 and was greatly relieved when the war ended in May 1936, but Vatican officials were distressed that the Lateran Accords were not extended to the new Italian empire.

For further reference: George W. Baer, *Test Case: Italy, Ethiopia and the League of Nations* (Stanford, CA, 1976); Peter C. Kent, ''Between Rome and London: Pius XI, the Catholic Church, and the Abyssinian Crisis of 1935–1936,'' *The International History Review*, 11:2 (May 1989): 252–271; Peter C. Kent, ''The Catholic Church in the Italian Empire, 1936–38,'' *Historical Papers of the Canadian Historical Association* (1984): 138–150.

Peter C. Kent

EUGENE I (654–657). Born into an aristocratic Roman family, at his election to the papacy Eugene was an aged cleric. At that time, POPE MARTIN I (649–653) had been placed under arrest by the emperor Constans II (654–668) for more than a year. Realizing that it was unlikely that Martin would be returning to Rome, the clergy of that city elected Eugene in August 654. The legitimacy of his tenure has been contested by scholars, some of whom place the start of his reign in 655, after Martin's death. During Eugene's reign, monothelitism continued to be the major theological controversy between Rome and Constantinople. Rome held that Christ had two wills, while the Eastern capital favored the belief in a single will.

At the behest of the patriarch Peter, Eugene agreed to a compromise formula. This stated that although Christ had one will for each of his natures, as a person or hypostasis he had only one. At its formal reading in St. Mary's Major on Pentecost in 655, the Roman clergy and people rejected it and forced Eugene to do likewise. Thus, the attempt at closing the SCHISM ended in failure. Constans II sought to arrest Eugene, but military campaigns against the Arabs prevented him from doing so.

In the meantime, Eugene I died and was buried at St. Peter's. He was later declared a saint.

For further reference: J. N. D. Kelly, *The Oxford Dictionary of the Popes* (Oxford: Oxford University Press, 1986); *New Catholic Encyclopedia*, vol. 5, pp. 624–625.

Patrick J. McNamara

EUGENE II (824–827). Eugene's election to the papacy was marked by existing divisions between the nobility and papal bureaucracy. With the support of a monk named Wala, an adviser to the Frankish emperor Louis I (the Pious) (814–840), the aristocrats triumphed in the election, and Eugène immediately swore allegiance to Louis while recognizing the emperor's sovereignty over the papal lands.

In August 824, Louis sent his son Lothair to Rome to conclude a CONCORDAT that solidified Carolingian control over Rome and restored the Roman people's right to participate in papal elections, a privilege suspended since 769. The agreement, finalized in November 826, required the presence of an imperial representative during consecration while requiring the POPE to swear allegiance to the emperor. Eugene, however, ignored Louis' condemnation of the papal position regarding iconoclasm, a HERESY that rejected as superstition the use of religious images and advocated their destruction, which was revived under the emperors at Constantinople, Leo V (813–820) and Michael II (820–829). The pontiff upheld the decision of NICAEA II (787), which permitted image veneration as an act of homage to the person it represented.

Internally, Eugene convened a council, which decreed a minimum level of education for the clergy in order to fulfill their duties, and he tightened CANON LAW pertaining to simony.

For further reference: Nicola Cheetham, *Keepers of the Keys: A History of the Popes from St. Peter to John Paul II* (New York: Charles Scribner's Sons, 1982); H. K. Mann, *The Lives of the Popes in the Early Middle Ages* (London: K. Paul, 1902–1932). The best beginning primary source remains the *Liber Pontificalis* (Paris, 1886–1892).

John C. Horgan

EUGENE III (1145–1153). This last of the papal reformers was born Bernard Paganelli, the son of the lord of Montemagno in the territory of Lucca. Paganelli began his career as vicar-general of the bishop of Pisa, became prior of St. Zeno in Pisa in 1128, and became administrator of that see in the late 1130s. He was influenced by the spiritual teachings of Abbot Bernard and became a monk at Clairvaux. On 15 February 1145, the day that LUCIUS II (1144–1145) died from the wounds he suffered during the assault on the Capitol, the cardinal-bishops and priests held a secret election in the monastery of St. Caesarius on the Palatine. The body, meeting secretly outside the Roman borders in fear of the reaction of the newly formed senate, unanimously elected Paganelli, who assumed the name Eugene III. Predictably, the senate refused to endorse him until he officially recognized the legitimacy of the new republican government.

Eugene was the first Cistercian to be elected POPE and retained the humble garb and manners of a simple monk, vowing to reform the church. Starting in 1147, he held important synods in Paris, Trier, and Rheims, enacting reforming canons and reviewing doctrinal issues. These accomplishments were over-shadowed by political turmoil that plagued his papacy and prevented him from residing in Rome for the majority of his reign. The first major event was the fall of the crusader outpost of Edessa in the Holy Land on 23 December 1144 to the Turks. An Armenian embassy was sent to the pope to request intervention.

Eugene utilized the persuasive rhetoric of St. Bernard of Clairvaux to promote a new crusade against Byzantium to Louis VII of France. He selected France for the mission rather than Germany in hope of reserving King Conrad's support to battle the Roman Senate. In a diplomatic misunderstanding, St. Bernard suc-cessfully enlisted the support of both Louis and Conrad, leaving Eugene de-fenseless, thus forcing him in 1147 to abandon Italy and flee to France. New problems were created by Arnold of Brescia during the pope's absence from Rome. INNOCENT II (1130–1143) had condemned him as a heretic and ban-ished him from Italy. He moved to France, where he studied under his former teacher, Peter Abelard. Eugene pardoned Arnold and allowed him to return to Rome, where he soon incited the Roman populace to revolt against the sover-eignty of the pope.

In 1151, hampered by conflicts with Roger and Arnold, Eugene appealed to King Conrad, who promised to support the pope and to travel to Italy within the year. Conrad died soon after, and his nephew, Frederick, duke of Swabia, was chosen as his successor. In 1153, through the signing of the Treaty of Constance, Frederick promised to defeat the republican government in Rome, support Eugene, and travel to Rome to be crowned. Before the coronation could take place, Eugene died in Tivoli on 8 July 1153 and was buried in St. Peter's. He was beatified in 1872 by PIUS IX (1846–1878).

For further reference: Eric John, *The Popes: A Concise Bibliographical History* (London: Burns and Oates, 1964); H. K. Mann, *The Lives of the Popes in the Early Middle Ages* (London: K. Paul, 1902–1932).

Christopher S. Myers

EUGENE IV (1431–1447). Gabriel Condulmaro was born in Venice c. 1383. As a nephew of the future GREGORY XII (1406–1415) he enjoyed the fruits of nepotism and became a cardinal in 1408. He struggled with the Council of BASEL, which he eventually transferred to Ferrara and then to Florence to negotiate with the Greek orthodox to end the SCHISM. The reunion was pro-claimed on 6 July 1439. Similar pacts were negotiated with the Armenians, the Copts of Egypt, and the Chaldeans and Maronites of Cyprus. He thus regained the allegiance of the princes who had supported Basel.

Eugene defended primacy against the assaults of the extreme conciliarists. But his conflict with the Council of Basel created the image of the papacy as the opponent of reform. In ecclesiastical affairs Eugene made many concessions to the princes that surrendered the "liberty of the church" for which GREGORY VII (1073–1085) and his successors had struggled. After ten years of exile he returned to Rome in 1443, where he died on 23 February 1447.

For further reference: J. Gill, *The Council of Florence* (New York: AMS Press, 1982); J. Gill, *Eugenius IV: Pope of Christian Union* (Westminster, MD: Newman Press, 1961).

Richard J. Kehoe

EULALIUS, ANTIPOPE (418–419). Eulalius' tenure as ANTIPOPE overlapped the pontificate of BONIFACE I (418–422). Perhaps even before Pope ZOSIMUS' death on 26 December 418, Eulalius, eldest of the Roman deacons, and his partisans in the city had locked themselves in the Lateran palace to cast their votes for Eulalius to succeed Zosimus. Once the votes were cast the following day (27 December), the Roman municipal prefect Symmachus enlisted the imperial support of Honorius in Ravenna. Meantime, the partisans of Boniface had met in the basilica of Theodora to elect their favorite, casting their votes on 28 December. On the next day, 29 December, both were consecrated, Boniface in the church of S. Marcello, with nine bishops attending, Eulalius, still in the Lateran palace, with the bishop of Ostia (traditional consecrator of POPES) officiating. Accepting Symmachus' report on the authenticity of Eulalius' prior election, Honorius recognized him as pope.

When conflicting accounts reached Ravenna, Honorius summoned a synod of local bishops in Ravenna to investigate. The local bishops quickly recommended that both Eulalius and Boniface leave Rome, that a more representative council be summoned in Spoleto in June of that year, and that in the interim the bishop of Spoleto, Achilleus, should assume the papal duties, in time to officiate in the Easter services on 30 March 419. Though both candidates initially withdrew, Eulalius and his partisans marched on Rome to take possession of the Lateran palace on 18 March. That provoked the wrath of Honorius, who, in April, ordered Eulalius' exclusion from Rome. Eulalius accepted the defeat, retiring to Anzio. After Boniface died in September 422, Eulalius accepted episcopal assignment in an unrecorded neighboring haven. His tenure as antipope ran from 27 December 418 to 3 April 419; he died in 423. His actions helped to establish a precedent for imperial intercession in papal elections.

For further reference: E. Caspar, *Geschichte des Papstums von den Anfängen bis zur Höhe der Weltherrschaft* (Tübingen: Verlag); J. N. D. Kelly, *The Oxford Dictionary of Popes* (New York: Oxford University Press, 1986).

Henry Paolucci

EUSEBIUS (310). While the dates for Eusebius' reign seem established in the Liberian Catalogue, the year of his papacy has been variously argued as 308,

309, or 310. The only facts that seem certain about Eusebius' reign are that the disputes over readmission of those who had apostacized during the persecution of Diocletian continued even after the banishment of Pope MARCELLUS I (306–308). The leader of the opposition was Heraclius, and conflict within the church grew so intense that the emperor Maxentius again resorted to banishment to alleviate the problem, sending both Eusebius and Heraclius to Sicily. Eusebius died in exile on 21 October. There is no evidence that he died as a martyr. His feast is celebrated on 17 August.

For further reference: Matthew Bunson, *The Pope Encyclopedia* (New York: Crown Trade Paperbacks, 1995); J. N. D. Kelly, *The Oxford Dictionary of Popes* (New York: Oxford University Press, 1986).

Bernard J. Cassidy

EUTHANASIA AND PAPACY. In the ancient Greco-Roman world, euthanasia referred to terminating a human life in order to give a person who was suffering a good death with or without the consent of the person whose life was terminated. Today it has come to mean terminating a human life with the consent of the involved individual and has been identified with suicide and assisted suicide. Many have also extended the term to include cases in which one can assume the consent of the individual euthanized, or the consent of the person to be euthanized is unattainable because he or she is unconscious or unable to communicate consent. One assumes that the individual would consent, if the individual could. This appears to be the rationale for many acts of euthanasia in Holland. Also acts of euthanasia have come to be described in the ambiguous terms of mercy killing or in terms of the tenuous distinction between passive and active euthanasia, where the withholding of standard medical procedures or water or nutrients is identified as passive euthanasia, and the direct doing of something to terminate a life is identified as active euthanasia. The church in *Jura et bona* of 5 May 1980 rejected the notion that active euthanasia and passive euthanasia are morally distinguishable. Those who draw such a distinction separate themselves from the teaching of the Catholic Church.

Secular culture with its notion of the absolute autonomy of the individual has proclaimed suicide a rational act that involves one individual, and therefore no one, not even God, has a right to condemn the choice. Within this context faith and hope in God are no longer virtues, and death is a passing into nothingness. Suffering in thus seen as futile. Within a Christian theocentric view of life, suicide can never be viewed as a good act since it represents a rejection of God's authority over life as a gift from God and the body as a temple of the Holy Spirit. The Christian view is that one's life is never absolutely one's own, and therefore an ethics rooted in the absolute autonomy of the human individual is rooted in a denial of the existence of God.

The church's condemnation of euthanasia defined it as ''an action or omission which of itself or by intention causes death, in order that suffering may in this way be eliminated.'' A patient can, but need not choose, extraordinary means to preserve health, and the patient can, if extraordinary means prove to fall short of expectations, interrupt their employment. When inevitable death is imminent, one need not choose means that would secure only a precarious and burdensome prolongation of life. This does not mean, as some have claimed, that one can cease to employ ordinary means or withhold food, water, and care and comfort. Nor can one increase the use of painkillers to the point that they cause the cessation of respiration. Ordinary care of the seriously ill must be sustained; otherwise, an injustice is done by way of omission.

In a theocentric Christian universe, where there is a recognition of a spiritual dimension to human life, suffering is not meaningless. This does not diminish the reality of human suffering or the responsibility to alleviate suffering through moral means. Suffering is not something to be sought after, but neither is it the ultimate evil to escape from by suicide. The ultimate evil is the rejection of God and the loss of eternal life. The ultimate good is the participation in the eternal life of God. For the saints unavoidable suffering in life is a reality that presents us with the most fundamental of human choices: either transcendence and transformation in Christ by participation in the redemptive mission of the mystical body of Christ or nihilistic despair. If one is moved toward transcendence in Christ, one is drawn into the mystery at the core of the Catholic faith.

In the end, suffering is about definitive good and evil, the attainment or loss of eternal life, the recognition of the emptiness of this life and the love of the things of this world so that one can come to love God, who is genuinely fulfilling. Euthanasia is a denial of the spiritual dimension of the human person.

For further reference: Joseph Califano, ''Human Suffering and Our Post-Civilized Cultural Mind,'' *The Twilight of Civilization*, ed. Peter Redpath (Notre Dame, IN: Notre Dame Press, 1990); *The HarperCollins Encyclopedia of Catholicism*, ed. Richard P. McBrien (San Francisco:HarperCollins, 1995); *Veritas Splendor* of 6 August 1993.

Joseph J. Califano

EUTYCHIAN (275–283). Little is known of the papacy of Eutychian. Most modern authorities accept the statement of the *Liber Pontificalis* that assigns an eight-year duration to Eutychian's papacy, but Eusebius notes that he was POPE for less than a year. He held the post of bishop of Rome in a time of peace for the church, between the persecutions of Valerian and Diocletian. Nothing else noted in the *Liber Pontificalis* can be relied on for information about this pope; even the statement of his martyrdom is generally believed to be erroneous. There is an inscription bearing his name in the Cemetery of Callistus. His feast is celebrated on 7 December.

For further reference: J. N. D. Kelly, *The Oxford Dictionary of Popes* (New York: Oxford University Press, 1986); J. Lebreton and J. Zeiller, *The History of the Primitive Church*, vol. 4 (London: Burns, Oates, and Washbourne, 1948).

Bernard J. Cassidy

EVARISTUS (c. 100–c. 109). Reigning from c. 100 to c. 109, during the period of the Antonine emperors, POPE St. Evaristus is the fourth pope after St. PETER (d. c. 64), succeeding LINUS (c. 66–c. 78), ANACLETUS (c. 79–c. 91), and CLEMENT I (c. 91–c. 101). Early sources differ as to the length of his reign, Eusebius referring to eight or nine years, the *Liber Pontificalis* about ten, and the fourth-century Liberian Catalogue, which also calls him Aristus, some fourteen years. The *Liber Pontificalis* mentions he was Greek, as his name suggests, but reports that his father was a Jew from Bethlehem. Supposedly, Evaristus was the first to assign Roman parishes to their various presbyters, and he instituted the practice of the bishop's being escorted by seven of his deacons. That source also claims that he was a martyr and was buried near St. Peter. The two letters and two fragments of decretals that were circulated under his name are regarded as apocryphal. There is, however, no reason to doubt that he was a leader of the Roman church, but the extent of his authority and influence in that early period can only be surmised. He feast is celebrated on 26 October.

For further reference: L. Duchesne, ed., *Liber Pontificalis* (Paris: E. de Boccard, 1955); Eusebius, *The History of the Church*, trans. G. A. Williamson (New York: Penguin Books, 1989).

William Roberts

EXARCH. SEE DONATION OF PEPIN.

EXCOMMUNICATION. Perhaps the most serious disciplinary action taken by the church, excommunication is the response given by church authorities to a baptized Catholic whose actions disturb the well-being and unity of the Christian community in a significant way. It is important to remember that the penalty or "censure" known as excommunication is occasioned by the action(s) of the offender and merely declared or affirmed by church officials. Canon 1257 of the 1917 Code of CANON LAW defined excommunication as a censure by which one is excluded from the communion of the faithful. Although the earliest traditions of the church apply the use of the term "excommunication" to any and all ecclesiastical punishments, the canonical expression itself has a very specific meaning and purpose.

As a censure, excommunication is intended to make the offender realize the seriousness of the actions involved while impressing upon him or her the urgent need for contrition and reunion with the Christian community, hence, the deprivation of certain activities ordinarily associated with membership in the church. In this sense excommunication is both punishment and "medicine" provided to heal and to cure the excommunicate. For that reason canon law classifies excommunication as a "medicinal penalty." This censure expresses a partial exclusion or, better, only an impaired ability to participate in the church's sacramental and ministerial life.

Canon law divides ecclesiastical penalties into several categories, among them the classification of those that are "automatic" or *latae sententiae*, with their effects immediately felt as a result of some most serious action; and those that must first be declared by competent ecclesiastical authority or *ferendae sententiae*, with their effects felt only after the intervention of, investigation, and judgment by, a person in authority. The 1983 Code of Canon Law provides that the penalty of excommunication is incurred automatically (*latae sententiae*) through commission of any of the following offenses: apostasy, HERESY, or SCHISM (canon 1364); violation of the Eucharistic species (canon 1367); physical attack on the POPE (canon 1370); absolution of a partner in a sexual sin (canon 1378); unauthorized ordination of a bishop (canon 1382); a confessor's violation of the secret of sacramental confession (canon 1388); procuring an ABORTION (canon 1398).

A person who is excommunicated may not participate in the reception of the Eucharist or other sacraments and may not perform any liturgical roles or official church actions (canon 1331). At the same time that the 1983 code describes what constitutes excommunication and its effects, canon law also indicates the circumstances that may exempt individuals from possible excommunication as well as other penalties, among them being a minor, especially under the age of sixteen; actions performed out of inculpable ignorance, inadvertence, error, physical force, or grave fear, being without the use of reason, and so on (canons 1323–1325).

Although the excommunicate is impeded from sacramental participation, he or she is still required to live the Christian life in every other way. Once the individual is aware of the censure, he or she has the obligation to seek its remission as soon as possible. Since excommunication is a medicinal penalty, its goal is the conversion and return of the sinner, which can occur only after repentance and reparation, once the censure is lifted by appropriate church authority.

For further reference: T. Lincoln Bouscaren and Adam C. Ellis, *Canon Law: A Text and Commentary* (Milwaukee: Bruce, 1957); James A. Coriden et al., eds., *The Code of Canon Law: A Text and Commentary* (New York/Mahwah, NJ: Paulist Press, 1985); Elizabeth Vodola, *Excommunication in the Middle Ages* (Berkeley: University of California Press, 1986).

David M. O'Connell

EXEQUATUR. The exequatur (Latin: "Let it be carried out") is the approval given by secular governments to papal bulls, briefs, and other documents required before they can be published and have binding force in their territories. Intended as a means of increasing the control of secular rulers over the church within their territories, at the expense of the papacy, it was introduced in the Middle Ages at different times in different states (e.g., in England c. 1078); by the seventeenth century it existed in almost all European states. The CONCOR-

DATS of the nineteenth and twentieth centuries gradually abolished the exequatur (e.g., in Italy, by the LATERAN ACCORDS of 1929).

For further reference: Charles H. Haskins, *Norman Institutions* (Cambridge: Harvard University Press, 1918).

Alan J. Reinerman

F

FABIAN (236–250). Eusebius recounts that, when the Christian electors were assembled in 236 to choose a successor to Pope ANTERUS (235–236), a dove alighted on the head of the priest Fabian, who was present but "came into nobody's mind." Immediately, the occurrence was taken as a sign from heaven, and Fabian was accordingly chosen bishop of Rome. Much of his reign fell under the tolerant rule of the emperor Philip the Arab (244–249), and Fabian is credited in the Liberian Catalogue with organizing Rome into ecclesiastical districts, each under a deacon.

Two events during the reign of Fabian demonstrate the increasing importance of the bishop of the Romans. First, Cyprian records that when Privatus of Lambaesis was censured by Donatus, bishop of Carthage, Fabian also wrote a letter of censure. St. Jerome reveals in one of his *Letters* that Origen, whose expulsion from Egypt and demotion from the priesthood had been approved by Pontian, wrote a letter to Fabian (as he did to other bishops) defending his orthodoxy. Fabian was an early victim in the persecution begun by the emperor Decius, and he died on 20 January 250. He was buried in the Cemetery of Callistus. His feast is celebrated on 20 January.

For further reference: J. N. D. Kelly, *The Oxford Dictionary of Popes* (New York: Oxford University Press, 1986); J. Lebreton and J. Zeiller, *The History of the Primitive Church*, vol. 4 (London: Burns, Oates, and Washbourne, 1948).

Bernard J. Cassidy

FASCISM AND PAPACY. In Italy, fascism was first a political movement, seeking to acquire and consolidate political power, and, subsequently, a dictatorial regime, seeking to preserve an existing power structure. Fascism was founded as a movement by Benito MUSSOLINI in 1919, amalgamating left- and right-wing antigovernmental elements. In 1920 and 1921, it was used by landowners and industrialists to reverse the spread of socialism, particularly in the countryside. Through adroit use of political violence, fascism both terrorized the countryside and induced the king to call Mussolini to become prime minister in 1922.

The rise of fascism coincided with Pope BENEDICT XV's (1914–1922) approval of the formation of a political party designed to represent the interests of Italian Catholics. Founded in 1918, the Partito Popolare Italiano (see Popular Party) (PPI) was led by reformist Christian democrats. The emergence of fascism as an antisocialist movement attracted the interest of socially conservative members of the PPI who wanted the party to join fascists and others in an antisocialist front. Once Mussolini became prime minister of Italy, these conservative Catholics favored PPI support of the regime, but, in so doing, they were opposed by the Christian democratic majority, which wanted to protect the democratic Constitution, under threat from legislation such as the Acerbo Election Act (1923), designed to give the largest party following an election a clear majority of seats in the Chamber of Deputies.

Pope PIUS XI (1922–1939), elected in 1922, supported the position of the conservative Catholics. The new pope did not favor Catholic political parties that were independent of church control. Pius XI believed that the various Catholic Action branches for women, men, and youth could infuse Italian society with Christian values in an apolitical fashion and eventually achieve the goal of the re-Christianization of modern society. In 1923, Pius XI forced the PPI to abstain in the crucial vote on the Acerbo Election Act and raised no objection to the dissolution of the PPI on the eve of the establishment of the fascist dictatorship.

Once prime minister, Mussolini sought Catholic support by restoring religious education to the schools and by reviewing anticlerical legislation. The conservative Catholics (or clerico-fascists as they came to be called), encouraged Mussolini and sought to serve as a bridge between fascism and the Vatican. Their efforts culminated in the LATERAN ACCORDS of 1929. Having permitted the dissolution of the PPI, Pius XI was able to protect the continued existence of Catholic Action through direct negotiations with the fascist regime.

With the institution of the dictatorship in 1928, fascism changed from a political movement to a totalitarian regime where every aspect of politics and society was expected to be subservient to the state. The Lateran Agreements, to the pope, represented a healthy injection of Christianity into modern Italian society and the basis for positive change in that society. To Mussolini and the Fascist Party, on the other hand, they represented the totalitarian co-optation of the church and the papacy. The stage was set for conflict. The independence of Catholic Action worried fascist leaders. Its professional sections questioned the operation of the fascist corporate state, and its youth sections were in direct competition with the fascist youth movement. Of even greater concern was the knowledge that Catholic Action was harboring many antifascist members of the former PPI and could be a potential threat to the continuation of the regime should the impact of the Great Depression worsen in Italy.

Under pressure from the Fascist Party, Mussolini closed the youth sections of Catholic Action in 1931, only to be attacked in the papal ENCYCLICAL *NON ABBIAMO BISOGNO*. A compromise between duce and pope was effected in September 1931 that reduced the expectations of each to control the other and allowed the continuation of the youth sections of Catholic Action with their activities severely restricted. The 1931 resolution endured until 1938, when the developing relationship with NAZI GERMANY caused a new totalitarian thrust in Italy, manifested by new party attacks on Catholic Action and by the introduction of anti-Semitic legislation. While PIUS XII (1939–1958) voluntarily put further restrictions on Catholic Action in 1939, only Italian entry into the war in 1940 saved the church from tighter control by the regime. Papal support of Catholic Action prevented fascism from achieving totalitarian control in Italy, and, because of this, the Catholic Action youth sections had the liberty to groom the future leaders of postfascist Italy.

For further reference: John F. Pollard, *The Vatican and Italian Fascism, 1929–32: A Study in Conflict* (Cambridge: Cambridge University Press, 1985); John F. Pollard, "Conservative Catholics and Italian Fascism: The Clerico-Fascists," in Martin Blinkhorn, ed., *Fascists and Conservatives: The Radical Right and the Establishment in Twentieth-Century Europe* (London: Unwin Hyman, 1990); Richard A. Webster, *The Cross and the Fasces: Christian Democracy and Fascism in Italy* (Stanford, CA: Stanford University Press, 1960).

Peter C. Kent

FEBRONIANISM. In the eighteenth century the bishops in Germany challenged the limitations of jurisdiction imposed by Rome. Gallican (see Gallicanism) and Jansenist (see Jansenism) authors provided a theoretical foundation for these complaints. These theories supported claims for the greater independence of the bishops, especially the prince-bishops of the empire. This movement became known as Febronianism because of a work, *On the State of the Church and the Legitimate Power of the Roman Pontiff*, published in 1763 under the pseudonym Justinus Febronius. The author was Johann Nikolaus Von Hontheim, auxiliary bishop of Trier, who called for the restoration of the rights of bishops that the Holy See had assumed over the centuries. Eager to limit papal authority in Germany, he appealed to the secular powers to support this effort. Hontheim also invoked a general council, or national synods, to pressure the Holy See.

The work created a sensation, and Rome placed it in the INDEX. Nonetheless, it went through several editions and appeared in translation. Hontheim was eventually identified, and Rome demanded a recantation, which was finally given. He died in 1790 in communion with the church. However, in 1786 the four archbishop-electors of the empire attempted to limit papal authority in Germany to purely spiritual matters. It likewise asserted that Roman documents had no legal effect until approved by the bishops, while criticizing Rome's courts, taxes, and granting of benefices in Germany. The French Revolution and the lack of support among the German bishops finally led to the collapse of the movement.

For further reference: H. Jedin, ed., *History of the Church*, vol. 6, trans. G. Holst (New York: Crossroad, 1981), pp. 449–469; T. Ortolan, "Febronianisme," *Dictionnaire de théologie catholique* (Paris: Letouzey, 1903–1950), vol. 5, Pt. 2, 2115–2124.

Richard J. Kehoe

FELIX I (269–274). Felix was elected to the papacy shortly after the death of DIONYSIUS (260–268), and it seems that he received the letter written by the synod of Antioch held in A.D. 268, at which Paul of Samosata was condemned because of his anti-Trinitarian and Adoptionist heresies. Despite this condemnation, Paul refused to leave his church for the new bishop, and the emperor Aurelian declared that the church should be given to those with whom the bishops in Italy and Rome should communicate in writing. Felix must have been the bishop responsible for deciding against Paul, for Eusebius recounts: "Thus, then, was the aforesaid man [Paul] driven with the utmost indignity from the church by the ruler of the world." This action of Aurelian, while indicating little about his attitude toward the church, does inform us of his recognition of the influential position enjoyed by the bishop of Rome.

The *Liber Pontificalis* tells us that Felix died a martyr, but the Roman calendar of 354 lists him under episcopal burials, not under martyrs. He was buried in the Cemetery of Callistus, and his feast is celebrated on 30 May.

For further reference: J. N. D. Kelly, *The Oxford Dictionary of Popes* (New York: Oxford University Press, 1986); J. Lebreton and J. Zeiller, *The History of the Primitive Church*, vol. 4 (London: Burns, Oates, and Washbourne, 1948).

Bernard J. Cassidy

FELIX II, ANTIPOPE (355–365). Felix II was alternately POPE and ANTIPOPE through almost all the pontificate of LIBERIUS, which ran from 17 May 352 to 24 September 366. An archdeacon at the time, he was raised to prominence by the Arian (see Arianism) partisans in Rome when Liberius was banished by Emperor Constantius II (337–361) for refusing to condemn Athanasius of Alexandria (d. 373). At first reluctant, professing loyalty to Liberius, Felix finally moved into the vacated Lateran palace only to find himself rejected by the laity, who would not stay to hear him when he presided. But Constantius II remained adamant, so that when he left Rome on 29 May 357, Felix was clearly "in possession."

But the imperial court soon learned that Liberius (352–366), under pressure, had finally compromised with his Arian foes, assenting to the "condemnation of Athanasius." Liberius' exile would end, it was ruled, on condition that he adopt a new "semi-Arian" creed, the "Third Formula of Sirmium," ambiguous enough to lend itself to diverse interpretations. By imperial fiat, there were now to be two "true" bishops in Rome, charged to rule jointly as popes. Against that situation, the popular cry was, One God, one Christ, one bishop. The popular favorite, however, was not Felix. Upon his return to Rome, Liberius was received with enthusiasm, and Felix found it necessary to retire without complaint. He died in Porto on 22 November 365. Historians have questioned whether Felix's election as pope was valid. Certainly, he was initially buried without ceremony. Rumors rose, however, that he had lived and died a martyr. At any rate, after a few years his body was exhumed and transported to a basilica that he had commissioned on Via Aurelia. He was later declared a saint.

For further reference: E. Caspar, *Geschichte des Papstums von den Anfängen bis zur Höhe der Weltherrschaft* (Tübingen: Verlag, 1956); J. N. D. Kelley, *The Oxford Dictionary of Popes* (New York: Oxford University Press, 1986).

Henry Paolucci

FELIX III (II) (483–492). Felix II—or Felix III, if the antipope Felix (355–365) is reckoned as Felix II—held the pontificate from 13 March 483 to 1 March 492. He was the son of a priest also named Felix and father of three children, through one of whom he qualifies as an ancestor of Pope GREGORY I, the Great (590–604). Early in his pontificate, Felix III faced the challenge of a decree by the emperor Zeno (pressed by Acacius, patriarch of Constantinople) that sought to appease the Eastern Monophysites by imposing Acacius' *Heneticon*, a doctrinal compromise on the "two natures of Christ" controversy, on all imperial subjects. In 484, the new POPE daringly cited Acacius to Rome to answer charges raised against him by John, patriarch of Alexandria. Rejecting the legality of the papal citation, Acacius found himself excommunicated (see Excommunication) by Felix. Felix III's act, of little direct practical effect in itself, stands as having produced the church's first East–West SCHISM—one that lasted from 484 to 519.

The bishops of Africa in the time of Felix III appealed to the bishop of Rome, as they had in the past, to exercise his pastoral care in their lands, where so many of his "sheep and lambs" had lain for half a century "at the mercy of the Arian Vandals." But in the end, on principle, he showed himself extremely severe toward rebaptized Africans, permitting priests, particularly, to be reconciled in the faith only on their deathbeds. When he died in the spring of 492, Felix III was buried in St. Paul's, sharing his grave with his father, wife, and children. His successor was GELASIUS I (492–496).

For further reference: E. Caspar, *Geschichte des Papstums von den Anfängen bis zur Höhe der Weltherrschaft* (Tübingen: Verlag, 1956); J. N. D. Kelly, *The Oxford Dictionary of Popes* (New York: Oxford University Press, 1986).

Henry Paolucci

FELIX IV (III) (526–530). Born in Samnium, Italy, he was ordained a deacon and in 519 sent to Constantinople. In July 526, following a vacancy of over 50 days, he was elected POPE with the approval of Theodoric, king of the Goths and master of Italy. Working closely with Theodoric's grandson and successor as well as the regent, he advanced the interests of the church and the papacy. Among other things, he secured the right to judge civil or criminal charges against the clergy, while ordaining a large number of men as priests. In Gaul he supported Caesiarius in his struggle against semi-Pelagianism by his "Capitula" drawn from Scripture and lent his support to the Augustinian position on original sin, grace, and free will at the synod of Valence in 528. In Rome he converted several buildings of the Forum for Christian worship. In one of these, the church of SS. Cosma and Damiano, adorned with a mosaic of Felix, we have the earliest survival of a papal likeness. As his death approached in 530, Felix tried to appoint his archdeacon Boniface as his successor, a move resisted by the senate, provoking a SCHISM.

For further reference: Matthew Bunson, *The Pope Encyclopedia* (New York: Crown Trade Paperbacks, 1995); J. N. D. Kelly, *The Oxford Dictionary of the Popes* (Oxford: Oxford University Press, 1986).

Francesca Coppa

FELIX V, ANTIPOPE (1439–1449). Duke Amadeus VIII of Savoy was born on 4 September 1383, ascending the Savoyard throne in 1391. Upon the death of his wife he retired in 1431 to embrace religious life but abdicated completely only in 1440. He enjoyed a reputation as mediator of political quarrels. After the Council of BASEL deposed Pope EUGENE IV (1431–1447), it elected Amadeus on 5 November 1439 as Felix V. He soon clashed with Basel, principally over finances, and withdrew to Lausanne and then Geneva. He was never widely recognized in Europe. Pressed by his family and the princes, Felix, the last ANTIPOPE, abdicated on 7 April 1449. Pope NICHOLAS V (1447–1455) treated him graciously, named him a cardinal-bishop, and granted him a pension and other privileges. He died in Geneva on 7 January 1451.

For further reference: M. Creighton, *A History of the Papacy from the Great Schism to the Sack of Rome* (New York: AMS Press, 1969); Marie Jose, *La Maison de Savoie: Amédée VIII. le Duc Qui Devient Pape* (Paris: Albin Michel, 1962).

Richard J. Kehoe

FILIOQUE. SEE SERGIUS IV.

FORMOSUS (891–896). Formosus, probably of Roman birth, was selected POPE on 6 October 891, commencing a tumultuous pontificate. Admired for his learning, Formosus was appointed bishop of Porto in 864. During the pontificates of NICHOLAS I (858–867) and ADRIAN II (867–872), he headed a mission to Bulgaria, where he so pleased King Boris I that the reigning popes were urged to make him the country's metropolitan bishop, despite the rule that bishops could not be "translated" from one see to another. Later, Pope JOHN

VIII (872–882) charged him to return to France but grew suspicious of Formosus, suspecting he was engaged in a conspiracy to replace him as pope. The result was EXCOMMUNICATION and exile, with Formosus forced to take an oath that he would never seek office in the church. John's successor, Pope MARINUS I (882–884), restored Formosus as bishop of Porto, in which capacity he served as a consecrator of Marinus' successor, STEPHEN V (885–891). Upon the latter's death, Formosus' partisans challenged the rule against "translation" of bishops from one see to another. His enemies, however, announced that Formosus was not qualified to be pope, stressing that he had been excommunicated by a previous pope. A rival candidate was advanced, Sergius Benedicti, who would later become Pope SERGIUS III (904–911).

As pope, Formosus involved himself in church matters in England, France, Germany, and distant Constantinople. Yet he could not extricate himself from the grip of local partisans, dominated by Guy or Guido of Spoleto, whose son Lambert he was forced to consecrate as emperor in 895. Deeming his position intolerable, he called on the German king Arnulf to intervene as papal protector. Arnulf seized Rome and received the imperial Crown at the hands of Formosus in 896. But before he could strike at Formosus' enemies in Spoleto, he was seized with paralysis and forced to return to Germany, where he died in February 896.

Formosus' death followed, on 4 April 896. But his body did not rest in peace. First there occurred a tumultuous election that elevated Pope BONIFACE VI (896), but he died after a few days. Next came Pope STEPHEN VI (896–897), whose short tenure included one monstrous act: wreaking upon the buried pope the vengeance of Lambert of Spoleto, who had by then regained control of Rome. Lambert forced Pope Stephen VI to "depose" the exhumed body of Formosus for a public trial. His corpse was propped up on a throne, to be "judged by a Roman synod for having invalidly occupied papal office." His vestments were torn away, the three fingers used for blessing were severed, and the body cast into the Tiber. All of Formosus' acts as pope were declared invalid; all ordained by him had to resign.

Later partisans of Formosus claimed that, miraculously, his body was found by fishermen and "carried back for burial" in St. Peter's and that, along the way, as the coffin passed, "all the images in the church bowed their heads." Countervengeance followed. Pope Stephen, tool of the Spoleto despots, was soon imprisoned and strangled. A series of shadowy popes passed in rapid succession. It has been aptly said that, with Formosus' election, the papacy entered a period of anarchy "when pontificates were gained by crime, and vacated by murder."

For further reference: J. N. D. Kelly, *The Oxford Dictionary of Popes* (New York: Oxford University Press, 1986); H. K. Mann, *The Lives of the Popes in the Early Middle Ages* (London: K. Paul, 1902–1932).

Henry Paolucci

FRANCISCANS. The Franciscans are a religious movement founded in Italy by St. Francis of Assisi (c. 1182–1226). After conversion in 1205 and living several years as a penitent, Francis di Pietro di Bernardone, inspired by the gospel account of Jesus' instructions to his apostles, began to preach penance and peace. With a group of male companions, he obtained from Pope INNO- CENT III (1198–1216) in 1209 approbation of a rule of life based directly on gospel texts and calling for a fraternal life of minority, poverty, and preaching. This "First Order," soon named by St. Francis the Order of Friars Minor (i.e., Little Brothers), was commissioned by Pope Innocent to preach penance throughout the world. Among those responding to the call of Francis was a young noblewoman of Assisi, Clare di Favarone di Offreduccio, St. Clare of Assisi (c. 1193–1253), with whom Francis founded the Franciscan "Second Order," the Poor Ladies of San Damiano, later renamed the Order of St. Clare, or popularly, the Poor Clares. Thousands of other men and women, married and single, clergy and laity, who were converted by the preaching of the friars to a God-centered life in the world, constituted a "Third Order," organized by St. Francis in 1221 with the help of Cardinal Hugolino dei Segni, later Pope GREG- ORY IX (1227–1241). Unlike the two religious orders, this was a secular order, known as the Order of the Brothers and Sisters of Penance.

The form of life Francis imparted to the Friars Minor incorporated elements of the contemplative life of hermits, the common life of monks, and the poor, itinerant, preaching life of the apostles. In the stress of adapting to changing circumstances, the unity of the friars suffered over the issue of poverty. Even within the lifetime of Francis, the rigorous poverty the saint envisioned was adapted in the final rule (1223) to allow for the education of preachers envi- sioned by the Fourth Lateran Council (see Lateran Council IV) (1215), though the friars completely rejected the use of money and the ownership of property. While unity was preserved under the wise administration of St. Bonaventure, general minister from 1257 to 1274, simmering discontent erupted after his death, and the Franciscan Spirituals separated from the community under Pope St. CELESTINE V in 1294. Zealots for poverty, the Spirituals' apocalyptic thought and rejection of papal authority resulted in their condemnation in 1317– 1318. Subsequent condemnation of the doctrine of the absolute poverty of Christ by Pope JOHN XXII (1323) and the imposition of monastic constitutions under BENEDICT XII (1336) transformed the Friars Minor for a time into a quasi- monastic order. Many friars lived in great urban convents attached to well- appointed and substantially endowed churches.

During the fourteenth century, a moderate reform movement, called the Ob- servance, sprang up in Italy, France, and Spain. Obedient to papal authority and zealous for poverty, the reform was at first encouraged by the order. Endorsed by the Council of CONSTANCE in 1416, supported by reform-minded popes, spurred by great popular preachers like St. Bernardine of Siena, St. John Cap- istran, and St. James of the March, the movement grew rapidly. Attempts to maintain unity failed, however, and in 1517 the order was divided into the Friars Minor of Regular Observance and the Conventual Friars Minor. The reformed friars could never agree, however, on the exact parameters of reform and fragmented further into Observants, Strictest Observants (Alcantarans or Discalced), Recollects, and Reformed, all of these combined by Pope LEO XIII in 1897 as the Order of Friars Minor. Still another reform group, the Friars Minor Capuchin, broke off from the Observants and became a separate order in 1528. Strongly supported by the Council of TRENT (1545–1563), the Capuchins were zealous preachers of Catholic orthodoxy in the sixteenth-century religious upheaval. The ministers general of the Friars Minor, the Friars Minor Conventual, and the Friars Minor Capuchin are recognized as successors of St. Francis, and friars of these three orders profess St. Francis' final rule for the Friars Minor (1223).

Although forced to accept the Benedictine Rule, St. Clare courageously sought and obtained a privilege of poverty and incorporated it into her own rule, approved by Pope INNOCENT IV, 9 August 1253, the first rule written by a woman to receive such approbation. The Order of St. Clare, however, received many rules throughout its history; no one rule ever gaining universal acceptance.

Within the lifetime of St. Francis, secular Franciscan fraternities began to develop into religious communities. An amalgamation of several male communities of Italy in 1447 resulted in the Third Order Regular. Female communities, frequently organized around a work of charity, also developed into religious communities, the oldest being the Franciscan Sisters of Dilligen-Donau, dating from 1241. A new rule for third order religious communities, of which there are many in the United States, was approved by Pope JOHN PAUL II on 8 December 1992. The Third Order Secular received a new rule and a new name, the Secular Franciscan order, from Pope PAUL VI on 24 June 1978.

Four Franciscan friars became pope: NICHOLAS IV (1288–1292) and the Conventual popes, SIXTUS IV (1471–1484), SIXTUS V (1585–1590), and CLEMENT XIV (1769–1774). Three Franciscans are honored as doctors of the church, St. Anthony of Padua, the evangelical doctor; St. Bonaventure, the seraphic doctor; and the Capuchin St. Laurence of Brindisi. Among the numerous other medieval Franciscan theologians of great importance were Alexander of Hales, Roger Bacon, John Pecham, Bl. John Duns Scotus, and William of Ockham.

Endowed by St. Francis with a missionary spirit, the friars came to the New World on Columbus' second voyage (1493) to evangelize the native population. In the territory of the United States they number 70 martyrs, including the Servants of God Peter of Corpa and his four companions, who died for the faith on the coast of Georgia in September 1597. A chain of Franciscan missions in Florida was destroyed by advancing British troops in the century preceding the Spanish evacuation of Florida in 1763. The eighteenth-century missions in California, founded by Bl. Juniper Serra, have lent their names to the geography of the United States. The Franciscan provinces in Anglo-America began with nineteenth-century Catholic immigration.

Post-Vatican II adaptation and renewal of religious life have taken various forms. Some important developments have been the internationalization of foreign mission efforts, de-emphasis on the clerical character of First order communities, focusing of apostolic activity among the poor, and new approaches to evangelization. Once again, adaptation has resulted in new reform movements such as the Franciscan Friars of the Immaculate and Franciscan Friars of the Renewal.

As of 1 January 1994, membership figures were the following—for the First order: Friars Minor 18,204; Friars Minor Capuchin 11,715; Friars Minor Conventual 4,400. For the Second order: Poor Clares 8,283; Capuchinesses 2,367; Urbanists 1,281; Colettines 882. For the Third order: Third order Regular 848. Other Third order male religious communities in the United States are Franciscan Friars of the Atonement 163, Franciscan Brothers of Brooklyn 116, Franciscan Brothers of the Holy Cross 57. There are 83 religious congregations of Franciscan sisters of the Second and Third orders of St. Francis in the United States Secular Franciscans worldwide number approximately 780,000. There are also Episcopalian and Lutheran Franciscan communities.

For further reference: Regis J. Armstrong, *Clare of Assisi: Early Documents* (St. Bonaventure, NY: Franciscan Institute, 1993); Ignatius C. Brady, *Francis and Clare: The Complete Works* (New York: Paulist Press, 1982); Arnaldo Fortini, *Francis of Assisi*, trans. Helen Moak (New York: Crossroad, 1981); Marion A. Habig, ed., *St. Francis of Assisi: Writings and Early Biographies: English Omnibus of the Sources for the Life of St. Francis*, 4th rev. ed. (Chicago: Franciscan Herald Press, 1983); Lazaro Iriarte, *Franciscan History: The Three Orders of St. Francis of Assisi* (Chicago: Franciscan Herald Press, 1982); Raoul Manselli, *St. Francis of Assisi*, trans. Paul Duggan (Chicago: Franciscan Herald Press, 1988); John Moorman, *A History of the Franciscan Order from Its Origins to the Year 1517* (Chicago: Franciscan Herald Press, 1988); Raffaele Pazzelli, *The Franciscan Sisters: Outlines of History and Spirituality*, trans. Aidan Mullaney, (Steubenville, OH: Franciscan University Press, 1993).

Conrad L. Harkins

FRANZ JOSEF AND THE PAPACY. Franz Josef (1830–1916), emperor of Austria from 1848 to 1916, proved favorable to the papacy, partly from personal piety, partly because he saw the Catholic Church as one of the traditional supports for the Hapsburg dynasty against the assaults of liberals and nationalists. In 1855 he agreed to the long-standing desire of the papacy to end the tight controls over the Austrian church that the emperor Joseph II (1780–1790) had established. The resulting CONCORDAT eliminated restrictions on free communication between Austrian clergy and the pope, abolished the PLACET and EXEQUATUR, eliminated state control over clerical appointments, and gave the church full control over the education of the clergy. Other concessions allowed the return of the Jesuits (see Society of Jesus) and other religious orders previously banned in the empire (1851) and gave the church increased control over education (1850), as well as control over marriage involving Catholics (1856).

During the following decades, however, the emperor's power was shaken by defeats in Italy (1859) and Germany (1866), and he had to conciliate the liberal middle class by granting a constitution in 1867. In the new parliamentary government, the anticlerical German liberals were at first predominant. Chief among their goals was the abolition of the concordat of 1855. Franz Josef staunchly opposed them but in 1870 was compelled to agree to its formal abolition. Most of its provisions remained in effect, however, although the church's control over education and marriage was weakened. By 1879 the German liberals were in decline, and later ministries were, in general, more sympathetic to Catholicism, with the emperor's blessing. Thereafter, relations between the emperor and the papacy were generally good: Franz Josef regarded Catholicism as one of the foundations of the empire to the end, while the papacy considered Austria the last Catholic Great Power, which it hoped to see preserved against the growing attacks of nationalism. Franz Josef's death, on 21 November 1916 in the midst of WORLD WAR I, was deeply regretted by the papacy, which lost a longtime ally.

For further reference: Friedrich Engel-Janosi, *Oesterreich und der Vatikan, 1846–1918*, 2 vols. (Vienna: Graz, 1958); Josef Redlich, *Emperor Francis Joseph of Austria* (Hamden, CT: Archon Books, 1969).

Alan J. Reinerman

FOURTH VOW. SEE SOCIETY OF JESUS.

FREEMASONRY AND PAPACY. Relations between the Catholic Church and Freemasonry have been stormy. Freemasonry assailed the papacy as tyrannical, while the Roman church denounced Freemasonry as satanic. Freemasonry's name, functions, and symbols were derived from medieval construction crafts, with later infusions from ancient Mithraism to Christianity. Influenced by the European Enlightenment, it transformed itself and expanded in the 1700s as a fraternal and intellectual association, dedicated to freedom of conscience and independent thought. Its more cultural version dates back to 24 June 1717, when the Grand Lodge of England was established. As it spread to the Continent and Great Britain's American colonies, it assumed local characteristics. In Presbyterian Scotland, the Bible was prominently displayed, although novices were at liberty to register their oaths on any religious book of their choice.

The movement was not immune to internal discord over principles and beliefs. On 3 September 1777, the Grand Orient of France removed belief in God and the immortality of the soul from the requirements for membership. Immediately, the Grand Lodge of England severed relations, as did its affiliates. Protestant

Holland in 1735 was the first state to ban the order on the grounds that Free-masonry's mysterious practices and strange ceremonies bordered on voodooism, alien to an open and progressive society. Belgian Freemasonry was stridently anti-Catholic, while in the American colonies and, later, the United States, no incompatibility was discerned between Freemasonry and traditional Protestant Christianity. A number of presidents across the Protestant Church spectrum en-joyed high rank in Freemasonry, including George Washington, Andrew Jack-son, Theodore and Franklin D. Roosevelt, and Harry S Truman.

Freemasonry penetrated the Italian states between 1720 and 1750, immedi-ately opposing the monopolistic control the Catholic Church exercised over im-portant segments of Italian culture and bitterly attacking the pope's temporal power. Both the Masonic movement's criticism of the church's strategic position in the peninsula as well as disagreement in principle motivated CLEMENT XII (1730–1740) on 28 April 1738 to promulgate *In Eminenti* (not to be confused with Urban VIII's [1623–1644] condemnation of JANSENISM in the bull of the same name, 19 June 1643). Freemasonry was repudiated because it was based on agnostic rationalism and because it was composed of an international network of conspiratorial personalities, which put both church and state in peril. Catholic involvement was proscribed on penalty of EXCOMMUNICATION.

There were moments in the later history of Freemasonry when its political outlook was hardly distinguishable from that of the republicans, socialists, left liberals, Social Democrats, and anticlericals. The observation has particular sig-nificance for France and Spain, but most of all, Italy. In the nineteenth century, French Freemasonry joined with republicans and socialists to mount a massive offensive for complete separation of church and state, finally realized by the laic laws enacted in 1904. During the wars of Italian unification, a number of democratic-republican nationalists enrolled in Garibaldi's militia were, like the general and his close collaborator and future premier Francesco Crispi, known Masons.

After Italy was unified (1861), the pioneer revolutionary anarchist Michael Bakunin arrived there in January 1864. The Russian, a member of the order of Freemasonry since his Paris days in 1840, recruited a strategic number of in-dividuals, such as Saverio Friscia, the Sicilian deputy, Sergio and Fanelli, the physician, Carlo Gambuzzi, Attanasio Dramis, and the ex-priest Raffaele Mileti, all members of the Neapolitan Masonic lodge, Vita Nuova, who, with the as-sistance of other converts, by 1872 established the nucleus and organizational framework of a national anarchist association. The Revolutionary Catechism, elaborated by Bakunin in 1866, made confession of atheism the first essential for membership. Italian Freemasonry's hostility to religion and the Catholic Church especially contributed to PIUS IX's (1846–1878) vitriolic assault on liberalism, the fountainhead of all HERESIES, and modern learning, codified in the SYLLABUS OF ERRORS, of 8 December 1864.

Under the successive leadership of Adriano Lemmi, Ernesto Nathan, and Et-tore Ferrari, grand masters between 1885 and 1919, Freemasons in Italy during the period expounded a militant type of anticlericalism, tagged "Jacobinism" by its enemies in and out of the church. It preached a secular state, unrestricted religious liberty for the country's Protestant minorities, the removal of Catholic teaching from the public school, and the right of divorce. Vatican reaction to the campaign unleashed by Masons for a laic Italy has been described as "pathological" by a servant of the church, as shown by the more than 400 damnations launched from Clement XII on, with many emanating from PIUS X (1903–1914).

Freemasonry's divisive effects on Italian life and institutions prompted a number of political parties to reject it. Groups as dissimilar and antagonistic as the Nationalist Association and the official Socialist Party formally rejected any connection with Freemasonry in 1912 and 1914. One of the major concessions the National Fascist Party was compelled to offer to effect its 1923 fusion with the Nationalist Association was the ouster of all unrepentant Freemasons from its ranks. Two years later, the fascist government outlawed Freemasonry, much to the delight of the Holy See, which hoped other countries would follow suit.

Freemasonry in Italy went underground, survived banishment and suppression, and participated in the antifascist Resistance. Postwar Freemasonry has turned from fundamental skepticism to the search for a supernatural-scriptural foundation. It has taken a more tolerant and amicable attitude toward God, the Bible, and Christianity, while the Catholic Church has itself become more understanding of modern culture and the evolving age. Formal dialogue was recently undertaken between Freemasonry and the Catholic Church, undoubtedly encouraged by Pope JOHN XXIII's (1958–1963) policy of *aggiornamento* (updating the church), enunciated in 1962. A growing mutuality has resulted between sectors of Freemasonry and the church, rendering the several hundred papal anti-Masonic pronouncements obsolete. On 17 July 1974, PAUL VI (1963–1978) abrogated Clement XII's excommunication decree of 28 April 1738.

For further reference: Rosario F. Esposito, *La Massoneria d l'Italia dal 1800 ai nostri giorni*, 5th ed. (Rome: Paoline, 1979); Robert F. Gould, *Gould's History of Freemasonry throughout the World*, ed. Dudley Wright, 6 vols. (New York: Scribner's, 1936); Albert G. Mackey and Harry L. Haywood, *Encyclopedia of Freemasonry*, ed. Robert I. Clegg, 3 vols. (Chicago: Masonic History, 1946).

Ronald S. Cunsolo

G

GAIUS (283–296). We know no more about the papacy of Gaius than about that of his predecessor, EUTYCHIAN (275–283). Two unreliable *Passions* link him with St. Suzanna and St. Sebastian, respectively, while further statements of the *Liber Pontificalis* about him bear no weight. Since he ruled in a period of peace for the church, there is no evidence to support the statement of his martyrdom. He was buried in the Cemetery of Callistus, although not in the old papal crypt, which may have been full. His feast is celebrated on 22 April.

For further reference: J. N. D. Kelly, *The Oxford Dictionary of Popes* (New York: Oxford University Press, 1986); J. Lebreton and J. Zeiller, *The History of the Primitive Church*, vol. 4 (London: Burns, Oates, and Washbourne, 1948).

Bernard J. Cassidy

GALLICANISM. Gallicanism encompasses a complex of doctrines, claims, and administrative and juridical practices that arose in France between the fourteenth and eighteenth centuries. Different groups formulated or appealed to rights that asserted the independence of the church or its members in the face of any challenge or limitation, normally from the See of Rome. Royal Gallicanism claimed power over temporalities of the church and a right to nominate to bishoprics and major benefices. Episcopal Gallicanism exalted the rights of bishops as successors of the apostles and the role of councils. Theological Gallicanism claimed the inerrancy and supremacy of councils, to which all, including the POPE, must submit. Finally, the Gallicanism of the *parlements* maintained that its courts were the supreme ecclesiastical courts and the juridic intermediary between the French church and Rome.

During the western schism (see Schism, Great Western) the University of Paris under the aegis of Jean Gerson and Pierre d'Ailly formulated the tenets of theological Gallicanism to justifiy the withdrawal of obedience by France

(1398, 1407) and the convocation of the Council of CONSTANCE. These theories provided the court with the basis for its right to grant benefices. The
concordat of 1516 replaced the Pragmatic Sanction of Burges (1438) but provided the constitutional foundation for royal Gallicanism by granting to the king
the right to nominate all French bishops (93) and holders of major benefices
(500).

Gallicanism received its classic formulation in Pierre Pithou's *Les Libertés
de l'Église gallicane* (1594). During the seventeenth century Louis XIV attempted to extend royal Gallicanism to new areas. The Assembly of the Clergy
supported the royal claims in the "Declaration of 1682," which affirmed the
independence of the king in temporal matters, the superiority of the council over
the pope, and that papal teaching was not irreformable until the church gave its
consent. Although withdrawn in 1693, it continued to be taught in universities
until the Revolution. Throughout these centuries the Gallicanism of the *parlements* asserted itself in the refusal to register papal acts, for example, the decrees
of the Council of TRENT and the condemnations of JANSENISM, thus making
them ineffective in France.

Gallicanism effectively came to an end with the Civil Constitution of the
Clergy (1790). A Neo-Gallicanism appeared in the Organic Articles added to
the CONCORDAT OF 1801. But these derived simply from a desire to control
the church rather than from the theological or historical reasons that grounded
traditional Gallicanism. Neo-Gallicanism lost support with the growth of ultra-
montanism among the French clergy during the nineteenth century and disappeared with the abrogation of the concordat and the separation of church and
state in 1905.

For further reference: C. Berthelot du Chesnay, "Gallicanism," *New Catholic Encyclopedia*, vol. 6, pp. 262–267; A-G. Martimort, *Le Gallicanisme de Bossuet* (Paris: Ed.
du Cerf, 1953); V. Martin, *Les Origines du Gallicanisme* (Paris: Bloud and Gay, 1939).
Richard J. Kehoe

GELASIUS I (492–496). Gelasius was born in Rome, apparently of African
descent, and was active there as archdeacon under his predecessor, FELIX III
(483–492). The Western empire was then under the control of Theodoric and
the Ostrogoths, and Gelasius appears to have developed a positive and beneficial
relationship with Theodoric. The church was split between East and West by
the Acacian SCHISM, which had arisen over the imposition of the so-called
Henoticon by the emperor Zeno. This document attempted to resolve issues that
had torn the church since the Council of CHALCEDON (451), but it was seen
by the Western church as a betrayal of the council and a concession to the
Monophysites. Felix III had excommunicated Acacius, patriarch of Constantinople, in 484, and Gelasius refused to reconcile with the patriarch Euphemius
until the East recognized the EXCOMMUNICATION of Acacius, who had died
in 489.

Gelasius upheld the primacy of Rome against Constantinople and was the first POPE to have been called "Vicar of Christ" (the title was used by a Roman synod in 495). He defended Chalcedon's teaching on the natures of Christ and opposed ARIANISM, Pelagianism, and Manichaeanism; against the latter, which looked upon wine as evil, he ordered the reception of the Eucharist under both species. He gave from his own estate to help the poor, regulated church discipline for the clergy, and established the ember seasons as the time for ordination.

In a letter to the emperor Anastasius, he enunciated a theory of two powers ruling the world: the spiritual authority embodied in the pope, which dealt with spiritual goods, and the temporal power represented by the emperor, which cared for earthly matters. Both were from God and were subject to Christ, and each was independent in its own area; but the spiritual authority of the pope was superior since it offered eternal salvation to the earthly power. This approach influenced medieval theories on kingship and on the relationship between church and state. About eighteen of the mass formulas found in the *Leonine Sacramentary* appear to come from Gelasius, but the *Gelasian Sacramentary* and the *Decretum Gelasianum* do not. Gelasius is second only to LEO I (440–461) in importance as a fifth-century pope, and he stands out in the development of the papacy and papal authority at his time in the line of Leo I and DAMASUS I (366–384). He was later declared a saint.

For further reference: Migne, *Patrologia Latina* 59, 13–190; J. Taylor, "The Early Papacy at Work: Gelasius I (492–496)," *Journal of Religious History* 8 (1974–1975): 317–332; A. K. Ziegler, "Pope Gelasius I and His Teaching on the Relation of Church and State," *Catholic Historical Review* 27 (1942): 3–28.

Gerard H. Ettlinger

GELASIUS II (1118–1119). A Benedictine monk and then papal chancellor since 1089, Gelasius was secretly elected POPE at a monastery on the Palatine Hill as Emperor Henry V (1106–1125) prepared to approve another candidate. Upon the public announcement of his election, Gelasius was attacked, dragged through the streets of Rome, and imprisoned by Cencius Frangipani, leader of an imperial faction. Released in the aftermath of a revolt protesting his treatment, Gelasius fled to Gaeta, where he was ordained a priest and consecrated cardinal and pope.

Gelasius' refusal to return to Rome, despite Henry's summons, prompted the emperor to confirm Maurice Burdinus of Braga as antipope GREGORY VIII (1118–1121), who had previously been excommunicated (see Excommunication) by PASCHAL II (1099–1118) for crowning Henry emperor. Gelasius retaliated by excommunicating both the emperor and his pope. When Henry departed Rome, firmly under the control of Burdinus, Gelasius returned briefly but was again attacked by the Frangipani. He fled to France, intending to convene a council to resolve the outstanding issues with the emperor, but frail health resulted in his death at Cluny before any action could be taken.

For further reference: Eric John, ed., *The Popes: A Concise Biographical Dictionary* (New York: Hawthorn Books, 1964); H. K. Mann, *The Lives of the Popes in the Early Middle Ages* (London: K. Paul, 1902–1932). The best beginning primary source remains the *Liber Pontificalis* (Paris, 1886–1892).

John C. Horgan

GEMELLI, FR. AGOSTINO. Fr. Agostino Gemelli was one of most controversial Catholic intellectuals of twentieth-century Italy. Born Eduardo Gemelli in Milan on 18 January 1878, he died there on 15 July 1959. From his parents and his secondary and university schoolmates, Gemelli absorbed the militant positivism and socialist convictions prevalent in turn-of-the-century Lombardy. After his conversion in 1903, however, Gemelli broke with materialist ideology, assuming the name Agostino upon entering the Franciscan novitiate at Rezzato (near Brescia) later that year. Henceforth, Franciscan spiritualism and neo-Scholasticism guided him through his long, productive public career.

Gemelli studied medicine at the University of Pavia, graduating in 1902. Specializing in experimental psychology, Gemelli did pioneering work in the areas of attitudinal and vocational testing, developmental psychology, and perception. More important was his broader educational contribution in opening Italian Catholic culture to modern science. In characteristic Thomist fashion, Gemelli argued that the ends and larger meaning of human existence were governed by Christ's message and by the church—but that the physical and psychological mechanisms of human behavior needed to be understood through empirical and reasoned scientific investigation.

In many respects, Gemelli deplored modern civilization. In the inaugural 1914 issue of their journal, *Vita e Pensiero*, he and two associates penned a manifesto entitled "Medievalism," urging their countrymen to join them in a return to the theocentric conception of the Christian Middle Ages. His crusade on behalf of church and science culminated in the founding of Milan's Catholic University of the Sacred Heart in 1921. As rector of the university, Gemelli supported the policies of the fascist regime throughout the interwar period but not the neofascist republic of Salò. Accused of clerico-fascism, he was briefly suspended from his rectorship by Allied authorities in 1945 but reinstated the following year. Beginning in 1937, Gemelli also presided over the newly established Pontifical Scientific Academy. Under the sympathetic patronage of Popes PIUS XI (1922–1939) and PIUS XII (1939–1958), Gemelli gathered an internationally renowned, ecumenical community of scholars in Rome for research and intellectual exchange.

For further reference: Giorgio Cosmacini, *Gemelli* (Milan: Rizzoli, 1985); Maria Sticco, *Father Gemelli: Notes for the Biography of a Great Man* (Chicago: Franciscan Herald Press, 1980).

Steven F. White

GERMAN–VATICAN RELATIONS, 1870–1933. Prior to unification in 1871, Germany was represented at the Holy See by a Prussian and a Bavarian legation, while the Vatican maintained a NUNCIO in Munich but none in Berlin. Church–state relations in Bavaria were regularized by the CONCORDAT of 1817, while those in Prussia were regulated by the papal bull *De Salute Animarum* (1821), which the Berlin government had approved. During the unification period, many Germans, including national liberal leader Rudolf von Bennigsen, equated Germanism with Protestantism and Prussianism. Suspicious that Catholics were pro-Austrian and seeing advantages to his foreign policy in allying with the new Italian kingdom, Bismarck distrusted the newly founded Catholic CENTER PARTY, which opposed his centralizing governmental tendencies and urged him to intervene in the Roman question and aid the POPE. Bismarck began his war on the church in Germany, the KULTURKAMPF. Restrictions were placed on the church, civil marriage was made obligatory, religious orders were expelled from the country, and ecclesiastics were arrested.

Tensions also increased in 1872, when PIUS IX (1846–1878) refused to appoint the Reich's candidate as first German ambassador to the Holy See. This rebuff and Pius' protests about the treatment of the church prompted Bismarck to end discussions over Reich representation at the Holy See and sever Prussian relations with the Vatican, which were not resumed until 1882. By 1878, when it was apparent there was no likelihood of German Catholics and Austria allying against the Reich, tensions eased. The new pope, LEO XIII (1878–1903), also sought to bring about a reconciliation. Restrictions against the church (the May Laws or Falk Laws of 1873) were gradually repealed in the following years. Until 1882, when Prussia once more resumed its diplomatic relations with the Holy See, the Bavarian legation and the nunciature in Munich dealt with most of the diplomatic communication between Germany and the Vatican. This enhanced Bavaria's particular and important status within the Reich.

In 1885 tension further lessened when Bismarck, in a dispute with Spain over the Caroline Islands, suggested the pope arbitrate the matter; Leo was flattered and undertook the task. During the period of the empire, most of German–Vatican relations dealt with ecclesiastical matters (e.g., the problem of papal INFALLIBILITY, the old Catholic SCHISM, the controversy over MODERNISM) and the removal of the remaining vestiges of the *Kulturkampf*. With the outbreak of WORLD WAR I with Catholics on both sides of the conflict, the Vatican strove to remain impartial. However, Rome entered into the arena of world affairs with the papal peace proposal of 1917. Germany, hoping for a military victory, rejected the papal efforts.

In 1919, diplomatic relations were finally established between the Reich and the Holy See (the nuncio did not take up residence in Berlin until 1925). Each government saw advantages in cooperating with the other. The Vatican believed that a strong Germany was necessary to block the spread of Bolshevism or secularist France's predominance on the Continent, while Germany hoped that Rome would use its influence to help moderate the conditions imposed by the Versailles Treaty. In questions about reparations, the Ruhr occupation, border alterations, and so, Berlin constantly sought Rome's support in presenting its case to the Allied powers.

The other major issue concerning Berlin and the Vatican during the entire Weimar period was the question of church–state relations. Efforts to negotiate a Reich concordat began almost immediately after the founding of the republic but continually foundered because of either Vatican demands, the objections of the individual states (*Länder*), or the opposition of the non-Catholic parties. The Holy See therefore adopted a policy of signing treaties with individual states (Bavaria 1924 (see Bavaria, Concordat of 1924), Prussia 1929 (see Prussian Concordat of 1929), Baden 1932). On 23 July 1933, in order to gain prestige by receiving international recognition for his government and to win support from German Catholics for his regime, Adolph HITLER, the new chancellor, had the Reich Concordat (see Germany, Concordat of 1933) quickly signed. What had occupied the legislators during the entire Weimar period was ironically concluded upon its demise.

For further reference: Georg Franz-Willing, *Die bayerische Vatikangesandtschaft, 1803–1834* (Munich: Ehrenwirth Verlag, 1965); Dieter Golombek, *Die politische vorgeschichte des Preussenkonkordats (1929)* (Mainz: Matthias Grünewald Verlag, 1970); Franciscus Hanus, *Die preussische Vatikangesandtschaft, 1747–1920* (Munich: Pohl Verlag, 1954); Wolfgang Steglich, ed., *Der Friedensappell Papst Benedikts XV* (Wiesbaden: F. Steiner Verlag, 1970); Stewart A. Stehlin, *Weimar and the Vatican, 1919–1933* (Princeton: Princeton University Press, 1983); Ludwig Volk, *Das Reichskonkordat vom 20. Juli 1933* (Mainz: Matthias Grünewald Verlag, 1972).

Stewart A. Stehlin

GERMANY, CONCORDAT OF 1933. The Holy See's interest in a CONCORDAT with Weimar Germany reflected the concern of the German episcopate and the Vatican with the position of the confessional schools in Germany. The Weimar Constitution of 1919 affirmed the right of parents to request the building of a confessional school. To the dissatisfaction of the Catholic and Protestant clergies, however, it stipulated that the interconfessional school should be normative. In the early 1920s the Catholic hierarchy initiated a petition calling on the national government to grant legal equality to the denominational schools. That campaign was successful, but only the Catholic Center (see Center Party) and the German Nationalist Peoples' Party, a party of the Protestant elites, supported a bill for equality to be accorded to those schools. That bill eventually died in committee in 1928.

The Vatican's concordat efforts initially appeared to have better prospects for success. In 1921–1922 the German president, Friedrich Ebert, a Social Democrat, and the chancellor, Joseph Wirth, a Catholic Centrist, welcomed concordat talks with the Holy See. Germany was then isolated, facing heavy reparations and seriously divided. The Holy See was the first foreign government to recognize it, doing so in 1920 and delegating its NUNCIO to Munich, Archbishop

Eugenio Pacelli, to represent it in Berlin as well. However, the Bavarian government insisted on its prior right to negotiate a concordat with the Vatican, and that pact was not concluded till 1924. By that time the German government had lost interest in concordat talks with nuncio Pacelli, for it was evident that the Reichstag would not approve such a treaty. Prussia did enter into a concordat with the Holy See in 1929, and Baden followed suit three years later, but neither pact contained articles on the schools.

In 1930–1931 Eugenio Pacelli, now the papal secretary of state, found new hope for a German concordat. The Reichstag had deadlocked in March 1930, and President Hindenburg appointed Heinrich Brüning, a Center Party conservative, to be chancellor and to govern by emergency degrees. Brüning was a close friend of Prelate Ludwig Kaas, the leader of the Center, who had an even closer friendship with Cardinal Pacelli, whom he had served as an adviser on German affairs for many years.

Pacelli was impressed by the rapid rise of the Nazi Party, which had won 107 Reichstag seats in the elections of November 1930. In April 1931 Hermann Göring paid a visit to the Vatican to express his party's goodwill toward the church. Cardinal Pacelli later urged Chancellor Brüning to bring some Nazis into his cabinet, only to be turned down by the chancellor. President Hindenburg, upset that Brüning could not win majority Reichstag support, dismissed him in May 1932, a fate that Brüning's successors, Franz von Papen, a Catholic ultraconservative nobleman, and General Kurt von Schleicher subsequently experienced. On von Papen's advice the president appointed HITLER to the chancellorship and von Papen to the newly created position of vice-chancellor in late January 1933.

The Nazi Party and its conservative nationalist allies failed to win a constitutional majority in the national elections of 5 March 1933, so Hitler needed the support of the Center in the Reichstag's voting on an enabling act. On 6 March Franz von Papen and Ludwig Kaas came together in a highly secret meeting. Circumstantial evidence suggests that the vice-chancellor assured the Center's leader that the regime would enter into binding concordat negotiations with the Holy See if Kaas would produce enough Center votes to ensure the passage of the Enabling Act in the Reichstag on 23 March. Most of the Center deputies did vote for that measure on that date, and Prelate Kaas would later take credit for its passage.

The concordat between the Holy See and NAZI GERMANY, signed on 20 July 1933, covered a wide range of issues and contained two major compromises. The pact guaranteed the legal equality of the confessional schools and their building where they did not exist. It also affirmed that German priests could not participate in political activity, which meant that the church was withdrawing its support of the Center Party. On learning of this concession, Heinrich Brüning, now the Center's leader, waited a few days and then with his colleagues dissolved his old party on 5 July. Within a few weeks a governmental decree declared that the Nazi Party was the only legal party in Germany. Within three years the Nazi regime began to convert the church schools into community schools, in which religion might be taught but in which the major emphasis would be on race.

For further reference: Stewart A. Stehlin, *Weimar and the Vatican, 1919–1929: German–Vatican Diplomatic Relations in the Interwar Years* (Princeton: Princeton University Press, 1983); Ludwig Volk, *Das Reickskonkordat vom 20 Juli Von den Ansatzen in der Weimarer Republik bis zur Ratifizierung am 10. September 1933* (Mainz: Matthias-Grunewald Verlag, 1973); John Zeender, "The Genesis of the German Concordat of 1933," in *Studies in Catholic History in Honor of John Tracy Ellis*, ed. Nelson H. Minnich, Robert B. Eno, and Robert F. Trisco (Wilmington, DE: Michael Glazier, 1985).

John K. Zeender

GNOSTICISM. Gnosticism, a term derived from the Greek word *gnosis*, meaning knowledge, describes an attitude, an approach to religion, a hermeneutic perhaps, that is often described as a movement but, in fact, has no reality apart from an established system such as Christianity or Judaism. The knowledge involved is not scientific or philosophical; it is spiritual knowledge derived from a special revelation that the gnostic teacher claims to have received. Through this knowledge one is enabled to obtain salvation that is denied those who do not possess it. Gnosticism appears in a variety of forms, which derive from its context in each case. In general most forms of gnosticism share as a basic principle a radical dualism that views spirit and matter as two utterly opposed realities.

Christian gnosticism, which appeared in the New Testament, flourished in the second and third centuries and survived in a modified form into the fifth century. At its height it was described in the late second and early third centuries by heresiologists such as Irenaeus, Hippolytus, Tertullian, and Clement of Alexandria, who treated it as a serious threat to Christianity. They considered it a HERESY that was dependent, for the most part, on ancient Greek philosophy, particularly on Platonism. The influence of Platonism can, indeed, be found in Christian gnosticism, but the same is true of elements from Judaism, pagan mystery religions, hermetism, and even religions of the Far East, especially India.

One cannot speak of gnostic teachings as fully organized systems, but since Irenaeus does describe the approach of several prominent gnostic teachers, including Valentinus and Bardesanes, a rough outline of their views can be made, although every element was not found in every teacher. Christian gnostics purported to offer a revelation that came from Jesus but had been kept secret and not handed on from the apostles or through the Gospels. To the heresiologists this seemed to attack the very heart of Christianity, and Irenaeus especially attempts to show that all Christian revelation came from Christ and was transmitted openly and fully through the apostles to all the churches down through time; for Irenaeus there were no secrets.

The gnostic god was described as absolutely unapproachable. Apart from, and beneath, this god was a heavenly realm populated by spiritual beings, sometimes known as Aeons, whose names corresponded to persons and aspects of Christianity; these beings multiplied, and at the lowest level one of them, in aspiring to unite with the transcendent god, produced the material universe as we know it, through a sin or an error. This being was often identified with the creator God of the Old Testament, so that a strongly anti-Jewish strain is often present.

From Christianity gnosticism took the idea of salvation for beings of this world, but seemingly only those who received sparks of the divine from the creator could achieve it; the process of salvation was, therefore, deterministic. Salvation sometimes came through a savior, but the savior, who was not always Jesus, usually needed salvation himself. If the savior was Jesus, he was not truly divine, since the heavenly realm was separated from the totally transcendent god, nor was he truly human, since the flesh, as matter, was inferior, if not actually evil. There are traces of a myth in which a savior (not Jesus) came from the heavenly realm to liberate those who were overwhelmed by this world; he was himself overwhelmed and required a call from above, and, having received it, he brought salvation to the elect. Throughout Christian history the heresiologists' picture of gnosticism was supplemented by texts found in apocryphal Gospels and Acts, some of which, such as the Song of the Pearl, lacked many of the bizarre qualities detailed by the heresiologists.

In 1945, however, a group of codices was discovered near the small Egyptian village of Nag Hammadi. These codices contain Coptic translations of over 50 texts with mostly Christian gnostic contents. The translations were made in the fourth century and may represent a library of a group of monks who lived in that area. Some of these works, such as the gospel of Thomas, provide us with sayings of Jesus that are similar to, or supplement, texts found in the synoptic Gospels. The gnostic elements of many of these writings are quite different from those found in the heresiologists, and this has raised questions about the accuracy of the latter and even about their intentions. It may be that Irenaeus and the others did not always understand what the gnostics were teaching, and it sometimes appears that they deliberately misrepresented them in order to suppress what was actually a legitimate form of Christianity.

These questions about the heresiologists were raised, on one hand, because of the fact that there was a great deal of latitude of expression allowed in the early, postbiblical church; the faith was professed in rather vague credal formulas called the rule of truth or the rule of faith, and there was no single, unified form of expression for all the details implied in these summaries. On the other hand, these considerations were further fueled by certain of the Nag Hammadi documents in which some aspects of the life and faith of the community they represent resonate with modern concerns. For example, women appear to have exercised authority and to have played an important role in community life, while church order seems far less structured and hierarchical than it was in the church of Irenaeus.

Final judgment on these issues remains to be passed. The Nag Hammadi documents leave no doubt that gnosticism was a far more complex reality than the heresiologists imagined and that they did not always fully understand what they were condemning. They also show that there were forms of Gnosticism that were not so perverse as those described by the heresiologists. These facts do not, however, serve to prove definitively that the heresiologists were acting out of bad will simply to suppress a legitimate form of Christianity that ran counter to their particular interests. The bulk of their attacks centered on issues that were the heart of Christian teaching and life; they concerned faith, morality, and, ultimately, salvation. They did touch upon church order, insofar as they were concerned to prove that the church hands on the truth revealed by Christ to the apostles, and the latter, in turn, handed on this truth to their successors. This was, however, an argument for authoritative teaching, not for hierarchical authority.

For further reference: R. M. Grant, *Gnosticism and Early Christianity*, rev. ed. (New York: Harper and Row, 1966); R. Haardt, *Gnosis. Character and Testimony* (Leiden: E. J. Brill, 1971); B. Layton, *The Gnostic Scriptures* (Garden City, NY: Doubleday, 1987); J. M. Robinson, ed., *The Nag Hammadi Library in English*, rev. ed. (San Francisco: Harper and Row, 1988); K. Rudolph, *Gnosis* (San Francisco: Harper and Row, 1983).

Gerard H. Ettlinger

GOLDEN ROSE. The golden rose is a sacred ornament artistically wrought in pure gold to represent a rose or rose bush, blessed annually by the POPES. They destined the golden rose as a token of favor to persons of note, especially sovereigns, to great centers of Catholic worship and pilgrimage, and to civic communities to render them public honor. The earliest form was that of a stem terminating in a single bloom, with a cusp concealed at the center of the petals, into which balsam and musk were inserted for fragrance. By the early fourteenth century the design tended to be more elaborate and incorporated entwined thorny stems with leaves and clusters of buds around the central flower. Precious stones were added to enhance its appearance and augment its value. In later centuries the golden rose appears complete with vase and supportive pedestal, both usually of silver gilt but richly decorated with bas-relief work and displaying the arms of the reigning pontiff.

The most renowned Italian goldsmiths were commissioned with making these ornaments, their value varying according to the generosity and economic circumstances of the donor. Few specimens of the golden rose have survived to present times, probably because they were melted down to recuperate the precious metals for monetary purposes, but examples can been seen in museums of Benevento, Congoli, Paris, Sienna, the Vatican, and Vienna.

It is impossible to establish with chronological accuracy the origins of the golden rose, but there is unanimous agreement that they go back to the early Middle Ages. The first certain mention is in 1049; the earliest record of the golden rose's being donated by the pope is on 1096. During the following century little information is to be had, but what records still survive all confirm the tradition that the popes proceeded with it in their hands on Laetare Sunday, the fourth Sunday of Lent, so called because the introit antiphon opens with the words *Laetare Jerusalem* but also known as Rose Sunday on account of the blessing that preceded the celebration of the papal mass that day.

The church has always used its prerogative of attaching a spiritual meaning to material objects, and the popes found the practice useful to encourage the recipients to cultivate those virtues consonant with their office or state of life. Great as may have been the artistic and monetary value of their gift, nevertheless, that was of secondary importance in comparison with that higher message the golden rose was intended to convey, as was invariably expressed in the letter accompanying the papal gift. In a sense, the rose, the fairest and most fragrant of all nature's flowers, represented Christ himself and was an assurance of eternal bliss, a source of joy and gladness, as was affirmed in the ritual formula of blessing.

In consultation with the cardinals, the pope decided to whom the golden rose should be given. Most often the recipient was not present at the papal court, and the precious gift had to be consigned to a royal ambassador in residence or to a papal LEGATE, specially commissioned to deliver it according to a precise protocol.

For further reference: C. Burns, *Golden Rose and Blessed Sword: Papal Gifts to Scottish Monarchs* (Glasgow, 1970); C. Burns, "Papal Gifts and Honours for the Earlier Tudors," *Miscellanea Historiae Pontificiae* 50 (1983): 173–197; E. Cornides, *Rose und Schwert im papstilichen zeremoniell* (Vienna, 1967); E. Muntz, "Les Roses d'Or pontificales," *Revue de l'Art Chretien* 44 (1901): 1–11.

Charles Burns

GREGORY I (590–604). Gregory the Great was born in Rome of a patrician family about 540 and died 12 March 604. One of the most important POPES, he has been designated the fourth (with Jerome, Ambrose, and Augustine) of four Latin fathers. A member of a prominent senatorial family, after a traditional course of study about 572 he was appointed prefect of the city, manifesting the talent for administration that would characterize his papacy. His conversion to the monastic life in 574–575 threw any future secular administrative career into question, as he turned his paternal estate in Rome into an urban monastery, St. Andrew's, on the Caelian Hill.

Gregory's influence on the monastic life of the Middle Ages was immense. The Doctor of Desire was an expositor of the process by which the soul is disengaged from the world and attached to God through compunction, detachment, and desire, the work of the Holy Spirit in the human heart. Gregory was subsequently ordained and in 579 was sent as emissary to Constantinople, where he represented papal interests at the imperial court and passed imperial instructions to Rome. He took a group of monks with him to the court, where he stayed until 585/586. At the court he re-created, as later he would as pope, a monastic community around him. Here he became acquainted with such figures as the brothers Leander and Isidore of Seville and began his greatest commentary, on the biblical book of Job, sometimes called the Moralia. Upon his return to Rome, he became secretary to Pope PELAGIUS II (579–590).

Gregory became pope in 590, a difficult time. In the two decades following 535, the emperor Justinian had attempted to reconquer the country, and in 568 a new invader, the Lombards, had crossed the Alps. The result of the Gothic and Lombard wars was unparalleled destruction, starvation, plague, decline of population, and economic recession. By the time Gregory became pope, the Lombards had destroyed much church property and threatened Rome itself from their strongholds less than forty miles away. In addition, the plague was raging, indeed, had been responsible for the death of Gregory's immediate predecessor as pope. Gregory was forced to deal with such immediate problems as trying to stave off starvation in Rome, where there remained a population of perhaps 30,000. He undertook many specific administrative initiatives, particularly the reform of the Patrimony of St. Peter, the papal properties. Here he restructured estates, pressing their clerical administrators to practice evangelical poverty and protect the rural population against oppression.

Gregory confronted other difficulties. Justinian had ruined the Roman economy in his attempted reconquest of Italy. The senate ceased to function. Having lost their political place in the world, the Romans did not restore their secular buildings, and Rome became a city of churches, saints, martyrs, and pilgrims. Gregory refused to accept this situation. Arian Christianity (see Arianism) had had a significant presence in Italy, as elsewhere, into the sixth century, and although the Lombards remained Arian into the seventh century, Gregory had the satisfaction of finally Catholicizing the Arian churches of Rome. Gregory continued to live the life of a monk and, in some degree, monasticized the papacy, attempting to oust laymen from the closest circle of papal advisers in favor of clerics or monks. His ideal was a life lived in, but not of, the world, and he was the first to use the title, still used today, *servus servorum dei* (servant of the servants of God).

Despite the Lombard presence elsewhere in Italy, Rome remained a part of the Byzantine empire, which maintained a garrison in the city. Yet, Gregory had repeatedly to negotiate the safety of Rome and Italy with the Lombards during his pontificate. Gregory's goal, the peaceful coexistence of Roman and barbarian, tacitly accepted the permanent presence of the barbarians in Italy and elsewhere and worked against the Byzantine goal of total recovery of their power in the West. Gregory recognized that the Byzantine presence in the West was feeble and accepted many temporal obligations, assuming secular tasks such as repair of the aqueducts and provision of food in time of famine.

Gregory gave himself to the task of evangelization and engaged in a widespread pastoral correspondence, often in difficult circumstances. Perhaps he is most remembered for the evangelization of England. Although Christianity had earlier found its way to Britain, where Irish monks had missionized, Gregory was the first pope to adopt the policy of sending missionaries beyond the boundaries of the Roman Christian world. In 596 he sent the missionary Augustine to England. Although the mission's success was largely limited to Kent, where a metropolitan bishopric was established at Canterbury, it came to be viewed as the foundation of English Christianity. In 601, Gregory sent Augustine the pallium. Until Gregory's day, Christianity had largely been a religion of urban populations centered in cities. Increasingly, as cities continued their decline, the missionaries—who commonly addressed their message to rulers—helped in the task of the conversion of the rural population.

In the midst of his many activities, Gregory continued to write. He was particularly interested in liturgical reform. The Gregorian Sacramentary as we have it contains not just his work but additions made to the Roman liturgy into the eighth century. Tradition also attributes a book of antiphons to Gregory. He wrote many homilies, commentaries on various books of Scripture, and the Pastoral Rule, influential beyond the Middle Ages as a guide for bishops.

For further reference: Jean Leclercq, *The Love of Learning and the Desire for God: A Study of Monastic Culture*, trans. Catharine Misrahi (New York: Fordham University Press, 1961); V. Recchia, "Gregory the Great," in *Encyclopedia of the Early Church*, vol. 1, ed. Angelo Di Berardino, trans. Adrian Walford (Cambridge, 1992); Bernhard Schimmelpfennig, *The Papacy*, trans. James Sievert (New York: Columbia University Press, 1992); Carole Straw, *Gregory the Great: Perfection in Imperfection* (Berkeley: University of California Press, 1988).

Glenn W. Olsen

GREGORY II (715–731). Born of a wealthy Roman family, while a deacon he accompanied Constantine I on a journey to Constantinople (709–711), where he participated in the negotiations with the Byzantine emperor over the decrees of the Quinisext Council of 692. Once POPE in 715, Gregory demonstrated his political skills in the demise of Byzantine power in Italy. In 716 Gregory persuaded the Lombard king, Liutprand, to return valuable patrimonies he maintained in the Cottian Alps. From 717 to 726, Gregory led the resistance to the crippling tax demands instituted by Emperor Leo III. His popularity led the government to call for his assassination or deposition. Gregory strove to prevent the Lombards from expanding, but Rome was threatened in 729 by an unexpected alliance of Liutprand and Eutychius, the exarch. Gregory survived and in his reamining years spread the faith in Germany.

For further reference: J. N. D. Kelly, *The Oxford Dictionary of Popes* (Oxford: Oxford University Press, 1986).

Patrick McGuire

GREGORY III (731–741). St. Gregory III reigned from 18 March 731 to 28 November 741 and was Syrian by origin. At the funeral of Pope GREGORY

II (715–731), he was spontaneously acclaimed pope at the Lateran by cheering Roman crowds and consecrated five weeks later, the last pope to obtain the approval of the Byzantine exarch.

As Gregory began his reign, the Iconoclastic Controversy was at its height, the prohibition against sacred images having been enacted by the Byzantine emperor Leo III (717–741) just a few months earlier. Eager to make peace with the Eastern empire, Gregory appealed to Leo to abandon this policy, offensive to Western practice. Receiving no response, he held a Synod of Bishops and excommunicated (see Excommunication) anyone destroying images, by implication including Leo and the patriarch of Constantinople. In retaliation the emperor sent a fleet to attack Italy. Later he transferred the ancient patrimonies of the See of Rome in Calabria, Sicily, and Illyricum in the Balkans to the jurisdiction of Constantinople. Gregory remained loyal to the Eastern empire because he regarded it to be the only legitimate authority. Thus, when Ravenna fell to the invading Lombards, he gave his support to the exarch Eutychius, who eventually retook the city. Both Leo and Eutychius concluded a truce with the pope. Gregory rebuilt the wall of Rome in defense against any further attacks by the Lombard king Liutprand and, as the Lombards grew stronger, sought help from the Franks, especially Charles Martel.

Gregory also undertook extensive missionary activity in Western Europe, fully supporting the work of Boniface (680–754), to whom he gave the rank of archbishop, and in Germany and strengthened relations between Rome and the English church. Gregory provided extensive support for the monastic movement in the Western church and was responsible for significant construction in Rome, beautifying its churches and decorating them with splendid images in defiance of the iconoclasts. His works in the city include an oratory in St. Peter's, where he would eventually be buried. His feast is 28 November.

For further reference: Matthew Bunson, *The Pope Encyclopedia* (New York: Crown Trade Paperbacks, 1995); L. Duchesne, ed., *Liber Pontificalis* (Paris: E. de Boccard, 1955).

William Roberts

GREGORY IV (827–844). Supported by the Roman nobility, this Roman-born, aristocratic cardinal assumed the pontificate during a period of turmoil within the Frankish kingdom. His consecration complied with the *Constitutio Lothari* (824), which not only allowed the Roman people and clergy participation in papal elections (a practice banned by Stephen III in 769) but also required the pope-elect to swear an oath of loyalty to the emperor. The POPE became embroiled in a series of conflicts between Emperor Louis I the Pious (814–840) and his sons, Lothar I, Pepin, and Louis the German.

When Lothar led a rebellion against his father in 833, Gregory, accompanying Lothar, interceded with the emperor to mediate a peaceful resolution to the conflict. Gregory's actions outraged the Frankish bishops, who accused the pope of supporting Lothar, which violated his oath of loyalty to Emperor Louis, and considered excommunicating (see Excommunication) the pontiff. Gregory responded by reminding the bishops of papal supremacy in matters temporal and secular. With an agreement in hand, Gregory soon realized he had been tricked by Lothar and his brothers, who secretly desired their father's removal. Events soured for the emperor when his soldiers deserted him, prompting his surrender and dethronement. The pope returned to Rome disappointed and angry with the machinations of Lothar. When Louis regained his throne in March 834, he initiated contacts with the papacy to resume normal relations. However, in 840, Louis' death plunged the empire into civil war, and Gregory's attempts to halt the bloodshed proved fruitless. The resulting breakup of the Frankish empire left the papacy without protection.

Gregory's reign was distinguished for two notable accomplishments. In response to Saracen raids along the Italian coast, a fortress was constructed at the mouth of the Tiber River (modern-day Ostia) for the defense of Rome. Additionally, with the cooperation of Louis during his reign, Gregory commenced the observation of the feast of All Saints' Day throughout the imperial lands.

For further reference: H. K. Mann, *The Lives of the Popes in the Early Middle Ages* (London: K. Paul, 1902–1932); Walter Ullman, *A Short History of the Papacy in the Middle Ages* (London: Methuen, 1972).

John C. Horgan

GREGORY V (996–999). The first German POPE, Gregory ascended the chair of St. Peter with the support of the German emperor Otto III (996–1002) and the Roman nobility. Otto had been summoned to Rome by JOHN XV (985–996) that spring to restore him to his rightful place and crush the tyranny of Crescentius Nomentanus, of Rome's powerful noble family. The advance of German troops proved sufficient to cause Nomentanus to recall John and beg the pontiff to prevent an attack by Otto. John's untimely death left the Roman noble exposed to Otto's planned retribution. The twenty-four-year-old Gregory interceded, obtaining a pardon for Nomentanus, an action he would regret. Gregory's first act was to crown Otto emperor and declare him the new protector of the church. Gregory possessed a degree of independence in deciding the thorny issue regarding the archbishopric of Rheims. At a synod in May 996, Gregory upheld the suspension, issued by his predecessor, John XV, of Gerbert as archbishop of Rheims.

The most divisive event of Gregory's pontificate occurred in June 996, when Crescentius Nomentanus, whom Gregory had earlier protected from Otto III, usurped the papal throne by leading a revolt against German influence in Rome. Gregory, forced to flee, pleaded for assistance from Otto, but the emperor was preoccupied with events in Germany, Gregory's two attempts to retake Rome failed, and, in February 997, he convened a synod at Pavia and excommunicated (see Excommunication) Crescentius. Meanwhile, Crescentius, supported by the

Byzantine emperor Basil II, elected and consecrated a Greek, John Philagathos, as Pope JOHN XVI (997–998), who relinquished temporal papal power to the Roman noble. This ANTIPOPE was also excommunicated by Gregory's synod. Otto intervened in February 998, easily recapturing Rome for his pope. The conspirators met a gruesome fate. John's eyes were gouged out, and his mutilated body paraded around Rome on a jackass. He was stripped of his rank by Gregory and imprisoned in a monastery, where he died in 1001. Crescentius Nomentanus was immediately beheaded. The restored pontiff eventually succumbed to malaria in February 999, although rumors suggested he may have been poisoned.

For further reference: Eric John, ed., *The Popes: A Concise Biographical Dictionary* (New York: Hawthorn Books, 1964); H. K. Mann, *The Lives of the Popes in the Early Middle Ages* (London: K. Paul, 1902–1932); Walter Ullman, *A Short History of the Papacy in the Middle Ages* (London: Methuen, 1972.)

John C. Horgan

GREGORY VI, ANTIPOPE (1012). Imperial absence from Rome encouraged hostility between the aristocratic families of the city. The Crescentii rose to challenge the Tusculan family, who, upon the death of SERGIUS IV (1009–1012), elected BENEDICT VIII (1012–1024). The Crescentii supported the candidacy of Gregory. This struggle eventually forced Gregory from Rome. The Saxon king, Henry II (1002–1024), assured Gregory that the issue would be settled provided Gregory not exercise the duties of his office pending a final decision. Unknown to Gregory, Henry had already settled upon Benedict, most likely due to the decades-long struggle between the Crescentii, Gregory's benefactors, and the German kings. There are no known records of Gregory's performing any official acts, nor is there any information regarding his whereabouts after leaving Henry's company.

For further reference: Joseph S. Brusher, *Popes through the Ages* (Princeton: D. Van Nostrand, 1964); Hans Kuhner, *Encyclopedia of the Papacy* (New York: Philosophical Library, 1958).

John C. Horgan

GREGORY VI (1045–1046). John Gratian, possibly interested in reforming the papacy, may have purchased Tusculan influence for his election. BENEDICT IX (1032–1044, 1045) resigned on 1 May 1045, and Gratian was consecrated as Gregory VI on 5 May; he resigned in December 1046. As Gregory VI he had to contend with two rivals—SYLVESTER III (1045), installed by the rival Crescentian family after Benedict IX fled Rome, and Benedict himself, who changed his mind shortly after resigning and wanted the office back. A possible sign of Gratian's desire to reform the papacy was his appointment of the Cluniac monk Hildebrand (the future GREGORY VII [1073–1085]) as his secretary. Hildebrand later persuaded Gratian to resign, because he was guilty of simony.

A series of synods called by the Holy Roman Emperor Henry III in 1046 accepted the resignation of Gregory VI, deposed Sylvester III, and rejected Benedict IX's effort to reclaim his office. The emperor nominated Suidger, bishop of Bamberg, for the papacy. He was elected on 24 December and consecrated on 25 December 1046 as CLEMENT II (1046–1047). Gratian was exiled to Germany, where he died at Cologne late in 1047 or early in 1048.

For further reference: Matthew Bunson, *The Pope Encyclopedia* (New York: Crown Trade Paperbacks, 1995).

Frank Grande

GREGORY VII (1073–1085). Hildebrand, the future Gregory VII, was born in Tuscany about 1021 and educated in the Lateran palace school in Rome. The 1040s found this cleric allied with an indigenous group of Roman reformers centered about GREGORY VI (1045–1046), whom Hildebrand served as chaplain. Following Gregory VI's deposition by the synod of Sutri (1046), he went into exile with the POPE. In exile he met the future LEO IX (1049–1054), joining his entourage in 1048 and living austerely. Hildebrand returned to Rome with the newly elected Leo IX in 1049, assisting Leo's reformist policies, including the reestablishment of papal power in the patrimony of St. Peter.

Hildebrand and his reform party believed that the entrance of the Germanic peoples into European life and conversion to Christianity had introduced some harmful customs, especially the notion that their monarch's rule in the name of God extended to supervision of the church and the papacy. Against ancient church law, they chose and invested in office the bishops of the regions subject to them—lay investiture. Hildebrand's party struggled against the practice, which commonly involved simony, a payment for the office received. As early as the Lenten synod of Rome of 1059, the reformers succeeded in prohibiting lay investiture, as well as clerical incontinence and simony.

Following his election as pope in 1073, Gregory VII's pontificate was dominated by a struggle for freedom of the church from the control of lay rulers. Around 1075, the *Dictatus papae*, entered in the papal register, gave special attention to the definition of papal powers. Within the church Gregory claimed to be the sole source of law, the sole figure able to appoint and remove prelates. Only those who followed the teachings of the Roman church could be considered Catholic. Gregory's group announced that the goal of Christianity was not just the formation of Christ-like individuals or communities living a life relatively secluded from society but the formation of a social or public life based on the Gospels. Thus, Gregory's pontificate was characterized by a struggle for "right order," for the formation of a social life that examined all customs and hierarchies in light of the Gospels.

Gregory's pontificate was filled with confrontation, particularly with Henry IV (1056–1106) of Germany over the issues of free episcopal elections and lay investiture. In 1075, Gregory reaffirmed the condemnation of lay investiture, which Henry continued to practice. In the succeeding years Henry twice had the German bishops depose Gregory and renounce obedience to him as pope, and Gregory twice deposed and excommunicated Henry. The brief reconciliation of 1077 at Canossa, after the first EXCOMMUNICATION, in which Henry submitted to Gregory, was followed by Gregory's support in 1080 for the anti-king elected in 1077 by the German nobility, Rudolf of Swabia. In response, Henry arranged for the election of an ANTIPOPE (Clement III, 1080, 1084–1100) and took control of Rome. Gregory, in turn, called upon his ally and vassal Robert Guiscard in 1084, but the Normans plundered Rome after dislodging Henry's forces, creating resentment among the Romans. Gregory thus was constrained to retire with the Normans when they returned home and died in exile in Salerno on 25 May 1085.

Although Gregory's struggle centered on Germany, there were other confrontations during his pontificate. In England, although William the Conqueror (1066–1087) refused to abandon lay investiture, he implemented many of the reforms sought by the papacy. In France, many of the papal goals were achieved in opposition to Philip I (1060–1108). Neither Gregory nor those around him intended to replace lay with clerical government but believed the clergy had the right to intervene to correct matters when a ruler seriously violated moral or ecclesiastical law. He believed the papacy should provide a moral and spiritual leadership, supervise European life, and serve as a court of last resort. Gregory has been variously judged in later historical memory. He seems to have been committed to the renewal of Christendom, the liberty of the church, and the advance of justice in society. He must be credited for a general religious reform and revival from his day into the twelfth century.

For further reference: Colin Morris, *The Papal Monarchy: The Western Church from 1050 to 1250* (Oxford: Oxford University Press, 1989); I. S. Robinson, *The Papacy, 1073–1198: Continuity and Innovation* (Cambridge: Cambridge University Press, 1990); Gerd Tellenbach, *Church, State and Christian Society at the Time of the Investiture Contest*, trans. R. F. Bennett (Oxford: Oxford University Press, 1959).

Glenn W. Olsen

GREGORY VIII, ANTIPOPE (1118–1121). Maurice Burdinus, the French-born archbishop of Braga, served as the third of a string of ANTIPOPES whose elections to the papacy centered around the ongoing dispute over investiture between the POPES and German emperors. Although Henry V (1106–1125) had reached agreement with PASCHAL II (1099–1118) in 1111 about investiture rights, with the pope agreeing to the emperor's retaining them, the firestorm of protest throughout the Western church caused Paschal to retract the agreement. In early 1118, Henry returned to Rome to settle the investiture issue with the new pope, GELASIUS II (1118–1119). Gelasius refused to negotiate. Henry, with the support of the noble Frangipani family in Rome, proceeded to have Maurice proclaimed pope, under the name of Gregory VIII. Gregory had no standing among his brethren in the church, in no small part due to a letter-writing campaign by Gelasius condemning his usurpation of the papacy.

Upon the death of Gelasius, Henry and his counselors, desiring better relations with the new pontiff, CALLISTUS II (1119–1124), withdrew their support for Gregory. Fleeing Rome for Sutri, Gregory was turned over to the pope's troops by the local townspeople after a period of siege. Callistus, in turn, humiliated the antipope by a mock procession through the streets of Rome. Gregory spent the remaining years of his life imprisoned in a series of monasteries until his death in 1140.

For further reference: Eric John, ed., *The Popes: A Concise Biographical Dictionary* (New York: Hawthorn Books, 1964); Walter Ullman, *A Short History of the Papacy in the Middle Ages* (London: Methuen, 1972).

John C. Horgan

GREGORY VIII (1187). The pontificate of Gregory VIII was one of the shortest in history, lasting only from 18 March to 28 November 1187. It was dominated by the fall of Jerusalem to Saladin.

Alberto de Morra, born in Benevento c. 1100, was both a holy and a learned man, serving as professor of law at Bologna. His church career began when ADRIAN IV (1154–1159) appointed him cardinal-deacon in 1157. He served as LEGATE to Hungary in 1167, and Alexander sent him on missions to England, Dalmatia, and Portugal. The purpose of his trip to England was to pronounce the absolution of Henry II after the murder of Thomas Becket. On 21 October 1187, Albert was elected by the cardinals at Ferrara to succeed URBAN III (1185–1187). He took the name Gregory VIII. Already 77 years old at his ascent, he had been selected, in part, to reconcile the differences between Frederic I, Barbarossa, and the Roman church.

Gregory made the focus of his pontificate the recovery of the Holy Land. Saladin had overrun Jerusalem on 2 October 1187, three weeks before the new POPE's election. Gregory began organizing a new crusade even before he was crowned. He first approached Frederick, who agreed to help with both the diplomatic and armed missions. Gregory sent emissaries to Germany, France, Denmark, Poland, and other Christian nations to enlist their support. The success of the crusade was premised, in great part, by a strong naval fleet. Since the powerful port cities of Pisa and Genoa were embroiled in a bitter struggle, Gregory sought to negotiate a peace between them so their combined fleets could be utilized in the crusade. He left Ferrara in mid-November, arriving in Pisa on 10 December to open negotiations with the city leaders. He died there a week later, on 17 December 1187. His remains were interred in the Duomo at Pisa.

For further reference: Eric John, *The Popes: A Concise Bibliographical History* (London: Burns and Oates, 1964); H. K. Mann, *The Lives of the Popes in the Early Middle Ages* (London: K. Paul, 1902–1932).

Christopher S. Myers

GREGORY IX (1227–1241). Reigning from 19 March 1227 to 22 August 1241, Ugo, a nephew of INNOCENT III (1198–1216), was chosen by the three cardinals delegated to select a POPE by the other members of the college. Trained in CANON LAW and theology at Paris and Bologna, at his election he was cardinal-archbishop of Ostia and 80 years old. He had served as a papal LEGATE and in 1220 presented the cross to Emperor Frederick at his coronation. He was energetic and unyielding and, like Innocent III, a "political" pope. Intensely religious, a friend of Francis of Assisi (1181–1226), and a staunch protector of the FRANCISCAN order, he was influential in encouraging its growth.

Early in his reign, he struggled with Frederick II following Frederick's abandonment of the Sixth Crusade in 1227. Although the emperor had fallen seriously ill, Gregory recalled his earlier procrastination and, rejecting Frederick's explanation, excommunicated him. In 1228, when he recovered, Frederick set out again and, despite the obstacles put in his way by Gregory, successfully negotiated the surrender of Jerusalem. But the pope maintained the ban. Gregory also set up a rival king to Frederick in Germany and released his Sicilian subjects from their allegiance to him, while raising an army to attack the imperial forces that had invaded the papal domains. Frederick, although undefeated by the papal forces, sought a reconciliation, and Gregory lifted the EXCOMMUNICATION. The truce lasted nine years, to their mutual benefit.

During his reign, Gregory canonized St. Francis and St. Dominic and, in 1234, published the *Liber extra*, the first authoritative collection of papal decretals, compiled by the Spanish canonist Raymond of Peñafort. It remained the basic source of canon law until the reforms of PIUS X and BENEDICT XV. The same year, Gregory also sought a reunion with the Eastern churches at a series of meetings at Nicaea, but no agreement was reached. He was also the pope of the INQUISITION and extended the death penalty to heretics.

In 1233 he founded a university at Toulouse, which had been the center of the Albigensian movement that he so zealously fought. In 1238, his conflict with Frederick was renewed, especially over control of Sicily. In 1239 he again excommunicated the emperor, who retaliated by calling for a general council to judge the pope. Then, in 1241, Frederick sent an army into papal territory, but, as the imperial forces surrounded Rome, Gregory died. The emperor then withdrew to Sicily.

For further reference: Matthew Bunson, *The Pope Encyclopedia* (New York: Crown Trade Paperbacks, 1995); L. Duchesne, ed., *Liber Pontificalis* (Paris; E. de Boccard, 1955).

William Roberts

GREGORY X (1271–1276). Tebaldo Visconti became POPE in 1276, assuming the name Gregory X, succeeding CLEMENT IV (1265–1268) after an interregnum of nearly three years caused by a split between the Italian and French cardinals. Two of the basic conditions for modern papal elections had already been determined—the electorate and the requisite majority. In 1059 NICHOLAS II (1058–1061) had restricted the right of election to the cardinal-bishops; in 1179 ALEXANDER III (1159–1181) had extended the vote to all cardinals and required a majority of two-thirds for election (increased by PIUS XII [1939–1958] in 1945 to two-thirds plus one, in order that no candidate might reach the two-thirds majority by his own vote). But what if the cardinals were split, as in this *sede vacante*?

When the sixteen cardinals were deadlocked at Viterbo in 1271, the people of the town walled up the entrance to the ecclesiastical palace. When this failed to produced agreement, they tore the roof off the building to expose the cardinals to the weather. The assembled cardinals appointed a commission of six to vote, and on the same day, 1 September 1271, they agreed on Tebaldo Visconti, who was serving as archdeacon with the crusaders at Acre, Palestine. He arrived in Italy in January 1272, was ordained on 19 March, and was consecrated on 27 March.

In 1274, at the Second Council of Lyons (see Lyons II, Council of), Gregory used the events at Viterbo to institute a third basic condition for papal elections—the conclave (from the Latin *conclave*, a room that can be locked). The seclusion of the electoral college to ward off external influence thereafter became a permanent part of the process for electing a pope. Gregory X also tried at this council to heal the rift between East and West. Michael VII Palaeologus sent representatives, but decisions of the council were rejected by the Greek and Slavic bishops.

Gregory died at Prezzo on 10 January 1276. Two short-lived popes were elected that year—INNOCENT V, who served only four months, and ADRIAN V, who became ill before his election and held the title less than six weeks. He never recovered sufficiently to be consecrated. They were succeeded by JOHN XXI (1276–1277).

For further reference: Matthew Bunson, *The Pope Encyclopedia* (New York: Crown Trade Paperbacks, 1995); B. Tierney, *The Crisis of Church and State, 1050–1300* (Englewood Cliffs, NJ: Prentice-Hall, 1964).

Frank Grande

GREGORY XI (1370–1378). Seventeen cardinals participated in the conclave to choose URBAN V's (1362–1370) successor. It took two days to unanimously agree on elevating 42-year-old Cardinal Pierre Roger de Beaufort to the chair of Peter. At the age of eleven, he was canon of Rodez and Paris and at the age of nineteen was named cardinal-deacon by his uncle, CLEMENT VI (1342–1352). Respected by many for his knowledge, he assumed a leadership position in the sacred college. It was there that Urban V relegated important responsibilities to Gregory. During the papacy of Gregory XI, three problems plagued him: the reform of religious orders, HERESY, and the most dominant one, peace. He, like Urban V, dreamed of returning the papacy to Rome. He left Avignon in September 1376, entering Rome in 1377 and thus bringing the Avignon papacy to an end. He died of exhaustion the following year.

For further reference: Matthew Bunson, *The Pope Encyclopedia* (New York: Crown Trade Paperbacks, 1995).

Patrick McGuire

GREGORY XII (1406–1415). Angelo Correr was born at Venice c. 1325. He became bishop of Castello (1380) and Latin patriarch of Constantinople (1390), adhering to the Roman obedience during the Western Schism (see Schism, Great Western), and was created a cardinal in 1405. When elected as Gregory XII in November 1406, he promised to resign if his rival, the antipope BENEDICT XIII (1394–1417), would do the same. Both claimants agreed to meet at Savona in November 1407 to heal the SCHISM by simultaneous resignations. As the day approached, Gregory vacillated. He asked for a change of site and multiplied conditions, all of which revealed a change of heart. The rivals never met.

When Gregory and Benedict failed to resign, the cardinals from both parties gathered at Pisa, deposed them, and elected ALEXANDER V, thus creating a third claimant to the papacy. Most Christians recognized the Pisan candidate. Gregory found support only in Rimini, Venice, and some places in Germany. He lived in exile under the protection of Carlo Malatesta, duke of Rimini. When the Council of CONSTANCE convened, Gregory notified it of his readiness to abdicate. After he had convened the council, Malatesta read Gregory's resignation on 4 July 1415. His resignation gained a final luster for Gregory's pontificate, which was marred by stubbornness and unbridled nepotism. Gregory died in Recanati, Italy, 18 October 1417.

For further reference: Louise R. Loomis, *The Council of Constance* (New York: Columbia University Press, 1961; L. Pastor, *History of the Popes*, vol. 1 (St. Louis: Herder, 1899).

Richard J. Kehoe

GREGORY XIII (1572–1585). Ugo Buoncompagni studied at Bologna, attaining degrees in canon and civil law at the age of twenty-eight and ordained at forty. PIUS IV (1559–1565) sent him as an expert on CANON LAW to Trent (see Trent, Council of) in 1561, where he played a significant role in drafting its decrees. Upon becoming POPE in 1572 he reconstructed the Roman College (see Colleges of Rome), which was later named the Gregorian University. Gregory's primary concern remained religious restoration, establishing colleges in Rome and other surrounding cities, entrusting their administration to the members of the SOCIETY OF JESUS.

Determined to preserve Catholicism, Gregory gave a militant slant to the COUNTER-REFORMATION. He celebrated the massacre of the French Huguenots with Te Deums and services of thanksgiving in the church's victory over infidelity as well as the defeat of political infidelity. The Catholic League's activities against the Huguenots were subsidized by Gregory. He encouraged Spain's Philip II to focus his attention on the Netherlands and Ireland, with the hope of an Irish invasion of England. When this failed, Gregory supported assassination plots against Elizabeth I. Gregory was instrumental in supporting the missionary work of the Jesuits in Europe as well as in China, Japan, India, and Brazil. In addition to fostering scholarship, Gregory succeeded in the completion of the building of the Gesù, the mother church of the Society of Jesus.

For further reference: Matthew Bunson, *The Pope Encyclopedia* (New York: Crown Trade Paperbacks, 1995).

Patrick McGuire

GREGORY XIV (1590–1591). Cardinal Niccolò Sfondrati, the most acceptable candidate during the stormy two-month conclave of 1590, was born at Somma in Lombardy in 1535. He was a student at Perugia, Padua, and Pavia before being ordained. An important influence on his life was his friendship with the theologian Charles Borromeo. At age twenty-five he was named bishop of Cremona by PIUS IV (1559–1565) and attended the Council of TRENT, where he argued for bishops to live in their dioceses and condemned the practice of pluralism. He devoted his energy to his own dioceses, where he put the council rulings into full effect. In 1583 GREGORY XIII (1572–1585) named him cardinal of St. Cecilia, and, while in Rome, he developed a friendship with, and stongly supported the work of, Philip Neri.

Noted for his piety when elected POPE, Gregory XIV lacked both curial and political experience. He entrusted church business to his nephew, Paolo Emilio Sfondrati, whom he made cardinal. His inexperience caused resentment in the CURIA, as he pursued the traditional policy of backing Spanish ambitions in Europe, believing that what was good for Spain was good for the church. Gregory also attacked the Protestant ruler of France, Henry IV, which only served to rally the moderate Catholic faction to the side of that king, who soon converted.

Within the city of Rome, Gregory was known for his charity and efforts to mitigate the plague, brigandage, and food shortages, which were prevalent, although his nephew's mismanagement, in part, contributed to these problems. He also issued rules forbidding mass to be said in private dwellings, arranged for the revision of the Vulgate issued under SIXTUS V (1585–1590), and banned betting on papal elections, on the length of pontificates, and on the creation of cardinals.

For further reference: W. D'Ormesson, *The Papacy* (New York: Hawthorn Books, 1959); T. Jalland, *Church and Papacy* (London: Society for Promoting Christian Knowledge, 1944).

William Roberts

GREGORY XV (1621–1623). Alessandro Ludovisi came from a noble family of Bologna, having studied liberal arts at the Roman College (see Colleges of Rome) in the Jesuit tradition and law at the University of Bologna. Subsequently, he assumed several responsible judicial positions and participated in sensitive diplomatic missions to Poland and Benevento. Largely through the efforts of Cardinal Borghese, PAUL V's (1605–1621) nephew, he was elected as his successor and took the name Gregory XV.

Gregory's pontificate made two significant contributions: designing the method of electing a POPE and establishing the Propagation of the Faith. Gregory wrote two bulls as a response to the widespread criticism of the elections and reorganized a detailed procedure suggesting that after the closure of a conclave, nominations and the election would occur. He also recommended voting by secret ballot. His revised system remains virtually unaltered to the present. The establishment of the Propagation of the Faith was to ensure authority over evangelization. The papal bull *Inscrutabili* was signed by Gregory in 1622, declaring the pontiff's responsibility for propagating the faith. Gregory, the first Jesuit-educated pontiff, strove to continue the spirit of renewing the church and regaining its lost ground. Although not a lengthy pontificate, Gregory's activities advanced the revival of the church. In 1622 Gregory authorized the canonization of several leaders: Ignatius Loyola, Francis Xavier, Philip Neri, and Teresa of Avila.

For further reference: Matthew Bunson, *The Pope Encyclopedia* (New York: Crown Trade Paperbacks, 1995).

Patrick McGuire

GREGORY XVI (1831–1846). Bartolomeo Alberto Cappellari was born at Belluno, Italy, 18 September 1765. This Camaldolese monk, whose religious name was Mauro, successively became a professor of science and philosophy, procurator general, then abbot of the San Gregorio on the Caelian Hill monastery in Rome. He also served as consultor to the Congregation of Extraordinary Ecclesiatical Affairs, the Holy Office, and other Roman congregations and examiner of prospective bishops. Publicly named a cardinal in 1826, he served as prefect to the Congregation for the Propagation of the Faith until his election as POPE. Before taking his position as pope, he was ordained to the episcopate.

During his papacy the church confronted serious problems. When he began his reign, Gregory viewed "rationalism" and "indifferentism" as major challenges to the faith and "liberalism," which opposed traditional, monarchical civil authority, as dangerous to society. He opposed these tendencies and dealt with them in firm statements of principles while attempting accommodation where possible. In 1831 Gregory published a small book called *Il trionfo*, which was directed against JANSENISM and its tendencies. In the book he rejected the notion that the state had the power to control religious matters. In Gregory's view, the papacy was a religious monarchy established by Christ and not open to modification. He believed the church to be independent of the civil power, and the pope enjoyed INFALLIBILITY (freedom from error) in matters of the faith when he speaks as head of the church.

Gregory XVI's encyclical Mirari vos (see Avenir Movement) (15 August 1832) was a response to two major concerns: (1) the followers of Lamennais, who, he believed, advocated complete separation of church from state, democracy even by revolution, and emphasized "natural" virtues and (2) serious political unrest in Italy, especially in his own area, the PAPAL STATES, where revolution broke out in 1831. The encyclical rejected complete separation of church and state, denounced revolutionary movements, and supported monarchy. In later letters Gregory denounced "rationalism," which elevated reason and undermined faith. Gregory condemned much of what was emerging as "the modern world," leaving the church in a difficult position to deal with the emerging civilization. Within the papal states Gregory maintained a firm hand, resisting changes in government structure and retaining clerics in most administrative positions. Economic difficulties mounted, and conditions became ripe for subsequent revolutions.

For further reference: James C. Livingston, *Modern Christian Thought: From the Enlightenment to Vatican II* (New York: Macmillan, 1971), p. 272; H. E. Wiseman, *Recollections of the Last Four Popes and of Rome in Their Times* (Boston: Patrick Donahue, 1858).

Loretta Devoy

H

HADRIAN, POPE. SEE ADRIAN.

HENOTIKON CONTROVERSY. SEE SIMPLICIUS.

HERESY. The word ''heresy'' derives from the Greek word meaning ''choice'' and in the ancient world conveyed the belief that an individual or a group had made a deliberate choice to follow a certain way of thought. In contemporary, non-Christian usage, therefore, it often was used to designate a ''sect.'' For the early Christians heresy was considered to be a rejection of the church's authority and a choice of one's own thoughts and interpretations as objects of faith in place of the true faith revealed by Christ and handed down in tradition through the apostles and their successors. Since true faith was the only means of achieving salvation, or union with God, heretical teaching was seen as a deliberate and malicious act that deprived those who adhered to it of eternal salvation. This explains why the originators of heresy were viewed in such a negative light and were often viciously attacked in the writings of those who represented what became the orthodox tradition; the latter generally attributed the development of an objectionable teaching to a deliberately evil intention and rarely considered the possibility that heresiarchs were sincere Christians seeking a solution for difficult problems.

The extant writings from the 200–300 years following the composition of the Bible indicate that Christian faith and life were expressed in a variety of forms that can be described as pluralistic. As the early followers of Christ sought to understand the true identity and significance of Christ and of the God whom he revealed, the details of their search were communicated in a variety of verbal formulations. This situation did not appear to be a problem: seemingly incompatible statements could exist side by side, along with assertions that would have been condemned a century or two later. But when beliefs or declarations of faith were perceived as totally at variance with authentic Christian teaching, then voices were raised against them. This is not to say that the so-called orthodox attacker was always correct or understood fully the intentions or the thought of the one accused, for there were often political or social issues involved in these conflicts. But if the defenders of "orthodoxy" possessed at least a minimum of honesty and sincerity, their opposition is understandable in light of the explanation given before about dangers to salvation.

Examples of individual and group teaching condemned in this way in the early church are GNOSTICISM, which was seen as a perversion of many areas of Christian faith; Arius and various forms of Arianism, which rejected the full divinity of the second and third persons of the Christian Trinity and therefore affected adversely the understanding of the person of Christ and the nature of salvation; Apollinarius, who was accused of downgrading the humanity of Christ; Nestorianism, which seemed to split Christ into two persons and therefore to deny that Jesus was truly divine; Monophysitism, which was accused of teaching that Christ had only one true nature, the divine, and was not therefore truly human. Most of these movements disappeared sometime after they were rejected, but Monophysitism, was embraced by a large group of Christians who considered themselves apart from the tradition that condemned their belief, and it is extant today in a number of Eastern churches, whose teaching is now viewed in a more favorable light by the very churches that once anathematized them.

It is important to understand the early conception of heresy, because it set the standard for the church's understanding of this phenomenon throughout most of its history. In the broadest terms, then, heresy is generally understood to be the acceptance or teaching of an expression of faith (a so-called doctrine) that is not acceptable to the mainstream tradition. Such a situation does not necessarily imply a complete or permanent split between the opposing parties, although in reality this is often the result. Since there is always some separation involved, every heresy can be called a SCHISM, which refers simply to a division within the church; but there is a technical sense of "schism" that is not necessarily verified in every heresy.

For further reference: W. Bauer, *Orthodoxy and Heresy in Earliest Christianity*, 2d ed. (Philadelphia: Fortress Press, 1971); H. O. J. Brown, *Heresies: The Image of Christ in the Mirror of Heresy and Orthodoxy from the Apostles to the Present* (Garden City, NY: Doubleday, 1984); A. H. M. Jones, *Were Ancient Heresies Disguised Social Movements?* (Philadelphia: Fortress Press, 1966); A. LeBoulluec, *La notion d'hérésie dans la littérature grecque, IIe-IIIe siècle*, 2 vols. (Paris: Augustiniennes, 1985); G. L. Prestige, *Fathers and Heretics. Six Studies in Dogmatic Faith with Prologue and Epilogue* (London: SPCK, 1940); H. E. W. Turner, *The Pattern of Christian Truth* (London: Mowbray, 1954); J. W. C. Wand, *The Four Great Heresies* (London: Mowbray, 1967).

Gerard H. Ettlinger

HIERARCHY. Derived from the Greek word *hierarches*, meaning "the presider at sacred rites," the English term "hierarchy" has come to refer to that group of persons within a community of religious faith entrusted to administer its sacred rituals and actions. Hence, the word "hierarchy" is used in the church to describe those who constitute the organized system of governance within the church as well as to designate those representatives of its clergy who possess both rank and order within the system because they are responsible for the church's ritual and related spiritual or sacred things.

Although the term "hierarchy" does not appear anywhere in the scriptural texts, both the Old and New Testaments bear witness to the fact that religious leaders of various ranks and responsibilities were commonplace among the ancient Jewish and Christian communities. The concept of an ecclesiastical hierarchy as it exists within the church today has its roots in the Scriptures as well as the experience of the early church. For example, St. Paul wrote in his First Letter to the Corinthians that God designated certain classes of people within the community—apostles, prophets, teachers, and so on—and assigned them both a rank and specific responsibilities (1 Corinthians 12: 28 ff.). The Gospels presented St. Peter in a prime leadership role among the other apostles and believers. The Acts of the Apostles also referred to specific roles of service to be performed within the fellowship of Christian believers, many of whom were not of apostolic rank.

Recognizing that some question its validity and origin, the current hierarchical structure of the church may be conveniently divided into two main classifications: a "hierarchy of orders" with its corresponding "power of orders" and a "hierarchy of jurisdiction" with its authority or "jurisdiction" attached. Simply stated, a "hierarchy of orders" refers to the experience of sacred ordination and the rank held by its recipient according to the particular order he receives at the hands of a validly ordained (power of orders) and legitimately deputed (power of jurisdiction) bishop, namely, deacon, priest, or bishop.

Holy orders, according to the church's sacramental theology, effects in the candidate an ontological as well as a theological change that separates him from those not ordained, or "the laity." This change is, by no means, an attempt to put the cleric on a higher level than the layperson. The church believes, however, that the change occurs by divine institution since the sacrament itself was instituted and intended by Christ. Ordination as a deacon is the first moment of holy orders as the individual proceeds toward priesthood; it can be, however, the only participation in the one sacrament of orders that the deacon receives. The ancient practice of the permanent diaconate was restored by the Second Vatican Council (1962–1965). Ordination to the priesthood is considered the ordinary goal of holy orders, with its fullest expression residing in episcopal ordination.

In addition to a "hierarchy of orders," a "hierarchy of jurisdiction" exists in the church. "Jurisdiction" and its accompanying power pertain to that level of authority and responsibility assumed by the ordained clergy according to their rank and office within the church. The offices of POPE and bishop, for example, exist by divine institution and, therefore, occupy the primary and secondary positions, respectively, within the hierarchical structure. All other ranks and offices exist by ecclesiastical design and, consequently, serve the higher levels of the hierarchical organization in virtue of a mandate or grant of jurisdiction given by those who have authority to govern the faithful, that is, the pope and the bishops.

In common parlance, the expression "hierarchy" has come to mean the governing body within the church and its powers. Included in the expression are the pope, the cardinals, and the bishops. Clergy of lesser rank, priests and deacons, are not usually intended when the term is used.

For further reference: P. J. Kenedy and Sons, *The Official Catholic Directory 1993* (New York: P. J. Kenedy and Sons, 1993); Robert Markus and Eric John, *Papacy and Hierarchy* (London: Sheed and Ward, 1969); Klaus Morsdorf, "Hierarchy," in *Sacramentun Mundi*, ed. Karl Rahner, vol. 3 (New York: Herder and Herder, 1969), pp. 27–29.

David M. O'Connell

HIERIA, COUNCIL OF. SEE STEPHEN III.

HILARUS (461–468). The son of the Sardinian Crispinus, Hilarus was the archdeacon of LEO I (440–461) and a LEGATE at the "robber council" of Ephesus. At Ephesus Hilarus publicly protested against the bishop of Constantinople Flavian's condemnation. Hiding in the burial chamber of John the Evangelist, Hilarus barely escaped alive to tell Leo of the disorderly proceedings. The successor to Leo I in 461, Hilarus saw his predecessor as a mentor. Little is known of Hilarus' activities with the East except for a papal decree he might have circulated among his brother bishops confirming the COUNCILS of Nicaea, Ephesus, and Chalcedon and condemning HERESIES. He was to have also confirmed Leo's *Tome*. The purpose of writing this decree, if authentic, was to suppress the growing Monophysite opposition to Chalcedon. Hilarus was also faced with the prospect of the widespread heresy of Arianism in Italy. He supported the patriarch of Constantinople, Flavian, thereby angering the patriarch of Alexandra, Dioscorus. Later declared a saint, his feast is 28 February.

For further reference: Matthew Bunson, *The Pope Encyclopedia* (New York: Crown Trade Paperbacks, 1995).

Patrick McGuire

HIPPOLYTUS, ANTIPOPE (217–235). Born c. 170, probably in the East, he died in Sardinia c. 235. It appears Hippolytus was ordained during the pontificate of VICTOR I (189–198). After studying the thought of Irenaeus of Lyons and the second-century apologists, he sought recognition as the chief intellectual of the Roman church. However, his writings raised several problems, and his offered solutions did not win universal acceptance among scholars. He was, some suspect, a man of violent temperament. He quickly condemned ZEPHYRINUS (198/199–217), the successor to Victor I, who chose the slave Callistus as his collaborator, by denouncing them as modalists in Christology. It has been suggested that Hippolytus established himself as bishop of a local schismatic group upon Callistus' election as POPE (217–222).

In 235, when Maximinus Thrax became emperor, he adopted a policy of striking at church leaders. As a result of this policy, Hippolytus was arrested and exiled to Sardinia, where he was subjected to inhumane conditions. It is surmised that before his death, in a Rome prison or in Sardinia, he reconciled with the Roman church. Unity was restored to the church when Hippolytus abdicated his claim as bishop and called for his schismatic followers to unite.

For further reference: Matthew Bunson, *The Pope Encyclopedia* (New York: Crown Trade Paperbacks, 1995).

Patrick McGuire

HITLER, ADOLF, AND CATHOLIC CHURCH. Born on 20 April 1889, Hitler was raised in a conventional Catholic milieu. But as a young man in Vienna, in the pre-1914 years, he abandoned his Catholic upbringing in favor of the frothy brew of anticlerical, nationalist, and pseudoscientific racist views, including virulent anti-Semitism, as propagated by radical extremists who found widespread support in the lower bourgeois circles of the Austro-Hungarian metropolis. Hitler's experiences during WORLD WAR I strengthened his indifference to the beliefs and practices of the established churches. His reaction to Germany's national defeat and humiliation and his belief that these were largely due to an alleged worldwide Jewish conspiracy led to his career as a political agitator.

In the early 1920s up to his abortive *putsch* attempt of November 1923, Hitler followed the lead of his patron, Field Marshal Ludendorff, in propagating a rabid anticlerical and anti-Christian stance. But his subsequent imprisonment and the writing of his book *Mein Kampf* led him to the opportunistic view that political success depended on recruiting both Catholics and Protestants to the Nazi ranks. Consequently, Hitler avoided any direct attacks on the Christian churches and disassociated himself from his more radical followers, such as Gauleiter Arthur Dinter or the editor of the party newspaper, Alfred Rosenberg.

Article 24 of the 1925 the Nazi Party program stated that the party stood for "positive Christianity," without defining this position more closely. A similar stance was adopted shortly after the Nazis came to power in public declarations stressing the importance of Christian churches in the maintenance of the national society. Hitler was careful to foster the illusion of the Nazi Party's benevolence. He never "left" the church, continued to pay the compulsory church taxes, and appeared occasionally at Catholic church services. Despite the Nazi determination to impose totalitarian control over all aspects of German life, the churches' official position and their institutional right to conduct public liturgies were never repudiated.

Privately, however, Hitler frequently expressed to his closest associates his fundamental antagonism to the "satanic superstition" of the "hypocritical priests" who were interested only "in raking in the money" and "befuddling the minds of the gullible" and his eventual intention of "stamping out Christianity root and branch." These views were cleverly disguised from the general public. Hitler's attitude toward the Vatican remained ambivalent throughout his years in power. On one side, he expressed envy and even respect for a body capable of preserving its influence for 2,000 years. On the other hand, his nationalist ambitions caused him to seek to curtail and thereafter eradicate any political authority the Vatican might seek to deploy in Germany or later in the German-held territories.

From Hitler's point of view, the 1933 Reich CONCORDAT (see Germany, Concordat of 1933) was designed to restrict the influence of the Vatican in German affairs, and the Nazis subsequent policy cleverly sought to diminish the Vatican's role still further. The numerous Vatican protests against breaches of the concordat or later in wartime diplomatic interventions were either ignored or circumvented. Nevertheless, Hitler never gave his approval for a formal breaking off of relations between Germany and the Holy See. Even on occasions, such as the foreign minister Ribbentrop's visit to the Vatican in March 1940 or following the Nazi attack on the "atheistic-bolshevik" Soviet Union in 1941, the Nazi government sought to gain Vatican support for its military plans. The failure of such attempts undoubtedly strengthened Hitler's resolve, after military victory, to abrogate the concordat and sever relations with the Vatican. As he told his entourage in the middle of WORLD WAR II: "When the war is over we shall tear up the Concordat. . . . I shall then consider that my life's final task will be to solve the religious question. Only then will the life of the German nation be guaranteed once and for all" (*Table Talk*, December 1941, July 1942).

For further reference: John S. Conway, "The Vatican, Germany and the Holocaust," in *Papal Diplomacy in the Modern Age*, ed. Peter C. Kent and John F. Pollard (Westport: Praeger, 1994); Hermann Rauschning, *Hitler Speaks* (London: Butterworth, 1939); Gordan Zahn, *German Catholics and Hitler's Wars* (New York: Sheed and Ward, 1962).

John S. Conway

HOLOCAUST AND THE PAPACY. Rolf Hochhuth's sensational drama *Der Stellvertreter* (The Deputy), produced in Germany in 1963 and translated into a score of languages, triggered a heated controversy about PIUS XII's (1939–1958) attitude toward the Jews and their plight during the Nazi Holocaust. Was Pius really the cold "POPE of silence" that Hochhuth depicted? Should he have spoken out more forcefully against Hitler's crimes? In the decades since Hochhuth's play, answers to some of the questions have been provided in published documents from the wartime archives of the Vatican, the United States, Britain, and Germany. In medieval times, the church taught that Jews bore collective guilt for Christ's Crucifixion. By the early twentieth century, such teachings had largely been abandoned. Nevertheless, many religious prejudices against Jews lingered on, especially in East-Central Europe. Not until 1965 at Vatican II were the old charges of Jewish collective guilt formally abjured, thanks to the insistence of Pope JOHN XXIII (1958–1963).

When HITLER and MUSSOLINI were imposing harsh anti-Semitic decrees in Germany and Italy in the 1930s, PIUS XI (1922–1939) spoke out sharply against them. On 20 September 1938, he declared to a throng of Belgian pilgrims: "Anti-Semitism is . . . a movement with which we Christians can have nothing to do. . . . It is inadmissible. Through Christ and in Christ we are the spiritual progeny of Abraham. Spiritually, we are all Semites." His strong encyclical *Mit brennender Sorge* (With Deep Anxiety, 14 March 1937), which condemned Nazi racism, was drafted with the help of his cardinal-secretary of state, Eugenio Pacelli.

In March 1939, Pacelli succeeded to the papal throne as Pius XII. He detested anti-Semitism and racism, but the austere new pontiff was temperamentally not inclined to be outspoken about such matters. While Pius XII encouraged a wide range of charitable activities to alleviate the sufferings of victims of WORLD WAR II, his rare public pronouncements in those years were usually turgid and vague. Moreover, he usually preferred to leave to local bishops decisions about formal pronouncements. Despite strong pressure from the wartime British and American governments that he condemn NAZI GERMANY, Pius XII refused to do so, as he nursed the hope (at least until 1942–1943) that by preserving strict Vatican neutrality in World War II (as Benedict XV [1914–1922] had done in WORLD WAR I), he might eventually be able to mediate the conflict. He was also reluctant to denounce Hitler's crimes unless he were also to denounce those of Stalin, who had become the wartime ally of the Anglo-Americans. Fears that a public condemnation of Germany might stir up worse reprisals against the Jews and also jeopardize his relief efforts in behalf of prisoners of war were also factors in his thinking.

Persecution of Germany's Jews accelerated after the Nazis' orgy of destruction on Crystal Night, 9/10 November 1938. Hitler's invasion of Poland in September 1939 led to the herding of hundreds of thousands of Jews into crowded Polish ghettos. In 1940 Hitler's troops seized control of much of Western Europe and began the hunt for Jews there. The German invasion of Soviet Russia in June 1941 opened the possibility for Hitler to gain control over most of Europe's Jews. The entry of the United States into the war a few months later ended any further thought by Hitler of deporting Europe's Jews to a distant place like Madagascar. At the Wannsee Conference in January 1942, Hitler euphemistically ordered a "Final Solution" for the "Jewish Problem." Hurriedly, the Nazis constructed death camps for the systematic gassing of millions of Jews, Gypsies, homosexuals, and others whom they brutally rounded up all over Europe. Altogether, some 6 million Jews and 3 million non-Jews were to be murdered by the Nazis during the war.

The first information about the extermination of Jews in the Nazi death camps in Eastern Europe was brought back to the West in the course of 1942, usually by German soldiers on leave from the eastern front but also by others. Almost certainly, such reports reached the Vatican. President Roosevelt's personal emissary to the Vatican, Myron C. Taylor, on 26 September 1942, transmitted to cardinal-secretary of state Maglione a memorandum from the Jewish Agency in Palestine containing precise information about mass extermination of Jews in Poland and mass deportations from Germany, France, the Low Countries, and elsewhere. Taylor asked whether the pope had any suggestion of how the power of civilized public opinion could be mobilized to prevent this barbarous behavior. On 10 October, Maglione replied that the Vatican could not be sure that these reports about events in Poland were accurate. A British historian, Anthony Rhodes, has observed that even if the Vatican considered suspect reports from foreign powers about extermination camps, it had reliable sources of information of its own. In VICHY FRANCE, Catholic bishops had spoken out loudly against persecution of the Jews. On 8 July 1942, Britain's cardinal Arthur Hinsley spoke on the BBC of crimes committed by Germans in Poland, citing that some 700,000 Jews had been massacred since the beginning of the war.

Why did the pope not publicly denounce or excommunicate Hitler? The answer was furnished by Pius XII himself in the wake of an appeal from Catholic bishops in Holland in 1942 that he protest German deportations of Dutch Jews. The pontiff explained that he had considered EXCOMMUNICATION but after much praying concluded that his condemnation would not only fail to help the Jews but might worsen their situation. The pope did decide, however, to make a brief reference to the plight of Jews in territories under German control when he delivered a Christmas radio message to the world in 1942. Near the end of this lengthy message, he inserted a sentence about "the hundreds of thousands of people who, through no fault of their own and solely because of their nation or their race, have been condemned to death or progressive extinction."

Although Pius XII was reluctant to speak out publicly about the persecution of the Jews, the published wartime documents in the Vatican archives reveal that he did sometimes "speak up" in private messages to various heads of state in Nazi-dominated Europe who were susceptible to papal influence. Thus, on 7 April 1943, in a message to the collaborationist Slovak government, he complained of the Slovak government's intention to proceed with the total removal of the Jewish residents of Slovakia. The Holy See deplored these measures, which gravely damaged a person's natural right, merely because these people belonged to a certain race. On 25 June 1944, at the height of the Hungarian-Jewish deportations, the pope cabled Hungary's leader, Admiral Nicholas Horthy, urging him to use all possible influence to cease the torments imposed on many solely because of their nationality or race.

In a letter of 30 April 1943 to his friend Bishop von Preysing of Berlin, Pius wrote: "It was for us a great consolation to learn that Catholics, in particular those of your Berlin diocese, have shown such charity towards the sufferings of the Jews. We express our paternal gratitude and profound sympathy for Msgr.

Lichtenberg who asked to share the lot of the Jews in the concentration camps, and who spoke up against their persecution in the pulpit.'' (Msgr. Licthenberg was sentenced to two years' imprisonment for this and died in Dachau.) ''As far as episcopal declarations are concerned,'' Pius continued, ''we leave to local bishops the responsibility of deciding what to publish for Our communications. The danger of reprisals and pressures—as well perhaps of other measures due to the length and psychology of the war—counsels reserve. In spite of good reasons for Our open intervention, there are others equally good for avoiding greater evils by not interfering. Our experience in 1942, when We allowed the free publication of certain Pontifical documents addressed to the Faithful justifies this attitude.''

Meanwhile, Hitler's contempt for the Vatican was boundless. After the Germans seized Rome in September 1943, he talked for a time of kidnapping the pope. On 16 October 1943, he ordered the roundup of 1,259 people residing in the old Jewish ghetto near St. Peter's basilica. Upon papal instructions, Msgr. Alois Hudal, the German rector of Santa Maria dell'Anima College in Rome, interceded with the German military commander. The cardinal-secretary of state Maglione followed this up with a personal protest to the German ambassador, Ernst von Weizsaecker. German authorities thereafter released 252 of the prisoners who were shown to be either ''Aryans'' or of mixed marriage. The remaining 1,007 Jews were hauled away in sealed freight cars to Auschwitz, where more than 800 of them met immediate death. Only 16 survived the war. Three thousand other Jews in Rome survived in convents and other sanctuaries that the pope opened up to them. At war's end, the World Jewish Congress expressed gratitude to Pius XII for his actions in behalf of Jews.

In 1987, the Vatican began work on drafting an official pronouncement regarding the church and the Holocaust. When it will be finished is uncertain. But in a highly visible ceremony on 17 April 1994, JOHN PAUL II, who had personally witnessed deportation of Jews in his native Poland, welcomed Elio Toaff, the chief rabbi of Rome, as his guest of honor at a concert in the Vatican in memory of the victims of the Holocaust. Five thousand invited guests filled the audience hall next to St. Peter's basilica for the unprecedented event. In a gesture to emphasize the equal dignity of the two faiths, the pope and the chief rabbi sat on identical gilt and brocade thrones next to the president of the Italian Republic, Oscar Luigi Scalfaro. The ceremony was perceived as an attempt by John Paul II to embrace the world's Jews as the ''elder brothers'' of Christians. It was also seen as his attempt to revive the revolution in Catholic–Jewish relations that had been set in motion at VATICAN II by JOHN XXIII (1958–1963). Meanwhile, the Vatican abandoned its long-standing anti-Zionist policy (see Zionism) and announced on 15 June 1994 the establishment of diplomatic relations between itself and the state of Israel.

For further reference: Pierre Blet, Robert A. Graham, Angelo Martini, and Burkhart Schneider, eds., *Actes et documents du Saint Siège relatifs à la seconde guerre mondiale,*

11 vols. (Vatican City: Libreria Editrice Vaticana, 1965–1982); Martin Gilbert, *The Holocaust: The History of the Jews in Europe during the Second World War* (New York: Holt, Rinehart, and Winston, 1985); Raul Hilberg, *The Destruction of the European Jews*, rev. ed., 3 vols. (New York: Holmes and Meier, 1985); J. Derek Holmes, *The Papacy in the Modern World, 1914–1978* (London and New York: Crossroad, 1981); John F. Morley, *Vatican Diplomacy and the Jews during the Holocaust, 1939–1943* (New York: KTAV, 1980).

Charles F. Delzell

HONORIUS I (625–638). A disciple of GREGORY I (590–604), Honorius was the son of the wealthy aristocrat Petronius. Little is known of Honorius' activities prior to his assuming the chair of Peter. In October 625 immediately after assuming the responsibilities of POPE, Honorius found himself entangled in Lombard politics. His involvement in Sardinia, Illyricum, and Spain seemed to prove fruitful, with Honorius' envoy urging the bishops to continue to convert the Jews at the Sixth Council of Toledo.

He called for a reformation in the education of the clergy as well as demonstrated success in assuming temporal duties civil authorities proved unable to handle. These include, but were not limited to, the revival of the Roman aqueducts and instructing governmental officials of Naples how to administer the city. His fiscal skills seem to have been Honorius' strength; during his pontificate he was able to refurbish several churches in Rome, most notably the complete restoration of St. Peter's and S. Agnese fuori le Mura, without depleting funds.

For further reference: Matthew Bunson, *The Pope Encyclopedia* (New York: Crown Trade Paperbacks, 1995).

Patrick McGuire

HONORIUS II (1124–1130). Cardinal Lamberto Scannabecchi was elected POPE after a stormy conclave, during which first the cardinal-priest Teobaldo was elected as CELESTINE II (1124) but was forced to resign by the influential Frangipani family, who imposed their candidate Cardinal Lamberto, who was installed as Honorius II. The new pope was born near Imola and had a reputation for learning. He was made cardinal-bishop of Ostia in 1117 by PASCHAL II (1099–1118), accompanied GELASIUS II (1118–1119) to France, and became a trusted adviser of CALLISTUS II (1119–1124), taking an important part in negotiating the Concordat of Worms in 1122. On becoming pope, he appointed his Roman supporter Aimeric, who also represented a younger, reforming element in the church, as his chancellor.

Honorius used the peace secured with the empire at Worms to strengthen his position and promote reform. In 1125, he backed Count Lothair III for the German Crown and anathematized his major rival, Conrad. In France, Honorius' diplomatic patience, which aroused the indignation of Bernard of Clairvaux (1090–1153), eventually led King Louis VI (1108–1137) to seek a resolution in his conflicts with the French HIERARCHY. This pope was able to secure the admission of papal LEGATES to England after 1125. However, in southern Italy he proved unable to prevent the formation of a Norman kingdom. In 1128 he had to recognize Roger II, count of Sicily (1095–1154) as duke of Apulia in return for his oath of fealty.

Church policies during his pontificate were directed by his powerful chancellor, Aimeric. A number of reformers were appointed to the College of CARDINALS. He also approved, through his legate at the council of Troyes in 1128, the rule of the Knights Templar, a move favored by Bernard of Clairvaux. In 1130, when Honorius became gravely ill, Aimeric had him brought to the monastery of St. Gregory on the Caelian Hill for protection and to secure the election of a favorable successor. After the pope's death in February of that year, he was hastily buried in the monastery, but his remains were later transferred to the Lateran.

For further reference: Matthew Bunson, *The Pope Encyclopedia* (New York: Crown Trade Paperbacks, 1995); Lo Duchesne, ed., *Liber Pontificalis* (Paris: E. de Boccard, 1955); H. K. Mann, *The Lives of the Popes in the Early Middle Ages* (London: K. Paul, 1902–1932).

William Roberts

HONORIUS II, ANTIPOPE (1061–1064). Honorius' "reign" occurred during a period when the church was attempting reforms on issues such as simony, investiture, concubinage, and papal election laws, as well as trying to assert its institutional independence from the German kings by allying itself with Norman troops in southern Italy against German imperial pressure. Honorius' election drew support from the German empress Agnes, regent for Henry IV (1056–1106), German and Lombard imperialists and antireformers, and the nobility of Rome. An ardent opponent of reform and the *Patarini* (an alliance of merchants and artisans struggling against the ruling oligarchy), Honorius' pontificate conflicted with the election of ALEXANDER II (1061–1073), who was backed by church reformers.

Assisted by Lombard troops, Honorius initially succeeded in his struggle against Alexander. Neither the Germans nor the Normans, Alexander's military allies, desired war. Duke Godfrey of Lorraine convinced Alexander and Honorius to retreat to their former archdioceses pending resolution of the impasse. That decision was left up to Anno, archbishop of Cologne and the new regent for Henry, who, motivated by his own sense of reform, sided with Alexander II. Honorius did not retire without a fight.

In May 1063, Honorius and his supporters attacked Rome. However, this time Alexander, with more vigorous Norman assistance, forced Honorius to retreat to Parma. Subsequently, a synod of German and Italian bishops met at Mantua, resolving the SCHISM in Alexander's favor. Honorius was deposed and retired to his bishopric at Parma, remaining there until his death in 1072.

For further reference: J. N. D. Kelly, *The Oxford Dictionary of Popes* (Oxford: Oxford University Press, 1986); H. K. Mann, *The Lives of the Popes in the Early Middle*

Ages (London: K. Paul, 1902–1932); Walter Ullman, *A Short History of the Papacy in the Middle Ages* (London: Methuen, 1972).

John C. Horgan

HONORIUS III (1216–1227). Elderly at the time of his election, Cencio Savelli was a Roman aristocrat who had been canon of Santa Maria Maggiore and a papal chamberlain. INNOCENT III made him cardinal-deacon in 1193, and in 1197 he became the tutor to the future emperor Frederick II. An able administrator, he sought to bring order into the church's finances by compiling, in 1192, the *Liber censuum*, a listing, by dioceses and provinces, of the spiritual and temporal institutions owing debts to the Holy See. Savelli was chosen as POPE in Perugia after the cardinals there appointed two of their number to chose a successor to Innocent III (1198–1216).

The major concern of his pontificate was the crusade that had been initiated by Innocent III at the Fourth Lateran Council (see Lateran Council IV) in 1215. To achieve support and unity for this endeavor, Honorius III negotiated peace between Philip II of France and James I of Aragon and pressured the French to abandon their plans to invade England, and he helped King John, who was still a minor, to obtain the English Crown. Nonetheless, the Fifth Crusade ended in failure. This was due, in part, to the errors of the papal LEGATE in charge, Cardinal Pelagius, but also to the change in policy of Frederick II, whom Honorius had crowned in Rome in 1120. Instead of joining the crusade as he had promised, Frederick turned his attention to southern Italy, where he sought to restore imperial power.

In other areas, Honorius was more successful. He encouraged missionary activity in the Baltic and, following policies of Innocent III, initiated crusades and brutal campaigns against the Moors in Spain and against the Albigensians in southern France. In this sense, he also set the groundwork for the INQUISITION, sanctioning the Dominicans as a preaching order and approving the definitive rule for the Franciscans and Carmelites. He also authorized the first official book of CANON LAW, compiled in his *Compilatio quinta*.

For further reference: Matthew Bunson, *The Pope Encyclopedia* (New York: Crown Trade Paperbacks, 1995); H. K. Mann, *The Lives of the Popes in Early Middle Ages* (London: K. Paul, 1902–1932).

William Roberts

HONORIUS IV (1285–1287). The former Giacomo Savelli, a Roman-born aristocrat, Honorius IV focused on political struggles for control of Sicily, a papal fief. The pontiff favored Charles of Anjou, count of Provence, over Aragon's King Pedro III (1276–1285). Pedro gained control over the island after defeating the French and Charles in the War of Sicilian Vespers (1282). Philip IV "the Fair," succeeding to the French throne, had no desire to engage in war with Aragon over Charles of Valois' claims to that throne, a process ignored by Alfonso III (1285–1291), who appointed his younger brother James as viceroy for Sicily. The Sicilians proclaimed James their new king in January 1286. James requested Honorius' recognition of his new title, which the POPE refused. Instead, he excommunicated (see Excommunication) James and the people of Sicily. Honorius threw his support behind a French military expedition in April 1287, but he died before it succumbed to the Aragonese forces led by Admiral Roger de Lauria.

Apart from the Sicilian affair, the pontiff provided generous support to the mendicant orders, particularly the Dominicans and FRANCISCANS, whose extended privileges included investigating grants of dispensation, examination of bishops-elect, and the review of qualifications of potential abbots and abbesses. More importantly, they received control over the INQUISITION. Honorius actively advanced the study of Oriental languages at the University of Paris not only to train missionaries for work in the East but also hoping to promote reconciliation between the churches. He also pursued the collection of tithes to raise revenues to launch a new crusade, hoping to free the Holy Land from Muslim rule and to unite all of Christendom, but it never came to fruition.

For further reference: Joseph S. Brusher, *Popes through the Ages* (Princeton: D. Van Nostrand, 1964); Eric John, ed., *The Popes: A Concise Biographical Dictionary* (New York: Hawthorn Books, 1964); Hans Kuhner, *Encyclopedia of the Papacy* (New York: Philosophical Library, 1958); Walter Ullman, *A Short History of the Papacy in the Middle Ages* (London: Methuen, 1972).

John C. Horgan

HORMISDAS (514–523). Although born in Frosinone in the Campania, he bore the name of the Zoroastrian god Ahura Mazda, or Ormisd. Perhaps his father was a Persian convert who settled in Italy? There was a Persian martyr named Hormisdas, but he was little known in the West. Before entering the priesthood, Hormisdas had been married and had a son, SILVERIUS, who later became a POPE (536–537) and was deposed by the Byzantine commander in Italy. During his papal tenure, Hormisdas, the designated successor of SYMMACHUS (498–514), devoted a great deal of energy to healing the Acacian SCHISM (484–519) by trying to persuade the emperor and the patriarch at Constantinople to accept the decree of the Council of CHALCEDON (451) on the two natures of Christ.

Hormisdas responded to the invitation of the emperor Anastasius I (491–518) to end the Acacian schism by sending two LEGATES to Constantinople in 515. They conveyed the conditions of reunion: the emperor and all bishops must publicly accept both the formula of the Council of Chalcedon (451) on the two natures of Christ and the *tome* of LEO I (440–461), accepted as definitive by the council. The *tome* argues not only for the two natures of Christ but also for the primacy of the bishop of Rome in matters of doctrine and jurisdiction. The Monophysite leaders also had to be condemned by name, and all cases of bishops who had been deposed or exiled had to be referred to the pope. Anastasius rejected these terms, but on his death in July 518 he was succeeded by Justin I

(518–527), who accepted the formula of Hormisdas, thereby bringing the Acacian schism to an end.

Hormisdas also commissioned an Egyptian monk in Rome, Dionysious Exiguus, to translate the canons of the Greek church into Latin. He reorganized the church in Gaul and Spain and began to restore the HIERARCHY in North Africa after the death (28 May 523) of the Vandal king, Thrasamund. Hormisdas died on 6 August 523 and was succeeded by JOHN I (523–526). Buried in St. Peter's, he was later proclaimed a saint.

For further reference: E. Caspar, *Geschichte des Papsttums* (Tübingen: J. C. B. Mohr, 1930–1933); F. Dvornik, *The Idea of Apostolicity in Byzantium and the Legend of the Apostle Andrew* (Cambridge: Harvard University Press, 1958); T. G. Jalland, *The Church and the Papacy* (London: SPCK, 1944).

Frank Grande

HYGINUS (c. 138–c. 142). Hyginus was the ninth POPE in the line begun by St. PETER. Estimates vary as to the length of his reign, the fourth-century Liberian Catalogue giving twelve years, but it was more likely the four years cited in both Eusebius (c. 260–c. 340) and the *Liber Pontificalis*. According to that latter source he was a Greek from Athens who previously had been a philosopher, as was his contemporary Justin Martyr (c. 100–c. 165), who was also a Christian apologist and had come from the East. It is unlikely, however, that, as the *Liber Pontificalis* claims, he had reorganized the clergy of Rome on a hierarchical basis and that he was buried near St. Peter. But most importantly, in terms of theologic and intellectual developments in the early church, during his reign, as is reported by Irenaeus, the gnostic (see Gnosticism) teachers Valentius and Cerdo came to Rome from Egypt and Syria. Although Hyginus is venerated as a martyr, there is little evidence to support this claim. His feast is 11 January.

For further reference: Matthew Bunson, *The Pope Encyclopedia* (New York: Crown Trade Paperbacks, 1995); Eusebius, *The History of the Church*, trans. G. A. Williamson (New York: Penguin Books, 1989).

William Roberts

I

ICONOCLASTIC CONTROVERSY. SEE GREGORY III.

INDEX OF FORBIDDEN BOOKS. As early as 150 the Council of Ephesus condemned an unauthorized biography of St. Paul the Apostle in circulation and prohibited Christians from reading it. Some twenty years later, with the appearance of the *Muratorian Canon* (170), the early church identified those books of the New Testament considered authentic and excluded certain other liturgical texts from being used. By the time of the Council of NICAEA'S (325) condemnation of the teachings of Arius (see Arianism) reflected in his book *Thalia*, the church had begun to develop a policy of censorship with regard to written expression.

Pope INNOCENT I (401–417) issued the first official list of forbidden books in 405. His condemnation included a set of apocryphal writings alleged to be missing from the authentic canon of Scripture as well as some other texts contrary to Christian teaching. At the end of the fifth century, Pope GELASIUS I (492–496) presented a decree to a synod in Rome (496) promoting the public and private reading of good literature while at the same time prohibiting heretical works. In addition to listing the texts of Scripture and the writings of the church fathers to be read, Gelasius banned certain books, a practice that was continued by popes and church councils for the next several centuries as a means of protecting the integrity of the Christian faith. He is often regarded as the "father of the Index," although he never actually used the term.

In the late fifteenth century Pope INNOCENT VIII (1484–1492) decreed that all written materials were subject to ecclesiastical review and approval prior to distribution to the public. Once approved, a "license to publish," the forerunner of the ecclesiastical imprimatur, was marked in each text by the local bishop. Pope LEO X (1513–1521) promulgated a similar policy at the Fifth Lateran

Council (see Lateran Council V) (1512–1517), thus establishing a pattern for, and practice of, censorship by the church.

The Council of TRENT (1545–1563) developed a rather comprehensive set of legislation designed to serve as the measure for evaluating all types of literature. Its laws remained in effect for the next three centuries. Pope PIUS IV (1559–1565) was the first Roman pontiff to actually use the expression "Index of Forbidden Books." As the Council of Trent drew to a close, the Index of Pius IV was revised and reissued in 1564, and the Tridentine legislation became available to the general public.

In 1571 Pope PIUS V (1566–1572) created the Congregation of the Index. It remained in existence until 1917, when it was merged with the Congregation of the Holy Office, which then assumed responsibility for both church censorship of books and the publication of the Index (see Congregations). Prior to this merger and at the request of the fathers of Vatican Council I (see Vatican Council I) (1869–1870), Pope LEO XIII (1878–1903) set about to adapt the church's rules regarding supervision of literature to the changing needs of the times. He established new policies and procedures that were promulgated in 1897 and published a completely revised Index in 1900.

In 1917 the first Code of CANON LAW was completed and approved. Its legislation included twenty-three canons (1384–1405, 2318) dealing with the examination of books, the prohibition of books and the Index, and the penalties incurred by those who did not observe the law. These canons were, for the most part, the very rules established by Leo XIII some twenty years earlier. The Congregation of the Holy Office continued to publish its Index of Prohibited Books throughout the first half of the twentieth century. With time, however, the practice of explicitly condemning specific books was significantly tempered.

In 1966, following the close of the Second Vatican Council (see Vatican Council II) (1962–1965), the Congregation for the Doctrine of the Faith (formerly, "of the Holy Office") announced the end of the publication of the Index as well as the termination of its associated canonical penalties. The last official revision and distribution of the Index had taken place in 1948. Although the Index itself has now become a "historical document," the church's ancient concern for the written word has continued to be demonstrated in the 1983 Code of Canon Law's treatment of the teaching office of the church, the canons on instruments of social communications, specifically, books (822–832). These canons represent a modification in tone from their 1917 counterparts. Rather than emphasizing the protection of faith and morals, the safeguarding of individuals from harm, and the dangers inherent in some texts, the 1983 code attempts to assure that writings that contain the church's prayer and beliefs do so authentically.

For further reference: Francis Betten, *The Roman Index of Forbidden Books* (St. Louis: B. Herder, 1920); T. Lincoln Bouscaren and Adam C. Ellis, *Canon Law: A Text and Commentary* (Milwaukee: Bruce, 1957); Redmond Burke, *What Is the Index?* (Milwaukee: Bruce, 1952); James A. Coriden et al., eds., *The Code of Canon Law: A Text and*

Commentary (New York and Mahwah, NJ: Paulist Press, 1985); John Goodwine, *Problems Respecting the Censorship of Books* (Washington, DC: Catholic University of America Press, 1950); J. M. Pernicone, *The Ecclesiastical Prohibition of Books* (Washington, DC: Catholic University of America Press, 1932).

David M. O'Connell

INFALLIBILITY, PAPAL. In general, infallibility is the privilege by which grace preserves the magisterium of the church from error when it proclaims doctrines of faith or morals binding on all the faithful. While infallibility is a gift to the church, it is exercised in several ways, each of which demands the concurrence of the person in the papal office. ''Papal'' infallibility rests with the office, for the faith of the church, not in the person who is POPE.

The grace of infallibility operates when the universal episcopate, under its head the pope, teaches that God has revealed a specific truth to the church. This grace operates also when an ecumenical council with the pope teaches a doctrine as true and revealed. A third way in which the grace of infallibility operates occurs when the pope alone, as supreme teacher of the church, pronounces a doctrinal definition that is binding on the whole church. This last operation of grace within the church is commonly called papal infallibility. First proclaimed in *Pastor Aeternus* (Vatican I, 18 July 1870), papal infallibility was further addressed in *Lumen Gentium* at VATICAN II (21 November 1964).

For further reference: Austin Flannery, ed., *Lumen Gentium,* in *Vatican Council II: The Conciliar and Post Conciliar Documents*, rev. ed. (New York: Costello, 1988), pp. 350–426; Jedin Hubert, *Ecumenical Councils of the Church: An Historical Outline* (New York: Herder and Herder, 1960); J. M. R. Tillard, *The Bishop of Rome* (Wilmington, DE: Michael Glazier, 1983).

Loretta Devoy

INNOCENT I (401–417). The son of, and successor to, ANASTASIUS I (399–401) seized the opportunity to assert the primacy of the Roman See at a time when barbarian attacks crumbled the Western empire. He thus proved to be one of the eminent popes of the early centuries, sometimes acclaimed as ''the first POPE.''

In 410, Innocent undertook a journey to Ravenna to arrange a truce between Emperor Honorius and Alaric the Goth. He was absent when the Gothic king pillaged Rome. His writings include thirty-six letters, categorized into three groups: to Western bishops, to Eastern bishops, and to African bishops. He wrote on such issues as discipline and the liturgy. He reiterated in his writings the prohibition of marriage for bishops, priests, and deacons and called for continence for those married before entering the clergy. Three of his letters in 417 condemned perverse views on grace, calling for the EXCOMMUNICATION of Pelagius and Caelestius unless they returned to the orthodox teachings of the church. He was pleased when his fellow brothers forwarded disputed matters to him and maintained the mandate they follow the ancient tradition. Innocent seemed to have been the first pope who strongly advocated that the apostolic see possessed the supreme teaching authority.

For further reference: J. N. D. Kelly, *The Oxford Dictionary of Popes* (New York: Oxford University Press, 1986).

Patrick McGuire

INNOCENT II (1130–1143). Gregorio Papareschi, of Roman patrician background, was cardinal-deacon of S. Angelo at the time of his election. When HONORIUS II (1124–1130) died, his chancellor Aimeric, with a minority of sympathetic cardinals, quickly elected Gregorio as Innocent II. However, the majority of cardinals, of the older Gregorian persuasion, elected his rival Pietro Pierleoni as ANACLETUS II (1130–1138).

This resulted in an eight-year SCHISM, with Anacletus having an initial advantage because of his control of Rome and the support of Roger II (1095–1154), to whom he granted the Crown of Sicily, Apulia, and Calabria. Innocent was forced to flee to France, but his claim was recognized almost everywhere except in Scotland, Aquitaine, and southern Italy. He also had the support of Bernard of Clairvaux, Louis VI of France, and Henry I of England, as well as the German episcopate and King Lothair III. Thus, by 1132 he felt sufficiently secure to reject Anacletus' proposals for arbitration, convinced that most of the Christian world had already decided in his favor. Innocent had already persuaded Lothair, with a promise of the imperial title, to march on Rome to depose Anacletus, and in 1133 they entered the city.

Lothair did not remain in Rome, and, when he left, Innocent was forced to retreat to Pisa, where he convened a synod to excommunicate (see Excommunication) both Anacletus and Roger II. In 1136, Lothair again invaded Italy, but his campaign against Roger proved indecisive, and he could not take Rome. Only the death of Anacletus in January 1138 ended the schism, as his successor, the antipope VICTOR IV (1138), resigned shortly after this. Innocent was back in the Lateran by March, having received the submission of the opposing cardinals and of the Pierleoni family. In April of the next year he called the Second Lateran Council (see Lateran Council II), which finally settled any problems arising out of the schism, annulling all decisions, acts, and ordinations performed under Anacletus. In 1140 Innocent confirmed the condemnation pronounced on the philosopher and theologian Peter Abelard. Innocent II's last years were beset by other problems. He was captured by Roger in 1139 and forced to recognize his title as king of Sicily, and in 1141, he fell out with Louis VII of France. In 1143, there were a riot and uprising in Rome, where the citizens established a commune with an independent senate.

For further reference: Matthew Bunson, *The Pope Encyclopedia* (New York: Crown Trade Paperbacks, 1995); T. Jallard, *Church and Papacy* (London: SPCK, 1944).

William Roberts

INNOCENT III (1198–1216). Lotario de' Conti di Segni was born in 1160 of the aristocratic Scotti family of the Roman Campagna. The *Gesta Innocentii* reports he studied at Rome, Paris, and Bologna. While it is clear that he studied theology at Paris, he appears to have spent less than two years at Bologna, insufficient time for a complete education in Roman and CANON LAW. In 1190, not yet a priest, he was made a cardinal, which was possible in his day. He still had not received holy orders in 1198, when he was elected POPE as Innocent III (1198–1216).

As pope, he introduced a number of innovations and was considered an excellent administrator. Appeals of ecclesiastical legal cases to Rome had been increasing since the pontificate of ALEXANDER III (1159–1181), and Innocent had to hear cases three times weekly in consistory. The more important of these he handled personally. To stem the flow of legal traffic to Rome, Innocent increased the use of judges sent to the various countries to hear cases locally in his name. Although Innocent recognized two new and influential religious orders—the Dominicans and FRANCISCANS—it was the Cistercians, the most important of the twelfth-century orders, whom he specially used as papal agents.

Innocent, who presented himself as an arbitrator between the kingdoms of Christendom, influenced events abroad as well as in Italy, marking the high point of papal power in Christendom. In 1194, he excommunicated (see Excommunication) King Sverre of Norway and in 1198, laid an interdict on the whole kingdom (an interdict prohibited the celebration of any Christian sacrament). With the death of Emperor Henry VI in 1197, Innocent asserted his right to arbitrate between the imperial claimants. He supported three men in turn, the third of whom, Henry VI's son, Frederick II (1215–1250), was elected on the condition that he do homage to Innocent for Sicily. In 1199 Innocent arranged a five-year truce between the kings of France and England, who had been disputing English control of lands on the Continent. Innocent's support of Philip II (1180–1223) of France was one factor in Philip's victory at Bouvines in 1214 over the former emperor, Otto IV of Brunswick.

Innocent was involved in two crusades, one against the Albigensians (see Albigenses) of southern France, and the other the Fourth Crusade for the Holy Land. The latter was diverted from its original goal and ended in the Latin conquest in 1204 of Constantinople and the Byzantine empire. Of the many interventions Innocent made in European life, those in England were especially striking, resulting in an interdict against King John of England (1199–1216), which lasted from 1208 until 1213. In England, as one element of the resolution of the quarrel over the appointment of Stephen Langton to be archbishop of Canterbury in 1207, King John accepted Innocent as his feudal overlord.

Innocent was a theoretician of the papal power. He wrote frequently of the papal *plenitudo potestatis* (fullness of power) and was the first pope to use the title Vicar of Christ. He portrayed papal authority as coming from Christ through the commission given to PETER (Matthew 16:18). In his most important statement on church and state, *Per venerabilem* of 1202, Innocent wrote that the pope, as Christ's vicar, held spiritual and secular jurisdiction. The pope's plenitude of power extended to judgment in secular affairs, and ambiguous cases, ecclesiastical or secular, should be submitted to him. According to Innocent, there is no human authority higher than that of the papacy, and thus there is no court of law that can contravene papal legal judgments. In certain cases, the pope holds temporal jurisdiction outside the PAPAL STATES. Innocent did not claim that the papacy had charge of the daily government of the world but that the pope was above all human political offices and was the judge of all Christians in matters of sin. Innocent insisted that where jurisdictions already existed for the judging of temporal matters, he did not intend to usurp such jurisdictions. Specifically, unless a matter of serious sin was involved, the pope had no intention of intervention.

Although the pontificate of Innocent III is usually understood to mark the high point of papal power in Christendom, as late as the thirteenth century, the popes were still not masters in Rome. The great families dominated political life there, keeping the city in turmoil and leading the pope to be concerned for his safety. Furthermore, in spite of much effort to make the papal states more efficient, in Innocent's day they provided only limited revenue and were not well governed. One of Innocent's problems was the insufficiency of revenues available for the projects he wished to sponsor. While Innocent ceaselessly exerted himself in the cause of advancing Christianity, composing more than 6,000 letters and decrees during his pontificate, the church was hampered by the slowness of communication, the inadequacy of revenue bases, and the relatively undeveloped state of basic administrative practices. The church, as an international institution, sought to influence events over vast distances from a very limited power base. In comparison, the developing national states had more compact territories and greater revenues.

Innocent took great interest in the development of education, especially in the cathedral schools on the threshold of university status and in the fledging universities that were emerging. The apparently limited nature of Innocent's own education leaves one unprepared for the high quality and wide range of the letters from his pontificate. Innocent's decretal letters deal with virtually every contemporary legal question. Doubtless, he had help in the composition of many of these, but Innocent's personal interest in the promotion of learning and of church reform through learning was genuine. The first officially sanctioned collections of canon law since the beginning of the twelfth-century revival of learning date from his pontificate.

Perhaps Innocent's greatest accomplishment was the convening of the Fourth Lateran Council (see Lateran Council IV) in 1215. It was the most comprehensive of church councils to its time and systematically organized the teachings and discipline of the church. This council defined the number and nature of the seven sacraments, described the Eucharist or mass in the terminology of transubstantiation, and legislated the obligation for all Christians annually to confess and take communion.

For further reference: C. R. Cheney, *Pope Innocent III and England* (Stuttgart: Hiersemann, 1976); Colin Morris, *The Papal Monarchy: The Western Church from 1050 to 1250* (New York: Oxford University Press, 1990); Kenneth Pennington, "Pope Innocent III's Views on Church and State: A Gloss to *Per Venerabilem*," in *Law, Church and Society: Essays in Honor of Stephan Kuttner*, ed. Kenneth Pennington and Robert Somerville (Philadelphia: University of Pennsylvania Press, 1977), pp. 49–67; Kenneth Pennington, *Popes, Canonists and Texts, 1150–1550* (Hampshire, England: Aldershot, 1993).

Glenn W. Olsen

INNOCENT III, ANTIPOPE (1179–1180). The church had been in SCHISM for twenty years at the time of Innocent's usurpation. Not only had the papacy offended the German emperor, Frederick I Barbarossa (1152–1190), with its alliance with the Normans, but, due to a mistranslation, it proclaimed its assertion to authority over secular rulers, provoking the emperor to recognize a series of ANTIPOPES. Lando of Sezza, from an Italian Lombard family, and cardinal-deacon of St. Angelo, was elected POPE by a group of pro-imperial cardinals opposed to Pope ALEXANDER III (1159–1181). Some of Innocent's supporters were relatives of antipope VICTOR IV, including Victor's brother, a knight, who provided protection for Innocent at his fortress in Palombara. Alexander dispatched his representative, Cardinal Hugo, to negotiate with the knight, negotiations that ended in bribery, prompting Innocent to be handed over to Alexander's envoy. The antipope was imprisoned in an abbey at La Cava until his death.

For further reference: J. N. D. Kelley, *The Oxford Dictionary of Popes* (Oxford: Oxford University Press, 1986); Hans Kuhner, *Encyclopedia of the Papacy* (New York: Philosophical Library, 1958).

John C. Horgan

INNOCENT IV (1243–1254). The Genoese Sinibaldo Fieschi, a brilliant canon lawyer who studied and later taught at Bologna and served as governor of Ancona, was elected after an eighteen-month vacancy following the death of his predecessor. Innocent was unscrupulous in pursuit of his ends and relied heavily on nepotism to create a widespread system of political support.

Like INNOCENT III (1198–1216), he held that the POPE was supreme over all earthly princes but recognized that this power was held de jure, not de facto. Under him, the conflict between the papacy and the Hohenstaufen reached its climax. Believing that the new pope would be favorable to him, Frederick gave his support after Innocent's election and began negotiations for the removal of his sentence of EXCOMMUNICATION. In 1244, a draft treaty provided for this on condition of the removal of imperial forces from papal territory. It was never ratified. In 1245, Innocent held the First Council of LYONS, originally planned by GREGORY IX (1227–1241). Its agenda included reform, recovery of the Holy Land, the Mongol invasions, and relations between the church and the imperial government. Frederick was found guilty of breach of peace, sacrilege, and HERESY and deposed.

The pope supported the move to replace Frederick, had a crusade preached against him, and even plotted his murder. Despite the efforts of Louis IX of France to mediate the conflict, it remained unresolved when Frederick died in 1250. Returning triumphant to Rome in 1251, Innocent continued the struggle against Frederick's son and successor, Conrad IV. The pope was determined to wrest Sicily from the Hohenstaufens and restore it as a papal fief and, for this reason, offered its Crown to Richard of Cornwall, Charles of Anjou, and finally to Henry III of England, who accepted it for his son Edmund. But when Conrad died in 1254, Frederick's bastard son Manfred, who served as regent of the kingdom, acknowledged the pope as his overlord. Innocent annexed the kingdom to the PAPAL STATES and took up residence in Naples. But Manfred soon revolted and defeated the papal forces at Foggia. The news of this defeat hastened the death of a seriously ill Innocent.

For some the reign of Innocent IV lowered the prestige of the papacy due to his nepotism, wasting of papal revenues, and political intrigues. He made the INQUISITION, in its most brutal forms, permanent in Italy and sent Louis IX on the ill-fated Seventh Crusade. Although he sought to send missionaries to convert the grand khan of the Mongols, a daring idea, and began reunion discussions with the Eastern church, neither endeavor succeeded. Nonetheless, he is considered a great jurist pope, publishing numerous official decretals, constitutions, and commentaries on CANON LAW.

For further reference: P. Hughes, *The History of the Church* (London: Sheed and Ward, 1955); J. A. Watt, *The Theory of Papal Monarchy in the Thirteenth Century* (New York: Fordham University Press, 1965).

William Roberts

INNOCENT V (1276). Born in France, Innocent was the first Dominican to become POPE. A respected theologian and preacher, he held a chair at the University of Paris; wrote a distinguished commentary on the *Sententiae* of Peter Lombard; with Thomas Aquinas and Albertus Magnus, drew up a plan of study that served as the basis for Dominican education; and served as archbishop of Lyons. Innocent played a prominent role at the Second Council of Lyons (see Lyons II, Council of) (1274), which healed the SCHISM with the Greek church when Emperor Michael VIII agreed to a reunion with Rome. The emperor fully accepted the Roman faith as well as Roman primacy but retained the Greek church's own symbols and rites.

Innocent was most active in external affairs. He planned to follow the program of his predecessor, GREGORY X (1271–1276), by launching a new crusade to capture Jerusalem. However, his short reign did not permit its implementation. Under pressure from King Charles of Sicily, the pope informed the Byzantine emperor of plans to retake Constantinople, a city that had been forcefully taken

from the West. Innocent also upset the delicate balance of power in Italy be-
tween King Charles and Rudolf I, the Hapsburg emperor, when he prevented
Rudolf's coronation in Rome until differences with Charles had been resolved.
In 1898, LEO XIII beatified Innocent. His feast day is 22 June.

For further reference: Joseph S. Brusher, *Popes through the Ages* (Princeton: D. Van
Nostrand, 1964); Hans Kuhner, *Encyclopedia of the Papacy* (New York: Philosophical
Library, 1958); H. K. Mann, *The Lives of the Popes in the Early Middle Ages* (London:
K. Paul, 1902–1932).

John C. Horgan

INNOCENT VI (1352–1362). Born Étienne Aubert, he served as distinguished
jurist and chief judge of Toulouse prior to assuming the papal responsibilities.
In 1338, after his ordination, he served as bishop of Noyon and then Clermont.
In 1352 he was installed as cardinal-bishop of Ostia, and later appointed administrator of the see of Avignon. In the conclave of Avignon in 1352, which
elected him POPE, the cardinals recommended that papal authority be curtailed,
while that of the sacred college be augmented.

The fifth Avignon pope, in 1353 Innocent overturned the preelection recommendation. He also corrected, in the spirit of BENEDICT XII (1334–1342),
numerous abuses in the papal CURIA. He called for a simplification of the
lifestyle in the papal household and a mandate to clergy to reside in their benefices, insisting that those aspiring to hold offices be required to submit evidence
of their ability. Nonetheless, Innocent's pontificate was plagued with repeated
disappointments. Negotiations between the English and French in 1354 failed
to prevent the resurgence in 1355 of the Hundred Years' War. Consumed with
debt from the wars in Italy, Innocent was forced to sell papal treasures in 1358.
Although unable to restore peace between Aragon and Castile, in 1360 he effected the Peace of Bretigny between France and England.

For further reference: Matthew Bunson, *The Pope Encyclopedia* (New York: Crown
Trade Paperbacks, 1995); J. N. D. Kelly, *The Oxford Dictionary of Popes* (New York:
Oxford University Press, 1986).

Patrick McGuire

INNOCENT VII (1404–1406). Cosimo Migliorati was born in Sulmona, Italy,
c. 1336. After his legal studies, he served in the papal CURIA and became
archbishop of Ravenna (1387) and then archbishop of Bologna and cardinal
(1389). When elected POPE in 1404, Rome was in turmoil, and he summoned
Ladislas Durrazzo to Rome as "defender of the church." Together with the
pope's nephew, Ladislas' efforts to pacify Rome led to riots and massacres in
the spring of 1405. Innocent sought refuge in Viterbo.

At this time BENEDICT XIII (1394–1417), the Avignon claimant, landed in
Genoa to meet with Innocent to end the SCHISM. With French military aid
Benedict was poised to march on Rome and end the schism by occupying the

Holy City. But the coolness of the French king to the project and the plague in Genoa forced Benedict to withdraw. In March 1406 Innocent returned to Rome in triumph. He planned to restore and expand the Roman University founded by BONIFACE VIII (1294–1303) in the hope of making Rome a center of learning. He died soon after on 5 November 1406.

For further reference: H. K. Mann, *The Lives of the Popes in the Early Middle Ages* (London: K. Paul, 1902–1932); L. Pastor, *History of the Popes*, vol. 1 (St. Louis: Herder, 1899).

Richard J. Kehoe

INNOCENT VIII (1484–1492). Giovanni Battista Cibo was born at Genoa in 1432. He studied at Rome and Padua and spent a profligate youth at the court of Naples, where he sired several illegitimate children. After entering clerical orders, his personal life improved. In 1467 he became bishop of Savona, which he exchanged for Molfetta in 1472. Through the influence of Cardinal Giuliano della Rovere, nephew of Pope SIXTUS IV (1471–1484) and later Pope JULIUS II (1503–1513), Cibo was made a cardinal in 1473.

In the conclave following the death of Sixtus, Cardinal della Rovere shamelessly bought votes and on 29 August 1484 secured the election of Cibo, who chose the name Innocent VIII. Under Innocent, Cardinal della Rovere exercised great influence. The papacy was involved in almost constant strife, primarily with the kingdom of Naples. As part of his diplomacy, Innocent's son, Franceschetto, was married to a daughter of Lorenzo the Magnificent of Florence in 1487. As a result, Lorenzo's son Giovanni, the future Pope LEO X (1513–1521), was made a cardinal at the age of fourteen.

Innocent's attempt to organize a crusade was unsuccessful, so he entered into an agreement with Sultan Bayezid II in 1489 under which the Turk agreed to pay the pope 40,000 ducats annually to keep his brother Djem confined in the Vatican. In 1492 the sultan made a present to Innocent of the Holy Lance of St. Longinus. Under Innocent VIII simony and other forms of fiscal corruption, which had been so scandalous under Sixtus IV, increased. After a long illness, Innocent died on 25 July 1492, after pleading with the cardinals to elect someone better than himself. In this, too, his efforts proved futile.

For further reference: William Raymond Bonniwell, "Innocent VIII, Pope," in *New Catholic Encyclopedia*, vol. 7 (New York: 1967), pp. 526–527; Ludwig von Pastor, *The History of the Popes*, vol. 5, 5th ed., ed. Frederick Ignatius Antrobius (St. Louis: B. Herder Book, 1949).

William C. Schrader

INNOCENT IX (1591). A favorite of the Spanish party, the election of Cardinal Giovanni Antonio Fachinetti to succeed GREGORY XIV (1590–1591) as pontiff was not surprising. Born in 1519 in Bologna of a family of Veronese origin, he studied law in Verona and in 1544 joined the staff of Cardinal Alessandro Farnese, who later became PAUL III (1534–1549) and who sent him first as representative to Avignon and then assigned him to Parma. In 1560 PIUS IV (1559–1565) made him bishop of Nicastro in Calabria, and shortly after he took an active part in the Council of TRENT. Under PIUS V (1566–1572), he served as NUNCIO in Venice and negotiated the anti-Turkish coalition that eventually defeated the Turks at Lepanto in 1571. Because of ill health he resigned his diocese in 1575 and returned to Rome, where GREGORY XII (1572–1585) appointed him to important posts in the CURIA and the INQUISITION. He was also made patriarch of Jerusalem and a cardinal.

Innocent IX, like his predecessor, followed a pro-Spanish policy, supporting Philip II and the Holy League against the still-Protestant king Henry IV of France. He sought to put papal finances on a firm basis and revealed a plan to establish a substantial reserve in Castel Sant' Angelo for emergency purposes. He also renewed Pius V's ban on the alienation of church property. An early act of his reign was to divide the Secretariat of State into different sections. He sought to repress banditry around Rome, improving sanitary conditions in the city. Something of a scholar, he wrote a commentary on Aristotle's *Politics*, which has never been published. He fell ill while making the pilgrimage to the seven churches of Rome and died on 18 December 1591.

For further reference: P. Hughes, *The History of the Church* (London: Sheed and Ward, 1955); T. Jalland, *Church and Papacy* (London: SPCK, 1944).

William Roberts

INNOCENT X (1644–1655). The Roman Giamattista Pamfili received degrees of doctor of civil law and CANON LAW at the University of Rome (see Colleges of Rome). His pontificate was troubled by several crises, including the final years of the Thirty Years' War (1618–1648), while his pro-Spanish position alienated the French. This POPE was displeased by the concessions granted the Protestants in the Peace of WESTPHALIA, 1648. He had to contend with the external enemies of Catholicism: the English, the Swedes, and the Turks as well as the Jansenists (see Jansenism). In 1653 he condemned the five propositions from the *Augustinus*. The ambitious Donna Olimpia Maidalchini-Pamphili, his brother's widow, exercised significant influence over the pope, who reportedly made no important decision without her input. He embellished Rome, and under his guidance the interior decoration of St. Peter's was completed, while the Piazza Navone was restored. A pioneer in prison reform, he helped reorganize those of the PAPAL STATES, installing a cell system.

For further reference: Matthew Bunson, *The Pope Encyclopedia* (New York: Crown Trade Paperbacks, 1995); J. N. D. Kelly, *The Oxford Dictionary of Popes* (New York: Oxford University Press, 1986).

Patrick McGuire

INNOCENT XI (1676–1689). In 1639 Benedetto Olescalchi, who studied with the Jesuits (see Society of Jesus), earned a doctorate in civil and CANON LAW.

He was appointed a cardinal by INNOCENT X (1644–1655), LEGATE to Ferrara in 1648, and bishop of Novara in 1650. Although favored for the chair of Peter in the conclave of 1670, Louis XIV's influence delayed his election until 1676. Prior to accepting the chair, he requested his colleagues to approve the "Summary Agreement," fourteen articles of ecclesiastical reform. This formed his program, which centered on three broad objectives: completion of the work initiated by the Council of TRENT, the defense of freedom and rights of the church, and the assurance of safety for Christians in Europe against the Islamic Turks. He worked tirelessly to unite the Christian princes, both Catholic and Protestant, against the growing threat of Turkish invasion. Beatified in 1956, this reformer is considered one of the leading POPES of the seventeenth century.

For further reference: Matthew Bunson, *The Pope Encyclopedia* (New York: Crown Trade Paperbacks, 1995); J. N. D. Kelly, *The Oxford Dictionary of Popes* (New York: Oxford University Press, 1986).

Patrick McGuire

INNOCENT XII (1691–1700). Antonio Pignatelli, a Neapolitan aristocrat and archbishop of Naples, ascended to the papacy as Innocent XII in a period of increasing turmoil between Rome and the French king, Louis XIV (1643–1715). Louis demanded recognition of the Gallican (see Gallicanism) Articles and extension of the *regalia* (collection of revenues from vacant bishoprics) in exchange for the French king's assistance in the extirpation of French Protestantism. Innocent settled on an uneasy compromise in which Louis promised the POPE he would no longer insist on the French clergy's unconditional adherence to the Gallican Articles, in exchange for the pope's promise to ratify the appointment of bishops made by the king and recognition of Louis' right to the *regalia* throughout his kingdom. This compromise resulted in Gallicanism's ruling the French church down to the Revolution.

Again in Franco–papal relations, Innocent declared his support for Louis' grandson, Phillip of Anjou, over the Austrian archduke Charles during the Spanish Succession. The pope deemed a French presence in Italy more palatable than an increased Austrian one. Innocent was also preoccupied with church reform. In addition to reducing the size of the papal court and clamping down on the practice of simony, the pope successfully addressed nepotism, an issue in which his predecessor, INNOCENT XI (1676–1689) had encountered opposition from the College of CARDINALS. On 22 July 1692, Innocent issued the papal bull *Romanum decet Pontificem*, forbidding the practice of nepotism and discontinuing some expensive offices while prohibiting the renewal of others.

For further reference: Joseph S. Brusher, *Popes through the Ages* (Princeton: D. Van Nostrand, 1964); Hans Kuhner, *Encyclopedia of the Papacy* (New York: Philosophical Library, 1958); H. K. Mann, *The Lives of the Popes in the Early Middle Ages* (London: K. Paul, 1902–1932).

John C. Horgan

INNOCENT XIII (1721–1724). Michelangelo dei Conti, son of the duke of Poli, was born in Rome on 13 May 1655. After studying with the Jesuits (see Society of Jesus) in Rome, he was introduced into the CURIA by Pope ALEXANDER VIII (1689–1691) in 1690. He served as a governor of several provinces in the PAPAL STATES and then was nominated as the NUNCIO at Lucerne, Switzerland (1695–1698), and at Lisbon, Portugal (1698–1709). CLEMENT XI (1700–1721) made him cardinal (7 June 1706) and bishop of the diocese of Osimo and later of Viterbo. In 1721, Michelangelo succeeded Pope Clement XI following a long and contentious conclave that was sharply divided between Bourbon and imperial supporters. His compromising nature helped get him elected, since many cardinals believed that the papacy needed a period of reconciliation after the controversial term of Clement XI. He chose the name Innocent XIII in memory of INNOCENT III, to whose lineage he belonged.

During his brief papacy, Innocent XIII attempted to improve relations with the major European powers. He tried to reduce tension with Emperor Charles VI, the bitter adversary of Clement XI, investing him with Sicily and Naples in June 1722. In July 1721 he satisfied the regent of France, Philip II of Orleans, by raising his powerful and corrupt minister, Guillaum Dubois, to the position of cardinal. Innocent XIII's conciliatory policy did not prevent Charles VI from asserting his supremacy over the Sicilian church, nor did it help in negotiating the withdrawal of imperial forces from the Comacchio, which they had occupied since 1708. Moreover, papal opposition to investing of the Spanish prince Don Carlos with Parma and Piacenza, traditional fiefs of the Pope, was ignored.

Like his predecessors, Innocent XIII recognized the English pretender as king of England and Scotland, granting him an annual income. In France, the Jansenists (see Jansenism) hoped that his opposition against the anti-Jansenist bull *Unigenitus* as a cardinal would make him friendlier toward them. However, he disappointed them when he ratified the bull. Innocent XIII raised his brother, Bernard, to the cardinalate but restricted his income to 12,000 *scudi*. The pope also opposed the use of Chinese rites among Catholic converts in China, supporting the Dominicans in their dispute with the Jesuits over that issue. His concern for the economic and cultural conditions of the papacy notwithstanding, his impact was limited due to his poor health and brief reign. Innocent XIII died in Rome on 7 March 1724.

For further reference: Matthew Bunson, *The Pope Encyclopedia* (New York: Crown Trade Paperbacks, 1995); Franco Venturi, *L'Italia nel Settecento dal 1714 al 1788* (Verona: Mondadori, 1971).

Alexander Grab

INQUISITION. The spread of HERESY in the twelfth century forced the church to develop ways of meeting this threat. POPES and councils reminded bishops of their obligation to suppress heresy. Lawyers reasoned that heresy constituted a serious attack on the church and the common good, likening action against heresy to a crusade. Heresy was seen as a form of lèse-majesté, which justified the use of force and even death to suppress it. Pope LUCIUS III (1181–1185) promulgated the procedure for the investigation and treatment of heretics. He required bishops to investigate reported cases of heresy and apply canonical sanctions where guilt was verified. The secular authorities had to cooperate under threat of EXCOMMUNICATION and deprivation of office. INNOCENT III (1198–1216) classified heresy as treason and incorporated the process of Lucius III into the decrees of the Fourth Lateran Council (see Lateran Council IV). These actions laid the foundation for the medieval Inquisition.

The twelfth century saw the spread of the Cathari and Albigensian (see Albigenses) heresies in southern Germany, northern Italy, and southern France. At first, the church followed the advice of St. Bernard that heretics must be won by persuasion and not by force. As the movement grew, the church appealed to the coercive power of the Inquisition. Innocent III supplemented the sometimes ineffective episcopal Inquisition by establishing the papal Inquisition, which grew under GREGORY IX (1227–1241) and INNOCENT IV (1243–1254). The papacy gradually assumed responsibility for the prosecution of all heretics. This Inquisition developed a juridical system that included courts and prisons, judges, clerks, and all the support personnel required by the courts. It operated as a circuit court, although in some places it acquired permanent sites. Upon arriving in a town the inquisitors preached a general sermon at which they explained the teaching of the church and refuted heretical teaching. They proclaimed a period of grace of fifteen to thirty days during which the guilty were reconciled. Secret heretics received private penances, while known heretics received canonical penances, for example, pilgrimages, fasts, or special prayers.

After the period of grace, the inquisitors cited those suspected of heresy on the basis of evidence collected from the laity, the local clergy, and admitted heretics. The accused were imprisoned, and their goods sequestered. They were interrogated and invited to repudiate their errors. Normally, the accused were not allowed counsel, and the names of accusers were kept secret for fear of retaliation. The process of interrogation had as its goal the uncovering of the truth and bringing the accused to repentance. Only the testimony of two eyewitnesses, apprehension in the very act, or the confession by the accused constituted full proof. At this point the use of torture became possible. This was introduced into the process by Innocent IV. Its use was closely defined by the jurists, and a confession obtained under torture had to be repeated the next day free of torture.

The process terminated in many ways. The sentences imposed on the guilty included fasts, fines, pilgrimages, and the wearing of distinctive clothing. Relapsed heretics could be confined to light imprisonment, house arrest, strict imprisonment, or solitary confinement. Imprisonment for life could be commuted to shorter periods. Those heretics who refused to repent were turned over to the secular arm for execution.

In fifteenth-century Spain a variation of the Inquisition was created. Rumor spread that *conversos*, recently converted Jews, secretly remained Jews. After initial papal hesitation a new court was established independent of the bishops and subject to the Crown. Over time its jurisdiction expanded to include Muslims who had become Christian, the *alumbrados*, and Protestants. During the sixteenth century, especially under the initiative of PAUL IV (1555–1559), the Roman Inquisition was activated to counter the spread of Protestantism. This rigid pontiff expanded the jurisdiction of the court beyond doctrinal matters to include the policing of morals and the silencing of his critics, for example, Cardinals Giovanni Morone and Reginald Pole.

When compared to other judicial systems of the time, the harsh procedures of the Inquisition were not singular. An age, however, sensitized to religious freedom and human rights finds odious a system that sanctioned the use of torture and did not allow cross-examination of witnesses or representation by counsel. Like any judicial system the Inquisition had its miscarriages of justice, for example, Joan of Arc and Galileo. The "Declaration on Religious Freedom" of VATICAN II speaks for another age and makes the Inquisition a historical anachronism.

For further reference: Y. Dossat, "Inquisition," *New Catholic Encyclopedia*, vol. 7 (New York: 1967), pp. 535–541; E. Peters, *Inquisition* (New York: Free Press, 1988); C. Roth, *A History of the Marranos*, reprint 1932 (New York: Meridian Books, 1959); E. Vacandard, "Inquisition," *Dictionnaire de théologie catholique* (Paris, 1903–50), vol. 7, pp. 2016–2068.

Richard J. Kehoe

INVESTITURE CONTROVERSY. This traced its origin to the practice of the proprietary church, whereby the founder of a parish or monastery and his heirs had the right to designate the pastor or abbot. By Carolingian times this was extended to bishoprics. With the development of feudalism, it became common for a bishop, abbot, or other cleric to receive from his patron some symbol of office and to swear an oath of homage. While this ceremony did not substitute for sacramental ordination, it placed the selection of clerics in the hands of laymen, while the swearing of an oath of homage implied the subordination of the church to the secular power.

Under the Saxon dynasty (919–1024) in Germany, Crown and church became allies against the secular nobility. The Crown endowed churches liberally and exempted them from the jurisdiction of dukes and counts and, in return, selected bishops and abbots. This reached a high point under Emperor St. Henry II (1001–1024), who personally invested 49 of the 50 bishops taking office during his reign, giving whole counties to some bishops. This situation was initially welcomed by the church, which sought to remain free of the rapacious grasp of feudal lords. The situation was worse in France, where the weakness of the kings allowed the feudal nobility to dominate the church.

In Rome itself, matters were out of hand as one noble faction strove with another to place its candidate on the chair of Peter. Finally, the reforming emperor Henry III (1039–1056) intervened to depose rival claimants and imposed a line of German reformers: CLEMENT II (1046–1047), DAMASUS II (1048), LEO IX (1049–1054), and VICTOR II (1055–1057). Leo IX traveled to France and Germany, where he held synods condemning simony, violence, moral laxity, and clerical concubinage. Under POPE NICHOLAS II (1058–1061), at the Lenten synod of 1059, a decree was adopted vesting the right to elect the popes in the College of CARDINALS, thus freeing the papacy from the domination of both the Roman nobility and the German emperors.

In 1061, on the death of Nicholas, the imperial government sought to regain the initiative by supporting the antipope HONORIUS II (1061–1072), while the reformers supported ALEXANDER II (1061–1073). The reformer Hildebrand was elected to succeed Alexander in 1073, contrary to the electoral decree of 1059, taking the name GREGORY VII. Relations between the new pope and Emperor Henry IV rapidly deteriorated. In the Lenten Synod of 1074 all simoniac clergy were deprived of office, and in that of 1075 the pope deposed several of Henry's bishops. In response Henry attempted to impose his bishops on Milan, Fermo, and Spoleto. At the Lenten Synod of 1076, Gregory pronounced Henry excommunicate and deposed. The German feudal lords made common cause with the pope, threatening to depose Henry in February 1077 if he did not reconcile himself with the pope. This prompted Henry to leave for Italy and venture to Canossa, where the pope had taken residence. There, on 28 January, the ban of EXCOMMUNICATION was lifted after the emperor had done public penance for three days.

Nonetheless, the feudal opposition elected a new king in Rudolf of Swabia, provoking civil war in Germany. Gregory VII in 1080 favored Rudolf, while claiming suzerainty over the empire. Henry named a rival pope in CLEMENT III in 1080 and in 1083 occupied Rome, where he was crowned emperor by Clement. Gregory VII was rescued from Rome by the Norman Robert Guiscard and retreated to Salerno, where he died on 25 May 1085. Despite Gregory's death, the reform party continued to resist lay investiture. Only in 1093 was Urban II (1088–1099) able to reside in Rome, although the SCHISM continued. Upon Urban's death he was succeeded by PASCHAL II (1099–1118). This pope renewed the excommunication of Henry IV, and in 1104 Henry's son, the future Henry V, rebelled against his father and was recognized as king by the German lords and the papal LEGATE. Henry IV died in captivity on 7 August 1106.

The papacy was winning the Investiture Controversy on other fronts as Ivo of Chartres (c. 1040–1116) introduced a clear distinction between a bishop's *spiritualia* and his *temporalia*. In 1098 Philip I of France accepted this distinction, renouncing his claim to invest with ring and crosier, and in 1107, Henry I of England and St. Anselm of Canterbury reached a similar agreement. On 4 February 1111, Henry V and Paschal II reached an accord in which the pope promised that in return for complete renunciation of investiture throughout the empire, Henry would receive back all the endowments given the church. The agreement collapsed when the bishops and nobles who accompanied Henry to Rome refused to accept it. In the ensuing tumult, Henry took Paschal prisoner and forced him to accept imperial investiture. However, as early as the Synod of 1112, the ban on lay investiture was renewed.

After much conflict in the autumn of 1121, negotiations resulted in the Concordat of Worms on 23 September 1122. Under its provisions Henry V renounced investiture with ring and crosier and guaranteed all bishoprics and monasteries in his realm free, canonical elections to be held, however, in the presence of the emperor or his representative. The elected, but not yet consecrated, prelate would receive the *temporalia*, symbolized by a scepter, from the emperor. This compromise, accepted by Pope CALLISTUS II (1119–1124), ended the Investiture Controversy but did not end the medieval conflict between papacy and empire. Strife over the respective bounds of spiritual and secular authority continues to our day.

For further reference: Geoffrey Barraclough, *The Medieval Papacy* (New York: Harcourt, Brace, and World, 1968); Marc Bloch, *Feudal Society: II—Social Classes and Political Organization* (Chicago: University of Chicago Press, 1961); Alfred Haverkamp, *Medieval Germany, 1056–1273* (Oxford: Oxford University Press, 1992).

William C. Schrader

IRISH NATIONALISM AND PAPACY. Although England had asserted overlordship of Ireland since the late twelfth century, not until the beginning of the sixteenth century was a consistent attempt made to impose Anglicization. As the newly established Protestant religion was a part of England's program, Irish resistance to the destruction of the traditional way of life automatically included an obstinate loyalty to Catholicism. Ireland became a battleground of the COUNTER-REFORMATION, with the papacy (in conjunction with Spain) supporting a series of Irish rebellions during the late 1500s. When the Irish Catholic Confederation was formed in 1642 to carry on an armed struggle against English policy, it received papal recognition and assistance. A special representative, Archbishop Rinuccini, took up residence in Ireland to "guide" the Confederates.

By the time that the next great surge of Irish national resistance was crushed in 1691, English policymakers and their Protestant supporters in Ireland were convinced of the inextricable identification of Catholicism with Irish "sedition." The pervasive anti-Catholic restrictions of the early eighteenth century reflected this perception. This program seemed validated by the papacy's recognition of the exiled Stuart dynasty, living under the POPE's protection in Rome, as the legitimate rulers of England and Ireland. These Jacobite monarchs were given the right to nominate bishops for Irish sees, and Irish priests were trained in Continental seminaries. Both priests and prelates were smuggled into Ireland in what, to England, was a clear papal support of treason.

Anglo–papal relations (see Anglo–Vatican Relations) changed dramatically during the late eighteenth century, as Rome abandoned the Jacobite cause and sought accommodation with London. The easing of anti-Catholic regulations was matched by endorsements of loyalty to the established authorities in Ireland from 1770 onward. During the era of the French Revolution, the papacy made common cause with the conservative, counterrevolutionary forces of Europe, including the Protestant regime in the British Isles. The nature of Irish nationalism, however, was undergoing a significant change at this time. Earlier, it had been essentially a cultural phenomenon, and Irish resisters had not demanded total independence from England, provided they were guaranteed preservation of their traditional way of life, including practice of the "old religion." If the rights of Catholicism were assured, the papacy had no objection to English rule in Ireland, and agreement on such an arrangement was developing in the 1790s. The birth of Irish political nationalism, based on republican doctrines derived from Revolutionary France, created a more radical program for future generations of Irish nationalists.

For the last 200 years, the papacy has generally remained supportive of the form of Irish nationalism that secures Catholic rights, while allowing some sort of compromise on the political relationship between Ireland and England. Thus, Rome was sympathetic to the Repeal movement of the 1830s and 1840s and the Home Rule movement of the 1870s and 1880s, which sought no more than Irish autonomy within the British imperial structure. On the other hand, the papacy vehemently opposed the radical revolutionaries of the United Irish Society during the era of the French Revolution because of their secular values and hostility to church guidance. Papal antagonism was also directed against the Young Ireland revolutionaries of 1848 and the Fenian Brotherhood of the 1860s and 1870s because of their identification with revolutionary and secret society policies the church deplored. While the Irish HIERARCHY throughout the nineteenth century remained, with few exceptions, firmly in line with Roman policy, there was always a certain proportion of the rank-and-file clergy willing to lend tacit or even open endorsement to radical nationalism. Such tendencies were more marked among Irish-born clergy in the United States, to which so many Irish Catholics had emigrated during the course of the century.

A revival of Irish revolutionary nationalism in the early 1900s produced the "Easter Rebellion" of 1916 and the Anglo-Irish War of 1919–1921. The papacy, concerned now about the status of the newly expanded church in England as well as of Catholicism in Ireland, found difficulty in maintaining a balanced position between the claims of British authority and Irish aspiration. The situation was all the more stressful because a greater number of Irish bishops and priests manifested strong nationalist sympathies during this period and failed either to condemn or to remain aloof from political activities. Following the creation of the Irish Free State and the separate Northern Ireland entity in 1922, the Vatican concentrated its attention on relations with the newly independent Dublin government. The special relationship between the southern regime and the Catholic Church that was enshrined in the new Irish Constitution seemed to confirm to Protestants the persistence of an identification between Catholicism and Irish nationalism. The Vatican, in fact, continued to reject the kind of automatic support of nationalism that would have further eroded the position of Catholics still under British rule in Northern Ireland.

A new stage in the history of Ireland's strained relations with England began in 1968, when demands for improved civil rights by Catholics in Northern Ireland precipitated Protestant persecution and the outbreak of an ongoing internal war between British forces and nationalist guerrillas. Vatican efforts during the period since 1968 have been directed toward the promotion of peace and reconciliation among all political, ethnic, and religious elements in Ireland. Repeated condemnations of terroristic violence by extreme nationalists and reprisals by Protestant militants have been uttered by most church leaders and all but a relatively small number of Irish and Irish-American clergy.

For further reference: S. J. Connolly, *Priest and People in Pre-Famine Ireland* (Dublin: Gill and Macmillan, 1991); Robert Kee, *The Green Flag: A History of Irish Nationalism* (New York: Simon and Schuster, 1990).

William D. Griffin

J

JANSENISM. Named after Cornelius Jansenius, Latinized version of Otto Jensen, the Flemish Roman Catholic theologian (1588–1638), it was concerned with the essential element of salvation. It surfaced in the Low Countries in the seventeenth century and spread as a heretical movement in the 1700s, particularly in France, where it became entangled in internal politics, the defense of the independent traditions of the Gallican church, and acrimonious debates over the respective roles of the papacy and councils (see Conciliar Movement) in the leadership of the church. When Jansenism appeared in Italy, it was judged a threat to the integrity of the church and papal institutions alike.

The roots of Jansenism are to be sought in the Protestant REFORMATION. Luther's belief that man could not be justified before God except by faith conveyed by the Word, combined with Calvin's extreme view of predestination and humankind's natural depravity, generated in Catholic circles spirited discussions on the parts played by divine initiative and human freedom in salvation. Before the Reformation, the Augustinian and Thomistic positions had prevailed, each complementing the other, however ambivalently. While the Augustinians unilaterally deferred to unmerited predestination and applied grace as the paramount factors in the gift of salvation, the Thomists expounded regeneration by revelation and confirmation by a person's power of reasoning under the immediate guidance of the church.

Led by the Jesuits, the Counter-Reformists (see Counter-Reformation) approached the teachings of Augustine and Aquinas in a balanced, flexible manner, conceding both to God's calling and to individual volition, while simultaneously subscribing to optimism regarding God and the human condition. Differences in emphasis became notorious in 1588 with the publication of the Jesuit Luis de Molina's *Concordia Liberi Arbitrii Cum Divinae Gratiae Donis*. It contended that predestination and grace became effective only in anticipation of personal surrender to God's will and provision in Christ. Both Augustinians and Thomists were scandalized. Molina's conclusion did not dislodge Augustinian ideas entrenched in many universities, including the French, but especially at Louvain, Belgium, then part of the Spanish Netherlands, where Jensen was professor of theology. Sometime in 1620, he determined to restate and defend Augustine's dictum on the indispensability of providential grace. Appointed bishop of Ypres in 1636, he died two years later, leaving his study unfinished. Completed by his followers, the work, in three volumes, was published posthumously in September 1640 as *Augustinus*. Through it, Jensen repudiated Molina's thesis and underscored God's redemptive love as the sole and active agent for salvation.

Augustinus sparked bitter polemics between Jansenists and the Jesuits (see Society of Jesus), who spurned Jensen for having cast Aquinas aside and, in doing so, deprived people of conscious choice in determining their destiny. The INQUISITION condemned the book on 1 August 1641, followed by POPE URBAN VIII's denunciation in the bull *In Eminenti*, dated 19 June 1643. To honor the urgings of French monarchs and high churchmen for decisive action, popes promulgated condemnations, INNOCENT X's *Cum Occasione* of 31 May 1653, and Pope ALEXANDER VII's *Regiminas Apostolici* in February 1665, but no decree of EXCOMMUNICATION was issued. To avoid another split in Western Christianity the popes refused to take a stronger stand, even though the minister of state Cardinal Richelieu and his successor Jules Mazarin, as well as most of the church HIERARCHY, openly opposed the Jansenists.

With the Second Dutch War pending (1673–1678), Louis XIV relaxed tensions. In February 1669, Jansenists imprisoned at Port-Royal were set free and allowed to participate in the sacraments. Likewise, the ascension of CLEMENT XI (1667–1669) bode well for reconciliation. Feelings, however, were aroused to fever pitch with the publication in 1694 of the Gallican, pro-Augustinian, Thomist, and allegedly anti-Jansenist scholar Parquier Quesnal's *Noveau Testament avec des Réflexions Morales*. It enlarged the arena of controversy with the argument that Christ did not vest supreme authority in the church in popes but in its devoted believers, acting through representative councils. Contrary to his intentions, Quesnal encouraged the Jansenists. Louis XVI, alarmed over the extent of Jansenist sentiment in his realm, confiscated Quesnal's papers following his arrest in 1707. CLEMENT XI (1700–1721) responded to the king's plea for a definitive statement with several bulls, the most noteworthy being *Unigenitus dei Filius*, announced in September 1713. It denounced 101 propositions from Quesnal's *Réflexions* as being of Jansenian inspiration. While the majority of clergy, "the Acceptants," demanded full compliance or outright expulsion from the church, "the Appellants," consisting of 3,000 priests, twelve bishops, including the archbishop of Paris, Noailles, and more than 100,000 clergymen in France, sponsored a statewide campaign to submit Clement's *Unigenitus* to a general church council. To prevent this, Clement excommunicated the Appellants, but the decree proved difficult to enforce. In 1773, the Jansenist Church of Holland was formed (the Great Schism of Utrecht) because church and state could not resolve the impasse.

The death of Archbishop Noailles of Paris in 1729 removed any influential Jansenist exponent from the French scene. His successor, Cardinal de Vintimille, a staunch Acceptant and partisan of royal divine right, succeeded in 1730 in convincing Louis XV (1715–1774) to compel all Appellants to bow to *Unigenitus* or lose their benefices and pensions. This resulted in obedience. Without any formal action of the pope, the Appellants, having repented, were restored to the church. Those who remained Jansenist in heart were won over when CLEMENT XIV (1769–1774), in July 1773, dissolved the Jesuit Order (see Society of Jesus, Abolition of), the arch foe of Jansenism. The remnant of the unconverted Jansenists became divided by the French Revolution of 1789 and largely disappeared during the Restoration.

In the Italian peninsula, Jansenism experienced a resurgence. Articulating the reformist impulse of the Gallican church, Italian Jansenists advocated, among other things, a reordering of church and papacy to resemble the simplified organizational framework exemplified by early Christianity. In 1786, Scipione de Ricci, the Florentine-born bishop of Pistoia-Prato, convoked a syndical conference at Pistoia to reconstitute the church in Tuscany along Jansenist lines. At the same time Jansenist thought managed to linger within certain sectors of society. Nationalists and unificationists, from Cavour to Mazzini, were influenced by their Jansenist upbringing. Within the Italian church, it had an important part in the emergence of a liberal Catholicism, which called for a separation of church and state.

For further reference: Nigel Abercrombie, *The Origins of Jansenism* (Oxford: Clarendon Press, 1936); *Jansenism: A Collection of Books and Pamphlets on Jansenism in Its Various Manifestations as They Existed Mainly in France and in the Netherlands* (Utercht: Beijers, 1956); Carlo A. Jemolo, *Il Giansenismo in Italia prima delle Rivoluzioni* (Bari: Laterza, 1928).

Ronald S. Cunsolo

JESUITS. SEE SOCIETY OF JESUS.

JOAN OR JOANNA, ALLEGED POPE (c. 855–c. 858). This legendary female occupant of the papal throne reportedly was born in England or in Germany of English parents and supposedly reigned as John Anglicus, known as Pope John VIII, between the pontificates of LEO IV (847–855) and BENEDICT III (855–858). Allegedly, her imposture was exposed while riding from St. Peter's to the Lateran, when she gave birth to a child in the narrow streets by the Colosseum. Her pontificate supposedly came to a bloody end when the angry Romans stoned her to death for her deception. The story was given a wide diffusion by the extremely popular and influential *Chronicle of Popes and Emperors*, compiled by the Dominican Martin of Troppau (d. 1297). Accepted in Catholic circles for centuries, she was written about by humanists such as Petrarch and Boccaccio, and her bust was included among those of other POPES in the cathedral of Sienna. During the REFORMATION some Protestants pointed to her shameful "pontificate" as part of their condemnation of the papacy in general. Another Protestant, the French Calvinist David Blondel, first challenged the authenticity of her papacy. In 1863 Johann Doellinger completely demolished the stories—some claimed her reign occurred in the ninth, the tenth, and eleventh centuries—as a fraud, without any substantiation. However, her legend remains of interest to many contemporary feminist writers.

For further reference: Matthew Bunson, *The Pope Encyclopedia* (New York: Crown Trade Paperbacks, 1995); J. N. D. Kelly, *The Oxford Dictionary of Popes* (New York: Oxford University Press, 1986).

Francesca Coppa

JOHN, ANTIPOPE (844). Internal struggles within Rome marked the election of John, a deacon, to the papacy supported by the citizens, who seized the Lateran and installed their candidate. Some questions arose as to whether John, in fact, led this rabble to the Lateran. Nevertheless, John stood in direct opposition to SERGIUS II (844–847), whose backing came from the lay aristocracy and clergy. The latter groups successfully removed John from the Lateran, while Sergius prevented John from being executed, banishing him instead to a monastery.

For further reference: H. K. Mann, *The Lives of the Popes in the Early Middle Ages* (London: K. Paul, 1902–1932); Walter Ullman, *A Short History of the Papacy in the Middle Ages* (London: Methuen, 1972).

John C. Horgan

JOHN I (523–526). Born in Tuscany, John I had earlier in his ecclesiastical career supported the antipope LAWRENCE (498/499, 501–506) but afterward submitted to the authority of Pope SYMMACHUS (498–514) in 506. Elderly at the time of his election, he was a senior deacon. Prior to his election, Emperor Justin I had resumed the persecution of Arians (see Arianism), closing down their churches in Constantinople and excluding them from employment in the imperial service. In response, Theodoric, the Ostrogothic king of Italy, took a less conciliatory stance toward Catholics in his domain. In 526, Theodoric sent John I to Constantinople with a delegation of bishops and senators to secure a reversal of the imperial policy toward Arians and to ensure that those forcibly converted to Catholicism be permitted to return to their original faith.

John received an elaborate reception from the emperor, much to the displeasure of Theodoric, who suspected the two of conspiring against him. Theodoric also suspected the Roman aristocracy of plotting with Justin to bring about his demise. He had already executed the philosopher Boethius (a friend of the pope's). Theodoric began to suspect the pope's goodwill toward him, and he ordered John to remain under house arrest in Ravenna. In 526, upon the advice of the canonist Dionysius Exiguus, John I introduced for common usage the

Alexandrian date of Easter. This method involved the numbering of years beginning from the birth of Christ, and it gradually gained acceptance throughout the Western world. Shortly afterward, the aged pontiff died from an illness that was most likely induced by maltreatment. He was buried in the nave of St. Peter's and at the time of his death was regarded as a martyr.

For further reference: J. N. D. Kelly, *The Oxford Dictionary of the Popes* (Oxford: Oxford University Press, 1986); *New Catholic Encyclopedia* (New York, 1967), vol. 7, pp. 1006–1007.

Patrick J. McNamara

JOHN II (533–535). The first POPE to change his name upon election, the Roman priest Mercurius was elected after a two-and-a-half-month vacancy in the papal office. During that period, attempts were made by various candidates to purchase the office. Following his election, Mercurius obtained from Athalaric, the Ostrogothic king, a confirmation of the Roman Senate's decree banning simony in papal elections.

Following a religious conference in Constantinople, the emperor Justinian I (527–565) published a dogmatic decree. Although this decree affirmed the teaching of the church's first four general councils, it also included the Theopacite formula, formerly rejected by Pope HORMISDAS (514–523) as both unnecessary and liable to misinterpretation. The inclusion of this formula met heated opposition from the Acoemetae (''sleepless'') monks of Constantinople, who appealed against it to John II. Justinian, who had referred to Rome as ''the head of all churches,'' urged John to approve the entire decree and to force the monks to do likewise. When the monks refused to do so, John excommunicated (see Excommunication) them as Nestorians in 534, after which he sanctioned the emperor's use of the formula. John II died in 532 and is buried in St. Peter's.

For further reference: Matthew Bunson, *The Pope Encyclopedia* (New York: Crown Trade Paperbacks, 1995); J. N. D Kelly, *The Oxford Dictionary of the Popes* (Oxford: Oxford University Press, 1986); *New Catholic Encyclopedia* (New York, 1967).

Patrick J. McNamara

JOHN III (561–574). The son of the Roman senator Anastasius, the cleric originally named Catelinus assumed the title John III upon his election to the papacy. He was not consecrated until four months later, following imperial approval. His reign, about which little information is extant, witnessed the Lombard invasion of Italy in 568 under King Alboin. The invaders met scant resistance from the Byzantine general Narses. One positive result of the invasion was the termination of the SCHISM between Rome and the churches of northern Italy in 572. This schism resulted from the refusal of those churches to accept Pope PELAGIUS I's (555–561) condemnation of the Three Chapters. The archbishop of Aquileia, however, obstinately rejected reconciliation.

In 571 John III persuaded Narses to defend Rome in the face of the Lombard advance. This action, nonetheless, made him unpopular with the Roman populace, which detested Narses. As a result, John was forced to reside outside the city until Narses' death in 573. During that time the pope continued to exercise all the duties of his office. John III died thirteen years after his election and was buried in St. Peter's.

For further reference: Matthew Bunson, *The Pope Encyclopedia* (New York: Crown Trade Paperbacks, 1995); J. N. D. Kelly, *The Oxford Dictionary of the Popes* (Oxford: Oxford University Press, 1986); *New Catholic Encyclopedia*, vol. 7 (New York: 1967).

Patrick J. McNamara

JOHN IV (640–642). Born in Dalmatia, John IV was a Roman archdeacon at the time of his election to the papacy. His consecration took place five months later, following imperial approval. During this period he addressed a letter to the Irish bishops and abbots admonishing them for observing the Easter feast on the day of the Jewish Passover and warning them to avoid tendencies toward Pelagianism. In January 641 John held a synod condemning monothelitism, the belief that Christ possessed one will. The emperor Heraclius (610–641) favored monothelitism in his *Ecthesis*, citing Pope HONORIUS I's (625–638) endorsement of it. John maintained, however, that Honorius meant that Christ, because of his sinlessness, did not experience a division of the wills as humans do. But according to John, Honorius never denied that Christ had two wills.

Mindful of the plight of Christians in his native Dalmatia, John IV devoted both time and money to free those taken captive by the Slavs and Avars. In addition, he endowed a chapel, adjacent to the Lateran baptistery, in honor of various Dalmatian saints.

For further reference: Matthew Bunson, *The Pope Encyclopedia* (New York: Crown Trade Paperbacks, 1995); J. N. D. Kelly, *The Oxford Dictionary of Popes* (Oxford: Oxford University Press, 1986); *New Catholic Encyclopedia*, vol. 7 (New York: 1967).

Patrick J. McNamara

JOHN V (685–686). John V, a Syrian, represented the first in a series of POPES of Greek or Syrian origin who sought to establish better relations with the Eastern church. He also was the first pope to be consecrated prior to receiving imperial confirmation. With the exception of reaffirming Rome's authority over Sardinia, John's short papacy did not achieve any notable accomplishments.

For further reference: Hans Kuhner, *Encyclopedia of the Papacy* (New York: Philosophical Library, 1958); H. K. Mann, *The Lives of the Popes in the Early Middle Ages* (London: K. Paul, 1902–1932).

John C. Horgan

JOHN VI (701–705). A native of Greece, John VI's reign coincided with the decline of the Byzantine empire and the release of its hold over Italy. Two incidents mark John's papacy: he saved the emperor's exarch of Ravenna, Theophylact, from a Roman mob intent on killing him and prevented a Lombard attack on Rome by paying ransom.

For further reference: Joseph S. Brusher, *Popes through the Ages* (Princeton: D. Van Nostrand, 1964); H. K. Mann, *The Lives of the Popes in the Early Middle Ages* (London: K. Paul, 1902–1932).

John C. Horgan

JOHN VII (705–707). A Greek, John VII was the first POPE born of a Byzantine official. The advent of his papacy also marks the return of Justinian II (685–695, 705–711) to the throne. The newly restored emperor suggested that John convene a synod of Western bishops to accept or decline individual decrees of the Quinisext Council (692), a council called by Justinian, whose final acts were anti-Western. Afraid of offending the emperor, John returned the decrees without his signature. In the West, John's excellent relations with the Lombards resulted in the return of the papal lands in the Cotian Alps (Liguria).

For further reference: Eric John, ed., *The Popes: A Concise Biographical Dictionary* (New York: Hawthorn Books, 1964); H. K. Mann, *The Lives of the Popes in the Early Middle Ages* (London: K. Paul, 1902–1932). The best beginning primary source remains the *Liber Pontificalis* (Paris, 1886–1892).

John C. Horgan

JOHN VIII (872–882). Born of a noble Roman family, John served as an archdeacon for twenty years before his election to succeed ADRIAN II (867–872) on 14 December 872. He spent much of his pontificate trying to protect Italy from the Saracens, regulating the succession to the emperorship, and mitigating the tension with Constantinople. Despite his age he conducted vigorous campaigns on all fronts, turning for assistance to the Holy Roman Emperor. He even conferred the Crown on Charles the Bald in 875 and Charles the Fat in 881, helping to establish the papacy as arbiter of the imperial title. John argued that the POPE, having been entrusted with the care of the *republica Christiana*, could bestow temporal rule on the emperor to protect and defend the church. But Charles the Bald died (877) before he could provide much help, and Charles the Fat proved incompetent. John fortified Rome and established a papal navy to protect the coast but had to contend with the Italian nobles, many of whom were prepared to reach an accommodation with the Saracens.

John appealed (878) to the Byzantine emperor, Basil I. In return, John agreed to recognize Photius, deposed in 867, as the successor to the late Ignatius, patriarch of Constantinople. This provided a temporary lull in the conflict between Rome and Constantinople. But Basil was in no position to help John militarily and advised him to bribe the Saracens. John died at the Lateran in 882, reportedly the first pope to be assassinated. According to contemporary gossip, he was poisoned, then clubbed to death by one of his advisers.

For further reference: Matthew Bunson, *The Pope Encyclopedia* (New York: Crown Trade Paperbacks, 1995); W. Ullman, *The Growth of Papal Government in the Middle Ages*, 2d ed. (London: Methuen, 1965).

Frank Grande

JOHN IX (898–900). A Benedictine monk, born at Tivoli, he had been ordained by the vilified Pope FORMOSUS (891–896). At first, on the death of Pope THEODORE II (897), the partisans of Pope Stephen who had posthumously condemned Formosus elected a rival, the bishop of Cerveteri, as pope with the name of Sergius. Although Sergius soon took possession of the Lateran, he was quickly expelled by Lambert of Spoleto, king of Italy, whom Formosus had crowned emperor in 892. Only then was John elected pontiff by the Formosan supporters.

With the support of the emperor, who controlled Rome and most of Italy, John immediately sought to end conflict between the pro- and anti-Formosan factions. John convened a synod at Rome, which annulled the ''cadaver synod's'' posthumous sentence on Formosus but pardoned those who took part after they pleaded that they had done so under duress. Ordinations performed by Formosus were recognized, as was his anointing of Lambert as emperor. But his anointing of Arnulf, king of the East Franks, as emperor was rejected. To prevent disorders at future papal elections it was decreed that while the pope should be elected by the bishops and clergy, at the request of the senate and people, his consecration could take place only in the presence of imperial emissaries.

In a synod at Ravenna under the protection of Emperor Lambert, these decisions were confirmed, and it was decreed that every Roman had the right to appeal to the emperor, whose supreme jurisdiction was reaffirmed. Lambert, in return, renewed the ancient privileges of the Holy See and guaranteed its territorial possessions. Unfortunately, the hopes that these agreements raised were dashed when the young emperor was killed in a hunting accident in October 898.

For further reference: Matthew Bunson, *The Pope Encyclopedia* (New York: Crown Trade Paperbacks, 1995); F. Dvornik, *The Photian Schism* (New York: Hawthorne Books, 1948).

William Roberts

JOHN X (914–928). Born in Tossignano and ordained at Bologna, he was elected, but not consecrated, bishop of Bologna. He held the position of archbishop of Ravenna from 905 to 914, when, at the insistence of the Roman nobility, John was elected POPE to succeed LANDUS. As pope John formed an alliance between the Byzantine emperor Constantine VII, Berengar I, and other Italian princes. He approved the strict rule of Cluny and promoted the conversion of the Normans as well as the claims of the church in Spain and

Slavic areas. He dispersed a delegation to the Synod of Hohenaltheim in 916 to lay the foundation in hopes of fostering a relationship between the church and the state of Germany.

One of John's unfortunate actions was his approval of Count Heribert's five-year-old son Hugh as archbishop of Rheims. This was approved to secure the release of King Charles the Simple, held in prison by Heribert. However, during his pontificate, the SCHISM between Rome and Constantinople over the issue of remarriage ceased. He died by suffocation in 929, a year after being deposed and virtually incarcerated in the Castel Sant' Angelo.

For further reference: Matthew Bunson, *The Pope Encyclopedia* (New York: Crown Trade Paperbacks, 1995); J. N. D. Kelly, *The Oxford Dictionary of Popes* (New York: Oxford University Press, 1986).

Patrick McGuire

JOHN XI (931–935/936). John was the son of the patrician and senatrix Marouzia of the powerful family of Theophylact and effective ruler of Rome. In his twenties he was already cardinal-priest of Sta. Maria in Trastevere and succeeded STEPHEN VII (928–931) through the influence of his family. According to the *Liber Pontificalis*, he was Marouzia's illegitimate son by Pope SERGIUS III (904–911).

John was interested in monastic reform, and one of his first acts was to confirm, on the petition of the abbot Odo, the privileges of protection by the Holy See and the free elections enjoyed by the reforming abbeys of Cluny and Déols. In 932, when the Eastern emperor Romanus I asked him to approve the appointment of his sixteen-year-old son, Theophylact, as patriarch of Constantinople, he readily granted a dispensation and sent two bishops as LEGATES to participate in the youth's consecration and enthronement. The consecration of this young patriarch shocked the Eastern church.

In that same year, Marouzia, still ambitious and newly widowed for a second time, married Hugh of Provence, the king of Italy. John most probably officiated at the wedding, which was uncanonical by the standards of the time since Hugh was Marouzia's brother-in-law. The marriage was unpopular in Rome, whose population was suspicious of foreign rule, and a riot, incited by Alberic II, Marouzia's son by her first marriage, ensued. An armed mob stormed the Castel Sant' Angelo, Marouzia's stronghold, where she resided with Hugh. He escaped with his life, but Alberic captured his mother and half brother, the pope, and imprisoned them. He then proclaimed himself prince of Rome, where he ruled until 954. Nothing more would be heard of Marouzia, while John was released but kept under guard at the Lateran, where he was restricted to ecclesiastical functions.

For further reference: J. Lebreton and J. Zeiller, *The History of the Primitive Church* (London: Burns, Oates and Washbourne, 1948); H. K. Mann, *The Lives of the Popes in the Early Middle Ages* (London: K. Paul, 1902–1932).

William Roberts

JOHN XII (955–964). Octavian was the bastard son of Alberic II, the powerful prince of Rome, who, on his deathbed, forced the leading Romans to swear that upon the death of the reigning POPE, AGAPITUS II (946–955), they would elect Octavian. Although this son was in holy orders, he was only eighteen, and contemporaries speak of his indifference to spiritual matters and debauched lifestyle.

Upon becoming pontiff, John XII asserted papal authority. In 958 he made an attempt to extend papal territory by attacking Capua and Benevento but failed. In 960 John asked Otto I, king of Germany, for help, in return offering him the imperial Crown. In 962, Otto reached Rome, where he and his wife, Adelaide, were anointed and crowned in St. Peter's, reestablishing the Holy Roman Empire, which was to last until 1806. At this time Otto published the "Ottonian privilege," which solemnly confirmed the donations of Pepin (see Donation of Pepin), adding territory to the papal state until it extended to about two-thirds of Italy. The Ottonian privilege also bound the emperor to defend the church's rights and possessions and reaffirmed the regulations for free papal elections, subject to imperial approval of the candidate.

Despite the treaty, John and Otto distrusted each other, and in 963 John began to intrigue against the emperor. An infuriated Otto returned to Rome, while the pope fled to Tivoli with the papal treasury. Otto then presided over a synod in St. Peter's, during which the clergy accused John of misbehavior, treachery, and perfidy. John was called to appear but refused and threatened the clerics with EXCOMMUNICATION. The synod, in retaliation, requested Otto to replace him. A Lateran official, Leo, was elected and consecrated as LEO VIII (963–965) two days later. However, Otto returned in April, and John fled to the Campagna. A month later, he suffered a stroke and died.

For further reference: Matthew Bunson, *The Pope Encyclopedia* (New York: Crown Trade Paperbacks, 1995); H. K. Mann, *The Lives of the Popes in the Early Middle Ages* (London: K. Paul, 1902–1932).

William Roberts

JOHN XIII (965–972). John was a Roman by birth, the son of John Episcopus and the grandson of Theophylact, as well as a relative of the Roman prince Alberic and of JOHN XI (931–945/946). Raised in the papal court, he was made bishop of Narnia in Umbria. After the death of LEO VIII (963–965) he was elected POPE with the consent of two bishops sent by the emperor Otto to represent imperial interests. His election finally put an end to the complicated issue of the status of the various rival popes. However, in December 965 a revolt broke out in Rome. John escaped and contacted the emperor.

A year later Otto arrived in Rome and restored John, who served under the protection of the emperor, who remained in Italy until the end of his pontificate. The two cooperated, and, at a synod at Ravenna in 967, Otto confirmed the restoration to the PAPAL STATE of large areas that had been lost. With the support of Otto, John also took measures to promote and enforce clerical celibacy and continued to encourage monasticism. John also reaffirmed the decision of his predecessor, John XII, regarding the status of the See of Magdeburg and its role as a center of conversion for the Slavs.

At Christmas in 967 John crowned Otto's young son, Otto II, as co-emperor. The pope also assisted in the imperial plan to improve relations with the Eastern empire and officiated at the marriage of Otto II and the princess Theophano, niece of the Byzantine emperor. Nonetheless, tension between the Eastern and Western churches continued. At the time of his death in 972 John was planning a synod for the reform of the church in Germany.

For further reference: Matthew Bunson, *The Pope Encyclopedia* (New York: Crown Trade Paperbacks, 1995).

William Roberts

JOHN XIV (983–984). Peter Canepanova, bishop of Pavia, was chosen POPE several months after the death of BENEDICT VII (974–983). When the saintly abbot of Cluny, Maiolus, declined the papal Crown, the choice, with the emperor Otto II's approval, went to his former archchancellor in Italy, Peter. Otto, however, apparently imposed the new pope, who took the name John XIV, on the Romans without consulting the city's clergy or people. Without allies among the Roman aristocracy and ruling classes, he had to depend on imperial protection. The two cooperated, and, for example, an early act of the pope was to grant the pallium to Archbishop Alo of Benevento in line with the emperor's policies in southern Italy.

However, at the very beginning of John's pontificate, Otto, who had just returned to Rome, died of malaria after receiving absolution, in the pope's arms. The empress Theophano was obliged to return to Germany to defend the interests of her son, Otto III, who was only three, and John, now without friends in Rome, was left defenseless. The Romans resented him for having been imposed upon them, and the city's powerful Crescentii family brought back BONIFACE VII, whom they had originally set up as ANTIPOPE in 974. Excommunicated (see Excommunication) by Benedict VII, he was in exile in Constantinople, awaiting an opportunity to return. In April 984 John was seized, deposed, and imprisoned in the Castel Sant'Angelo. No record of the trial exists, and within four months he died, according to some accounts, of starvation or poisoning. His epitaph in St. Peter's does not mention the details of his death.

For further reference: L. Duchesne, ed., *Liber Pontificalis* (Paris: E. de Boccard, 1955).

William Roberts

JOHN XV (985–996). This Roman author, son of a priest, and cardinal-priest owed his election to the support of the Crescentii, Rome's most powerful family. Abiding by an agreement reached with Theophano, widow of Otto II (973–983) and regent for Otto III (996–1002), John limited himself to ecclesiastical matters.

He successfully negotiated a treaty preventing war between King Aethelred of England (978–1016) and Duke Richard I of Normandy (946–996). John also received the entire realm from Duke Mieszko I of Poland (960–992), who desired protection from the papacy against the Germans. John was the first POPE to formally canonize a saint, the bishop of Augsburg, Ulrich, in January 993, placing John in good stead with the German emperor. This period also marked the beginning of the conversion of the Russians to Christianity. Emperor Vladimir (972–1015), although subject to the authority of the patriarch at Constantinople, recognized the pope in Rome as head of the Catholic Church.

The most contentious issue John confronted concerned the French bishops and their king, Hugh Capet (987–996). At the Synod of Mouzon (995), John reversed the actions of both the bishops and the king when they placed Gerbert (the future pope SYLVESTER II) in the See at Rheims. John's repudiation of the French claims and his suspension of Gerbert prevented further independence on the part of the French church from Rome. In 995, John was forced to flee from the tyranny of Crescentius Nomentanus, who had gained control of Rome upon the death of his brother. The displaced pope turned for assistance to the young German emperor Otto III, who proved obliging. Just the threat of a German invasion caused Crescentius to invite John's return. The Roman aristocrat then begged the pope to prevent an attack on the city by Otto. Unfortunately for Crescentius, the pope died of a fever before Otto reached the city limits.

For further reference: Hans Kuhner, *Encyclopedia of the Papacy* (New York: Philosophical Library, 1958); H. K. Mann, *The Lives of the Popes in the Early Middle Ages* (London: K. Paul, 1902–1932); Walter Ullman, *A Short History of the Papacy in the Middle Ages* (London: Methuen, 1972).

John C. Horgan

JOHN XVI, ANTIPOPE (997–998). The Greek John Philagathos had served as chancellor of Italy. As tutor to Otto III (996–1002) and bishop of Piacenza, John journeyed to Constantinople to procure a bride for the young emperor Otto. He returned to Italy shortly after Crescentius Nomentanus, head of the ruling family of Rome, led a revolt against German influence and forced Pope GREGORY V (996–999), Otto's cousin and court chaplain, from Rome. Crescentius, along with his newly elected POPE, John XVI, sought the protection of the emperors at Constantinople.

John and Crescentius further conspired to share power among themselves when John relinquished temporal papal power to Crescentius. These actions resulted in John's being excommunicated (see Excommunication) by Gregory in March 997. John, unsure of his precarious relationship with Crescentius, attempted to establish relations with Otto, but his efforts failed. Regrouping his forces and accompanied by his pope, Otto marched on Rome in February 998. The German forces quickly captured both Crescentius and his ANTIPOPE. John, after a brief imprisonment, had his eyes gouged out, his body was mutilated, and he was paraded around Rome on a jackass. He was later put on trial by Gregory, where he was stripped of his rank and pontifical robes. John subsequently died in 1001 while a prisoner in a Rome monastery. Crescentius' fate was no less horrible: upon his capture, he was beheaded.

For further reference: Hans Kuhner, *Encyclopedia of the Papacy* (New York: Philosophical Library, 1958); H. K. Mann, *The Lives of the Popes in the Early Middle Ages* (London: K. Paul, 1902–1932).

John C. Horgan

JOHN XVII (1003). A native of Rome, married, and the father of three children, John's ascension to the papacy occurred during the struggle between the Roman nobility and the German emperors for control of the church. John proved unable to establish a meaningful relationship with the new German king Henry II (1002–1024), who was preoccupied with gaining control in Germany. The most significant development during his short papacy was granting Benedict, a Polish missionary, the right to evangelize among the Slavs.

For further reference: Joseph S. Brusher, *Popes through the Ages* (Princeton: D. Van Nostrand, 1964); H. K. Mann, *The Lives of the Popes in the Early Middle Ages* (London: K. Paul, 1902–1932).

John C. Horgan

JOHN XVIII (1003–1009). The Roman Giovanni Fasano became POPE with the support of the patrician John II of the powerful Crescentii family. Unlike his predecessor, JOHN XVII (1003), who likewise owed his appointment to the Crescentii, Fasano showed himself both more vigorous and independent. Among other things, he established the See of Bamberg, reestablished the See of Meresburg, and consented to the Roman Synod of 1007. He canonized the five Polish martyrs: Benedict, John, Isaac, Matthew, and Christian and is credited with the diffusion of Christianity among the Slavs. The patriarch of Constantinople refused to recognize him as anything more than bishop of Rome, but his papal authority was recognized in the West. The last years of his reign are shrouded in mystery, as he withdrew to the Monastery of St. Paul's outside the walls.

For further reference: Mathew Bunson, *The Pope Encyclopedia* (New York: Crown Trade Paperbacks, 1995); J. N. D. Kelly, *The Oxford Dictionary of Popes* (New York: Oxford University Press, 1986).

Francesca Coppa

JOHN XIX (1024–1032). Romanus, of the Tusculan family, held the office of counsel, dux, and senator during his older brother BENEDICT VIII's (1012–1024) pontificate. Upon his brother's death and while still a layman, Romanus assumed possession of the papacy, allegedly by bribery. Despite canonical regulations, he received all orders on the same day, shocking many. It appears John was an ineffectual pontiff yet was able to strengthen his office by being instrumental in uniting noble families. In the presence of Burgundy's king Rodolphe III and King Cnut of England and Denmark, John, in Rome, crowned Conrad II emperor at Easter 1027. The new emperor did not renew the Ottonian privilege granted by his predecessors or swear allegiance to protect the church.

John had been considered an inconsistent administrator, interested only in securing financial gain by demanding money for positions in the HIERARCHY. According to some, his contributions to the chair included his support to Guido of Arezzo, to the Cluniac reform, and to the Truce of God.

For further reference: Matthew Bunson, *The Pope Encyclopedia* (New York: Crown Trade Paperbacks, 1995); J. N. D. Kelly, *The Oxford Dictionary of Popes* (New York: Oxford University Press, 1986).

Patrick McGuire

JOHN XX. No such pope held office.

JOHN XXI (1276–1277). Following the death of ADRIAN V in 1276, Cardinal Pedro Juliao was elected POPE as John XXI. A prolific writer, scholar, and philosopher, he had studied in Paris and taught medicine in Italy at the University of Sienna. Having no intentions of abandoning his scholarly pursuits and having little experience in curial business, John retired to a cell in the rear of his palace. He was criticized by some for an alleged ill favor toward the religious orders and moral instability. In fact, John relinquished most of the decisions to Cardinal Orsini. He died from injuries sustained when the ceiling of his study collapsed.

For further reference: Matthew Bunson, *The Pope Encyclopedia* (New York: Crown Trade Paperbacks, 1995); J. N. D. Kelly, *The Oxford Dictionary of Popes* (New York: Oxford University Press, 1986).

Patrick McGuire

JOHN XXII (1316–1334). In May 1314, four months after the death of CLEMENT V (1305–1314), the cardinals (see Cardinals, College of) proved unable to elect a POPE. After three months, they were forced to disperse amid violence. In March 1316, they met in Lyons, selecting Jacques Duèse, the bishop of Porto, two years after Clement's death. He chose the name John XXII. The second of the Avignon popes, John spent nearly two decades grappling with the FRANCISCANS. Because of this conflict, as well as charges of overspending, laxity in the court, nepotism, and HERESY, the reign of John XXII is viewed by many as a disaster.

Soon after his coronation, extremist Franciscans refused to submit to papal requirements regarding the lawful use of money and property. John excommunicated the rebels and demanded their immediate submission, which he received from all but a small group, eventually remanded to the INQUISITION. A larger controversy soon brought John into a heated conflict with Michael of Cesena, master general of the order. In a meeting of the general chapter of the order in Perugia in May 1322, the clerics claimed that Christ and the apostles maintained the absolute rule of poverty and proclaimed the denial of this rule to be heresy. John countered that the decision, proclaimed in defiance of the Inquisition, was heresy.

In 1316, John invited Louis IV and Frederick the Fair of Austria to his court to help settle their disputed elections to the throne after the death of Henry VII. When they declined, John applied the doctrine that the empire reverted to the Holy See when vacant and confirmed the appointment of Robert of Naples as imperial vicar in Italy. In September 1322, Louis defeated his rival and marched to Italy, where he was crowned emperor. When Louis supported the political ambitions of the pope's rivals in Italy, the conflict intensified, eventually leading to Louis' EXCOMMUNICATION in 1324.

While preaching in Avignon in 1331, John created a new controversy by claiming that the souls of the just did not enjoy the full vision of God and that the souls of the condemned were not immediately damned but that both awaited the final judgment. This drew sharp criticism from theologians, and he was denounced as a heretic. John eventually assembled a commission, which concluded that although his preaching was not in accordance with traditional doctrine, he was expressing an opinion as an individual and not in his capacity as pontiff. In December 1344, John fell ill and died a few days later on December 4 at the age of 90. At his death in 1334, the papacy was virtually bankrupt.

For further reference: Eric John, *The Popes: A Concise Bibliographical History* (London: Burns and Oates, 1964); J. N. D. Kelly, *The Oxford Dictionary of the Popes* (Oxford: Oxford University Press, 1986).

Christopher S. Myers

JOHN XXIII, ANTIPOPE (1410–1415). Baldassarre Cossa was born in Ischia and pursued a military career. Later he studied at Bologna, entered the papal service, and became a cardinal in 1402. Cossa joined the revolt against GREGORY XII (1406–1415) that led to the Council of Pisa. In May 1410, he succeeded ALEXANDER V (1409–1410), the Pisan candidate, in an election allegedly marred by simony. He pacified the PAPAL STATES and further eroded the support for his rival, Gregory XII. Bowing to pressure from Emperor Sigismund, John summoned the Council of CONSTANCE for 1 November 1414. The council concluded that the only way to unity lay in the resignation of all three papal claimants. John agreed to resign but imposed conditions the council refused. The beleaguered prelate stole out of Constance on the night of 20 March and fled to Germany. He returned to Constance a prisoner to stand trial and was deposed on 29 May 1415. He accepted the decision and was imprisoned in Germany. Released in 1419, Pope MARTIN V (1417–1431) graciously named him cardinal-bishop of Tusculum in June 1419. He died on 22 December 1419 in Florence.

For further reference: E. J. Kitts, *Pope John XXIII and Master John Hus* (New York: AMS Press, 1978); Louise R. Loomis, *The Council of Constance* (New York: Columbia University Press, 1961); John H. Smith, *The Great Schism 1378: The Disintegration of the Papacy* (New York: Weybright and Talley, 1970).

Richard J. Kehoe

JOHN XXIII (1958–1963). Born Angelo Giuseppe Roncalli on 25 November 1881 in Sotto il Monte in northern Italy, John XXIII, who summoned the Second Vatican Council (see Vatican Council II) in 1959, brought the papacy to new heights of popularity among Catholics and non-Catholics alike during the course of his four-and-one-half-year reign. Following on the heels of the formal and aristocratic pontificate of PIUS XII (1939–1958), John's person and papacy were seen by many as a breath of fresh air. His manner was naturally open and friendly, and much was made of his peasant origins. Rather than cultivate an aura of separateness from people, he worked hard to remain simple and humble throughout his clerical career.

Ordained in Rome in 1904, Roncalli served his home diocese of Bergamo for sixteen years as a parish priest, seminary professor, and active member of Catholic Action. In 1925, he was appointed archbishop by Pope PIUS XI (1922–1939) and embarked upon a diplomatic career, serving in Bulgaria and Turkey. In 1944, he was given the important post of NUNCIO to France, where he remained until 1953. In that year, he was recalled to Italy and, after twenty-three years as a Vatican diplomat, Archbishop Roncalli was made primate of Venice and elevated to the College of CARDINALS. Already 72 years old, Roncalli's appointment to Venice was seen as a just reward for a loyal prelate in his final years.

At the death of Pius XII, however, a consensus appeared to emerge among members of the College of Cardinals that the church had need of a ''transitional'' POPE who would put the church more in touch with the world but would do nothing remarkable until a successor (many believed Archbishop Montini of Milan) was ready to assume the papal throne without the immediate baggage of Pius XII's reign. Cardinal Roncalli seemed to fit the description. He was old, known, supported by the French cardinals, the second largest national group, and had a strong following among the Italians. In 1958, Cardinal Roncalli was chosen the 259th pontiff.

His warm personality and the ease with which he approached the outside world convinced many in the college that Roncalli would be the pope who could bring the church into greater contact and relevance with the secular world. At the same time, he was conservative in many ways. As primate of Venice, he had a reputation as a tough leader among his priests; he discouraged his religious from watching television and was extremely strict with them in matters of personal morality. He himself had always demonstrated absolute obedience to his clerical superiors and expected nothing less from his subordinates. Unlike either Pius XII or PAUL VI (1963–1978), Roncalli seldom agonized over important decisions. His decisions, no matter how momentous, were made quickly and in the simple faith that he was nothing more than the instrument of the Holy Spirit.

The most significant achievement of John's papacy was his decision to call an ecumenical council, known as VATICAN II. Even this act was taken, according to John's own words, without a great deal of thought. The pope was apparently discussing with Cardinal Tardini the sorry state of the world, and he simply suggested a "council." Taken aback, Tardini is said to have quickly agreed; and the Second Vatican Council was born. In John's mind, the council was a bold, decisive effort to open the church to the world, to look objectively at the strengths of the church, and to offer broad guidelines to the new "opening outward."

The pope also departed radically from Pius XII's policy of strong and direct involvement in Italian politics. John was less likely to see the world divided starkly into camps of good and evil (noncommunist and communist) than his predecessor. He was more willing to work with various forms of governments and, as a result, received strong criticism from conservative circles, particularly in Italy, for his decision to receive Nikita Khrushchev's son-in-law in March 1963. Italian conservatives blamed the pope's gesture toward a high-level communist for the improvement of Italian communists at the polls that year.

At any rate, none of these ripples during the course of his four-and-one-half-year papacy diminished Papa Roncalli's tremendous popularity. Upon his death on 3 June 1963, John XXIII left the unfinished work of his ecumenical council to a strong supporter and devoted follower, Cardinal Giovanni Battista Montini of Milan, who took the name Paul VI.

For further reference: Ernesto Balducci, *John the Transitional Pope* (New York: McGraw-Hill, 1965); Loris Capovilla, "Giovanni XXIII, trent'anni dopo," *Humanitas* (June 1993); Alberto Melloni, *Fra Istanbul, Atene e la guerra: La missione de A. G. Roncalli, 1935–1944* (Genoa: Casa Editrice Marietti, 1992).

Richard J. Wolff

JOHN PAUL I (1978). Albino Luciani, elected POPE on 26 August 1978, died one month later, on 28 September. Born into a working-class family at Forno di Canale (now Canale d'Agordo), near Belluno, Italy, he was ordained in 1935 by the local bishop. In 1946 he earned his doctorate from the Gregorian University (see Colleges of Rome) with a dissertation on the thought of Antonio Rosmini. After 1937 Luciani taught at the Belluno seminary and served in that diocese until becoming the bishop of Vittorio Veneto (1958). In 1969 Pope PAUL VI (1963–1978) named him patriarch of Venice, and in 1973 he received the cardinal's hat. From 1972 to 1975 he served as vice president of the Italian Episcopal Conference. In Venice, Luciani acquired a popular reputation for his work on behalf of the handicapped, for his close attention to pastoral work in the industrial suburb of Mestre, and for his ambitions to transfer superfluous church wealth to the poor and to the Third World. His early reputation as an advocate of Catholic–communist dialogue, however, was transformed into one of confrontation by the 1970s.

In the important and charged Italian elections of 1976, the patriarch advocated that voters follow the recommendations of the Episcopal Conference, and he chastised rebellious priests who had taken sides with the Marxist Left. After the death of Paul VI, Luciani was elected to the throne of St. Peter on the third ballot, to the surprise of many, particularly as a candidate from outside the CURIA. His tenure ended after only thirty-three days when his corpse was discovered in bed on the morning of 29 September; he had suffered a heart attack the previous evening. The circumstances of his death were later tainted by unfounded speculation that he had been murdered in connection with improprieties surrounding the scandal-ridden Banco Ambrosiano and the *Istituto di Opere Religiose*. His pontificate was too brief to be remembered for noteworthy achievements, but his gentle personality and reassuring smile left strong and fond impressions among many, particularly in the sadly terror-stricken Italy of 1978.

For further reference: Matthew Bunson, *The Pope Encyclopedia* (New York: Crown Trade Paperbacks, 1995); Peter Hebblethwaite, *The Year of Three Popes* (Cleveland, OH: William Collins, 1979).

Roy Palmer Domenico

JOHN PAUL II (1978–). He was born Karol Wojtyla on 18 May 1920 in Wadowice, Poland, son of a retired army lieutenant. Educated in state schools in Poland, Wojtyla demonstrated a love for theater and literature early in life. He had just entered the university in Cracow when the Nazis invaded Poland, effectively shutting down higher education. During WORLD WAR II, Wojtyla worked in a stone quarry, faithfully attended weekly religious meetings, and reportedly engaged in anti-Nazi resistance and helped Jews to escape. At this time Wojtyla studied in an ''underground'' seminary under the tutelage of Prince-Bishop Sapieha. On 1 November 1946, Wojtyla was ordained a priest.

After a short time in parish work, Wojtyla was sent to Rome, where he received his doctorate in theology. Having studied Thomism under Père Garrigou-Lagrange, Wojtyla did his thesis on faith in St. John of the Cross. Later, he completed a doctorate in philosophy at the Jagellonian University, with a dissertation on Max Scheler. Wojtyla's theses have both been published as full-length books. In addition, he is the author of numerous articles in theological and philosophical journals and of several plays and books of poetry. The latter were often published under the name ''Jawien.'' Consecrated auxiliary bishop of Cracow on 28 September 1958, he became archbishop of Cracow in 1964 and cardinal in 1967. As bishop, Wojtyla participated in the Second Vatican Council (see Vatican Council II) in 1962. Although his public interventions were few, Wojtyla is often credited with effecting the compromise that produced the Pastoral Constitution, ''The Church in the Modern World'' (*Gaudium et Spes*, 7 December 1965).

As POPE, John Paul II has distinguished himself by his efforts in ecumenism, especially with the Jewish community in Rome and with the orthodox. Frequent trips from the Vatican have brought him to more lands than any other pope in history. At the same time, world leaders have come to the Vatican in increasing numbers. Theologically, John Paul II has continued the restoration begun in Vatican II, although his approach has been controversial. He is the author of numerous ENCYCLICALS, in which he has focused on Christ, human dignity, and a variety of social issues. On 13 May 1981 John Paul II was the victim of an assassin's bullet after a general audience in the Vatican. He survived the attack and has gone on to become very active in securing peace throughout the world.

For further reference: Lord Longford, *Pope John Paul II: An Authorized Biography* (New York: William Morrow, 1982); George Hunston Williams, *The Mind of John Paul II: Origins of His Thought and Action* (New York: Seabury Press, 1981).

Loretta Devoy

JOSEPHISM. Empress Maria Theresa and her son and successor, Joseph II, inherited a policy of church–state relations developed by their predecessors in the Hapsburg lands. During the eighteenth century, however, this policy underwent radical transformation. The defeats Maria Theresa suffered at the hands of Frederick the Great convinced her of the need to reorganize her kingdom. To this end she recruited Prince Wenzel Anton von Kaunitz and other administrators imbued by the Enlightenment. The empress and her advisers sought to use the wealth and personnel of the church in this reorganization. When the papacy failed to second their projects, they took unilateral action. The civil authorities closely monitored monastic life, used the property of the suppressed Jesuits to improve education, and revamped theological faculties. Maria Theresa, because of her piety and sensitivity to local customs, moderated or delayed some of the reforms.

When Joseph II succeeded as sole ruler in 1780, all restraint disappeared. With Kaunitz he overhauled the state–church system. Joseph granted toleration to Protestants and Jews. He suppressed many monasteries and used their wealth to fund schools, parishes, charitable institutions, and pensions for the religious. Clerical salaries were standardized, begging was outlawed, and religious communities were forbidden to recruit candidates. In order to assure a clergy formed according to the mind of the state, Joseph closed all diocesan seminaries and founded general seminaries that all seminarians had to attend. The academic program aimed at producing good servants of the state, minions of the enlightened monarch.

To create a national church, Joseph eliminated foreign clergy from bishoprics in Hapsburg lands. He monitored the contacts the clergy had with Rome and regulated the publication of papal documents. At their installation bishops had to swear allegiance to the secular authorities. Diocesan boundaries were redrawn to conform to civil ones. Imperial oversight reached even into the parishes. Joseph ordered that all "unnecessary" church decorations be eliminated, for example, relics, statues, and votive offerings and lamps. The number and length of religious services were regulated, as were church music, the candles used at services, and processions. He standardized the shape of coffins and then ordered that cloth burial bags be used. Such regulations won him the sobriquet "Joseph the Sacristan."

The reform stirred much opposition. PIUS VI (1775–1799) traveled to Vienna in a vain attempt to modify the imperial program. Bishops complained of the encroachments on their authority. At times popular protest forced the cancellation of some measures. In Hungary and Belgium the protests sparked revolts. Joseph II was a pious Christian sincerely committed to the basic beliefs and practices of the Catholic Church. He regarded HERESY with contempt. He did not share the antireligious sentiments of many of his contemporaries and ministers. He practiced his faith regularly and frequented the sacraments. As an enlightened monarch, however, he saw in the church a resource for realizing his social reforms. Many of these measures did not long outlive him, but some affected the church in Austria into the twentieth century.

For further reference: Paul P. Bernard, *Jesuits and Jacobins. Enlightenment and Enlightened Despotism in Austria* (Urbana: University of Illinois Press, 1971); Paul P. Bernard, *Joseph II* (New York: Twayne, 1968); F. Maass, *Der Josephinismus*, 5 vols. (Vienna: Verlag Herold, 1951–1961).

Richard J. Kehoe

JULIUS I (337–352). Julius I, a native Roman, was elected POPE on 6 February 337. Some three months after his accession, on 22 May, the ancient world witnessed the death of its first Christian emperor, Constantine the Great. Julius I is remembered chiefly for his defense of the orthodox creed defined at the First Council of NICAEA (325) against the Arian (see Arianism) "restorations" that Constantine I seemed to favor during the decade before his death. The central event of Julius I's pontificate was the Council of Sardica, convened in 343 on the urging of Julius by the emperor Constans, youngest of Constantine's three sons. Conspicuously absent in both instances was the bishop of Rome, who sent representatives. At Nicaea in 325 the central dispute proved to be between the champion of orthodoxy, Anathasisus of Alexandria, and the tireless partisans of the doctrine of Arius who denied the divinity of Christ as "son of God." Aware that Athanasius had the support of the absent bishop of Rome, Constantine, in the end, ruled in favor of Athanasius. But, if supporting Athanasius against the Arians had pleased the emperor in 325, that had ceased to be his pleasure some ten years later, in 335/336, when he convened a regional council of African bishops at Tyre, where an Arian majority voted to condemn Athanasius for his "unscrupulous partiality." An imperial order of banishment quickly followed, again with the full force of law. The experience at Arles,

Nicaea, and Tyre made it clear that, in the end, great church controversies could not be settled by a majority vote of "representative" bishops. A single focused will had to be added. The remaining question was, Would it always be the will of a Christian emperor presiding in law enforcement, or might it increasingly become the will of a bishop of Rome?

Constantine the Great had hoped for ecclesiastical unity by the time of his death so as to secure a comparable unity in his tottering imperial state. But he left three ambitious sons as his successors: Constantine II (age twenty-one), Constantius II (twenty), and Constans (some three to five years younger)—each with a distinctive imperial will of his own. The Eastern bishops, foes of Rome's Pope JULIUS and of Athanasius, exiled bishop of Alexandria, became embroiled in the conflict. To settle their differences, it was agreed to assemble all the bishops at a site convenient to both East and West, namely, Sardica, in 343.

The council split in two unequal parts, a pro-Athanasian majority backed by Julius I and Constans remaining in Sardica, and an anti-Athanasian minority backed by Constantius II. In 350, Constans was murdered, and Constantius II remained as sole ruler of the empire. Julius, however, was left undisturbed in Rome, where he died 12 April 352 and was buried in the Callistus Cemetery. He was later pronounced a saint.

For further reference: E. Caspar, "Julius I. (337–352) und das Konzil von Sardica (343)," in *Geschichte des Papstums von den Anfängen bis zur Höhe der Weltherrschaft* (Tübingen: Verlag von J. C. B. Mohr, 1930–1933); J. T. Shotwell and L. P. Loomis, *The See of Peter* (New York: Columbia University Press, 1927).

Henry Paolucci

JULIUS II (1503–1513). Giuliano della Rovere was born of poor parents near Savona on 5 December 453. Through his uncle Francesco, who later became POPE SIXTUS IV (1471–1484), he was educated at Perugia by the FRANCIS-CANS and took orders. When his uncle became pontiff in 1471, he named Giuliano bishop of Carpentras and cardinal-priest of S. Pietro in Vincoli. In 1480–1482 Giuliano served as LEGATE in France. He was prominent during the reign of INNOCENT VIII (1484–1492), whose election he managed, but was opposed by ALEXANDER VI (1492–1503), during whose pontificate he fled to France. While in France, he met Charles VIII and encouraged him to attempt the conquest of Naples. He accompanied Charles on that campaign, but his attempt to have Alexander deposed failed. At the subsequent conclave of 1503 he was not chosen, but the next pope, PIUS III (1503), reigned only twenty-six days, and upon his death Giuliano was unanimously elected with the help of lavish bribes.

A strong and ruthless ruler, Julius forsook nepotism and personal aggrandizement as he sought to extend papal territory and power. He hoped to restore what had been lost under the Borgias and regain the papacy's independence in Italy. He quickly drove Cesare Borgia into exile and then, in 1503, in alliance with France and Germany, won the Romagna back from Venice. In his 1506 campaign, which he personally led, the pope took Perugia and Bologna. In 1508 he retook the remaining papal territory of Rimini and Faenza earlier seized by Venice. But, not wanting to weaken Venice, which was indispensable in any conflict with the Turks, he quickly made peace and turned his forces against France, which had become powerfully established in northern Italy. By 1511 he had taken Ferrara and other areas allied with France. Julius II's military exploits would be caricatured in Erasmus' "Praise of Folly" and described by the historian Guicciardini, who said that there was nothing of the priest about him but his garb and his name.

To retaliate against him, the French king Louis XII encouraged the Council of Pisa to depose the pontiff. That council decreed the pope's suspension. To counter this move, Julius called the fifth Lateran council (see Lateran Council V) in 1512. He had already formed the Holy League with Spain and Venice to defend the papacy, and the league was soon joined by Henry VIII of England. After an initial defeat of the league's forces at Ravenna, it eventually drove the French from Italy. Parma, Reggio-Emilia, and Piacenza were then added to an enlarged PAPAL STATE.

In ecclesiastical matters, he issued the dispensation for Henry VIII's marriage to Catherine of Aragon, published a bull declaring papal elections achieved by simony to be invalid, and founded the first sees in Latin America. At the Fifth Lateran Council he condemned both the Council of Pisa and the Pragmatic Sanction of Bourges. He was an important patron of artists, most notably Michelangelo, whose painting of the Sistine Chapel he commissioned, Raphael, and Bramante. He commissioned the last to begin plans for a new St. Peter's and, in 1506, assisted at the laying of the cornerstone. The cost would be defrayed by the sale of indulgences, which angered Protestant reformers in Germany. Known sometimes as "il terrible," despite his expensive wars and campaigns, Julius left a full papal treasury and at his death was considered a liberator of Italy from foreign rule.

For further reference: W. D'Ormesson, *The Papacy* (New York: Hawthorn Books, 1959); L. Pastor, *The History of the Popes from the Close of the Middle Ages* (London: Herder, 1953).

William Roberts

JULIUS III (1550–1555). Giovanni Maria Ciocchi del Monte was chosen after a long conclave marked by divisions between French and imperial factions. Born in Rome in 1487, the son of a jurist, he studied law at Perugia and Sienna before becoming chamberlain to JULIUS II (1503–1513), the patron whose name he took. In 1520 he became bishop of Pavia and served as governor of Rome under CLEMENT VII (1523–1534). He was later made cardinal-bishop of Palestrina. He was one of the copresidents who opened the council of TRENT in 1545 and was responsible for transferring the council to Bologna in 1547.

An able canon lawyer, Julius was also a Renaissance POPE (see Renaissance Papacy), excessive in his love of pleasures and his nepotism, with a fifteen-year-old protégé, for example, being made a cardinal. But he also was aware of the need for reform and, for this reason, reconvened the Council of Trent, which had been suspended, in 1551. It met for several sessions, some of which were attended by Protestant theologians from Germany. Henry II of France, however, refused to allow his nation's representation, and the council fell victim to the French–imperial conflict.

Following the defeat of his policies, Julius retired to his villa outside Rome, where he devoted himself to pleasurable diversions. He would try, but without success, to arrange a peace between Henry II and Charles V, and he carried out some further church reforms, limiting pluralism, reforming the CURIA, and reaffirming monastic discipline. He encouraged and confirmed the constitution of the newly formed SOCIETY OF JESUS in 1550 and in 1552 established the Collegium Germanicum for the training of German priests. His greatest success would be the short-lived return of England to Catholicism.

Julius was also a patron of the arts and humanism and made Michelangelo the architect of St. Peter's and the scholar Marcello Cervini, who was later to become pope MARCELLUS II (1555), the librarian of the Vatican and named the composer Palestrina choirmaster of the Cappella Giulia. Julius also built the church of S. Andrea to commemorate his own escape after being held hostage by the emperor during the Sack of Rome in 1527. Julius died in 1555, while the council was again suspended and unable, as he had hoped, to restore Germany to allegiance to the Holy See.

For further reference: W. D'Ormesson, *The Papacy* (New York, Hawthorn Books, 1959); P. Van Lierde, *The Holy See at Work* (New York; Hawthorn Books, 1962).

William Roberts

K

KULTURKAMPF. In 1871 an alliance of the Prussian–imperial monarchy and the liberal parties commenced a prolonged and bitter conflict with the Catholic Church in Prussia. A limited part of its legislation was federal in origin and scope. In March 1873 Rudolf Virchow, a left-liberal, would eulogize the contest as a *Kulturkampf* (struggle for civilization), a name that would also be accepted by the Catholics.

The liberals had always been dissatisfied with the Prussian state's union with the two major Christian churches and their control over the school system. In the early 1860s, however, they became involved in a seemingly irreconcilable struggle with the Prussian monarchy over the army's reorganization, suspecting that the Crown intended to promote Prussia's territorial ambitions rather than the cause of a German national state. After Prussia had expelled Austria from Germany in 1866, Otto von Bismarck, the first minister, assured the liberals that he wanted to create a national federal state under Prussia's leadership but in which the other monarchical states and a national Parliament would have some influence. At that point the liberals were already in a press war with the Catholic Church over the papal SYLLABUS OF ERRORS, which they deemed a categorical rejection of their principles. Their antagonism toward the Catholic Church, in particular the papacy, grew after the First Vatican Council (see Vatican I, Council) proclaimed the doctrine of papal INFALLIBILITY a dogma in July 1870.

When the new Reichstag and the Prussian Landtag met in early 1871, Bismarck and the Catholic leaders had an imperfect understanding of each other's major concerns. The Catholic leadership worried about their church's future in a national state governed by the Protestant Prussian monarchy in league with anti-Catholic or anticlerical liberals. Bismarck thought the church should feel more secure because of the Prussian monarchy's correct relations with it and the constitutional systems that existed in most German states. He was concerned that nothing should take place that would interfere with the Prussian monarchy's ability to govern the new Reich, a creation that many German states had not wanted and that Austria and France had unsuccessfully tried to prevent. So the German chancellor was disturbed when he found a new Catholic party, the CENTER PARTY, in the Reichstag in March 1871 and saw in its ranks some old opponents of Prussia's ambitions. He became distressed when the center moved that the government should add provisions in the new Constitution for religious freedom and called upon it to recover the city of Rome, which the Italian monarchy had seized in September 1870.

The *Kulturkampf* began when the Prussian government refused to remove from their teaching positions priests and teachers who had refused to accept the new dogma of papal infallibility. Next, the Federal Pulpit Act of 1871 prohibited clergymen from treating politics in their sermons. The Prussian School Inspection Law of 1872, a more severe blow to the church, transferred control over Prussian schools from the churches to the state. The Federal Anti-Jesuit Law of 1872 dissolved the Jesuit order (see Society of Jesus) and exposed its members to expulsion from their communities. This reflected the liberals' hostility toward the Jesuits but was also designed to prevent the Protestant conservatives from making a coalition with the center since the conservatives, knowing the widespread Protestant fear of the Jesuits, felt constrained to vote for the bill.

The worst attacks on the Catholic Church's freedom would come in the Prussian May Laws of 1873 and 1874. They required each bishop to report new pastoral appointments to the state, implying that the regime could veto them (*Anzeigepflicht*). They also stipulated that all candidates for the priesthood had to study at a state university for three years and pass a national test in three secular disciplines. They also provided that the state could declare an episcopal see vacant if its holder had not complied with a law and that the same would be true for a pastorate under the same circumstances. In 1875 the Prussian Landtag passed legislation denying salaries to all church officials in violation of the laws and dissolving the remaining nonnursing religious orders. Soon afterward, all of the Prussian bishops were in custody or in exile, many priests were in the same situation, and over 1,400 churches and chapels were closed.

Nonetheless, Bismarck had increasing doubts about the *Kulturkampf*'s value to the state. The Catholic Church had not given in to the regime, and the Center Party had grown significantly in Reichstag mandates. The chancellor was increasingly annoyed with the left-liberals, who wanted more places in the Prussian ministerial council and who insisted on a continuation of the Reich's free trade policies, even though they denied needed income to its government. He was also worried about the increase in votes for the Social Democrats. He was unwilling, however, to deal with Ludwig Windthorst, the center's able leader, who insisted that a peace settlement would have to be based on the status quo of 1871, preferring to negotiate with the conciliatory new POPE, LEO XIII (1878–1903). He also expected to be able to influence the center's policies on secular matters through Prussia's diplomatic channels with the Vatican. The pontiff himself hoped, in turn, that Bismarck would use his influence with other governments to secure the return of Rome to the papacy. Still, the Prussian–papal negotiations were at a standstill until the German and Spanish governments, at Bismarck's initiative, invited the pope to arbitrate their differences over the Caroline Islands in late 1885. Soon afterward Leo XIII agreed to final negotiations with Prussia in which the church's representative would be, on Bismarck's recommendation, Bishop George Kopp of Fulda and not Ludwig Windthorst and in which the church's representative agreed to accept the *Anzeigepflicht* and not raise the thorny school question.

The peace settlement of 1886–1887 between the Prussian state and the Catholic Church revised the May Laws of 1873 and 1874 in ways acceptable to the Prussian episcopate and restored peace in the life of the Prussian Catholic Church. There would be some additional revisions in 1891–1892, but there would be no withdrawal of the Prussian School Inspection Law of 1872, and most of the religious orders, including the Jesuits, would be barred from Germany till 1916–1917. Ironically, Leo XIII and Bismarck would be disappointed that their relationship would be brief and not fully productive. The pope was deeply disillusioned when he learned in 1887 that Germany had renewed its alliance with Austria-Hungary and Italy. Bismarck had already found that he could not direct the Center Party with the papacy's aid. At his urgent request Leo XIII had twice asked Ludwig Windthorst in the winter of 1886–1887 to provide his party's support for a major government army bill, but the center's leader insisted on keeping his party on an oppositional course till 1890. The center was the only middle-class party that did not capitulate to Bismarck after 1871.

For further reference: Margaret L. Anderson, *Windthorst, a Political Biography* (Oxford: Oxford University Press, 1982), Chapters 6, 7, 12, 13; Gordon A. Craig, *Germany 1866–1945* (Oxford: Oxford University Press, 1980), pp. 72–78; Thomas Nipperday, *Deutsche Geschichte, 1866–1918*, vol. 2 (Munich: C. H. Beck Verlag, 1992), b; *The New Catholic Encyclopedia*, vol. 8 (New York: McGraw-Hill, 1967), pp. 267–269.

John K. Zeender

L

LANDUS (913–914). Landus, or Lando, was born in the Sabine area northeast of Rome and was the son of a wealthy Lombard count, Taino. Of his pontificate, little is known. A benefaction dedicated to the memory of his father remains, inscribed in the cathedral of Sabina, S. Salvatore in Fornovo, and a flattering epitaph of Landus himself also exists but contains few details of his reign. Most likely, Landus was a candidate put forward with the approval of the powerful Theophylact family. The ambitious and energetic Senatrix Theodora of this family led an oligarchy that effectively controlled Rome and the affairs of the papacy at this time.

For further reference: J. Lebreton and J. Zeiller, *A History of the Primitive Church* (New York Burns, Oates and Washbourne, 1948); H. K. Mann, *The Lives of the Popes in the Early Middle Ages* (London: K. Paul, 1902–1932).

William Roberts

LATERAN ACCORDS. These were three pacts signed between the Holy See and the government of Italy on 11 February 1929. They consisted of the Conciliation Treaty, the CONCORDAT, and the Financial Convention. The Lateran Accords became a part of the 1948 Constitution of the Italian Republic, but the concordat was revised in 1984. These accords ended the troublesome ROMAN QUESTION which had poisoned church–state relations since the unification of Italy at the expense of the papacy. However, even before MUSSOLINI came to power in 1922, both the kingdom of Italy and the Holy See were disposed to reach an accommodation. The victory and swift consolidation of FASCISM accelerated the process. Mussolini saw in peace with the church a means of strengthening his regime, while Pope PIUS XI welcomed the opportunity of obtaining guarantees for the free expression of Catholicism. The Popular Party was a casualty of the reconciliation.

Secret negotiations for the pacts began in August 1926, with Francesco Pacelli, legal consultant to the Holy See and brother of Msgr. Eugenio Pacelli (then apostolic NUNCIO to Germany and later Pope PIUS XII), representing the papacy and Domenico Barone, councillor of state, representing the Italian government. The negotiations moved slowly because of numerous disagreements, such as the status of Catholic youth organizations in a fascist regime and sovereignty over Villa Doria Pamphili, territory behind the Janiculum. Eventually, the disagreements were resolved through compromises.

Under the Conciliation Treaty Article I, Italy reaffirmed "the Catholic, Apostolic and Roman faith [as] the only religion of the state." VATICAN CITY, an area of about 110 acres, was established as a sovereign and independent state with the pope as sole ruler. The new state was to be "neutral and inviolable" but with all the characteristics and powers of secular sovereign states. The Holy See recognized the kingdom of Italy, with Rome as its capital, and the Roman question was declared settled. Finally, the treaty recognized the right of the Holy See to communicate freely with the clergy and laity of the Catholic community, both at home and abroad.

The concordat guaranteed to the church in Italy the free exercise of spiritual power, public worship, and ecclesiastical jurisdiction. Ecclesiastics in the employ of the state were required to have the permission of their respective bishops. All bishops were required to swear loyalty to the head of state. Canonical marriages were to be accorded civil validity. Religious instruction was to be provided in state elementary and secondary schools by teachers who had the approval of ecclesiastical authorities. Italian Catholic Action and its auxiliary organizations were recognized by the state, but such organizations, as well as the religious, were forbidden to engage in the activities of political parties.

The Financial Convention, designed to provide partial compensation for the papal territories annexed by Italy during the process of unification, pledged the Holy See 750 million lire in cash and 1 billion lire in government bonds.

The Lateran Accords enhanced the prestige of Mussolini but did not end disputes between church and state. The most serious conflict occurred in 1931 concerning Italian Catholic Action. Negotiations for a modification of the concordat began in 1975 and were completed in 1984. The revised concordat reaffirmed that church and state, each in its own sphere, were sovereign and independent. However, a protocol stated that "the principle of the Catholic religion as the sole religion of the Italian State, originally reaffirmed by the Lateran Pacts, is considered to be no longer in force." Other modifications in the concordat made religious instruction in the state schools a matter of choice and altered the procedure whereby the government provided financing for the clergy and religious institutions. The revised concordat was signed on 18 February 1984 by Premier Bettino Craxi for Italy and Cardinal Agostino Casaroli for the Holy See.

For further reference: Daniel Binchy, *Church and State in Fascist Italy* (New York: Oxford University Press, 1941); Franscesco Margiotto Broglio, *Italia e Santa Sede dalla grande guerra alla conciliazione* (Bari: Laterza, 1966); Maria Elisabetta de Franciscis, *Italy and the Vatican: The 1984 Concordat between Church and State* (New York: Peter Lang, 1989).

Elisa A. Carrillo

LATERAN COUNCIL I (1123). In the middle of the eleventh century a reform movement emerged to eradicate the evils in the church. Inspired by the monastic reform of Cluny, the movement captured the See of Rome when Emperor Henry III appointed a series of reform POPES beginning with Pope CLEMENT II (1046–1047). With imperial support these popes fought to rid the church of the scourges of simony and clerical concubinage. Following the death of Henry III, the movement claimed autonomy with the election of Pope STEPHEN IX (1057–1058). The reformers sought to reclaim the freedom of ecclesiastical elections. Hilderbrand, a member of the CURIA since the beginning of the reform, was elected pope as GREGORY VII (1073–1085) and spearheaded the movement.

Emperor Henry IV clashed with Gregory VII over the issue of freedom in ecclesiastical elections. If deprived of the right of investiture, the emperor would lose control of the church in the empire and much of his authority. For 50 years the Investiture Controversy embroiled relations between the papacy and the empire. Succeeding popes tried to resolve this controversy without success. Finally, Pope CALLISTUS II (1119–1124) reached a compromise with Emperor Henry V enshrined in the Concordat of WORMS (23 September 1122), by which the emperor renounced investiture with ring and staff but retained the right to investiture with the "regalia" (see Investure Controversy). Henry granted free canonical election and consecration, although elections were to take place in his or his representative's presence.

Callistus II summoned a council to ratify the concordat. Several hundred prelates and abbots gathered in Rome at the Lateran in March–April 1123 and approved the concordat. They also treated other issues, for example, simony, clerical marriage, the Crusades, and the Truce of God. This synod became known as the First Lateran Council.

For further reference: Raymonde Foreville, *Latran I. II. III. et Latran IV* (Paris: Ed. de l'Orante, 1965); I. S. Robinson, *The Papacy 1073–1198. Continuity and Innovation* (New York: Cambridge University Press, 1990).

Richard J. Kehoe

LATERAN COUNCIL II (1139). Pope HONORIUS II (1124–1130) died on the night of 13–14 February 1130. With the support of the Frangipani clan, a few cardinals immediately elected INNOCENT II (1130–1143). Another faction led by Cardinal Peter Pierleoni gathered a majority of the cardinals and elected Pierleoni as ANACLETUS II (1130–1138), who attracted support in Rome, in some Italian cities, and from Roger II of Sicily. Innocent, forced to flee, found allies in France, England, and Germany. His success was largely due to the support and eloquence of St. Bernard of Clairvaux. The death of Anacletus in 1138 opened the way to end the SCHISM. His successor, VICTOR IV (1138), renounced his title almost immediately, submitting to Innocent, who returned to Rome. Innocent summoned a synod to deal with the effects of the schism. More than 500 prelates gathered in the Lateran in April 1139. Innocent dealt harshly with the followers of his dead rival, deposing them and ordering them to surrender their episcopal rings and croziers. The synod not only forbade clerical marriages but declared them invalid. This council became known as the Second Lateran Council.

For further reference: Raymonde Foreville, *Latran I. II. III. et Latran IV* (Paris: Ed. de l'Orante, 1965; I. S. Robinson, *The Papacy 1073–1198. Continuity and Innovation* (New York: Cambridge University Press, 1990).

Richard J. Kehoe

LATERAN COUNCIL III (1179). The stormy papal conclave of 7 September 1159 produced a double election. A majority of the cardinals voted for Roland Bandinelli, who took the name of ALEXANDER III (1159–1181). A minority cast ballots for Octavian of Monticello, who styled himself VICTOR IV. Alexander's partisans opposed the designs of Emperor Frederick I to extend imperial claims in Italy, while Victor's supporters generally supported these aspirations. The emperor convened a Council at Pavia (5–11 February 1160), which declared for Victor. Alexander rejected the decision, claiming the Roman See could be judged by no one. Except for Germany and northern Italy most of Christendom recognized Alexander. For seventeen years Alexander and Frederick sought to resolve the impasse. Reconciliation finally occurred in Venice in July 1177, when Alexander withdrew his EXCOMMUNICATION of Frederick, and the emperor renounced the ANTIPOPE. The POPE summoned a COUNCIL at Rome for March 1179 to heal the effects of the SCHISM. The council decreed that papal elections be determined by a two-thirds majority of the cardinals in the conclave. It also nullified the actions of the antipopes and their ordinations. This synod became known as the Third Lateran Council.

For further reference: Marshall W. Baldwin, *Alexander III and the Twelfth Century* (New York: Newman Press, 1968), pp. 186–207; Raymonde Foreville, *Latran I. II. III. et Latran IV* (Paris: Ed. de l'Orante, 1965); I. S. Robinson, *The Papacy 1073–1198: Continuity and Innovation* (New York: Cambridge University Press, 1990).

Richard J. Kehoe

LATERAN COUNCIL IV (1215). INNOCENT III (1198–1216) succeeded his uncle, CELESTINE III (1191–1198), as POPE on 8 January 1198, continuing the Gregorian reform movement. During his pontificate Innocent reorganized the CURIA and PAPAL STATES, reanimated the crusading ideal, and called for the extirpation of HERESY and the reform of both clergy and laity. His programs were not always realized, as the tragedies of the Fourth Crusade and the crusade against the ALBIGENSES attest. Innocent sought to rally Christendom behind him by means of a general COUNCIL. More than 400 bishops, 800 abbots and priors, and the representatives of secular rulers answered his call to gather in Rome in November 1215 for the greatest of the medieval councils, the Fourth Lateran Council. In three sessions the council approved 70 decrees, which can be considered as the legislative summary of the pontificate of Innocent III.

The council's decrees open with a profession of faith to counter the errors of the Albigenses and Waldenses. It contains the term "transubstantiation," which became the traditional understanding of the Eucharistic change. The council called for a new crusade for June 1217. Provisions for provincial councils and clerical discipline sought to reform the clergy. Legislation concerning matrimony and the annual reception of penance and Holy Communion looked to the spiritual life of the faithful. Regulations for distinctive dress for both Jews and Muslims aimed at limiting social contacts with these groups. The impact of the council on the church is seen in the flurry of synods it spawned and the adoption of 59 of the council's decrees into the church's CANON LAW.

For further reference: Raymonde Foreville, *Latran I. II. III. et Latran IV* (Paris: Ed. de l'Orante, 1965); W. Ulmann, *A Short History of the Papacy in the Middle Ages* (London: Methuen, 1972).

Richard J. Kehoe

LATERAN COUNCIL V (1512–1517). In response to the COUNCIL assembled by Louis XII of France in Pisa (1511), Pope JULIUS II (1503–1513) convoked a council in Rome on 10 May 1512. Julius II struggled to nullify the effects of Pisa and secure the recognition of the Lateran Council by the European states. With the danger of SCHISM averted, his successor, Pope LEO X (1513–1521), turned the attention of the council to the reform of the church. Egidio of Viterbo, the general of the Augustinians, had sounded the call for reform in the opening address of the council. Tommaso Giustiniani and Vincenzo Quirini detailed areas needing reform, for example, the papacy's preoccupation with secular, rather than spiritual, matters, the benefice system, and clerical education and discipline. Unfortunately, the reform decrees of the council failed to eliminate these abuses. It limited pluralists to no more than four incompatible benefices and preserved the papal right to dispense from this regulation. In effect, it institutionalized the abuse.

Leo negotiated the CONCORDAT of Bologna (1516), which gave the French king the right to nominate all the bishops (93) and most of the abbots and priors (500) in France. The council included this agreement in its legislation and thus gave the Gallican church a constitutional base. The council ended on 12 March 1517, having failed to realize the reform that Martin Luther called for just six months later.

For further reference: O. de la Brosse et al., *Latran V et Trent* (Paris: Ed. de l'Orante, 1975); H. Jedin, *The History of the Council of Trent*, vol. 1, trans. E. Graf (London: T. Nelson and Son, 1957), pp. 127–138; N. H. Minnich, *The Fifth Lateran Council. Studies on Its Membership Diplomacy and Proposals for Reform* (Brookfield, VT: Ashgate, 1993).

Richard J. Kehoe

LAWRENCE/LAURENTIUS, ANTIPOPE (498/499, 501–506). The fifth century drew to a close with both church and empire in turmoil. In 482, the Byzantine emperor Zeno (474–491) issued an edict, *Henotikon*, which opposed CHALCEDON. It recognized the emperor as the divinely appointed spokesman for Christ on earth. With the assistance of Acasius, patriarch of Constantinople, Zeno attempted to force this imperial decree on the church and empire, creating a new SCHISM. The elevation of Lawrence to the papacy was a direct result of the Acacian schism. Lawrence, desiring accommodation with the empire, was prepared to accept a modified version of the *Henotikon*. Pope SYMMACHUS (498–514), consecrated simultaneously, championed Leonine-Gelasian principles that recognized the authority of the bishop of Rome as the supreme head of Christendom. Both sides appealed to the Gothic king, Theodoric (493–526).

Theodoric selected Symmachus as the "real" pope since he had been elected first and had the support of the Roman clergy. Although Lawrence reluctantly accepted the decision of the king, antagonism between the two sides lingered. To his credit, within months of the election, Lawrence affixed his signature to a new statute regulating future papal elections. Henceforth, the papal successor received automatic acceptance if chosen unanimously; otherwise, the pontificate devolved upon the person who received the majority of votes.

The rivalry between the two sides reemerged within three years. In 501, Festus, a Roman senator and the most vocal of Lawrence's supporters, leveled charges against Symmachus that included celebrating Easter on the wrong day, misuse of church funds and property, and the selling of church offices. Symmachus retreated to St. Peter's, where he remained until 505. The schism reached its peak when Lawrence took up residence in the Lateran and placed his portrait alongside those of past bishops of Rome. In 505, Theodoric, seeking to enhance his own power, removed Lawrence from the papacy, definitively declared for Symmachus, and ordered Lawrence to retire to Festus' estate. Lawrence ultimately succumbed to the effects of a fast in which he had engaged as a sign of protest over the king's decision.

For further reference: H. K. Mann, *The Lives of the Popes in the Early Middle Ages* (London: K. Paul, 1902–1932); Walter Ullman, *A Short History of the Papacy in the Middle Ages* (London: Methuen, 1972).

John C. Horgan

LAZARISTS. SEE CONGREGATION OF THE MISSION.

LEGATES, PAPAL. As early as the fourth century, POPES appointed individuals to serve as personal representatives to particular churches, governments, or other assemblies throughout the world. These representatives, known as "legates," have the responsibility to gather information for the Roman pontiff and to handle those church concerns within their competence. The Council of Arles (314) was the first occasion where papal representation by "legates" is clearly in evidence. Such representatives were also present at the COUNCILS of NICAEA (325) and EPHESUS (431). Their principal responsibility was "to preside" at these councils, whether particular or general, in the name of, and with the same faculties as, the pope who appointed them. Theirs was exclusively an ecclesiastical role, with explicit powers delegated to them by the pope. The concept of "vicars apostolic" also developed around this time with the Roman pontiffs' dispatching representatives to various dioceses and provinces to watch over the faithful living there, to maintain peace, to correct abuses in doctrine, and to settle conflicts among bishops. Once again, the vicars played a religious role within a region.

In 458, Pope LEO I (440–461) began sending envoys called *apocrisarii* to the imperial court at Constantinople. These papal legates served many functions, ranging from that of mere papal messenger gathering information about the court for the Roman pontiff, to that of personal papal representative, conveying papal desires and intentions to the emperor. From the fifth through the eighth centuries, therefore, the role of the papal legate developed and expanded from one of representing the pope exclusively at ecclesial gatherings to one that included some involvement in temporal affairs. As the influence of papal representatives became more significant in both ecclesiastical and civil society from the ninth through the eleventh centuries, the church reserved such appointments to cardinals.

Pope GREGORY VII (1075–1085), in an effort to carry out his reforms and to vindicate the prestige of the papacy, continued to utilize and expand the services of papal legates in both the church and civil arena. For the next six centuries, a system of organized papal diplomacy steadily developed. One year before he died, Pope GREGORY XIII (1572–1585) strengthened this diplomatic system by establishing a series of strict regulations to be followed in the appointment of papal legates and in the duties they were to perform. Pope Gregory XIII differentiated roles and responsibilities among the individuals who represented him before the officials of church and state.

From the mid-seventeenth century forward there appeared to be a gradual decline in the prestige attached to the role of papal legate both within and outside the church. Although representatives of the Roman pontiff continued to be appointed and dispatched throughout the remote provinces of the world, their significance seemed to diminish until after WORLD WAR I. In the years between the world wars, papal diplomacy witnessed a revival in importance. The role of the papal legate has continued to be an important one, not only within the church but among nations as well. The growing significance attached to the position, however, became a cause for concern among some of the church's bishops who felt that, despite protests to the contrary, the presence of a papal legate in their territories diminished their own authority. Some papal legates were also accused of meddling in political affairs.

In response to these concerns, the fathers of VATICAN COUNCIL II (1962–1965) addressed the role of the papal legate in their decree on the Bishops' Pastoral Office in the Church, *Christus Dominus* (28 October 1965). In article 9 of that document they called for the office of legates of the Roman pontiff to be more precisely determined. The bishops also asked that legates of the Roman pontiff be drawn more widely from the various geographical areas of the church so that its universal character might become more evident (article 10).

In 1969, Pope PAUL VI (1963–1978) responded to the concerns of the council fathers with a *motu proprio* letter entitled *Sollicitudo omnium Ecclesiarum* (24 June 1969). In it, Pope Paul VI sustained the four main classifications of papal legation traditionally employed in the church: the APOSTOLIC DELEGATE; the NUNCIO; the pronuncio; and the internuncio. Following the recommendations of Vatican II and the *motu proprio* of Paul VI, the 1983 Code of *CANON LAW* devoted five of its canons, 362 through 366 inclusive, to the role and responsibilities of papal legates. Canon 362 affirms the right of the pope to nominate and employ legates, while canon 363 states, ''To legates of the Roman Pontiff is entrusted the responsibility of representing him in a stable manner to particular churches and also to states and public authorities to which they are sent.'' The code indicates in canon 364 that the principal obligation of a papal legate is ''to work so that day by day the bonds of unity which exist between the Apostolic See and the particular churches become stronger and more efficacious.''

The canon then describes the legate's areas of competence on behalf of the Roman pontiff and Apostolic See to include information gathering, providing assistance to local bishops without prejudice to their authority, fostering close relations between the Vatican and conferences of bishops, presenting the names of potential bishops and reviewing their histories, promoting peace and harmony among people and churches, protecting the church's mission, and, finally, fulfilling any mandates given him by the pope.

If the papal legate also has a responsibility toward civil governments, canon 365 states that he must foster relations with the nation concerned, deal with issues of conflict between church and state, and keep local bishops informed regarding the progress of these matters. According to canon 366, a papal legate ceases in office when he has fulfilled his mandate from the pope, when he has been recalled, or when his resignation has been accepted by the pope.

The four ranks of papal legate can be described as follows:

1. The apostolic delegate is a prelate, usually an archbishop, appointed by the pope as his representative to the church of a region. Although in the present day there will obviously be some interaction with national governments or civil officials, the apos-

tolic delegate has no formal diplomatic status. Hence, the authority and responsibilities exercised by the apostolic delegate are purely ecclesiastical and religious in nature. He would be considered the pope's "internal representative."

2. The nuncio, in addition to the internal, ecclesiastical duties performed by the apostolic delegate, has the added distinction of being a member of the diplomatic community before a government with the rank of ambassador. Usually an archbishop, the nuncio serves as dean of the diplomatic corps according to the protocol established at the Congress of VIENNA in 1815. He exercises certain external, civil responsibilities in the region where he serves on behalf of the pope and for the good of the local church.

3. The pronuncio is likewise a prelate. He performs all the responsibilities of the apostolic nuncio and possesses the same rights and privileges within a region except that he does not serve as dean of the diplomatic corps.

4. The internuncio performs functions similar to the other papal legates described. The apostolic internuncio is a member of the diplomatic corps but enjoys no special diplomatic status before his peers. Also a prelate, he is considered to be an extraordinary envoy on behalf of the Roman pontiff.

It should be noted that, regardless of rank or diplomatic status, the papal legate serves the spiritual purposes of the church and represents the pope in virtue of the spiritual and pastoral mission of ecclesiastical governance with which he has been entrusted.

For further reference: Walter M. Abbott, ed., *The Documents of Vatican II* (New York: Herder and Herder, 1966); Lamberto de Echeverria, "The Popes' Representatives" in *The Roman Curia and the Communion of Churches*, ed. P. Huizing and Knut Walf (New York: Seabury Press, 1979), pp. 56–63; Isidoro Martin, "The Church's Relations with Foreign Governments," in *Structures of the Church*, ed. Teodoro Jimenez Urresti (New York: Herder and Herder, 1970), pp. 94–103; Mario Oliveri, *The Representatives: The Real Nature and Function of Papal Legates* (Gerrards Cross: Van Duren, 1981); Gino Paro, *The Right of Papal Legation* (Washington, DC: Catholic University of America Press, 1947); Paul VI, *motu proprio Sollicitudo omnium Ecclesiarum*, 24 June 1969, *Acta Apostolicae Sedis* 61 (1969): 473–484.

David M. O'Connell

LEGATIONS. The Legations were the northern provinces of the PAPAL STATES, so-called from the LEGATES sent from Rome to govern them. They had first come under papal rule after the collapse of Byzantine authority there in the eighth century, and though at times over the following centuries they came temporarily under other rulers, papal authority was always reestablished eventually. In 1797, Napoleon annexed them, first to his newly created CISALPINE REPUBLIC and later to his kingdom of Italy. After the fall of Napoleon, the papacy secured their return at the Congress of VIENNA. However, two decades of French rule had accustomed the people to efficient secular government, and there was little enthusiasm for a return to the inefficient ecclesiastical papal administration. The papal secretary of state, Cardinal CONSALVI, saw the potential danger and introduced reforms intended to reconcile the legations to papal rule, but reactionaries in the papal government sabotaged his plans.

Discontent with the unreformed papal government grew rapidly, to break out in open revolution in February 1831. Only Austrian military intervention saved the papal regime, and Austrian forces occupied the legations down to 1838 to prevent another uprising. During these years the legations became a stronghold of the *Risorgimento* and took a leading role in the revolutions of 1848 and 1859. In 1860 they became part of the united Italian state, where they now make up the region of Emilia-Romagna.

For further reference: Moritz Brosch, *Geschichte des Kirchenstaats*, 2 vols. (Gotha: Herder, 1882); E. E. Y. Hales, *Revolution and Papacy* (Garden City, NY: Hanover House, 1960).

Alan J. Reinerman

LEO I (440–461). The Tuscan deacon Leo exerted great influence on his predecessors CELESTINE I (422–432) and SIXTUS III (432–440). He was elected POPE in 440 while in Gaul on a diplomatic mission for the imperial court. He was a dominant figure in his world both ecclesiastically and politically at a time when both the church and the Roman empire were in turmoil. He is known for his confrontations with Attila the Hun and with Gaiseric, leader of the Vandals; the former he apparently induced to withdraw during his pillage of Italy in 452; they sacked Rome, but Leo persuaded him not to ravage the city and its inhabitants.

Leo labored to strengthen the papacy, which he believed descended from PETER. He centralized papal authority and claimed jurisdiction over the entire Western church. His tenure stands out as a watershed in the development of the doctrine of papal primacy. He opposed many HERESIES. Manichaeism, Pelagianism, and Priscillianism were recurring problems throughout the early fifth century; Nestorianism and Eutychianism, the latter leading to Monophysitism, were more intense during his pontificate. Eutyches, who was accused of teaching that Christ had only one divine nature, created serious problems. In 449 Leo sent Flavian, the bishop of Constantinople, an exposition called the *Tome*, which condemned Eutyches and explained the doctrine of the two natures in the one person of Christ.

When Emperor Theodosius II called a COUNCIL at Ephesus in August 449, Leo sent three delegates with the *Tome* to represent his position. The council rejected Leo's position and restored Eutyches to good standing. Leo refused to endorse this council. A new emperor, Marcian, convened a council in 451 at Chalcedon, and Leo's *Tome* was accepted by the assembled bishops as the voice of Peter. Leo supported the doctrinal assertions of this council and fought to have them accepted during the remainder of his tenure. But he delayed his endorsement for two years and even then rejected as invalid canon 28, which reaffirmed the decree of the Council of CONSTANTINOPLE I (381), giving

Rome and Constantinople equal prerogatives because they both possessed imperial power.

Leo was not a brilliant or original theologian, but he possessed the power to bring material together and express it clearly. This is evident in the *Tome* and in his extant writings (96 sermons and more than 120 letters), which offer rich witness to the Christian life and the liturgical practice of his time. Leo's episcopacy also took giant strides toward the more universal primacy that developed during the medieval papacy. He and GREGORY I (590–604) are the only two popes to be called "the Great." He was later proclaimed a saint.

For further reference: A. Chavasse, ed., *Tractatus (Sermones)*, Corpus Christianorum, Series Latina (1957), pp. 138–138A; T. G. Jalland, *The Life and Times of St. Leo the Great* (London: SPCK; New York: Macmillan, 1941); E. Schwartz, ed., *Acta Conciliorum Oecumenicorum*, vol. 2 (Strasbourg, 1932), p. 4; N. P. Tanner, ed., *Decrees of the Ecumenical Councils*, vol. 1 (London: Sheed and Ward; Washington, DC: Georgetown University Press, 1990), pp. 99–100 (canon 28); W. Ullman, "Leo I and the Theme of Papal Primacy," *Journal of Theological Studies*, n.s. 11 (1960): 25–51.

Gerard H. Ettlinger

LEO II (682–683). Leo's consecration was delayed by the Byzantine emperor Constantine IV (668–685) until the Sixth General COUNCIL (see Constantinople III, Council of) completed its deliberations regarding the monothelite HERESY and freed the church from obtaining imperial confirmation of papal elections. Leo confirmed the decrees of the Sixth Council, which condemned the monothelite heresy, a doctrine that recognized the two natures of Christ within a single will. Leo also censured POPE HONORIUS I (625–638) for undermining the faith of the church for failing to denounce the heresy at an earlier date. The pope actively urged the bishops in the West to accept the recommendations of the council. Leo's reign opened a period of cooperative and friendly relations between Rome and Constantinople. Proclaimed a saint, his feast date is celebrated on 3 July.

For further reference: Joseph S. Brusher, *Popes through the Ages* (Princeton: D. Van Nostrand, 1964); H. K. Mann, *The Lives of the Popes in the Early Middle Ages* (London: K. Paul, 1902–1932).

John C. Horgan

LEO III (795–816). Leo III, an Italian of modest southern stock, was elected POPE in December 795. He brought to a culmination the scheme of his aristocratic predecessor, ADRIAN I (772–795) to unite all the Germanic tribes under the sway of a single regime that, though Germanic, could function in the West with the authority that Roman emperors earlier enjoyed.

The Roman aristocracy was hostile to him, and, fearing their hostility, he early recognized the "inconvenience" of having to deal with diverse Germanic tribes without an imperial protector. Leo soon began to treat Charlemagne as if he were an emperor, as Adrian I had indeed done, after his vision of a providential transformation of Charlemagne into another Constantine the Great. Leo reaffirmed Charlemagne's status as a Roman *patricius*, sending him the traditional standard of that office, as well as the keys of St. Peter's tomb. Still, when Leo asked that special emissaries be sent to witness the Roman citizenry's swearing of an oath of loyalty to the Frankish king, Charlemagne frowned on the idea. He said that customary Germanic "fellowship law" sufficed as authorization for his actions.

On 26 December 795, Leo was attacked by thugs, acting for relatives of Adrian, who attempted to tear out his eyes and tongue and disqualify him from serving as pope. Leo appealed in vain for help from the Frankish king Winichis of Spoleto. He next sent an emissary across the Alps to Charlemagne's court, but again, no help came. Finally, the pope himself took flight to Paderborn to make a direct plea but found agents of his Roman foes already present, demanding a royal trial.

Fortunately, Charlemagne's counselor, Alcuin, intervened to insist that no one, not even the king of the Franks, was qualified to sit in judgment on a pope. Leo and Charlemagne then conferred privately. Subsequently, Leo was sent back to Rome with an escort of Frankish prelates. Late in 800, Charlemagne abruptly appeared in Italy, determined to hear the charges against Leo for himself. Welcoming Charlemagne's presence, Leo eagerly purged himself of the charges against him with a solemn oath. His accusers were condemned to death, but Leo pleaded for mercy in St. Peter's basilica on 23 December 800.

Two days later, on Christmas Day, while he and Charlemagne were kneeling in prayer at the altar, Leo boldly placed an imperial crown on the Frankish king's head. Charlemagne was then "enthroned and anointed with holy oil, and worshipped by the pope." The overall impression had been that such an act could have occurred only in Rome in St. Peter's and, by grace of God, only as the prerogative of the pope. The event marked the refounding of the Christian Roman empire on a new ethnic basis. Charlemagne's crowning as emperor put a strain on what had been improving relations with the Eastern court. Leo tried to ease the strain theologically in 809, when he confirmed the correctness of the *filioque* clause in the orthodox Nicene Creed, while at the same time urging that the creed not be sung in the public liturgy. Charlemagne died in 814; and once again, as after the death of Constantine the Great, there was a division of authority. Leo died shortly afterward, on 12 June 816.

For further reference: E. Caspar, *Das Papstums unter fränkische Herrschafft* (Darmstadt: Wissenschaftliche, 1956); T. J. Jalland, *The Church and the Papacy* (London: SPCK, 1944).

Henry Paolucci

LEO IV (847–855). Leo Radoaldi, a pious priest living a monkish life, was chosen POPE as Leo IV on 19 April 847. The approval of the emperor Lothair was, however, withheld, so that his consecration was delayed some six weeks and finally completed without imperial consent. He seemed a suitable choice to succeed SERGIUS II (844–847) after the debacle of the previous pontificate, which had ended with a menacing army of Muslims at the gates of Rome. Despairing of imperial help, Leo IV ordered reinforcement of the old walls and the construction of new towers at key points. After the Saracens were temporarily driven off by Lothair's son Louis, Leo extended the circle of Rome's walls around the entire Vatican hill, including St. Peter's and St. Paul's. In his honor the new enclosure of safety came to be called the ''LEONINE CITY.''

After 850, when Lothair's son Louis became emperor, crowned and anointed by Leo IV at Eastertime in Rome, the papacy acted with increasing self-confidence. To reaffirm papal authority, Leo firmly intervened to discipline high prelates in the Eastern church, like Ignatius, patriarch of Constantinople. He died on 17 July 855, being much revered and honored thereafter in popular legend. In later centuries, a conviction appears to have risen that in 855 a woman was secretly made pope commonly called Pope JOAN.

For further reference: J. N. D. Kelly, *The Oxford Dictionary of Popes* (Oxford: Oxford University Press, 1986); H. K. Mann, *The Lives of the Popes in the Early Middle Ages* (London: K. Paul, 1902–1932).

Henry Paolucci

LEO V (903). This Italian-born POPE another in a long line of medieval popes whose reigns were cut short due to political infighting. A simple priest, Leo appears to have been a compromise choice between the clergy and nobility of Rome. His only action during his one-month pontificate was to issue a bull granting tax exemptions to Bologna and its environs. Deposed and imprisoned by a cardinal-priest named Christopher, who subsequently claimed the papacy and ruled as an ANTIPOPE until 904, Leo met his death in prison, possibly at the hands of a successor, SERGIUS III (904–911).

For further reference: J. N. D. Kelly, *The Oxford Dictionary of Popes* (Oxford: Oxford University Press, 1986); *Liber Pontificalis* (Paris, 1886–1892); H. K. Mann, *The Lives of the Popes in the Early Middle Ages* (London: K. Paul, 1902–1932).

John C. Horgan

LEO VI (928). In 928 this Roman nobleman was already an elderly man when elected to succeed JOHN X (914–928) as POPE Leo VI. Leo owed his election to Marouzia, head of the oligarchic family of Theophylact, who, under the titles *senatrix* and *patricia*, was, with her second husband, Guido, the marquis of Tuscany, the real ruler of Rome. Leo was considered an interim pontiff until Marouzia's son John was of age to succeed to the papal throne. Little is known of Leo's reign, save for a single surviving letter sent to the bishops of Croatia and Dalmatia instructing them to be content with their territorial boundaries and to be obedient to their archbishop, John of Spalato. In most matters Leo was dependent on Marouzia's group.

For further reference: P. Hughes, *The History of the Church* (New York: Sheed and Ward, 1955); H. K. Mann, *The Lives of the Popes in the Early Middle Ages* (London: K. Paul, 1902–1932).

William Roberts

LEO VII (936–939). Leo, the successor to JOHN XI (931–935/936), owed his elevation to Alberic II, prince of Rome, who was absolute ruler of the city from 932 to 954. Leo's monastic background may have appealed to Alberic, who supported monastic reform. Restricted by Alberic to purely ecclesiastical functions, Leo was able to pursue this reformism without restriction and at the beginning of his reign invited Odo of Cluny to Rome to negotiate a peace between Alberic and King Hugh of Italy. While there, Odo, who sought to end lay control over monasteries, was entrusted with the reform of Rome's religious houses and those of the surrounding area, beginning with St. Paul's basilica. At the same time Leo renewed the privileges of the restored abbey of Subiaco, some distance from Rome, which was the site of the grotto of St. Benedict, and also renewed the privileges that had been granted to the abbeys of Cluny and Déols by his predecessor. Similar honors were granted to the revived abbey of Gorze, near Metz, which was the center of a different reforming movement in Lorraine.

For further reference: H. K. Mann, *The Lives of the Popes in the Early Middle Ages* (London: K. Paul, 1902–1932); J. R. Palanque, *The Church in the Christian Roman Empire* (New York: Macmillan, 1953).

William Roberts

LEO VIII (963–965). Pope Leo VIII was chosen after a Roman synod in December 963 deposed JOHN XII (955–964). Favorable to the imperial house and an official of the Lateran, this layman was quickly installed with the lower orders in one day, after which he was consecrated by the bishops of Ostia, Porto, and Albano. Most likely Leo swore an oath of fealty to Otto before the ceremony, the so-called Ottonian privilege.

In Rome neither Otto nor Leo was popular, and in January 964 John instigated a revolt that was suppressed by imperial troops. Leo, seeking to avoid further violence, persuaded Otto to release the hostages taken and to accept an oath of loyalty from the Romans. However, as soon as the emperor and his forces left the city, disturbances erupted, forcing Leo to seek refuge with Otto as John returned. At a synod held in February in St. Peter's, John excommunicated (see Excommunication) Leo and deposed him. Following the death of John, the Romans petitioned the emperor to allow the election of the cardinal-deacon Benedict. Although Otto refused, the Romans elected and enthroned BENEDICT V (964). However, they surrendered him after Otto's army besieged the city. In June Otto triumphantly entered Rome and reinstated Leo, who, at a synod held a few days later, deposed and humiliated Benedict. In ecclesiastical matters, little survives from Leo's reign. Documents attributed to him that granted Otto and his successors various concessions, such as the right to nominate and install bishops, were later proven to be forged in the eleventh century by supporters of Henry IV during the INVESTITURE CONTROVERSY.

For further reference: H. K. Mann, *The Lives of the Popes in the Early Middle Ages* (London: K. Paul, 1902–1932); W. Ullmann, *The Growth of Papal Government* (London: Methuen, 1970).

William Roberts

LEO IX (1049–1054). Born Bruno in June 1002, this son of Count Hugh of Egisheim, Alsace, was related to the imperial house. In 1027 he was appointed bishop of Lombardy, where he sought to reform the clergy and monasteries and served in the emperor's diplomatic service. Upon the death of Pope DAMASUS II in 1048 he was the emperor's choice to succeed. Arriving in Rome in February 1049, he was crowned pontiff, selecting a name that would recall the ancient, pure church.

Among his first acts Leo called a synod in April 1049 to rule against simony and clerical unchastity. Leo soon gathered around him capable and reform-minded individuals to assist in carrying out his policies, including Hildebrand (later, GREGORY VII) and Frederick of Liège (later, STEPHEN IX). To encourage support for his policies Leo adopted the unprecedented practice of visiting European sites to emphasize the need for reform, visiting Rheims, Mainz, Salerno, Vercelli, Mantua, Bari, and Siponto. He sought to suppress simony and clerical unchastity and to affirm the pontiff's unique role as primate of the universal church.

The latter years of Leo's reign were marked by disappointments. In 1053, seeking to protect the papal territories from the Norman raids in southern Italy, he led a small and ill-equipped force against them. Leo's army was defeated, and he was captured. He was held for nine months, although the Normans treated him with respect and allowed him to have contact with the outside world. He was widely criticized by reformers for leading such an expedition, which led also to another important development of his reign, the break with the Eastern church. The strongly anti-Latin patriarch Michael Cerularius, angered by Leo's interference in areas claimed by Byzantium in southern Italy, including the appointment of Humbert as archbishop of Sicily, closed the Latin churches in Constantinople and launched an attack on Western liturgical practices such as the use of unleavened bread in the Eucharist.

On 16 July 1054 Leo's agent placed a bull excommunicating the patriarch and his supporters on the altar of Hagia Sophia. The patriarch responded with counteranathemas, and the SCHISM between East and West became final. Leo returned to Rome in March of that year and died the next month, his last prayer recited in his native German. He would be considered a precursor of the later

Gregorian reformers, having restored the prestige of the papacy. He was soon declared a saint, and in 1087, because of miracles attributed to him, his remains were disinterred at the order of VICTOR III (1086–1087) and placed over an altar in St. Peter's. His feast day is 19 April.

For further reference: S. Runciman, *The Eastern Schism: A Study of the Papacy and the Eastern Churches during the XIth and XIIth Centuries* (Oxford: Clarendon Press, 1955); W. Ullmann, *Medieval Papalism: The Political Theories of the Medieval Canonists* (London: Methuen, 1949).

William Roberts

LEO X (1513–1521). After considerable service to the church, at an early age Giovanni de' Medici took up studies in theology and CANON LAW at Pisa. He was tonsured at the age of seven and at the age of thirteen appointed cardinal-deacon. In 1492, at the age of seventeen, he became a member of the College of CARDINALS, where he took up residence. Exiled in 1494, he traveled to France, Holland, and Germany but restored the Medici control of Florence in 1512. Upon his brother's death in 1503, he succeeded him as the head of the Medici family. He intended to maintain Italy and Florence from outside influences as well as advance the Medici family outside Florence. The thirty-seven-year-old cardinal Giovanni de' Medici was elected to the chair in March 1513.

Leo enjoyed the arts and music and restored Rome as the cultural center of the Western world. Allegedly a reckless extravagant, he collected books, manuscripts, and gems with little regard for price. To acquire money for his pleasures, it was rumored that Leo sold his furniture. Supposedly to meet his financial responsibilities of the projected crusade and construction of the basilica, Leo restored the abuses of selling indulgences authorized by JULIUS II (1503–1513). When the Dominican friar John Tetzel renewed the preaching of the use of indulgences, Martin Luther, the Augustian monk, reacted by nailing the 95 theses of protest on a Wittenberg church (see Reformation). Leo made several, but unsuccessful, attempts to silence Luther, publishing a papal bull *Exsurge Domine*, condemning Luther on 41 counts. Luther responded by publicly burning the papal bull and was excommunicated (see Excommunication) in Leo's bull *Decet Romanum pontificem*.

For further reference: Matthew Bunson, *The Pope Encyclopedia* (New York: Crown Trade Paperbacks, 1995).

Patrick McGuire

LEO XI (1605). Alessandro Ottaviano de' Medici was born in Florence in June 1535 to a collateral branch of that powerful Florentine family. Through his mother, Francesca Salviati, he was a great-nephew of LEO X (1513–1521) and was also related to the French queen Marie de' Medici. For several years he served as Grand Duke Cosimo I's ambassador in Rome, where he became the leading disciple of Philip Neri. GREGORY XIII (1572–1585) named him bishop of Pistoia (1573), archbishop of Florence (1574), and cardinal (1583). Deeply devout, he had close ties with the Dominicans of S. Marco in Florence and was responsible for introducing the Tridentine reforms into his dioceses. As LEGATE in France in 1596–1598 he helped to persuade CLEMENT VIII to lift the EXCOMMUNICATION on King Henry IV and sought to restore discipline in the French church. He was unsuccessful, however, in persuading Henry to have the decrees of the Council of TRENT published in his kingdom, as had been promised, but was able to successfully negotiate the peace treaty of Vervins between France and Spain in 1598.

With French backing in 1605 he was elected to succeed Clement VIII. He chose the name of his uncle, Leo. Although popular, the new POPE was in poor health and elderly, dying within the month. Not being able to establish a policy, he settled a dispute between the clergy of Castile and Leon and the Jesuits. He also was a strong opponent of nepotism, refusing the requests of both family and friends to raise a popular great-nephew, whom he had brought up and educated, to the cardinalate.

For further reference: P. Hughes, *The History of the Church* (London: Sheed and Ward, 1955); T. Jalland, *The Church and the Papacy* (New York: Morehouse, 1944); L. Pastor, *A History of the Popes from the Close of the Middle Ages* (London: Herder, 1953).

William Roberts

LEO XII (1823–1829). Annibale Della Genge was born at Castello della Genga, near Spoleto, Italy, on 22 August 1760. Although in poor health, he was elected POPE by a largely conservative conclave in 1823 and took the name Leo XII. In his first encyclical, *Ubi primum* (3 March 1824), Leo indicated his intention of following a reform program in education and discipline, especially for the clergy and the PAPAL STATES. Unfortunately, little was accomplished.

During Leo's reign, revolutions in South America effectively blocked Spain's plans for a Spanish restoration there. Leo XII began filling South American bishoprics, despite the discontent of Madrid. In the papal states, Leo encouraged laws, such as preventing Jews from owning real property, that controverted the Napoleonic Code. In 1825 Leo XII celebrated the only Jubilee Year of the nineteenth century. Centered in Rome, the year gained momentum after a disappointing start, revealing the difficulties of pilgrimages over long distances. Leo XII was instrumental in returning the Jesuits (see Society of Jesus) to some strength. He gave the Jesuits back their previous exemptions, again placing them in charge of the Roman College (1826).

For further reference: Owen Chadwick, *The Popes and European Revolution* (Oxford: Clarendon Press, 1981); Nicholas Wiseman, *Recollections of the Last Four Popes and of Rome in Their Times*, intro. John C. Reville (New York: Wagner, 1858).

Loretta Devoy

LEO XIII (1878–1903). Gioacchino Vincenzo Pecci was born in Carpineto, central Italy, 10 March 1810. Although Leo's pontificate was not expected to last long because of his age (68) at election, it lasted twenty-five years and had an important impact. He is noted for his efforts to embrace the workers' movement, bringing the church's teachings to bear on behalf of workers in industrialized society.

Leo gave significant attention to missionary activities at the start of his pontificate. To expedite the abolition of African slavery he issued two encyclicals: *In plurimus* (5 May 1888) and *Catholicae Ecclesiae* (20 November 1890). On 4 August 1879, Leo issued the encyclical *Aeterni Patris*, which sought, among other things, to bring Thomism back to the center of philosophical and theological teaching in the church. Leo's pontificate coincided with the beginning of a crisis in the church called "MODERNISM." Modernism had begun as an attempt to bring the church up-to-date in biblical and dogmatic scholarship. Leo issued the encyclical *Providentissimus Deus* on 18 November 1893, in which he outlined what Rome considered to be legitimate methods in biblical study as distinct from what the Vatican authorities considered unacceptable methods. His *Testem Benevolentiae* of 1899 condemned AMERICANISM, the ill-defined movement to adopt Catholicism to the American culture. Further, in 1902 he established the Pontifical Biblical Commission, which, in effect, set the limits for biblical scholarship and exegesis. Originally viewed as restrictive, the biblical commission would bear fruit in the late twentieth century, when it assisted in promoting Catholic biblical scholarship after PIUS XII's *Divini Afflante Spiritu* (1943).

Pope Leo XIII was one of the first POPES in the history of the church to be involved publicly and vitally in topics usually called "social questions." His *Rerum Novarum* (1891), which defended the workers' right to protection against economic and social exploitation, has been deemed the Catholic "magna carta" of labor. Other of his encyclicals related to the organization and relations between church and state are *Diuturnum* (29 June 1888), *Immortale Dei* (1 November 1885), *Libertas* (20 June 1888), and *Sapientiae Christianae* (10 January 1890).

For further reference: E. E. Y. Hales, *The Catholic Church in the Modern World: A Survey from the French Revolution to the Present* (Garden City, NY: Doubleday, 1958), Chapters 16, 17; René Füllöp Miller, *Leo XIII and Our Times*, trans. Conrad M. R. Bonacina (London: Longmans, Green, 1937).

Loretta Devoy

LEONINE CITY. The Leonine City is that part of Rome, including the Vatican, Castel Sant' Angelo, and the Borgo, that Pope LEO IV (847–855) surrounded with a defensive wall after the Saracen raid of 846. In 860, Pope NICHOLAS I (858–867) transferred the papal residence from the Lateran palace to the more defensible Vatican. Thereafter, the Leonine City became the center of papal administration and of Roman religious life. After the Italian occupation of Rome in 1870, the Italian government offered to allow the papacy to retain the Leonine

City, but PIUS IX (1846–1878) refused the offer, which would have implied his acceptance of the loss of the rest of the PAPAL STATES. In 1929, the LATERAN ACCORDS returned political authority over the Vatican to the pope as the VATICAN CITY, but the rest of the Leonine City remained under Italian jurisdiction.

For further reference: Moritz Brosch, *Geschichte Kirchenstaats*, 2 vols. (Gotha: Verlag, 1882).

Alan J. Reinerman

LIBERATION THEOLOGY. This is a term used to describe a particular direction and method in theology that emerged in Latin America in the mid-1960s as a response to VATICAN II's challenge to bring the church into the modern world. The modern world of liberation theology, however, is a world of the political, social, and economic oppression that characterizes so much of the Latin American experience. Liberation theology understands evangelization as the church's mission and responsibility to transform the world in accordance with the spirit of the gospel. It works on the prophetic assumption that "the protests of the poor are the voice of God."

The General Conference of the Latin American Episcopacy (CELAM II) held at Medellín, Colombia, in 1968 unequivocally declared the church's commitment to a "preferential option for the poor." It also called attention to the realities of "economic colonialism" and of "institutional violence," to which the poor and the powerless are continually subjected by "those who have a greater share of wealth, culture and power." Church historian Enrique Dussell has fittingly called CELAM II the "Vatican II of Latin America." A follow-up meeting of Latin American bishops was held in 1979 at Puebla, Mexico. This second conference (CELAM III), despite strong opposition from conservative church leaders, succeeded in endorsing all the major liberation themes that had been put forward at Medellín, including the recognition of systemic societal evil, the option for the poor, and the important role of the popular base communities among the Christian poor (*communidades ecclesiales de base*).

The first systematic expression of the new theology had already appeared in 1971 with the publication of Gustavo Gutierrez' *A Theology of Liberation*. Gutierrez, a Peruvian priest, had been a powerful theological influence at Medellín and later at Puebla. His book was soon be recognized as the "Magna Carta" of liberation theology, and he quickly became the leading exponent of the movement. Gutierrez and other champions of liberation theology insist on the thoroughly ecclesial nature of the movement. They emphasize its close ties to the concrete, grassroots experience of the thousands of small, basic, Christian communities of the poor and dispossessed that are found throughout Latin America. While it has a strong academic component, it is not primarily a theology of the schools. In the words of Gutierrez, it is a "theology in search of the poor of Jesus Christ."

On the whole, liberation theology stands firmly opposed to the capitalist system, which it sees as the main source of the ongoing economic dependency and oppression of the vast majority of Latin Americans. As a form of social criticism, it is usually tied to some variety of Marxist–Leninist theology of dependency, whereby the underdevelopment of the poor countries is seen as a by-product of the development of the rich ones. Accordingly, it routinely supports efforts to establish economic and political socialism—if necessary, through revolution. As a rule, it favors close cooperation with humanistic Marxists, who are also committed to the struggle for liberation from dependency and the creation of a just social and economic order. Liberation theologians routinely rely on Marxist analysis of history and society for their interpretation of the social ills that keep Latin America trapped in what Lenin called "the net of financial and diplomatic dependence."

While liberation theologians claim that they are able to disassociate the Marxist–Leninist analysis from its underlying atheistic and materialistic ideology, Vatican authorities have remained unconvinced and have insisted that the Marxist analysis is inseparable from its ideology and from the practice of class struggle that it enjoins. Cardinal Joseph Ratzinger, prefect of the Sacred Congregation for the Doctrine of the Faith, has cautioned liberation theologians against the danger of a "confusion of the biblical horizon with the Marxist view of history." The Vatican "Instruction on Certain Aspects of the 'Theology of Liberation,' " issued by the same congregation in August 1984, censures "certain forms" of liberation theology for an uncritical use of Marxist analysis that "seriously departs from the faith of the church, and, in fact, actually constitutes a practical negation." But, as the instruction clearly implies, not all theologies of liberation fall under this critique.

In order to throw light on the positive contributions of liberation theology, the Vatican issued a second document, which it called "Instruction on Christian Freedom and Liberation" (March 1986). In this document the congregation calls for an authentic theology of liberation to meet the needs and challenges of our time. It applauds the "theologies of liberation" for having restored a place of honor to "the great texts of the prophets and of the gospel in defense of the poor," while continuing to warn against any reduction of the gospel message to a purely this-worldly hope.

While liberation theology has deep roots in the experience of Christian communities in Latin America, it has also exerted an enormous impact worldwide, especially in India, Sri Lanka, the Philippines, Taiwan, and Africa. The themes and goals of liberation theology have also profoundly affected the consciousness and the methods of theology as practiced in First World, industrialized countries. Liberation theology continues to inspire a number of significant Christian movements of liberation, including feminist, black, and Latino theologies. At its best, liberation theology serves as a continual reminder to the church of "the mystery of the presence of Christ in the poor" (Cardinal Lercaro).

For further reference: Gustavo Gutierrez, *A Theology of Liberation: History, Politics and Salvation*, trans. and ed. Caridad Inda and John Eagleson (Maryknoll, NY: Orbis Books, 1973); Alfred T. Hennelly, ed., *Liberation Theology: A Documentary History* (Maryknoll, NY: Orbis Books, 1990).

Raymond F. Bulman

LIBERIUS (352–366). Liberius assumed the papacy under trying conditions, which included the exiling of St. Athanasius and the energetic activity of the Arians. It has been suggested that Liberius, the successor to Pope JULIUS I (337–352), assumed a contradictory stance and allegedly accepted the emperor Constantine's attempt to impose a modified ARIANISM on the church, while accepting the condemnation of Athanasius. However, toward the close of his pontificate Liberius affirmed that the Nicene Creed encompassed the entire truth of the church.

For further reference: Matthew Bunson, *The Pope Encyclopedia* (New York: Crown Trade Paperbacks, 1995).

Patrick McGuire

LINUS (c. 66–c. 78). According to Irenaeus of Lyons and Hegesippus and confirmed by Eusebius, Linus was the first successor to PETER. Eusebius and Irenaeus suggested Linus was a companion of Paul. The actual dates of Linus' leadership in the church remain unknown; some suggest he reigned for approximately twelve years. Likewise, we are uncertain of his responsibilities and papal activities, since we can surmise that the monarchical episcopate had not yet emerged in Rome.

For further reference: Matthew Bunson, *The Pope Encyclopedia* (New York: Crown Trade Paperbacks, 1995).

Patrick McGuire

LUCIUS I (253–254). Born in Rome, Lucius was elected in 253 to succeed CORNELIUS (251–253) as bishop of Rome and was exiled almost immediately after his consecration. The favor of the new emperor Valerian supposedly allowed him to return to Rome, where Cyprian of Carthage wrote him a letter (letter 61) congratulating him and praising him for his suffering. Little is known of the life of Lucius before and after his election as bishop of Rome. In letter 68 to STEPHEN I (254–257), the successor of Lucius, Cyprian indicates that Lucius had acted in the tradition of Cornelius by allowing those who had fallen during persecution to be restored to communion after doing appropriate penance; he therefore seems to have maintained the opposition shown by Cornelius to Novatian, whose SCHISM continued during his tenure. He ruled less than one year, from June 253 to March 254. He is called a martyr by Cyprian in letter 68, but it is not certain that he was actually put to death for his faith. He was later declared a saint.

For further reference: Cyprian of Carthage, *Letters* 61, 68; Eusebius of Caesarea, *The History of the Church*, trans. G. A. Williamson (New York: New York University Press, 1966); J. N. D. Kelly, *The Oxford Dictionary of Popes* (Oxford: Oxford University Press, 1986).

Gerard H. Ettlinger

LUCIUS II (1144–1145). The brief pontificate of Gerard Caccianemici of Bologna was the first of a series to be plagued by internal Roman political strife during the mid- to late 1100s. Gerard was appointed cardinal-priest of St. Croce in Gerusalamme by CALLISTUS II (1119–1124) in 1123 and afterward served as papal LEGATE in Germany and papal governor of Benevento in 1130. He was a close friend of Pope INNOCENT II (1130–1143), who appointed him to succeed Aimeric as chancellor and librarian of the Apostolic See in 1141.

Little is recorded about his election except that he assumed the name Lucius II and that he was consecrated on Sunday, 12 March 1144. His papacy was burdened by ongoing political upheavals in southern Italy. Among Lucius' supporters was King Roger of Sicily. While it appeared that this would prove helpful to the papacy, since Roger had proven to be an adversary to prior popes, no solution to the ongoing conflict over southern Italy could be found. Tensions were ultimately increased, culminating in Roger's invasion of Campania. The Romans, distressed at the destruction of their territories, empowered Lucius to declare a truce in 1144.

A popular commune had been declared in Rome that aimed to establish a republican government, thus ending papal sovereignty in the city. Giordano Pierleoni, brother of the late antipope ANACLETUS II (1130–1138), was appointed as leader of the new independent senate, with the title of patrician. Lucius appealed to the king of Germany, Conrad III, but was unsuccessful in securing aid, since Conrad was involved in a civil war within his own country. Lucius thus took matters into his own hands, leading an attack on the stronghold of the senate. The assault was repelled, and Lucius was injured during battle. He died from his wounds on 15 February 1145 in the monastery of St. Gregor. His body was buried in the Lateran basilica.

For further reference: Eric John, *The Popes: A Concise Bibliographical History* (London: Burns and Oates, 1964); H. K. Mann, *The Lives of the Popes in the Early Middle Ages* (London: K. Paul, 1902–1932).

Christopher S. Myers

LUCIUS III (1181–1185). An old man at the time of his ascent, Ubaldo Allucingoli of Lucca became Pope Lucius III in 1181. A POPE who craved peace, he failed to achieve this goal. Allucingoli's involvement in the church began with his appointment to the Cistercians by order of Bernard of Clairvaux. He was then made cardinal-deacon by INNOCENT II (1130–1143) and cardinal-bishop of Ostia and Velletri by ADRIAN IV (1154–1159) in 1159. He was a trusted friend and negotiator for ALEXANDER III (1159–1181) and was instrumental in arranging the Treaty of Benevento in 1156 and the Peace of Venice in 1177. He also enjoyed the favor of Frederick I, Barbarossa.

Confronted by ongoing disturbances in Rome, Lucius III decided to be crowned in the city of Vetri. Soon after, in an attempt to establish peace between the church and the empire, he instituted negotiations with Frederick to resolve their differences. Lucius authored the constitution *Ad abolendum*, after agreeing with Frederick that the spread of HERESY needed to be stopped. The constitution required that all heretics would be excommunicated (see Excommunication) by the church and then turned over to the state for punishment. Second, Frederick agreed to make preparations for a new crusade in response to the growing power of Saladin, sultan of Egypt, in the Holy Land.

The last period of his pontificate was marked by a divided election to the See of Trier, which had a profound impact on a number of European countries. Furthermore, Frederick, in the interest of assuring the succession of his son Henry, asked Lucius to crown him emperor. Lucius refused on the grounds that there could not be more than one emperor at a time. A more tangible reason may have been that in 1185, Henry married Constance, daughter of Roger II of Sicily and aunt of William II, king of Sicily. Fearing the union of Germany and Sicily, Lucius refused to crown Henry. He died soon after, leaving instructions to his successor not to crown Henry as long as Frederick lived. Lucius died in Verona on 25 November 1185 at the age of 78. He was buried in the cathedral of Verona.

For further reference: J. N. D. Kelly, *The Oxford Dictionary of the Popes* (Oxford: Oxford University Press, 1986); H. K. Mann, *The Lives of the Popes in the Early Middle Ages* (London: K. Paul, 1902–1932).

Christopher S. Myers

LYONS I, COUNCIL OF (1245). Emperor Frederick II dreamed of an empire on the scale of the ancient Roman empire. From his position in Sicily and southern Italy, he planned to extend his power throughout the peninsula. This project threatened the PAPAL STATES. Thus, until his death in 1250, Frederick found the Roman pontiffs his determined opponents. GREGORY IX (1227–1241) excommunicated (see Excommunication) Frederick in 1227 for his failure to lead the crusade as he had vowed. Absolved but again excommunicated in 1239, the emperor appealed to a COUNCIL that Gregory convened. It never opened, in part due to imperial obstruction. Pope INNOCENT IV was elected on 25 June 1243, but Frederick forced him to flee Rome for Lyons, where he summoned Christendom to a council on 26 June 1245.

In his opening address Innocent outlined the task of the council, the healing of the "five wounds of the church," clerical immorality, the fall of Jerusalem, the plight of the Latin empire of Constantinople, the Mongol incursion, and the persecution of the church by Frederick. The pope charged the emperor with HERESY, alliance with infidels, breach of contract, and perjury. The council approved measures to heal the wounds of the church and the deposition of Frederick. It closed on 17 July 1245. Frederick continued to rule after the council. The papal and imperial courts maneuvered to gain partisans. Many princes remained neutral. After the death of Frederick, Innocent returned to Rome. However, the struggle between the papacy and the Hohenstaufens ended only with the death of the last of that dynasty in 1268.

For further reference: T. C. Van Cleve, *The Emperor Frederick II of Hohenstaufen. Immutator Mundi* (New York: Oxford University Press, 1972); H. Wolter and H. Holstein, *Lyon I et Lyon II* (Paris: Ed. de l'Orante, 1966).

Richard J. Kehoe

LYONS II, COUNCIL OF (1274). Pope GREGORY X (1271–1276) was elected on 1 September 1271 after a vacancy of almost three years. The POPE sailed from Acre, the last crusader stronghold in the Holy Land, to assume his office. He returned with a keen awareness of the plight of the crusader states and a desire to heal the SCHISM separating the Greek and Latin churches. He convoked a COUNCIL to meet these pressing needs on 7 May 1274. Gregory set the three goals of the council: Christian moral reform, aid for the Christian states of the Holy Land, and the reunion of the churches. Some 300 bishops attended the council, but the Greek delegation sent by the Byzantine emperor, Michael VIII, did not arrive until 24 June.

The council raised measures to remedy some of the abuses that plagued the church, for example, contested ecclesiastical elections, absence from benefices, and prolonged vacancies of benefices. It also sought to eliminate prolonged papal conclaves by requiring that the conclave begin within ten days of the death of the pope. The electors were to be sequestered, and the longer the conclave lasted, the harsher the diet would become. After three days the cardinals would receive only one dish at midday and an evening meal; after five more days the fare consisted of bread and water. Provisions were made for the reconquest of the Holy Land by the imposition of a tax and forbidding all commerce with the Saracens.

The Greek delegation met all the demands of the Latins. They accepted the *filioque* in the creed, the use of unleavened bread, and papal supremacy. Michael VIII had sent a delegation of pro-union prelates and dignitaries to facilitate agreement in the hope that the pope would curb the aggressive designs of Charles of Anjou on Constantinople. The union proved short-lived. Gregory died on 10 January 1276 and was unable to meet with Michael VIII. Pope MARTIN IV (1281) excommunicated (see Excommunication) Michael and approved the plans of Charles of Anjou to capture Constantinople. Moreover, the Byzantine clergy and populace never accepted the union of Lyons, although Michael VIII remained faithful to it until his death in 1282.

For further reference: D. J. Geanokoplos, *Emperor Michael Palaeologus and the West (1258–1282)* (Cambridge: Cambridge University Press, 1959); J. M. Hussey, *The Orthodox Church in the Byzantine Empire* (Oxford: Clarendon Press, 1986); H. Wolter and H. Holstein, *Lyon I et Lyon II* (Paris: Ed. de l' Orante, 1965).

Richard J. Kehoe

M

MANICHAEISM. SEE ALBIGENSES.

MARCELLINUS (296–?304). Most of the reign of Marcellinus fell in the period of peace preceding the persecution of Diocletian. However, in February 303, Diocletian published his first edict ordering, among other things, the destruction of churches throughout the empire and the burning of the Scriptures. The *Liber Pontificalis* records that, when Marcellinus was compelled to offer sacrifice, he did so. A century later the Donatists charged him with having handed over the sacred books and implicated his presbyters Marcellus, Miltiades, and Sylvester—all of whom later became POPES. By the end of the fifth century, his guilt seems to have been accepted. The *Liber Pontificalis*, probably following a later tradition, notes that, after he offered sacrifice, Marcellinus was filled with remorse and was subsequently beheaded.

In the confused chronology of the time, it seems that his handing over of the sacred books occurred in May 303, and, since such an act in the West would disqualify a man from the priesthood, the Roman See was left without a bishop. According to the length of his reign as expressed in the Liberian Catalogue, Marcellinus probably died on 25 October 304. His feast is celebrated on 2 June.

For further reference: Timothy D. Barnes, *Constantine and Eusebius* (Cambridge: Harvard University Press, 1981), pp. 38, 303, n.100; J. N. D. Kelly, *The Oxford Dictionary of Popes* (New York: Oxford University Press, 1986), pp. 24ff.

Bernard J. Cassidy

MARCELLUS I (306–308). Marcellus was probably elected shortly after peace was restored to the church at the accession of Maxentius. He was immediately faced with the problem of how the *lapsi* (Christians who had apostacized during the persecution of Diocletian) were to be accepted back into the church and apparently took a hard line, requiring the imposition of a heavy penance. Although the Donatists in the early fifth century accused him of complicity in the apostacy of Marcellinus, he seems to have removed Marcellinus' name from the lists of his predecessors.

Marcellus is credited by the *Liber Pontificalis* with subdividing the church of Rome into *tituli* under the supervision of priests. Opposition to Marcellus' strict policy with regard to the *lapsi* led to bloodshed and his expulsion by the emperor Maxentius; he died in exile on 16 January 308, according to the *Liber Pontificalis*. Some scholars have argued that Marcellus should be identified with his predecessor, Marcellinus, because of the omission of one name or the other from certain records. His separate existence, however, seems to have been more likely. His feast is celebrated on 16 January.

For further reference: J. N. D. Kelly, *The Oxford Dictionary of Popes* (New York: Oxford University Press, 1986), pp. 25ff.; J. Lebreton and J. Zeiller, *The History of the Primitive Church*, vol. 4 (London: Burns, Oates, and Washbourne, 1948).

Bernard J. Cassidy

MARCELLUS II (1555). Reigning only from 9 April to 1 May 1555, Marcellus II was chosen after a short, but contentious, conclave in which the reforming element prevailed. Marcello Cervini was chosen to succeed JULIUS III (1550–1555). Born near Sienna, Marcello, whose sister would be the mother of St. Robert Bellarmine, was the son of an official of the Sacred Penitentiary. He was a bibliophile, erudite scholar, and friend of leading humanists.

Upon returning to Rome in 1531, he was noticed by Cardinal Farnese, who, upon becoming Pope PAUL III (1534–1549), made him tutor to his nephew Cardinal Alessandro. Through Alessandro, who became Paul III's close adviser, Marcello's influence rose, and between 1539, when he was named cardinal-priest of Sta. Croce, and 1544, he was appointed successively bishop of Nicastro, Reggio Emilia, and Gubbio. During his years as bishop he was often on diplomatic missions, especially to France and to the imperial court, to which he was made LEGATE in 1543.

In 1545 he was chosen one of the three copresidents of the Council of TRENT, where he upheld papal policy over the disapproval of the emperor. Later, in 1548, he was given the welcome assignment of reorganizing the Vatican Library and was also made a member of Paul III's reform commission. Marcellus, who broke with tradition and kept his own name, once pope, showed a reformist zeal. He immediately reduced the expenses of his coronation and court. Acting against nepotism, he forbade his many relatives from venturing to Rome. But, after a twenty-two-day reign he suffered a stroke and died. To honor him and his reforms, the great composer Palestrina wrote the ''Missa Papae Marcelli.''

For further reference: T. Jalland, *The Church and the Papacy* (New York: Morehouse, 1944); L. Pastor, *A History of the Popes from the Close of the Middle Ages* (London: Herder, 1953).

William Roberts

MARCUS OR MARK (336). Sandwiched between the long reigns of ST. SYL-
VESTER I (314–335) and ST. JULIUS I (337–352), Marcus' short pontificate
has been characterized as marking a lull between the church's First ecumenical
COUNCIL convened by Constantine the Great at NICAEA in 325 and the death
of that emperor on 22 May 337, when governance of the empire was divided
among his three sons. Marcus' pontificate is important because it was the first
to run its course after the removal of the imperial capital to Constantinople in
330. What the imperial absence from Rome meant for the new synodal system
of universal church governance introduced by Constantine would become clear
only under Marcus' successor, Julius I during and after the Council of Sardica
(343).

Instead of having to battle imperial power during his pontificate, Marcus enjoyed imperial endorsement in pursuing his aims. He continued the work of
bringing the church as well as its meeting places, cemeteries, and martyr commemorations out of hiding. Marcus is the first POPE credited with converting
private-house meeting places into churches, proclaiming them as such with titles
(*tituli*) inscribed over their public entrances. Marcus also appears to have initiated the compilation of two major lists that have ever since shaped the church's
calendars. They were lists of popes' names and dates of death and of dates and
names of places of annual commemorations of Roman martyrs.

For further reference: E. Caspar, *Geschichte des Papstums von den Anfängen bis zur
Höhe der Weltherrschaft*, vol. 1 (Tübingen: Verlag von J. C. B. Mohr, 1930), pp. 131–
133, 142; T. J. Jalland, *The Church and the Papacy* (London: Society for Promoting
Christian Knowledge); J. T. Shotwell and L. P. Loomis, *The See of Peter* (New York:
Columbia University Press, 1927).

Henry Paolucci

MARINUS I (882–884). An Italian and son of a priest, Marinus was sent by
Pope ADRIAN II (867–872) to lead the Eighth General Council (see Constantinople IV, Council of) (869–870), which condemned Photius, patriarch of
Constantinople (858–867, 878–886), who had excommunicated (see Excommunication) Pope NICHOLAS I (858–867) over Rome's assertion of supremacy
in Bulgaria. Marinus upheld the condemnation as POPE. Upon the assassination
of JOHN VIII (872–882), Marinus was elected pope by the Roman people in
violation of CANON LAW, which forbade translations of bishops from one see
to another, although this action was not unprecedented. The irregularity of his
election, his involvement in the Eighth General Council, and his consecration
without the consent of the emperor led both patriarch and Eastern emperor from
recognizing his election.

Marinus pardoned and restored Formosus of Porto, a bishop whom John VIII
suspected of conspiring against him to acquire the papacy. He also initiated and
maintained excellent relations with Emperor Charles III (the Fat) (881–887) and
Alfred the Great of England (849–899).

For further reference: Joseph S. Brusher, *Popes through the Ages* (Princeton: D. Van
Nostrand, 1964); Eric John, ed., *The Popes: A Concise Biographical Dictionary* (New

York: Hawthorn Books, 1964); H. K. Mann, *The Lives of the Popes in the Early Middle Ages* (London: K. Paul, 1902–1932).

John C. Horgan

MARINUS II (942–946). Marinus, who is sometimes mistakenly listed as Martin III, was born in Rome and at the time of his election was cardinal-priest of S. Ciraico. Little else is known of his early life, and, like his two predecessors, he owed his election to the prince of Rome, the powerful senator and patrician Alberic II of Spoleto. He was apparently also completely under the control of Alberic; coins issued in his name show on one side his monogram with St. Peter's, but the other side reveals the name and title of Alberic.

Baronius describes this POPE as devoted exclusively to the reform of the clergy and monasteries, the care of the poor, and the restoration of churches, while avoiding any warlike conflicts. Those acts of his reign that are recorded bear this out. A bull of 946 confirms the appointment of Archbishop Frederick of Mainz as papal vicar and envoy in Germany with authority to call synods and to enforce reform among the clergy and monks.

For further reference: L. Duchesne, *The Beginnings of the Temporal Sovereignty of the Popes* (London: International Catholic Library, 1908); H. K. Mann, *The Lives of the Popes in the Early Middle Ages* (London: K. Paul, 1902–1932).

William Roberts

MARSHALL PLAN AND PAPACY. George C. Marshall, President Truman's secretary of state, on 5 June 1947 delivered a speech at Harvard University announcing that the United States was ready to rebuild the war-torn economies of Europe, if these countries worked out cooperative priorities among themselves. Pope PIUS XII (1939–1958) endorsed the plan immediately. In his letter of 19 July 1948 to Truman, Pius wrote, "The European Recovery Program must succeed." The pope went on to emphasize three points: (1) whether or not Russia decides to participate, the United States must stabilize the rest of Europe; (2) the program must be long-term and rest on the inalienable right of everyone to life, liberty, and the pursuit of happiness; and (3) the question of immigration and free movement of people within the European Cooperation Administration must be worked out through international agreements that respect rights of the family. The papacy subsequently approved Western European economic groupings such as the European Coal and Steel Community (1953) and the European Economic Community (1958), all of which had strong backing from Christian democratic parties.

For further reference: Ennio di Nolfo, *Vaticano e Stati Uniti 1939–1952 (Dalle carte di Myron C. Taylor)* (Milan: Franco Angeli Editore, 1978).

Charles F. Delzell

MARTIN I (649–653). The successor to THEODORE I (642–649), Martin's primary concern was to clarify the church's teaching on the Christological HERESY monothelitism. Independent in spirit, he was consecrated without receiving the necessary imperial ratifications, which, in turn, infuriated Emperor Constans II, who refused to recognize Martin as the true pontiff. Smuggled out of Rome, Martin arrived in Constantinople in 653, where he received an unpleasant welcome from the people. Brought before the court, he was charged with treason. After being stripped of his episcopal robes and tunic and publicly flogged, Martin was condemned to death. At the request of the dying patriarch Pyrrhus I he was exonerated and exiled to Crimea.

For further reference: J. N. D. Kelly, *The Oxford Dictionary of Popes* (New York: Oxford University Press, 1986); Matthew Bunson, *The Pope Encyclopedia* (New York: Crown Trade Paperbacks, 1995).

Patrick McGuire

MARTIN II. SEE MARINUS I.

MARTIN III. SEE MARINUS II.

MARTIN IV (1281–1285). Chancellor of France under Louis IX, Simon de Brion was elected—through the efforts of Charles of Anjou—to the Holy See on 22 February 1280 and took the name Martin IV (misnumbered because two earlier POPES, Marinus I (882–884) and II (942–946), had erroneously been listed as Martin II and III). Unswerving in his commitment to the French, he was bent on establishing Charles D'Anjou on the throne of Sicily.

Supporting Charles' projected attack on the Eastern empire, Martin excommunicated its emperor Michael VIII Palaeologus, thereby destroying the unity of the Latin and Byzantine churches that had been achieved at the Second Council of Lyons (see Lyons II, Council of) in 1274. This plan to gain control of the Eastern empire was thwarted by the rebellion against the French in Sicily in 1282 ("Sicilian Vespers"), which forced Charles to abandon plans to reconquer Constantinople. When the pope refused their pleas for papal suzerainty, the Sicilians turned to Peter of Aragon and, following their EXCOMMUNICATION by the pope, declared Peter king of Sicily. A campaign organized by the pope against Peter under the leadership of Philip III of France failed.

Bold and energetic in his campaign to solidify the French position in Italy, this "most French of 13th-century popes" proved equally forceful and perhaps overly zealous in authorizing the mendicant orders to preach and hear confessions and to argue their position in university debates—what many saw as a dangerous intrusion on the rights and duties of the secular clergy. In 1300 BONIFACE VIII (1294–1303) modified this extension of privileges, which had also come under fire in the biting, humorous tales of Boccaccio. Martin died in

Perugia on 28 March 1285, less than two months after the death of his great patron, Charles I, on 7 January 1285.

For further reference: E. John, ed., *The Popes* (New York: Hawthorn Books, 1964); H. K. Mann, *The Lives of the Popes in the Early Middle Ages* (London: K. Paul, 1902–1932).

Anne Paolucci

MARTIN V (1417–1431). Oddo Colonna was born in 1368 of Roman nobility. He entered papal service and supported the Roman claimant during the Western Schism (see Schism, Great Western), joining his fellow cardinals in the attempt to settle the SCHISM at the COUNCIL of Pisa. He was one of the last to abandon JOHN XXIII (1410–1415) and join the Council of CONSTANCE. The council unanimously elected Colonna as Martin V, to end the schism. He answered the call for reform by convoking the Council of Pavia-Sienna (1423), which dissolved without accomplishment. Reluctantly, he convoked a council for BASEL in 1431 but died before the council convened. Martin did much to restore Rome and the papacy following the chaos of the Western Schism, but some of his policies, for example, his nepotism and failure to implement reforms, created problems for his successor.

For further reference: K. Fink, "Martin V," in *New Catholic Encyclopedia*, vol. 9 (New York: McGraw-Hill, 1967), pp. 300–302; P. Partner, *Papal States under Martin* (London: British School at Rome, 1958).

Richard J. Kehoe

MEDICAL SCIENCE AND THE PAPACY. Christ's concern for the sick and suffering has influenced the church's views on medicine. Disease is recognized as an evil, and humanity is obliged to employ whatever moral means available to eliminate it. Thus, the Catholic Church, from the ancient time of the *xendochia*, houses for the sick, to the building of modern hospitals, has long provided medical treatment and comfort for the sick as part of its redemptive mission. Within this context, the medical profession is viewed as a vocation in service of life.

Hippocrates determined that medical science and practice could be good only if human life was considered to be an unconditional good to be preserved. He rejected the taking of a human life by a physician, including the unborn, without exception. He also rejected the notion, prevalent in his time, that the art of medicine was to be put in the service of the king by preserving the life of those the king wanted to live and taking the lives of those the king wanted to die. Thus, the political use of medical knowledge to solve social problems was excluded from the practice of medicine.

A duality in the medical profession is concerned with both developing scientific knowledge and practicing the art of preserving health and treating diseases. As a science, the medical profession is concerned with making discoveries about the nature of the human body and mind that will enable the practitioner to understand the causes of diseases of the body and mind. As an art, the medical profession is concerned with developing methods of preventing diseases and the practical, therapeutic means of treatment to restore health. The church, in its long history, has always had a deep respect for the medical profession, maintaining that genuine science and good medical practice cannot be in conflict with the faith and moral teaching of the church.

Nonetheless, the church has long recognized that the means employed to obtain scientific knowledge can present moral problems, and the use of medical knowledge likewise involves moral issues, for every medical choice made by a doctor, in conjunction with his or her patient, is also a moral decision concretizing or rejecting fundamental human values. Thus, the notion of a physician as a moral person who is concerned with the good of the whole human being and who is aware of the spiritual needs of the patient as well as the physical needs, is to be distinguished from the narrow notion of a medical doctor as someone who is technically proficient in treating the body in an impersonal way. The church perceives the moral physician as one who integrates the various roles of counselor, teacher, and therapist and recognizes the spiritual needs of the patient as essential to the practice of good medicine. To be a good physician, lawyer, teacher, or priest, one must first be a moral person.

The moral physician must be aware of the unity of the person, understanding that health involves spiritual and mental, as well as physical elements. The physician must also be aware of the dignity of the human beings who come under his or her care. Therefore, a physician's direct taking of human life, from the moment of conception until a natural death, has no place in the practice of a good physician. Surgery is morally acceptable only when a pathological condition exists and when, for example, tissue must be removed in order to remove the pathology; or when repair is necessary to restore normal appearance and function. The good surgeon does not mutilate the body or remove healthy tissue in order to render a healthy organ unable to perform its normal functions, for example, sterilization. Further, the moral physician recognizes the right of the patient to participate in an informed manner in his or her treatment as essential to sound medical practice. Informed consent requires that a patient be made to understand the risks and benefits of undergoing any procedure, without any coercion by the physician.

Patients should not be made to undergo experimental procedures that are not directly related to improving their health, since that would reduce them to a means for the profession to obtain knowledge. However, the introduction of a properly tested vaccine where there is an established epidemic is directly related to the health of those who might contract the disease. An experimental procedure that is directly related to improving the health of a patient can be performed only if the patient freely consents, after fully understanding the risks and benefits of such a procedure.

Scientific knowledge of the human body is invaluable, but it cannot be gained by reducing a human being to laboratory experimentation for the sake of obtaining such knowledge. Thus, a canon of loyalty must be accepted by the physician who would respect the life and rights of the patients who come under his or her care that the physician will always act for the good of the patient and never act out of self-interest. The good physician does not permit personal desire to be the first to do a study or to reduce people to instruments of research or publication.

The use of medical techniques to produce human embryos for purely scientific research is perceived as a perversion, forgetting the fact that science and medicine exist for the sake of human beings, rather than human beings existing for the sake of science. The church has, on numerous occasions, especially in the twentieth century, called physicians to remember the principles at the foundation of their profession. The practice of medicine concentrates a great deal of power in the person of a physician and therefore there is a great responsibility to use that power justly. A scalpel in the hands of a physician can be used to save a life or take a human life. The proper practice of medicine requires that a physician will always act with the best interest of the patient in mind, while providing the patient with the best, up-to-date, moral means of preserving his or her health that is available. Medicine exists for the sake of men and women, and not the reverse. The papacy has called physicians and health care providers to become a higher witness to intrinsic goodness of human life.

For further reference: Monks of Solesmes, eds., *The Human Body, Papal Teaching* (Boston: Daughters of St. Paul, 1979); Kevin O'Rourke and Philip Boyle, eds., *Medical Ethics, Sources of Catholic Teachings* (St. Louis: Catholic Health Association of the United States, 1989).

Joseph J. Califano

MEMORANDUM OF 1831. The Memorandum of 1831 was a plan for the reform of the PAPAL STATES drawn up by the Great Powers. The backward-looking and inefficient papal government set up after the restoration of the papal states in 1815 aroused growing discontent, which exploded in February 1831 in revolution. Only the intervention of the Austrian army repressed the uprising and restored papal authority. However, France, Austria's traditional rival for influence in Italy, opposed the intervention, and the resulting international crisis threatened to lead to war. The crisis was settled peacefully, but it had brought home to the powers the dangers of popular discontent in the papal states, which could lead to a new revolution and another crisis. To prevent this danger, the powers (Austria, France, England, Prussia, and Russia) sent representatives to Rome in April 1831 for a conference to devise reforms that would end popular discontent.

On 21 May 1831, the diplomats presented to Pope GREGORY XVI (1831–1846) a memorandum listing the reforms they considered most urgent: admission of laymen to most posts in the civil government; reform of the judicial system; municipal self-government by elected city councils; provincial councils to express local wishes to the POPE; and a council of laymen at Rome to supervise state finances. Though it would not have satisfied dedicated liberals, the memorandum would have done much to satisfy public opinion in the provinces. Unfortunately, Rome failed to implement much of the memorandum; it thus lost an opportunity to win over moderate opinion and made inevitable the growth of revolutionary discontent that ultimately led to the end of the temporal power.

For further reference: Mario Caravale, *Lo Stato Pontificio da Martino V a Pio IX* (Turin: UTET, 1978); Alan J. Reinerman, *Austria and the Papacy in the Age of Metternich*, vol. 2 (Washington, DC: Catholic University Press, 1989).

Alan J. Reinerman

METTERNICH, PRINCE VON, AND THE PAPACY. Clement von Metternich-Winneburg (1773–1859) was born in Coblenz of an aristocratic Rhineland family. Driven from his home by the armies of Revolutionary France, he entered the Austrian diplomatic service in 1794. In 1809 he was appointed foreign minister, and after Napoleon's disaster in Russia in 1812, he was able to regain Austria's freedom of action. At the Congress of VIENNA, his diplomatic skill secured the restoration of Austria's prerevolutionary possessions, as well as hegemony over Italy and Germany. For the next thirty years, he managed to defend this favorable position. By the 1840s, however, the growing strength of liberalism and nationalism was becoming too much for him. In March 1848, revolution broke out in the Austrian empire, as in most of Europe, and the old chancellor was driven into exile. He returned to Vienna in 1851, but never held office again. He died in Vienna on 11 June 1859.

The papacy played an important role in Metternich's system. First and most fundamentally, he wished to enlist it in his lifelong struggle to defend the empire and the conservative order of Europe against the challenge of the liberal-nationalist revolutionary movement. The papacy should join with Austria in a "Union of Throne and Altar," in which Rome would contribute its moral authority, and Austria its material strength to the defense of the established order. On a second level, the PAPAL STATE was the second largest in Italy, occupying the strategic center of the peninsula; its cooperation was vital for the maintenance of Austrian hegemony. It was also important that the papal state follow the domestic policy that Metternich considered best suited to avoid revolution, nonpolitical reforms that would eliminate the grievances that fed revolutionary discontent. Finally, the papacy bitterly resented JOSEPHISM, the religious system introduced by the emperor Joseph II (1780–1790), which placed the Austrian church under close state control at the expense of papal authority. Metternich feared that papal resentment might burst out in an open attack on Josephism, leading to a church–state quarrel that would disrupt the union of throne and altar; he therefore assured Rome that if it would cooperate with Austria he would be able to gradually dismantle the Josephist system.

Metternich's success in pursuing these policies was mixed. During 1815–1820, cooperation was at a high point, but during the 1820s, papal distrust of Austrian hegemony in Italy and the coming to power at Rome of reactionaries who disliked his stress on reform led to cooler relations. The 1831 revolution in the papal states, repressed only by Austrian military intervention, brought home to Pope GREGORY XVI (1831–1846) papal dependence on Austria for protection, while at the same time Metternich's campaign against Josephism had begun to have some success. Consequently, Rome's attitude toward Austria became more favorable, and Gregory XVI cooperated closely with the empire throughout his pontificate. The election of Pope PIUS IX in 1846 brought an abrupt reversal. The new POPE (1846–1878) believed that his predecessor had compromised the independence of the papacy by his dependence on Austria; he was also disillusioned by Metternich's inability to overthrow Josephism against the resistance of the Vienna bureaucracy and was inclined to be sympathetic to the demands of the growing liberal-nationalist movement. He therefore abandoned the union of throne and altar and made clear his sympathy with the Italian cause, an attitude that, exaggerated by Italian patriots, paved the way for the outbreak of the revolutions of 1848 in Italy.

For further reference: Alan J. Reinerman, *Austria and the Papacy in the Age of Metternich, 1809–1848*, 2 vols. (Washington, DC: Catholic University Press, 1979–); Heinrich von Srbik, *Metternich*, 3 vols. (Munich: Bruckmann, 1925–1954).

Alan J. Reinerman

MIGUELITE WAR AND PAPACY. This civil war is an early nineteenth-century conflict between Portuguese liberals and conservatives and derives its name from Dom Miguel (1802–1866), younger son of Joao VI of Portugal. The royal family had fled to Brazil in 1807 during the Napoleonic invasion. Following the ouster of the French, a regency council governed until 1820. In that year, Portuguese liberals, inspired by an uprising in Spain, proclaimed a democratic Constitution and demanded the return of the absentee king. Leaving his elder son, Pedro, to govern Brazil, Joao returned to Portugal with Miguel. The absolutist and Catholic faction, rejecting constitutionalism, looked to Miguel as its leader. He attempted a coup against his father in 1824 and after its failure was banished to Austria.

On the death of Joao VI in 1826, Pedro, by now ruler of an independent Brazil, succeeded to the Portuguese throne. He decided to remain in Brazil and to hand over the sovereignty of Portugal to his seven-year-old daughter, Maria da Gloria (Queen Maria II). Pedro reaffirmed the Constitution but sought to appease conservatives by offering his brother Miguel the regency during the minority of Maria da Gloria, on the condition that Miguel marry her. Miguel accepted this arrangement, returned to Lisbon in 1827, and took an oath of loyalty. But he soon rallied his old supporters and early in 1828 persuaded a majority of the Parliament to repudiate the young queen and proclaim him King

Miguel I. The stage was now set for a civil war, pitting liberal backers of the constitutional monarch against the champions of absolutism, who declared the whole religious and social tradition of Portugal to be at stake. In this conflict, the liberals would receive the support of Britain and France, and the conservatives were endorsed by Spain, Austria, and the papacy.

With the Constitution abolished and the queen finding sanctuary in Britain, the absolutists carried out a triumphant persecution of their opponents during the next several years. But then, in April 1831, Pedro abdicated the Brazilian throne in favor of his son and returned to Europe to fight for Maria da Gloria's restoration with the aid of the British and the French. Pedro struck a decisive blow in July 1832, when he captured Oporto. At the beginning of 1834, with his resources exhausted, Miguel surrendered and was allowed to go into exile. Immediately following the end of the Miguelite War, Portugal joined the liberal, anticonservative bloc in Europe, claiming the Portuguese throne. The downfall of the Portuguese absolutists represented a significant defeat for the cause of European political and religious conservatism.

For further reference: A. H. Oliveria Marques, *History of Portugal* (New York: Columbia University Press, 1990).

Julia L. Ortiz-Griffin

MILTIADES (311–314). Following the banishment of Eusebius, Miltiades, a former presbyter of Marcellinus, was elected to the papacy in July 311. In the early fifth century, the Donatists charged that he was implicated in Marcellinus' handing over of the sacred Scriptures during the persecution of Diocletian, but apparently his contemporaries did not share this suspicion. Early in the year 313, there was a challenge to the validity of the ordination of Caecilianus, bishop of Carthage, whose opponents appealed to the emperor Constantine. Constantine appointed three bishops of Gaul as arbitrators, and they were to hear the case at Rome, with the bishop of Rome presiding. Miltiades added fifteen Italian bishops to the commission, transforming it into a regular church synod. The synod found for Caecilianus and excommunicated (see Excommunication) Donatus, who had been elected bishop as a rival to Caecilianus.

The strong condemnation of Donatus reflects the position of the Roman church that the validity of the sacraments of baptism and ordination was permanently conferred, and rebaptism and reordination were not required in the cases of those laity and bishops who had lapsed. Donatus and his followers, however, insisted on rebaptism of laity and reordination of bishops under these circumstances. An appeal was made to Constantine, who summoned a COUNCIL of bishops of the Western provinces to meet at Arles on 1 August 314. This council affirmed the decision rendered by the council held at Rome in the previous year, but Miltiades had died in July. His confrontation with the Donatists, however, probably led to their implicating him a century later in the lapse of Marcellinus. He is buried in the Cemetery of Callistus, and his feast is celebrated on 10 December.

For further reference: Timothy D. Barnes, *Constantine and Eusebius* (Cambridge: Harvard University Press, 1981); J. N. D. Kelly, *The Oxford Dictionary of Popes* (New York: Oxford University Press, 1986).

Bernard J. Cassidy

MIT BRENNENDER SORGE. SEE TOTALITARIANISM AND THE PAPACY.

MODALISM. SEE ZEPHYRINUS.

MODERNISM. Modernism is the name accorded to the disciplinary and doctrinal crisis in the Catholic Church in the first decade of the twentieth century. It had been manifest in some theological and philosophical works toward the end of the nineteenth century and into the early part of the twentieth century. It was a complex phenomenon rendered deceptively simple in the condemnation by the Holy Office of the Vatican under PIUS X (1903–1914) in *Lamentabili* (3 July 1907) of 65 propositions concerning criticism and dogma and in Pius X's encyclical *Pascendi* (8 September 1907).

The general notions associated with Modernism are that the Bible may be subjected to historical-critical study; an immanentist-evolutionary view of God and dogma; that doctrine develops within history; and a notion of the church as a purely societal phenomenon. The ideas condemned in *Pascendi* were compilations, and all had never been held at one time by any one Modernist. In a Europe in the process of transformation, thinking that conflicted with the traditional classical view of monarchy as appropriate hierarchical ordering and change as a "lack of perfection," was suspect. Vatican authorities reacted severely to Modernism's extreme elements and failed to grasp the reality that some scholars, for example, Maurice Blondel and Jules Lebreton, were trying to engage the church in dialogue with Modernity. Two famous Modernists whose ideas were condemned were Alfred Loisy and George Tyrrell. Many of the notions of the moderate Modernists came to reasoned discussion during the Second Council of the Vatican (see Vatican Council II) (1962–1965).

For further reference: René Marlé, *Au Coeur de la Crise Moderniste: le dossier inédit d'une controverse* (Paris: Aubier, 1960); Alec Vidler, *The Modernist Movement in the Roman Church* (London: Cambridge University Press, 1934).

Loretta Devoy

MONOPHYSITISM. SEE SEVERINUS.

MONOTHELITISM. SEE CONSTANTINOPLE III, COUNCIL OF; THEODORE I.

MURRI, ROMOLO. An early founder of the Christian democratic movement, Murri was born 27 August 1870 in the Marches and died in Rome 12 March 1944. In 1887 he graduated from the seminary in Fermo and then went on to more advanced studies in Rome at the Gregoriana and the Sapienza (see Colleges of Rome) (1888–1894). He received a degree in theology from the Gregoriana, but at the Sapienza his vision of life was broadened by his contacts with anticlerical students and by the course he took under the Italian Marxist Antonio Labriola.

In 1894 Murri was ordained a priest. Founder of the journal *Cultura Sociale*, he hoped the journal would be the mouthpiece of those university-educated Catholics who would be in the forefront of the moral regeneration of society. In 1899, when the Christian democrats published their ''programma sociale della democrazia cristiana,'' it was enthusiastically acclaimed by Murri's adherents, who called for the formation of a Catholic party, despite the objections of Pope LEO XIII (1878–1903).

In June 1903 Pope Leo XIII asked Murri to withdraw from the Christian democratic movement and to accept a teaching position in the seminary in Narni. Though Murri accepted the position, he remained active in the Christian democratic movement. The dissolution of the Opera dei congressi by Leo's successor, Pope PIUS X (1903–1914), did not distress Murri; rather, he saw it as an added opportunity for the formation of a Christian Democratic Party free of ecclesiastical interference. In 1906 Murri terminated *Cultura Sociale* and substituted *Rivista di Cultura* to further expound his theory of social activism and political independence for Italian Catholics. In April 1907 Pope Pius X suspended Murri *a divinis*. Efforts at reconciliation failed, but Murri's final break with the church was occasioned by a disciplinary matter, not dogma. In the general elections of 1909 Murri, in flat defiance of the pope, ran for the Chamber of Deputies and was excommunicated (see Excommunication). Subsequently, Murri began to espouse MODERNISM, which the pope had condemned in his ENCYCLICAL *Pascendi* (September 1907).

In Parliament Murri voted with the extreme Left, composed of radicals, republicans, and socialists. His marriage in 1912 added to the isolation that was now enveloping him. The balance of Murri's life was characterized by loneliness and ideological ambivalence. During the fascist era, Murri was employed in the Rome office of the Bolognese daily *Il Resto di Carlino*, and he wrote occasionally for *Critica Fascista*. A few months before his death in 1944, Murri was reconciled with the church. No abjuration of his previous writings or ideas was required of him.

Murri made two major contributions to Italian Catholic thought in the years before WORLD WAR I. The first was in raising the consciousness of Italian Catholics with respect to the needs of the proletariat. The left wing of the Christian Democratic Party of the post–WORLD WAR II era would carry on this tradition. The other contribution, later reflected in the political thought of Don Luigi Sturzo and Alcide DE GASPERI, was his distinction between the Catholic as citizen of the state and the Catholic as a member of the Roman Catholic Church.

For further reference: Maurilio Guasco, *Il caso Murri dalla sospensione alla scomunica* (Urbino: Argalia, 1978); Romolo Murri, *La Chiesa e i nuovi tempi* (Rome: Direzione della Scuola Teolgica Battista, 1917); Pietro Scoppola, *Crisi modernista e rinnovamento cattolico in Italia* (Bologna: Il Mulino, 1961).

Elisa A. Carrillo

MUSSOLINI AND PAPACY. Benito Mussolini ruled Italy from 1922 to 1943, frequently in close collaboration with the papacy, the Italian HIERARCHY, and the Catholic laity. Yet, when Mussolini's ambitions led to his association with Hitler in the Rome-Berlin Axis, the papacy withdrew active support, assumed a neutral position, and protected the future founders of the Christian Democratic Party. Mussolini started his political career as an anticlerical, revolutionary socialist. Expelled by the Socialist Party in 1914 for supporting intervention in WORLD WAR I, Mussolini created fascism out of an amalgam of revolutionary and nationalist interests in 1919. Fascism was adopted by landed and business interests as an antidote to socialism in 1920 and 1921, causing Mussolini to find political advantage in shedding his anticlericalism. In his first address to the Chamber of Deputies in 1921, he called for reconciliation between church and state.

While the Fascist Party was a useful tool to frighten the authorities, Mussolini's appointment as prime minister in October 1922 owed as much to his acceptability to the traditional governing elites—army, monarchy, business interests, and landed classes—as to his revolutionary initiatives. Once in power, Mussolini saw an opportunity of acquiring the support of the Italian church and the papacy for his regime by resolving the "ROMAN QUESTION." In 1870, Italian troops seized Rome from the papacy and ended the POPE's temporal power. Consequently, the papacy refused to recognize the kingdom of Italy or to encourage Catholics to participate in its political process. Where a series of anticlerical governments had refused to discuss the restoration of the temporal power, the appointment of Mussolini as prime minister with a stated willingness to resolve the Roman question opened new prospects for the papacy.

Pope PIUS XI (1922–1939) responded to Mussolini's initiatives, and secret negotiations began. The pope believed that the needs of Italian Catholics could best be served by the development of Catholic Action, the nonpolitical association of the Catholic laity that operated under the hierarchy of the church. Negotiations would allow the pope to protect Catholic Action in Italy. The negotiations culminated in the Lateran Agreements of February 1929, which consisted of a treaty, a CONCORDAT, and a financial agreement. In the treaty, the papacy recognized the kingdom of Italy, and, in return, Italy recognized VATICAN CITY as an independent state, thereby renewing the temporal power of the papacy. The concordat regulated the role of the Italian church and protected Catholic Action.

The LATERAN ACCORDS meant that it was no longer unpatriotic for an Italian to be a practicing Catholic, and consequently they were very popular. Both Mussolini and the papacy benefited. The support of the Vatican secured the Catholic Church as a buttress of the fascist regime and was instrumental in creating Mussolini's domestic consensus of the early 1930s. At the same time, the Vatican became influential in Italian education, while the membership of Catholic Action expanded rapidly. Fearing its popularity, the Fascist Party forced Mussolini to impose tighter controls on Catholic Action in 1931, but relations between church and state nevertheless remained close until after the ETHIO-PIAN WAR.

The Ethiopian War of 1935–1936 was used by Mussolini to free himself from reliance on the traditional institutions of Italy. Hence, he would not reward the church for its support during the war and make the new Italian empire officially Catholic by extending the Lateran Agreements to it. Nor was Mussolini's post-war cooperation with Adolf Hitler and the German Nazis well received by the Vatican. While Hitler concluded a concordat (see Germany, Concordat of 1933) in 1933, he did not respect its terms, as Mussolini had done. The Vatican feared that the 1936 Rome–Berlin Axis would result in Mussolini's adoption of the Nazi attitude toward the church.

Mussolini's subservience to Hitler was made manifest in 1938, when Italy accepted the German occupation of Catholic Austria. Pius XI had protested strenuously against the new relationship with Germany, even leaving Rome when Hitler visited in May 1938. The introduction of Italian anti-Semitic legislation in the summer of 1938 was strongly opposed by the pope, both because it aped Nazi racism and because it reflected the policy of racial and religious apartheid, which was being practiced in the Italian empire. In 1938, the active support of the papacy for Mussolini's regime came to an end, and the Vatican assumed a more neutral stance in its dealings with the fascist government. Hitler's influence with Mussolini increased as that of the Vatican declined. The Vatican kept its own counsel in WORLD WAR II and sheltered antifascist Catholic leaders within the walls of Vatican City. When Mussolini was ousted from power in 1943, these Catholics emerged from hiding to create the Christian Democratic Party, which soon dominated the postfascist governments of Italy.

For further reference: Peter C. Kent, *The Pope and the Duce: The International Impact of the Lateran Agreements* (London: Macmillan, 1981); Peter C. Kent, "A Tale of Two Popes: Pius XI, Pius XII and the Rome-Berlin Axis," *Journal of Contemporary History* 23 (1988): 589–608; John F. Pollard, *The Vatican and Italian Fascism, 1929–1932: A Study in Conflict* (Cambridge: Cambridge University Press, 1985); Anthony Rhodes, *The Vatican in the Age of the Dictators, 1922–45* (London: Hodder and Stoughton, 1973).

Peter C. Kent

N

NATO AND THE PAPACY. During the COLD WAR, PIUS XII provided moral support to a number of associations formed to safeguard the West against possible communist aggression. Among these were the Western European Union (1948) and the North Atlantic Treaty Organization (NATO) (1949). The United States was anxious to include Italy as a charter member of NATO because of its strategic location in the Mediterranean and its proximity to communist Yugoslavia and Albania. Alberto Tarchiani, Italy's ambassador to the United States, seconded this call but met considerable resistance among some left-wing currents of Italy's ruling Christian Democratic Party. Vatican pressure on Premier Alcide DE GASPERI helped persuade the party to approve ratification of the treaty in April 1949. Subsequently, the papacy raised no objections to including Greece and Turkey (1952), West Germany (1955), and Spain (1982) in NATO. In the Netherlands in the early 1980s, certain Catholic peace groups (though apparently without support from the papacy) objected to deployment by NATO of intermediate-range nuclear weapons in response to Soviet deployment of analogous weapons.

For further reference: G. Di Capua, *Come l'Italia aderì al Patto atlantico* (Rome: EBE, 1971); Ennio di Nolfo, "La Civiltà Cattolica e le scelte di fondo della politica estera italiana nel secondo dopoguerra," *Storia e Politica* (1970): 230–239; Eric O. Hanson, *The Catholic Church in World Politics* (Princeton: Princeton University Press, 1987).

Charles F. Delzell

NAZI GERMANY AND THE VATICAN. The rise of the Nazis to power in January 1933 led to a rapid change in relations between the German government and the Vatican. Prompted by a desire for international legitimation from Europe's oldest diplomatic entity and by a need to thwart any possible resistance from clerical forces in Germany, HITLER, in contrast to the hesitations of the previous governments of the Weimar Republic, offered to conclude a *Reich CONCORDAT* (see Germany, Concordat of 1933) with the Vatican. Leading officials, including the Catholic vice-chancellor, von Papen, were dispatched to Rome in April 1933, prepared to make far-reaching concessions to the Catholic Church in such matters as education and to offer the prospect of a legal treaty applicable to the whole country. The German bishops warmly supported this move, hoping thereby to obtain a legally guaranteed status that would remove any danger of a renewal of Bismarck's ill-fated *KULTURKAMPF*. This offer was quickly taken up by the Vatican authorities, especially by the cardinal-secretary of state, Pacelli, who had served as NUNCIO in Germany for twelve years (1917–1929) but whose efforts to obtain such an agreement had been consistently thwarted. The concordat was signed in July 1933 and ratified in September.

The haste with which the concordat was drafted, however, left many issues unresolved, in particular, the future of Catholic organizations. As the Nazi Party consolidated its power, its more radical members sought to interpret the treaty to their advantage and to place restrictions on the freedom of expression, which was supposedly guaranteed. The Nazis' incessant nationalist propaganda campaigns advanced claims to a totalitarian control, which contradicted the Vatican assumption that Catholic rights and privileges would remain protected. Conflict over the issue of youth activities became increasingly obvious. Expressions of Catholic dissent were ruthlessly suppressed by the secret police or by administrative measures.

The Vatican's expectations that the Nazi regime would turn out to be a traditional nationalist and conservative force were soon disillusioned. By the middle 1930s, the more dangerous elements in Nazism, with their explicit anticlerical and anti-Christian bias, seemed to be uppermost. The numerous and lengthy remonstrances against breaches of the concordat sent from Rome were either ignored or sidestepped. The Vatican's concordat with such a regime now proved to be decisively compromising and hindered the mobilization of Catholic resistance to Nazi pretensions. No less inhibiting was the Vatican's awareness that the majority of German Catholics readily supported Hitler's nationalist and racialist goals.

In March 1937, Pope PIUS XI issued a strongly worded encyclical, *Mit brennender Sorge*, protesting against the anti-Christian beliefs of the Nazi Party, which was smuggled into Germany and read from almost every pulpit. The results proved disappointing. Hitler abandoned his tactically motivated stratagem of using the Catholics to bolster his regime and encouraged his officials to step up their attacks on Catholic institutions and activities. On the other hand, no full-scale *Kulturkampf* was reinstated. Hitler shrewdly calculated that he could retain the loyalty of German Catholics so long as no open breach with the Vatican took place.

With the looming threat of a renewed war in Europe, the Vatican, especially after Pacelli's election as Pope PIUS XII (1939–1958) in March 1939, threw its efforts into the attempt to maintain peace. Pius XII's belief that the Vatican should exercise its influence and diplomatic skills to bring hostilities to an end lasted throughout WORLD WAR II. Despite the growing evidence of German aggression and war crimes, the Vatican's political stance precluded any open condemnation. This proved to be the case even after 1942, when awareness of the horrendous genocide of the Jews of Europe was brought to the Vatican's attention by its nuncios. The nadir of German–Vatican relations came in 1943–1944, when Rome was occupied by German troops, the Vatican was surrounded, and officials feared they would be carried off into captivity. Despite his evident malevolence, Hitler nevertheless decided that such a step would reap few benefits. On the other side, despite the clear evidence of the Nazi regime's criminal character, the Vatican still adhered to its peacemaking task. Relations were never broken off.

In the aftermath, Pius XII and his Vatican officials were widely reproached for their failure to oppose Nazism more vigorously and, in particular, to protest the mass murder of the Jews. The subsequent publication of the numerous diplomatic protests made by the Vatican to the German government did little to disarm critics who believed the Vatican's reputation had been dangerously compromised. On a deeper level, Nazi Germany's relations with the Vatican provide a graphic picture of the diminished moral and political authority of all religious institutions, including the Vatican, in an age of uncontrolled political dictatorship fired by national and racist ambitions for universal hegemony.

For further reference: Pierre Blet et al., eds., *Actes et documents du Saint Siege relatif à la seconde guerre mondiale*, 11 vols. (Vatican City: Libreria Editrice Vaticana, 1965–1981); Peter Kent and John Pollard, eds., *Papal Diplomacy in the Modern Age* (Westport: Praeger, 1994).

John S. Conway

NAZI RACIALISM AND THE VATICAN. The ideological position of the National Socialist Party, as developed during the 1920s and clearly expressed in Adolf HITLER's book *Mein Kampf* (1925), was based on a concept of history dictated by racial conflict. The calling of the German people to be the dominant race was threatened by "lesser races," especially Jews. Hitler readily accepted the current view in the 1920s, ascribing Germany's catastrophic defeats and, indeed, all social evils to a deliberate conspiracy organized by the powerful forces of world Jewry. In contrast to earlier religiously based antagonism to Judaism, Nazi racialism stressed the biological danger of interracial breeding, the pernicious social impact of racist coexistence, and the necessity of stringent measures to protect the national purity of the German race. Nazi propagnada was to develop this image of the menace to public health of the Jewish race, frequently using metaphors drawn from pathology, veterinary science, or parasitology.

Hitler was not an original thinker. His skill lay in his oratorical ability to mobilize such diffuse ideas into a dynamic political creed in emotional and semireligious language, which offered a plausible explanation of Germany's post-1918 predicament. Skillfully organized by the party's chief propagandist, Josef Goebbels, the Nazi crusade for national regeneration on racial lines satisfied the aspirations of millions of Germans unwilling to face the reality of their new political situation.

Despite warnings issued by church leaders against the dangers of this political idolatry, the Nazi call for national unity and racial "purity" proved highly successful. After 1933, all organs of the Nazi Party received state support in a continuous and relentless campaign of denigration of "lesser races," especially the Jews, and in the propagation of an ersatz religion of blood and soil. No adequate measures were taken by the churches to counteract the political consequences of the ideological onslaught. In part, this failure can be attributed to the unwillingness or inability of European churchmen to confront their followers with the need to be prepared to take up arms against state-organized injustice and violence. But, in part, the impact of entrenched, theological anti-Semitic prejudice must be held responsible for the lack of any coherent Christian defense of Judaism or the Jewish people.

The Vatican's stance on Nazi racialism or on anti-Semitism was, at best, ambivalent. The fact that the Holy See had not opposed the rise of FASCISM in Italy, had concluded a concordat with the new Nazi regime in 1933, and had failed to denounce the frequent anti-Semitic utterances of church leaders in such countries as Poland and Hungary leads to the conclusion that the protection of the Catholic communities' political position outweighed concern for the Jewish victims of racially inspired policies. The Vatican's most notable challenge came in the papal encyclical *Mit brennender Sorge* of March 1937, which denounced the totalitarian pretensions of Nazi racialism and called for the restoration of the inalienable rights of the individual. But no explicit reference was made to Nazi anti-semitism or to the Nazi persecution of the Jews. The political impact was negligible.

Anti-Semitism continued to be regarded as the product of pagan secularism. There is no evidence that the Vatican was prepared to acknowledge the Christian component in the formation of anti-Semitic attitudes or to adopt a revised theological stance to counteract such deeply entrenched dogmatic tendencies. Considerable, if insufficient, efforts were made by the Vatican to assist Jewish refugees, which were, however, often frustrated not only by Nazi countermeasures but also by the worldwide indifference to the Jewish plight. This inauspicious climate undoubtedly contributed to the Vatican's failure to recognize the full consequences of the Nazi genocidal policies, let alone the implications for Christianity and the church. In short, the Vatican's protests against Nazi racism were made more to safeguard traditional respect for Catholic nationalism or to identify the church with the victims of brutal treatment than from any other conscious rejection of anti-Semitic ideologies in the name of Christian theological insights.

For further reference: Guenter Lewy, *The Catholic Church and Nazi Germany* (New York: McGraw-Hill, 1964).

                                                                    John S. Conway

NICAEA I, COUNCIL OF (325). The First Council of Nicaea was the first ecumenical COUNCIL of the Christian Church and was convened by the emperor Constantine not long after he won control of the Eastern part of the empire in 324. The intensity of the Arian controversy (see Arianism) threatened the unity of the Eastern church, and it is almost certain that Constantine was as determined to preserve peace as he was to ensure doctrinal rectitude. He had earlier sent his ecclesiastical adviser, Bishop Hosius of Cordova, to Alexandria to investigate the conflict between Bishop Alexander and Arius, and his report appears to have roused Constantine to call a council. According to a synod held at Antioch in late 324 or early 325, the original plan was to have the council meet in Ancyra, but Nicaea was more convenient for the Western bishops and closer to the emperor's residence.

The exact number of bishops who attended is impossible to ascertain, but it has traditionally been fixed at 318, which is surely a symbolic figure. The commonly accepted opening date has always been 20 May 325, but recent scholarship shows that it was actually 19 June of that year. It is impossible to verify whether Hosius of Cordova, Eustathius of Antioch, or possibly Alexander of Alexandria presided over the sessions; the name of Hosius, however, together with the names of Vitus and Vincentius, the representatives of the Roman bishop, appears before the names of the other bishops in the list of participants, among whom were the three just mentioned, as well as the young deacon Athanasius of Alexandria, Eusebius of Caesarea, and Eusebius of Nicomedia, a supporter of Arius.

The council commenced with a discussion concerning the nature of the Son and his relationship to the Father. Constantine formally opened the proceedings with a welcoming address, and the first order of business was the rejection of an Arian profession of faith offered by Eusebius of Nicomedia. Eusebius of Caesarea then presented a creed that was used in his own community; although Constantine, who favored Eusebius, may have preferred this creed, which was accepted as orthodox, the council did not use it in formulating its own profession of faith. It is now generally agreed that the creed that was promulgated at Nicaea derived from that used in the church of Jerusalem. This creed, together with a list of anti-Arian condemnations, was signed by all the bishops present except two, who were deposed and sent into exile.

A series of twenty canons dealt with a variety of ecclesiastical issues: the life and ordination of clergy and bishops, the primacy of certain sees, penitential practice, viaticum, treatment of apostates and of the followers of Paul of Samosata and the Cathars, and the requirement to pray standing (not kneeling) on Sundays and during the season of Pentecost. A letter from the council was sent to the church of Alexandria, informing it of the council's actions; the council also attempted to settle the Melitian SCHISM in Alexandria, and it ordered that the Eastern churches should follow the method employed by Rome and Alexandria in fixing the date of Easter.

The bishop of Rome approved the council's actions, but after the council Eusebius of Nicomedia withdrew his signature, and Eusebius of Caesarea interpreted the creed in such a way that he withheld full support of the Nicene teaching. Arius had been condemned, but the Arian controversy would continue for another 50 years before drawing to a close.

For further reference: L. D. Davis, *The First Seven Ecumenical Councils (325–787): Their History and Theology* (Wilmington, DE: Michael Glazier, 1987); I. Ortiz de Urbina, *Nicée et Constantinople*, Histories des Conciles, vol. 1 (Prais: Editions de l'Orante, 1963); E. Honigmann, "The Original Lists of the Members of the Council of Nicaea," *Byzantion* 16 (1942–1943): 20–28; J. N. D. Kelly, *Early Christian Creeds*, 3d ed. (London: Longmans, 1972), pp. 205–262; T. E. Pollard, "The Creeds of A.D. 325: Antioch, Caesarea, Nicaea," *Scottish Journal of Theology* 13 (1960): 278–300; N. P. Tanner, ed., *Decrees of the Ecumenical Councils*, vol. 1 (London: Sheed and Ward; Washington, DC: Georgetown University Press, 1990), pp. 1–19.

Gerard H. Ettlinger

NICAEA II, COUNCIL OF (787). The Seventh Ecumenical Council met at Nicaea in 787 to halt the iconoclastic movement, which had raged in the Eastern church throughout the eighth century. In 754 a synod in Hieria affirmed the iconoclastic position against icons and veneration of the saints, giving rise to a renewed and bitter persecution of those who opposed it. In 784 Tarasius, the new patriarch of Constantinople, suggested to the empress Irene, acting as regent for her minor son Constantine VI, that a council be convened. An invitation was sent to Pope ADRIAN I (772–795), who accepted and agreed to send two LEGATES on the condition, among others, that the Synod of Hieria be condemned.

The council was summoned in early 786 and met in August in the presence of the empress and her son; it was disrupted, however, by an attack of iconoclastic soldiers and was unable to meet again until September 787. Under the presidency of Tarasius and in the presence of the papal legates, the council participants professed their faith in the church's traditional teaching concerning the cult of sacred images as expressed in a letter of Adrian I, which was read at one of the sessions. They declared that the veneration offered to pictorial representations was not the absolute worship given to God but reverence and honor directed to the person represented by the image. Four anathemas on this topic were appended to the declaration of faith, as were twenty-two disciplinary canons concerning bishops, clergy, and monks. The papal legates signed the declaration, but Tarasius sent word to Adrian I about the council's actions. Although Adrian I did not reply, his defense of the council against Charlemagne in 794 indicates his acceptance of its decree. The iconoclastic movement was slowed by the council's declaration, but it continued to flourish in the military, broke out again with renewed strength in 814, and was stopped officially only in 843.

For further reference: P. Brown, "A Dark Age Crisis: Aspects of the Iconoclastic Controversy," *English Historical Review* 80 (1973): 1–34; L. D. Davis, *The First Seven Ecumenical Councils (325–787): Their History and Theology* (Wilmington, DE: Michael Glazier, 1987); G. Dumeige, *Nicée II*, Histoire des Conciles, vol. 4 (Paris: Editions de l'Orante, 1978); N. P. Tanner, ed., *Decrees of the Ecumenical Councils*, vol. 1 (London: Sheed and Ward; Washington, DC: Georgetown University Press, 1990), pp. 131–156.

Gerard H. Ettlinger

NICHOLAS I (858–867). Born in Rome in 800, Nicholas became a counselor to BENEDICT III (855–858), whom he succeeded. Nicholas devoted his term to defending the moral prerogatives of the papacy. In his decretals, he advanced the writings on papal power of LEO I (440–461), GELASIUS I (492–496), and GREGORY I (590–604), arguing that secular princes, as well as ecclesiastics, must recognize the POPE as final arbiter in all matters concerning morality. Three events dominated the papacy of Nicholas I: he prevented the brother of the Holy Roman Emperor from obtaining a divorce, forced metropolitans in the West to acknowledge the supremacy of the pope, and intervened in the succession to the patriarchate of Constantinople.

When the archbishop of Ravenna asserted he had ultimate authority over local bishops in his province (861), Nicholas forced him to relent by excommunicating (see Excommunication) and deposing him. Nicholas insisted that the metropolitans could not override the direct link between all bishops and the pope. Nicholas also forced the archbishop of Rheims, the most powerful metropolitan in the empire, to reinstall (865) a bishop he had deposed (861) without papal permission. In his dispute with the Byzantine emperor Nicholas may have alluded to the "False Decretals," which exalted the powers of the papacy in matters of ecclesiastical discipline. These Frankish forgeries were a series of thirty-nine false decrees and acts of spurious councils interpolated (c. 850) into a collection of genuine conciliar acts compiled by Isidor of Seville (d. 636).

When the Byzantine emperor deposed the patriarch Igantius (862) in a political dispute and replaced him with Photius, a learned layman, Nicholas, declared: "We, by the power committed to us by our Lord through St. Peter, restore our brother Ignatius to his former station" and pronounced anathema on anyone who attempted to contravene this order. Ignoring the anathema, Photius retaliated by excommunicating and deposing the pope (867), but Nicholas died on 13 November 867, before news of the Photian SCHISM reached Rome. The schism was not healed until the twentieth century. Nicholas was later proclaimed a saint.

For further reference: F. Dvornik, *The Photian Schism* (Cambridge: Cambridge University Press, 1948); W. Ullmann, *The Growth of Papal Government in the Middle Ages*, 2d ed. (London: Methuen, 1965).

Frank Grande

NICHOLAS II (1058–1061). Born in French Burgundy, Gerard de Bourgogne became bishop of Florence in 1045 and, under the influence of Hildebrand (the future GREGORY VII) and St. Peter Damien, allied himself with the reform cardinals. After STEPHEN IX (1057–1058) died in March 1058, the Tusculan family, seeking to regain control of Rome and the papacy, moved quickly to name a successor. On 5 April they proclaimed John Mincius, bishop of Velletri, Pope BENEDICT X. But the reform cardinals refused to recognize him and moved to Sienna, where they elected Gerard in December 1058 as Nicholas II. Once POPE, he devoted himself to securing the independence of papal elections from lay control.

In April 1059, at a Lateran Council, Nicholas issued the decree *In nomine Domini*, in which the election of the pope was reserved for the cardinal-bishops, to be confirmed by the other cardinals and the lesser Roman clergy. An honorary, but not automatic, right to confirm the election was given to the German emperor. By the time Henry IV reached his majority, two more popes had been elected under the new rule. In 1179 ALEXANDER III would extend the vote to the other orders of cardinals (priests and deacons) and introduce the requirement of two-thirds majority for election. Election in this manner by the College of CARDINALS would remain the rule down to 1945, when PIUS XII added the requirement of two-thirds plus one (to prevent any candidate from reaching the two-thirds majority through his own vote).

Nicholas II also sought other reforms, issuing decretals against simony, lay investiture, clerical marriage, and easy annulments. To gain a political ally, Nicholas recognized Robert Guiscard (1015–1085) as duke of Apulia and Calabria and lord of Sicily, thereby confirming the conquests he had already made. In turn, the Normans helped break the control over Rome and the papacy exercised by the Tusculan family since 1012. Nicholas died in Florence on 27 July 1061.

For further reference: C. Morris, *The Papal Monarchy: The Western Church from 1050 to 1250* (Oxford: Oxford University Press, 1989); B. Tierney, *The Crisis of Church and State, 1050–1300* (Englewood Cliffs, NJ: Prentice-Hall, 1964).

Frank Grande

NICHOLAS III (1277–1280). Giovanni Gaetani of the powerful Orsini family of Rome was elected POPE on 25 November 1277 and consecrated under the name of Nicholas III. From the beginning Nicholas was bent on recovering papal political independence. His ambitious plans included a CONCORDAT with the Hapsburg Holy Roman Emperor Rudolph of Germany that added the Romagna and the exarchate of Ravenna to the papal territories. Nicholas determined to oust the French from Sicily, aided in his effort by the Greek emperor Michael Paleologus, who provided him with funds for that purpose. This culminated in the so-called Sicilian Vespers of 1282. The inevitable consequence was the loss of that entire territory to the house of Anjou when the French retaliated in force.

A born politician, Nicholas increased the patrimony of the church during his pontificate. Dante praises Nicholas for his efforts to join the houses of Anjou and Hapsburg, hoping for a strong empire with Germany as its hereditary center and Burgundy, Lombardy, and Tuscany in a favored status within it. Nicholas III had other schemes at the time of his unexpected death in Soriano, near Viterbo, on 22 August 1280.

For further reference: J. N. D. Kelly, *The Oxford Dictionary of Popes* (Oxford: Oxford University Press, 1986); H. K. Mann, *The Lives of the Popes in the Early Middle Ages* (London: K. Paul, 1902–1932); Paget Toynbee, *Concise Dante Dictionary* (Oxford: Clarendon Press, 1914).

Anne Paolucci

NICHOLAS IV (1288–1292). Eleven months elapsed between the death of HONORIUS IV (1285–1287) and the election of Girolamo Masci, a FRANCISCAN friar, as a compromise candidate. The first Franciscan to be elected POPE, this Italian-born cleric had previously served as provincial of Dalmatia, papal LEGATE at Constantinople and the COUNCIL of Lyons in 1274, general of the Franciscan order, and cardinal-bishop of Palestrina. Like many of his predecessors, Nicholas was submerged in the ongoing struggles between competing Roman noble families. He favored the Colonna family, appointing members to various administrative posts within the papacy and elevating one to the position of cardinal.

Nicholas' reign was noteworthy for his foreign involvements, particularly the Sicilian issue. The pontiff demanded that Aragon return control of Sicily, a papal fief, to the Angevins, despite the latter's loss of the territory resulting from the War of Sicilian Vespers in March 1282. Aragon's refusal to abide by the pope's request prompted Nicholas to promote a military alliance between Castille and France against Aragon. Alfonso III (1285–1291), king of Aragon and James' older brother, made peace with the pope, abandoned James' claim to Sicily, and ended the war between Aragon and France. Unfortunately for Nicholas, Alfonso died suddenly, leaving James king of both Aragon and Sicily.

Nicholas' setback in Sicily was not his only foreign failure. The fall of Tripoli in Lebanon in April 1289 convinced the pontiff that a new crusade was necessary. His issuance of a call to the Christian monarchs of Europe was met with many promises but no action. Instead, Nicholas' reign witnessed the end of the crusading impulse when Acre, the last remaining Christian enclave in the Holy Land, fell to the sultan of Egypt. This failure in the Near East, however, was redeemed by an important success in the Far East. Nicholas appointed Giovanni di Monte Corvino, a Franciscan friar, as missionary to the court of the Chinese emperor Kubla Khan (1260–1294). Nicholas' most notable internal action occurred on 18 June 1289, when he issued *Coelestis altitudo*. This constitutional bull not only divided papal revenues with the College of CARDINALS but also provided for a separate administration, thus granting the assembly greater independence.

For further reference: Eric John, ed., *The Popes: A Concise Biographical Dictionary* (New York: Hawthorn Books, 1964); H. K. Mann, *The Lives of the Popes in the Early Middle Ages* (London: K. Paul, 1902–1932); Walter Ullman, *A Short History of the Papacy in the Middle Ages* (London: Methuen, 1972).

John C. Horgan

NICHOLAS V, ANTIPOPE (1328–1330). After the conflict that erupted between JOHN XXII (1316–1334) and the FRANCISCANS, the pontiff grappled for power with Emperor Louis IV. In an attempt to take over the church, Louis arranged to have a group of Roman clergymen elect Pietro Rainalducci on 18 April 1328. He took the name Nicholas V. Under the direction of Louis, Nicholas created a CURIA of Franciscans and Augustinian friars who opposed John XXII's rule. He found it beneficial to stay close to the emperor's side and departed Rome with him on 4 August 1328. By this time, the popularity of the ANTIPOPE and the influence of Louis in Italy had waned. In April, Nicholas decided to part company with Louis and went into hiding. When John learned of his presence, he demanded that Nicholas be turned over. Nicholas appealed to the POPE, who allowed him to travel to Avignon, where he renounced the title of antipope and pledged loyalty to John. The pontiff forgave him and detained him in honorable confinement at the papal residence until Pietro's death on 16 October 1333.

For further reference: Eric John, *The Popes: A Concise Bibliographical History* (London: Burns and Oates, 1964); J. N. D. Kelly, *The Oxford Dictionary of the Popes* (Oxford: Oxford University Press, 1986).

Christopher S. Myers

NICHOLAS V (1447–1455). Tommaso Parentucelli was born in Sarzana, Italy, 15 November 1397. After his studies he joined the household of Cardinal Nicholas Albergati of Bologna, becoming bishop of Bologna in 1444 and cardinal in 1446. Following his election Nicholas V's first task was to secure papal authority in the face of the Council of BASEL. He won the support of Emperor Frederick III with the CONCORDAT of Vienna and the promise of the imperial Crown. He dealt leniently with Basel's leaders and accepted his election by the council, its final act before its dissolution. He withdrew all its censures, confirmed the benefices it had granted, and restored the titles and benefices its adherents had lost.

The same conciliatory attitude guided his governance at home. He made generous concessions to Roman families to pacify the PAPAL STATES. The Jubilee of 1450 brought thousands to the Holy City and enhanced papal authority. He also planned to transform the dilapidated medieval city into the city that greets the visitor today. In addition, he recruited scholars for the papal chancery and the Vatican Library. His efforts to enrich the library make him the founder of that institution. Not all of Nicholas' projects were crowned with success. Cardinal William d' Estouteville's efforts in France and St. John Capistran's in

Bohemia ended in failure. His efforts to aid Constantinople before its fall like-wise failed. His call for a crusade fell on deaf ears. He had to deal with the conspiracy of Stefano Porcaro to assassinate him and overthrow papal authority. Despite these failures, when he died, Nicholas had done much to restore the moral authority of the papacy and set it on a course that would define it for the next several centuries.

For further reference: J. Gill, "Pope Nicholas V," *New Catholic Encyclopedia*, vol. 10, pp. 443–445; L. Pastor, *The History of the Popes*, vol. 2 (New York: B. Herder, 1899).

Richard J. Kehoe

NON ABBIAMO BISOGNO. An encyclical letter written in Italian by Pope PIUS XI (1922–1939), dated 29 June 1931 but not published until 7 July 1931, *Non abbiamo bisogno* was issued during a bitter controversy between Italian Catholic Action and fascist officials. In this encyclical the pope protested against the physical violence and verbal abuse directed by the Fascist Party against Catholic youth organizations and the attempt to establish a fascist monopoly over Italian youth.

The pope also denied MUSSOLINI'S allegation that Italian Catholic Action was dominated by former members of the Italian POPULAR PARTY. He char-acterized the fascist regime as "based on ideology which clearly resolves itself into a true and real pagan worship of the state." This ideology, asserted the pope, was incompatible with Catholicism. While not condemning the Fascist Party as a whole, the pontiff made it clear that certain elements of FASCISM ran counter to Catholic doctrine and practice. The controversy over Italian Cath-olic Action ended in a compromise. The integrity and independence of Italian Catholic Action were preserved.

For further reference: D. A. Binchy, *Church and State in Fascist Italy* (London: Ox-ford, 1941); Liliana Ferrari, *Una Storia dell'Azione cattolica* (Genoa: Marietti, 1989); Angelo Martini, *Studi sulla Questione Romana e la conciliazione* (Rome: Edizioni 5 Lune, 1963).

Elisa A. Carrillo

NOVATIAN, ANTIPOPE (251–258). The details of Novatian's early life are unknown, but he was one of the leading figures in the Roman church after the death of FABIAN in January 250. The election of Fabian's successor was de-layed by the continuing persecution under Decius, but in June 251 an election was finally held, and Cornelius was chosen as bishop. Novatian then had himself consecrated bishop by three Italian bishops; his disaffection was further evi-denced in his shift from an apparently moderate to an extremely rigorist position regarding the treatment of repentant apostates. Cornelius espoused a gentle ap-proach that allowed them to return to the sacraments after completing an appropriate penance, but Novatian flatly rejected any form of reconciliation for such sinners.

Once Cornelius was established as bishop, he called a synod, which excommunicated (see Excommunication) Novatian and his followers. They formed their own church, whose doctrine was orthodox but that taught the rejected rigorism just described. It spread to both East and West and survived for several centuries. Although Cornelius expressed strong reservations and even dislike for him, Novatian was once very respected, and his writings were among the best of his time. His treatises on the Trinity, Jewish foods, public shows, and the advantages of chastity are extant and admired, even today, for both their literary style and their contents. The fifth-century historian Socrates says that Novatian died in 258 during the persecution of the emperor Valerian.

For further reference: R. J. De Simone, *The Treatise of Novatian the Roman Presbyter on the Trinity* (Rome: Institutum Patristicum Augustinianum, 1970); R. J. De Simone, trans., *Novatian. The Trinity, the Spectacle, Jewish Foods, in Praise of Purity*, Fathers of the Church (1974), vol. 67.

Gerard H. Ettlinger

NUNCIOS AND INTERNUNCIOS. The titles of "nuncio" and "internuncio" refer to those prelates within the church who serve as LEGATES on behalf of the Roman pontiff. What distinguishes them from an "APOSTOLIC DELEGATE" and from one another is the rank they hold within a country's diplomatic community. The apostolic nuncio is equivalent in rank to an ambassador and serves as the dean of the diplomatic corps. He performs both ecclesiastical and civil functions for the Apostolic See in the region to which he has been assigned. The apostolic internuncio, also a prelate appointed by the POPE, is equal in rank and responsibility to the nuncio with the exception that he is not the dean of the diplomatic corps.

For further reference: Richard P. McBrien, ed., *The Harper Collins Encyclopedia of Catholicism* (San Francisco: Harper, 1995).

David M. O'Connell

O

OFFICE, ECCLESIASTICAL. Canon 145 of the 1983 Code of CANON LAW defines an ecclesiastical "office" as "any function constituted in a stable manner by divine or ecclesiastical law to be exercised for a spiritual purpose." The same canon continues that "the obligations and rights proper to individual ecclesiastical offices are defined in the law by which the office is constituted or in the decree of a competent authority by which it is at the same time constituted and conferred." The code then devotes canons 146 through 196 inclusive to a description of the manner in which ecclesiastical offices are conferred and lost.

The 1983 code's description of ecclesiastical office, formulated in light of the deliberations of the Second Vatican COUNCIL (see Vatican Council II) (1962–1965), represents a change from the way the 1917 Code of Canon Law defined the same canonical institute. The 1917 code noted that when the term "ecclesiastical office" appeared in the text of its law, it is to be understood in the strict sense unless the law itself claimed otherwise. What is noteworthy in the change of definition that appears in the 1983 code is that the revised law no longer describes ecclesiastical office as including "some participation in the power of orders or jurisdiction," a phrase that would traditionally restrict the holding of ecclesiastical offices to members of the ordained clergy. Canon 228 of the later code explicitly states that "qualified lay persons are capable of assuming from their sacred pastors those ecclesiastical offices and functions which they are able to exercise in accord with the prescriptions of law."

The source of these innovations can be found in Vatican II's Dogmatic Constitution on the Church, *Lumen Gentium* (21 November 1964). Article 33 of that constitution decreed that "laymen have the capacity to be deputed by the HIERARCHY to exercise church functions for a spiritual purpose." Article 37 encourages church authorities to assign duties for the service of the church to members of the laity. At the same time that the Second Vatican Council and the 1983 code foster and encourage lay participation in official church activities, canon 274 of the code continues to restrict those offices that require the powers of orders or ecclesiastical governance to members of the ordained clergy.

Examples of those offices restricted to the clergy would include the diocesan bishop and his episcopal vicars, the judicial vicar, the vicar forane, the pastor of a parish, the rector of a church, the religious superior in an exempt clerical institute, chaplains, and the rector of a seminary. Among the ecclesiastical offices available to qualified members of the laity are that of the diocesan chancellor, diocesan notaries, the diocesan finance officer and members of the diocesan finance council, and judges in a collegiate tribunal.

For further reference: The 1917 and 1983 Codes of Canon Law; Walter M. Abbott, ed., *The Documents of Vatican II* (New York: Herder and Herder, 1966); James A. Coriden, *An Introduction to Canon Law* (New York and Mahwah, NJ: Paulist Press, 1991; James A. Coriden et al., eds., *The Code of Canon Law: A Text and Commentary* (New York and Mahwah, NJ: Paulist Press, 1985).

David M. O'Connell

OPUS DEI. *Opus Dei* is a prelature of lay and clergy members founded in Spain in 1928 by Josemaria Escriva de Balaguer y Albas (1902–1975). Restricted at first to men, Escriva's young society inaugurated a women's branch in 1930. In 1943 his work received sanction from the Holy Office in Rome for the creation of a parallel organization, the Priestly Society of the Holy Cross, permitting diocesan priests to identify with *Opus Dei*. Pope PIUS XII (1939–1958) approved the *Opus Dei* constitution in 1950. In 1982 Pope JOHN PAUL II awarded the institution the stature of "personal" prelature in that it is not organized territorially or along diocesan lines but rather on an individual, or personal, basis. Thus, while loyal to their local bishops, lay members submit to the jurisdiction of the prelate of *Opus Dei* who resides in Rome. Local bishops, nevertheless, enjoy a measure of supervision over *Opus Dei* activities that occur within their diocese. Some priests in the movement, furthermore, have been appointed as bishops, particularly in Latin America.

The society's history has been brief but stormy. It has been dominated, in death almost as much as in life, by Escriva, who was declared "venerable" in 1990 and was beatified on 17 May 1992. Born in Barbastro, Spain, he studied at Logrono and Zaragoza and was ordained in 1925. From the beginning, Escriva's ability to elicit a strong loyalty from *Opus Dei* members, combined with much secrecy around the society's internal affairs, has fostered a degree of suspicion among outsiders. Along with Escriva's writings, specifically his *Camino*, much of the public knowledge about the society has stemmed from accidental leaks of information or from the writings and claims of former members.

Controversy has also touched on *Opus Dei*'s alleged right-wing political activities. Initially and in particular, its close identification with Francisco Franco and the nationalist cause in Spain's civil war has occasioned speculation. Escriva's intense animosity toward the political Left has been well documented.

Spain's Communist Party, in fact, condemned him to death during the conflict. But *Opus Dei*'s numerical insignificance during the 1930s and some Francoist suspicions that it fronted Masonic activity (a few members were, in fact, arrested for this in Barcelona in 1940), render somewhat inflated claims of its significance for the nationalist victory. By the 1950s and 1960s, however, a stronger and more mature *Opus Dei* had attained a clear prominence in Franco's regime. Yet the nature of this relationship remained unclear since, while many of Spain's most important ministers, particularly in the economic chairs, were *Opus Dei* members, others, such as Calvo Serer and Escriva, himself, publicly argued with Falangist ideologues.

By the end of WORLD WAR II *Opus Dei* had expanded to about twenty Spanish cities and abroad, to Portugal (Coimbra in 1945), to Italy, and to the United Kingdom (1946). It subsequently enjoyed particular success in Mexico, Colombia, Peru, Chile, Kenya, Germany, the United States, Canada, and the Philippines. Nevertheless, *Opus Dei* continues to be dogged by accusations of political and economic intrigue. In the 1970s and 1980s, for example, members were linked to Augusto Pinochet's authoritarian regime in Chile and to the Masonic P-2 scandal in Italy. But *Opus Dei* has also earned repute for the construction and administration of high schools around the world and of universities in Spain and Latin America.

For further reference: Peter Berglar, *Opus Dei, Life and Work of Its Founder, Josemaria Escriva De Balaguer* (Princeton: Scepter Press, 1993); Rocca Giancarlo, *L' "Opus Dei," Appunti e documenti per una storia* (Rome: Edizioni Paoline, 1985).

Roy Palmer Domenico

OSSERVATORE ROMANO, L'. A Vatican newspaper, the current *Osservatore Romano* was founded as a daily in 1861, although it had predecessors in 1849 and 1851. Begun as an independent "moral-political newspaper," after 1870 it became the authoritative but unofficial organ of the Holy See, publishing the Italian texts of papal speeches and pronouncements as well as other official Church announcements. Its editors are appointed by the Secretariat of State, and the *Osservatore*'s editorials and major articles are presumed to reflect the Vatican's views. During the Fascist dictatorship and the German occupation, *L'Osservatore Romano* was frequently the source of information not found in any other Italian publication.

For further reference: Richard P. McBrien, ed., *The HarperCollins Encyclopedia of Catholicism* (San Francisco: Harper, 1995).

Salvatore Saladino

P

PAPAL BULL. The expression "papal bull" is derived from the Latin term *bulla*, which refers to any object made round through artistic endeavor. Its use with regard to papal writings originated in the rounded, leaden seal used to authenticate these documents. The practice of marking papal documents with a spherical, lead seal seems to have been established by the sixth century in the papal chancery. On one side of the seal appeared the names of ST. PETER and St. Paul, while the other side of the medallion bore the name of the papal author himself. Initially a reference to the papal seal, the expression "bull" gradually became a widely used description for the papal document itself.

By the pontificate of Pope INNOCENT IV (1243–1254), the expression "papal bull" referred only to the most important documents written by the POPE. These writings, reserved for matters of great moment, were characterized by a formal, stylized penmanship. Written in Latin and borrowing their title from the first two words of the text itself, papal bulls began with the name of the pope and the title, *Servus servorum Dei*, servant of the servants of God. They were dated according to the year of the pontificate in which they appeared (e.g., "in the tenth year of our pontificate").

Pope LEO XIII (1878–1903) introduced the practice of using modern literary script within the papal bull and replaced the leaden seal with a red stamp bearing the same information contained on the previous type of seal. Pope Leo XIII reserved the use of papal bulls to only the most solemn circumstances. His successor, Pope PIUS X (1903–1914), began to date the papal bulls with the year, month, and day of their issuance in addition to the year of the pontificate in which they appeared. In general, papal bulls contain papal decrees, ordinances, precepts, and rescripts as well as announcements of hierarchical titles, canonizations, and decisions requiring explicit papal approval.

For further reference: Francis G. Morrisey, *The Canonical Significance of Papal and Curial Pronouncements* (Washington, DC: Canon Law Society of America, 1978).

David M. O'Connell

PAPAL GUARANTEES, THE LAW OF, 1871. The Law of Papal Guarantees was passed by the Italian Parliament on 13 May 1871 to regulate relations with the papacy following the Italian occupation of Rome on 20 September 1870 and the final liquidation of the POPE's "temporal power," the territorial sovereignty that he had exercised over the PAPAL STATES of central Italy. Despite repeated rejections of the law by successive pontiffs, it formed the basis of church–state relations until the resolution of the "ROMAN QUESTION," as the church–state conflict was called, by the signing of the Lateran Pacts in 1929.

The law was based on the proposals made to PIUS IX (1846–1878) in the winter of 1860–1861 by Count Camillo Cavour, first prime minister of Italy, following the incorporation of the northern and central sections of the papal states into the newly unified kingdom. The pope had rejected the proposals, refused to recognize the new state, and excommunicated (see Excommunication) its rulers. Despite Pius IX's continuing refusal to negotiate and despite the fierce criticisms of the bill by the more anticlerical opposition party, the Left, the governmental majority, secured passage of the legislation.

The Law of Papal Guarantees was built around the principle that the pope would be allowed unhindered exercise of his spiritual powers. To this end, it provided that the pope should be accorded all the honors and privileges of a sovereign ruler in Italy, that he should have free communication with the church in Italy and the world, that the envoys to his court should enjoy the same privileges and immunities as diplomats accredited to Italy, and that St. Peter's basilica and the Apostolic Palace ("VATICAN CITY") and other papal palaces and offices in and around the city of Rome should enjoy extraterritorial status.

In addition, the Italian government guaranteed that general COUNCILS of the Roman Catholic Church and conclaves to elect the pope were to be free from outside interference, and the pope was to be granted an annual payment of 3.25 million lire as compensation for the loss of revenues from the former papal states. Finally, in regard to church–state relations in Italy, the law provided for the eventual enactment of legislation for the abolition of state control over episcopal appointments (the *EXEQUATUR* and *PLACET regium*) and for "the re-organization, conservation and administration of ecclesiastical property throughout the Kingdom."

Both Pius IX and his successor, LEO XIII (1878–1903), rejected the law because it was not achieved through free negotiation and because it had no standing in international law, being merely an act of the Italian Parliament, which could unilaterally amend or repeal it. Over the years suggestions were made that the law should be "internationalized," that is, effectively turned into a bilateral treaty between the Holy See and Italy with additional guarantees from other powers. But the proposals foundered on objections that this arrangement would constitute interference in Italy's internal affairs.

Despite their rejection of the law, successive popes insisted on its strict observance by the Italians. They also deplored the fact that the legislation promised for the abolition of the *exequatur* and the *placet* and for the reorganization of ecclesiastical property was never passed. In fact, after the coming to power of the Left in 1876, legislation was introduced further restricting church influence over such matters as charities, and there were fears that the Law of Guarantees might be drastically amended or even repealed. Under the fiercely anticlerical prime minister Francesco Crispi church–state relations deteriorated, and on more than one occasion the pope considered leaving Rome. Nevertheless, by the end of the 1890s almost all Italian political forces had come to accept the necessity of the law.

Though Italian governments had been at pains to demonstrate their strict application of the law in regard to the papal conclaves of 1878, 1903, and 1914, after Italy's entry into WORLD WAR I in May 1915 there were serious violations of the spirit and letter of the law. The German and Austro-Hungarian envoys to the Holy See were banished to Switzerland for the duration of the hostilities, and the embassy of the Austro-Hungarian envoy was confiscated by the Italian state.

The end of World War I saw an attempt to find a solution to the "Roman question" on the basis of the transformation of the extraterritoriality granted by the Law of Guarantees into outright sovereignty for the Vatican City. The negotiations between Vittorio Emmanuele Orlando, prime minister of Italy, and Msgr. Cerretti, the papal envoy, took place behind the scenes at the Versailles Peace Conference in 1919. They failed due to Orlando's fall from power soon afterward.

In November 1919, Benito MUSSOLINI, the leader of the new fascist movement, declared that "there is only one possible revision of the Law of Guarantees and that is its abolition, followed by a firm invitation to his Holiness to quit Rome." Ironically, ten years later, it fell to Mussolini to achieve the long-sought-after reconciliation between the Holy See and Italy by signing the Lateran Pacts and repealing the Law of Guarantees on which, in so many of their aspects, the pacts were based.

For further reference: D. A. Binchy, *Church and State in Fascist Italy* (Oxford: Oxford University Press, 1970); A. C. Jemolo, *Church and State in Italy, 1850–1950* (Oxford: Basil Blackwell, 1960); J. F. Pollard, *The Vatican and Italian Fascism, 1929–1932* (Cambridge: Cambridge University Press, 1985), Appendix I (text of the law).

John F. Pollard

PAPAL STATES. The papal states were the territories in central Italy where the POPES were political as well as religious rulers. They took definite shape in the eighth century, when the lands that the popes had usually ruled de facto since the collapse of the Roman empire were confirmed to them by the Frankish rulers who then dominated Italy. The short-term justification for the papal state was that it provided Rome with the revenue necessary for its religious activities. The long-term justification was that it was necessary if the papacy were to have freedom of action to carry out its religious mission. Effective papal power ebbed and flowed: during the tenth century the papal state was controlled by the Roman aristocracy, and during the Avignon papacy (1305–1377) and the Great Western Schism (see Schism, Great Western) (1378–1418), papal authority nearly vanished. After each decline, however, there came a revival, usually marked by a further expansion of the states.

During the RENAISSANCE, the drawbacks of the papal states for the papacy became evident, as the popes became increasingly preoccupied with political activities, to the detriment of their spiritual role. Thereafter, doubts began to grow that the papal states were an asset rather than a liability for the papacy and the church, though down to at least the nineteenth century, most Catholic leaders remained convinced of their indispensability—how could the popes be truly free to perform their spiritual mission if they were under the control of some other ruler?

The French Revolution brought about the crisis of the papal states, a crisis that lasted, with intermissions, until their final disappearance in 1870. Napoleon invaded the papal states in 1797 and annexed the LEGATIONS; in February 1798, another French army occupied Rome, arrested Pope PIUS VI (1775–1799), and set up a Roman Republic that proclaimed the end of the temporal power. The republic was overthrown in 1799 by the Army of the Holy Faith (see Sanfedisti), a peasant force aroused by Fabrizio RUFFO, and the papal state once again revived, only to be again occupied and annexed to France in 1809.

The Congress of VIENNA restored the papal states in 1815. However, after years of progressive and secular French administration, the educated classes were hostile to the revival of the inefficient ecclesiastical regime. The papal secretary of state, Cardinal CONSALVI, tried to appease this discontent with a reform program but was driven from power by reactionaries who feared change. The reactionary policies that prevailed after his fall in 1823 led to the revolution of 1831, which was repressed only by Austrian intervention. The powers, concerned that discontent would lead to a new revolt, urged reform and drew up the MEMORANDUM OF 1831 as a guide; but nothing substantial was done to implement it, and discontent continued. By 1846, when PIUS IX (1846–1878) came to power, it was too late for his program of moderate reform to satisfy public opinion. In November 1848, he had to flee a radical uprising and was restored only by French intervention. Thereafter, the Papal States were clearly dependent on foreign protection, especially after the unification of most of the rest of Italy in 1859–1860. When in 1870 the French army withdrew, the Italian army occupied Rome. With the formal annexation of Rome to Italy on 6 October 1870, the papal states came to an end.

For further reference: Moritz Brosch, *Geschichte Kirchenstaats*, 2 vols. (Gotha: Herder, 1882); Mario Caravale, *Lo Stato Pontificio* (Turin: UTET, 1978).

Alan J. Reinerman

PASCHAL, ANTIPOPE (687). Paschal is one of the more than thirty claimants to the throne of Peter and has not received official recognition by the Roman Catholic Church as a legitimate POPE. This archdeacon of Rome sought to succeed CONAN (686–687) as pope in 687 and to this end sought and secured the support of the Imperial exarch or representative at Ravenna. Despite his bribes and imperial support, Paschal's election was contested by the Roman archpriest, Theodore, who emerged as a rival claimant. These two candidates occupied different parts of the Lateran palace with their respective supporters. Outside the Lateran, however, the clergy and people of Rome gathered at the imperial palace at the Palatine and secured the election of a compromise candidate, the titular priest Sergius of Sta Susanna. Paschal invoked the intervention of the exarch, who ventured to Rome from Ravenna. However, once in the city, the imperial representative deemed it prudent to uphold the election of SERGIUS I (687–689), deposing the two rival claimants. While Theodore accepted the decision, Paschal did not; he continued to intrigue to replace Sergius. For this and other reasons, he was imprisoned in a monastery, where he died in 692.

For further reference: Matthew Bunson, *The Pope Encyclopedia* (New York: Crown Trade Paperbacks, 1995); J. N. D. Kelly, *The Oxford Dictionary of Popes* (Oxford: Oxford University Press, 1986).

Francesca Coppa

PASCHAL I (817–824). Prior to the succession of STEPHEN IV (816–817), Paschal was ordained a priest by LEO III (795–816). He served for an extended period in the CURIA, followed by his appointment as abbot of St. Stephen's monastery. He was then elected POPE and consecrated the following day, fearful of opposition from the Holy Roman Emperor, the protector of the Holy See. The most significant contribution of his papacy was his ongoing effort to define a relationship between the newly formed Frankish empire and the papacy. During his pontificate, Paschal made numerous enemies and was despised by many in Rome. Upon his death, burial was prevented by the chaos in Rome. His successor, EUGENE II (824–827), entombed him in one of Paschal's newly built churches, Sta Prassede.

For further reference: Matthew Bunson, *The Pope Encyclopedia* (New York: Crown Trade Paperbacks, 1995); T. Jalland, *Church and Papacy* (London: SPCK, 1944).

Patrick McGuire

PASCHAL II (1099–1118). Rainerius, son of Crescentius, of a noble, but not wealthy, family, was born near Viterbo, Italy, around 1050. As a child he was offered as an oblate. Sent to Rome on business of his house, his abilities were recognized by GREGORY VII (1073–1085), who made him cardinal-priest of St. Clement. Later, he served URBAN II (1088–1099) in Spain and became abbot of St. Paul-outside-the-Walls. His sanctity led to his election to succeed Urban on 13 August 1099.

Although Paschal hoped to reach accord with Emperor Henry IV, the latter refused to abandon his claims to invest bishops, so that his EXCOMMUNI-CATION was renewed in 1102. Meanwhile, Ivo of Chartres had prepared the theoretical ground for a settlement by drawing a distinction between a cleric's *spiritualia* and his *temporalia*, refusing lay claims to confer the former but allowing the latter. In 1107 this distinction formed the basis for a settlement signed by Paschal with Philip I of France and another settlement that same year negotiated between St. Anselm of Canterbury and Henry I of England.

Emperor Henry IV was overthrown by his son in 1105, who succeeded as Henry V. Although supported by Paschal, Henry V also refused to abandon his claims to invest with ring and crosier and was condemned by the pope at synods held in 1106, 1107, 1108, and 1110. Henry marched on Rome, seeking imperial coronation. Prior to his arrival, Paschal II and Henry V agreed to the remarkable CONCORDAT of Sutri on 9 February 1111. By this pact, the church in the empire would return to the emperor all *temporalia* given by previous emperors and kings, retaining only the tithes and gifts bestowed by private patrons. Paschal would also crown Henry as emperor. In return, Henry would abandon all claims to investiture.

The reaction among the aristocratic following was intense, and Henry refused to abide by the concordat. Eventually, Paschal was taken prisoner, forced to crown Henry, and in April to concede investiture to the emperor. Freed from confinement, the pope repudiated the privileges forced from him (1112) and renewed the condemnation of lay investiture (1116). Paschal died in Rome on 21 January 1118, without having reached agreement with the empire, but his pontificate prepared the way for the Concordat of Worms in 1122.

For further reference: John Thomas Gilchrist, ''Paschal II, Pope,'' *New Catholic Encyclopedia*, vol. 10 (New York: McGraw-Hall, 1967), p. 1049; Alfred Haverkamp, *Medieval Germany, 1056–1273*, 2d ed., trans. Helga Braun and Richard Mortimer (Oxford: Oxford University Press, 1992); H. K. Mann, *The Lives of the Popes in the Early Middle Ages* (London: K. Paul, 1902–1932).

William C. Schrader

PASCHAL III, ANTIPOPE (1164–1168). Guy of Crema, cardinal of St. Callistus, was a partisan of the Roman empire. His election on 22 April 1164 as Paschal III, two days after the death of antipope VICTOR IV (1159–1164), dispelled the hope that the SCHISM, started in 1159, would end at Victor's death. Emperor Frederick Barbarossa's chancellor rushed to elect Guy, so the electoral process lacked the appearance of legality.

Pope ALEXANDER III (1159–1181), the northern Italian communes, and the

Norman king, William I of Sicily, allied to the papacy by the Treaty of Bene-
vento of 1156, resisted the emperor's designs. Moreover, members of the
German episcopate that since 1159 had supported the emperor in their adhesion
to the ANTIPOPE were showing disaffection toward the new one and upholding
Alexander instead. Frederick sought to bolster the antipope's position by winning the king of England Henry II, a supporter of Alexander, to the cause of
Paschal. To strengthen the antipope's position, he held a diet at Wurzburg on
Pentecost 1165, and during its course the emperor and the secular and ecclesiastical princes took an oath that they would recognize only the schismatic Paschal.

Nonetheless, the imperial cause deteriorated in Italy. The cities subjected to
the emperor during his 1158 campaign rose in revolt in 1164. In 1165 Paschal
took residence at Viterbo, while Lombard resistance encouraged Alexander to
take possession of Rome. Barbarossa prepared a new Italian expedition and
captured Rome in 1167, while Alexander evaded imperial control by retiring to
Benevento. Paschal, who was crowned as POPE at St. Peter's on 22 July 1167,
crowned Frederick and his wife on 1 August. By then the imperial army fell
victim to a ravaging infection, probably malaria, that took the life of many.
Barbarossa, unable to eliminate Alexander or to resist the definite formation of
a Lombard League in December 1167, pulled back from Italy in a disastrous
retreat in the spring of 1168. At his departure the Lombards founded a fortified
city, named Alexandria in honor of the pope. Paschal's death on 20 September
1168 followed the defeat of the imperial policies.

For further reference: Marshall W. Baldwin, *Alexander III and the Twelfth Century*
(Glen Rock, NJ: Newman Press, 1968); Colin Morris, *The Papal Monarchy: The Western
Church from 1050 to 1250* (Oxford: Clarendon Press, 1989).

Elda G. Zappi

PAUL I (757–767). Pope STEPHEN II's (752–757) brother, Paul, played a
significant role in establishing the states of the church in Italy by the Frankish
king Pepin III. Two secular leaders, Desiderius, the new king of the Lombards,
and Constantine V Copionymos, the Byzantine emperor, challenged Paul's leadership skills during his early pontificate. Desiderius was determined to regain
the land his predecessor was forced to surrender to the church and Constantine.
He believed the pope was an obstacle to iconoclasm.

Throughout his papacy, Paul called for Pepin's assistance in defending the
chair. Initially, Desiderius posed the greatest threat to Paul by attacking papal
territories. Paul, again, called for Pepin's military assistance. Pepin, however,
did not send military assistance but sent emissaries to restrain the forces of
Desiderius and subsequently forced him to surrender the lands to the PAPAL
STATE. Paul encouraged the reform movement within the church in the Frankish kingdom. The Frankish ruler was, however, receptive to Paul's guidance,
thereby joining the papacy and the Franks in a closer relationship. Although

little is known of Paul's papacy, several sources claim his leadership was unyielding and rigid. It is quite possible Paul ruled with such an iron hand to meet the challenges he experienced in the newly acquired land, now under the reign of the papacy.

For further reference: Matthew Bunson, *The Pope Encyclopedia* (New York: Crown Trade Paperbacks, 1995); H. K. Mann, *The Lives of the Popes in the Early Middle Ages* (London: K. Paul, 1902–1932).

Patrick McGuire

PAUL II (1464–1471). Pietro Barbo, the future Paul II, was born in Venice on 23 February 1417 and was educated by his uncle Gabriel Condulmaro, who became Pope EUGENE IV (1431–1447). Originally trained for a mercantile career, by the age of twenty-three he was bishop of Cervia and Vicenza and cardinal, amassing a fortune. His ecclesiastical career was undistinguished, although he gained a reputation as a generous patron and lavish host.

In the brief conclave following the death of PIUS II (1458–1464), Barbo emerged as victor on 30 August 1464. He wanted to be called Formosus II, but the cardinals dissuaded him, saying it might be regarded as vanity on the part of the handsome pontiff. Finally, he chose the name Paul II. As POPE, he was extravagant in his support of public displays. Although he did not have a new tiara made for his coronation, he later commissioned one costing 200,000 scudi. The visual and architectural arts found in him a munificent patron, and his reign saw the end of Gothic construction in Rome. The arches of Titus and Septimius Severus were restored, along with the equestrian statue of Marcus Aurelius. Paul was especially interested in his collection of gems as well as rare treasures of Italian and Flemish gold work. His hoarding to afford this expensive hobby was so extreme that when ecclesiastical benefices fell vacant, Paul frequently allowed them to go long unfilled in order to accumulate the revenues.

Paul's support for the arts did not extend to literature. No intellectual himself (he never mastered Latin), he began his pontificate by dismissing a number of humanists appointed by Pius II. The resentment of the dismissed clerks convinced the suspicious pontiff that a conspiracy against his life was being plotted in the Roman Academy, where humanists gathered to discuss antiquity and philosophy. Paul dissolved the academy, seized many of its members, and accused them of treason. Under torture several died, but no evidence of a conspiracy was uncovered. Paul then accused the prisoners of HERESY, but the inquisitors found no evidence of this either. Paul simply kept the remaining humanists imprisoned. He failed to improve the position of the papacy in Italy or organize resistance to the encroachments of the Turks. He died on 26 July 1471 at the age of 53, after gorging himself on melons.

For further reference: John F. D'Amico, *Renaissance Humanism in Papal Rome: Humanists and Churchmen on the Eve of the Reformation* (Baltimore: Johns Hopkins University Press, 1983); Michel Francois, "Paul II, Pope," *New Catholic Encyclopedia*, vol. 11 (New York: McGraw-Hill, 1967), pp. 12–13; Ludwig von Pastor, *The History of the*

Popes, vol. 4, 5th ed., ed. Frederick Ignatius Antrobius (St. Louis: B. Herder Book, 1949); John Addington Symonds, *The Age of the Despots* (New York: G. P. Putnam's Sons, 1960).

William C. Schrader

PAUL III (1534–1549). Alessandro Farnese was born at Canino on 29 February 1468, a member of a powerful *condottiere* family. He pursued a humanist education and in 1492 was made treasurer of the Roman church and the next year a cardinal-deacon by Pope ALEXANDER VI (1492–1503). His sister Giulia was that pope's mistress, and Alessandro, although not ordained a priest until 1519, held several bishoprics and rich benefices. He was made bishop of Parma in 1509 by JULIUS II (1503–1513) and took the responsibilities of that office seriously, putting the reform decrees of the Fifth Lateran Council (see Lateran Council V) into effect. In 1513 he began to reform his private life, ending his liaison with his mistress, and, after being ordained in 1519, he quickly became associated with the reforming party in the CURIA. At the time of CLEMENT VII's (1523–1534) death he was the dean of the sacred college, respected for his experience, learning, and spirit of reform. After a two-day conclave he was elected unanimously.

Paul III was a RENAISSANCE pope and a patron of the arts and scholarship. He restored the university at Rome and added extensively to the collection in the Vatican Library. He commissioned such artists as Michelangelo to complete the *Last Judgment* scene in the Sistine Chapel and to supervise the building of the new St. Peter's and began his own family residence in Rome, the Palazzo Farnese. Reviving the carnival in Rome in 1536, the Vatican became a center of festivities. He did not shun nepotism, raising two young grandsons to the cardinalate. He saw the need to constructively meet the challenge posed by Protestantism, and, although technically not the first reforming POPE, he took steps to encourage renewal in the church. The chief plan of this program was the calling of a general COUNCIL.

The council was convened at TRENT. Paul already had reduced the expenses of the sacred college and made a series of significant appointments to that body, including Gasparo Contarini, Giovanni Carafa (later, Paul IV, 1555–1559), Reginald Pole, and Marcello Cervini (later, MARCELLUS II, 1555). A commission had already been set up in 1536 to examine the affairs of the church, and in the next year a report, *Consilium de emendenda ecclesia*, was issued, which became the basis for the council's work. Paul III also encouraged reforms within the religious orders and established the new orders of the Ursilines, Barnabites, Theatines, and Somaschi. In 1540 he approved and established the SOCIETY OF JESUS and in 1542 the Congregation of the Roman Inquisition, or the Holy Office, with powers to censor and to attack HERESY.

The Council of Trent began in 1545 with the pope represented by three LEGATES. It was not, however, the council of all Christendom as requested by the Protestants, but neither was it to be merely one dealing only with reform and discipline. From the beginning, it was decided that both dogma and reform would be discussed, and, in the first seven sessions, decrees on the sacraments, justification, original sin, and Scripture and tradition were elaborated. Then in 1547, renewed conflict between the pope and emperor caused the council to be moved, on the pretext of an outbreak of typhus, to Bologna, which was within papal territory. But, as Charles refused to allow bishops subject to him to attend, Paul had to suspend the eighth session early in 1548 without any further decrees being issued.

During his pontificate Paul III dealt with other matters of church and state, notably, his EXCOMMUNICATION of Henry VIII in 1538, at which time he placed England under interdict. He sought to maintain a neutral position between France and the empire but still regarded France as the natural counterbalance to Charles V's influence in Italy. The constant rivalry and fighting between these two powers prevented the papacy from organizing an effective action against the Ottoman Turks. Paul also supported Charles V's war against the German Protestant princes' Schmalkaldic League and encouraged Francis I to persecute the Huguenots in France. Conflicts between Charles and the pope developed, however, over a dispute regarding the papal territories of Parma and Piacenza, both of which Paul sought to bestow on his son, the irresponsible Pierluigi Farnese. After Pierluigi's murder in 1549 Charles claimed these duchies for his own son-in-law, Ottavio, who was the pope's grandson. Paul soon became ill, his death hastened by this family dissension.

For further reference: W. D'Ormesson, *The Papacy* (London: Hawthorn Books, 1959); T. Jalland, *Church and Papacy* (London: SPCK, 1944); L. Pastor, *The History of the Popes from the Close of the Middle Ages* (St. Louis: Herder, 1898).

William Roberts

PAUL IV (1555–1559). The noble Neapolitan Giampietro Carafa was born at Benevento on 28 June 1476 and was educated in the classics. He rose rapidly in the church HIERARCHY; from 1505 to 1524 he was bishop of Chieti and during the period also served as LEO X's (1513–1521) LEGATE to Henry VIII of England (1513–1514), archbishop of Brindisi (1518), and NUNCIO to Flanders and Spain (1515–1520). A reformer and humanist, he practiced a strict asceticism and corresponded with Erasmus. Politically, his Neapolitan background made him suspicious of Spanish influence in Italy. Back in Rome, he joined the Oratory of the Divine Love and sought to promote diocesan reform.

In 1524 he renounced his episcopal holdings and with Gaetano di Thiene founded and became the first superior of the Theatines, an order dedicated to its apostolic poverty and the reform of ecclesiastical abuses. He was named cardinal in 1536 and proved a zealous leader of the reform party. He became the head of the INQUISITION and was noted for his severity and brutality. In 1549 he became archbishop of Naples, in 1533 dean of the sacred college, and in 1555 was chosen to succeed MARCELLUS II (1555).

As POPE, he came under the influence of his nephew Carlo Carafa, who urged closer ties with France and declaration of war on Spain. However, his forces were defeated by the viceroy of Naples, the duke of Alba, and Paul IV was forced to accept the terms of the Peace of Cave in 1557. Although the PAPAL STATES had been overrun by the Spanish forces, the peace terms were not severe. Autocratic in his rule, he condemned the Peace of Augsburg (1555), which admitted to a coexistence between Lutherans and Catholics in Germany as HERESY and refused to recognize either the abdication of Charles V in 1556 or the election of Ferdinand I in 1558. His relations with England were not good either. He quarreled with Mary I of England, insisting that confiscated church property be restored, and later demanded that Elizabeth I acknowledge his supremacy. He thus facilitated the advance of the English Protestant movement.

Dedicated to a sense of personal reform and virulently anti-Protestant, he would not recall the suspended Council of TRENT but instituted a special commission in 1556 under his direction to carry out papal policies. While this never materialized, he devoted his energies to the Inquisition, placing it under the direction of Michele Ghislieri (later, PAUL V) and greatly increasing the scope of its authority. He personally attended its sessions and, in his zeal for orthodoxy, imprisoned the innocent Cardinal Giovanni Morone in the Castel Sant'Angelo and deprived the capable Reginald Pole of his post as legate to England. Through the Congregation of the Inquisition he also created in 1557 the INDEX of Forbidden Books.

Believing that the Jews were responsible for the growth of Protestantism, the pope ordered them restricted to ghettos in Rome and the papal territories and forced them to wear a distinctive headdress. In terms of a future renewal of the church, he established the basis by carefully selecting new cardinals, ordering bishops to reside in their dioceses, reducing the number of bishops resident in Rome from 113 to 12, and extending discipline and limiting secular influence in the monasteries. He appointed a commission to reform the missal and the Roman breviary and took measures to improve the celebration of the divine service in Rome.

Having earlier succumbed to nepotism and suffering its effects through the damage done by his nephew Carlo, the pope in 1559 belatedly expelled his relatives from Rome. The damage, however, had been done, and Paul and his family became unpopular in Rome. On his death riots ensued, and mobs destroyed the headquarters of the Inquisition and released its prisoners, while the statue of the pontiff on the Capitol was torn down.

For further reference: M. Creighton, *A History of the Papacy from the Great Schism to the Sack of Rome* (New York: AMS Press, 1969); W. D'Ormesson, *The Papacy* (London: Hawthorn Books, 1959); T. Jalland, *Church and Papacy* (New York: SPCK, 1944).

William Roberts

PAUL V (1605–1621). Camillo Borghese was born in Rome of a Sienese family. He joined the clergy and rose quickly in papal service. The untimely death of LEO XI (1605) forced a new conclave, with a split between the French and the Spanish cardinals. They turned to a compromise candidate, Camillo Borghese, who became Paul V.

Paul devoted his attention to strengthening and reforming the church. One of his first acts was to enforce the requirement of the Council of TRENT (1545–1563) that all bishops reside in their sees. He also sought to enforce discipline in the various orders and approved some important new ones, such as the Congregation of the Oratory (1612), founded by St. Philip Neri, and the Capuchins (1618), a branch of the FRANCISCANS. Paul V also advanced the cause of many saints: he canonized Charles Borromeo (1538–1584) and beatified Ignatius Loyola (1491–1556), Francis Xavier (1506–1552), Theresa of Avila (1515–1582), and Philip Neri (1515–1595). He promoted the missions, including the use of the vernacular in liturgy in China (1615).

Paul proved less successful in politics. The Venetian Republic passed laws prohibiting the construction of any new religious buildings or the alienation of any real property to the church without the permission of the senate. In 1606 Paul excommunicated (see Excommunication) the doge and the members of the senate and put Venice under an interdict. Paul tried to stir up a war against Venice, but Henry IV of France managed to mediate a settlement: the bishop and abbott were released from jail and the interdict was lifted (1607). Still no definitive agreement was reached with Venice. In England, the Parliament passed an oath of allegiance (1606), affirming the authority of the king against the POPE. In Russia Paul supported the claim of Dimitri, son of Ivan IV, a convert to Catholicism, who seized the throne from Fedor, successor to Boris Gudunov. Obviously, Paul hoped for a reunion of Russia with Rome, but Dimitri was assassinated, and Paul gained only opprobrium from the Russians.

In France Paul fared better. In 1611 Edmond Richer, dean of the Sorbonne, published *Libellus de ecclesiastica et politica potestate*, in which he reaffirmed the Gallican theory that COUNCILS were superior to the pope. But by 1615 the French clergy affirmed the decrees of the Council of Trent. In the conflicts between France and Spain, Paul tried to remain neutral. When the Thirty Years' War (1618–1648) broke out, Paul with his concern for the law, did not want to appear to break with the Peace of Augsburg (1555).

In Rome, Paul pressed for the completion of the new St. Peter's. When he assumed the papacy, the treasury was empty, and he hoped to reform papal finances. He never did and borrowed until the end of his reign. Paul V established the SECRET VATICAN ARCHIVES, for which modern scholars have praised him. In 1616 he censured Galileo (1564–1642) for teaching the Copernican system and suspended Copernicus' *De revolutionibus* ''until corrected,'' for which scholars have often reviled him.

On 21 January 1621, Paul suffered a stroke during a procession celebrating the victory (1620) of imperial forces at White Mountain, near Prague, and died in a week.

For further reference: A. C. Crombie, *Styles of Scientific Thinking in the European Tradition* Vol. 1 (London: Duckworth, 1994); W. Reinhard, *Papstfinanz und Nepostismus unter Paul V*, 2 Vols. (Stuttgart: A. Hiersemann, 1974).

Frank Grande

PAUL VI (1963–1978). Born Giovanni Battista Montini on 26 September 1897 in Brescia, Paul VI became pontiff in 1963. Swept by the winds of change from VATICAN COUNCIL II and from the cultural transformations of Western societies in the 1960s and 1970s, Paul's pontificate was perhaps the most turbulent of the twentieth century. His years in the Vatican were marked by challenges to papal and church authority by an increasingly restless laity, defections of thousands of priests, nuns, and brothers from religious life, and demands for a greater role for women in the church.

Strongly committed to the principles and teachings of Vatican II, Pope Paul sought to maintain the spirit of the council, while preserving the discipline and relevance of the church in the modern world. His historic travels around the globe brought the papacy face-to-face with Catholics and non-Catholics alike on a scale never before achieved by a Roman pontiff. He tended to be sympathetic to the problems of the poor and was an eloquent champion of the peoples of the Third World against what he perceived as exploitation by both communist and capitalist systems.

The tragedy of Paul's pontificate was that he was criticized by conservative and liberal Catholics alike. Conservative Catholics viewed him with suspicion for his strong support for reforms of Vatican II that swept away familiar rituals and liturgical practices and held him responsible for declining church attendance and the exodus from religious life. From the conservative wing of Catholicism emerged a powerful challenge to papal authority, the movement of Archbishop Marcel Lefebre, a French prelate who refused to accept many of the reforms of the COUNCIL and would not subject himself to papal discipline. At the same time, the extreme liberal elements of Catholicism criticized the POPE for his stand against birth control (see Abortion), and homosexuality, and his refusal to sanction married priests or the ordination of women.

Throughout his career, including the years of his papacy, Paul demonstrated a decided preference to lead by example and moral suasion, rather than by exercising clerical authority. He was extremely intelligent, quiet, and scholarly, and his asceticism (he wore a hair shirt under his papal robes in later years, as he anguished over the problems confronted by the church) generally passed unnoticed by his contemporaries. In the last years of his pontificate, the pope curtailed his travels and increasingly divided his time between the Vatican and Castel Gondolfo, his summer residence. Only months before he died, the pope was shaken by the kidnapping and assassination of former Italian prime minister Aldo Moro, his longtime friend and collaborator in Catholic Action.

By all standards, Giovanni Battista Montini was well prepared and trained to assume the papal throne. Montini came from a family active in Catholic politics;

his father was a prominent newspaper editor and an adviser to Pope BENEDICT XV (1914–1922). Young Montini entered the seminary in 1916, was ordained in 1920, and entered the Vatican diplomatic corps. He served for many years in the Vatican Secretariat of State and, simultaneously, as the *assistente ecclesiastico* of the national association of Catholic university students (Federazione Universitaria Cattolica Italiana). In the 1920s and 1930s, Montini quietly opposed the FASCIST regime. In 1937, he was appointed undersecretary of state by PIUS XII (1939–1958), a position that afforded him an influential role in Vatican wartime diplomacy. In 1954, he was made archbishop of Milan, where he interested himself in the lot of workers and the poor of his large diocese. In 1958 he was appointed to the College of CARDINALS by JOHN XXIII (1958–1963). Upon the death of Pope John in 1963, in the midst of the Vatican Council, Montini was elected the 260th Roman pontiff. On 6 August 1978, after a turbulent fifteen-year reign, Pope Paul VI, in the end weakened and dispirited by his long confrontations with both conservative and liberal extremists within the church, died at Castel Gondolfo.

For further reference: Giselda Adornato, ed., *Giovanni Battista Montini. Arcivescovo di Milano. Al Mondo del Lavoro. Discorsi e scritti (1954–1963)* (Rome: Edizioni Studium, 1988); W. E. Barrett, *Shepherd of Mankind* (New York: Doubleday, 1964); Antonio Fappani and Franco Molinari, eds., *Giovanni Battista Montini giovane. Documenti inediti e testimonianze* (Turin: Marietti, 1979); Richard J. Wolff, "Giovanni Battista Montini and Italian Politics, 1897–1933," *The Catholic Historical Review* (April 1985).

Richard J. Wolff

PELAGIUS I (556–561). Pelagius is remembered as much for his rise to the papacy as for his reign as POPE. In 537, Pelagius was suspected of involvement, at the bequest of Empress Theodora, in the exile and death of SILVERIUS (536–537), to secure the papacy for Silverius' successor, VIGILIUS (537–555). While serving as Vigilius' apocrisiarius in Constantinople, Pelagius became a confidant of Emperor Justinian (527–565), a relationship that facilitated his ascending to the papacy.

Disagreement arose between the emperor and Vigilius over the latter's refusal, initially supported by Pelagius, to ratify Justinian's condemnation of the Three Chapters at the Fifth General Council, CONSTANTINOPLE II, in 553. The Three Chapters supported the idea of a two-nature Christology and was anti-Monophysite. Upon Vigilius' death, in which Pelagius was allegedly involved, he received Justinian's nomination to the papal chair. However, Pelagius' election was delayed for nearly a year due to the opposition of many Western bishops when he declared his support for the emperor's position on the Three Chapters. Eventually, only two bishops agreed to consecrate his papacy. Almost immediately following his ordination, Pelagius affirmed his support for Chalcedon and the previous general councils while denying any role in the death of Vigilius.

His most significant act as pope was to restore order in Italy (after the invasions of the Goths) with the backing of Justinian's Pragmatic Sanction (554), which had confirmed the temporal power of the papacy and firmly established the pope's temporal domains. Despite his active role in relieving poverty and overhauling papal finances and the judicial system in Rome, Pelagius was constantly engaged in struggles with various parts of Gaul, Africa, and northern Italy that refused to recognize his authority due to his condemnation of the Three Chapters. SCHISMS developed and lasted well into the seventh century.

For further reference: Hans Kuhner, *Encyclopedia of the Papacy* (New York: Philosophical Library, 1958); H. K. Mann, *The Lives of the Popes in the Early Middle Ages* (London: K. Paul, 1902–1932). The best beginning primary source remains the *Liber Pontificalis* (Paris, 1886–1892).

John C. Horgan

PELAGIUS II (579–590). Born in Rome, Pelagius was the second Gothic POPE. On the death of BENEDICT I (575–579), he was elected and consecrated without imperial confirmation, because Rome was under siege by the Lombards. He devoted his papacy to securing recognition of the supremacy of the See of Rome by all bishops. Pelagius appointed his deacon, who later became his successor, GREGORY I (the Great, 590–604), apocrisarius to Constantinople from 579 to 585, in order to obtain help against the Lombards. Emperor Tiberius II (578–582), beset by the Persians, suggested that Pelagius bribe the Lombards and seek help from the Frankish king. The appeal to the Franks was fruitless but set a precedent that was to have a great impact in the future. By 585 Smargadus, the Byzantine exarch of Ravenna, was able to negotiate a truce with the Lombards.

Gregory was then brought back from Constantinople to help negotiate an end to the SCHISM of north Italian bishops who had broken with Rome after VIGILIUS (537–555) had acquiesced in the condemnation (543) by Justinian of the "Three Chapters." The efforts to heal this Aquileian schism failed. But by 589 the Visigoths in Spain had been converted. When the patriarch of Constantinople, John IV ("the Faster"), assumed the title of "ecumenical patriarch" in 588, Pelagius wrote that no patriarch could claim to be universal. The letter of Pelagius has not survived. But some historians have suggested that he overreacted, that the title, originally used by Acacius in the fifth century, may simply have meant supreme within his own patriarchate, rather than "worldwide." Pelagius is generally credited with having the high altar of St. Peter's built directly above the shrine of the apostle. He died of the plague in Rome during February 590 and was buried in St. Peter's.

For further reference: E. Caspar, *Geschichte des Papsttums* (Tübingen: J. Mohr, 1930–1933); T. G. Jalland, *The Church and the Papacy* (London: SPCK, 1944).

Frank Grande

PEPIN, DONATION OF. SEE DONATION OF PEPIN.

PETER THE APOSTLE (d. c. 64). The papacy traces its origins to the apostle Peter, traditionally commissioned by Jesus to lead the church. Peter's life is known through the New Testament and other ancient sources. Originally named Simon, or Simeon, he was from Bethsaida, a village on the Sea of Galilee (see Matt. 16:17). With his brother Andrew and with James and John, he was summoned by Jesus to become a disciple. All are described as having earlier been the disciples of John the Baptist. The four Gospels agree that from that point Peter was recognized as the leader of the apostles. He is mentioned with great frequency and is always the first in the lists of the twelve and was present at such significant events as the Transfiguration (Matt. 17:1), the raising of the daughter of Jairus (Matt. 9:18), and the Agony in the Garden (Matt. 26:37). He was with Jesus at the wedding feast at Cana. Simon always answered for the other Apostles and in reply to his identifying Jesus as the Messiah was given the Aramaic name Cephas, or rock, which translates as Peter in Greek.

He was the "rock" upon whom the church would be built, and to him were given "the keys to the kingdom of heaven," with the powers of "binding and loosing." At the Last Supper he was charged by Jesus to strengthen the others (Luke 22:32), and even though his courage failed during Jesus' trial and death, to the point of denial (Mark 8:31 and Matt. 26:69), Peter was the first disciple to enter the empty tomb and the first to see the risen Christ (see Luke and John).

The Acts of the Apostles note that after the Ascension Peter was the uncontested leader of the early church. He presided over the choice of a successor to Judas, led the apostles at Pentecost, healed the sick and lame, pronounced the sentence on Ananias and Sapphira, and brought the Gentiles into the church by baptizing Cornelius (see Acts: 1,2,3). He aggressively preached and spread the word of the new church, visiting the early Christian communities that had emerged. He was arrested by Herod Agrippa I but was miraculously freed and, at the subsequent COUNCIL of Jerusalem, successfully supported a more open policy toward the Gentiles. Peter was the first source of information for Paul after his conversion about Jesus and the faith, and although they at times disagreed, it is clear that Paul held him in great respect. In his missionary role Peter would be especially active in regions that were largely Gentile, like Asia Minor and Corinth. Early tradition notes that he was the first bishop of Antioch.

It is rather conclusive that Peter spent his final years in Rome, but there is little or no indication of how he got there or when, how long he stayed, or even the exact role that he played. But, although not mentioned directly in the New Testament, the reference to "Babylon," a code name for Rome, in the Acts as well as strong implications in the gospel written by Mark, who was Peter's companion, makes the fact that he was in the city certain. Also, early reliable writers such as Clement of Rome (c. 95), Ignatius of Antioch (c. 107), and Irenaeus (c. 180) all attest to his presence in the city, noting that it was common knowledge. With Paul, he had special authority over the church there. It was there that, with Paul, he was martyred, about the year 64. Tertullian reports that he was crucified, as is also implied in the gospel of John. By the second century there is reference to his burial place on the Vatican Hill, as is mentioned by the Roman presbyter Gaius (c. 200). At first a small memorial, fragments of which still remain, was erected to him, and in the fourth century the emperor Constantine built the first great basilica on the site. The *confessio* of the present basilica rises over this traditional burial place. Excavations done in 1939 and 1949 and in 1965 seem to bear this out, clearly indicating that the locations of Peter's tomb had been found there. The feast day of this saint, along with St. Paul, is 29 June.

For further reference: P. Hughes, *The History of the Church* (London: Sheed and Ward, 1955); M. Winter, *St. Peter and the Popes* (London: Helicon Press, 1960).

William Roberts

PETRINE DOCTRINE. The Petrine Doctrine is the basis for the claims of the bishops of Rome to primacy over the universal church. It is the belief that the apostle PETER was designated by Christ to be the leader of the church and Christ's chief representative (vicar) on earth following the Ascension and that this dignity was passed on to Peter's successors, the bishops of Rome. The scriptural basis for this doctrine is found in Matthew 16: "Thou art Peter, and upon this rock I will build my church, and the gates of hell shall not prevail against it. And I will give unto thee the keys of the Kingdom of Heaven: whatsoever thou shalt bind on earth shall be bound also in heaven; and whatsoever thou shalt loose on earth shall be loosed also in heaven." It might be noted, too, that at the COUNCIL of Jerusalem, recounted in Acts 15, Peter made the final decision, announcing to the faithful that "the Holy Spirit and we have decided."

A distinct, but related, aspect of this doctrine is the claim of the POPES to "the plentitude of power." This claim to hold whatever authority is necessary to carry out the functions of their office and even (during medieval times) to exercise a papal monarchy over the Christian world rests on the word "whatsoever" in the quotation from Matthew's gospel—"whatsoever thou shalt bind ... whatsoever thou shalt loose." In considering the position of the popes in the church, a distinction must be made between their position as Christ's vicar, chief bishop, and guardian of doctrinal purity, on one hand, and papal bureaucracy and administrative jurisdiction, on the other. The latter demonstrably rose in historical times.

Whether the apostle Peter was ever in Rome cannot be decided from Scripture. There is no contemporary evidence for the belief that St. Peter suffered martyrdom during the persecutions of Nero in A.D. 64–67. However, within a generation this belief was widely accepted in liturgical practices and in the First Epistle of Clement. Other early sources for the belief that St. Peter (sometimes combined with St. Paul) was the founder of the church in Rome include the writings of St. Ignatius of Antioch, St. Justin Martyr, St. Clement of Alexandria, and St. Hegesippus, all from the second century. From that same century we have the statement of St. Irenaeus that "it is necessary that every church agree with this church [Rome] because of its pre-eminent authority." Tertullian, early in the third century, confirms the currency of Roman claims to hold the authority of St. Peter when he complains that Callistus I (217–222) presumed to claim for Rome alone the authority given in Matt. 16 to "all churches of Petrine origin."

Archaeological evidence for the burial of St. Peter on Vatican Hill, where the present basilica is located, is strong but inconclusive. Constantine believed this tradition when he ordered the construction of the original basilica early in the fourth century, and it persists to the present. The evidence of the shovel does indicate a memorial, called the Aedicula, on the appropriate location. This discovery of the bones of an elderly man on this site in the 1960s also strengthens the case for a burial of Peter, but it is not definitive.

Recognition of the Roman claims was sporadic in the early church. The church of Corinth appealed to Clement I (c. 91–101) late in the first century. A century later, Victor I (189–198) intervened in Ephesus and Byzantium in the Easter controversy. Fabian (236–250) was appealed to by Origin after the latter had been condemned by his bishop, Demetrius of Alexandria. The advice of STEPHEN I (254–257) was sought by Spanish and Gallic bishops and by Cyprian of Carthage following the persecution of Decius. Although SYLVESTER I (314–335) enjoyed a significant reputation in medieval times as the contemporary and, according to some accounts, converter of Constantine the Great, it was actually the Spanish bishop Hosius who exercised the greatest influence on this first of the Christian emperors. It is significant that Sylvester did not attend the Council of NICAEA (325) in person but was represented by agents, a precedent followed by later popes, setting them apart from the other bishops.

JULIUS I (337–352) convoked the Council of Sardica (343), which recognized his primacy and his claim to the authority to annul decisions of councils. However, Sardica does not have ecumenical status, and its decisions were not accepted in the East. Unequivocal conciliar recognition of Rome's claim to primacy would not come until a century later, when the Fourth Ecumenical Council at CHALCEDON (451) accepted Pope LEO I, the Great's (440–461) position on the Monophysite controversy, recognizing his primacy and greeting his theological treatise, the *Tome*, with the words, "this is the faith of the Fathers, this is the faith of the Apostles, this is the faith of us all. Peter has spoken through Leo."

For further reference: Anon., *Liber Pontificalis*, the books of the popes from Peter to Gregory the Great; Daniel William O'Connor, *Peter in Rome: The Literary Liturgical and Archaeological Evidence* (New York: Columbia University Press, 1969); Jaroslav Pelikan, *The Christian Tradition: A History of the Development of Doctrine*, vol. 1, *The*

Emergence of the Catholic Tradition (100–600) (Chicago: University of Chicago Press, 1971); John E. Walsh, *The Bones of St. Peter* (New York: Doubleday, 1982).

William C. Schrader

PHILIP, ANTIPOPE (768). Anarchy befell Rome when Lombard troops, upon the request of Archdeacon Christopher, who led the Roman clergy, invaded the city to remove the antipope CONSTANTINE II (767–768). A Lombard priest, Waldipert, an intimate of the Lombard king Desiderius (757–774), proclaimed Philip the new pontiff. Upon receiving the news, Christopher's men marched to the Lateran and removed Philip, returning him to his monastery.

For further reference: Eric John, ed., *The Popes: A Concise Biographical Dictionary* (New York: Hawthorn Books, 1964); H. K. Mann, *The Lives of the Popes in the Early Middle Ages* (London: K. Paul, 1902–1932).

John C. Horgan

PIUS I (c. 142–c. 155). Pius was the tenth POPE in the line of succession begun by St. PETER. Early accounts differ about the dates of his reign, and some mistakenly place him after his successor, Anacletus (c. 71–c. 91). The *Liber Pontificalis* notes that he was an Italian from Aquileia, the son of Rufinus. The later Muratorian Canon, which dates from the second century and is the oldest extant canon of New Testament writings, reports that he was the brother of Hermas, the former slave who was the author of *The Shepard*, a visionary and much popularized statement on repentance. Although this book proclaimed forgiveness and pardon for grave sins such as apostasy, at a time when reconciliation with the church was denied to penitent adulterers, murderers, and apostates, it was not condemned by Pius. The book's passages reveal that a central, monarchical episcopate already existed in Rome. As it would have been unusual for one brother to have a Greek name and the other a Latin one, possibly Pius and Hermas were half brothers, or perhaps this pope changed his original name to one less suggestive of pagan mythology.

During Pius I's pontificate the leading gnostics Cerdo and Valentinus, as well as Marcion of Pontus, who taught that the God of the Old Testament was to be rejected in favor of the New Testament Deity as revealed through Christ, were all in Rome developing their respective theological positions. Pius certainly must have presided over the synod of presbyters that in July 144 expelled Marcion from the orthodox church. Although Pius is mentioned as a martyr in the martyrology of Ado of Vienne, compiled in 858, there is no other earlier source that indicates this was so. His feast day is 11 July.

For further reference: J. Lebreton and J. Zeiller, *The History of the Primitive Church* (New York: Burns, Oates, and Washbourne, 1948); M. Winter, *St. Peter and the Popes* (London: Helicon Press, 1960).

William Roberts

PIUS II (1458–1464). A Tuscan from the impoverished nobility, Aeneas Sylvius Piccolomini was born on 18 October 1405 near Sienna. He pursued legal studies at Sienna and classical studies at Florence. In 1431 he accompanied the humanist Cardinal Capranica to the COUNCIL of BASEL as a secretary and remained in the north for most of the next twenty years. Supporting the radical conciliarists in their quarrel with Pope EUGENE IV (1431–1447), Piccolomini gave his allegiance to the antipope FELIX V (1439–1449).

In 1442 Emperor Frederick III crowned Aeneas Sylvius poet laureate, and shortly thereafter he entered the service of the Hapsburgs. During his stay in the north Piccolomini wrote a wide variety of works. During this period he acquired a sense of the Turkish danger threatening Christendom, which, along with personal sufferings, wrought a significant change in his life. In 1445 Aeneas Sylvius was reconciled with Pope Eugene and conducted the negotiations leading to the emperor's abandonment of the Council of Basel. Piccolomini received holy orders in 1446 and in the following year was named bishop of Trieste by NICHOLAS V (1447–1455). He became a cardinal in 1456.

Upon the death of CALLISTUS III (1455–1458) a strenuous conflict took place in the conclave, described by Piccolomini in his *Commentaries*. On 19 August 1458, he became Pope Pius II. The humanists flocked to Rome upon hearing of Pius' election, but they found a reformed man, concerned more with the Turkish menace than with liberality toward men of letters. This explains many of the negative judgment's these men of letters passed on Pius after his death. In October 1458, he convoked a congress to meet at Mantua, intended to establish peace throughout Christendom, in order to focus the attention of the West on a new crusade. Disappointed with the attendance and results, Pius attributed the decline in papal influence to the conciliar movement and in 1460 issued the bull *Execrabilis*, asserting papal authority and condemning appeals to future councils.

The discovery of alum mines at Tolfa gave Pius needed revenues, leading the frustrated pontiff to head the crusade himself. The ailing pope took the cross in a ceremony in St. Peter's on 14 June 1464 and set out for the Adriatic to make contact with the Venetian fleet. He died at Ancona on 15 August. Pius II was, in the words of John Addington Symonds, "the last Pope of the Renaissance period whom we can regard with real respect."

For further reference: Eugenio Garin, *Portraits from the Quattocento*, trans. Victor A. and Elizabeth Velen (New York: Harper and Row, 1963); Iris Origo, "Pope Pius II," in J. H. Plumb, *The Italian Renaissance* (Boston: Houghton Mifflin, 1987); Ludwig von Pastor, *The History of the Popes*, vol. 3, 5th ed., Frederick Ignatius Antrobius (St. Louis: B. Herder Book, 1949); John Addington Symonds, *The Age of the Despots*, originally published 1875, Capricorn ed. (New York: G. P. Putnam's Sons, 1960).

William C. Schrader

PIUS III (1503). Reigning from 22 September to 18 October 1503, Francesco Todeschini, a nephew of PIUS II (1458–1464), was born at Sienna in 1439. The uncle, who allowed him to take his family name and arms of Piccolomini, sponsored his legal studies at Perugia. Upon receiving his doctorate, he made him archbishop of Sienna when he was only twenty-one, elevating him thereafter to cardinal-deacon. Pius II then appointed him LEGATE to the March of Ancona and in 1464 left him in charge of Rome and the PAPAL STATE when he left to lead a crusade. Francesco was also for many years cardinal protector of both Germany and England and came to be a trusted friend to both nations.

Pope PAUL II (1464–1471) made him legate to Germany, where his fluency in the language allowed him in 1471 to defend the church's interests before the emperor and the diet of Regensburg. He continued to have influence under Pope ALEXANDER VI (1492–1503), who had sent him on a short-lived mission to Charles VIII of France in 1494, but he also kept a distance from that pope, having angrily refused to accept bribes to vote for him at the conclave in 1492.

Francesco was elected at the conclave as a neutral candidate to break the deadlock caused by the rivalry between foreign powers and the interference of Cesare Borgia. He was selected on the basis of his experience and abilities, having been seriously considered at earlier conclaves. His poor state of health also played a part in his selection, for an interim pontiff was desired. In fact, he was so ill that the usual ceremonies at his coronation on 8 October had to be canceled, and he died soon after. Many contemporaries regretted this short pontificate, as it had been expected that, had he lived, he would have called a general council to initiate needed reforms.

For further reference: M. Creighton, *A History of the Papacy from the Great Schism to the Sack of Rome* (New York: AMS Press, 1969); T. Jalland, *Church and Papacy* (London: SPCK, 1944); L. Pastor, *A History of the Popes from the Close of the Middle Ages* (London: Herder, 1897).

William Roberts

PIUS IV (1559–1565). In 1559 Giovanni Angelo Medici was chosen after a conclave of almost four months, deadlocked by French and Spanish factions. A third group, led by Cardinal Carafa, supported Medici to succeed PAUL IV (1555–1559). Born at Milan on 31 March 1499, Medici, not related to the Florentine house, was a notary's son. Under PAUL III (1534–1549) he served as governor of the PAPAL STATE and vice-LEGATE to Bologna. When his older brother married into the POPE's family, he rose rapidly and, although he was the father of three children, was in 1545 made archbishop of Ragusa and in 1549 a cardinal.

Upon his election, the affable Pius IV reversed many of Paul IV's repressive policies. He freed and rehabilitated Cardinal Giovanni Morone, who had unjustly been accused of HERESY, restricted the authority of the INQUISITION, removed the ban on vagrant monks, and began a revision of the INDEX of Forbidden Books. He ended Paul's anti-Hapsburg policy and initiated friendly relations with Emperor Ferdinand I and Philip II of Spain. The nunciatures to

Vienna, Florence, and Venice, long vacant, were filled and, in response to the hatred for Paul IV's nephews, Cardinal Carlo Carafa and Giovanni, duke of Palino, had them tried and executed for murder. But Pius indulged in nepotism himself and in 1560 nominated the youthful Carlo Borromeo as cardinal-archbishop of Milan. This proved to be a blessing for the church, for his nephew influenced his worldly uncle in favor of reform.

In 1560 Pius reconvened the COUNCIL of TRENT, suspended since 1552, and brought it to a successful conclusion. Pius kept control of the council largely through the diplomatic ability of Cardinal Morone, whom he made president in 1563. Late that year the bull *Benedictus Deus* confirmed its decrees. He then sought to have the council accepted in Catholic areas, reserving to himself interpretation of its decrees. Enforcement began immediately in Italy, where bishops were now required to reside in their dioceses. Soon after, the council's Index of Forbidden Books was published. As the council left the issue of communion in both kinds to his discretion also, the chalice was allowed in Germany, Hungary, and Austria in an effort to counter the influence of Protestantism. In late 1564, all bishops, superiors, and doctors were required to subscribe to the new "Profession of the Tridentine Faith," and a new catechism was initiated.

Under Pius IV the papacy regained much of its prestige in terms of the church's program of reform and Pius revival of the humanistic and Renaissance tradition that had ended with Paul IV. Pius was a generous patron of the arts and scholarship and set up a printing press in Rome. In administering the papal states, however, he was not so successful, nor did he succeed in stemming the tide of Protestantism, especially in England, Germany, and France.

For further reference: P. Hughes, *The History of the Church* (New York: Sheed and Ward, 1955); T. P. Neil and Raymond Schmandt, *History of the Catholic Church* (Milwaukee: Bruce Publishing Co., 1965).

William Roberts

PIUS V (1566–1572). Antonio Ghislieri was born to a humble family outside Alessandria on 17 January 1504 and was a shepherd until the age of fourteen, when he entered the Dominicans. Ordained in 1528, he was made inquisitor for Como and Bergamo. His zeal brought him to the attention of Cardinal Giampietro Carafa, upon whose recommendation he was appointed to the commissary general of the Roman INQUISITION in 1551 by JULIUS III (1550–1555). When Carafa became Pope PAUL IV (1555–1559), Ghislieri was made inquisitor general.

He fell into disfavor under PIUS IV (1559–1565), who was opposed to the Carafas, and devoted himself to reform in his diocese of Mondovi and of the Barnabite order, of which he was protector. His personal asceticism made him a leading candidate for the vacant See of Rome. He was chosen POPE after a nineteen-day conclave through the efforts of the reforming faction led by Cardinal Charles Borromeo. Continuing to wear a monk's robe even as pope and to practice personal spiritual discipline, Pius V as pope sought to implement the reforms decreed at TRENT. He imposed strict standards on his greatly reduced papal court and sought to eliminate immorality and profanation of holy days in Rome. Contemporaries complained he wanted to change the city into a monastery. Although he made a grand-nephew, the Dominican Michele Bonelli, a cardinal and used him as his secretary of state, Pius was opposed to nepotism and gave his other relatives little financial support. He enforced the rules of clerical residence and reformed and even abolished religious orders, like the Humiliati in 1571, that had become degenerate.

Pius relied on the Inquisition, especially in his efforts to attack HERESY. Under him the number of persons accused and sentenced increased enormously, seeking especially to keep Italy free of Protestantism. The Jews also suffered as a result of his policies, almost all being expelled from papal territory. In 1571 he established the Congregation of the INDEX as a new branch of the Inquisition with the result that hundreds of printers fled north to Switzerland and Germany. In 1576 he condemned the main teachings of Michael Baius, the Flemish precursor of JANSENISM and, in the same year, named Thomas Aquinas, the great Dominican scholar, a doctor of the church.

Pius V's political efforts often proved unsuccessful. His attempt to free the church of state influence alienated most of the Catholic rulers whose support he needed. His EXCOMMUNICATION of Elizabeth I, the last such sentence issued against a reigning monarch by a pope, alienated England and made matters worse for English Catholics. His efforts to attack the Huguenots in France were thwarted when they were granted freedom of religion in 1570 by the Peace of Saint-Germain, and his relations with the emperor Maximilian II were damaged over his policies toward Protestantism, and even Philip II of Spain, who would have been a natural ally, was alienated because of clashes over control of the church there.

Pius V's most successful political enterprise was the formation a Holy League with Venice and Spain against the Turks. A combined naval force defeated the Turkish fleet at Lepanto in 1571, ending Turkish control of the Mediterranean. Pius was beatified in 1672 by CLEMENT X (1670–1676) and canonized in 1712 by CLEMENT XI (1700–1721).

For further reference: W. D'Ormesson, *The Papacy* (New York: Hawthorn Books, 1959); T. Jalland, *Church and Papacy* (London: SPCK, 1944); L. Pastor, *A History of the Popes from the Close of the Middle Ages* (London: Herder, 1953).

William Roberts

PIUS VI (1775–1799). Born Giannangelo Braschi in Cesena, Italy, on 25 December 1717, Pius VI was elected to the papacy at a critical time for the papacy. After earning the degree of doctor of laws, he had a distinguished career in the church under three pontificates. He served as private secretary to Cardinal RUFFO at Ostia and Velletri until 1753. In recognition of his diplomatic skills

Pope BENEDICT XIV (1740–1758) nominated him one of his secretaries and canon of St. Peter's. In 1766 Pope CLEMENT XIII (1758–1769) appointed him treasurer of the apostolic chamber, and in 1773 Pope CLEMENT XIV (1769–1774) made him a cardinal. At the latter's death, Braschi became POPE after a four-month conclave, taking the name Pius VI.

Coming to the papal throne only four years after the Catholic powers of Portugal, Spain, and France had forced his predecessor, Clement XIV, to suppress the SOCIETY OF JESUS, Pius VI had to try to achieve reconciliation with, and reestablish the authority of the papacy over, recalcitrant monarchs. The Jesuit controversy had revealed the impotence of the church when faced by determined opposition. Its prestige further undermined by the criticism of the *philosophes*, the church faced the arduous task of reassessing its position in the changing political balance of the age and introducing some measure of spiritual and institutional reforms to counter the secular thought of the century.

Pius, however, proved unable to introduce any fundamental reforms. There were hostility to change within the church itself and lack of interest on the part of the rulers concerned with controlling the national churches. In Austria, Emperor Joseph II, the prototype of the "enlightened" monarch, granted tolerance to all religions within the Hapsburg dominions in 1781, despite the pope's personal visit to Vienna. With the outbreak of Revolution in France Pius faced growing hostility from its new political leaders. In 1790 the Civil Constitution of the Clergy brought priests under state control, demanding they take an oath of allegiance to the new French Constitution. The French clergy divided between those who accepted the new state directives and those who remained loyal to Rome. Pius VI denounced both the Civil Constitution and the Revolution in a brief on 10 March 1791.

After war broke out between Revolutionary France and the European powers, Pius VI sided with the anti-French coalition, only to find himself at the mercy of the French army that invaded Italy under Napoleon Bonaparte. In 1796 the PAPAL STATE was occupied by republican soldiers, and the pope was forced to sue for peace in 1797. In that year the French general Duphot was killed by rioters in Rome. The French reoccupied the city, and in 1798 a Roman Republic, professing revolutionary principles, was proclaimed. Taken prisoner, Pius VI was incarcerated in France, where he died at Valence on 29 August 1799. Thus ended a pontificate that saw the fortunes and prestige of papacy and church reduced to a low point. An able prelate, as pope Pius VI proved unable to introduce a modicum of reform within the church and to survive the revolutionary storm that swept away the base of the church's power in France and then in the papal state itself.

For further reference: Owen Chadwick, *The Popes and European Revolution* (Oxford: Clarendon Press, 1981).

Emiliana P. Noether

PIUS VII (1800–1823). Born Luigi Barnaba Chiarmonte at Cesena, Italy, on 14 August 1740, he succeeded to the papacy after a seventh-month interregnum following the death of PIUS VI in captivity. With Rome in turmoil, the College of CARDINALS met in conclave at Venice under the protection of Austria and elected Chiarmonte on 14 March 1800. Chiarmonte chose the name Pius VII. A member of the Benedictine order, he had taught at various Benedictine colleges in Parma and Rome. In 1782 he was appointed bishop of Tivoli and in 1785 bishop of Imola and cardinal. As newly elected POPE in 1800, he faced a precarious situation. Pius VII was perhaps more favorably disposed toward the new order than some of the church's allies. Three years before his election he had publicly proclaimed that true democracy and the church were not incompatible.

Consequently, he replied positively to Napoleon's overtures to regularize relations and entrusted the ensuing negotiations to his astute secretary of state, Cardinal CONSALVI. The resulting CONCORDAT OF 1801 resolved many of the outstanding problems between France and the church. It recognized Catholicism as the religion of the majority of the French people (but not as state religion). Agreement was reached on the position of the French clergy and confiscated church property. In sum, the CONCORDAT regularized and legitimated the position of the church in France, but a new source of discord emerged in the "Organic Articles" appended unilaterally to the concordat by Napoleon in 1802. These drastically restricted the authority of the church in France. Napoleon rejected Pius' protests, and the pope's further attempts failed when he journeyed to France for the coronation of Napoleon as emperor in 1804. Relations soon deteriorated. Occupied by the French in 1808, Rome was incorporated into France. Pius VII countered by excommunicating (see Excommunication) those responsible. Taken prisoner, he remained in French hands until Napoleon's final defeat in 1814. During this time he was forced to accept a French-dictated concordat at Fontainebleu on 25 January 1813, which he repudiated shortly thereafter.

With the end of Napoleonic power and the restoration, Pius VII returned to Rome, to be received with great joy in May 1814. At the Congress of VIENNA Cardinal Consalvi secured the restoration of the PAPAL STATE. Disenchanted with liberalism, Pius VII set about reestablishing the papal administration. He restored the Jesuits and worked to strengthen the church's position in concordats with the European powers. He found, however, that, while paying lip service to the church, the latter had no intention of ceding their authority over the national churches to Rome. Pius VII and Cardinal Consalvi sought to gloss over the differences by strategic compromises. Thus, by the time of Pius' death on 20 August 1823, the dignity and prestige of the church as a spiritual force had been reestablished, and its sovereignty over the papal states in Italy assured. A new alliance between throne and altar emerged to counter the unrest that began to seethe throughout Europe before 1848.

For further reference: Owen Chadwick, *The Popes and European Revolution* (Oxford: Clarendon Press, 1981).

Emiliana P. Noether

PIUS VIII (1829–1830). Born Francesco Saverio Castiglioni at Cingoli, Italy, 20 November 1761, Castiglioni possessed an uncommonly fine intellectual ability. Trained in CANON LAW, Pius VII (1800–1823) relied on Castiglioni advice when he encountered delicate questions with the French emperor. In 1808 he was imprisoned for refusing to take the oath of allegiance to Napoleon I. In 1829, despite very poor health, Castiglioni was elected POPE and took the name Pius VIII. As pope he confronted the following problems: religious indifferentism, opposition to Christian education, secret societies, a program of Catholic liberalism sponsored by Lamennais, and attempts by European monarchs to control the church. Pius VIII achieved some measure of independence for the church in France, thus paving the way for the growth that would take place in the 1840s and 1850s.

For further reference: E. E. Y. Hales, *Revolution and Papacy, 1769–1846* (Garden City, NY: Doubleday, 1960); H. E. Wiseman, *Recollections of the Last Four Popes of Rome in Their Times* (Boston: Patrick Donahoe, 1858).

Loretta Devoy

PIUS IX (1846–1878). The longest reigning POPE, Giovanni Maria-Mastai Ferretti was born into a family of the lower nobility in Senigallia on 13 May 1792. He played an important part in nineteenth-century Italian and European developments, shaping the character of the Catholic Church and the papacy prior to VATICAN II. Ruler of the PAPAL STATES until their dissolution in 1870 and head of the church from 1846 to 1878, he influenced both the risorgimento and counter-risorgimento. This pope had an impact on the diplomatic events of his day, influencing the policies of FRANZ JOSEF's Austria, Bismarck's German empire, and Napoleon III's France, while intervening in the conflict between liberalism and conservatism. Commencing his pontificate on a progressive note, he ended it by waging war against liberalism, nationalism, and the separation of church and state, condemning the Italian kingdom and Bismarck's *KULTUR-KAMPF*.

Although his studies at the College of Volterra in Tuscany were interrupted by an attack of epilepsy, he was ordained in 1819. His first assignment as a priest was at the Roman orphanage of Tata Giovanni, where he remained until 1823. From 1823 to 1825 he took part in a papal mission to Chile and Peru, the first figure who occupied the chair of PETER to visit America. Upon returning to Rome, he served as the director of the hospice of San Michele. Archbishop of Spoleto from 1827 to 1832, he became bishop of Imola in 1832 and was made a cardinal by GREGORY XVI (1831–1846) in 1840. In 1846 he was elected to succeed Gregory, assuming the name Pius in honor of PIUS VII (1800–1823).

Pius IX was perceived as the patriotic pope who would forge Italian unity. He confirmed this opinion by appointing a leading liberal as his secretary of state, followed by his 16 July 1846 amnesty of political prisoners, which won the heart of Italians. In 1847 Pius introduced a consultative chamber and a Council of Ministers. In January 1848, when Rome received word that Ferdinand II of Naples had granted a constitution, Pius was petitioned to do the same. On 10 March the pope announced the formation of a liberal ministry presided over by Cardinal Giacomo ANTONELLI. Four days later the Roman constitution was published, creating two deliberate councils for the formation of law. To safeguard the position of the church, the councils were prohibited from discussing the diplomatic-religious relations of the Holy See or limiting its rights.

Shortly thereafter, Rome received word of the revolution in Vienna, the outbreak against Hapsburg control in Milan and Venice, and the opening of a war of national liberation, spearheaded by Carlo Alberto of Piedmont-Sardinia. Pius was called upon to join the Italian crusade against Austria but hesitated, fearing a German SCHISM. In his allocution of 29 April 1848, he announced that as common father of all Catholics, he could not wage war upon Austria. The reaction to this pacific policy, which was contrary to that of his constitutional monarchy, provoked a revolution in Rome in mid-November. The imposition of a radical, anti-Austrian ministry led Pius to flee his capital for the Kingdom of the Two Sicilies on the evening of 24 November 1848 and subsequently to call for the intervention of the Catholic powers (France, Austria, Spain, and the kingdom of the Two Sicilies) to crush the Roman Republic formed early in 1849.

Although Cardinal Antonelli orchestrated the pope's successful flight from Rome and the diplomacy that led to the papal restoration, he did not initiate the antinational, illiberal policy pursued by Rome after 1849, which was inspired by Pius. The events of 1848 turned the pope against constitutionalism as well as his earlier reformism. The ''liberal'' pope of 1846–1848 turned into the conservative of the second restoration. Following the French destruction of Mazzini's Roman Republic and the pope's return to Rome in 1850, Pius refused to negotiate on the issue of the temporal power, which he deemed essential for the preservation of the church. Offended by the anticlericalism of the Turin government, he refused to negotiate with the Piedmontese and, after 1861, refused to recognize the kingdom of Italy. A priest first and a prince second, Pius left diplomatic and political affairs in the hands of his secretary of state, as he focused on ecclesiastical matters, reestablishing the HIERARCHY in England (1850) and the Netherlands (1853), while his devotion to Mary led him to proclaim the Immaculate Conception on 8 December 1854. In April 1855 the pope escaped injury when the floor in the Convent of Sant' Agnese collapsed.

Determined to safeguard the church, Pius favored neo-Scholasticism and centralization. In 1864, he issued the encyclical *Quanta cura*, to which was appended the "SYLLABUS OF ERRORS," which denounced the notion that the temporal power should be abolished and condemned liberalism, nationalism, and the separation of church and state. Some charged that the pope had opened a war on the modern world and its ideologies. Pius' counteroffensive was continued by the calling of the VATICAN Council (1869–1870), which culminated in the declaration of papal INFALLIBILITY, 18 July 1870. Following the loss of Rome in 1870, Pius declared himself a "prisoner in the Vatican," where he died on 7 February 1878.

For further reference: Frank J. Coppa, *Pope Pius IX: Crusader in a Secular Age* (Boston: Twayne, 1979); August Bernard Hassler, *How the Pope Became Infallible: Pius IX and the Politics of Persuasion*, trans. Peter Heinegg (Garden City, NY: Doubleday, 1981); Giacomo Martina, *Pio IX*, 3 vols. (Rome: Università Gregoriana, 1974–1990); Alberto Giovanni Serafini, *Pio IX Giovanni Maria Mastai Ferretti dalla giovinezza alla morte nei suoi scritti e discorsi editi inediti—I: Le vie della Divina Providenza (1792–1846)* (Vatican City: Tipografia Poliglotta Vaticana, 1958).

Frank J. Coppa

PIUS X (1903–1914). Born into a large family of modest means in the Italian village of Riese (Treviso) on 2 June 1835, Giuseppe Melchiorre Sarto was elected POPE on 4 August 1903 and died on 20 August 1914. Pius X was only the second pope since Sergius IV (1009–1012) not to be an aristocrat. Canonized in 1954, he was also the only pope since 1712 to be declared a saint. The pontificate of Pius X established several basic doctrinal, juridical, and institutional underpinnings of twentieth-century Catholicism that characterized the church until VATICAN II and beyond. These included a rigidly pyramidal ecclesiology that stressed papal and priestly authority rather than episcopal collegiality or the role of the laity, a standardized catechism, a uniform code of CANON LAW, and a streamlined central government. A prolific, if conservative, reformer, Pius X was suspended between reaction and renewal, and his papacy has consequently been an object of controversy and of conflicting interpretations.

Between his ordination in 1858 and the conclave of 1903, Giuseppe Sarto held a series of ecclesiastical posts located almost entirely within his native region of the Veneto: curate in Tombolo (1858), pastor in Salzano (1867), chancellor of the diocese of Treviso (1875), bishop of Mantua (1884), cardinal-patriarch of Venice (1893). Certain interests as pope, such as concern for sacred music and seminary reform, were adumbrated during the course of this long pastoral experience. Sarto's staunch opposition to secular liberalism and to any compromise between rationalism and religion also developed during this period. However, because of his practical sense of the possible, Sarto always established a respectful modus vivendi with local authorities. This same pragmatism led Cardinal Sarto to orchestrate a coalition between Catholics and moderate liberals in the Venetian municipal elections of 1895. An additional factor in his support for clericomoderate alignments, continued under his pontificate during Italian national elections, was Sarto's distrust of autonomous Catholic political parties.

As regards the internal life of the church, Pius X was the greatest reformer since the COUNCIL of TRENT. In the first five years of his pontificate, Sarto's reforms aimed at a renewal of structures and revitalizing Catholic faith and spirituality. In 1904, the right of veto held by Catholic powers over papal elections was abolished, and absolute secrecy was imposed regarding the deliberations of future conclaves. That same year, Sarto initiated the first codification of canon law. The central government of the church, or Roman CURIA, was reorganized in 1908. In 1904, candidates to the priesthood were finally obligated to attend a seminary, and in the following years (1905–1908) a thorough reform of the internal organization and curriculum of seminaries was undertaken. With reference to faith and devotion, a new standard catechism was promulgated in 1905; papal decrees encouraged frequent communion (1905) and lowered the minimum age for reception of the Eucharist (1910); a *motu proprio* of 1903 provided norms for music used in religious services and rehabilitated Gregorian chant.

On 3 July 1907, the Holy Office issued a decree, *Lamentabili sane exitu*, condemning 65 propositions ascribed to the so-called Modernist current (see Modernism) of progressive Catholic thought. This action was followed on 8 September 1907 by an encyclical, *Pascendi Dominici gregis*, in which the pope denounced Modernism as "the synthesis of all heresies" and outlined a series of measures designed to extirpate it (the expulsion of all suspect professors from seminaries, the appointment of censors in every episcopal curia, the institution of vigilance committees in each diocese). The most far-reaching and controversial step was the imposition of an anti-Modernist oath on all clerics and seminarians (1 September 1910). The anti-Modernist crusade lasted five years (1907–1912). It absorbed the pope's energies, and he was directly compromised in some of its more inquisitorial aspects (e.g., backing Msgr. Umberto Benigni's Sodalitium Pianum, a secret espionage network outside the HIERARCHY), and the reformist thrust of the earlier part of his papacy was brought to a halt.

Four factors conditioned Pius X's actions regarding the laity's participation in social and labor organizations: his conservative view of class relations, his insistence upon strict doctrinal orthodoxy, subordination to ecclesiastical authority, and, consequently, his distrust of interconfessional trade unions. These principles resulted in the condemnation of Romolo MURRI's Christian democratic movement in Italy (1903) and the Sillon of Marc Sangnier in France (1910), while they informed the ENCYCLICAL *Il fermo proposito* (11 June 1905), which laid the basis of Catholic Action.

In external relations, in spite of his antiliberalism and a personal sympathy for the Hapsburg monarchy, Sarto freed the Holy See from temporalist preoccupations, maintained a strict neutrality regarding international alignments, and facilitated the integration of Catholics into the Italian political system.

His renunciation of temporal claims, his pragmatism, and his diffidence toward Catholic parties all led Sarto to encourage electoral coalitions in Italy between clerical forces and, as he wrote in 1908, "other honest defenders of order." In dealing with national governments, Pius X's sole concern was the religious interest of the church as he understood it. This was particularly evident in his reaction to the 1905 separation of church and state in France, in which the compensatory arrangement offered by the government was rejected by the pope in favor of the liberty of the church (encyclical *Gravissimo officii munere* of 10 August 1906).

For further reference: Girolamo Dal Gal, *Il papa santo. Pio X* (Padua: Il Messaggero di S. Antonio, 1954); Rafael Merry del Val, *Memories of Pope Pius X* (Westminister, MD: Newman Press, 1951); Carlo Falconi, *The Popes in the Twentieth Century from Pius X to John XXIII* (Boston: Little, Brown, 1967); Gianpaolo Romanato, *Pio X. La vita di papa Sarto* (Milan: Rusconi Libri, 1992); Annibale Zambarbieri, "Pio X," *Dizionario storico del movimento cattolico in Italia, 1860–1980*, vol. 2 (Casale Monferrato: Marietti, 1982), pp. 486–495.

Andrew M. Canepa

PIUS XI (1922–1939). On 6 February 1922, Achille Cardinal Ratti, archbishop of Milan, was elected to the papal throne, taking the name Pius XI. Ratti's career path to the Vatican was somewhat unusual. He had been appointed to the Milan See only seven months before he was chosen POPE and his career as a Vatican diplomat, although eventful, began only in 1919. In that year, he was appointed apostolic visitor and later NUNCIO to Poland, as that country sought to establish its independence in the wake of WORLD WAR I. Thus, his diplomatic and pastoral experience was limited for a new pope, but his understanding of the Vatican was not.

Born on 31 May 1857 in the town of Desia in the hills of Lombardy, Ambrogio Domiano Achille Ratti, under the influence of his uncle-priest, entered the minor seminary of St. Peter the Martyr in Seveso at the age of ten. He was ordained in 1877, after completing his studies in Rome at the Lombard College. Ratti also graduated from the Gregorian University and the Academy of St. Thomas, coming under the influence of important Italian Jesuits and the growing Thomist movement.

The new priest served only four months as a curate in a small village in Lombardy before being called to Milan by the archbishop to become a professor at the diocesan seminary. In 1888, the young scholar was asked to join the staff of the Ambrosiana Library, a well-known Catholic research center. He rose to be director of the library and, in 1913, was appointed to the additional duties of director of the Vatican Library. His career as a research librarian and scholar was marked by the publication of many scholarly articles and monographs under his own name and pseudonyms. He counted among his friends many scientists and intellectuals, including those who professed liberal, anticlerical sentiments.

It came as some surprise that BENEDICT XV (1914–1922) called upon Ratti to go to Poland on a delicate diplomatic mission, as national and diocesan boundaries were being redrawn, and the Bolshevik threat loomed in the East. But, in fact, Ratti had always interested himself in politics and had many political friends in his circles in Milan and Rome. His stay in Poland was a brief two years, but he was in Warsaw in the midst of the Russo-Polish War and did not forget the experience. In June 1921, Benedict conferred the red hat upon him and installed him in Milan. Seven months later, he was elected pope.

Pius XI was considered by many contemporaries an authoritative leader. Even his admirers admitted that he minced few words and led forcefully but pointed out that he was always kind and considerate of others. As pope during most of the fascist years in Italy, Ratti effected the *conciliazione* between church and state in 1929, establishing the Vatican as an independent state. He then moved to give the Vatican all the elements of a genuine state, building the Vatican radio and the railroad station and establishing a lay governor of the city-state. He also created the Papal Academy of Science, which elected, under his direction, eminent scholars around the world, irrespective of their religious beliefs.

On the political front, the pope's record was more mixed. Although he worked with MUSSOLINI to return Catholicism to prominence in the Italian state, he drew the line on the education of the youth. His lack of support spelled doom for the Catholic POPULAR PARTY and its leader Don Luigi Sturzo, but he staunchly supported the growth and development of Catholic Action throughout Italy and Europe. His insistence on the rights of the church in society and education caused an open clash with Mussolini in 1931, culminating in Pius's harsh encyclical *NON ABBIAMO BISOGNO*. In 1937, he issued an equally harsh condemnation of Nazism's treatment of the church with his encyclical *Mit Brennender Sorge*. In international relations, he put his faith in a diplomacy of CONCORDATS designed to give the church juridical protection of its rights in individual nations. Pius XI died at the age of 82 on 10 February 1939, only months before the outbreak of WORLD WAR II.

For further reference: Marc Agostino, *Le Pape Pie XI et l'opinion (1922–1939)* (Rome: Ecole Francaise de Rome, 1991); Carlo Confalonieri, *Pio XI visto da vicino* (Turin: SAIE, 1957).

Richard J. Wolff

PIUS XII (1939–1958). Eugenio Maria Giuseppe Giovanni Pacelli, the conservative and controversial Roman pontiff who reigned during WORLD WAR II and the early years of postwar reconstruction, was born within the Aurelian walls of Rome on 2 March 1876. This third child of Filippo and Virginia Pacelli, members of the papal or ''black nobility,'' studied at the Gregorian University (see Colleges of Rome), earning a degree in law and theology. In 1899 he was ordained a priest. Brought into the Vatican Secretariat of State, Pacelli was named (1914) secretary of the Congregation for Extraordinary Affairs.

In 1917, in order to further the Vatican's peace effort to end the Great War,

Pacelli was named apostolic NUNCIO to Bavaria. During the Spartacist rising in Munich in 1919, communists burst into his nunciature with revolvers in their hands. Pacelli stood his ground and ordered them to leave—which they did. The harrowing encounter made an unforgettable impression upon him. In 1920 he became the first apostolic nuncio to the new German Republic and remained there until 1929. He was fluent in German and developed great love for the German people. He was a strong believer in the principle of the concordat (see Germany, Concordat of 1933), aiming to preserve the church's privileges and freedom of action, even with regimes hostile to Christian principles. He helped to negotiate CONCORDATS with BAVARIA (1924), PRUSSIA (1929), Baden (1932), Austria (5 June 1933), and, finally, Hitler's Third Reich (20 July 1933). Pacelli was created cardinal in 1929 and next year replaced Cardinal Pietro Gasparri as secretary of state. In 1935 he was appointed camerlengo, holding both of these important posts simultaneously.

He traveled widely on papal missions to North and South America and to France. The principal adviser to PIUS XI on how to deal with the Nazi regime, the secretary of state helped draft the anti-Nazi encyclical *Mit Brennender Sorge* (With Deep Anxiety), 14 March 1937, which rejected the myths of race and blood (but made no explicit mention of anti-Semitism). Nazi programs of euthanasia and sterilization were also denounced. The austere Vatican secretary of state received Nazi foreign minister Ribbentrop coldly when he came to Rome, and in 1938 he was sharply critical of HITLER's annexation of Austria.

After Pius XI's death, Cardinal Pacelli was elected his successor on 2 March 1939, in the shortest conclave since 1623. He took the name Pius XII and was soon called the "POPE of peace," as he tried to dissuade the European governments from embarking on conflict.

The first ENCYCLICAL of the new pope was *Summi pontificatus* (On the Limitations of the Authority of the State), issued on 20 October 1939, a few weeks after hostilities began. Seeking to keep Italy from joining the war, Pacelli turned directly to King Victor Emmanuel III in a vain attempt to restrain Benito MUSSOLINI, who entered the war on Hitler's side, 10 June 1940.

Pius XII delivered a noteworthy series of Christmas broadcasts during the war in which he envisioned a new order that would supersede selfish nationalism. Though he was technically impartial in his relations with the Axis and the Allies, Pius' policies were colored by uncompromising anticommunism. Although he established the Vatican Information Service to distribute aid to, and information about, thousands of refugees during the war and had instructed the church to give discreet aid to the Jews, the pontiff was sharply criticized after the war for having often appeared to be a "pope of silence" in the face of the HOLOCAUST.

Pius tried unsuccessfully to spare Rome from aerial bombardment. When German troops occupied the city after Italy's surrender to the Allies in September 1943, Pius proclaimed it to be an "open city" and came to be known as *defensor civitatis.* Several thousand antifascist politicians and Jews found refuge in Vatican buildings during the occupation. Far less fortunate were 1,259 Romans rounded up in Jewish homes in Rome on the sabbath, 16 October 1943. The Vatican managed to secure the release of 252 who were either entirely Aryan or of mixed marriages. The 1,007 who were Jewish were quickly hauled off to Auschwitz, where more than 800 met immediate death.

Like his predecessor, Pius XII strongly supported Catholic Action, but he did not, at first, favor creation of a separate postwar Italian Christian Democratic Party. However, when the Christian Democratic Party organized itself in 1942–1943, Pius accepted it. The precarious postwar balance between Christian democrats and the extreme Left in Italy led him later to encourage Catholic Action to intervene in parliamentary politics. Christian democratic premier Alcide DE GASPERI protested successfully against this in 1949, earning disfavor at the Vatican.

Clerical intrusion in Italian public life reached a high pitch in the 1950s, when Pius' failing health left power increasingly in the hands of conservative cardinals. Pius also stirred up resentment in the 1950s, when he denounced the new ministry of French "worker-priests." He endorsed postwar Western European integration, and he adamantly condemned the expansion of COMMUNISM into Eastern Europe but stopped short of advocating a crusade against the Soviets. On the other hand, the Holy Office in 1949 excommunicated (see Excommunication) Italian Catholics who joined the Communist Party.

Pius was gifted and deeply spiritual, but he could hardly be called a creative pope. He was especially conservative in his attitude toward marital sexual relations, making a number of pronouncements about the "safe period" but without carrying discussion of it much beyond the position of his predecessor. Nor did he do much to further ecumenism. One of Pius XII's greatest encyclicals was *Divino Afflante Spiritu* (1943; With the Help of the Divine Spirit), which gave fresh impetus to the study of Scriptures in their historical setting. Such studies had been hampered by the inquisitorial atmosphere persisting since Pius X's denunciation of MODERNISM. Subsequently, however, the conservative encyclical *Humani generis* (1950; Of the Human Race) sought to restrain the theological speculation that *Divino Afflante Spiritu* had seemed to encourage. *Mystici Corporis Christi* (1943) was a profound study of the church as the Mystical Body of Christ, while *Mediator Dei* (1946; Mediator of God) forwarded the liturgical movement. In 1950, Pius proclaimed the dogma of the Bodily Assumption of Mary, and in 1954 he promulgated the Marian Year.

In failing health, Pius XII died at Castel Gandolfo on 11 October 1958 at the age of 82. His death marked the end of a conservative era for a church that was about to embark on major reforms under JOHN XXIII.

For further reference: Carlo Falconi, *The Popes in the Twentieth Century* (English trans., London: Weidenfeld and Nicolson, 1967); Saul Friedlander, *Pius XII and the Third*

Reich (English trans., New York: Knopf, 1966); Oscar Halecki and J. F. Murray, *Pius XII: Eugenio Pacelli, Pope of Peace* (New York: Farrar, Straus, and Young, rev., 1954); Nazareno Padellaro, *Portrait of Pius XII* (English trans., London: J. M. Dent, 1956).

Charles F. Delzell

PLACET. The placet (Latin: "it pleases") denotes the approval given by a secular ruler or government to eccelsiastical acts or enactments, required for them to go into effect in his territories. It originated in the Middle Ages, when bishops were often lords of important fiefs, so that their selection and conduct were of great importance to the king; papal pronouncements could have major repercussions. Consequently, in France by the eleventh century kings had begun to claim the power to supervise episcopal elections and to prevent any papal bull or papal LEGATE from entering the country without their permission. The placet was introduced into England after the Norman Conquest. The placet had spread to virtually all Europe by the sixteenth century. The papacy always condemned it as an abuse, since it threatened to lead to the creation of national churches in which the king had greater power than the POPE; but the bulls that condemned the placet were themselves forbidden entry into the states concerned. Only with the CONCORDATS of the nineteenth and twentieth centuries was the placet gradually abolished. Today CANON LAW decrees the EXCOMMUNICATION of anyone using the placet, with absolution reserved to the Vatican.

For further reference: H.E.A. Feine. *Kirchliche Rechtsegeschichte* (Cologne: Verlag, 1964).

Alan J. Reinerman

PONTIAN I (230–235). EUSEBIUS tells us that Pontian succeeded URBAN I (222–230) and ruled for six years; the Liberian Catalogue says that his reign lasted a little more than five years. In any event, after some five years of the tolerant policies of Alexander Severus, Pontian was exiled to the island of Sardinia under the persecution initiated against church leaders by the new emperor Maximin.

It is believed that the "Yppolitus presbyter" exiled with Pontian was HIPPOLYTUS (217–235), the ANTIPOPE, who had confronted two of Pontian's predecessors as bishop of Rome and that the two were reconciled during their ordeal. Both Hippolytus and Pontian died in exile, and their bodies were brought back to Rome by Pope FABIAN (236–250). Pontian was interred in the Cemetery of Callistus. St. Jerome records that the church of Rome approved the actions of two Egyptian synods that banished Origen and deprived him of the priesthood. This approval had to have come while Pontian was bishop of Rome. Interestingly, the Liberian Catalogue indicates that Pontian resigned his position as bishop on 28 September 235. Presumably, he realized that he would not return from his exile on Sardinia. His feast is celebrated on 13 August.

For further reference: J. N. D. Kelly, *The Oxford Dictionary of Popes* (New York: Oxford University Press, 1986); J. Lebreton and J. Zeiller, *The History of the Primitive Church*, vol. 4 (London: Burns, Oates, and Washbourne, 1948).

Bernard J. Cassidy

POPE. The term "pope" is an English word that has its roots in an ancient Greek colloquial expression used by children, *papas*, when referring to their fathers. By the third century A.D., this Greek word was used to identify priests, more specifically, bishops, who exercised a certain spiritual paternity over their ecclesiastical subjects. All bishops eventually enjoyed exclusive use of this title until the sixth century, when its popular use was reserved to the bishop of Rome as head of the Catholic Church. GREGORY VII (1073–1085) established it as the official title of the successor to St. PETER.

The pope, also known as the Roman pontiff, exercises supreme, full, and immediate jurisdiction over the universal church. As bishop of Rome, the pope is Vicar of Christ, successor of Peter, prince of the apostles, supreme pontiff, patriarch of the West, primate of Italy, archbishop and metropolitan of the Roman province, and sovereign of the state of VATICAN CITY. Although Jesus did not appoint specific successors to the prime leadership role exercised by Peter or by any of the other apostles, for that matter, the authority traditionally attached to the Petrine office in the church is rooted in the divine mission of Christ entrusted at the Ascension (Matt. 28: 18 ff.) to the apostles, for whom Peter appears to have been spokesperson, leader, and first in rank, according to the New Testament. In this sense, by divine law and succession to its legitimate exercise, apostolic power was seen to reside in the office and person of the one whom the church designates as pope, successor of Peter and bishop of Rome. This has been the experience of the church from the very beginning.

Including JOHN PAUL II's pontificate (1978–), 262 people have assumed the papal office. The story of the papacy is filled with diversity and contrast, corresponding to history's rich and varied cultural and political movements as well as to the individual personalities that have shaped the history of the church. From apostolic times there has been a consciousness of the primacy of the Roman pontiff among the members of Christian community that has developed with the expansion of the church into a hierarchical structure. Despite this consciousness, however, the full extent of papal authority was never so explicitly defined as it was by the fathers of VATICAN COUNCIL I (1869–1870), who affirmed:

Because the Roman Pontiff is, by divine right of the apostolic primacy, head of the whole Church, we also teach and declare that he is the supreme judge of all the faithful, to whose judgment appeal can be made in all matters which come under ecclesiastical examination. But the verdict of the Apostolic See may be rejected by no one, since there is no higher authority, and no one may pass judgment on its judgment. (Vatican I, Denzinger, p. 1827; Denzinger-Schonmetzer, pp. 3060–3064)

Without any lessening of the pope's power of primacy over all, pastors as well as the general faithful, Vatican Council II (see Vatican Council II) (1962–1965) devoted a great deal of energy to the concept of the relationship of "the college" or body of bishops to the pope in the exercise of authority within the church. In Vatican II's Dogmatic Constitution on the Church, *Lumen gentium*, article 22, the fathers of the council stated:

The order of bishops is the successor to the college of the apostles in teaching authority and pastoral rule; or, rather, in the episcopal order the apostolic body continues without a break. Together with its head, the Roman Pontiff, and never without this head, the episcopal order is the subject of supreme and full power over the Universal Church. But this power can be exercised only with the consent of the Roman Pontiff.

The most recent canonical expression of the long tradition of the church and the developments of the Second Vatican Council regarding the office of pope, the scope of his authority, papal election, and episcopal communion may be found in canons 330 through 335 inclusive of the 1983 Code of Canon Law.

For further reference: George A. Bull, *Inside the Vatican* (New York: St. Martin's Press, 1982); Friedrich Gontard, *The Chair of Peter: A History of the Papacy* (New York: Holt, Rinehart, and Winston, 1964); Patrick Granfield, *The Papacy in Transition* (Garden City, NY: Doubleday, 1980); Patrick Granfield, *The Limits of the Papacy: Authority and Autonomy in the Church* (New York: Crossroad, 1987); Robert Markus and Eric John, *Papacy and Hierarchy* (London: Sheed and Ward, 1969); Peter J. McCord, ed., *Pope for All Christians? An Inquiry into the Role of Peter in the Modern Church* (New York: Paulist Press, 1976); Michael Schmaus and Georg Schwaiger, "Pope," in *Sacramentum Mundi*, vol. 5, ed. Karl Rahner (New York: Herder and Herder, 1970).

David M. O'Connell

POPULAR PARTY. This party was the political expression of CHRISTIAN DEMOCRACY in Italy between 1918 and 1926. It was officially organized in Rome in November 1918, after the Vatican proved willing to rescind its long-standing prohibition against Catholic participation in political life.

Don Luigi Sturzo, the party's major founder, promoted a party that was interclass in structure, nonconfessional in character, though of Christian inspiration, and open to all Italians willing to accept its platform. The platform included an elective senate, proportional representation, corporatism, agrarian reform, woman suffrage, political decentralization, independence for the church, and social legislation. The strongest support for the party came from Catholic trade unions and the lower clergy. In the general elections of 1919 the Popularists won 100 seats out of 508, an amazing feat for a new party. After his election to the Chamber of Deputies in 1921, Alcide DE GASPERI became the president of the Popularist parliamentary group.

During 1922 fascists repeatedly assaulted the headquarters and printing presses of the Popular Party. It was ineffective in halting the advance of FASCISM due to inexperience on the part of most party leaders, division within the party into right and left wings, and an ideological incompatibility with the Socialist Party, fascism's major opponent. Popularists joined the ministry formed by MUSSOLINI in late October 1922, hoping that the realities of government would tame Mussolini and force him to follow the path of constitutionalism. This expectation was not realized. Fascist violence did not diminish, and when the party boldly asserted its autonomy, Mussolini expelled it from his ministry. The party also encountered papal diffidence, for Pope PIUS XI (1922–1939) feared that a Catholic party would antagonize Mussolini and prevent or delay the settlement of the ROMAN QUESTION. Vatican pressure resulted in the resignation of Don Sturzo from the party secretaryship and his exile from Italy. In May 1924 Alcide De Gasperi was chosen by the party's National Council as the secretary. By this time the right wing of the party, the so-called clerico-moderates, were supporting Mussolini.

Popularists participated in the Aventine Secession, but the parliamentary boycott, stemming from the Matteotti murder, was a political failure. On 28–30 June 1925 the Popular Party, under the leadership of De Gasperi, held its fifth and last National Congress. De Gaspari conceded that the battle for Christian democracy had been lost, but he sketched plans for the party's future renewal. In 1926 all members of the Aventine Secession were deprived of their parliamentary seats, and the Popular Party was dissolved. It was reborn during WORLD WAR II and became known as the Christian Democratic Party. In 1994 the Christian Democratic Party renamed itself the Popular Party but bears scant resemblance to Sturzo or De Gasperi's party.

For further reference: Elisa A. Carrillo, *Alcide De Gasperi: The Long Apprenticeship* (Notre Dame, IN: University of Notre Dame Press, 1965); Gabriele De Rosa, *Storia del Partito Popolare* (Bari: Laterza, 1958); Gabriele De Rosa, *Sturzo* (Turin: Unione Tipografico-Editrice Torinese, 1977); Richard A. Webster, *The Cross and the Fasces* (Stanford, CA: Stanford University Press, 1960).

Elisa A. Carrillo

PRUSSIAN CONCORDAT (1929). Negotiations for a Reich CONCORDAT (see Germany, Concordat of 1933) had been going on since the beginning of the Weimar Republic. In the early 1920s the Vatican had also begun discussions with officials of the various German states. When it became apparent by 1922 that a Reich concordat would not be signed in the near future, the Vatican began to concentrate on negotiating state concordats.

Discussions with Prussia, in which most German Catholics lived, became serious only in 1925, once Bavaria had signed a concordat (see Bavaria, Concordat of 1924). NUNCIO Eugenio Pacelli and Prussian minister of religious affairs Carl H. Becker represented their respective governments in these negotiations. In addition to several domestic and external concerns that faced the Berlin government, progress in the concordat discussions was also delayed for several years as both parties waited to see if the Bavarian Treaty would be ratified and whether a national school bill, providing for some of the points concerning religious education about which the negotiators disagreed, would be enacted. An understanding was reached only after the Vatican, for the sake of obtaining its other demands, reluctantly agreed to omit the school question from the final draft. The treaty, signed on 14 June 1929 and ratified on 9 July with a vote of 243 to 172, was supported by the Center Party, the Social Democrats, and the Democrats, with the communists and the rightist parties—the nationalists, the German People's Party, and the Nazis—opposing its passage. To placate the Vatican's unhappiness about the omission of the school question, Prussia assured Rome that it would continue to safeguard the position of confessional schools and religious instruction in public schools.

The treaty superseded the papal bulls of 1821 that had regulated Prussian–Vatican relations up until then. The concordat guaranteed the free exercise of the Catholic faith in Prussia, fixed diocesan boundaries in conformity with the postwar political boundaries, created two new dioceses (Aachen and Berlin), and raised Breslau and Paderborn to the rank of archdioceses. Changes were made in the procedure for episcopal appointment and the rights of the government in the selection process, state subsidies to the church were increased, bishops and clergy were required to be German citizens and in general to have most of their training in German institutions, and bishops were to be consulted on the selection of members of Catholic theological facilities in state universities.

The concordat brought advantages for both parties. For Prussia, by legally defining diocesan boundaries and establishing new sees in both the East and West, the treaty helped strengthen Germany against territorial claims of some of its Eastern neighbors and its position against French influences in the Rhineland. It also solved some of the many church–state problems that had distracted the government for the last decade and ended some of the tension between the socialists and the Center Party within the ruling coalition. For the church, the agreement demonstrated that Rome could negotiate a treaty with a state that was not predominantly Catholic and have it serve as a model for future international negotiations. The concordat also guaranteed the rights and legal status of the church and its institutions, gave it more control over theological facilities and the episcopal selection process as well as increasing state subsidies to the church, and strengthened Catholic influence in north Germany by the elevation of Breslau and Paderborn to archepiscopal rank and in the nation's capital by the establishment of a bishop's seat in Berlin.

In 1933 the Reich concordat confirmed the legality of the state concordats and supplemented some of their provisions. After 1945, despite the fact that Prussia no longer existed, the Western zones and the Federal Republic of Germany generally accepted the legal opinion that the concordat remained valid for territories of the former Prussian state, whereas in the East neither the Soviets nor the German Democratic Republic recognized its validity.

For further reference: Dieter Golombek, *Die politische Vorgeschichte des Preussen-konkordats (1929)* (Mainz: Matthias Grünewald Verlag, 1970); Ernst Helmreich, *The*

German Church under Hitler (Detroit: Wayne State University Press, 1979); ''Zur Geschichte des Preussischen Konkordats und der Errichtung des Bistums Berlin,'' in *Wichmann-Jahrbuch*, nn. 19–20 (1965–66), pp. 64–89; Stewart A. Stehlin, *Weimar and the Vatican, 1919–1933* (Princeton: Princeton University Press, 1983).

Stewart A. Stehlin

Q

QUIETISM. The seventeenth century witnessed a revival of Catholic spirituality. This movement was dominated by the problem of grace. The Jansenists (see Jansenism), emphasizing fallen human nature, called for a rigorous moral code, while those included under the heading of quietism opened the way to a contemplative union with God as pure gift. Both groups fell under the criticism of advocates of other spiritualities, especially the Jesuits (see Society of Jesus).

While elements of quietism found an echo in traditional Christian spirituality, the movement derives essentially from the life and writings of Miguel de Molinos, a Spanish priest who gained a great reputation in Rome in the latter part of the seventeenth century. His admirers included INNOCENT XI (1676–1689). Molinos urged all to open themselves to the gift of passive contemplation in which God alone is present to the soul. To achieve this, one must be emptied of self through the destruction of desire, will, and consciousness so that God might fill the void. Once granted, the gift of passive contemplation begets a permanent state of prayer. When this occurs, the higher part of the soul is separated from the body and the lower part of the soul and is no longer responsible for their actions.

This teaching drew criticism for several reasons. It appeared to open the way to sensuality. In addition, the emphasis on passivity made useless and even harmful the exercise of the moral virtues, the traditional forms of prayer and asceticism, and the ministrations of the church. Cited by the INQUISITION, Molinos' teaching was condemned, and he was imprisoned for life. The movement found a second life in France due to the activities of the eccentric Madame Guyon, who spread it by her books and teaching. Arrested for suspicion of HERESY in 1687, she was released due to royal intervention. At this time F. Fenelon, the future archbishop of Cambrai, became her director and defender. He engaged in a bitter controversy with J. Bossuet, bishop of Meaux, who eventually succeeded in securing the condemnation of Madame Guyon (1695) and Fenelon (1699). These condemnations damaged Christian mysticism and caused it to enter a period of regression.

For further reference: M. de la Bedoyere, *The Archbishop and the Lady. The Story of Fenelon and Madame Guyon* (New York: Pantheon, 1956); R. Knox, *Enthusiasm* (New York: Oxford University Press, 1950).

Richard J. Kehoe

R

RALLIEMENT. In the early 1890s, the Vatican and a small number of influential French Catholics sought a rapprochement (the *Ralliement*) between French Catholics and the anticlerical Third French Republic. European trends as well as the histories of the Vatican and the Third Republic explain the *Ralliement*. The policy partially failed in the short term but had significant impact over time.

By 1890, as liberalism, democracy, and socialism gained more adherents, the Catholic Church became one of the primary targets of the nineteenth-century rebellion against the traditional order. Responding to the loss of temporal authority in Italy, Pope PIUS IX (1846–1878) renounced the new ideas emerging. Committed to similar values as Pius IX, Pope LEO XIII (1878–1903), his successor, changed strategy. He repositioned the church in modern society in order to more effectively fight for Catholic perspectives. As early examples, the papal encyclicals *Immortale Dei* (1885), *Libertas* (1888), and *Sapientiae Christanae* (January 1890) suggested that the forms of states mattered less than the content of their legislation. Increasingly, the attention of the Vatican focused on France.

Founded between 1870 and 1875, the early Third Republic defined itself as fundamentally anticlerical. Many of its strongest proponents were positivists, who were committed to political liberty, individualism, faith in science, and the idea of progress and perceived the Catholic Church as an enemy. In addition, anticlericalism was one of the few issues upon which many republicans could agree. Thus, during the 1880s, the leaders of the Third Republic established secular education, replacing priests as teachers in public schools. They also restricted Catholic associations, made seminarians liable to military service, and reestablished divorce. These laic laws became bêtes noires for many French Catholics. Representatives of two different worldviews, schoolmaster and curé, faced each other across the barricades in French towns and cities.

French Catholics adapted to the Third Republic with difficulty and diversity. During the mid-1880s, Count Albert de Mun, a leading French Catholic and

Social Catholic, sought to establish a Catholic party, which the Vatican opposed. Still tempted by antirepublicanism, many French conservatives supported General Boulanger's abject failure to overturn the republic.

In this historical context, the *Ralliement* flowed from French Catholic and Vatican sources. In March 1890, Jacques Piou, a deputy and former supporter of Boulanger, established the *droite constitutionnelle* (the Constitutional Right), a new group that would accept the republic in order to influence it in a conservative direction. After meeting with leaders of the Third Republic and with Leo XIII in Rome, on 12 November 1890, Cardinal Lavigerie spoke to officers of the French Mediterranean fleet. Probably on his own initiative but with papal approval, Lavigerie urged his royalist-leaning audience to recognize "a great need for unity." The officers' stony faces presaged opposition by intransigents.

At first Pope Leo XIII did not publicly back the cardinal, although his sympathy is not in doubt. In 1889, Msgr. Ferrata, a papal adviser and future NUNCIO to France, had advocated the *Ralliement* policy, and shortly after Lavigerie's address, Cardinal Rampolla, Vatican secretary of state, backed the cardinal in a letter to a French bishop. Neither *Rerum Novarum*, Leo XIII's famous encyclical of 1891, nor the small Christian democratic and Social Catholic currents springing up in French Catholicism were exactly equivalent to the *Ralliement* policy, but they all reflected the same reorientation occurring within some elements of Catholicism and the Vatican. In February 1892, the encyclical *Au milieu des sollicitudes* put the POPE's weight behind the *Ralliement*. Leo XIII was not a liberal but perceived the adherence of French Catholics to the monarchist cause counterproductive. He wished to strengthen conservatives within the republic in order to better preserve Catholic beliefs and interests and to compete more effectively against socialists and radicals. The pope also hoped improvement in relations with France might bolster the Vatican's position in the world at large and in Italy with reference to the ROMAN QUESTION.

The *Ralliement* achieved limited success. There were prominent converts to the policy, for example, Count Albert de Mun in 1892. Inside the republic, some conservative republicans responded affirmatively. A relatively small number of *ralliés* (thirty six), but not the major leaders, were elected in 1893. In French politics during the 1890s, the Opportunists (also called Progressistes and Moderates), conservative republicans, predominated, with the help of votes from conservative Catholics. Nonetheless, resistance and mistrust against the *Ralliement* remained strong among clericals and anticlericals. The Dreyfus affair intensified these hostile sentiments and, in 1905, led to the demise of the concordat and to the separation of church and state. After a sharp reversal of the *Ralliement* policy under Pope PIUS X (1903–1914), during and after WORLD WAR I the *Ralliement* continued.

For further reference: Oscar Arnal, *Ambivalent Alliance: The Catholic Church and the Action Francaise 1899–1939* (Pittsburgh: University of Pittsburgh Press, 1985); Maurice Larkin, *Church and State after the Dreyfus Affair: The Separation Issue in France* (London: Macmillan, 1974); Benjamin F. Martin, *Count Albert de Mun: Paladin of the Third*

Republic (Chapel Hill: University of North Carolina Press, 1978); Harry Paul, *The Second Ralliement: The Rapprochement between Church and State in France in the Twentieth Century* (Washington, DC: Catholic University of America Press, 1967); Alexander Sedgwick, *The Ralliement in French Politics 1890–1898* (Cambridge: Harvard University Press, 1965).

Joel Blatt

REFORMATION. During the Middle Ages the call for reform echoed constantly in Christendom. Spiritual renewal formed part of the agenda of all the medieval COUNCILS. Since this movement frequently assumed an antipapal stance, the POPES viewed it with reserve. Nonetheless, many recognized the need for reform on the eve of the Reformation. The opening speaker at the Fifth Lateran Council (see Lateran Council V) (1512) considered reform the chief task of the council. The council presented Pope LEO X (1513–1521) with a bold reform program, which he never implemented. Pope ADRIAN VI (1522–1523) publicly acknowledged the need for reform of the clergy and CURIA. These voices were inspired by the spiritual renewal fostered by the *Devotio Moderna* and Christian humanism.

Martin Luther (1483–1546), who belonged to a reformed branch of the Augustinian Friars, was deeply affected by these currents. His critique of the preaching of indulgences in Germany (1517) highlighted abuses that others had earlier attacked. He quickly became the spokesman for the discontent with church practices and papal leadership that circulated in Germany. Luther gathered a sympathetic following, which included some political leaders. The support of the latter at the Diet of WORMS (1521) assured his personal survival and, at the Diet of Augsburg (1530), the survival of the movement of which he had become the leader. During the last fifteen years of his life Luther presided over the consolidation and spread of the church, which eventually took his name. Outside Germany Lutheranism took root in the Scandinavian countries.

Ulrich Zwingli (1484–1531) gave voice to the humanistic reform movement that arose in Switzerland. John Calvin (1509–1564) left his native France and assumed leadership of the reform in Switzerland. From Geneva he sent disciples throughout Europe to proclaim his message and organize churches in conformity with his teaching. In France his disciples, the Huguenots, challenged the Catholic monarchy, leading to the wars of religion that convulsed the country for thirty years. In the Netherlands, Calvinism struck deep roots as one of the rallying points of the nationalist movement that overthrew Spanish domination. John Knox (1513–1572), an ardent disciple of Calvin, profited from the volatile political situation in Scotland and organized the national ''kirk'' on the Genevan model. Calvinism influenced churches that did not derive directly from it. The Church of England reflects this influence in the Thirty-Nine Articles, as do the German and Hungarian reformed churches through the *Heidelberg Catechism*.

England felt the impact of the Continental Reformation. But the proximate cause of the reform in England was the desire of Henry VIII to divorce his wife,

Catherine of Aragon. When the pope refused his request, Henry withdrew the church in England from obedience to Rome and established the Church of England. Under his first successors, Edward VI and Mary Tudor, the church fell under the influence of the Continental reformers and then returned to union with Rome. With the accession of Elizabeth I the Church of England once again became independent and, during the long reign of the last of Henry's children, established its unique identity among the churches of the Reformation.

The Reformation impacted the Roman Catholic Church profoundly. The reform movement, which had stagnated under the RENAISSANCE PAPACY, found expression in humanists like Erasmus, who remained Catholic, and in individuals and groups in Italy and Spain influenced by humanism and the *Devotio Moderna*. Ignatius Loyola, a Spanish nobleman and founder of the SOCIETY OF JESUS, was nurtured by these currents and became an advocate for Catholic reform. Renewal eventually penetrated the Roman Curia and the College of Cardinals. The latter urged Pope PAUL III (1534–1549) to convoke a council to effect the necessary reforms. After many delays the Council of TRENT (1545–1563) opened and over its life structured the plan for the renewal of the Catholic Church.

A movement as profound and extensive as the Reformation cannot be explained by one cause alone. The rise of nationalism at the end of the Middle Ages challenged the universalism of the church led by the pope. It is impossible to understand the Reformation in Germany apart from the struggle between Emperor Charles V and the German princes. Technology, especially the invention of the printing press, provided the means for the rapid spread of the Reformation, which would have been inconceivable 50 years earlier. The spread of learning fostered by humanism created literate consumers of the books and pamphlets generated by the religious controversies. While the political, technological, cultural, and social contexts had a profound and undeniable impact on the rise and development of the Reformation, at its center the Reformation was a religious movement. Most of those involved, despite distractions from many quarters, strove to restore both the church and its practices to their pristine spiritual and religious purposes. The causes of the Reformation are multiple, but religion must be seen as its primary cause.

For further reference: H. Hillerbrand, *Christendom Divided: The Protestant Reformation* (Philadelphia: Westminster Press, 1971); D. L. Jensen, *Reformation Europe. Age of Reform and Revolution* (Lexington, MA: D. C. Heath, 1981); J. Lortz, *How the Reformation Came* (Montreal: Palm, 1964); S. Ozment, *The Age of Reform 1250–1550* (New Haven, CT: Yale University Press, 1980).

Richard J. Kehoe

RENAISSANCE PAPACY. By the middle of the fifteenth century the papacy emerged victorious over the reform councils that encroached on its authority. The resignation of the last ANTIPOPE, FELIX V (1439–1449), and the dissolution of the COUNCIL of BASEL ended conciliarism's (see Conciliar Movement) challenge to the papacy. NICHOLAS V (1447–1455) set about restoring its tarnished reputation. Papal LEGATES attempted to respond to the call for reform that continued to echo in the church. Nicholas strove to restore Rome as the center of the Catholic world with the Jubilee Year of 1450. He began the transformation of Rome into the Renaissance city of today as papal patronage drew humanist scholars to its court.

CALLISTUS III (1455–1458) devoted his energies to vain efforts for a crusade. He did not foster the Renaissance, but his nepotism burdened the church for a half century with his two cardinal nephews, Juan-Luis Mila and Rodrigo Borgia, whose sensuality and intrigue scandalized the church. PIUS II (1458–1464) pursued fruitless efforts for a crusade. Nepotism also tarnished his reign. Two of his relatives became cardinals, and he used his office to advance their families. PAUL II (1464–1471), a product of the nepotism of EUGENE IV (1431–1447), brought to the papal throne mediocre talents and a suspicious and authoritarian personality. Under him the Renaissance suffered a temporary setback because of the POPE's sometimes violent suppression of humanist gatherings.

With SIXTUS IV (1471–1484) the high Renaissance settled in Rome. Before his election he signed a capitulation, an agreement by which the cardinals, if elected pope, swore to follow certain policies. Capitulations, part of most of the conclaves of the era, required the new pope to war against the Turks, call a council to reform the church, limit the number of cardinals, guarantee the cardinals' share in papal revenues, and seek their consent on certain issues. These pacts witnessed the efforts of the cardinals to limit papal authority and enhance their role in the governance of the church. Under Sixtus IV the papacy sank to new depths. He dedicated himself to strengthening the papacy within the PAPAL STATES and in Italy and to placing his numerous relatives in positions of wealth and power through systematic nepotism. He named six nephews, almost all unworthy, cardinals. Like a typical Renaissance prince he resorted to deception, intrigue, and violence to achieve his goals. While he contributed much to the rebuilding of Rome and generously supported humanist projects, he financed these by fiscal practices that denigrated his office, for example, the creation of new, marketable posts and the granting of indulgences for the sake of revenues. As one historian observes, at his death "he left the papacy hated as a power where before it had merely been mistrusted."

A conclave stained by bribery and simony elected INNOCENT VIII (1484–1492), a weak, vacillating pope who had neither the will nor the energy to stem the moral decline of the papacy. It appears that simony also assured the election of Rodrigo Borgia as ALEXANDER VI (1492–1503). This man of great ability lacked all moral qualifications for his office. He devoted his energy to providing for his illegitimate children, using force and ecclesiastical sanctions to achieve his goals. He struggled shrewdly to protect the papal states in the face of French aggression. The death of his son awakened in him a moral sense, and a commission of cardinals produced a plan for church reform. But it remained a dead letter.

JULIUS II (1503–1513) gained the see of Peter in a conclave again corrupted by simony. More a *condottiere* than a priest, he set about reconquering the papal states. For this he formed alliances and broke them at will. He aimed at driving all non-Italians from Italy. His policies caused Louis XII of France and a group of cardinals to call a council at Pisa to depose him. In response, Julius convoked the Fifth Lateran Council (see Lateran Council V) (1512) to forestall their plans. Hardly a year passed without Julius marching off to war. He left his mark on Rome by engaging Michelangelo, Bramante, and Raphael in rebuilding and beautifying the city. The energy and skill of Julius restored the political fortunes of the papacy but were not used for the primary task of the papacy, the spiritual renewal and leadership of the church.

The election of LEO X (1513–1521) brought the Renaissance in Rome to its apogee. This son of Lorenzo the Magnificent, ruler of both the papal states and Florence, struggled to stabilize Italy by excluding foreign rulers. He lived as a Renaissance prince, loving pageantry and luxury and using his office to advance his family in Rome and elsewhere, spending lavishly to promote the arts in Rome. To support this program he emptied the Vatican treasury and multiplied the deplorable fiscal practices of the CURIA. The calls for reform from the Fifth Lateran Council and Martin Luther failed to evoke in him a genuine religious response. Like his predecessors, he had lost the sense of the religious mission of the church.

The Renaissance papacy depended on practices most in need of reform in the church: pluralisms and exemptions that sanctioned the holding of several incompatible benefices, the failure to reside in benefices that entailed the care of souls, and the image of church property as a source of personal wealth rather than a means to provide for the care of souls. The multiplication of taxes, indulgences, and offices to be sold created an atmosphere of venality at the heart of the church. A College of CARDINALS created by nepotism and political favor could not provide the leadership to heed the call for reform (see Reformation) that echoed loudly in Europe.

For further reference: H. Jedin, *History of the Church*, vol. 4 (New York: Crossroads, 1986), pp. 521–566; L. Pastor, *The History of the Popes*, vols. 2–8 (St. Louis: B. Herder, 1899–1908); C. L. Stinger, *The Renaissance in Rome* (Bloomington: Indiana University Press, 1985); J. F. Thomson, *Popes and Princes, 1417–1517* (London: George Allen and Unwin, 1980).

Richard J. Kehoe

ROMAN QUESTION. The "Roman question" was the impasse in church–state relations in Italy resulting from the annexation of most of the states of the church by the kingdom of Italy, proclaimed 17 March 1861. Although Turin served as the first capital of the Savoyard state from March 1861 to June 1865, and Florence from June 1865 on, nationalists had always assumed that the Eternal City was destined to become the new nation's capital. This occurred during the Franco–Prussian War, which prompted Italy's seizure of Rome, 20 September 1870, and its designation as the Italian capital.

Calling himself "the prisoner of the Vatican," PIUS IX (1846–1878) on 1 November 1870 issued the bull *Respicientes la Omnia*. Without specifying personalities, he excommunicated (see Excommunication) all the Italian patriots who had been involved in the spoliation of the states of the church. The Italian government responded by formulating the Law of Guarantees of 13 May 1871. Drafted without the Holy See's input, this legislation was designed to place church–state relations on a stable and equitable foundation. The person of the POPE was accorded royal status. Unfettered communications were assured with Catholics and states throughout the world, while no restrictions were imposed on clerical activities except in violation of Italian law, and prelates were exempt from the oath of loyalty to the secular regime. The Vatican and its holdings in Italy were granted extraterritoriality. To cover the loss of income from the confiscation of the church's lands and annexation of its states, 3,225,000 lire were to be deposited annually in Italian banks to the Holy See's account.

On 15 May the law was repudiated by Pius IX. Don Giacomo Margotti's 1861 prescription, *Ne' eletti, Ne' elettori* (neither deputies or electors) was reinforced by the pope's September 1874 *Non Expedit* (it is not expedient for Catholics to participate in national elections), invoking a Catholic boycott of the electoral process. On the other hand, anarchists, independent anticlericals, Freemasons, and freethinkers decried the Law of Guarantees for having accorded the pope a statutory reverence.

The Roman question was gradually diffused of its superheated overtones by the understanding of segments of the liberal ruling classes and ecclesiastical officials that the deadlock served neither well but only encouraged the ultras within the parties of the extreme Left: socialists, radicals, and republicans, enemies of both church and state. Practical evidence of this new realism was given by PIUS X's (1903–1914) suspension of the *Non Expedit* for the general elections of 1904, to spur Catholics to the polls in behalf of the candidates of order, the conservative liberals, against the entries of the Left. The high point of the evolving and informal mutuality was the unofficial support tendered Catholic moderates to the liberal premier Giovanni Gioliiti and his tickets, especially during the political elections of 1913, allegedly negotiated through Count Ottavino Gentilone's Unione Elettorale Cattolica. Nonetheless, Premier Antonio Salandra and Foreign Minister Sidney Sonnino insisted on inserting a protocol in article 15 of the Secret Treaty of London, signed 26 April 1915, that disallowed the pope a seat at the peace conference at the conclusion of WORLD WAR I, fearing he might reopen or pursue the Roman question.

The fact that Italian Catholics participated in the war with the same nationalistic zeal and febrile expectations as other Italians was not lost on either state or church. There was an interest in accommodation and the final breakthrough achieved with the advent of Benito MUSSOLINI and FASCISM to power, 28 October 1922. Although there was always an undercurrent of diffidence in both camps, fascism and Catholicism alike favored a paternalistic order of society and were certain that COMMUNISM was the more virulent foe. Begun in 1926 and carried on in secret, negotiations were concluded in 1929 under the watchful eyes and guidance of Mussolini and Cardinal Pietro Gasparri, Pope PIUS XI's secretary of state.

The LATERAN ACCORDS consisted of three pacts between the kingdom of Italy and the Holy See. As announced by the Conciliation Treaty, the Law of Guarantees was abrogated, and the Roman question was declared resolved. The papacy recognized the kingdom of Italy under the House of Savoy as a historical fact, with Rome as its capital, while Roman Catholicism was acknowledged to be the religion of the state. VATICAN CITY was created from a portion of Rome as an autonomous entity, having the privileges and responsibilities of a sovereign state.

The CONCORDAT intended to regulate church–state relations, assured the church free exercise of spiritual functions, complete jurisdiction in internal matters, and unabridged accessibility of parishioners to houses of worship. Prior state approval was required for appointment of bishops to serve in Italy, who also had to take an oath of allegiance to the Italian head of state. No prelate or nun could be in the employment of the state without diocesan sanction. Religious instruction was mandated for primary and secondary education, with the teaching personnel reviewed by the church for suitability. Clergymen were forbidden to have membership or take part in the activities of a political party.

As monetary compensation for the territories seized in the unification struggle, the Financial Convention provided the church 750 million lire in cash and 1 billion lire in government bonds. The bonds may have had the intent of creating a Catholic stake in the survival of the fascist state.

For further reference: S. William Halperin, *Italy and the Vatican at War* (Chicago: University of Chicago Press, 1939); Carlo A. Jemolo, *Church and State in Italy, 1850–1950*, trans. David Moore (Oxford: Basil Blackwell, 1960); Angelo Martini, *Studi sulla Questione Romana e la conciliazione* (Rome: Cinque Lune, 1963).

Ronald S. Cunsolo

ROMANUS (897). Italian-born and hailing from the same hometown as MARINUS I (882–884), Romanus' brief pontificate was highlighted by his declaration invalidating the acts of his predecessor, STEPHEN VI (896–897). Apart from this, no other significant acts or events are known.

For further reference: Joseph S. Brusher, *Popes through the Ages* (Princeton: D. Van Nostrand, 1964); H. K. Mann, *The Lives of the Popes in the Early Middle Ages* (London: K. Paul, 1902–1932).

John C. Horgan

RUFFO, CARDINAL FABRIZIO. Ruffo was born in June 1744 in Calabria of an aristocratic family that had given many important prelates and cardinals to the church. He took holy orders and entered papal service in 1765, where with the patronage of his uncle Cardinal Tommaso Ruffo he rose rapidly. In 1785 he became treasurer of the Camera Apostolica, but his efforts to prevent the property of the church from being misappropriated by the aristocracy aroused strong hostility toward him. Eventually, in 1791 Pope PIUS Vl (1775–1799) asked him to resign but named him a cardinal. He retired to Naples. When the French invaded Naples in 1798 and set up the Parthenopean Republic, he fled to Sicily with the king. Early in 1799 he returned to the mainland, where he aroused a holy war of the devout peasantry against the French and their liberal Italian supporters. His "Army of the Holy Faith" (the *SANFEDISTI*) rapidly reconquered the mainland. At Naples he negotiated the surrender of the liberals on condition that their lives be spared. However, the king was persuaded by Admiral Nelson, who arrived with a British fleet, to ignore the agreement and carry out a bloody repression. In disgust, Ruffo abandoned politics, devoting himself to religious affairs. He died at Naples on 12 August 1827.

For further reference: Harold Acton, *The Bourbons of Naples* (London: Methuen, 1956); Benedetto Croce, *La Riconquista del Regno di Napoli nel 1799* (Bari: Laterza, 1943); Gerardo Marotta, *La notte comincia ancora una volta* (Cosenza: ENEL, 1985).

Alan J. Reinerman

S

SABINIAN (604–606). Italian-born, Sabinian served as GREGORY I's (590–604) ambassador to Constantinople. Upon his election as POPE, he reversed Gregory's earlier policy by staffing his administration with the secular clergy rather than monks. His reign witnessed renewed hostilities with the Lombards, and he was accused of profiteering while selling grain from the papal stores during a famine in Rome.

For further reference: Eric John, ed., *The Popes: A Concise Biographical Dictionary* (New York: Hawthorn Books, 1964); Hans Kuhner, *Encyclopedia of the Papacy* (New York: Philosophical Library, 1958).

John C. Horgan

SANFEDISTI. The name was first applied to the armed bands of peasants, deeply Catholic and devoted to the traditional order, that Cardinal Fabrizio RUFFO organized into the ''Army of the Holy Faith'' in 1799 to overthrow the French satellite republic in Naples and restore the monarchy. The *Sanfedisti* represented the spontaneous resistance of the southern peasants to a regime that had offended their deepest convictions and was seen as an alien intrusion. After 1815 the term was also applied to the various conservative secret societies that were organized to oppose those of the liberals. The name was also frequently applied by liberals and by some later historians to supporters of throne and altar in general against the liberal revolutionary movement.

For further reference: E. E. Y. Hales, *Papacy and Revolution* (Garden City, NY: Hanover House, 1960); Francesco Leoni, *Storia della Controrivoluzione in Italia* (Naples: Guida, 1975).

Alan J. Reinerman

SAPIENZA. SEE COLLEGES OF ROME.

SCHISM. "Schism" is derived from the Greek word *schisma*, meaning a "split," a "rent," a "division." In its earliest usage a schism was seen as dividing the unity of the one church of Christ, an evil to be avoided. It was distinguished from HERESY, which was concerned with dogmas or doctrines of the faith. While heresies often resulted in splits within the church, in its technical sense schism was normally used to describe divisions that often began with a personal conflict based on church discipline or order. An early example is Novatianism (c. 251). NOVATIAN challenged Cornelius, the bishop of Rome, on the issue of the penance required of people who had committed apostasy during persecution, and it led to the proclamation of Novatian as ANTIPOPE. In the fourth century Donatism, which insisted that the personal holiness of the church's ministers was necessary for the validity of the sacraments, developed into a separate church that survived for at least a full century.

Common to these movements is the formation by their leaders of a fringe church separated from the so-called mainstream or orthodox church. Faith issues, namely, sacramental theology and ecclesiology, were also involved, but these cases differ from a heresy such as ARIANISM, which explicitly denied a major element of faith, the divinity of the second and third persons of the Christian Trinity. Unlike heresies, schisms do not in themselves imply anathemas or EX-COMMUNICATION, although such penalties are sometimes applied because of other circumstances. In a schism ordained clergy may continue to exercise their ministry validly, if not licitly. The "Great Schism" between the Eastern and Western churches stemmed from theological differences, for example, the *filioque*, as well as from personal and political considerations and issues of church order; the two sides excommunicated one another in 1054, but these anathemas were annulled in 1965 by Pope PAUL VI (1963–1978) and Athenagoras, the ecumenical patriarch. From 1378 to 1417 the Western church experienced the "Great Western Schism," which had no theological or doctrinal basis but during which there were two and even three claimants of the papacy. In the "Great Schism" two churches already in existence formalized their separation; the outcome of the "Great Western Schism" was not a separate church but an open division in the unity of church order.

For further reference: D. Baker, ed., *Schism, Heresy, and Religious Protest* (Cambridge: Cambridge University Press, 1972), S. L. Greenslade, *Schism in the Early Church*, 2d ed. (London: SCM, 1964).

Gerard H. Ettlinger

SCHISM, GREAT WESTERN. This was the greatest internal crisis (1378–1417) experienced by the church short of the Protestant REFORMATION. During its course three rival POPES ruled from Rome, Avignon, and Pisa.

Pope GREGORY XI (1370–1378) died on 27 March 1378, within fourteen months of his return to Rome, ending the Babylonian captivity of the church. As a protest against the transplanting of the papacy to Avignon and to safeguard it in the future, Italians in Rome demonstrated for a pope of Italian ancestry who would publicly pledge to keep the papal seat in Rome. Yielding to local sentiment, the College of CARDINALS, predominantly French, named an Italian cardinal with the title URBAN VI (1378–1389). The newly elected pontiff immediately announced that a reform of the College of Cardinals would be the first of many sweeping transformations contemplated for the church. Having interpreted Urban's determination as a threat to their position of power, thirteen cardinals, all but one French, proceeded, on 30 September 1378, to declare Urban's selection void and chose "Clement VII" (1378–1394), a cardinal from their ranks and cousin of the French king, Charles V.

URBAN VII refused to abdicate. Instead, he appointed an all-Italian College of Cardinals and remained in Rome. Confronted by the deadlock, "Clement VII" and his ministers abandoned Rome for Avignon. All the church institutions, from the College of Cardinals, to the CURIA, to monasteries and monastic orders, were torn in allegiance between the two sees. The death of one or another pope did not relieve the situation, since each College of Cardinals chose a pope of its own nationality as successor. The stalemate had Continental repercussions. France and the countries friendly to it, Aragon, Castille, Naples, and Scotland, were pro-Avignon; England, Flanders, the Holy Roman Empire, Hungary, Poland, and Portugal were pro-Rome.

The shocking incident spurred the development of the CONCILIAR MOVEMENT, whose main idea was that at critical crossroads a general council of broad representation was to be convoked to guide the church. The rival cardinals were finally persuaded to call some 500 prelates and delegates of the European states to meet in solemn session in Pisa. The COUNCIL of Pisa (1409–1410) examined the contesting popes, deposed both, and elevated ALEXANDER V (1409–1410). Following the unexpected death of this ANTIPOPE in 1410, the Pisan councillors honored the local cardinal Baldassare Costa as the new pope. Assuming the title "JOHN XXIII" (1410–1415), he was known more for his martial ardor than for religious fervor. Neither of the two prior popes in Rome and Avignon gave way. A triple split ensued. It remained for the Council of CONSTANCE (1414–1417) to resolve the issue.

For further reference: George Jeffries Jordan, *The Inner History of the Great Schism of the West; A Problem in Church Unity* (London: Williams and Norgate, 1930); Gail Marzieh, *The Three Popes: An Account of the Great Schism When Rival Popes in Rome, Avignon, and Pisa Vied for the Rule of Christendom* (New York: Simon and Schuster, 1969).

Ronald S. Cunsolo

SECRET VATICAN ARCHIVES. The Secret Vatican Archives form an intrinsic component of the Holy See, with the specific purpose of serving the Roman pontiff and his CURIA in the pastoral guidance of the universal church. All aspects of this supreme ministry are reflected in the doctrinal, canonical, constitutional, and juridical, as well as purely administrative nature of the records that have emanated from the diverse departments of the central government throughout the centuries and are preserved *ad perpetuam rei memoriam*.

The Vatican Archives are designated ''secret'' simply because the first nucleus of the present institution originated in the *bibliotheca secreta* of SIXTUS IV (1471–1484). Moreover, that term was already applied to the archives of other European sovereigns to denote the fact that they were private and not by their nature accessible for consultation. The interest lies not in their secrecy but rather that they are the principal and indispensable source for the history of the papacy and the church from the High Middle Ages until the present day and fulfill a cultural role of primary importance because of the exceptional historical value of the documents amassed there.

This vast collection of records occupies 130 rooms of the Vatican Palace with a surface area of approximately four acres. The cardinal archivist of the holy Roman church is the patron of the Vatican Archives, an honorary, rather than executive, position. The effective organizing and running of the institution are entrusted to the prefect, assisted by professional and subaltern personnel employed in administrative, secretarial, and ancillary services.

The Vatican Archives are open to bona fide researchers without discrimination of nationality or religious affiliation. They may request material for the period inclusive of the pontificate of BENEDICT XV (1914–1922). Although only select scholars were admitted previously, since 1880, the papal archives have been open for general consultation, and they have become the mecca of countless researchers intent upon investigating these original sources for the ecclesiastical, political, and social history of their respective nations. Such were the international range and richness of the information contained in the archival collections that soon afterward several historical institutes were founded in Rome before the end of the last century, the availability of this fresh material being the determining factor. The editorial enterprise for the publication of the Vatican sources has been undertaken almost exclusively by these and by the many other national institutions founded afterward.

The Holy See is the only contemporary institution that has had a continuous existence since the time of the early Roman empire. Even in the primitive church, there is reason to believe that papal decrees were being copied for retention at the seat of central government, similar to the archives of the state. The existence of such official records can be proved positively from the late fourth century, while in the fifth allusion is made to the chancery practice of copying outgoing correspondence into registers following an arrangement that was planned and not haphazard. The papal chancery was slow, however, to change from the use of traditional, but fragile, papyrus to more durable parchment, and this explains why those early records were not destined to survive.

The extant regular series of *Registra Vaticana* begins only with INNOCENT III (1198–1216), though further losses occurred during the thirteenth to fifteenth centuries due to the mobility of the POPES. During prolonged absences from

Rome, their archives followed the itinerant curia as it moved between Viterbo, Anagni, Orvieto, Montefiascone, Perugia, and Assisi. After the popes had established their permanent residence at Avignon, all the earlier records were reunited there finally in 1339.

Meantime, the system of record conservation had been extended beyond the chancery to other offices of the curia, such as the Camera, the Datary, the Penitentiary, the Rota, and the emerging secretariates. Original, incoming documents were now preserved, as well as the registration of the outgoing material. The GREAT WESTERN SCHISM (1378–1417) gave rise to three rival "obediences," which generated corresponding parallel series of records. By the time Christendom was reconciled under MARTIN V (1417–1431), "papal" archives were dispersed in many locations of Southwestern Europe, and it required repeated efforts before the bulk of this material was recuperated and brought to Rome.

In the sixteenth century, under PIUS IV (1559–1565), the concept of a central archive of the Holy See began to evolve, but it was much later, under PAUL V (1605–1621) that they materialized. In 1611 the pope instituted the new Secret Vatican Archives for the express purpose of containing all the proceedings and documents concerning the government of the universal church.

Very great losses were sustained by the archives in the wake of the Napoleonic occupation of the PAPAL STATES. In 1810 it was decided to bring all the material to Paris, involving the transport over the Alps of some 200,435 items, packed in 3,239 chests and weighing over 400 tons! Losses occurred en route, many items disappeared in France, and whole sections were deliberately destroyed at the order of the papal commissioners entrusted with organizing the return of the archives to the Vatican, in 1817, after the Congress of VIENNA.

The short sojourn of the papal archives at Paris was not altogether negative. Of primary importance was the fact that the richness of the Vatican collections was now revealed to historical researchers for the first time, and this dictated a change of policy regarding accessibility, after their restitution to the Holy See.

Although greater liberality was used in permitting consultation, only in 1880 did LEO XIII (1878–1903) make the formal decision to open the Vatican Archives in general to qualified researchers. A more dynamic policy has been followed regarding new accessions of the Holy See, even if some departments of the Roman Curia have remained autonomous and preserve their records at the source of creation.

For further reference: L. E. Boyle, *A Survey of the Vatican Archives and of Its Medieval Holdings*, vol. 1 (Toronto: Pontifical Institute of Medieval Studies: Subsidia Mediavalia, 1972); "Saint Siège—*Archivio Segreto Vaticano*," *Archivum* 15 (1965): 305–310.

Charles Burns

SECRETARIATS, PAPAL. Prior to Pope JOHN PAUL II's (1978–   ) efforts to reorganize the Roman CURIA with the publication of his apostolic constitution *Pastor Bonus* (28 June 1988), there existed within the Apostolic See four major agencies known as ''secretariats'': the Secretariat of State or Papal Secretariat, headed by the cardinal secretary of state; the Secretariat for Christian Unity; the Secretariat for Non-Christians; and the Secretariat for Non-Believers.

The Secretariat of State is the department that provides the most immediate assistance to the Roman pontiff in his governing the church throughout the world. In addition, this secretariat serves to coordinate the internal workings of the other dicasteries of the Apostolic See. The cardinal appointed by the POPE as secretary of state is his ''prime minister,'' personally overseeing all curial operations. He handles all matters entrusted to him by the pope and any other concerns that do not fall within the ordinary competence of other congregations or offices.

The responsibilities and activities of the other three ''secretariats'' have been assumed by specific pontifical councils of the Roman Curia. The Secretariat for Christian Unity, established by Pope JOHN XXIII (1958–1963) in 1960 as an agency to help prepare for Vatican Council II (see Vatican Council II) (1962–1965) and raised by him to ''commission'' status in 1962 during the Vatican Council's first plenary session, was given responsibility for handling all relations with other Christian churches and for promoting ecumenical dialogue with them. Also included in the work of this secretariat was the promotion of dialogue with members of the Jewish faith. Following Vatican II, the secretariat was charged with the implementation of the COUNCIL's ecumenical decrees and directives. The reorganization of the Roman Curia occasioned by *Pastor Bonus* took effect on 1 March 1989, and the activities of the Secretariat for Promoting Christian Unity became the responsibility of the Pontifical Council for Promoting Christian Unity.

The Secretariat for Non-Christians established by Pope PAUL VI (1963–1978) in 1964 was authorized to promote studies concerning, dialogue with, and understanding of, peoples of religious beliefs who were not Christians, particularly Muslims. Its activities became part of the competence of the Pontifical Council for Interreligious Dialogue in 1989.

The Secretariat for Non-Believers, established by Pope Paul VI in 1965, was given responsibility for studying atheism and related philosophies as well as promoting dialogue with those who profess no religious belief. Its activities were assumed by the Pontifical Council for Non-Believers with the publication of *Pastor Bonus*, made effective in 1989.

For further reference: Peter A. Baart, *The Roman Court* (New York: F. Putet, 1985); Peter Huizing and Knut Walf, eds., *The Roman Curia and the Communion of Churches* (New York: Seabury Press, 1979).

David M. O'Connell

SERGIUS I (687–701). One of a line of Greek clerics elevated to the papacy to facilitate relations with the Eastern church, Sergius, a Syrian from Antioch, was a compromise choice for pontiff. Divisions within the church led to the nomination of two candidates prior to Sergius' election, but both men were rejected by the Romans, who proclaimed for Sergius. The exarch withheld his recognition of the new pontiff until Sergius paid him a bribe.

Sergius' most notable accomplishment was preventing the implementation of reforms demanded by Emperor Justinian II in the Second Trullan or Quinisext COUNCIL (692). The council issued over 100 reforms, many which contradicted Western CANON LAW, including the banning of specific practices, for example, clerical celibacy, the Saturday fast during Lent, and legalizing married clergy. Furthermore, Justinian reestablished the twenty-eight canon of CHALCEDON (451), which had elevated Constantinople to patriarchical status, thus setting it on an equal footing with Rome. Although Sergius' representatives in Constantinople were forced to signed the decrees, the pontiff refused to recognize the new canons. Sergius' action angered the emperor, who dispatched troops to Rome with instructions to either force the pope to sign or capture him. Neither scenario occurred. Justinian's soldiers were defeated by imperial troops who defended the POPE.

Sergius' pontificate was marked by a program of intense church building and restoration. Many of the new churches were dedicated to Eastern saints, which reflected the influence of Greek-speaking personnel in the administration of the church. Additional characteristics of Greek culture, for example, art, education, and Greek monasticism, also permeated the church.

For further reference: H. K. Mann, *The Lives of the Popes in the Early Middle Ages* (London: K. Paul, 1902–1932); Walter Ullman, *A Short History of the Papacy in the Middle Ages* (London: Methuen, 1972).

John C. Horgan

SERGIUS II (844–847). This Roman-born, aristocratic priest was old and in frail health when he was elevated to the chair of St. PETER with the support of the Roman nobility. Sergius' election was opposed by both the Roman people and clergy, who selected the ANTIPOPE John (844). Sergius' backers forcibly removed John from the Lateran palace and installed Sergius on the papal throne. Defying the wishes of his supporters, Sergius prevented John's execution, choosing to confine the antipope to a monastery.

Sergius' consecration, without the approval of the Frankish emperor Lothar, was in violation of the 824 *Constitutio Lothari*, which required imperial confirmation of the POPE-elect and the swearing of a loyalty oath to the imperial LEGATE. Lothar dispatched his son Louis, viceroy of Italy, to Rome with an army to reassert imperial control. Rather than lay waste to Rome, Louis agreed to Sergius' pacific pleas to a hearing before a council of twenty Italian bishops, which subsequently ratified Sergius' election. In deference to the emperor, Sergius immediately swore his loyalty to Lothar, crowned Louis, king of the Lombards, and appointed Louis' great-uncle, Archbishop Drogo of Metz, as apostolic vicar for all countries north of the Alps.

Sergius' tenure was marked by corruption. His brother Benedict, whom Sergius appointed bishop of Albano, influenced the pontiff's administration. Allegations persisted that accused Benedict of usurping ecclesiastical and civil authority from the ill pope. The moneys that allowed for Sergius' restoration and church-building projects in and around Rome resulted from Benedict's unscrupulous methods of revenue collection by engaging in simony, extortion, and the selling of church offices. The Roman people directly attributed the excesses of Sergius and Benedict to the looting and sacking of St. Peter's and St. Paul's by 10,000 Saracens in 846.

For further reference: H. K. Mann, *The Lives of the Popes in the Early Middle Ages* (London: K. Paul, 1902–1932); Walter Ullman, *A Short History of the Papacy in the Middle Ages* (London: Methuen, 1972).

John C. Horgan

SERGIUS III (904–911). Sergius, of Roman, noble background, had been consecrated bishop of Cerveteri by FORMOSUS (891–896). He took part in the "cadaver synod" presided over by STEPHEN VI (896–897) that posthumously condemned Formosus, annulling all his ordinations. Sergius at that point considered himself reduced to the diaconate and submitted to reordinaton as a priest by Stephen VI (896–897).

In 897, following the death of THEODORE II (897), this leader of the anti-Formosan faction had been elected POPE and installed in the Lateran but had to give way to the pro-Formosan JOHN IX (898–900), who had the support of Emperor Leopold of Spoleto. He remained in exile for seven years when a faction of the Formosan party in Rome overthrew Leo V (903). With the help of Duke Alberic I of Spoleto, Sergius took the city and was proclaimed pope. He then allegedly had LEO V murdered in prison. Dating his reign from 897, he considered all his predecessors since John IX as illegitimate, overturning their decrees and reaffirming the condemnation of Formosus.

There was opposition to Sergius throughout Italy but little in Rome, where he held power. He had the support of the noble Roman families, such as that of Theophylact and his wife, the senatrix Theodora. It was reputed, in fact, that Sergius had a son, the future pope JOHN XI (931–935/936), by their young daughter Marouzia, and for several decades the papacy would be dependent on this oligarchy.

Little is known of Sergius ecclesiastical activities. He sought the support of the Frankish episcopate in arguing the issue of "*filioque*" clause in the credo with the Eastern church and passed a judgment in favor of the fourth marriage of the Byzantine emperor Leo VI after Nicholas, the patriarch of Constantinople, refused to recognize the union. As a result Nicholas was deposed, and the Eastern church was thrown into confusion. Sergius also completed the restoration of St. John Lateran, which had been damaged by earthquake during the "cadaver synod," and was the first pontiff since ADRIAN I to put his image, wearing the miter, on papal coinage. He was buried in St. Peter's.

For further reference: L. Duchesne, *The Beginnings of the Temporal Sovereignty of the Popes* (London: K. Paul, 1908); H. K. Mann, *The Lives of the Popes in the Early Middle Ages* (London: K. Paul, 1902–1932).

William Roberts

SERGIUS IV (1009–1012). The son of a Roman shoemaker, Sergius, as bishop of Albano (1004–1009), was chosen by John Crescentius, the ruling nobleman of Rome, to ascend to the seat of St. PETER. The patriarch of Constantinople refused to recognize the election and later excommunicated (see Excommunication) the new POPE, as Sergius had included the *filioque* in his profession of faith accompanying his election announcement. The *filioque* was a matter of contention between the Eastern and Western churches. A Latin word, it translates as "and from the Son," indicating the transmission of God as the Holy Spirit from the Father and the Son. It had been added to the Nicene Creed, but the Greeks viewed its addition as unorthodox.

Sergius was instrumental in granting spiritual exemptions and papal privileges whereby the pope extended protection toward places or persons in exchange for an annual tax, which freed many monasteries from local control, thereby allowing them to elect their own authorities. Upon receiving the news of the destruction of the Church of the Holy Sepulchre in Jerusalem by the caliph of Egypt (1010), Sergius called for the Christian West to unite and launch a crusade to restore the church. He unsuccessfully attempted to free Sicily from Arab domination.

For further reference: Hans Kuhner, *Encyclopedia of the Papacy* (New York: Philosophical Library, 1958); H. K. Mann, *The Lives of the Popes in the Early Middle Ages* (London: K. Paul, 1902–1932). The best beginning primary source remains the *Liber Pontificalis* (Paris, 1886–1892).

John C. Horgan

SEVERINUS (640). A Roman elected in 638, Severinus' consecration was delayed by the Byzantine emperor Heraclius (610–641). Having just reconquered Eastern portions of the empire from the Persians, inhabited by adherents to Monophysitism (a doctrine that recognized Christ as having only one nature), Heraclius needed a means for retaining their allegiance. The means, in the form of a compromise, was supplied by the emperor's patriarch of Constantinople, Sergius, who devised the idea of monothelitism (two natures of Christ within one will). Heraclius subsequently issued an edict, *Ecthesis*, commanding all of his subjects to adhere to the new doctrine.

Severinus refused to agree to *Ecthesis*, believing that monothelitism contradicted the conclusions reached at the COUNCIL of CHALCEDON (451) that recognized Christ as having two distinct natures, both true God and true man, therefore two distinct wills. The emperor's exarch in Ravenna, Isaac, approved the invasion of the Lateran palace to force Severinus' consent to *Ecthesis* while simultaneously plundering the treasury. This action mistakenly led Heraclius to believe that Severinus became more favorable toward the new doctrine and permitted his consecration to occur. Severinus' condemnation of monothelitism, along with his successors in the following forty years, prevented the church from falling into HERESY. Regarding internal church affairs, Severinus opposed the promonastic policies of GREGORY I (590–604).

For further reference: Joseph S. Brusher, *Popes through the Ages* (Princeton: D. Van Nostrand, 1964); H. K. Mann, *The Lives of the Popes in the Early Middle Ages* (London: K. Paul, 1902–1932). The best beginning primary source remains the *Liber Pontificalis* (Paris, 1886–1892).

John C. Horgan

SILVERIUS (536–537). Silverius Hormosdae of Frosinone was the legitimate son of Pope HORMISDAS (514–523), who had fathered him before becoming a priest. Silverius' predecessor was Agapitus I (535–536), who had died in Constantinople. The Ostrogothic king Theodahad, who had sent Agapitus to Constantinople to talk Justinian out of invading Italy, hastened to elect a new POPE favorable to his people. His choice was the subdeacon Silverius. Meanwhile, the imperial court in Constantinople had named a candidate of its own: the Roman deacon Vigilius, who had accompanied Agapitus to Constantinople. Vigilius had courted the friendship of the empress Theodora, offering to rehabilitate her local favorite, Anthimius, the Monophysite patriarch of Constantinople. But Vigilius returned to Rome too late; Silverius was already pope. However, the Byzantine general Belisarius was in Italy, and it was left to him to accomplish Theodora's purpose.

Fearful of Belisarius, Silverius sought to win his favor while at the same time maintaining good relations with Theodahad. But Belisarius charged him with treasonous dealings with the Goths, summarily stripped him of his treasured pallium, and deported him to Patara in Anatolia. VIGILIUS was hastily elected pope in Silverius' place. Appeals were made to Justinian, who ordered Silverius' return to Rome and reconsideration of the charges against him. However, Belisarius saw to it that Silverius was delivered into the hands of Vigilius, who instantly reconvicted him. He was then sent to Palmaria, an island near Gaeta, where he was forced to abdicate as pope on 11 November 537, an abdication validated retroactively to legitimate the earlier election of Vigilius. Silverius was tortured and starved to death, dying on 2 December 537. It has been aptly said that the forced abdication of Silverius and the prior elevation of Vigilius, pliant slave of the empress Theodora, ''completed the degradation of the Roman see'' on the eve of the Justinian restoration.

For further reference: E. Caspar, *Geschichte des Papstums von den Anfängen bis zur Höhe der Weltherrschaft* (Tübingen: Verlag von J. C. B. Mohr, 1930–33); T. J. Jalland, *The Church and the Papacy* (London: Society for Promoting Christian Knowledge, 1944).

Henry Paolucci

SILVESTER I, II, III, IV. SEE SYLVESTER I, II, III, IV.

SIMPLICIUS (468–483). Simplicius was born in Tivoli, some fifteen miles northeast of Rome. The most notable fact of his pontificate was the final fall of the Western empire in September 476, when the young Roman puppet emperor, Romulus Augustus, was deposed. The real Roman ruler at the time was Augustus' father, Orestes, commander of the Roman army in Gaul, who had deposed the legitimately consecrated Roman emperor Julis Nepos (473–475), to whom he had sworn allegiance. Thus, when the German Arian (see Arianism) tribal chief Odoacer, a mutinous captain in the Roman border service, seized power in Italy in 476, Orestes was slain, while his young son, forced to "abdicate" his throne, was simply "sent to dwell in freedom with his family in Campania," generously supported by an annual pension.

Odoacer extinguished the office of emperor in the West, accepting for himself, with Constantinople's approval, the title of Roman *patricius*, designated head of administration and imperial vicar in the West. The title remained a link between barbarian power and Roman authority in the West down through the coronation of the *patricius* Charlemagne as emperor by Pope LEO III in 800. Simplicius unsuccessfully attempted to intervene in support of Pope LEO I's condemnation of the design of Acacius, patriarch of Constantinople, to assume the same status in the East that the bishops of Rome enjoyed in the West. The same is true of his involvement in the substance of the *henotikon* controversy, the so-called decree of union, probably prepared by Acacius for the emperor Zeno, which sought to purchase ecclesiastical unity by means of grossly misleading simplifications. Again Simplicius' opinions were ignored. He died in March 483 and was buried in St. Peter's. He was later declared a saint.

For further reference: E. Caspar, *Geschichte des Papstums von den Anfängen bis zur Höhe der Weltherrschaft* (Tübingen: Verlag von J. C. B. Mohr, 1930–33); T. J. Jalland, *The Church and the Papacy* (London: Society for Promoting Christian Knowledge, 1944).

Henry Paolucci

SIRICIUS (384–399). Roman-born Siricius Tiburti had served under Popes LIBERIUS (352–366) and DAMASUS I (366–384), before being elected bishop of Rome in December 384. The open approval of the emperor Valentinian II sufficed to quell the challenge of Ursinus, who had figured as an ANTIPOPE during Damasus' pontificate. Siricius' election represented a victory over St. Jerome and his supporters, whom he looked upon as rivals. Although he did not order the expulsion of Jerome, who left Rome for Bethlehem, Siricius consented to it.

Siricius' pontificate is notable for his having formalized the developing papal tradition of assuming responsibility for church matters at home and abroad. His intervention took the form of letters providing focused pronouncements, which came to be known as decretals. Typical of his tone and language is this sentence at the close of the first paragraph of his famous, often-quoted letter to Himerius, bishop of Tarragona, which ranks as the first papal decretal: "We bear the burdens of all who are heavy laden; nay rather, the blessed Apostle PETER bears them in us, he who, as we hope, protects and guards us as the sole heirs of his office." Siricius first stressed the impersonality of the papacy, its institutional character with a living identity of its own, apart from the particular occupants, except to the extent that they are perceived as successive reincarnations of St. Peter. Such pronouncements marked his intervention in the Melitian SCHISM and his active opposition to Priscillianism and to extremist doctrines of all kinds. He is remembered for having consecrated the basilica of St. Paul. He died on 26 November 399 and was later declared a saint.

For further reference: E. Caspar, "Julius I. (337–352) und das Konzil von Sardica (343)," in *Geschichte des Papstums von den Anfängen bis zur Höhe der Weltherrschaft*, vol. 1 (Tübingen: Verlag von J. C. B. Mohr, 1930–33), pp. 257–285; J. T. Shotwell and L. P. Loomis, *The See of Peter* (New York: Columbia University Press, 1927).

Henry Paolucci

SISINNIUS (708). A Syrian, Sisinnius was crippled with gout at the time of his election, a malady to which he would succumb within weeks of his election in January 708. His election, despite his frail health, may have been due to the fact that the electors did not realize the severity of his condition or, as some scholars suggest, that the reign of POPES from the Orient (with the exception of the Roman GREGORY II, 715–738) was due to the machinations of the exarch at Ravenna on behalf of the Byzantine emperor. Sisinnius' only known act as pope was the consecration of a bishop for Corsica. He did recommend the restoration and strengthening of the walls of Rome, a policy that proved beneficial against later attacks by the Lombards and Saracens.

For further reference: Hans Kuhner, *Encyclopedia of the Papacy* (New York: Philosophical Library, 1958); Horace K. Mann, *The Lives of the Popes in the Early Middle Ages* (London: K. Paul, 1902–1932).

John C. Horgan

SIXTUS I (c. 116–c. 125). Sixtus, in the earliest lists of papal succession, is the seventh POPE after St. PETER. While the exact dates of his reign are uncertain, early sources agree that it lasted about ten years. According to the *Liber Pontificalis*, he was a Roman, the son of Pastor, and his name in its original form, "Xystus," suggests a Greek origin. Some speculate that the name is derived from the Latin "sextus" (sixth), as he was the sixth successor to the apostle, but this is not corroborated in the early sources. Little is known of the actual activities of his pontificate, however, and the information noted in the *Liber Pontificalis* regarding various liturgical and disciplinary innovations for this period are clearly anachronistic. At any rate, as in the case of the other earliest popes, it is difficult to form a clear view of the actual role of the leaders of the Roman church and the exact nature of his government and jurisdiction. Later traditions represent him as a martyr, and he was commemorated with the apostles and other martyrs in the ancient canon of the mass. However, in the list compiled by Irenaeus of early Roman bishops, the fact that only Telesphorus is listed as a martyr suggests that Sixtus was not. Although the *Liber Pontificalis* also notes that he was buried on the Vatican Hill near St. Peter, there is no other substantiation for that fact. His feast day is 3 April.

For further reference: L. Duchesne, ed., *Liber Pontificalis* (Paris, 1955); J. Lebreton and J. Zeiller, *The History of the Primitive Church* (London: Burns, Oates, and Washbourne, 1948); M. Winter, *St. Peter and the Popes* (Baltimore: Helicon Press, 1960).

William Roberts

SIXTUS II (257–258). Sixtus was probably Greek by nationality and was elected to the papacy at the beginning of Valerian's persecution of the church at Rome. He managed during his short reign to improve relations with Cyprian of Carthage, whom Sixtus' predecessor, STEPHEN I (254–257), had alienated by his uncompromising position regarding the validity of baptism administered by heretics. The *Liber Pontificalis* erroneously indicates that Sixtus was once a philosopher, possibly because of confusion with a Pythagorean philosopher named Sixtius whose *Sententiae* Rufinus translated into Latin. Seized during a religious service in the Cemetery of Praetextatus, Sixtus was martyred on 6 August 258, along with four of his deacons. His body was interred in the Cemetery of Callistus, and his feast is celebrated on 7 August.

For further reference: J. N. D. Kelly, *The Oxford Dictionary of Popes* (New York: Oxford University Press, 1986), pp. 21ff.; and J. Lebreton and J. Zeiller, *The History of the Primitive Church*, vol. 4 (London: Burns, Oates, and Washbourne, 1948).

Bernard J. Cassidy

SIXTUS III (432–440). Following CELESTINE I's policies (422–432) and the ecumenical COUNCIL of EPHESUS, Sixtus encouraged ongoing dialogue between John of Antioch and Cyril of Alexandria, who disagreed over theological issues. They came to an agreement, confessing to the two natures of Jesus Christ. Sixtus had a reputation of being sympathetic to Pelagius, and in return the Pelagians claimed he was their ally. However, in 418, with the publication of the *Tractoria*, Sixtus publicly anathematized Pelagianism. Little is known of Sixtus' activities during the pontificate of BONIFACE I (418–422), but letters written to Celestine I indicate he played a role in the Council of Ephesus.

During his pontificate, Sixtus erected several monuments in Rome. In the rebuilding of the Lateran baptistery, Sixtus had engraved on the font the theology of baptism, announcing the triumph of the church over the heretical teachings of Pelagius. He also was responsible for the reconstruction of the Liberian Basilica of Saint Mary Major.

For further reference: Matthew Bunson, *The Pope Encyclopedia* (New York: Crown Trade Paperbacks, 1995); J. N. D. Kelly. *The Oxford Dictionary of Popes* (Oxford: Oxford University Press, 1986).

Patrick McGuire

SIXTUS IV (1471–1484). Francesco della Rovere of Savona was elected POPE on 9 August 1471, ruling as Sixtus IV until his death on 12 August 1484. A member of the FRANCISCAN order, Sixtus, whose reputation before becoming pope was blameless, was to begin the flagrant nepotism that distinguished the papacy for the next 75 years. In addition, his pontificate was marked by an increased preoccupation with Italian and European politics. Both of these phenomena helped transform Sixtus from a Franciscan reformer to an Italian prince. Following his unsuccessful call for crusade against the Turks, Sixtus organized the papacy to look after the territorial affairs of the church and the aggrandizement of his own family.

Although Lorenzo de'Medici had come to Rome to honor the new pontiff, relations between the Medici and Sixtus quickly deteriorated. In creating a territorial state for his extended family, Sixtus came into conflict with Medicean interests. He, therefore, schemed to remove the Medici from power in Florence, seeking help from Florentines who were discontented with the Medici role. Sixtus called upon the Pazzi, who, though related to the Medici by marriage, were anxious for a larger role in Florence and a bigger share of the papal banking business in Rome, and also Francesco Salviati, the archbishop of Pisa.

The real leader of the plot, however, was Girolamo Riario, one of the pope's ruthless nephews, who was willing to sacrifice his cousin the young cardinal Raffaelle Sansoni to further Sixtus' desires. Although Sixtus forbade the murder of Lorenzo and Giuliano de'Medici, he wanted their power reduced and the family out of Florence. Because the original assassin Giovanni Battista Montesecco was unwilling to commit the murder in church, Riario was forced to employ others, including two priests and other Florentine citizens, to commit the murders. The attempt against the Medici took place on 26 April 1478 in the Florentine Duomo at the mass in honor of Cardinal Sansoni. Although Giuliano was slain, the plot failed when Lorenzo was able to evade the knives of the priestly assailants and when the people refused to follow the Pazzi in forsaking the Medici. We know of the involvement of Sixtus and Riario as well as the Pazzi and Salviati families through Montesecco's confession after the plot failed. War between Sixtus and Florence followed the attempted assassination—a war that eventually involved the entire Italian peninsula and took several years to settle.

Sixtus' campaign against the powerful Roman families of the Colonna and Orsini as well as his war with Ferrara are examples of his desire to rule as a temporal leader as well as a spiritual one. Even though much of his energy was devoted to Italian politics, Sixtus also poured money and support into beautifying Rome by broadening streets, building bridges, paving streets, building

churches, bringing water to the Trevi Fountain, and other forms of urban renewal, the creation and decoration of the Sistine Chapel, and the building of
the Vatican Library. Sixtus was among the most worldly popes of the quattro-
cento. Throughout his pontificate, ambition and nepotism were the guiding principles of his policies. Sixtus set the stage for ALEXANDER VI (1492–1503),
who was even more ruthless and secular than his predecessor.

For further reference: H. Acton, *The Pazzi Conspiracy: The Plot against the Medici*
(London: Thames and Hudson, 1979); M. Creighton, *A History of the Papacy from the
Great Schism to the Sack of Rome*, vol. 4 (London: Longmans, Green, 1923); M. A.
Ganz, "The Humanist as Citizen: Donato di Neri Acciaiuoli, 1428–1478," Ph.D. diss.,
Syracuse University, 1979; F. Gregorovius, *History of the City of Rome in the Middle
Ages*, trans. A. Hamilton, vol. 7, part I (London: George Bell and Sons, 1900).

Margery A. Ganz

SIXTUS V (1585–1590). Felice Peretto, the son of a field laborer, was born in
the March of Ancona on 13 December 1520. He entered the Franciscan order
at the age of twelve and earned a doctorate in theology from the University of
Fermo. His talent for preaching led Cardinal Carpi to bring him to Rome. PIUS
V (1566–1572) named him vicar-general of the FRANCISCANS and bishop of
Sant' Agata dei Goti and in 1570 made him a cardinal. In 1585 he was unanimously elected POPE and assumed the name Sixtus V. In his allegiance to the
church reform movement, Sixtus' pontificate called for the imposition of strict
discipline on the clergy, not only in Rome but throughout the church. He also
called for the strict enforcement of the rulings of the COUNCIL of TRENT
against simony and the plurality of benefice. However, it was widely feared
Sixtus might be guilty of nepotism in his decision to elevate his fourteen-year-
old grandnephew to the cardinalate.

Prior to his death, Sixtus pondered whether or not to require the Jesuits (SO-
CIETY OF JESUS) to be renamed and considered appointing a commission to
review the constitution of the Jesuits. In an attempt to settle a dispute over the
theological teaching on grace, Sixtus imposed a mutual silence between the
Dominicans and Jesuits. An avid supporter of the missions, Sixtus was aware
of the dialogue in China and Japan. Likewise, he was attentive to the FRAN-
CISCAN and Dominican missions in the Philippines and in South America.
During his pontificate, Sixtus attempted to eliminate Protestantism. He also
sought to maintain a political balance so that Spain would not dominate all of
Europe. A talented and energetic administrator, Sixtus was able to enforce public
order. However, his true love seemed to be art and learning.

For further reference: Matthew Bunson, *The Pope Encyclopedia* (New York: Crown
Trade Paperbacks, 1995); J. N. D. Kelly, *The Oxford Dictionary of Popes* (Oxford: Oxford University Press, 1986).

Patrick McGuire

SOCIALISM AND THE PAPACY. Socialism emerged from the perception that the political, social, and economic developments of the modern world were radically unjust. While socialists agreed on the injustices of the modern world, they disagreed on solutions, having fundamentally different socioeconomic and political viewpoints. They provided different answers to the questions, What is the nature of a human being? Does God exist? What is the nature of justice? How should a modern society be organized, and what means are to be employed to bring about social justice? Some socialists were atheists; others were Christians. Socialism claimed to offer a solution to the economic and social injustices created by the Industrial Revolutions of the eighteenth to the twentieth centuries and the capitalistic individualism and the accumulation of wealth in the hands of the few to the detriment of the many. They criticized a socioeconomic system that produced an abundance of material goods and monetary wealth but distributed these in a way that resulted in the most abject forms of poverty for those who produced these goods.

Some socialists advocated the nationalization of the means of production and the government's control through centralized planners of the production and distribution of goods and services. Others have advocated a system of decentralized, self-governed, producer-communities that would be controlled by the workers. For example, anarchism, Nazism, and communism have all claimed to be forms of socialism. In the Third World, after WORLD WAR II, military dictatorships and one-party systems, as well as many diverse systems of governments, have likewise claimed to be socialistic.

Socialism can be said to have its origin in the rejection of the assumptions of eighteenth-century classical economic theory, which assumed that industrialized economies would operate at maximum production and employment because of ever-expanding markets. Even if national markets were to become saturated, they did not recognize the possibility of unemployment or depression in an industrial economy because they saw labor as having an endless capacity to migrate and modern economies as having an endless capacity to find new markets for goods abroad. Thus, the wealth of a nation is increased and maintained by creating a sizable imbalance of foreign trade in favor of one's own nation-state. This created a break within the nominally Christian European community between the traditional Catholic view of economic activity and the new laissez-faire view.

Bernard de Mandeville claimed that private vices, like greed, worked for the public benefit on the assumption that all actions are equally vicious because all are founded on self-interest, thus eliminating justice from the consideration of economic matters. Adam Smith, while not agreeing with Mandeville, provided a rationale for laissez-faire capitalism as the natural order of things, claiming that competition would be the best means of increasing the wealth of nations. The existence of unemployment and cyclical depressions was a reality that classical economists could not explain, contributing to the emergence of a socialist perspective in England.

David Ricardo provided a more exact anaylsis in the labor theory of value, equating the value of a product with the labor it took to produce it, while William Thompson proposed that only force and fraud kept labor in the capitalistic system of inequality. Thomas Hodgskins concluded that capitalism was not a natural state of affairs but an artificial and unacceptable situation that produced a powerless proletariat and the social evils of modern societies. This led some to conclude that the capitalistic distribution of wealth is neither natural nor just and should be changed.

Similar developments occurred in eighteenth-century France. Rousseau declared that social institutions were the cause of all evil, especially the institution of private property, which came into existence when some made a claim to property that went unchallenged by others. Rousseau's social contract theory became the basis for Gabriel de Mably's (1768) call for an equality of goods and the management and ownership of all property by a differently conceived state. Gracchus Babeuf in his *Manifesto of Equals* (1796) advocated a revolution that would take possession of all property and create a central committee to institute a common life and administer an egalitarian communist state. In his *Défense devant la Haute-Court* (1797), he declared the doctrine of class struggle a historical necessity.

In 1803 Henri de Saint Simon advocated a totally secular organization of society and the replacing of priests with elite scientists as the solution to social problems. He offered a secularized version of Christian social teaching. Saint Simon is considered by some to be the father of socialism, as distinct from modern communism. In his work appeared the notion of the proletariat, which he borrowed from Mallet du Pan. Auguste Comte systematized many of the thoughts of Saint Simon into what he claimed was the basis for the systematization of all positive scientific knowledge. A new discipline was projected that was modeled after mathematical physics with a deterministic view of human behavior. This new science was called sociology and supposedly provided a synthesis of all truth. He also conceptualized a dialectical model of human history having three stages of human development.

In the second half of the nineteenth century, socialism split into secular state socialism and Christian socialism. The first assumed a materialistic, deterministic model of human nature and history with an a priori assumption of atheism or agnosticism. It made the material world absolute in light of its presuppositions of naturalism, determinism, rationalism, and scientism, which led to the view that all religious beliefs are an aberration of the natural order. Secular state socialists declared that private property had to be eliminated, and most concluded that violence was necessary to bring about the desired social change.

Christian socialists sought to correct the injustices of the industrial world without eliminating the right to property and without advocating violence as the means of bringing about the desired social developments. While rejecting the assumptions of eighteenth-century classical economic theories and the assumptions and presuppositions of state socialism, they believed that the proper application of Christian principles would lead to progress. Many Catholic socialistic thinkers, such as Wilhelm Emmanuel Ketteler in Germany and Comte Adrien Albert Marie de Mun (1841–1914) in France, tried to employ the Christian notion of solidarity of all human beings and the Thomist principles of the proper use of property to bring about social justice. They worked to institute communities where private property would be used in light of the Christian notion of the responsibilities of ownership. Thus, social insurance, minimum hourly wage, and many other types of social legislation were sought, while state socialism was rejected.

When Giovanni Maria Mastai Ferretti became PIUS IX in June 1846, he confronted a world divided by conflicts in the political and socioeconomic orders, as well as conflicts in the philosophical, religious, and spiritual life of Christianity. The years from 1848 to 1870 were characterized by numerous revolutions in Europe, originating mostly from national aspirations, and were later followed by secularistic, Marxist, socialistic, and anarchistic movements directly opposed to Catholic teaching. Pius IX found he could not condone means contrary to faith and morals to obtain political and religious unity. POPE Pius IX condemned the notions of both economic liberalism and socialism in his SYLLABUS OF ERRORS of 1864.

Pius IX, LEO XIII, and their successors recognized that the assumptions of modernity had created an environment that inhibited a proper understanding of the nature of social justice and the proper means of achieving it. The acceptance of such presuppositions caused many to perceive the issue in terms of the false alternatives of accepting either eighteenth-century classical economic theory or secularistic state socialism. Socialism correctly identified the injustices of the capitalistic economic systems that modernity had wrought, but the Holy Fathers recognized that the solutions that were offered by state socialism would result only in the exchange of one set of evils for another. The papacy understood that the church had to offer a genuine means of bringing about social justice without violating the faith.

For further reference: the following Vatican documents in historical order: *Qui Pluribus*, Pius IX, 11/9/1846; *Singulari Quadam*, Pius IX; *Quanta Cura* (Syllabus), Pius IX, 12/8/1864; Documents of Vatican I, 1870; *Sapientiae Christianae*, Leo XIII, 1/10/1890; *Rerum Novarum*, Leo XIII, 5/15/1891; *Graves de Communi*, Leo XIII, 1/18/1901; *Pascendi*, Pius X, 9/8/1907; *Quadragesimo Anno*, Pius XI, 5/15/1931; *Caritate Christi Compulsi*, Pius XI, 5/3/1932; *Summi Pontificatus*, Pius XII, 7/20/1939; *Mater et Magistra*, John XXIII, 5/15/1961; *Pacem in Terris*, John XXIII, 4/11/1963; *Ecclesiam Suam*, Paul VI, 8/6/1964; *Gaudium et spes*, Vatican II, 1966; *Dignitatis Humanae*, Vatican II, 1966; *Populorum Progressio*, Paul VI, 3/26/1967; *Laborem Exercens*, John Paul II, 9/14/1981; *Sollicitudo Rei Socialis*, John Paul II, 12/30/1987; *Centesimus Annus*, John Paul II, 5/1/1991; *Veritatis Splendor*, John Paul II, 8/6/1993; *Catéchisme de l'Église Catholique* (Vatican City: Libreria Editrice Vaticana 1993).

Joseph J. Califano

SOCIAL JUSTICE AND PAPACY. From its inception the church has affirmed humanity's dignity, flowing from the fact that it is made in the image of God. Charity provides the only genuine context in which we can comprehend human rights and produce a world where peace and justice can be realized. While material things are necessary to sustain human life, to make material things the center of one's life distorts our sense of justice and our relationship to God and others. The apostles and fathers of the church have always declared that we should meet the needs of those who live under the scourge of poverty, freeing them of their suffering.

In *Rerum Novarum* (1891), LEO XIII responded to modern society's development of a new form of labor for wages and the new form of malignant poverty. Labor had become merely a commodity, the value of which was determined by supply and demand. There was no consideration of whether wages were sufficient to provide a worker and his or her family with a decent life befitting a human. Thus, a new form of de facto slavery became institutionalized and rationalized as the natural order of things. Usury was widespread as workers were forced in many circumstances to loan money against future earnings at high interest rates in order to survive. As a result, workers were caught up in a vicious cycle of ever-increasing debt, even if their whole family worked excessive hours. PIUS XI, in *Quadragesimo Anno*, noted that twentieth-century finance capitalism only intensified the lack of the sense of responsibility of executives to their employees.

Pope Leo and his successors proclaimed the evils that modernity had wrought in the lives of men and women and proposed solutions to these evils by applying the principles of justice of the faith. Leo declared that workers had to be given a just wage as the first step toward distributive justice, which is a principal part of social justice. A just wage is a wage that will support a worker and the worker's family in a decent life, enabling the worker to save enough money, if frugal, to acquire some property. The wage must be sufficient to enable mothers the freedom to nurture their children properly. Workers have the right to organize and bargain collectively for just wages and working conditions. The external appearance of agreement to work at an unjust wage does not satisfy the demands of justice. For if the workers agree to unjust wages, either out of ignorance or the desperation of their situations, the contract is fundamentally flawed.

A decent life enables a person to develop one's God-given talents to the fullest, physically, socially, and spiritually in an environment befitting a human being. JOHN XXIII, in *Pacem in Terris*, further elaborated the human rights that must be granted, if local society or the global community is to be viewed as achieving social justice. Human life must be viewed as a good to be preserved and properly developed. One has the right to food, clothing, shelter, rest, medical care, and the social services that guard one from sickness, an inability to work, widowhood, old age, and unemployment. All people have the right to an education and the pursuit of truth. These rights are directly related to what constitutes a just or living wage, whether provided directly to the laborer through salary or through taxes that provide various social services. A just wage and ethical nature of the work are not determined by the kind of work being performed, in the physical or economic meaning of these terms, but by the dignity of the one who is performing the work (JOHN PAUL II: *Laborem Exercens*).

Because men and women are intelligent by nature and are endowed with liberty, they have the right to freely participate, through the use of moral means, in the political activities of the community and nation. In a socially just society, all men and women have the right to worship God both privately and publicly. Worshiping God is directly related to social justice on earth because knowing God, his truth, his laws, and our relationship with him is essential to our understanding of our relationship with one another and the living of a just life. Each of the human rights contained in the papal teaching is an essential aspect of the common good, which presupposes respect for persons and their rights.

John Paul II subsequently declared the global application of the preceding. Thus, international corporations that seek to exploit the natural resources of less developed countries and pay less than a just wage to desperate people in those countries by coercing them to work at substandard wages violate the demand of justice. Governments that permit this to occur are coconspirators in depriving their own people of their rights; such activities in the name of maximizing profit are unjust. They coerce workers in developed countries to accept unjust wages in competition with workers in less developed countries who have accepted unjust wages. Social justice can be achieved only if inordinate desire to acquire enormous wealth is corrected, and the abundance of the modern world is used for the common welfare.

For further reference: *Quanta Cura*, Pius IX, 12/8/1864; *Rerum Novarum*, Leo XIII, 5/15/1891; *Quadragesimo Anno, Pascendi*, Pius X, 9/8/1907; Pius XI, 5/15/1931; *Summi Pontificatus*, Pius XII, 7/20/1939; *Mater et Magistra*, John XXIII, 5/15/1961; *Pacem in Terris*, John XXIII, 4/11/1963; *Ecclesiam Suam*, Paul VI, 8/6/1964; *Populorum Progressio*, Paul VI, 3/26/1967; *Laborem Exercens*, John Paul II, 9/14/1981; *Sollicitudo Rei Socialis*, John Paul II, 12/30/1987; *Centesimus Annus*, John Paul II, 5/1/1991; *Veritatis Splendor*, John Paul II, 8/6/1993; *Catechisme de l'Église* (Vatican City: Catholique Libreria Editrice Vaticana, 1993).

Joseph J. Califano

SOCIETY OF JESUS. After being wounded in battle and undergoing a conversion during convalescence, a Spanish nobleman and soldier named Ignatius of Loyola (c. 1491–1556) and his six companions founded this order of clerics regular in 1534. Through their highly developed spirituality, rooted in the conversion of Ignatius and related in his text *The Spiritual Exercises*, the order grew rapidly to become the largest Catholic religious order of men in the world. In part due to its exemption from episcopal jurisdiction and its special "Fourth Vow," the order developed a complex relationship with the papacy.

Ignatius and his companions explained their way of life in a document called the *Formula of the Institute*. That description received confirmation in the papal decree *Regimini militantis ecclesiae* (27 September 1540) and elaboration in *Constitutions*, which Ignatius composed between 1544 and 1556. These documents reveal the notable similarities between the society and older religious orders but also its distinctive characteristics. The order places routine executive power in a superior general, with supreme authority vested in a general congregation of professed members. The superior general, however, receives a lifetime appointment, and general congregations are held only to elect a new general or in the context of matters defined in the *Constitutions* as "long-lasting," "important," or "very difficult." A religious habit is worn, but not a distinctive one, rather, one modeled on the dress of secular clergy in any given area. Members who are priests are to recite the divine office, but not in common, so that they might be free to focus on diverse pastoral ministries. In addition, the "Fourth Vow" of willingness to undertake any mission considered necessary by the papacy highlights the distinctive stress Ignatius placed upon obedience. Although never conceived by its founding members as a battalion of papal "shock troops" dedicated to reform (see Reformation and Counter-Reformation) of the Roman church or to the extirpation of Protestant HERESY, the order gained that reputation due to misunderstanding of this vow and certain Jesuit documents like the "Rules for Thinking with the Church."

Members of the order engaged in a wide variety of ministries throughout its history. From open-air preaching and sacred lecturing, to devout conversation with individuals in prisons and marketplaces, to administration of houses for repentant prostitutes and promotion of Marian devotions, to catechetical instruction and administration of the sacraments, to guidance of nonmembers through the *Spiritual Exercises* and theological consultation for POPES and curial officials, the society gradually adopted education as its principal work. Colleges and the attached churches and residences for Jesuit staff they required became centers for the continuation of all these ministries plus education and scholarship. The best known of these, the Roman College, was founded in 1551 and eventually became the Gregorian University (see Colleges of Rome). By 1749, the order ran 669 colleges and 176 seminaries. Members also undertook widespread missionary activities in both the Old and the New Worlds, perhaps best exemplified by the work of Peter Canisius (1521–1597) to reconvert Protestants in Germany and that of Francis Xavier (1506–1552) to spread the faith among non-Christians in Asia. Jesuits both in the age of Ignatius and beyond identified two basic ideals in their pastoral practice: accommodation to the needs and situation of those served and active promotion of spiritual consolation.

Novelties in the organization of the group—and some of the ministries' members engaged in such services as confessors of absolute monarchs—generated jealousy, then animosity and outright enemies. Concerted efforts of the latter led to the suppression of the order, first through gradual expulsion from Western European nations and then universally by decree of CLEMENT XIV (1769–

1774) in 1773. He issued no blanket condemnation, and the order was never fully suppressed due to the religious and political policies of the Russian empress Catherine II. Many members continued to work as secular priests, and PIUS VII (1800–1823) revoked the bull of suppression and restored the order in 1814, after the political climate changed following the fall of Napoleon.

In the modern history of the order, Jesuits have made education, scholarship, and missionary activity their most common enterprises. The order now runs some 5,000 educational institutions worldwide and at all levels: elementary, secondary, and higher. Twentieth-century Jesuit scholars have made important contributions in virtually every discipline. They can be found in academic fields like philosophy and theology but also in sciences like astronomy and seismology as well as in the social sciences. Jesuit theological reflection contributed to both the inspiration behind VATICAN COUNCIL II's *aggiornamento* and to the development of its declarations, constitutions, and decrees. Members continue to engage in extensive missionary activity, now chiefly in Asia and Africa. The most extensive growth of the order during the twentieth century took place in the United States, and by 1964 they outnumbered German, French, Italian, Austrian, Belgian, and Dutch Jesuits combined. The picture of twentieth-century Jesuit vitality must be balanced with recognition of the persecution members have faced in this era, suffering property confiscation, banishment, and even physical violence, particularly in Latin America. The motto of the order is *ad majorem Dei gloriam* (to the greater glory of God).

For further reference: William V. Bangert, *A History of the Society of Jesus* (St. Louis: Institute of Jesuit Sources, 1972); George E. Ganss, ed., *Ignatius of Loyola: Spiritual Exercises and Selected Works* (New York: Paulist Press, 1991); George E. Ganss, trans., *The Constitutions of the Society of Jesus* (St. Louis: Institute of Jesuit Sources, 1970); Joseph de Guibert, *The Jesuits: Their Spiritual Doctrine and Practice, a Historical Study*, trans. W. J. Young (St. Louis: Institute of Jesuit Sources, 1972); Martin Harney, *The Jesuits in History: The Society of Jesus through Four Centuries* (Chicago: Loyola University Press, 1962); John W. O'Malley, *The First Jesuits* (Cambridge: Harvard University Press, 1993); Louis J. Puhl, ed., *The Spiritual Exercises of St. Ignatius* (Chicago: Loyola University Press, 1951).

William V. Hudon

SOCIETY OF JESUS, ABOLITION OF (1773). On 21 July 1773, after some three decades of acrimonious criticism and censure, the Society of Jesus was abolished by Pope CLEMENT XIII (1758–1769) in the apostolic brief *Dominus ac Redemptor*. Their wealth confiscated, their houses and seminaries closed, their members dispersed, the remnants of the once-powerful order ironically survived in Protestant Prussia and orthodox Russia. A number of factors—some resulting from the modus operandi of the Jesuits themselves, and others from the natural consequence of the changing political and intellectual climate in eighteenth-century Europe—caused their undoing.

Jesuit interests in the overseas colonies of Spain, Portugal, and France aroused enmity within and without the church and played a prominent role in the order's final disgrace. In 1741 Pope BENEDICT XIV (1740–1758) first reprimanded Jesuit policies. His bull *Immensa pastores* denounced the Jesuits as slaveholders and "missionary tricksters" in South America, where they controlled vast land-holdings worked by Indians. The settlement in 1759 by Spain and Portugal of a boundary dispute in South America further threatened Jesuit power. Moreover, rumors circulated in the two courts that the Jesuits had hoarded vast caches of wealth in South America. Royal commissions were convened to investigate the charges. Though no treasure was unearthed, the Jesuit missions were disbanded in 1766, and the Jesuits were expelled from the colonies.

A different economic controversy undermined Jesuit prestige in France. Again, the conflict originated overseas in the French colony of Martinique, where the Jesuit mission had amassed a large debt. In attempting to recoup the losses and acquire fiscal stability, Father Antione La Valette, despite orders to the contrary from his superiors in Rome, borrowed heavily to expand the order's landholdings on the island, hoping to generate added revenue from the exports of coffee, indigo, and sugar to France to liquidate the mission's debts and to continue its work. Successful at first, La Valette's activities foundered during the 1750s as Anglo–French conflicts crippled trade between Martinique and France. Creditors continued to demand payment. When La Valette was unable to meet his obligations, they forwarded their claims to the Office of the Superior General of the Order, who refused to accept any responsibility for La Valette's dereliction and repudiated the debt. The case eventually came before the anti-clerical Paris Parlement, which extended its inquiry into the very bases of the Jesuit organization, finding much to censure in the constitutions regulating its conduct.

After 1750 criticism of Jesuit power and influence increased throughout Catholic Europe. Three sources of anti-Jesuit distrust can be identified. The first can be traced back to seventeenth-century Jansenist censures of the Jesuits in Blaise Pascal's *Lettres provinciales*. While the Jansenists (see Jansenism) had been publicly suppressed, their ideas continued to inspire many Catholics. Second, Enlightenment anticlericalism attacked presumed omnipotence. Finally, the drive during the eighteenth century toward consolidation of the national state's power and authority over its subjects saw in the supranational Jesuit order a threat to its success. Moreover, governments coveted Jesuit wealth to finance expanded state obligations. That the Jesuits occupied influential positions as religious advisers and confessors to kings and teachers of the ruling class did not endear them to the nation builders. Each of these strands of thought conspired to discredit the Jesuits and bring about their resulting suppression.

Suppression of the Jesuit order commenced in Portugal. Under the leadership of its absolute and reform-minded prime minister, the marquis do Pombal, Portugal was laying the bases of a modern, absolutist state. In 1756 Pombal attacked the Jesuits in a white paper distributed to the pope and the courts of Europe. An assassination plot against the king Jose I prompted Pombal to name the

Jesuits as its instigators. On 19 January 1759 a decree was promulgated denouncing the Jesuits as "traitors, rebels, and enemies" of Portugal, confiscating all their property, and ordering their immediate expulsion from all Portuguese territory at home and overseas.

The next expulsion came in France. Its immediate cause was the La Valette case. On 6 August 1762 the Paris Parlement reached its final judgment on the order, condemning it for endangering the Christian faith, disturbing the peace of the church, and outraging the laws of nature. The Paris Parlement, however, had no enforcing power. Its resolutions required the king's signature to become effective. Louis XV was reluctant to sign, and the Jesuits survived this first attack. Two powerful personalities, however, rallied to the Parlement: the duc de Choiseul, the current prime minister, and Madame de Pompadour, the king's mistress, who had suffered slights and humiliations from the court Jesuits. After much agitation, the anti-Jesuit forces won. By royal edict in November 1764, the society was proscribed throughout France, but former Jesuits were allowed to remain in the country as "good and loyal subjects" under the spiritual guidance of the bishops. Deprived of shelter and most sources of income, many French Jesuits faced destitution.

The third country to suppress the Jesuits was Spain. As in Portugal, a dramatic incident focused attention on the Jesuits and gave their enemies the opportunity to move against them. On 26 March 1766 rising food prices and despotic government regulations provoked popular riots in Madrid. In the resulting inquiry on the disturbances, the Jesuits were accused of having fomented them. On 27 February 1767 Charles III signed a secret decree expelling the Jesuits from the Spanish lands. The sentence was carried out swiftly and mercilessly on the night of 2–3 April as Jesuits throughout Spain were summarily evicted from their communities, allowed to take with them only the clothes on their backs and a few necessities. In all more than 5,000 Jesuits were forcibly expelled from Spain and its overseas colonies. The states of Naples and Parma, with close ties to Spain, followed their mentor's examples, abolishing the order and banishing its members.

Pope Clement XIII protested the drastic measures taken by his Catholic subjects in vain. To the king of Spain he wrote: "We testify before God and man that the Society as a whole, its Institute, and its spirit are completely guiltless, and not merely not guilty, but pious, useful, holy, both in its objectives and in its rules and principles." Clement XIII succumbed to a heart attack on 2 February 1769. The Jesuit questions dominated the conclave. Anti-Jesuit forces supported the candidacy of the Franciscan Giovanni Vincenzo Antonio Ganganelli, who on being elected on 18 May 1769 took the name CLEMENT XIV (1769–1774).

The new pope deliberated for four years the portentous step urged upon him by the anti-Jesuit coalition. Finally, in July 1773 he advised the order of its dissolution in two briefs, *Dominus ac Redemptor* and *Gravissimis ex causis*. Throughout Catholic Europe Jesuit property was confiscated. The order survived only in non-Catholic countries, particularly Prussia and Russia. On 7 August 1814, as Europe tried to put its revolutionary and Napoleonic past behind, Pope PIUS VII (1800–1823) restored the Society of Jesus in the bill *Sollicitudo Omnium Ecclesiarum.*

For further reference: William V. Banger, *A History of the Society of Jesus,* 2d ed., rev. (St. Louis: Institute of Jesuit Sources, 1986); Manfred Barthel, *The Jesuits. History and Legend of the Society of Jesus,* trans. and adapt. Mark Howson (New York: William Morrow, 1984); Henri Daniel-Rops, *The Church in the Eighteenth Century,* trans. John Warrington (London and New York: Doubleday, 1964); Magnus Morner, ed., *The Expulsion of the Jesuits from Latin America* (New York, 1965).

Emiliana P. Noether

SOTER (c. 166–c. 174). Soter was the twelfth POPE in the succession begun by St. PETER. The *Liber Pontificalis* notes that he was an Italian from Campania, but the early sources disagree regarding the exact dates of his pontificate. It is known that at some point he sent a letter to the church in Corinth urging a firm profession of faith and union with bishops and presbyters. The church historian Eusebius (c. 260–c. 340) has preserved fragments of an acknowledgment, filled with praise, from Dionysius, the bishop of Corinth, thanking him profusely for alms and promising that this letter would be read at services in the church there. Interpretations of other letters from Dionysius have led to the speculation that Soter may have disapproved of that bishop's laxity in judging matters of sexual continence and the restoration of sinners to communion and that his effusive tone in them may have been an attempt to placate Soter. Although Soter's original letter has been lost, some scholars believe it may be the letter wrongly called the Second Epistle of Clement.

In other ecclesiastical matters, it was a singular event that, under Soter, the celebration of Easter as an annual festival was introduced in Rome. It had not been so previously, and the date chosen, in contrast to the quartodeciman practice of the churches of Asia Minor, was the Sunday following the fourteenth day of the Jewish month of Nisan, the day of the Passover. It was also noted that Soter wrote against Montanism, the ascetic and prophetic movement begun by the prophet Montanus in Phrygia, but this is not corroborated. He is venerated as a martyr, with his feast day on 22 April.

For further reference: L. Duchesne, ed., *Liber Pontificalis* (Paris: E. de Boccard, 1955); J. Lebreton and J. Zeiller, *The History of the Primitive Church* (London: Burns, Oates, and Washbourne, 1948).

William Roberts

SPAIN AND THE VATICAN, 1814 TO THE PRESENT. Relations between the Holy See and Spain since the beginning of the nineteenth century have been shaped by two factors: the heritage of the *patronato real* (royal patronage), which gave the state the privilege of selecting the upper clergy in return for the state's promotion and upkeep of the church; and the extreme and often violent changes of government during most of the early nineteenth century and during the SPANISH CIVIL WAR in the twentieth century.

At the beginning of the nineteenth century, the Spanish church was almost completely under the domination of the absolutist Bourbon monarchy, a relationship called regalism. By the terms of the CONCORDAT of 1753, the Crown was confirmed in the privilege of naming the upper clergy, and it took advantage of the weakness of the papacy to seize control of the church's finances and to discipline the clergy. Succeeding constitutional governments in the nineteenth century managed to continue this relationship despite their secular and anticlerical biases. From the end of the Napoleonic War in 1814 until the end of the First Republic in 1874, conservative governments alternated with liberal governments in what was a 60-year-long civil war. But both liberal and conservative governments viewed the church in the same regalistic manner. The papacy generally approved of conservative governments because they did not attempt the anticlerical reforms the liberal governments did, specifically, limitations upon the numbers of clergy, regulation of clerical education, and confiscation of church property. Moreover, the liberal governments often were unable or unwilling to prevent violent anticlericalism—the killing of clergy and the burning of churches. Nevertheless, despite their anticlericalism, liberal governments still insisted upon keeping the regalistic privileges: they intended to reform the clergy by using the privileges granted to the absolutist eighteenth-century state. This approach led to numerous diplomatic conflicts with the papacy. Nor were papal relations with the conservative/absolutist governments that alternated in power with the liberals free of conflict.

The two collided over the independence of the Spanish colonies in Latin America: the POPES wanted to select the bishops in the newly independent states, while the Spanish Crown, refusing to recognize the new states, maintained that it still had the right of nomination. This controversy was settled in 1836, when Pope GREGORY XVI (1831–1846) recognized the new states, and the liberal government in Spain was caught up in civil struggle. A final bone of contention between the two was the unwillingness of the papacy to recognize Isabella II as the legitimate monarch during the Carlist War's (see Carlism) dynastic struggle for succession.

After 1843, when more moderate governments came to power after a decade of anticlericalism in which priests were killed, and clerical lands were nationalized by liberal governments, a settlement became possible, especially after the papacy recognized Isabella II after the end of the first Carlist War. As a result, the two agreed on the Concordat (see Concordats) of 1851, a document that governed relations until 1931. The concordat reaffirmed the state's right to nominate bishops, and the pope accepted the sale of clerical properties; in return, the state undertook the obligation to pay the clergy salaries. While there were tense relations during liberal and revolutionary upheavals in 1854–1856 and 1868–1873, the concordat remained in force.

From the time the monarchy was restored in 1875 until 1931, a long period of relative stability in church–state relations ensued. The only major issue between the papacy and the restoration monarchy was the status of the regular clergy. The mildly liberal governments wanted to restrict their growth, and the conservative governments resisted such attempts, with the support of the papacy, but the issue was not resolved. By the turn of the century both church and state were faced with more serious problems with the rise of socialist and anarchist working-class movements and the consequent threat of violent anticlericalism. The popes and the restoration governments bridged their difficulties in view of these new fears.

In 1931 the fears became reality when the monarchy was overthrown, and the Second Spanish Republic was proclaimed. The new government unilaterally abrogated the Concordat of 1851 and in a new Constitution separated church and state, dissolved the Jesuits, and announced its intention of abolishing clerical salaries and prohibiting the regular clergy from teaching. The government was also unable or unwilling to prevent anticlerical incendiarism. As a result, Pope PIUS XI (1922–1939) condemned the government's anticlericalism in an encyclical in 1933 and urged Catholics to political unity. While maintaining diplomatic relations with the anticlerical republic, the pope refused to accept their ambassador until 1934. Conservative governments suspended much of the anticlerical legislation in 1933–1935, but a Popular Front government elected in 1936 began implementation of the anticlerical laws, and violent anticlericals again threatened church incendiarism.

When the Spanish Civil War broke out in the summer of 1936, Pope Pius XI was deeply shocked by the violent anticlericals who killed nearly 8,000 priests, monks, and nuns; he was also offended by the Franco government's execution of Basque separatist priests. The Vatican did not break diplomatic relations with the anticlerical republicans, but in 1938 it recognized Franco's government. After the war, Franco wanted to regain the privileges of the 1851 concordat, but the new pope, PIUS XII (1939–1958), resisted. Finally, in 1941, the two agreed upon a restoration of the principal provisions of the 1851 concordat, and these were finalized in a concordat in 1953. Within a decade, the new concordat was an anachronism because of the reforms of VATICAN II. Even before the death of Franco, the Spanish bishops were pulling away from support of the regime, and with the accession of King Juan Carlos in 1975, the status of the church became free for the first time in centuries. In agreements with the papacy in 1976 and 1979, the new monarchy renounced the nominating privileges of the Concordat of 1953 but agreed to continue clerical salaries on a voluntary basis. In return, the papacy implicitly came to recognize the secularistic legislation of the modernized Spanish state.

For further reference: William J. Callahan, *Church, Politics, and Society in Spain, 1750–1874* (Cambridge: Harvard University Press, 1984); Frances Lannon, *Privilege, Persecution and Prophecy* (Oxford: Oxford University Press, 1987); Vicente Cárcel Ortí, *Historia de la Iglesia en España: V: La Iglesia en la España contemporánea (1808–*

1975) (Madrid: BAC, 1979); Stanley G. Payne, *Spanish Catholicism* (Madison: University of Wisconsin Press, 1984).

José M. Sanchez

SPANISH CIVIL WAR AND PAPACY. The Spanish civil war began in July 1936, when the army rebelled against the left-wing government of the Spanish Republic. The republic had been created in 1931 following the abdication of King Alfonso XIII and had become increasingly polarized between ideologues of Left and Right. In its uprising, the army was supported by the HIERARCHY of the Roman Catholic Church, by the landed classes, and by the political Right. The rebels became known as nationalists and were led by General Francisco Franco. The government side, known as loyalists, was supported by the working and peasant classes, by the political Left, and by the Basque and Catalan regional interests.

From the start, the nationalists received foreign assistance from fascist Italy and NAZI GERMANY. While the loyalists looked to the democracies for assistance, the latter preferred to isolate the Spanish conflict through an international Non-Intervention Agreement, signed by all the European powers. When this agreement was not respected by HITLER and MUSSOLINI, the Soviet Union intervened to support the Spanish government and encouraged voluntary participation by members of the international Left, both communist and noncommunist. The government held Madrid and the southeast throughout the war, while the nationalists progressively increased their control over the rest of the country. The capture of the northern Basque country in 1937 was an important victory for the nationalists. The fall of Catalonia in 1939 finally induced the surrender of the government.

The Spanish civil war had a wider significance because it served as an ideological battleground in the 1930s, pitting the armies of anticommunism led by Hitler and Mussolini against the forces of antifascism led by Stalin. Since the rise of Hitler in 1933, the communist and noncommunist Left in Europe had rallied to stop FASCISM by cooperating in a series of POPULAR FRONT electoral coalitions. One of these coalitions was elected in Spain in February 1936, and many interpreted the July 1936 rising of the Spanish generals as a fascist attack on the Popular Front. The Left intended that Spain should become the graveyard of fascism.

The Vatican was ambivalent about the Spanish civil war because there were Catholics on both sides of the conflict. Spanish Catholics had divided over the 1931 republic. The hierarchy of the church remained loyal to the monarchy, while other Catholics, led by the Jesuits, had been willing to work within the republic. The papal NUNCIO had also been willing to accept the republic and had encouraged the formation of a Catholic political group to contest the 1933 elections. Because the republican Constitution recognized the autonomy of the regions, it secured the loyalty of the strongly Catholic Basque country.

The divisions among the Catholics continued with the outbreak of the civil war. The hierarchy supported the army uprising as a means of destroying the republic. Other Catholics supported the nationalists because they questioned the republican government's ability to restrain radicals from destroying the persons and property of the church. Only the government supported regional autonomy, and, for that reason, the entire population of Catalonia and the Basque country remained loyal to the republic. Under these circumstances, the Vatican refused to give official sanction to the nationalists at the beginning of the war, and a nuncio was not named to nationalist Spain until May 1938, after the fall of the Basque country.

Not wishing to see the polarization of Europe enhanced by this war, the Vatican was also distressed by the foreign intervention. While recognizing that communism, represented by the Popular Front coalition and the Soviet intervention, was a danger to Christian civilization, the Vatican would not sanction an anticommunist crusade led by Hitler and Mussolini. Mussolini had resolved outstanding problems between church and state through treaty and CONCORDAT in 1929, and the church had enjoyed a privileged position in Italy since that time. Hitler, on the other hand, had concluded a concordat in 1933 (Germany, Concordat of 1933) but had violated its terms by constantly limiting and persecuting the church in Germany. The Spanish civil war represented the beginning of a phase of cooperation between Mussolini and Hitler, characterized as the Rome–Berlin Axis, which followed a period of discord.

POPE PIUS XI (1922–1939) feared that increased cooperation between Hitler and Mussolini would result in the latter's adopting the anti-Catholic practices of the former. Since the Spanish civil war was driving the two dictators into the same camp, the Pope was reluctant to sanction the crusade mounted by the fascist powers in support of General Franco. In March 1937, to distance himself from both extremes, the pope denounced first the communists and then the Nazis in two consecutive encyclicals, *Dilectissima Nobis* and *Mit Brennender Sorge*. The Vatican assumed a middle position in the international civil war that centered on Spain.

For further reference: Peter C. Kent, "The Vatican and the Spanish Civil War," *European History Quarterly* 16 (1986): 441–464; José M. Sanchez, *Reform and Reaction: The Politico-Religious Background of the Spanish Civil War* (Chapel Hill: University of North Carolina Press, 1962).

Peter C. Kent

SPANISH INQUISITION. This papally created, but state-controlled, tribunal, initially charged with the investigation of HERESY later had a wider jurisdiction. Although inquisitorial bodies had been created in the church as far back as the fourth century and were to be found in virtually every country in Christian Europe, the most noted of all such bodies was established in 1479 in response to an appeal by Queen Isabella of Castile. Pope SIXTUS IV (1471–1484), although reluctant to concede the sweeping powers sought by Isabella and her consort Ferdinand, agreed to the creation of a tribunal to root out "false Christians." The papal bull authorized the monarch to appoint a panel of bishops, theologians, and canon lawyers to investigate charges of heresy. A similar jurisdiction was shortly granted to the Crown of Aragon, and these two bodies, operating separately, came to be known as the Spanish Inquisition.

From its beginning, the Inquisition was a state-controlled body, ranking as one of the administrative councils of the realm. Although its decisions were theoretically sanctioned by the papacy, it functioned as an arm of the government, with little input from Rome during most of its existence. The inquisitor-general was a high-ranking cleric appointed by the sovereign and presided not only over the tribunal and its numerous assistants but over an ever-expanding army of policemen, informants, and jailers. While the original cause of Queen Isabella's concern had been secret Jewish religious loyalties among supposedly converted Jews, the expulsion and harassment carried out against the Spanish Jewish population from 1492 onward gradually led to covert Muslims or Protestants becoming the chief targets for heresy investigations. By the mid-sixteenth century, the government's concern with the extirpation of heresy had turned the Inquisition into one of the principal instruments of state policy.

Those denounced to the Inquisition by paid spies or voluntary informers were subject to arrest, interrogation, imprisonment, and, in some cases, torture or execution. While evidence shows that many of the cases were dismissed as the product of frivolous or malicious charges, a sufficient number were carried to the punishment stage to create an air of dread around the operations of the Inquisition. Recantation or confinement was deemed a sufficient penalty in most instances, but enough prisoners were "relaxed" to the secular authorities for physical chastisement to give the Inquisition a reputation for bloodthirstiness. No accurate figures on the number of persons executed over the course of the three and a half centuries of the tribunal's existence survive, but estimates range from a few hundred to more than 10,000.

After the close of the sixteenth century, with its public mass burnings of heretics and other manifestations of violence against dissident elements, the activities of the Holy Office of the Inquisition became more routine. Although it had interpreted investigation of heresy in the widest terms ever since its foundation, the tribunal in later days concerned itself with a multitude of unorthodox or merely immoral types of behavior, such as allegations of priests' seducing penitents in the confessional. Among the offenses against the stability of society judged and punished on a regular basis were polygamy, usury, and smuggling, as well as assumption of false identity and calumny. Censorship of books, always a major concern, was directed against not only heretical propositions but unorthodox or politically subversive ideas of any sort. Frontier guard posts were manned not only by regular troops but by agents of the Inquisition charged with confiscating foreign books that appeared too dangerous to be allowed free circulation in Spain. The Spanish Inquisition maintained its own INDEX of prohibited books and allowed many works forbidden by the pope to be read in Spain as long as offending passages had been crossed out by inquisitors.

The Spanish Inquisition was not limited to the Iberian Peninsula. As the colonial empire grew, local tribunals were established in the principal cities of the Americas to regulate behavior and thought among transplanted Spaniards and to carry out trials of foreign heretics who fell into their hands. English seamen (all of whom were deemed pirates in Spanish waters) were frequently convicted as *luteranos* and executed. These outposts of the Inquisition survived in Spanish America until the wars of independence at the beginning of the nineteenth century.

The Inquisition redoubled its efforts during the era of the Enlightenment, striving to keep the effects of that phenomenon from "infecting" Spanish territory. It fell victim to the spread of the French Revolution, the "enlightened" regime of Joseph Bonaparte abolished the Inquisition in 1808, and its reestablishment by the restored Bourbon dynasty in 1814 was greeted with indignation by all but the most conservative elements of Spanish society. Viewed now as a complete anachronism, the Inquisition served as a weak and ineffectual institution for two decades. Following the death of the reactionary king Ferdinand VII, the Inquisition was permanently dissolved in 1834.

For further reference: Jean Plaidy, *The Spanish Inquisition: Its Rise, Growth and End* (Edinburgh: McIntosh, 1991); Cecil Roth, *The Spanish Inquisition* (New York: Norton, 1990).

Julia L. Ortiz-Griffin

STEPHEN I (254–257). Stephen was apparently born in Rome and was bishop there from May 254 to August 257. He was involved in three major disputes with Cyprian of Carthage; two of them dealt with problems in Spain and Gaul, while the third had ramifications for the theology and practice of the universal church. Two bishops in Spain were condemned by the local bishops for denying their faith during the Decian persecution. They represented their case to Stephen, who reinstated them; Cyprian called a synod of North African bishops and wrote a letter reaffirming their condemnation and excusing Stephen on the grounds that he had been deceived by them. Stephen and Cyprian came into conflict again over Marcian, the bishop of Arles, who was accused of following the schismatic antipope NOVATIAN in his harsh treatment of repentant apostates.

The third controversy stemmed from the issue of the validity of baptism conferred by heretics. Cyprian, along with most of the North African bishops and some from Asia Minor, denied its validity on the grounds that valid sacraments could be administered only within the church, from which heretics had excluded themselves; he insisted, therefore, that those who had received such a baptism must be rebaptized. Stephen, on the other hand, maintained that heretical baptism was valid and rejected rebaptism in such cases as contrary to tradition. In 255 and 256 Cyprian convened several synods in North Africa; they supported his position, but attempts to communicate this to Stephen were frustrated when the latter refused even to meet with Cyprian's representatives. Cyprian's comments concerning Stephen and his role in this controversy are harsh, but Stephen does not appear to have countered in a similar vein, and Cyprian's status suffered no ill effects from his struggle with the bishop of Rome. The personal battle ended when Stephen died, and by the end of the third century his position was generally accepted in North Africa as well as in Rome.

Stephen is one of the first bishops of Rome to become seriously involved in the affairs of other lands, such as Spain and Gaul, and among the first proclaimed a saint. He may also have been the first bishop of Rome to claim primacy over the church on the basis of Christ's words to Peter in Matthew 16: 18–19. Stephen's episcopate, therefore, marks a new phase in the church's evolving self-consciousness concerning the episcopacy and the role of the bishop of Rome. At the same time, however, Cyprian's bold attacks on Stephen and the latter's lack of effectiveness in countering or silencing his opponent show that the level of real power exercised by this POPE was decidedly inferior to that wielded in succeeding centuries by a DAMASUS I (366–384) or a Leo the Great LEO I, (440–461).

For further reference: Cyprian of Carthage, *Letters* 67–75; E. Dekkers, "Symbolo Baptizare," *Fides Sacramenti Sacramentum Fidei, Studies in Honour of Pieter Smulders,* ed. H. J. auf der Maur et al. (Assen: Van Gorcum, 1981), pp. 107–112; Eusebius of Caesarea, *Church History* 7, 2–5; S. G. Hall, "Stephen of Rome and the One Baptism," *Studia Patristica* 17:2 (1982): 796–798.

Gerard H. Ettlinger

STEPHEN II (752). This elderly Roman priest was elected POPE by the population of the city following the death of Pope ZACHARIAS (741–752). Installed in the Lateran, he suffered a stroke three days later and died before his consecration. The *Liber Pontificalis* and medieval documents did not consider him a valid pope, insisting that consecration was deemed essential to be included on the official list of popes. Afterward some argued that election sufficed to be included among the popes, and the *Annuario Pontificio* included him until 1960. Subsequently, his name was again removed, throwing into disorder the numbers assigned to the succeeding popes bearing that name, so that Stephen II (752–757) has been listed as Stephen II (III), and STEPHEN IX (1057–1058) is listed as Stephen IX (X).

For further reference: Matthew Bunson, *The Pope Encyclopedia* (New York: Crown Trade Paperbacks, 1995); J. N. D. Kelly, *The Oxford Dictionary of Popes* (New York: Oxford University Press, 1986).

Francesca Coppa

STEPHEN II (III) (752–757). Stephen was a Roman of noble birth who, orphaned in childhood, was raised with his younger brother Paul in the Lateran. Pope ZACHARIAS (741–752) made them deacons. When the elderly priest named Stephen, who succeeded Zacharias, died after only four days (752), the younger Stephen was unanimously elected to succeed him. As the elder Stephen was duly installed but not consecrated, as was essential to the CANON LAW of the period, he is not listed as POPE by the *Liber Pontificalis* or other early sources. Only after the sixteenth century, when it was deemed that valid election is all that is required for one to become pontiff, would he be listed as Stephen (II). More recent listings, including the *Annuario Pontifico*, dropped his name. Thus, his successor is identified as Stephen II (III).

During this latter Stephen's pontificate the papacy passed from Byzantine to Frankish protection, and the PAPAL STATE was formed. Shortly after his election Rome was menaced by Aistulf, the Lombard king who had just conquered Ravenna. He regarded Rome as his fief, and, despite appeals to the Byzantines, Stephen found himself defenseless. He turned to Pepin III, king of the Franks, seeking his protection. Receiving a favorable response, Stephen set out to meet Pepin and crossed over the Alps (being the first pontiff to do so) through the St. Bernard Pass, to be ceremoniously received by Pepin at Ponthion. There in penitential garb, Stephen and his clergy besought the king to protect them and the Roman people from the Lombards. As a result, Pepin promised that he and his sons would protect the Roman church and, in the "Donation of Pepin," which he put in writing, to guarantee papal possession of extensive areas in central and northern Italy. In return, Stephen solemnly anointed Pepin and his family, thereby legitimating their dynasty, and granted them the title of "patrician of the Romans."

Pepin sought first to negotiate with Aistulf, but when this failed, he defeated him after a short campaign and made him swear, in the Peace of Pavia, to return the conquered territory to the pope. Stephen was then accompanied back to Rome by Pepin's army, where he received a tumultuous welcome. But as soon as the Franks crossed over the Alps and returned home, Aistulf broke the treaty and besieged Rome. Pepin returned and again defeated the Lombards and, after a second peace treaty, left a small force to ensure protection. However, officials of the Byzantine government soon protested that territory given to the pope by Pepin actually belonged to them. Pepin replied that what he had conquered he would not hand over to anyone except to the successor to St. PETER. He then presented Ravenna and various other areas that had formed part of the Byzantine exarchate to the Roman church in perpetuity, the document of donation being deposed on the tomb of the apostle by Pepin's representative. The papal state had come into existence.

For further reference: L. Duchesne, *The Beginnings of the Temporal Sovereignty of the Popes* (London, 1908); H. K. Mann, *The Lives of the Popes in the Early Middle Ages* (London: K. Paul, 1902–1932).

William Roberts

STEPHEN III (IV) (768–772). A Benedictine monk of Sicilian origin, Stephen succeeded two ANTIPOPES, CONSTANTINE II (767–768) and PHILIP (768), and his reign coincided with the beginning of Charlemagne's rule (768–814). The problems created by the elections of antipopes were addressed by the church at the Lateran Council (769) presided over by Stephen. The COUNCIL decreed that only cardinals could be elected POPE. Laymen were not permitted to participate or observe such elections. The council also reversed all appointments made by the antipopes. Stephen sanctioned the veneration of images while condemning the decrees of the Byzantine emperor Constantine, who, at the Council of Hieria (754), declared the use of icons as heretical.

For further reference: Eric John, ed., *The Popes: A Concise Biographical Dictionary* (New York: Hawthorn Books, 1964); H. K. Mann, *The Lives of the Popes in the Early Middle Ages* (London: K. Paul, 1902–1932). The best beginning primary source remains the *Liber Pontificalis* (Paris, 1886–1892).

John C. Horgan

STEPHEN IV (V) (816–817). Born of a noble Roman family, Stephen was the first POPE elected following the establishment of the Carolingian empire. He did not seek imperial approval prior to his consecration because of the confusion as to who was the legitimate emperor. Before LEO III (795–816) the popes had never questioned the legitimacy of the Byzantine emperors as heirs to the classical empire. However, the Eastern empire had recently been entangled in HERESY with the church, a position from which it had not completely recovered. Additionally, Leo had recognized Charlemagne as the emperor in the West, compounding the confusion.

It was generally recognized that, ultimately, the pope created the empire; only he could crown an emperor, and his papal authority legalized the status of emperor. Furthermore, whoever held the title of emperor was, in effect, the secular leader of Christendom. Stephen resolved the confusion when he made the Romans swear an oath of allegiance to Charlemagne's successor, Louis the Pious (814–840). Subsequently, he traveled to Rheims to crown the emperor, while confirming relations between the empire and the papacy by receiving guarantees from Louis regarding the autonomy of the PAPAL STATE and freedom of papal elections.

For further reference: Hans Kuhner, *Encyclopedia of the Papacy* (New York: Philosophical Library, 1958); H. K. Mann, *The Lives of the Popes in the Early Middle Ages* (London: K. Paul, 1902–1932).

John C. Horgan

STEPHEN V (VI) (885–891). Born of a noble Roman family, Stephen was elected without the consent of Emperor Charles III, the Fat (881–888). Although not Charles' choice for the papacy, the emperor grudgingly accepted the new POPE after Stephen convinced the emperor's representatives that he received unanimous support for his election. Upon the death of Charles and in the midst of the crumbling Carolingian empire, Stephen crowned Count Guido III of Spoleto the new emperor in order to provide needed protection against the Saracens, although the emperor, distracted by events in the north, failed to provide troops when the Saracens actually attacked.

Stephen also became immersed in an ongoing dispute between Rome and the Byzantine empire when he refused to recognize Photius as patriarch of Constantinople (858–867, 878–886). Photius objected to papal influence in Bulgaria and accused Rome of HERESY for its toleration of the *filioque* to the Nicene Creed, a doctrinal dispute that indicated the transmission of God as the Holy Spirit from the Father and the Son. Photius' abdication in 886 resolved the conflict, and the pope recognized the new patriarch, Stephen I.

For further reference: Hans Kuhner, *Encyclopedia of the Papacy* (New York: Philosophical Library, 1958); H. K. Mann, *The Lives of the Popes in the Early Middle Ages* (London: K. Paul, 1902–1932).

John C. Horgan

STEPHEN VI (VII) (896–897). A Roman and son of a priest, Stephen's election and pontificate was marred by the struggle between two factions for power in Rome. He was supported by Lambert, the duke of Spoleto, whose family was a longtime enemy of the papacy. Lambert hated Stephen's predecessor, FORMOSUS (891–896), for crowning Arnulf emperor. In January 897, at Lambert's insistence, Stephen ordered the exhumation of Formosus' body to stand trial on charges of perjury, for violating the canons prohibiting the translation of bishops, and for coveting the papacy. The body was dressed in papal vestments and propped up on a throne with a bishop acting as his defense attorney. This rigged trial resulted in Stephen's annulling Formosus' ordinations, excommunicating (see Excommunication) the dead POPE, and chopping off three of his fingers while disposing of the remainder of the corpse in the Tiber River. Furthermore, Stephen required all members of the clergy ordained by Formosus to submit letters renouncing their orders. These actions spurred Formosus' supporters to imprison Stephen, depose him, and finally strangle him to death.

For further reference: Eric John, ed., *The Popes: A Concise Biographical Dictionary* (New York: Hawthorn Books, 1964); H. K. Mann, *The Lives of the Popes in the Early Middle Ages* (London: K. Paul, 1902–1932).

John C. Horgan

STEPHEN VII (VIII) (928–931). Roman by birth, when elected to succeed LEO VI (928), he was priest of S. Anastasia. At the time of his elevation the earlier pontiff JOHN X (914–928) was still alive in prison. Like his predecessor Leo, Stephen owed his election to Marouzia, the senatrix and patrician of Rome who was the head of the Theophylact family and therefore, with her second husband, Guido, the marquis of Tuscany, the city's all-powerful ruler. They had, in fact, deposed and imprisoned John X. In this sense, when Stephen became POPE, he was considered an interim pontiff, to reign until Marouzia's son John was of age to succeed to the papal throne. Under the complete control of this dynasty, Stephen had little power and could act independently only in very narrowly defined ecclesiastical matters. Records of this period are scanty, and his only known actions concern the confirmation or extension of privileges to various religious houses in France and Italy.

For further reference: P. Hughes, *The History of the Church* (London: Sheed and Ward, 1955); H. K. Mann, *The Lives of the Popes in the Early Middle Ages* (London: K. Paul, 1902–1932).

William Roberts

STEPHEN VIII (IX) (939–942). Stephen was Roman by birth and at the time of his election was cardinal-priest of SS. Silvestro and Martino. Later sources erroneously described him as of German background, imposed on the Holy See by Otto I, king of Germany. In fact, he owed his position, as did his predecessor, LEO VII (936–939), to Alberic II, the prince of Rome, senator, and patrician, who was the city's absolute ruler during this period. Alberic, like his mother, the senatrix and patricia, Marouzia, leader of the family and Roman oligarchy of Theophylact, appointed the pontiffs of his choice. Personally, Stephen was considered a holy and learned man, devoted to peace and meditation.

As POPE he had little independence; even his ecclesiastical acts, such as his support for the Cluniac reform movement, had to have Alberic's approval. But Stephen did on occasion act on his own initiative, as in 942, when he intervened in favor of Louis IV d'Outremer, the son of Charles the Simple, who had been crowned as king of France but then faced a major rebellion. Stephen sent Bishop Damasus as papal LEGATE to urge the French and Burgundian nobility and people to accept Louis on pain of EXCOMMUNICATION, providing Louis strong moral support against his dangerous rival, Hugh the Great. As a conciliatory gesture in that same year he sent the pallium to Archbishop Hugh of Rheims, restoring him to the see from which he had been displaced several years earlier. During the last years of his reign, Stephen seems to have taken part in a conspiracy to depose Alberic, for which he was imprisoned. Reportedly, the pope was brutally treated during this imprisonment and died of his injuries.

For further reference: L. Duchesne, ed., *Liber Pontificalis* (Paris: E. de Boccard, 1955); H. K. Mann, *The Lives of the Popes in the Early Middle Ages* (London: K. Paul, 1902–1932).

William Roberts

STEPHEN IX (X) (1057–1058). Stephen was chosen POPE following the unexpected death of VICTOR II (1055–1057). When the leaders of the reform party in Rome asked Frederick of Lorraine, the abbot of Monte Cassino, for advice about possible successors, he proposed five individuals. However, Frederick was himself elected on 2 August, taking the name of St. Stephen I, whose feast day it was. No effort had been made to consult with the German imperial family to prevent various Roman families from interfering in the election. At any rate, the new pope could rely on the support of his powerful brother Godfrey, the duke of Lorraine and count of Tuscany. Soon after the election, a delegation led by Hildebrand went to the imperial court at Pohlde in Saxony and obtained official approval for the choice.

Stephen's background indicated he would be a progressive and active pope. The youngest son of Duke Gozelon I of Lorraine, he had been educated at Liège, where he served as canon and archdeacon. He probably met Pope LEO IX (1049–1054) at the reforming synod of Mainz and followed him to Rome, becoming one of Leo's closest collaborators. He accompanied Leo on his campaign against the Normans and was one of the LEGATES to the important meeting at Constantinople in 1054. But in 1055, because of the visit to Rome of the emperor Henry III, one of his brother's enemies, he found it prudent to retire as a monk to Monte Cassino.

As pope, Stephen, who remained abbot of Monte Cassino, undertook a reform program, appointing the saintly Italian monk Peter Damiani, a proponent of reform, cardinal-bishop of Ostia. Humbert of Silva Candida, who was probably the greatest power in Rome after the pope and who strongly supported the independence of episcopal sees from lay control, was his chancellor, and Hildebrand was a close adviser. Stephen often denounced clerical marriage and stressed the practice of evangelical poverty and, through Hildebrand, made contact with the reforming movement of Milan, which opposed simony and clerical unchastity.

In 1058 Stephen was planning to renew Leo IX's campaign against the Normans in southern Italy and was considering crowning his brother Duke Godfrey as emperor to enlist his support. In March of that year he traveled to Florence to consult with Godfrey and died there. Before he left Rome, he had bound the clergy and the people of the city by a solemn oath not to elect a successor in the event of his death until Hildebrand had returned from Germany, where he had gone on a mission to the royal court. He was buried in S. Reparata in Florence.

For further reference: L. Duchesne, ed., *Liber Pontificalis* (Paris: E. de Boccard, 1955); H. K. Mann, *The Lives of the Popes in the Early Middle Ages* (London: K. Paul, 1902–1932).

William Roberts

SWORD AND HAT, BLESSED. The sword and hat were ceremonial regalia, blessed annually by the POPES and awarded, almost exclusively, to emperors and kings as an incentive to defend the rights of the church. The sword took the form of a cross-handed sword, with intricate engraving on the blade and elaborate repoussé work on the guard, grip, and pommel. The scabbard also was richly decorated and provided the silversmiths with an ideal opportunity for showing their originality in design and ability in execution. The sword belts were in keeping with the rest of this costly gift.

The hat had a stiff, high crown with a deep brim, which curved upward to a point at the front, and two lappets hung from the back similar to those of a liturgical miter. It was made of dark crimson, gray, or even black velvet and was lined with ermine. The dove, symbolic of the Holy Spirit, was embroidered in gold thread on the right-hand side and was ornamented with pearls. From the top of the crown, rays alternately straight and wavy, in gold thread work filled with seed pearls, descended toward the brim.

The sword and hat formed an expensive gift, and the recorded payments to the various ateliers still bear witness to this. From the entries noted in the accounts of papal exchequer at different times it is possible to compile an itemized statement that provides the approximate cost of the various components. Early examples of the blessed sword and hat have not survived. With the hat this is understandable, given the less durable nature of the fabric; the swords have withstood the ravages of times slightly better. Ten swords of the fifteenth century still exist in various museums and private collections and about a dozen from the sixteenth century. Two hats of the sixteenth century are preserved in Vienna.

It is difficult to disentangle what may be the origins of this papal gift from the long association that swords had throughout the Middle Ages with the liturgical ceremonies connected with knighthood and the coronation of kings. Gregorovius says that the tradition originated in 758 with the sword that Pope PAUL I (757–767) gave to Pepin, king of the Franks. The first certain mention of the blessed sword and hat, as a gift of the popes, is an entry for payment contained in the accounts ledger for 1357. Confirmation can be found in a similar entry in 1365, when already it seems to have been regarded as a long-established practice. Whatever may be the real origin, by the sixteenth century several hundred years of tradition had lain behind this gift, and it made a strong appeal to the highest ideals of chivalry.

The blessed sword and hat were designed to show the confidence the popes placed in any given person to defend the rights and liberties of the church and of the papacy in particular, sometimes awarded as recognition of services already performed or as an incentive to prompt him to take up the sword. Political motives played their part. It took the ritual blessing of the sword and hat to attach a spiritual symbolism to the gift and make it a guarantee of divine protection. This blessing always took place at Christmas and was incorporated into the liturgical ceremonies of the feast.

The sword was intended to represent that temporal power invested in the popes in virtue of their supreme jurisdiction (based on those theories of medieval canonists in allusion to the two swords produced by St. PETER, when the officials of the high priests came to arrest Christ), which they, in turn, entrusted to secular rulers to exercise in their name and on their behalf. The blessed hat was taken to represent the unfailing protection of the Holy Spirit, which would accompany every valiant defender of the Catholic faith.

If the prince whom the pope wished to honor happened to be present at the blessing, then the investiture with the sword and hat took place immediately, and he had a special place in the procession that followed. More often, however, the honor was conferred away from the papal court, and a special envoy was deputed to consign it in accordance with a minutely regulated ceremony.

For further reference: C. Burns, *Golden Rose and Blessed Sword: Papal Gifts to Scottish Monarch* (Glasgow: Burns, 1970); C. Burns, "Papal Gifts and Honours for the Earlier Tudors," *Miscellanea Historiae Pontificiae* 50 (1983): 173–197; E. Cornides, *Rose und Schwert im papstlichen zeremoniell* (Vienna: Heinemann, 1967); E. Muntz, "Les epees d'honneur distribuees par les papes pendant les XIVe, XVe et XVIe siecles," *Revue de l'Art chretien* 39 (1889): 408–411; 40 (1890): 281–292.

Charles Burns

SYLLABUS OF ERRORS. During the pontificate of PIUS IX (1846–1878) many urged him to condemn the errors that threatened religion and the church in the nineteenth century. A list of 61 propositions to be condemned was drawn up and submitted to the bishops gathered in Rome in 1862. When it was leaked to the press, it created a furor and was withdrawn. After the occupation of the papal LEGATIONS by Piedmont and the convention of September 1864 between France and Piedmont, Pius felt no need to appease governments by which he felt betrayed. Eighty propositions on various modern errors were gathered from papal addresses and letters for condemnation.

The list was added to the encyclical *Quanta Cura*, issued on 8 December 1864 and became known as the "Syllabus of Errors." The syllabus contains ten sections touching many areas: (1) pantheism, (2) rationalism, (3) indifferentism, (4) socialism, communism, and secret societies, (5) the rights of the church, (6) civil society, (7) ethics, (8) Christian marriage, (9) the civil power of the papacy, and (10) modern liberalism.

The syllabus provoked a storm of criticism. Enemies of the church saw in it another sign of its demise. Some Catholics and papal sympathizers were astounded by some of the propositions, while ultramontanes rejoiced in what they saw as their vindication. The interpretation of the propositions became the center of controversy. To be rightly understood, each statement must be read in its original context. Read out of context and as absolute statements, they can be misinterpreted. Few faulted the condemnations of atheism (1), pantheism (2), or rationalism (10). But some statements touching toleration (15, 77) and the separation of church and state (55) appeared to condemn the practice of contemporary governments. Moreover, the condemnation of the proposition that "the Roman Pontiff can, and ought to reconcile himself to and agree with, progress, liberalism, and modern civilization" (80) appeared to confirm the conviction of many of the incompatibility of the Catholic Church and modern society. A pamphlet by Antoine Dupanloup, bishop of Orleans, that explained the propositions calmed the storm to a degree.

More than a century later the syllabus still raises questions. It is certainly not infallible teaching since it fails to meet the conditions for INFALLIBILITY formulated by VATICAN I. The papal secretary of state, not the POPE, issued the text. Although part of the teaching of the church, it must be read in the context of the ROMAN QUESTION and the encroachments of the government of Piedmont on the PAPAL STATES.

For further reference: R. Aubert, *Le Pontificat de Pie IX* (Paris: Bloud and Gay, 1952); F. Coppa, *Pope Pius IX: Crusader in a Secular Age* (Boston: Twayne, 1979); C. Hollis, "The Syllabus of Errors: Its Genesis and Implications," *Twentieth Century Catholicism*, ed. L. Sheppard (New York: Hawthorn Books, 1965).

Richard J. Kehoe

SYLVESTER I (314–335). The successor to Pope MILTIADES (311–314), Sylvester's pontificate correlates with Constantine I's reign, exercising a dominant role in the political and ecclesiastical activities of the Roman empire. Eusebuis tells us Constantine I assumed the authority in calling COUNCILS, often engaged in dogmatic discussions, and occasionally assumed the title of "bishop of external affairs." In the tradition of the Roman state, Constantine authorized the use of religion as an instrument of state policy: Christian clergy were exempt from public service, he authorized local churches to accept legacies, and, in specific areas, the decisions of episcopal courts were held equal to those of civil courts. After the defeat of Lincinius of Adrianople, the marriage of the state with the church, later known as caesaropapism, was intensified. In May 325, Adrianople Constantine summoned approximately 250 bishops to the first ecumenical council in NICAEA to denounce Arius' heretical teachings and approved the Roman teaching of homoousios.

For further reference: Matthew Bunson, *The Pope Encyclopedia* (New York: Crown Trade Paperbacks, 1995); J. N. D. Kelly, *The Oxford Dictionary of Popes* (Oxford: Oxford University Press, 1986).

Patrick McGuire

SYLVESTER II (999–1003). Born sometime between 940 and 945 of humble parents in Auvergne (in today's France), Gerbert as a boy was sent to the monastery of St. Geraud at Aurillac, where he acquired a reputation for learning and became a monk. When he traveled to Rome, his learning impressed Pope JOHN XIII (965–972). In 972 he went to Rheims, where he studied logic and became master of the cathedral school. His reputation spread, and Otto II presented him with the abbacy of Bobbio, but he did not remain there long, returning to Rheims. There he supported Hugh Capet against the last of the Carolingians and in 991 was chosen archbishop of Rheims by King Hugh but was denied the recognition of Rome. After years of strife he fled to the court of Emperor Otto III and in 998 became archbishop of Ravenna.

Upon the death of GREGORY V (996–999) in February 999, Gerbert became POPE as Sylvester II. His choice of name revealed his bond to the emperor and the Roman heritage, for stories then prevalent indicated that Pope SYLVESTER I (314–335) had helped to create harmony between church and state during the reign of Constantine. However, the feudal disorder in Italy following the death of Otto III in 1002 precluded any significant improvement in the condition of the West. Sylvester, the first Frenchman to ascend the throne of Peter, furthered the church's missionary effort: establishing the HIERARCHY in Poland and Hungary, furthering the Christianization of Scandinavia, and pursuing good relations with St. Vladimir of Kiev. He died in Rome 12 May 1003 and was buried in the cathedral of St. John Lateran.

For further reference: Eleanor Shipley Duckett, *Death and Life in the Tenth Century* (Ann Arbor: University of Michigan Press, 1967); H. K. Mann, *The Lives of the Popes in the Early Middle Ages* (London: K. Paul, 1902–1932); Harriet Pratt, "Sylvester II, Pope," *New Catholic Encyclopedia*, vol. 13, pp. 858–859.

William C. Schrader

SYLVESTER III (1045). In September 1044, rioting broke out in Rome, and BENEDICT IX fled, briefly ending the first of the three periods in which he occupied the papacy (1031–1044, 1045, 1047–1048). The Crescentian family, hoping to regain control of the city they had lost to the Tusculans in 1012, secured the election of a native Roman, Bishop John of Sabina, who accepted reluctantly. He reigned as Pope Sylvester III, beginning 20 January 1045. Benedict, who had never been formally deposed, excommunicated (see Excommunication) Sylvester and returned with an army in March to reclaim the city and the papacy. Sylvester III returned to Sabina under the protection of the Crescentian family. Sylvester III was formally deposed by the COUNCIL of Sutri in 1046 and confined to a monastery. Apparently, this sentence was lifted, because there are references to his continuing service as bishop of Sabina. He died about 1063.

For further reference: Matthew Bunson, *The Pope Encyclopedia* (New York: Crown Trade Paperbacks, 1995); J. D. Kelly, *The Oxford Dictionary of Popes* (Oxford: Oxford University Press, 1986).

Frank Grande

SYLVESTER IV, ANTIPOPE (1105–1111). This former archpriest of St. Angelo served as a pawn between the warring factions of Rome's nobility for control of the city and the struggle between the papacy and the German emperors over the investiture issue (see Investiture Controversy). He was elected by supporters from the Roman nobility, assisted by Count Werner of Ancona, who accused Pope PASCHAL II (1099–1118) of simony and HERESY. Initial clashes between Sylvester and the pope's troops favored the usurper, but as finances dwindled, Sylvester found himself abandoned, forcing him to flee under the protection of Werner to an estate at Ancona.

The German emperor, Henry V (1106–1125), used Sylvester as a bargaining ploy against Paschal in an attempt to resolve the investiture issue. Henry threatened to forcibly impose Sylvester if Paschal refused the emperor's bidding. Paschal eventually reached a compromise with the emperor, whereby Henry retained rights of investiture as well as a promise from the pope he would never be excommunicated (see Excommunication), in exchange for the emperor's promise not to interfere in canonical elections. Henry promptly forced Sylvester to renounce his claim to the pontificate. Sylvester remained at Ancona under the protection of Werner.

For further reference: Eric John, ed., *The Popes: A Concise Biographical Dictionary* (New York: Hawthorn Books, 1964); J. N. D. Kelly, *The Oxford Dictionary of Popes* (Oxford: Oxford University Press, 1986).

John C. Horgan

SYMMACHUS (498–514). Born in Sardinia and baptized as an adult in Rome, Symmachus (498–514) consistently asserted the independence of the papacy. He was elected at the Lateran on 22 November 498 in the midst of the Acacian SCHISM (482–519), which divided the clergy in Rome into two factions—those who looked to the Gothic rulers in Ravenna and those who looked to Constantinople and favored conciliation with the Monophysites, which had been the policy of Symmachus' predecessor, ANASTASIUS II (469–498). At S. Maria Maggiore, a sizable minority elected LAWRENCE who became an ANTIPOPE. When street fighting broke out, both sides appealed to Theodoric, the Ostrogothic king. He ruled in favor of Symmachus and then called for a synod, which met in 499. The members voted to bar discussion of the succession during a POPE's lifetime and confirmed the right of the pope to designate his own successor by appointing him as archdeacon. Lawrence accepted this formula.

By the end of the year 500, however, new quarrels broke out. Laurentius revived his claims to the papacy, and Theodoric, having shifted allegiances, called for a new synod to try Symmachus on charges of alienating church property to secure his election, fornicating, and celebrating Easter on the wrong date. But this *Synodus palmaris* declared in its final session (23 October 502) that no humans were competent to try the pope; he must be judged by God alone.

Theodoric allowed Lawrence to return to Rome, where he tried to rule as pope from the Lateran. Street fighting broke out again, and Symmachus took refuge in St. Peter's, beginning a precedent that would eventually lead to the transfer of the papal staff from the Lateran to the Vatican. By 507 Theodoric was persuaded to order Lawrence to step aside and return control of all churches in Rome to Symmachus. The second recension was favorable to the pope but relied on forgeries. These forgeries concocted a series of decrees dating back to the early fourth century, claiming that the power of the pope was not derived from those who had elected him, and the pope was totally independent of the clergy as well as of secular rulers. There is no evidence that the pope was involved in these so-called Symmachan forgeries. Even before these forgeries, the principle that the first see is judged by no one had been upheld by Popes ZOSIMUS (417–418) and BONIFACE I (418–422).

Apart from the controversies over papal power, Symmachus worked hard, driving the Manichaeans out of Rome and supporting the bishops persecuted by the Arians (see Arianism) in North Africa. He also built new churches in Rome and added to others, particularly St. Peter's. Relations with Constantinople worsened until Emperor Anastasius I (491–519), faced with internal revolts, asked Symmachus to convene a COUNCIL to settle the doctrinal disputes. But Symmachus died (19 July 514) before the invitation arrived. He is buried in St. Peter's. Nearly a thousand years later, two Carthusians bestowed on Symmachus the title of "saint."

For further reference: *The Book of Pontiffs, Liber Pontificalis*, trans. R. Davis (Liverpool: Liverpool University Press, 1989); E. Caspar, *Geschichte des Papsttums* vol. 2 (Tübingen: J. C. B. Mohr, 1930–33), T. G. Jalland, *The Church and the Papacy* (London: SPCK, 1944).

Frank Grande

T

TELESPHORUS (c. 125–c. 136). Telesphorus is described in the earliest succession lists of bishops of Rome beginning with St. PETER as the eighth POPE. Although the dates of his reign are uncertain, the sources agree that it was for a period of eleven years. The *Liber Pontificalis* notes that he was a Greek, as his name indicates, and that he had been an anchorite. The latter is an anachronism. It also reports that he introduced such practices as the seven-week fast before Easter and the use of the "Gloria in excelsis" in the Christmas midnight mass, but these, too, were developed in later centuries.

Irenaeus more accurately recounts (c. 180) that Telesphorus suffered martyrdom, bearing "witness gloriously." Eusebius (c. 300) records that he was martyred under Emperor Antoninus Pius (138/139), but more likely this occurred earlier, during the reign of the emperor Hadrian (117–138). He is, at any rate, the only second-century pope whose martyrdom can be reliably confirmed. As is the case with other early popes, it is difficult to determine the nature and extent of his authority and role. His feast is 5 January.

For further reference: L. Duchesne, ed., *Liber Pontificalis* (Paris: E. de Boccard, 1955); H. K. Mann, *The Lives of the Popes in the Early Middle Ages* (London: K. Paul, 1902–1932).

William Roberts

THEODORE, ANTIPOPE (687). At the time of JOHN V's (685–686) death, twin struggles were occurring affecting the stability of the papacy. The Eastern empire had suffered losses of territory to the Arabs and Bulgars, thus threatening its overall integrity, while the emperors continued to contend with the POPES for primacy within the church and Christendom. Theodore, a Roman archpriest, probably of Greek or Syrian origin, competed with a rival, Peter, for the papal chair. Theodore's candidacy was supported by the Rome militia, while Peter was backed by the clergy. The ensuing stalemate resulted in the election of a compromise candidate, CONON (686–687). Upon the death of Conon, the succession was once again disputed, and Theodore faced a challenge from a new rival, Paschal (ANTIPOPE, 687). Both candidates, along with their respective supporters, occupied the Lateran. As before, this standoff ended in the election of another compromise candidate, SERGIUS I (687–701), whom Theodore accepted.

For further reference: Eric John, ed., *The Popes: A Concise Biographical Dictionary* (New York: Hawthorn Books, 1964); J. N. D. Kelly, *The Oxford Dictionary of Popes* (Oxford: Oxford University Press, 1986).

John C. Horgan

THEODORE I (642–649). A Greek from Jerusalem, son of a bishop, and a refugee of Arab invasions, Theodore's reign (24 November 642–14 May 649) was marked by the struggle with monothelitism (a doctrine that recognized the two natures of Christ but within a single will). His opposition to this HERESY, as well as his ties to critics of it, guaranteed his election to the papacy. Theodore's position received the support of the bishops of Cyprus, Palestine, and Africa, while confronting staunch opposition from the Eastern emperor Constans II (641–648). The Arab invasions were eroding the emperor's authority, and his continued support for monothelitism was necessary to prevent alienating his remaining Eastern subjects. Although Constans refused to withdraw *Ecthesis* (an edict issued by his predecessor, Heraclius (610–641), commanding subjects of the empire to adhere to the heresy), he instead issued *Typos* (648), forbidding discussion of one or two wills of Christ. This edict was not acceptable to Rome.

A second controversy marking Theodore's papacy was his refusal to recognize Paul II (641–653), a monothelite, as patriarch of Constantinople. His predecessor, Pyrrhus (638–641), had been illegally deposed for political reasons and, although a monothelite, would convert back to orthodoxy, aided by St. Maximus the Confessor. Paul's refusal to prove his orthodoxy resulted in his EXCOMMUNICATION by the POPE. Just prior to Theodore's death, Pyrrhus renounced his conversion, returned to the monothelite heresy, and was promptly excommunicated.

For further reference: Hans Kuhner, *Encyclopedia of the Papacy* (New York: Philosophical Library, 1958); H. K. Mann, *The Lives of the Popes in the Early Middle Ages* (London: K. Paul, 1902–1932). The best beginning primary source remains the *Liber Pontificalis* (Paris, 1886–1892).

John C. Horgan

THEODORE II (897). A Roman, Theodore's pontificate lasted a brief twenty days in December 897. However, in that time, he held a synod that reversed the actions taken by his predecessor, STEPHEN VI (896–897), by recognizing the validity of Pope FORMOSUS' ordinations and reinstated the clerics expelled by Stephen. Additionally, Theodore retrieved the body of Formosus and had it reburied in St. Peter's. Despite his actions, he was unable to resolve the differences between the supporters and enemies of Formosus.

For further reference: Joseph S. Brusher, *Popes through the Ages* (Princeton: D. Van Nostrand, 1964); Eric John, ed., *The Popes: A Concise Biographical Dictionary* (New York: Hawthorn Books, 1964).

John C. Horgan

THEODORIC, ANTIPOPE (1100–1101). A cardinal-deacon in Sta Maria in Via Lata in 1084, Theoderic became the successor of Antipope CLEMENT III (1080, 1084–1100) in a clandestine nomination, election, consecration, and enthronement process at night in St. Peter's. In the absence of Pope PASCHAL II (1099–1118), Theoderic assumed this leadership position for 105 days. He attempted to flee to Emperor Henry IV when Paschal II returned but received no sympathy from him. Paschal's supporters arrested Theoderic and sentenced him to a monastery in LaCava near Salerno, where he became a monk. The Normans were available to ensure Theoderic's confinement. He died in 1102.

For further reference: J. N. D. Kelly, *The Oxford Dictionary of Popes* (Oxford: Oxford University Press, 1986).

Patrick McGuire

TOTALITARIANISM AND THE PAPACY. Three violently "totalitarian" dictatorships emerged in Europe after WORLD WAR I. On the ideological Left was the communist dictatorship in Soviet Russia (1917–1991), while on the right were MUSSOLINI's fascist regime in Italy (1922–1943) and HITLER's Third Reich in Germany (1933–1945). Mussolini coined the term "totalitarian" to describe his fascist state, which asserted "total" control over all aspects of life. In retrospect, however, historians regard Hitler's Nazi regime as being more brutal and intrusive than Mussolini's fascist one. Most totalitarian of all was the communist regime of Lenin and Stalin. The more totalitarian the regime, the greater likelihood it would clash with the Roman Catholic Church, which claimed the right to educate its youth and look after the souls of the faithful.

Communist Russia. At first sight, the papacy's stance toward communist Russia and its ideology was intransigent. In the encyclical "On Atheistic Communism" (*Divini Redemptoris*), PIUS XI declared on 18 March 1937: "Communism is intrinsically wrong and no one who would save Christian civilization may collaborate with it in any field whatsoever." A similar theme was sounded by PIUS XII in his 1956 Christmas message, in which he warned against coexistence and the tendency of some Catholics to engage in "dialogue" with the communists in the post-Stalin era. But one can also find more conciliatory pronouncements about totalitarianism. Thus, in a dispute with Mussolini over education in Italy, Pius XI explained (14 May 1929), "When there is question of saving souls, or preventing greater harm to souls, we feel the courage to treat with the devil in person."

Concerned about several hundred thousand Roman Catholics in the western sectors of Russia, the papacy tried several times after 1917 to achieve an accommodation with the Kremlin. The principal effort occurred in 1921 during the international economic conference in Genoa. Vatican emissaries also worked in Russia alongside Herbert Hoover's American Relief Administration from 1922 to 1924, hoping this humanitarian gesture might ease tensions. During the "thaw" of 1924, when France, Italy, Britain, and other countries recognized the Soviet Union, at least some churchmen hoped for a Kremlin–Vatican accord, but again to no avail. The situation worsened in 1926, when a French priest, Fr. d'Herbigny, was secretly consecrated a bishop in the chapel of the papal NUNCIO in Berlin by Eugenio Pacelli (the future Pius XII) and dispatched to Moscow to consecrate new bishops. The Kremlin quickly imprisoned many of these.

In 1929, Stalin embarked upon the most brutal antireligious campaign yet. Pius XI in March 1930 transformed the Pontifical Commission for Russia into an independent organ reporting directly to himself. At the sixteenth Congress of the Communist Party of the Soviet Union in June 1930, Stalin denounced the alleged "clerical 'crusade' headed by the Pope against the USSR." The Kremlin had clearly rejected any accommodation. As the danger of communism grew worldwide during the Great Depression, Pius XI in 1937 delivered his strongest denunciation of the Soviet Union with the encyclical "On Atheistic Communism."

The Papacy and Italy. The Vatican had experienced problems with the liberal kingdom of Italy since 1870, when the newly unified state dispossessed Pius IX of his temporal power in Rome. For the next half century no formal ties existed between the papacy and the Italian state. In 1918, however, Benedict XV perceived that continued Catholic political isolation in Italy was only making things easier for the rising tide of Marxist socialism. He allowed Fr. Luigi Sturzo to form a centrist Catholic party (PPI; Partito Popolare Italiano). In the 1919 election it came in second to the socialists. Meanwhile, in the postwar turmoil, Italy's liberal system of government rapidly disintegrated, while on the far Right a new violent and ultranationalist movement, Benito Mussolini's FASCISM, was attracting growing support from war veterans, youth, and many frightened middle-class people. By 1922, in a bid to win support from the monarchy and church, Mussolini suddenly repudiated his earlier republican and anticlerical program. This quickly paid off. When the fascists marched on Rome in late October of that year, King Victor Emmanuel III asked Mussolini to form a coalition government. The fascist duce transformed this into a single-party, totalitarian regime after the coup d'état of 3 January 1925.

By this time, Pius XI had decided to dissolve the PPI and work with the fascists who, in his judgment, were a stronger bulwark against communism and might be willing to resolve the long-festering "ROMAN QUESTION." He was also intrigued by fascism's espousal of the "corporative state," inspired by national-syndicalist and Catholic corporatist thought and organized on the basis

of socioeconomic syndicates and "corporations" (guilds). In 1925, secret negotiations got under way between Mussolini's regime and the Vatican for a
treaty to resolve the Roman question, a CONCORDAT to define the church's
legal status in Italy, and a financial agreement. All three goals were achieved
in the LATERAN ACCORDS signed on 11 February 1929 by Mussolini and
cardinal secretary of state Pietro Gasparri. The treaty gave the pope sovereignty
over VATICAN CITY, thus satisfying his insistence on having at least a measure of "temporal power," and proclaimed Roman Catholicism the official religion of Italy. Delighted by the "Conciliation," Pius referred to the duce as
"a man whom Providence has caused us to meet."

The inescapable rivalry between totalitarian fascism and an authoritarian papacy was clearly revealed in a dispute in 1931 over the status of *Azione Cattolica*
(Catholic Action), a powerful organization of Catholic laymen. The squabble
extended into rival university student organizations, the Fascist University
Groups (GUF) versus the University Federation of Italian Catholics (FUCI). The
dispute reached its climax on 29 June 1931, when PIUS XI issued the encyclical
NON ABBIAMO BISOGNO ("We have no need"), flatly rejecting fascist accusations regarding Catholic Action. A shaky compromise was worked out by
2 September. Catholic Action would be placed under the direct control of the
bishops, who would select leaders not connected with the outlawed PPI. Catholic
Action would not have any syndical functions, and its youth groups would stay
out of sports. The fascists appeared to have won. However, Catholic Action
survived and helped to prepare a new generation of Catholic politicians who
would assume leadership in the postfascist era.

In another development, Pius XI issued the encyclical *Quadregesimo anno*
on 15 May 1931, the fortieth anniversary of Leo XIII's *Rerum novarum*. It
updated the corporatist philosophy in that document and at the same time expressed mild criticism of the fascist model of the corporative state. Many church
leaders enthusiastically supported Mussolini's war against Ethiopia (see Ethiopian War) (1935–1936) and his intervention on behalf of General Francisco
Franco in the SPANISH CIVIL WAR (1936–1939). But friction emerged again
in 1938, when Mussolini, who by then had linked his regime to Hitler's in the
Rome-Berlin Axis, issued very unpopular anti-Semitic decrees. Pius XI criticized these unequivocally on 21 July. On 20 September he explained to Belgian
pilgrims, "Spiritually we are Jews." Amid ensuing recriminations, fascists confiscated several issues of the Vatican newspaper. As the tenth anniversary of the
Lateran pacts neared, Pius XI planned to use that occasion to speak to the Italian
episcopate criticizing Mussolini's actions. But death struck him first on 10 February 1939.

His successor, Pius XII, tried to improve relations with the fascist regime in
the hope of preventing World War II. After Hitler launched that war in September 1939, the pope urged King Victor Emmanuel III to restrain Mussolini from
entering the war. But by 10 June 1940, that strategy, too, had failed. Italy's

series of military defeats led to the successful Allied invasion of Sicily in July 1943. Two weeks later (24/25 July), a coup d'état by the king and Marshal Pietro Badoglio easily overthrew Mussolini's by now unpopular fascist regime. The papacy shed no tears for the deposed dictator, turning quickly to Catholic Action and the new Christian Democratic Party to defend its interests in Italy.

Nazi Germany. In Germany popular dissatisfaction with the postwar Weimar Republic intensified during the depression and led to huge gains by Adolf Hitler's racist National Socialist Party on the far Right and by communists on the far Left. Hitler maneuvered himself into the chancellorship of Germany on 30 January 1933 by cleverly allying with Franz von Papen (a conservative former chancellor) and with Alfred Hugenberg's Nationalist Party. But to achieve full "emergency" powers, Hitler needed a two-thirds majority in Parliament. To this end, he called for a new parliamentary election in March. Even after that, he needed the votes of the powerful Center Party, which, with the Bavarian People's Party ally, represented a large proportion of the 30 million German Catholics and accounted for 13.9 percent of the popular vote. As soon as Hitler secured Catholic support for passage of the required Enabling Act, he dissolved Parliament and set about implementing his totalitarian dictatorship.

In light of what followed, the Center Party bore a grave responsibility for giving Hitler the necessary votes in March 1933. But at that time party leaders did not see it that way: for them, as for most Germans, the choice seemed to be Hitler or the communists, and Hitler was preferable because he stood for Germany, discipline, and private property. Moreover, Vice-Chancellor von Papen was a zealous Catholic and former member of the Center Party. Most Catholics felt that surely von Papen, together with President Paul von Hindenburg, the aged national hero who had appointed Hitler chancellor, could civilize and control him.

The Nazi führer needed civilizing. His *Mein Kampf* was a thoroughly un-Catholic book, and the bishops had banned Catholic membership in the Nazi Party in several German states. On 28 March 1933, however, that ban was lifted so that von Papen could start negotiations with the Catholic leadership for a national concordat—something that had eluded the leaders of the Weimar Republic. Hitler saw the concordat as a means of neutralizing Catholic political hostility—as was soon proved by the willingness of the CENTER PARTY to dissolve itself on 4 July 1933. The concordat was completed with unusual speed and signed on 20 July. Cardinal Eugenio Pacelli, Pius XI's secretary of state, was largely responsible for its content. Pacelli understood the evil nature of Nazism but believed that a national concordat would give the church more legal standing and might strengthen moderates around the führer. By terms of the concordat, the government retained the right to veto episcopal appointments and to require an oath of loyalty to Hitler. Catholic political and social organizations that competed with Nazi ones would be eliminated. In return, the government guaranteed freedom of religion, protection of church institutions, the right to

disseminate papal letters and encyclicals, permission to establish Catholic theological faculties at universities, and the preservation of Catholic public primary
education.

Within five days after the signing of the concordat, Hitler, without regard for
Catholic teaching, promulgated a law calling for the compulsory sterilization of
certain categories of people. In 1934, when Rome placed *The Myth of the Twentieth Century*, written by Alfred Rosenberg, on its INDEX, Hitler replied by
suppressing the pastoral letter in which the German bishops refuted Rosenberg's
theories. Between 1933 and 1939 the Vatican dispatched 105 notes of protest
to Berlin. In 1935 Hitler established a Ministry of Church Affairs, and "immorality" trials of priests and nuns began to take place. Meanwhile, in 1935–
1936, Nazism's ideological fervor increased as doctrines of race, blood, and
conquest were expounded by Joseph Goebbels, Martin Bormann, and other fa-
natics. Intimidation and persecution of Jews began in April 1933 and were intensified by the discriminatory Nuremberg Laws (15 September 1935) and
especially by the pogroms and mass arrests that followed Crystal Night (9/10
November 1938). Although most Germans (both Catholics and Protestants) did
not oppose Hitler's anti-Semitic and racist policies, at least a handful of religious
leaders began to speak out against them. On the Catholic side, Cardinal Faulhaber of Munich defended in sermons the Jewish "ancestors of all Christians
according to the spirit," while Bishops Galen of Munster and Preysing of Berlin
condemned not only the Nuremberg Laws, which forbade intermarriage between
Aryans and Jews, but the whole racist HERESY.

In 1936 the German episcopate, meeting in Fulda, sent an urgent appeal to
Pius XI for an encyclical exposing the plight of Catholicism in Hitler's Germany. The pope responded on 14 March 1937 with an encyclical in German,
Mit brennender Sorge (With Deep Anxiety). Drawn up with the assistance of
Cardinals Pacelli and Faulhaber, it was printed secretly in Germany and read
from the pulpits on Palm Sunday. It was the most serious public denunciation
of Hitler's regime and its ideals to which the dictator was ever subjected at
home. The pope spoke of "the vain attempt to imprison God, Creator of the
Universe . . . within the confines of a common blood or a single race," of "aggressive neopaganism," of a "war of extermination" waged against the church.
Hitler was furious and forbade the encyclical to be circulated. But he stopped
short of a complete breach with the Catholic Church.

Many German Catholics still imagined that an accommodation was possible.
Von Papen was one of these. In 1934, Hitler appointed him ambassador to
Austria to prepare the climate there for German annexation of that Catholic
country. When the anschluss (merger) finally occurred in March 1938, Cardinal
Innitzer, the archbishop of Vienna and primate of Austria, enthusiastically welcomed the German takeover. His action incurred the wrath of Pius XI. The Nazis
lost no time in launching a campaign to convert the Austrians to Nazi beliefs
and attacked Catholic education at all levels. But only after Hitler invaded Poland in September 1939 did Nazi persecution of the Catholic Church in Germany

and especially in the German-conquered territories to the east reach the intensity of a second *KULTURKAMPF.*

For further reference: Daniel A. Binchy, *Church and State in Fascist Italy* (London: Oxford University Press, 1941, reprinted with new preface, 1970); John S. Conway, *The Nazi Persecution of the Churches 1933–45* (New York: Basic Books, 1968); Guenter Lewy, *The Catholic Church and Nazi Germany* (New York: McGraw-Hill, 1964); Anthony Rhodes, *The Vatican in the Age of the Dictators, 1922–1945* (London: Hodder and Stoughton, 1973); Hansjakob Stehle, *Eastern Politics of the Vatican, 1917–1979,* trans. Sandra Smith (Athens: Ohio University Press, 1981).

Charles F. Delzell

TOURS, BATTLE OF. SEE DONATION OF PEPIN.

TRENT, COUNCIL OF (1545–1563). Regarded as the nineteenth general COUNCIL of the Roman Catholic Church, its assignment was the healing of the division of Western Christianity caused by the Protestant REFORMATION, agreement on genuine reform that would rid the church of worldliness, and the encouragement of harmony among all Catholic princes. Although Pope PAUL III (1534–1549) was alternately engaged and hesitant, the clamor of the conciliarists and of such new organizations as the Capuchins (1530s) and the SOCIETY OF JESUS (1540), the advance of Protestantism even into Italy, and the incessant pressure of Charles V of the Holy Roman Empire ultimately aroused Paul, who was obliged, in the summer if 1541, to call for a council.

Inaugurated on 13 December 1545 (and closed on 4 December 1563), it was scheduled for Trent, a city northwest of Venice. The Tridentine Council occupied the pontificates of four popes, and held twenty-five plenary sessions, seventeen substantive and eight ritualistic. Because of the decrees' liturgical and juridical significance, the session's meetings were in the Cathedral of St. Vigilius, where the opening ceremonies had taken place, or at another prominent church nearby. Voting rights were restricted to the 229 ''Fathers of the Council,'' interpreted as the bishops and the generals in command of the mendicant orders. Together, they determined the agenda in compliance with the original papal charge. The presiding officer was the senior officer of the legateship. The most proficient of the LEGATES was Cardinal Giovanni Marone, selected by PAUL IV, in March 1563. A staunch papal spokesman, Marone, with his acute mind and tireless energies, brought Trent to a climax, marked by a last-minute passage of reform measures and the reassertion of papal supremacy.

Political rivalries and opposing interests of major personalities and groups impeded the council's labors. Emperor Charles V favored fundamental change in creed, structure, and practice, if need be, to win back the Protestants, locked in his realm in a series of devastating religious wars with the Catholics. Since he assumed that accelerating religious conflict would seriously weaken Charles' capacity to wage war, Francis I of France had been neither enthusiastically disposed toward the idea of a council nor prepared when it eventuated to collaborate fully for its success. Chagrined over their failure at Pisa (1409–1410), CONSTANCE (1414–1417), and BASEL (1431–1449) to place the source of church authority in a council of broad representation, the conciliarists were determined to exploit the general indignation stemming from the split in Latin Christendom to vindicate their stance. With total submission to the pope as an indispensable requirement for membership, the SOCIETY OF JESUS, founded by Ignatius de Loyola in Rome in 1534 and approved by Paul III in 1540 could be counted upon to counter any conciliar plan that would diminish papal power. As for the Protestants, Pope Paul's delaying tactics in summoning a council and his approval and extension of the Draconian tribunals and methods of the Holy Office of the INQUISITION (1542) combined to make his sincerity suspect. From its inception, Protestants did not acknowledge Trent as an authentic council. Protestant states may have sent ambassadors and theologians, granted safe passage by Emperor Charles, but they were present only as observers during the second phase, 1551–1552.

The council's work was interrupted several times due to deaths of popes. Trent was coincidental with the reign of Paul III (1534–1549), JULIUS III (1550–1555), PAUL IV (1555–1559), and PIUS IV (1559–1565). Upon taking office, each pope reinstated the council. Besides the distractions of open religious controversy, the city of Trent proved too small to accommodate a vast assemblage of dignitaries on a scale to which they had become accustomed, so many councillors periodically absented themselves from Trent.

In its most important decisions, the council rejected all Protestant viewpoints, thus eliminating any possibility of compromise and reunion. Institutional salvation was reaffirmed in Trent's Profession of Faith's reference to "the Holy Mother Church." Traditions from apostolic times were coequal and as authoritative as the Scriptures. The essential role of the priesthood was underscored, and higher prelates were to be revered as "the Fathers of the Church." Following prolonged debate on Luther's doctrine of justification by faith alone, the Tridentine Council, with few dissenting votes, denounced it and allowed works to be coupled with faith in the experience of salvation. The dogmatic nature of the seven sacraments was defined and upheld, as was their crucial meaning in the unfolding life of the devout Christian. Similarly, by the Euchartist Decree of 11 October 1551, the character of the mass as sacrificial was emphasized, as was Christ's actual presence in the bread and the wine (transubstantiation). The existence of purgatory as a transitional stage, veneration of the saints, respect for relics, and monastic vows were all affirmed as irrefutable manifestations of religious beliefs, as well as marriage and its indissolubility, in contrast to the doubts and denials circulated by Protestant Reformers. In summary form, the "Six Canons" of 17 June 1556 condemned the Protestant position on original sin. On the subject of indulgences, which had sparked the REFORMATION, the adherents to Trent settled the issue not by decree but by simple pronouncement. Indulgences represented a legitimate spiritual exercise but were not to be pursued as miraculous in themselves.

Administratively, the council agreed on the setting up of seminaries for a stricter training of the clergy. After several postponements, the council placed all religious societies and their constituencies under the immediate supervision of local bishops. To prevent accumulation of sinecures and benefices by CURIA officials residing in Rome, cardinals and bishops were to dwell in their dioceses. Unable, however, to spell out precisely the nature of the obligation, a substitute proposal was then enacted, recommending that priests and bishops preach every Sunday and on holy days to their parishioners. Trent confirmed the Inquisition and accepted the Index of Forbidden Books (1559) to include all the writings of Protestant heretics but also of such anticlericals as Machiavelli and Baccaccio and of novelists whose characters did not portray Christian virtue at its best.

On the constitutional issue, whether the church was a monarchy, and the pope ruled by right of apostolic succession or a community of believers governed by a council representative of broad cross-sections of the universal church, with the pope the executor of its will, the question was resolved clearly in favor of monarchy and papal reign. True, it was decided by a bare majority, on 20 April 1562, that bishops held their rank independent of the pope, and at the last session, 3–4 December 1563, each of the 229 fathers extended his placet (endorsement) to all Trent had accomplished, but the popes convoked, suspended, and recalled the council. Pro-papal elements, led by Marone and the Jesuits, argued that any transfer of power from the supreme pontiff to a general council would severely undermine the momentum of the Catholic Reformation, then in full force. In spite of the agreement reached at Constance for stated periodic convening of general councils, the next council, known as VATICAN COUN-CIL I, was not summoned until 1869 by Pius IX, over 300 years after Trent.

For further reference: Hubert Jedin, *Geschichte das Konzils von Trent*, 4 vols. in 5 (Freiburg: Herder, 1951–1975); Herbert T. Mayer, *The Story of the Council of Trent* (St. Louis: Concordia Publishing House, 1962); Sforza Pallavicino, *Storia del Concilio di Trento*, 3 vols., ed. Mario Scotti (Turin: UTET, 1968); Paolo Sarpi, *Storia del Concilio Tridentino*, 2 vols. (Florence: Sansomi, 1982).

Ronald S. Cunsolo

TRIBUNAL. An ecclesiastical tribunal or "church court" is any person or persons who exercise judicial power within the church. A tribunal can be, for example, the Roman pontiff himself, who alone exercises supreme judicial power for the universal church, a diocesan bishop, who exercises judicial power for his particular diocese, or any person or persons constituted as a "tribunal" with the POPE or the bishop and who share in his judicial power. According to CANON LAW, judicial power is to be exercised in the manner prescribed by law (canon 135.2). The existence of such tribunals has been in evidence within the church since earliest times. Their presence within the Christian community has been demonstrated in the Scriptures, for example, in the Gospel of Matthew (18:15–18), where wrongdoers are encouraged to be referred to the church for judgment, and in the writings of the early church fathers. As the church community grew, and its discipline became increasingly defined, ecclesiastical tribunals began to appear and served an important decision-making role among the believers. With this historical development also came the establishment of certain judicial procedures, heavily influenced by ancient Roman law, which governed the administration of justice by the church courts.

The organization of the church's judicial power into a tribunal or court system is rather simple, although the procedures to be observed by tribunals are quite complex. Unlike American civil courts, ecclesiastical tribunals neither operate on a system of precedents nor create new law through the interpretive judgments they render. Their main responsibility is to reconcile the norms of church law with the controversies brought before them for resolution. Over the centuries, the church has developed an intricate system of laws and procedures to exercise its jurisdiction and to adjudicate matters presented to its tribunals. Most of the currently used procedures and legislation may be found in Book VII of the 1983 Code of Canon Law. These complicated procedures prescribed by ecclesiastical law and followed within church tribunals are designed to assist the court in rendering its decisions in a way that balances the common good of the Christian community with the rights of the individual(s) concerned.

At present, the object of most tribunal activity in the church is the resolution of questions relating to the validity of marriages. The work of a tribunal, however, is not limited to handling marital disputes. The prosecution or vindication of ecclesiastical rights as well as the imposition or declaration of ecclesiastical penalties are also the concern of church tribunals. According to the 1983 Code of Canon Law, the church claims jurisdiction over all spiritual matters as well as any infraction of ecclesiastical law "by proper and exclusive right (canon 1401)." Anyone, whether a baptized member of the church or not, has access to a church tribunal for the resolution of any legal controversy involving some ecclesiastical concern (canon 1476). The judgments of church courts, however, have no civil effects whatsoever but, rather, pertain to the spiritual welfare of those in need of the tribunal's services.

Depending on the nature of the need itself, an appropriate or "competent forum" exists where that issue may be addressed. Unless the matter is reserved by ecclesiastical law to another tribunal, most issues requiring ecclesiastical adjudication are presented at the diocesan level. The diocesan bishop alone or those he associates with himself in the exercise of judicial power (the judicial vicar and the diocesan judges) are constituted as the "tribunal of first instance." Usually, although not always, this tribunal is composed of three judges as a "collegiate court." Although by past law and tradition, the exercise of judicial power had been reserved to the ordained clergy, in certain cases the 1983 Code of Canon Law permits qualified members of the laity to act as judges along with the clergy in a collegiate court.

If canon law requires the review of the decision of the tribunal of first instance before it is considered binding, or if a party or parties involved should appeal that decision, the matter is forwarded to a "tribunal of second instance," constituted in the same way as the lower court, only with a different composition of judges. This tribunal exists under the jurisdiction of the metropolitan archbishop of a region and functions in the same way as its first instance counterpart. In addition to these ecclesiastical courts, there exist "tribunals of the Apostolic See." These tribunals are considered the courts of the Roman pontiff and include (1) the Sacred Penitentiary, whose jurisdiction is limited to those matters of the internal forum: absolutions, dispensations, penal sanctions, and the like; (2) the Roman Rota, whose jurisdiction includes all judicial cases submitted to the Apostolic See as a first instance court or as an appeal from lower-level decisions; and, (3) the Supreme Tribunal of the Apostolic Signatura, whose jurisdiction involves cases decided by the Roman Rota and appealed by the parties concerned or cases introducing charges against the judges of the Roman Rota.

Any controversy ordinarily presented to a lower-level court may be presented directly to the Roman Rota or the Apostolic Signatura, but their activity is more frequently confined to the resolution of appeals of lower-level decisions. The Roman pontiff also uses these courts for matters reserved by law to his jurisdiction. The Apostolic Signatura also monitors the activities of all lower-level tribunals throughout the world. There is usually no appeal of a decision pronounced by a tribunal of the Apostolic See.

For further reference: William Basset and Peter Huizing, eds., *Judgement in the Church* (New York: Seabury Press, 1977); James A. Coriden et al., *The Code of Canon Law: A Text and Commentary* (New York and Mahwah, NJ: Paulist Press, 1985).

David M. O'Connell

TÜBINGEN, UNIVERSITY OF. The University of Tübingen, founded in 1477, contains several faculties, including a faculty of Protestant theology and a faculty of Catholic theology, founded in 1817. In the nineteenth century both faculties played an important role in theological discussion. As one of the oldest universities in Germany, Tübingen has gone through several periods in its growth. In Catholic Tübingen speculative and historical theology became mutually enriching and influenced many other Catholic faculties in Europe. Soon the phrase "the Tübingen School" referred to the method and contributions of the faculties of theology, both Protestant and Catholic.

By the middle of the nineteenth century the Catholic faculty at Tübingen was appreciated as the leading exponent of the "romantic" school of theology, that is, a method that attempts to view Catholicism as an organic whole. This view was later influential in the documents (on the church) of VATICAN II. Among its most famous theologians was Johann-Adam Möhler. In the course of Möhler's career, he entered into spirited discussion with F. C. Baur, the famous Protestant Tübingen theologian, who inaugurated a historical-critical method that has endured until contemporary times. Several of the theologians and bishops present at the first COUNCIL of the Vatican (1869–1870) had been students of the Catholic faculty at Tübingen. The Catholic faculty still publishes *Theologische Quartalschrift*, which began publication in 1819. The Protestant faculty continues to have a major influence on biblical scholarship in the United States.

For further reference: Horton Harris, *The Tübingen School* (Oxford: Clarendon Press, 1975); R. W. Mackay, *The Tübingen School and Its Antecedents* (Edinburgh: Williams and Norgate, 1863).

Loretta Devoy

U

UNITED NATIONS AND THE VATICAN. Although extremely active diplomatically before and during WORLD WAR II, the Vatican was not directly involved in the establishment of the United Nations (UN). In the first place, the UN was created by the Allies on the verge of victory, and the Vatican had attempted to remain "neutral" through much of the war in order to protect Catholics on both sides of the conflict. Second, the Vatican's "CONCORDAT policy," embarked upon by PIUS XI (1922–1939) and refined by PIUS XII (1939–1958), received a great deal of criticism in the postwar period as having put Catholicism in the position of "treating with the devil" to advance its diplomatic goals.

The Vatican did have a permanent observer to the United Nations Educational, Scientific, and Cultural Organization (UNESCO) and to the Food Agricultural Organization, both UN organizations, but no representation at the new international body itself. Under Pius XII, the Vatican interested itself only sparingly in the UN, except for the organization's charitable and humanitarian activities. Pius had little use for international organizations, and he preferred to continue to treat with individual states in order to protect the church's rights in societies around the globe. Pius infrequently addressed the United Nations in his elocutions; and when he did so, he directed his remarks to specific UN organizations, not to the UN itself. When the pontiff directed his remarks to these organizations, such as the Relief and Rehabilitation Administration and the International Labor Organization, he invariably focused on their humanitarian work and usually repeated his belief that individual states must respect the rights of the church.

This aloof Vatican stance toward the United Nations changed dramatically with the accession of Cardinal Giovanni Battista Montini to the papal throne in 1963 as PAUL VI (1963–1978). Paul quickly pressed for official representation at UN headquarters, which was granted in 1964, when the Vatican sent its first permanent observer. In 1965, the pontiff marked the new diplomatic direction toward the UN by delivering a speech to the General Assembly in New York. The pope's historic speech was a ringing endorsement of the United Nations as an institution. Paul saw the UN as the mirror image of what the Catholic Church intends to be in the spiritual order: one and universal. He said that the goals of the UN and those of Vatican diplomacy were one and the same: to be against war and for peace. Throughout the Pauline papacy, the UN was seen as a natural forum for solving problems, for keeping the peace, and for ensuring the rights of the less developed world, all within a supranational organization, unencumbered—much like the Vatican—by petty nationalistic jealousies and arrogance.

Strong support of the UN has, however, been lacking when the organization has taken on questions of population control. In 1974 and 1984, the Vatican refused to consent to the collective views expressed at the decennial world population conferences that suggested artificial birth control as a strategy. In 1994, the Vatican led a spirited and largely successful offense against language that would have suggested that abortion was an acceptable means of birth control and even a human right. However, these clashes with the UN did not weaken overall Vatican support for the United Nations and much of its work around the world, support that began in earnest under Paul VI and continues under JOHN PAUL II.

For further reference: Matthew Bunson, *The Pope Encyclopedia* (New York: Crown Trade Paperbacks, 1995); Peter Nichols, *The Politics of the Vatican* (New York: Praeger, 1968).

Richard J. Wolff

UNITED STATES AND THE VATICAN. The United States and the Holy See had their first official contacts in the early days of the republic during the last troubled days of the pontificate of PIUS VI (1775–1799), when the United States sent a consular official to Rome. The consular relationship was elevated in 1848, during the early years of the pontificate of Pope PIUS IX (1846–1878), when the United States established a diplomatic mission to the PAPAL STATES. The first diplomatic representative of the United States accredited to the pope was Jacob I. Martin. This relationship between the United States and the papal states ended in 1867, when the U.S. Congress prohibited the financing of any diplomatic post to the papal states.

The closing of the U.S. diplomatic mission in 1867 initiated a long interregnum of 72 years, when the United States had no diplomatic representative to the pope. The absence of diplomatic representation coincided with the period of strong anti-Catholicism in the United States. It was a time when an increasing number of immigrants from predominantly Catholic countries were arriving, and there was a strong negative reaction against the Irish, the French, Italians, Poles, Spanish, and Germans. The contemporary literature was full of highly intemperate and, in some cases, vicious characterizations of the leadership of the

Catholic Church. It is difficult to imagine that there would have been any kind of approval by the American Congress for diplomatic representation to the pope in the circumstances of the late nineteenth and early twentieth centuries in the United States.

This absence of diplomatic relationship ended in 1939, when President Franklin Roosevelt dispatched a "personal envoy" of the president that would represent him in conversations with the pope. Myron Taylor, the first special envoy, was not a diplomatic representative of the U.S. government but an agent of the president. Following WORLD WAR II, especially with the onset of the COLD WAR, the U.S. government saw the advantages of some regular diplomatic relationship with the papacy. Both the Holy See and the United States had an anticommunist focus. This resulted in a convergence of interests in many cases in the post–World War II period. The Holy See emerged as a major supporter of the UNITED NATIONS since its foundation in 1945. Indeed, when the support of the United States for the United Nations was reduced in the 1960s and 1970s, the Holy See continued to give moral support to the world organization.

The 1984 proposal of President Reagan for the establishment of full diplomatic relations started a public debate on the questions of such a relationship. William A. Wilson was confirmed by a landslide vote, serving as U.S. ambassador from 1984 to 1986, when he was succeeded by Frank Shakespeare, who served until 1989. Dr. Thomas P. Melady was U.S. ambassador from 1989 to 1993, and he was succeeded by Raymond L. Flynn. Archbishop Pio Laghi was the NUNCIO of the Holy See to the United States from 1984 to 1991. He was succeeded by Archbishop Agostino Cacciavillan. The cornerstone of diplomatic cooperation between the Holy See and the United States is the mutual respect for religious freedom and human rights and concern for humanitarian affairs. This convergence was a main factor in the United States–Vatican cooperation that played a major role in the ending of communist control in Poland, Czechoslovakia, and the other Eastern European countries. Similar cooperation occurred when violations of religious freedom and/or human rights occurred in Sudan, Malawi, Ethiopia, South Africa, Liberia, Indonesia, Vietnam, and China.

One area where the Holy See and the United States have not converged is in the use of force to solve international problems. In the case of the Gulf War, the Holy See, recognizing the illegality of Iraq's takeover of Kuwait in 1990, opposed the use of war to free Kuwait. The Holy See in the past has been supportive of the "just war" theory but, with the advent of the pontificate of JOHN PAUL II (1978–   ), proved increasingly reluctant to justify the use of war under any circumstance. With the ending of the Soviet Union's superpower status in the early 1990s, the anticommunist aspect that had, in some cases, energized the convergence of the Vatican and Washington disappeared. Other issues assumed increasing importance. The pope, in addition to being the head of the government of the Holy See, is first and foremost head of the universal Catholic Church. This fact did not complicate United States–Vatican relationships during the more conservative Reagan–Bush presidencies. Starting with the

Clinton presidency in 1993, however, the American president and the pope differed sharply on several moral issues, above all, abortion.

Despite these differences it appears likely that the Holy See and the United States will find many areas of convergence in the world. The United States, as the world's superpower, and the Holy See, as the world's universal moral power, will confront many challenges where their cooperation will serve their vital interests while being of service to the world community.

For further reference: Daniel G. Babis and Anthony J. Maceli, *A United States Ambassador to the Vatican* (New York: Pageant, 1952); Gerald B. Fogarty, *The Vatican and the American Hierarchy from 1870 to 1965* (Wilmington, DE: Michael Glazier, 1985); Thomas Patrick Melady, *The Ambassador's Story* (Huntington, IN: Our Sunday Visitor, 1994); Leo Francis Stock, ed., *United States Ministers to the Papal States: Instructions and Despatches 1848–1868* (Washington, DC: Catholic University Press, 1933).

Thomas Patrick Melady

URBAN I (222–230). Eusebius indicates that Urban succeeded CALLISTUS I (217–222) and that he was bishop of the church of the Romans for eight years. The Liberian Catalogue gives the length of his rule as almost nine years. Little is known about Urban since the references in the *Liber Pontificalis* are either anachronistic (e.g., his being a confessor in the time of Diocletian) or confused (e.g., his connection with the conversion of St. Cecelia's husband). There is no evidence that the Antipope HIPPOLYTUS came into conflict with Urban, although he had confrontations with Urban's two immediate predecessors and lived through the reign of Urban's successor, PONTIAN (230–235). Furthermore, there is no reason to believe that Urban was a martyr, since the church enjoyed a period of peace under Alexander Severus, the emperor at the time. Urban was buried in the Cemetery of Callistus. His feast is celebrated on 25 May.

For further reference: J. N. D. Kelly, *The Oxford Dictionary of Popes* (Oxford: Oxford University Press, 1986), pp. 15ff.; J. Lebreton and J. Zeiller, *History of the Primitive Church*, vol. 4 (London: Burns, Oates, and Washbourne, 1948).

Bernard J. Cassidy

URBAN II (1088–1099). Urban II (Odo of Lagery), successor to Victor III (1086–1087), was born in Chatillons-sur-Marne, France, and studied at Rheims under St. Bruno (c. 1030–1101), founder of the Carthusians. In 1068 the future POPE became a monk at Cluny and later its prior. He was appointed cardinal-bishop of Ostia by GREGORY VII (1073–1085). Urban was elected in 1088, but the opposition of the Holy Roman Emperor Henry IV and the election of an ANTIPOPE, Clement II, forced Urban to spend the early years of his pontificate in southern Italy, under the protection of the Normans. He was unable to occupy the See of Rome until 1093.

The aims of Urban were to eliminate lay influence in determining ecclesiastical appointments and church policy, strengthen the priesthood by requiring celibacy, and heal the split with Byzantium. In 1095 he deposed the bishop of Cambrai because he had received his office from Henry IV and excommunicated (see Excommunication) Philip I of France for adultery. But he was unable to obtain all the back revenues from England.

Urban's most far-reaching act was to launch the First Crusade. At the COUNCIL of Clermont (1095) the pope issued a call for an army to defeat the Muslims. In doing this, he took up the theme of Gregory VII's unsuccessful call to drive the Muslims out of Spain and the East. Urban probably envisioned the reunion of East and West, with recognition of the primacy of Rome. His exact words at the Council of Clermont have not survived, but his call struck a response. Thousands moved eastward. Normally, the kings would have been the natural leaders of such an expedition, but the rulers of England, France, and the Germanic states were estranged from the papacy. By default, therefore, the pope became the titular head of a polyglot army that swarmed toward Jerusalem. This international movement continued, off and on, for nearly 200 years (1095–1291).

Urban apparently also issued one of the earliest general indulgences in the medieval church: word spread that he had granted to the crusaders remission of temporal punishment for their sins. He also promised that they could retain any lands they conquered. Urban died less than one month after the crusaders won Jerusalem, before the news reached Rome. Urban was beatified in 1881.

For further reference: C. Erdmann, *The Origins of the Idea of Crusade*, trans. M. W. Baldwin and W. Goffart (Princeton: Princeton University Press, 1977); H. E. Mayer, *The Crusaders*, trans. J. Gillingham, 2d ed. (Oxford: Oxford University Press, 1988); S. Runciman, *The Eastern Schism: A Study of the Papacy and the Eastern Churches during the XIth and XIIth Centuries* (Oxford: Oxford University Press, 1955).

Frank Grande

URBAN III (1185–1187). In his two-year reign as Pope Urban III, Umberto Crivelli was best known as a bitter enemy of Emperor Frederick I, Barbarossa. Crivelli was archdeacon of Bourges and archbishop of Milan, in 1182 was appointed cardinal-deacon of St. Lorenzo by LUCIUS III (1181–1185), and became archbishop of Milan in 1185. Upon the death of Lucius III, he was unanimously elected pope in Verona. Urban inherited the major problems that originated during Lucius' time as pope, most notably, the dilemma of Prince Henry's marriage to Roger II of Sicily's daughter, the SCHISM created by the split vote to the archbishopric of Trier, and the issue of crowning Henry as emperor while Frederick was still head of state. Unlike his predecessor, however, Urban was an avowed enemy of Frederick's and spent his time as pontiff wrangling over matters between church and empire.

Urban could not prevent the marriage of Henry and Constance in 1186, but he maintained his refusal to crown Henry while his father was emperor. In retribution, Frederick arranged for the patriarch of Aquileia to crown Henry king of Italy. To further complicate relations, Urban promised Frederick that he would not oppose the consecration of the emperor's candidate, Rudolph, to the see of Trier, but he went back on his word. At the end of 1186, Frederick went on the offensive. First, he instructed his son to occupy the PAPAL STATES and isolate Urban and the CURIA from the outside world. At the same time, Frederick convened an assembly of German bishops at Gelsenhausen in November to protest the hostility of the papacy toward the Crown. The bishops sided with Frederick and sent a mission to advise Urban to put aside hostilities. Infuriated, Urban planned for Frederick's EXCOMMUNICATION, but the event never took place. Urban, at the insistence of the city fathers, left Verona. On 20 October 1187, he died of dysentery in Ferrara while on his way to Venice. He was laid to rest in the Duomo in Verona.

For further reference: Eric John, *The Popes: A Concise Bibliographical History* (London: Burns and Oates, 1964); H. K. Mann, *The Lives of the Popes in the Early Middle Ages* (London: K. Paul, 1902–1932).

Christopher S. Myers

URBAN IV (1261–1264). Jacques Pantaléon de Court-Palais, born of a shoemaker in Troyes, France, worked his way up to archdeacon of Liège. He was summoned to the papal court at Lyons by INNOCENT IV (1243–1254), who sent him as LEGATE to Poland, Prussia, and northern Germany before making him bishop of Verdun in 1252. In 1255, his predecessor, ALEXANDER IV (1254–1261), named him patriarch to the Latin monarchy in Constantinople, and, in that capacity, he was on business in Rome when Alexander died at Viterbo on 26 May 1261. Elected POPE on 29 August, those who selected him shared his fear of Hohenstaufen power. Within a few months of his election, Urban had managed to install secular rulers dependent on the Roman See and to recover the papal territories lost by Alexander IV. He also quickly filled fourteen vacant posts with cardinals, six of whom were decisive and supportive Frenchmen.

Urban offered the Crown of Sicily to the French king in his effort to oust the Hohenstaufens. When Louis IX refused the offer, Urban approached the king's brother, Charles of Anjou, who accepted. In the process, he liquidated the claims of the English; but Manfred, the bastard son of Frederick II, stood in the way of Urban's plans for Sicily. Posing as a papal champion with Eastern imperial support, Manfred blocked Urban's plans; and when he learned of the plots to dispossess the Hohenstaufens, he attacked the papal territories, thus forcing Urban to flee from Rome to Orvieto and then to Perugia, where he died on 2 October 1264.

Urban's failure to stop the Hohenstaufens from gaining control of Sicily was only a temporary setback in the power struggle between the German imperial house and the Angevins. Ultimately, the Angevins won out, and the Hohenstaufen claims in Italy were permanently undermined. Urban has the dubious distinction of having created the Angevin problem and having "stacked" the College of CARDINALS with French supporters of his cause. Yet he is honored for his bull *Transiturus* (1264), universalizing the celebration of the feast of Corpus Christi (Body of Christ), which he brought from France.

For further reference: E. John, *The Popes* (New York: Hawthorn Books, 1964); J. N. D. Kelly, *The Oxford Dictionary of Popes* (Oxford: Oxford University Press, 1986); H. K. Mann, *The Lives of the Popes in the Early Middle Ages* (London: K. Paul, 1902–1932).

Anne Paolucci

URBAN V (1362–1370). After the death of INNOCENT VI (1352–1362), the cardinals first elected Hugues Roger, who declined the office. The cardinals then chose Guillaume de Grimoard, a humble Benedictine monk who was not a member of the CURIA. He was crowned in Avignon in December 1362 as Urban V, the sixth of the Avignon POPES. Urban was a pious and learned man who continued to wear the black monastic garb from his days in the abbey. He confessed daily and, with his detachment from wealth, wished for a more austere court. He reduced the mandatory tithes and took measures to reduce the greed within the church. He subsidized hundreds of students and contributed his vast collection of books to the Vatican Library.

Urban established two goals for his pontificate: the return of the papacy to Rome and the reunion with the Byzantine church. Both were formidable tasks. The PAPAL STATES had been dominated for years by Bernabò Visconti and his allies, but in April 1363 the long campaign of Albornoz was capped by a victory that returned Italy to the control of the pope. To the chagrin of the French cardinals and court, Urban announced that he would move back to Rome and left Avignon on 30 April 1367. He first went to Orvieto and then entered Rome with a large military escort on 16 October. Urban immediately set about rebuilding the dilapidated churches and other buildings. St. John Lateran, which had been burned down in 1360, during the papacy of Innocent VI, was reconstructed.

In April 1363, Urban declared a new crusade against the Turks in the Holy Land. Ultimately declared a failure, the Western forces were led by King John II of France, who died a year later. Pierre de Lusignan, the king of Cyprus, briefly conquered Alexandria in October 1365 but was unable to hold it. In 1364, the pontiff purchased peace with Bernabò Visconti by paying a huge sum in return for the surrender of Bologna; Urban believed that Bernabò could be persuaded to turn his forces toward the Holy Land and join the fight against the Turks. Urban also held out hope of a reunion between his court and the Byzantine church by receiving the Byzantine emperor, John V Palaeologus. John appealed to the pontiff for aid in battling the Turks in Constantinople and converted to the Latin Catholic Church.

In 1370, Urban returned to Avignon, arriving there on 27 September. He died on 19 December of that year. Initially interred in the cathedral at Avignon, his remains were ultimately placed at his beloved abbey of St. Victor. He was beatified in 1870 by PIUS IX (1846–1878).

For further reference: Eric John, *The Popes: A Concise Bibliographical History* (London: Burns and Oates, 1964); J. N. D. Kelly, *The Oxford Dictionary of the Popes* (Oxford: Oxford University Press, 1986).

Christopher S. Myers

URBAN VI (1378–1389). Bartholomeo Prignano was born in Naples c. 1318. He entered papal service in Avignon and was named archbishop of Acerenza (1363) and Bari (1377). He returned to Rome with GREGORY XI (1370–1378) from Avignon in 1377. In the conclave of 1378, at which a Roman mob demanded "a Roman or at least an Italian," the votes fell unexpectedly on Prignano on 3 April 1378. He took the name of Urban VI but soon alienated cardinals and princes by his abusive manner.

In the following months the cardinals left Rome and gathered at Anagni, where on 2 August 1378 they declared Urban's election invalid because of coercion. Attempts at reconciliation failed, and on 20 September 1378 the cardinals elected Robert of Geneva as CLEMENT VII (1378–1394). Urban quickly created a new College of CARDINALS and CURIA, and the forty years of confusion known as the Western Schism (see Schism) began. The nations of Europe sided with one or the other claimant as politics dictated. Urban found support principally in Italy, Germany, and England. He strove to secure wider recognition and to impose his will on the kingdom of Naples by force. With time his actions became more bizarre and unpredictable. Some cardinals, judging Urban incapable of ruling, planned to form a council that would serve as a check on his actions. Informed of this plot, Urban tortured the cardinals to uncover the conspirators. Five cardinals were eventually murdered; only an English cardinal escaped with his life. Urban died in Rome on 15 October 1389.

Controversy has swirled around the validity of Urban's election. The cardinals originally questioned Urban's capacity to rule the church, a charge that was not clear at the beginning of his reign but that finds justification even in the reports of supporters at the end of his pontificate.

For further reference: John H. Smith, *The Great Schism 1378: The Disintegration of the Papacy* (New York: Weybright and Talley, 1970); W. Ulmann, *The Origins of the Great Schism* (London: Burns, Oates, and Washbourne, 1948).

Richard J. Kehoe

URBAN VII (1590). Reigning only from 15 to 27 September 1590, Urban was chosen to succeed SIXTUS V (1585–1590) largely through the influence of Spain. He was born Giambattista Castagna at Rome on 4 August 1521, the son of a Genoese nobleman and a Roman mother. Educated at Padua and Perugia, he graduated doctor of laws at Bologna and, in 1551, served on the staff of his uncle, Cardinal Verallo, when the latter went to France as papal LEGATE to Henry II. In 1553 Castagna was named archbishop of Rossano in Calabria. He served briefly as governor of the PAPAL STATE under PAUL IV (1555–1559) and played an active role in the last meetings of the Council of TRENT. In 1564 he was assigned by PIUS IV (1559–1565) to accompany Cardinal Boncompagni, who was later to become GREGORY XIII (1572–1585), and Felice Peretti, the future Sixtus V, on their legation visit to Spain, where he remained as NUNCIO until 1572. After resigning the See of Rossano in 1573, he was named nuncio to Venice and then governor of Bologna. Gregory XIII in 1583 elevated him to the position of cardinal-priest. Sixtus V, whose election he had not initially supported, confirmed him as governor of Bologna and appointed him inquisitor-general.

A popular figure in Rome, he was elected amid great rejoicing and raised hopes that he would prove to be a moderate and experienced pontiff. He was known for his charity and opposition to nepotism and upon his election vowed that his relatives would not be granted high positions or privileges. He promised to supplement the income of the cardinals, who had felt themselves impoverished due to Sixtus V's rigorous economic policy. But, although in good health, he was struck down with malaria the evening after his election and died before his coronation could take place.

For further reference: P. Hughes, *The History of the Church* (London: Sheed and Ward, 1955); L. Pastor, *A History of the Popes from the Close of the Middle Ages* (London: Herder, 1953).

William Roberts

URBAN VIII (1623–1644). Maffeo Barberini was chosen POPE after a contentious conclave. Born at Florence in 1568 of a wealthy merchant family, he was educated by the Jesuits (see Society of Jesus). He became a doctor of laws at Pisa in 1589 and began a successful career in the CURIA. In 1601 he was sent to France as envoy extraordinary to Henry IV and in 1604 returned to serve as NUNCIO. For his service PAUL V (1605–1621) in 1606 named him cardinal and in 1608 bishop of Spoleto. He was made LEGATE of Bologna in 1611 and prefect of the Signatura in 1617.

Upon becoming pontiff, Urban VIII ruled as an authoritarian, rarely discussing important matters with his cardinals. He was a cultured individual and literary connoisseur who composed and published Latin verses. A nepotist, he raised several brothers and nephews to the cardinalate and enriched them. He spent lavishly on the rebuilding of Rome and in November 1626 consecrated the new St. Peter's on the 1300th anniversary of the dedication of the first basilica. Earlier in his pontificate Urban had taken the bronze from the great portico of the Pantheon to construct the huge baldachin over the high altar. Urban also fortified Rome and, in strengthening the Castel Sant' Angelo, again allowed the Pantheon bronze to be looted, this time to be used to provide cannons.

His reign coincided with the Thirty Years' War (1618–1648), during which he struggled to maintain an uneasy neutrality. However, because of his fear of the Hapsburgs, his policy proved pro-French. Even when Richelieu allied with Protestant Sweden, he took no effective action. He only mildly rebuked the French, while severely blaming the emperor Ferdinand for the war. A result of his anti-Hapsburg policy was to bring the COUNTER-REFORMATION in the empire to a close.

Although a political pope, his ecclesiastical activities are of note. In 1634 he confirmed the canonical procedures for canonization and beatification, giving both their final form. He was a strong supporter of the missions and founded the Collegio Urbano (see Colleges of Rome) for the training of missionaries, especially in the Far East. He gave sanction to several new religious orders, including the Lazarists and the orders of the Visitation and of St. Vincent de Paul, and he reaffirmed the decrees of the COUNCIL of TRENT that bishops should reside in their dioceses. Under Urban, Galileo Galilei, who was actually a personal friend, was condemned and forced to recant his Copernican theory of the solar system. He also censured the teaching of Cornelius Jansen in his *Augustinus*, setting off a theological debate that was to last for decades over the questions of grace and predestination.

For further reference: J. N. D. Kelly, *The Oxford Dictionary of Popes* (Oxford: Oxford University Press, 1986); L. Pastor, *A History of the Popes from the Close of the Middle Ages* (London: Herder, 1953).

William Roberts

URSINUS, ANTIPOPE (366–367). The details of Ursinus' early life and the date of his death are unknown. He was a deacon under Pope LIBERIUS (352–366), who returned from exile in 358 and ruled, along with an ANTIPOPE, FELIX II (355–365), until the latter's death in 365. When Liberius died on 24 September 366, his supporters met in the Julian basilica (Santa Maria in Trastevere), elected Ursinus, and had him immediately consecrated. An equally dedicated group of Felix's adherents elected DAMASUS (366–384), who was consecrated in early October after violent clashes between the two factions. Ursinus was exiled to Gaul, while many of his clergy and supporters were arrested.

The bishops of Italy refused to condemn Ursinus; but the government supported Damasus and in 370 decreed that the Ursinians could worship only outside the city walls. An uneasy peace ensued, and Ursinus and his followers were allowed to return to Italy, but not to Rome. They settled in the north, whence he and his followers continued to harass Damasus, to the point of bringing a false charge of adultery against him in 371. Through the intervention of civil authority the charges were dismissed, and Ursinus was again exiled, this time to Cologne. He did not withdraw from active life, however, and was periodically accused of fomenting trouble against Damasus. At the latter's death in 384, Ursinus offered himself for election as bishop but was rejected.

For further reference: Ambrose, *Letter* 11; J. N. D. Kelly, *The Oxford Dictionary of Popes* (Oxford: Oxford University Press, 1986), pp. 34–35; A. Lippold, "Ursinus and Damasus," *Historia* 14 (1965): 105–128; Ammianus Marcellinus, *Rerum gestarum libri* 27, 3; Rufinus, *Church History* 2, 10.

Gerard H. Ettlinger

V

VALENTINE (827). The son of an upper-class Roman family, Valentine entered the clergy during the pontificate of PASCHAL I (817–824), rising to the position of archdeacon. His succession to the chair of St. PETER, following the death of EUGENIUS II (824–827), received unanimous endorsement from the clergy, nobility, and people of Rome. The participation of the nobility and people in his election, although in violation of the decree of the Roman Council (769) that forbade the laity's involvement in papal elections, more accurately reflected the struggle for authority between the church and the Western kings. Lothar, son of the Frankish emperor Louis, had concluded an agreement, the *Constitutio Lothari*, with Eugenius II requiring imperial confirmation as well as swearing oaths of loyalty to the imperial envoy and the Roman people prior to a newly elected POPE's consecration. Valentine's death within three weeks of his consecration permitted little time for him to officiate, and no known acts of his pontificate are recorded.

For further reference: H. K. Mann, *The Lives of the Popes in the Early Middle Ages* (London: K. Paul, 1902–1932); Walter Ullman, *A Short History of the Papacy in the Middle Ages* (London: Methuen, 1972).

John C. Horgan

VATICAN CITY. This is an independent and sovereign member of the international community, with the POPE as its sovereign. Known juridically as Lo Stato del Vaticano, the state was established in 1929 under the terms of the LATERAN ACCORDS (Conciliation Treaty). The 1948 Constitution of the Italian Republic confirmed the Lateran Accords.

Under the Conciliation Treaty a state of 108.7 acres under the sovereignty of the pope was created. Vatican City is in the shape of a trapezoid within the city of Rome and near the right bank of the Tiber River. Vatican City includes buildings and lands that physically are outside the trapezoid and in the Republic of Italy. These buildings and lands also enjoy extraterritoriality, immunity from expropriation, and tax exemption. They are the Basilicas of St. John Lateran, St. Mary Major, and St. Paul Outside the Walls; the buildings of the Chancery, Datary, Holy Office, Propaganda, and Vicariate of Rome; the papal palace at Castel Gandolfo; and the transmission center of Vatican Radio at Santa Maria di Galeria.

Citizenship in Vatican City is accorded to individuals who reside permanently in Vatican City because of their work or papal authorization. Immediate relatives, such as wives and children, who also reside in Vatican City are also considered citizens; so, too, are curial cardinals who reside outside Vatican City. Citizenship is terminated when the conditions for its acquisition no longer obtain.

Though there is a Constitution, Vatican City is an absolute monarchy, at least in theory, with all legislative, executive, and judicial powers residing in the pope. He may, however, delegate some of his powers to others. Thus, his authority in governing Vatican City is entrusted to the Papal Commission for Vatican City, made up of three cardinals. Ordinances and regulations are issued by a governor, who is assisted by a central COUNCIL. For defense purposes Vatican City possesses four armed corps: the Noble Guard, the Palatine Guard of Honor (these first two are largely ceremonial), the Swiss Guards, and the Gendarmerie. The police of the Republic of Italy patrol St. Peter's Square.

Vatican City is required to extradite to the republic individuals accused of crime in either state who take refuge in Vatican City or in any of its extraterritorial possessions. The official language of Vatican City is Italian. The city has its own postage and postal system, coinage, seal, and flag. The Vatican's postal, telephone, telegraph, radio, and railroad services are connected to the outside world. The pope represents Vatican City in its international relations. In accordance with the treaty that created it, Vatican City is perpetually neutral and inviolable. Though not a member of the United Nations, Vatican City may maintain official observers at the United Nations. It has full membership in many international organizations, such as the Universal Postal Union and the Berne Convention for the Protection of Literary and Artistic Works.

For further reference: D. A. Binchy, *Church and State in Fascist Italy* (London: Oxford University Press, 1940); Maria Elisabetta de Franciscis, *Italy and the Vatican* (New York: Peter Lang, 1989); A. Martini, *Studi sulla Questione Romana e la conciliazione* (Rome: Edizioni 5 Lune, 1963); Robert Neville, *The World of the Vatican* (New York: Harper, 1962).

Elisa A. Carrillo

VATICAN COUNCIL I (1869–1870). This twentieth ecumenical COUNCIL of the Roman Catholic Church was convoked by Pope PIUS IX (1846–1878) in 1868 and solemnly convened on 8 December 1869. The council aimed to confront the growing challenge of MODERNISM and liberalism within the church and society. At the time the council began, the former PAPAL STATES had been reduced to Rome and the surrounding area. The French forces were required to protect the remaining papal territory from the designs of the Italian risorgimento. Approximately 800 prelates—cardinals, patriarchs, archbishops, bishops, abbots, and superiors general of religious orders—attended the council. These official representatives were accompanied by teams of theological consultants or experts.

Preparation for the council was the primary responsibility of a Central Preparatory Committee. This committee directed five subordinate commissions, dealing with questions of church doctrine, discipline, religious orders, Eastern churches and missions, and politico-religious affairs. Once the council got under way, these various deputations came under the direction of newly appointed official committees headed by cardinals and bishops, which were charged with presenting issues and drafting documents for the general assemblies of the council.

In the course of 86 meetings, the general assemblies prepared 51 documents, but only 6 of these were discussed at the four public sessions of the council. Despite this cumbersome procedure, the council was able to give solemn approval to two significant dogmatic documents: the constitution *Dei Filius*, which examined the meaning of revelation and the relation of faith to reason and the constitution *Pastor Aeternus*, which dealt with papal authority and INFALLIBILITY. After much debate and revision, the council gave its solemn approval to *Dei Filius* at the third public session (24 April 1870) and to *Pastor Aeternus* at the fourth and final session (18 July 1870).

The doctrine of papal *infallibility*, which was adopted in *Pastor Aeternus*, proved to be the most controversial and divisive issue from the moment the council was announced right until the final vote. The idea of papal infallibility had occasioned very heated debate not only in theological circles but also in the public, political arena, where the doctrine was viewed by many as a defense of autocratic absolutism and a rejection of liberal progress. *Pastor Aeternus* was originally intended as the first of two proposed constitutions on the church. In fact, the question of papal prerogatives was pushed up on the agenda, so that it would be sure to reach the council floor. As a result papal primacy and infallibility were presented outside the intended context of the authority of the whole church. Other aspects of the doctrine of the church, such as the authority of the bishops, were supposed to be taken up in the second proposed constitution, which, in fact, failed to materialize after the council came to an abrupt conclusion. This result was a one-sided emphasis on papal authority. A more balanced exposition of papal prerogatives without the fuller context of church authority and collegiality would have to wait until VATICAN COUNCIL II (1962–1965).

The anti-infallibilitist bishops at the council had opposed the declaration of papal infallibility primarily on the grounds of inopportuneness. Specifically, they maintained that the formulation of the doctrine was still imprecise, that it was in conflict with the historical record of the doctrinal errors of previous POPES, and that it had an unbalancing effect on delicate church–state relations. Complaining of "high-handed tactics" on the part of Pope Pius IX and the Roman CURIA, some 60 anti-infallibilist fathers refused to attend the fourth session of the council, which approved *Pastor Aeternus* and the doctrine of papal infallibility with a vote of 533 to 2. Ultimately, all the minority bishops did submit to the council decrees, but small groups of Swiss, German, and Austrian Catholics, led by university professors, rejected the doctrine of papal infallibility, sparking the "Old Catholic Schism" from the church.

Italian troops occupied Rome on 20 September, and Pius IX adjourned the council sine die on 20 October 1870. The council had sown seeds of resentment within the Catholic ranks and paved the way for exaggerated Roman centralization. At the same time, its intellectual achievements were substantial and played a central role in subsequent theological discussion, especially over the next century.

For further reference: Roget Aubert, *Vatican I* (Paris: Plon, 1964); Edward Cuthbert Butler, *The Vatican Council: 1869–1870* (based on Bishop Ullathorne's letters), 2d ed., 2 vols. (Westminster: Newman Press, 1964); Frank J. Coppa, *Pope Pius IX: Crusader in a Secular Age* (Boston: Twayne, 1979); James Hennesey, *The First Council of the Vatican: The American Experience* (New York: Herder and Herder, 1963).

Raymond F. Bulman

VATICAN COUNCIL II (1962–1965). Vatican II, the twenty-first ecumenical COUNCIL of the church, was convoked by Pope JOHN XXIII (1958–1963) on 25 January 1959. Because of its size, universality, and radical impact on Catholic thought and practice, it is considered one of the most significant councils in church history. The council met for one session under Pope John and for three under Pope PAUL VI (1963–1978). The three main goals of the council were church renewal, dialogue with the modern world, and the promotion of unity among the Christian churches. In his address opening the council on 11 October 1962, Pope John made it clear that the council was to be pastoral rather than dogmatic, with the explicit commission of finding new ways to express the ancient deposit of faith.

The historical context of the council was that of a radically changing world marked by the end of colonialism, the rapid spread of industrialization, and major advances in communications. The council's call for modernization or updating (aggiornamento) was an attempt to respond to this situation through a more positive approach to modern secular culture as well as a more open stance toward the other Christian communities. At the same time, an effective response in both these areas seemed clearly to require a profound renewal of church life. Pope John appreciated the radical implications of the council, deeming it a "new epiphany" for both the church and the world.

In June 1960 Pope John had appointed ten preparatory commissions to draft documents that would be submitted to the council fathers. The drafts were then reviewed by a central commission over which the pope presided. Altogether, the preparatory commissions produced 70 documents, 7 of which were distributed to the bishops throughout the world prior to the opening of the council. The council was attended by over 2,000 Catholic bishops, approximately 80 non-Catholic observers from the major Christian denominations, and as many as 480 experts, mainly theological advisers to the bishops. According to Pope Paul VI's *Ordo Concilii Oecumenici Vaticani Secundi*, the conciliar experts (who had been summoned by the pope) were to be carefully distinguished from private advisers to the bishops. Only the first group had a right to attend discussions in the council sessions or to work on the conciliar commissions. About 1,000 members of the press were present at the council but were not permitted to attend any official meetings.

At the first general congregation or working session (13 October 1962) the ten preparatory commissions were constituted as the official ten conciliar commissions. At the insistence of the majority of bishops, however, election to these working bodies was postponed until the various regional groups could consult so as to choose their most qualified candidates. This decision did much to democratize the proceedings from the outset and guaranteed a more representative membership on the council commissions.

First Session (Fall 1962). The discussions of the opening session centered primarily on liturgical reform, with the issue of the use of Latin or the vernacular as the main point of contention. These debates over the liturgy immediately called attention to a deep rift among the council fathers, which the press characterized as a struggle between "traditionalists" and "progressives." The liturgical controversy continued till the end of the second session, when the use of the vernacular as well as the greater participation of the laity were solemnly approved in the dogmatic constitution *Sacrosanctum Concilium* (4 December 1963). The first session witnessed an even more heated debate over the issue of Divine Revelation, a matter that touched the core of Catholic doctrine. The original scheme of the Theological Commission was rejected as inadequate in its approach to Scripture and tradition. Subsequent drafts were debated until the final approval of *Dei Verbum* (the Dogmatic Constitution on Revelation) toward the very end of the fourth session (18 November 1965). Few documents had actually been approved by the end of the first session, but the democratization of the proceedings was enhanced through the establishment of a new central committee, which now included some of the leading theologians from Germany, France, Belgium, and America.

Second Session (Fall 1963). Pope John XXIII had died in June 1963, and Giovanni Battista Montini, the cardinal-archbishop of Milan, was elected to the papacy as Pope Paul VI. Pope Paul immediately announced his commitment to the council, ordering an opening for the second session (29 September 1963). At his opening address to the council he strongly endorsed John's goals in convoking the council and insisted that the schema on the church be placed at the top of the new session's agenda. The most controversial question to emerge in this discussion was that of *collegiality*—the responsibility of the bishops to share with the pope in the governance of the church. Other issues to be resolved included membership in the church, the exercise of church authority, the apostolic role of the laity, and the reestablishment of a married diaconate.

During this session the Theological Commission (chaired by Cardinal Ottaviani, the principal proponent of traditionalism) was required to prepare amendments regarding all disputed questions, rather than to present a single text for consideration by the council fathers. With the approval of the pope, the conciliar commissions were further expanded, with the effect that they now included a larger representation of progressive bishops. The second session ended on 4 December with the promulgation of "The Constitution on the Sacred Liturgy" and "The Decree on Social Communications."

The Third Session (Fall 1964). While the *schema* on the church was once again the main focus of attention, the sensitive issue of "religious liberty" became an additional source of contention. Cardinal Ruffini, supporting a traditional stance, argued that the notion of "religious liberty" had no foundation in Revelation and should be replaced by the term "religious tolerance." His view was rejected by the majority. Other key topics taken up at this session were the relation of the church to the Jews and the role of the laity in apostolic activity. The conservatively oriented Theological Commission attempted to water down a proposed declaration on the Jews and to endorse an ambiguous document on the laity but was unsuccessful on both counts.

By the end of October the debate had begun in earnest on the controversial *schema* 13, which dealt with the central conciliar theme of "the church in the modern world." The draft covered a wide range of issues, including racial justice, the purpose of marriage, the autonomy of science, the value of technological culture, and the global threat of modern warfare. The last days of the session were devoted to final arguments over the schema on the church, which by now had evolved into the conciliar document "The Dogmatic Constitution on the Church" (*Lumen Gentium*). After vigorous debate and a significant amount of compromise, the final draft was approved by a margin of 2,156 to 5. *Lumen Gentium* was solemnly promulgated at the closing public session (21 November), together with the two derivative documents, "The Decree on Ecumenism" and "The Decree on the Oriental Churches." *Lumen Gentium* is widely regarded as the centerpiece document of the entire council.

Fourth Session (Fall 1965). At the opening of the final session, Pope Paul VI announced the establishment of the long-awaited Synod of Bishops—a concrete implementation of the principle of collegiality. The council fathers immediately resumed discussion of *schema* 13, which by now had been designated as a "pastoral constitution" on relating the church to the modern world. Other areas under discussion included priestly ministry, religious life, and the status of non-Christian religions. At the insistence of many Eastern bishops the previously formulated draft on the Jews had become incorporated into a more comprehensive document, "The Declaration on the Relation of the Church to Non-Christian Religions" (*Nostra Aetate*), which was officially approved on 28 October 1965. Several other important documents, such as the declaration on religious liberty (*Dignitatis Humanae*), a decree on the church's missionary activity (*Ad Gentes*), and a decree on the ministry of priests (*Presbyterorum Ordinis*), received final approbation at the last public session held on 7 December. By far the most dramatic moment of this same session was the resounding acclamation given by the council fathers to the approval of "The Pastoral Constitution on the Church in the Modern World" (*Gaudium et Spes*). This longest document produced by the council was an explicit expression of its concern of relating the church to modern culture. On 8 December Vatican Council II came to a close with the celebration of a solemn liturgy of thanksgiving in St. Peter's basilica.

Altogether the council had produced sixteen documents: four constitutions, nine decrees, and three declarations. The four constitutions, on the liturgy, on the church, on revelation, and on the modern world, are considered the doctrinal pillars of the council. In 1985 on the occasion of the twentieth anniversary of the closing of the council, an extraordinary Synod of Bishops assembled in Rome solemnly renewed the commitment of the church to the principles of Vatican II. In 1994 Pope John Paul II (1978–   ) dedicated the new universal catechism of the Catholic Church to "the work of renewing the whole life of the Church, as desired and begun by the Second Vatican Council."

For further reference: *Acta Synodalia S. Concilii Oecumenici Vaticani II*, 26 vols. (Rome: Typis Polyglottis Vaticanis, 1970–1986); Austin Flannery, ed., *Vatican Council II: The Conciliar and Post Conciliar Documents*, 2 vols., rev. ed. (Northport, NY: Costello, 1992); Giacomo Martina, "The Historical Context in Which the Idea of a New Ecumenical Council Was Born," in *Vatican II: Assessment and Perspectives*, ed. Rene Latourelle (New York and Mahwah, NJ: Paulist Press, 1988); Michael J. Walsh, "The History of the Council," in *Modern Catholicism: Vatican II and After*, ed. Adrian Hastings (New York: Oxford University Press, 1991).

Raymond F. Bulman

VATICAN DIPLOMACY. The Holy See has one of the largest diplomatic establishments in the world, maintaining relations with 150 states and international organizations. Almost all of the great and medium-size powers, including the United States, Russia, Britain, France, Germany, and Japan, have relations with the Vatican. The only Great Power that does not is China, but Castro's Cuba continues its links. The major Islamic states, including Iran but excepting Saudia Arabia, are represented in the Vatican.

In recent years, the Holy See has been able to reestablish links with many Eastern European and Baltic states: in addition, a number of newly independent territories of the former Soviet Union in the Caucasus and Central Asia have opened relations with the Vatican. The Holy See has also succeeded in reestablishing links with Mexico, by tradition a strongly anticlerical state, and in December 1993 it agreed to exchange envoys with the state of Israel. Finally, the Vatican sends permanent representatives to the UNITED NATIONS (and some of its individual agencies), the European Union and the Organization of American States.

The Nature and Organization of Vatican Diplomacy

States send envoys to the POPE in his spiritual role as head of the Roman Catholic Church and not as sovereign of the state of the Vatican City. Any territorial sovereignty that they have exercised has usually been a secondary consideration. Thus, between September 1870, when Italian troops occupied the city of Rome and brought to an end the PAPAL STATES of central Italy, and February 1929, when the Lateran Pacts signed with Italy created the Vatican state, several Catholic states and a few non-Catholic ones continued to maintain diplomatic relations with the Holy See.

For its part, the Holy See conducts diplomatic relations with national states for largely spiritual objectives. Thus, a papal envoy's first concern is to ensure the best conditions of life for the Roman Catholic Church within a given country, and matters affecting church–state relations such as education, marriage and property law, and ecclesiastical appointments may well be regulated by a bilateral agreement known as a CONCORDAT. Another important function of the envoy is to act as the most direct link between the Holy See and the local HIERARCHY of the church and, in particular, to advise the Holy See about episcopal appointments.

The papal envoy also has the task of seeking the support of the government to which he is accredited for those causes that the Roman Catholic Church seeks to promote throughout the world, respect for life, family values, international social justice, and peace. In recent years Vatican representatives at international conferences have been especially zealous in arguing against the use of artificial contraception as a means of population control.

Until 1967 responsibility for the conduct of diplomatic relations with states was shared between the Vatican Secretariat of State and the Sacred Congregation for Extraordinary Affairs. In that year Pope PAUL VI (1963–1978) abolished the congregation and established the COUNCIL for the Public Affairs of the Church. In 1988 this council was, in its turn, absorbed into the Secretariat of State under the title of the "Section for Relations with States." Inasmuch as the Secretariat of State deals with other major areas of the government of the Roman Catholic Church and Vatican City, the cardinal secretary of state is the pope's "prime minister," and the secretary of the Section for Relations with States, is effectively his "foreign minister."

The Vatican's envoys are known as NUNCIOS or pronuncios. The former title is used where the papal envoy is the doyen of the diplomatic corps. Where he is not, especially in predominantly Protestant or Islamic ones, he is known as a pronuncio. In those countries with which the Holy See does not have diplomatic relations, there is usually an APOSTOLIC DELEGATE, a papal envoy to the local hierarchy of the Roman Catholic Church without diplomatic status. Sometimes apostolic delegates unofficially act as diplomatic links between the Holy See and national governments. Moreover, they carry the same ecclesiastical rank of a titular archbishop.

The History of Vatican Diplomacy

From the earliest centuries of its existence, the Holy See has sent envoys, LEGATES of different grades, or nuncios to local branches of the Roman church, to Eastern churches, and to states. When the Holy See consolidated its temporal power in central Italy and around Avignon in France, some diplomatic representations to and from the Holy See assumed a more permanent character. In the fifteenth, sixteenth, and seventeenth centuries, as the ruler of a substantial Italian principality, the pope was directly involved in international power diplomacy and even war—the Renaissance pope JULIUS II (1503–1513) led his armies into battle!

Modern Vatican diplomacy could be said to have started in the late eighteenth century. The REFORMATION and the French Revolution had created situations in which large numbers of Catholics were under Protestant control in Germany and anticlerical, if not downright anti-Christian, in the case of Republican/Napoleonic France. The acquisition of Polish lands by Russia led to Catholics there being ruled by an orthodox monarch. For this reason the notion that only Catholic monarchs could be represented in Rome came to an end.

The Congress of VIENNA of 1815 was the last major peace conference at which the Holy See was represented. At Vienna the temporal power of the popes, which had been taken away by Napoleon, was restored. Henceforth, the further defense of papal states against the rising forces of Italian liberalism and nationalism would be one of the main aims of papal diplomacy. But in 1870 the Holy See lost its last shred of temporal power as a result of the conquest of Rome by the Italians, who made the city the capital of their recently unified kingdom.

Thanks to the Law of Papal Guarantees, the Holy See was able to maintain relations with other powers, though in this period both Great Britain and the United States felt compelled to withdraw their envoys to the Vatican. The church–state conflict in France also led to the breaking off of links with the republic in 1904. On the eve of WORLD WAR I, with relations with only three Great Powers, Austria, Russia, and Prussia, the Vatican's limited diplomatic influence seemed to mirror its religious and political isolation.

World War I dramatically changed the Holy See's diplomatic position. In December 1914 Great Britain attached a "special mission" to the Holy See and was followed by France, which sent an "unofficial" envoy in the same year to combat the apparently overwhelming influence of Austria-Hungary and Germany. During the course of the war, Pope BENEDICT XV (1914–1922) proclaimed the Holy See's neutrality, gave succor to the victims of war and in his "Peace Note" of 1917, suggesting the bases for an honorable and comprehensive peace, and claimed for the Holy See a peacemaking role that was to be continued by successive popes: PIUS XII (1939–1958) in WORLD WAR II; PAUL VI (1963–1978) during the Vietnam War; and JOHN PAUL II (1978–   ) in the Gulf conflict.

The 1919 peace settlement further boosted the Vatican's diplomatic standing. Despite the collapse of its last major "ally," the Catholic Austro-Hungarian empire, the Holy See quickly adapted itself to the postwar territorial setup in Europe. By the end of the 1920s, the Holy See had established relations with all of the "successor states" to the empire and had signed concordats or modi vivendi with the majority of them. New states, even predominantly Protestant ones such as Estonia and Finland, hurried to gain recognition from one of Europe's oldest powers. Even secular France reestablished full diplomatic relations in 1921.

In the 1930s PIUS XI (1922–1939) struggled to defend the Roman Catholic Church against the totalitarian (see Totalitarianism) pretensions of Nazism and fascism and against the persecution by anticlerical and/or Marxist regimes in Spain, Mexico, and the USSR. These efforts cannot be entirely separated from his wider strategy of seeking to prevent the emergence of intransigent, ideologically based power blocs in Europe. His successor, Pius XII, struggled to defend the neutrality of the Vatican after the outbreak of World War II, which he had tried to prevent, and the war in Italy brought the threat, in the shape of the German armies and Allied bombardment, to his doorstep in Rome.

For a short interval, during the COLD WAR, the Vatican's neutrality between the contending power blocs was compromised by communist persecution of the church in Eastern Europe and by Pius XII's anticommunist crusade.

But the accession of his successor, JOHN XXIII (1958–1963), marked a turning point in the development of Vatican diplomacy. In particular, John XXIII not only sought to build on the work of Benedict XV and Pius XI and to develop relations with the decolonized, emergent nations of the Third World but also initiated a cautious, but thoroughly genuine and generous, "opening to the East." On this basis Cardinal Agostino Casaroli developed his *Ostpolitik* toward the communist states in the reigns of John XXIII's three successors.

One novelty of his immediate successor, PAUL VI (1963–1978), was his journeys to at least four continents, including visits to Jerusalem and New York; this was to set the pattern for a new policy of personal papal diplomacy that has been continued in the present pontificate of John Paul II. The latter's Polish origins, his sympathy for the American position during what turned out to be the very last phase of the Cold War, and his personal contribution to the downfall of the communist system mark his pontificate as one of enormous importance in the history of papal diplomacy.

In the postcommunist world of the 1990s the Holy See and therefore Vatican diplomacy enjoy enormous, unprecedented international standing, but major problems remain. The policy of *Ostpolitik* has not proved successful in relations with communist China: the situation of Chinese Catholics remains pitiable, torn as they are between a state-sponsored, schismatic church and a persecuted, underground church. A further problem is the militant zeal of Islamic fundamentalism, which threatens Christian minorities in Asia, the Middle East, and Africa. Paradoxically, in its moment of "triumph" over COMMUNISM, Vatican diplomacy faces probably its most serious and insidious enemies in the materialism and secularism of Western capitalist society in Europe, North America, and other developed countries.

For further reference: *Annuario Pontificio* (Vatican City: Libreria Editrice Vaticana); H. E. Cardinale, *The Holy See and the International Order* (Gerrards Cross, England: Collin Smythe, 1976); Robert A. Graham, *Vatican Diplomacy: A Study of Church and State on the International Plane* (Princeton: Princeton University Press, 1957); B. J. Hehir, "Papal Foreign Policy," *Foreign Policy* 78 (Spring 1990); Peter C. Kent and John F. Pollard, eds., *Papal Diplomacy in the Modern Age* (New York: Praeger, 1994); Hansjacob Stehle, *The Eastern Politics of the Vatican, 1917–1979* (Athens and London: Ohio University Press, 1981).

John F. Pollard

VICHY FRANCE AND THE VATICAN. The French HIERARCHY, the Vatican, and many French Catholics greeted the Vichy regime enthusiastically. Vichy valued the support of the Catholic Church and shared many of the same enemies. Tensions emerged, though, particularly over Vichy's policies toward Jews and toward compulsory labor by French workers in Germany. The major leaders of the French church remained sympathetic to Petain until the end, but French Catholics played a prominent role in the Resistance.

A dramatic change in regime followed the catastrophic French defeat of May–June 1940. While NAZI GERMANY ruled directly over three-fifths of France, a new government emerged at Vichy under the aegis of Marshal Philippe Pétain. The new regime proclaimed a national renewal, blaming the disaster on the sins of the anticlerical Third Republic. Vichy sought a prominent place in Nazi Europe, often acting on its own initiative and looking to French Catholicism for support.

For the French Catholic Church, Vichy posed a great temptation. French Catholics perceived the regime's slogan of *travail, famille, patrie* ("work, family, nation") as their own. They were attracted to Pétain, who claimed to restore order based on traditional values. Prominent clergymen lauded Pétain as a gift of providence. During the summer of 1941, French church leaders affirmed that *sans infeodation* (without subservience), they would "practice a sincere and complete loyalty towards the established power." The French hierarchy sympathized with Vichy, not Nazi Germany, but the ties to Vichy ultimately compromised the French church. Vichy offered tangible, but limited, concessions to the Catholic Church, particularly in education. There was talk of a CONCOR-

DAT between Vichy and the Holy See, but no serious movement toward it; the Vatican and some members of the French hierarchy expressed caution about Vichy's longevity.

The existence of Catholic youth groups and Catholic labor unions raised potentially contentious issues. Two other crucial subjects of dispute also arose. Vichy's policies toward Jews ultimately posed wrenching moral questions for Catholics. In 1940 and 1941, on its own initiative, Vichy promulgated anti-Jewish laws that evicted Jews from jobs and schools, confiscated property, and ordered a census. Before WORLD WAR II, Pope PIUS XI (1922–1939) and leading French clerics had condemned anti-Semitism forcefully, yet in 1940–1941 Catholics largely greeted Vichy's evisceration of Jewish emancipation with public silence. The Jesuit Gaston Fessard's public condemnation of the anti-Jewish laws was remarkable for its rarity. Father Fessard also authored the first number of the *Cahiers du Témoignage Chrétien*, a resistance journal, which warned, "France, be careful not to lose your soul."

In August 1941 Pétain asked León Bérard, Vichy's ambassador to the Holy See, to ascertain the Vatican's perspective. Bérard responded that the Vatican accepted restrictions on Jews; however, the Holy See insisted converted (baptized) Jews were Catholics and that the Statut des Juifs be applied with "justice and charity." Pétain interpreted Bérard's report as condoning Vichy's actions. In response to the papal NUNCIO, Valerio Valeri, who disapproved of the laws, the papal secretary of state, Cardinal Maglione, acknowledged the overall accuracy of Bérard's report but found Pétain's conclusions excessive.

During the summer 1942 Vichy's active participation in the HOLOCAUST created a brief spasm of condemnation by prominent members of the hierarchy in the unoccupied zone. Although the initiative came from the Nazis, French police carried out the mass roundup of Jews in the Paris region in July and in the unoccupied zone in August 1942. As thousands of Jews, including more than 4,000 children, were packed by French authorities into the Vélodrome d' Hiver (Vel d' Hiv), an indoor sports facility in Paris, prior to being sent to the French concentration camp at Drancy and to death at Auschwitz, and as Pierre Laval pressed the Germans to take children under sixteen, a small number of leading Catholic clergymen spoke out. Msgr. Jules-Gérard Saliegè, archbishop of Toulouse, affirmed the existence of a "Christian morality, a human morality," emanating from God that could not be "suppressed." He asserted the common humanity of Jewish men and women and foreigners (Jews from abroad were Vichy's primary targets), "our brothers."

In another pastoral letter, Bishop Pierre-Marie Théas of Montauban protested with outraged "Christian conscience" "the most barbarous savagery" against Jews. Msgr. Delay, bishop of Marseilles, and Cardinal Pierre-Marie Gerlier, archbishop of Lyon, criticized the deportations forcefully; however, both alleged a real Jewish problem facing Vichy. Nevertheless, these public protests helped swing Catholic public opinion toward the victims and away from Vichy.

The intensity of these protests was not sustained. No public outcries emanated from high church officials in the occupied zone. Laval brought up Pope PIUS XII's (1939–1958) "silence," cautioned the French church against weakening France's international position, and offered subsidies for Catholic higher education and other carrots. In February 1943, Cardinal Emmanuel Suhard, archbishop of Paris, greeted renewed deportations with an anemic private request to Pétain to alter the "manner" of the operations. In contrast, in August 1943, the French hierarchy expressed their opposition to the deportations that would follow withdrawal of the nationalizations of Jews in France back to 1927.

Catholics (and Protestants) in France also helped Jews survive the massive hunt of human beings. In 1940–1941, Abbé Alexandre Glasberg, a Ukrainian Jewish convert to Catholicism, raised the consciousness of Cardinal Gerlier about conditions in the notorious internment camp of Gurs, leading to protests by Frs. Pierre Chaillet, Glasberg, and others. Amitié Chrétienne hid Jewish children in 1942. Ultimately, Cardinal Gerlier resisted pressure to reveal the locations of their hiding places. Frequently, humble Catholic men and women, lay and clergy, aided Jews. The stunning loss of approximately one-quarter of the Jews in France, between 76,000 and 80,000 people, many of whom were foreign Jews, and the survival of approximately three-quarters and the Catholic Church's roles in each require explanation.

The Service du Travail Obligatoire (STO), established in February 1943 to draft French laborers for work in Germany, raised an even more divisive issue between the regime and French Catholics. Cardinal Liénart, archbishop of Lille, advised French workers that service in Germany was not a "duty of conscience" and could be rejected; however, it could also be interpreted as a Christian act, sparing someone else the obligation.

The princes of the French Catholic Church remained loyal to Pétain until the end. As late as April 1944, Cardinal Suhard and crowds greeted Pétain in Paris. Cardinal Suhard gave the absolution for Philippe Henriot, the prominent Vichy minister assassinated in June 1944. Reflecting their acute fear of COMMUNISM, church leaders regarded the Resistance with distrust. Nonetheless, French Catholics, lay and even some lower clergy, joined it, fighting for values and a national renewal different from Vichy's.

The hierarchy's close ties to Vichy ultimately discredited traditional conservatism within the French church. Charles de Gaulle forbade Cardinal Suhard's participation in the Te Deum mass in Notre Dame at the liberation of Paris. In December 1944 the Vatican appointed Angelo Roncalli (the future Pope JOHN XXIII, 1958–1963) as papal nuncio to France, and with his good sense he helped soothe relations. The post–World War II Catholic Church in France became more pluralistic. Echoes of the past resurfaced recently during the case of Paul Touvier, a Frenchman convicted of murdering Jews during World War II. For diverse motives, French Catholic networks sheltered Touvier for decades. Because relations between the Catholic Church and Vichy took place within the context of perhaps the gravest moral crisis in the history of the West, the subject retains compelling significance.

For further reference: Renée Bédarida, *Les Armes de l'Esprit: Temoignage Chretien (1941–1944)* (Paris: Les Editions Ouvrieres, 1977); Jacques Duquesne, *Les Catholiques français sous l'occupation* (Paris: Editions Bernard Grasset, 1966); *Eglises et chrétiens dans la IIe guerre mondiale*, ed. Xavier de Montclos et al., 2 vols. (Lyon: Presses Universitaires de Lyon, 1978, 1982); *Le régime de Vichy et les français*, ed. Jean-Pierre Azéma and François Bédarida (Paris: Fayard, 1992); René Remond, "Le catholicisme français pendant la seconde guerre mondiale," *Revue d' Histoire de l'Eglise de France* 64 (1978): 203–213; René Rémond et al., *Paul Touvier et l'église* (Paris: Fayard, 1992); Richard J. Wolff and Jorg K. Hoensch, eds., *Catholics, the State, and the European Radical Right, 1919–1945* (Highland Lakes, NJ: Social Science Monographs; Boulder, CO: Atlantic Research, 1987); Susan Zuccotti, *The Holocaust, the French, and the Jews* (New York: Basic Books, 1993).

Joel Blatt

VICTOR I (189–198). African by birth, Victor was the first POPE not of Graeco-Oriental background. Coming from the West, he probably was responsible for the Latinization of the church, which had hitherto been dominated by Eastern influences. Certainly, he was the most dynamic of the second-century pontiffs. Early in his reign he used his position to bring other churches in line with the Roman practice of celebrating Easter on the Sunday following the fourteenth day of the Jewish month of Nisan, which was the day of Passover. This was in contrast to the age-old quartodeciman practice, prevalent elsewhere, which observed Easter on the fourteenth of Nisan no matter the day of the week. At his instigation synods were held in Rome and in various centers, from Gaul to Mesopotamia, to decide the issue, and the majority agreed with Rome. The churches of Asia Minor, however, refused to abandon the quartodeciman custom, and Victor promptly excommunicated (see Excommunication) them from communion with Rome and the church.

Victor's action marks an important point, going far beyond the impersonal example of CLEMENT I (c. 91–c. 101) and the church at Corinth, for instance, of a pope's claiming the right to intervene in the affairs of other churches. With similar confidence Victor in or about 192 excommunicated Theodotius of Byzantium, the leader of the Adoptionsits, who taught that Jesus had been an ordinary, but extremely pious, man who was adopted as the son of God when the Spirit descended on him at baptism. Victor is also the first to have had dealings with the imperial Roman household. He was able to give Marcia, the mistress of Emperor Commodus, who was herself a Christian, a list of Christians who had been condemned to the mines in Sardinia. They were subsequently released, and among them was a future pope, CALLISTUS I (217–222), whose name Victor had deliberately withheld. It is unclear if the reports of his martyrdom and burial near St. Peter are true. His feast is 28 July.

For further reference: J. N. D. Kelly, *The Oxford Dictionary of Popes* (Oxford: Oxford University Press, 1986); J. Lebreton and J. Zeiller, *The History of the Primitive Church* (London: Burns, Oates and Washbourne, 1948).

William Roberts

VICTOR II (1055–1057). Gebhard of Dollnstein-Hirschberg, son of the Swabian Count Hartwig, was the last of the four German POPES nominated by Emperor Henry III. In 1042, when still in his twenties, he was made bishop of Eichstatt and became an indispensable adviser to the emperor. Then upon LEO IX's death in 1054, after long discussions with a Roman legation headed by the deacon Hildebrand (later, GREGORY VII, 1074–1085), Henry named Gerhard pope. But Gebhard hesitated for several months until the emperor agreed to restore certain territories and properties that had previously been taken from the Holy See. Finally, almost a year after Leo's death, he was enthroned as Victor II.

Concerned with reform, he called a synod at Florence in 1055 to condemn simony, clerical unchastity, and the alienation of church property. Similar decisions were published in France in 1056 by local synods presided over by French bishops, with Hildebrand as papal LEGATE. At the same time the emperor sought to consolidate his political position in Italy, where he had come to specifically drive out Godfrey of Lorraine. This he accomplished while holding Godfrey's wife and his stepdaughter, the future Countess Matilda of Tuscany, as hostages and forcing Godfrey's brother Frederick, who was chancellor of the Roman church, to retire to Monte Cassino as a monk. Then, to strengthen his ally Victor's position in Italy, Henry appointed him duke of Spoleto and count of Fermo, but, after the emperor's departure from Italy, the pope had to confront the Norman presence in the south without imperial reinforcements. After Henry's death late in 1056, Victor, who was in Germany seeking military help, was able to secure at Aachen the succession of Henry's five-year-old son, Henry IV, with his mother, the empress Agnes, as regent.

Upon returning to Italy in February 1057, Victor held a synod in the Lateran, and, to further gain the support of Godfrey of Lorraine, who had now become a power in Italy, he had Godfrey's brother Frederick (the future STEPHEN IX, 1057–1058) named abbot of Monte Cassino and cardinal-priest of S. Crisogono. A few months later Victor, after completing a synod at Arezzo, was stricken with fever and died. The German members of his court sought to take him back to Eichstatt for burial, but the citizens of Ravenna interred his body in Sta. Maria Rotonda, the huge mausoleum of Theodoric the Great, just outside the city walls.

For further reference: J. N. D. Kelly, *The Oxford Dictionary of Popes* (Oxford: Oxford University Press, 1986); H. K. Mann, *The Lives of the Popes in the Early Middle Ages* (London: K. Paul, 1902–1932).

William Roberts

VICTOR III (1086–1087). The death of GREGORY VII (1073–1085) in exile at Salerno in May 1085 threw the reformist party in Rome, already weakened by desertions to the antipope CLEMENT III (1080, 1084–1100) into confusion. Finally, after a year, through pressure from the Norman prince Jordan of

Capua, the cardinals elected Desiderius, the abbot of Monte Cassino, on 24 May 1096. Selected against his will, he seemed to be the right choice because of his influence with the Normans and because it was possible that he might bring about a reconciliation with Emperor Henry IV.

Born in 1027, his original name was Daufer, and he was related to the Lombard rulers of Benevento. Early in his life he had been a hermit and, after serving as adviser to LEO IX (1049–1054), became a monk of Monte Cassino, taking the name Desiderius, and in 1058 became abbot. His leadership at Monte Cassino marked one of its greatest periods. In 1059 he was named cardinal-priest and vicar of southern Italy by NICHOLAS II (1058–1061). In that capacity he negotiated the alliance between the papacy and the Normans. He also reconciled Gregory VII and the Norman duke of Apulia, Robert Guiscard, but in 1082 incurred that POPE's anger when he tried to effect a reconciliation between the pontiff and Henry IV.

Four days after his own election in 1086, Victor was forced by riots to flee from Rome. He put aside the papal insignia and retired to his abbey. At the instigation of Jordan of Capua, he convened a synod at Capua, in the capacity as papal vicar rather than pope. Finally, in March 1087 he was recognized as pontiff and in May was able to return briefly to be crowned in St. Peter's. Despite the support of his powerful friends, Jordan of Capua and Countess Matilda of Tuscany, it was impossible for him to rule from the city where his opponents had the backing of the forces of the antipope, Clement III. Only in July did Victor's supporters, with the help of Norman troops, retake the Leonine section of the city, but Victor, now seriously ill, returned to Monte Cassino, where he served as abbot until his death. In August, as pontiff, he presided over an important COUNCIL at Benevento, and among its decrees were a restatement of Gregory VII's prohibition of lay investiture (see Investiture Controversy), a declaration against simoniac ordinations and clerical marriage, and the anathematizing of Clement III and the extreme Gregorians. During his reign a large Genoese and Pisan naval expedition attacked the Saracen base in Tunisia, presenting part of the spoils to the basilica of St. Peter's. He died at Monte Cassino on 16 September 1087. He was beatified by LEO XIII (1878–1903) in 1887. His feast day is 16 September.

For further reference: L. Duchesne, *The Beginnings of the Temporal Sovereignty of the Popes* (London: K. Paul, 1908); J. N. D. Kelly, *The Oxford Dictionary of Popes* (Oxford: Oxford University Press, 1986).

William Roberts

VICTOR IV, ANTIPOPE (1138). Gregorio Conti was born in Frosinone and became cardinal-priest SS. Apostoli. In 1138 he was elected successor of antipope ANACLETUS II (1130–1138) with the support of Roger II, king of Sicily, but proved to be in a weak position. This election prolonged for four more months the SCHISM that had started in 1130 with the dual election of Pope INNOCENT II (1130–1143) and Anacletus II.

Meanwhile, St. Bernard of Clairvaux had been ceaselessly campaigning on behalf of Pope Innocent II, winning over many of those who had pledged to Victor's cause. After only two months in power, the antipope decided to negotiate the terms for surrendering his dignity, using the intercession of St. Bernard, and, on 29 May 1138, Victor and the schismatic clergy proclaimed their submission to Innocent II. The Second Lateran COUNCIL (see Lateran Council II) held in 1139 deposed all the cardinals who had supported Anacletus, thus removing the last traces of the eight-year-old schism.

For further reference: H. K. Mann, *The Lives of the Popes in the Early Middle Ages* (London: K. Paul, 1902–1932); T. F. Tout, *The Empire and the Papacy, 918–1273* (London: Rivingtons, 1958).

Elda G. Zappi

VICTOR IV, ANTIPOPE (1159–1164). The aristocratic Cardinal Octavian of St. Cecilia was elected POPE on 7 September 1159, but the simultaneous election of Cardinal Roland of Sienna as ALEXANDER III (1159–1181) produced an eighteen-year SCHISM. The diplomatic revolution of 1156, enshrined in the Treaty of Benevento, prepared the ground for the 1159 breach. By this treaty the pope, departing from the policy of cooperation with the Roman empire, signed an alliance with William I, the Norman king of Sicily.

The emperor sought to build up a Central European kingdom that included Lombardy and attempted to assert his authority over ecclesiastical nominations. Moreover, Barbarossa entered into relations with the unruly citizens of Rome, who were generally hostile to the popes, especially to those who were foreigners in the city. Tensions grew when he sent one of his military commanders to Rome, which led to the formation of two factions in the CURIA and in the College of CARDINALS. The majority of the college adhered to the Norman alliance, while the minority advocated an arrangement with the emperor. At Adrian's death on 1 September 1159 the hostilities came to a climax. The pro-Norman cardinals elected Roland, but the enraged opposition, supported by Frederick's ambassadors, resorted to a dual election by demanding that Octavian be elected pope. During Alexander's investiture, Octavian snatched the papal mantle from his rival's neck and put it on himself. The crowd burst into St. Peter's, put Alexander III and his followers to flight, and acclaimed Octavian as Pope Victor IV.

With no precise rules governing papal elections, Frederick decided to arbitrate between the rivals and invited them and the episcopate to a COUNCIL at Pavia in February 1160. Many bishops as well as Alexander, who had excommunicated (see Excommunication) the emperor, refused to appear. The council decided that Victor was the canonical pope. But he was recognized as such only in Germany and in some parts of northern Italy, where he took residence. The surrender of Milan to the imperial army in 1162 strengthened Frederick's military position and Victor's support in the region. Alexander was acknowledged by the rest of the Christian world. Victor's death in Lucca on 20 April 1164 was a setback for the imperial cause but did not put an end to the schism.

For further reference: *Boso's Life of Alexander III*. Intro. Peter Munz (Totowa, NJ: Rowman and Littlefield, 1973); I. S. Robinson, *The Papacy, 1073–1198, Continuity and Innovation* (Cambridge: Cambridge University Press, 1990).

Elda G. Zappi

VIENNA, CONGRESS OF, AND THE PAPACY. The Congress of Vienna, held in 1814–1815, was the greatest international conference of the nineteenth century. Over twenty years of war and revolution had disrupted the political order of Europe, and after the fall of Napoleon, the victorious Allies realized the urgent need for a new international settlement. Their main goal at the congress was a stable international order that would ensure the peace of Europe; they hoped to achieve this aim by establishing a balance of power, by redistributing territory so as the satisfy the ambitions of the powers, and by creating a ring of strong states around France to restrain it from future aggression. All the states of Europe were represented, but the settlement was largely worked out among the Great Powers, Austria, France, England, Russia, and Prussia. Their work was not easy, and the congress lasted far longer than anticipated.

The papacy was represented at the congress by the secretary of state, Cardinal Consalvi, one of its greatest diplomats. His was not as easy task, since many other states had their own ambitions for the lands that Napoleon had taken away from the papacy. Consalvi concentrated on winning the support of the Austrian leader Prince METTERNICH, with success, since the prince wanted papal cooperation with Austria in a union of throne and altar as a means of defending the conservative order against the threat of revolution. With Metternich's backing, Consalvi was able to beat off attempts by Naples, France, and Russia to appropriate papal lands for themselves or their clients. In the end, virtually all the prerevolutionary PAPAL STATES were regained. The territories that Rome had held in France before the Revolution, Avignon and Venaissin, were not regained, but Consalvi had resigned himself to their loss before the congress. He realized that any attempt to regain them would sour Franco–papal relations and would stir French nationalist passions against the peace settlement. Religious questions were not much discussed at the congress; a possible CONCORDAT for the new German Confederation was considered, but no agreement could be reached among the German states. However, Consalvi did make contracts with European statesmen that later helped him to negotiate concordats and other agreements to regulate church–state relations in several countries.

For further reference: Harold Nicolson, *The Congress of Vienna* (London: Constable and Co., 1946); Alan J. Reinerman, *Austria and the Papacy in the Age of Metternich*, vol. 1, *Between Conflict and Cooperation, 1809–1830* (Washington, DC: Catholic University of America Press, 1979); Charles K. Webster, *The Congress of Vienna* (New York: Barnes and Noble, 1964).

Alan J. Reinerman

VIENNE, COUNCIL OF (1311–1312). After an eleven-month conclave. Pope CLEMENT V (1305–1314), the former archbishop of Bordeaux, was elected on 5 June 1305. The new pontiff began his rule under the shadow of the king of France, Philip the Fair. At the king's request he scheduled the papal coronation for Lyons, reinstated two cardinals who had been excluded from the college because of their pro-French dealings, shifted the balance in the College of CARDINALS by naming nine Frenchmen at his first consistory, and revoked or reinterpreted the acts of BONIFACE VIII (1294–1303), which nettled Philip.

In a flagrant breach of clerical immunity, Philip arrested the members of the Knights Templars in France on suspicion of HERESY. Under torture, some Templars admitted their guilt, which they later denied. With his eye on the wealth of the Templars, Philip pressured the timorous pope to call a COUNCIL to deal with this matter. Clement called a council in Vienne to deal with heresy, the reform of the church, and the affair of the Templars. Not all bishops were invited to the council. It appears that the French government approved those who attended. The conciliar commission established to examine the Templars doubted the charges brought against them. Philip marched to Vienne and intimidated Clement, forcing the pope to dissolve the Templars by apostolic decree on 3 April 1312.

Its main work done, the council reviewed other matters touching the practice of poverty among FRANCISCANS and the instruction in Arabic, Hebrew, and other Oriental languages at universities to facilitate missionary work in the Middle East. The council ended its deliberations on 6 May 1312. It stipulated that the wealth of the Templars should be transferred to the Knights of St. John. In Aragon and France the bulk of the wealth found its way into the royal treasury. The guilt of the Templars remains an open question, with a majority of historians declaring them innocent.

For further reference: J. Lecler, *Vienne* (Paris: Ed. de l'Orante, 1964); Georges Lizerand, *Le Dossier de l'Affaire des Templiers* (Paris: Société d'Edition "Les Belles Lettres," 1964); Peter Partner, *The Murdered Magicians. The Templars and Their Myth* (New York: Oxford University Press, 1982).

Richard J. Kehoe

VIGILIUS (537–555). Vigilius gained the papacy with the support of Justinian and Theodora and spent most of his reign trying to uphold the doctrine of the hypostatic union against the Monophysites. Vigilius was appointed as apocrisiarius to Constantinople. He was there with Pope AGAPITUS I (535–536) when the latter died and gave Theodora the impression that he would support conciliation with the Monophysites if she would help him gain the papacy. By the time Vigilius returned to Rome, however, SILVERIUS (536–537), son of

HORMISDAS (514–523), had already been elected. After Justinian's forces regained the city from the Goths, the Byzantine commander, Belisarius, deposed Silverius and secured the election of Vigilius as his successor.

Justinian had never actually rejected CHALCEDON and was also aware that the Roman emperor had given up the title of *pontifex maximus* in 379. But he felt he had to mediate the Christological controversies in order to ensure the support of the Monophysite bishops in Egypt and Syria. In 543 Justinian issued an edict that condemned the writings of Theodore of Mopsuestia, who had espoused Nestorianism, but died (428) before Nestorius was condemned, and the writings of Theodoret of Cyrus (d. c. 458) and Ibas of Edessa (d. 457), anti-Monophysites recognized as orthodox by the Council of Chalcedon. Justinian's edict, which referred to the ''Three Chapters'' (headings) of these writers, did not specifically repudiate Chalcedon but diminished its importance. Vigilius, who refused to accept this, was arrested by Byzantine police in 545. By Easter 548 he capitulated and condemned the Three Chapters, while trying to uphold the orthodoxy of Chalcedon. This judgment was rejected in the west, and the bishops in North Africa even excommunicated (see Excommunication) the pope (550). Vigilius publicly annulled his *Iudicatum* (verdict) but privately assured the emperor of his support of the condemnation of the Three Chapters. Pope and emperor agreed to hold a council to settle the dispute.

Since the pope took no action to convene the council, Justinian issued a new condemnation of the Three Chapters in 551. On 4 May 553 Vigilius issued a *Constitutum* in which he pronounced anathema some passages from Theodore's writings but not the man himself. At the same time, Vigilius reaffirmed the orthodoxy of Theodoret and Ibas. Justinian, tired of waiting for papal action, convened his own council (553), which came to be known as the Fifth Ecumenical Council. Vigilius refused to attend. In their final session, the bishops condemned the Three Chapters in accordance with Justinian's edict of 551.

The pope was isolated. In a letter to the patriarch (8 December 553), Vigilius retracted his *Constitutum*. But the emperor demanded more, and in a second *Iudicatum* (23 February 554), Vigilius largely accepted the decrees of the Fifth Ecumenical Council. In return, he received the Pragmatic Sanction of 13 August 554, giving the church various rights under the restored imperial government in Italy but also requiring confirmation of papal elections by the emperor. In the spring of 555 he finally started back to Rome but died at Syracuse on 7 June 555.

For further reference: T. G. Jalland, *The Church and the Papacy* (London: SPCK, 1944); J. N. D. Kelly, *The Oxford Dictionary of Popes* (Oxford: Oxford University Press, 1986).

Frank Grande

VITALIAN (657–672). A native Roman, Vitalian assumed a conciliatory stance toward the East–West SCHISM that had troubled his predecessors. In a letter to Emperor Constans II, Vitalian deliberately downplayed the monothelitist controversy. His attempts to promote positive relations between the two cities, largely through the avoidance of controversy, proved successful. In fact, his name was inscribed upon the diptychs in Constantinople as proof of his good standing in the Eastern capital. Nonetheless, in 666 the emperor upheld the archbishop of Ravenna's rebelliousness against Rome. Constans granted Ravenna the authority to elect its own bishop, who might be consecrated by three of his own suffragans (a Roman practice). During the reign of Constantine IV (668–685), Vitalian was able to more stridently voice his opposition to monothelitism.

With regard to the English church, Vitalian supported the introduction of Roman practices on that island, especially with regard to the substitution of the Roman date for Easter instead of the Celtic. In 668 he consecrated Theodore of Tarsus as archbishop of Canterbury, in the hope that he might facilitate the move toward Romanization. During Vitalian's reign, King Wulfhere of Mercia endowed a monastery at Peterborough, making it one of the first monastic institutions to be placed directly under papal protection.

For further reference: J. N. D. Kelly, *The Oxford Dictionary of the Popes* (Oxford: Oxford University Press, 1986); *New Catholic Encyclopedia*, vol. 14 (1967), p. 724.

Patrick J. McNamara

W

WESTPHALIA, PEACE OF (1648). Although preliminaries for this conference, which marked one of the significant turning points in modern diplomatic history, commenced in May 1643, only in December 1644 did serious negotiations begin, and only in October 1648 was the peace signed. It ended the Thirty Years' War, which had included almost every major European power. Beginning, in large measure, as a war of religion when the Bohemian Protestants revolted against the threatened imposition of the COUNTER-REFORMATION, by its conclusion the struggle marked the victory of German particularism over Hapsburg centralization, of Dutch capitalism over Spanish mercantalism, and of Bourbon over Hapsburg dynastic interests.

The peace congress was attended by 111 German delegates and thirty-seven representatives of the other powers. All except the Swedes and Danes were accredited to Münster, but most of the German Protestants found more congenial quarters with the Scandinavians at Osnabrück. The church witnessed the end of the Hapsburg emperors' attempts to impose religious uniformity on Germany and the fact that Calvinists were to share in the privileges of the Peace of Augsburg (1555) equally with Catholics and Lutherans. The church lost two archbishoprics, fourteen bishoprics, and hundreds of monasteries, collegiate churches, and parishes in Germany. Much of this dismayed the papal NUNCIO, Cardinal Fabio Chigi, later Pope ALEXANDER VII (1655–1667), who protested the decisions that had already been made. At the conclusion of peace Pope INNOCENT X (1644–1655) condemned many portions of the settlement, but his protests were ignored by both the Catholic and Protestant powers. In the words of Sir Charles Petrie, "from that time" the POPE's "direct influence in international affairs may be said to have ceased." For this reason the Peace of Westphalia has a place in the history of the papacy.

For further reference: Hans Galen et al., *Münster 800–1800: 1000 Jahre Geschichte der Stadt* (Münster: Stadtmuseum Munster, 1984); Charles Petrie, *Earlier Diplomatic*

History, 1492–1713 (London: Hollis and Carter, 1949); Cecilly Veronica Wedgwood, *The Thirty Years War* (London: Penguin Edition, 1957).

William C. Schrader

WORLD WAR I AND THE VATICAN. Shortly after the beginning of World War I, Giacomo Della Chiesa (21 November 1854–22 January 1922) ascended the papal throne (3 September 1914) as BENEDICT XV (1914–1922). Faced by a disastrous war, the cardinals, it is thought, chose a candidate of great diplomatic skill. Benedict XV followed a policy of Christian pacifism and impartiality in the pursuit of peace. Declining to choose sides, he repeatedly condemned the slaughter, cruelty, and injustices of the war.

Benedict's numerous condemnations of the war and pleas for peace started with his message of a 8 September 1914. "There is no limit," he wrote, "to the ruin and slaughter: every day the earth is steeped in fresh blood and covered anew with dead and wounded." Appealing to the governments of the warring states not to pursue a military victory, he implored them to end the conflict with a just peace. Denying the applicability of the just war theory, the POPE believed that neither side fought from a position of justice. As the Vicar of Christ and messenger of peace, he proclaimed war an immoral way for Christians to resolve their conflicts. It was destructive not only of society but of the cause of Christ. Far from creating security, he feared that a lengthy war would inevitably lead to social revolution. He challenged the militaristic nationalism of Europe with his proposals for mutual disarmament and the abolition of general conscription. An international court of arbitration, freedom of communication and of the seas, and the establishment of an international organization of states were proposed to preserve peace.

Not unexpectedly, these were rejected, and the pope was mistrusted and denounced by both sides. When the Vatican sought to keep Italy (1915) and the UNITED STATES (1917) neutral, the Allies accused the papacy of favoring the Central Powers. Though the pope had actually condemned the violation of Belgium neutrality with his categorical condemnation of violations of international law, the Allies considered this insufficient. The Germans received their share of papal criticism for sinking the *Lusitania* and the use of poison gas; impartially, the pope chastized the perpetrators of both land and aerial bombardment of unfortified towns and the deportation of civilians. In 1915 Benedict's renowned prayer for world peace was recited thoughout the world, yet it was not favorably received in France, where it was considered a threat to military morale.

The pope was deeply distressed by the suffering that the war inflicted. Called a "second Red Cross," the Vatican administered extensive charity in the form of hospitalization and large gifts of money, food, and medicine. In 1914 the money from "Peter's Pence" was designated for Belgian relief. The plight of children and civilian deportees was of particular concern. Prisoners were traced and exchanged, a missing persons bureau was established in the Vatican, and the sick and wounded were given care through newly established agencies in

Switzerland and Germany. Gifts were distributed throughout Europe from France to Lithuania. Relief efforts were especially extensive in Russia. It is estimated that the Vatican contributed 82 million gold lire during the war.

Benedict's most important peace initiative was his famous peace note of 1 August 1917. Not a detailed proposal, the note was a list of points, which included the renunciation of the use of force, mutual disarmament, freedom of the seas, renunciation of reparations, the restoration of occupied territories, and international arbitration. The aim of Vatican diplomacy was to elicit a German promise of the restoration of Belgian independence and the Austrian cessation of the Trentino to Italy. The new NUNCIO in Munich, Msgr. Eugenio Pacelli, was sent to Berlin to determine the German conditions for peace negotiations and was encouraged by the kaiser's response.

While the Allies were ''cautious,'' and the German emperor was in favor of peace by Christmas, the appeal failed, chiefly due to the German government and Richard von Kuhlmann of the Foreign Office for their refusal to restore the independence of Belgium. The Vatican's participation in the Peace Conference was prevented by the Italian government. The dictated Treaty of Versailles was contrary to the ideals and goals of Benedict. He favored the disarmament of both sides and a return to the Germans of their colonies. Although he favored the League of Nations, its restricted membership increasingly made him skeptical of its potential.

While the efforts of the Holy See to bring about a negotiated peace had failed, Benedict's impartial Christian stand raised the stature of the papacy in the international community. Had the peace appeal of 1917 been accepted, millions of lives would have been spared. A Bolshevik dictatorship in Russia might have been avoided as well as the rise of fascism and Nazism.

For further reference: Robert Althann, ''Papal Mediation during the First World War,'' *Studies* 61:243 (Ireland) (1972): 219–240; Charles Herber, ''Eugenio Pacelli's Mission to Germany and the Papal Peace Proposals of 1917,'' *Catholic Historical Review* 65:1 (1979): 20–48; J. Derek Holmes, *The Papacy in the Modern World* (New York: Crossroad, 1981); Walter H. Peters, *The Life of Benedict XV* (Milwaukee: Bruce, 1959); Anthony Rhodes, *The Power of Rome in the Twentieth Century: The Vatican in the Age of Liberal Democracies, 1870–1922* (London: Scagwick and Jackson, 1983); Stewart H. Stehlin, ''Germany and the Proposed Vatican State, 1915–1917,'' *Catholic Historical Review* 60:3 (1974): 402–426.

Joseph A. Biesinger

WORLD WAR II AND THE PAPACY. PIUS XII (1939–1958), who came to the throne 2 March 1939, aspired to be a ''POPE of peace,'' desperately attempting to prevent World War II. In mid-March, HITLER repudiated the Munich Pact of 1938 and carved up Czechoslovakia. Britain and France thereupon renounced Munich-style appeasement and promised help to Poland if Germany attacked. Pius XII sought, nevertheless, to promote a new five-power conference to press Poland to make concessions to Germany. The refusal of

Britain and Germany to support such a conference caused the pope to abandon the plan on 10 May. Next, he offered his good offices for bilateral talks between Germany and Poland and between France and Italy—again to no avail. Instead, Hitler and MUSSOLINI forged their Pact of Steel alliance in May, while on 23 August Hitler and Stalin reached a startling nonaggression treaty that enabled them to partition Poland.

On 24 August, Pius made an anguished radio appeal to the world. An advocate of peace at any price, he argued that "nothing is lost by peace, but everything may be lost by war." At the same time, he again urged Poland to make concessions to Germany. On 1 September 1939 Hitler invaded Poland; World War II had begun. On 20 October, Pius issued his first encyclical, *Summi pontificatus* ("On the Limitations of the Authority of the State"), in which he sketched a possible path to peace. In December he broadcast the first of his wartime Christmas messages and expressed hope for an end to the selfish nationalism that had led to the war. He also protested Nazi euthanasia and sterilization policies (December 1940 and February 1941). However, most of Pius' attention that first winter focused on keeping Italy neutral. Pius' most sensational action was to arrange an unprecedented exchange of Christmas visits between himself and Italy's royal family. This was obviously designed to increase pressure on Mussolini to stay out of the war. But on 18 March 1940, the fascist dictator decided otherwise. In a meeting with Hitler, he secretly promised that Italy would soon join the war.

When Hitler invaded Denmark and Norway in April 1940, *L'OSSERVATORE ROMANO* condemned this extension of the war, whereupon Mussolini tried to prevent distribution of the Vatican newspaper. The pope also made a new appeal to the duce to stay neutral; but on 30 April, Mussolini informed him he could no longer guarantee that. Early in May, Pius learned from army officers in the anti-Nazi underground that Hitler was about to invade the Low Countries. He quickly forwarded this news to those countries, and in the wake of the actual invasion, he sent telegrams on 10 May to the Benelux sovereigns, expressing sorrow that their lands had been invaded "against [their] will and right" and assuring them of his paternal affection and of his prayers that full freedom and independence would soon be theirs again. These telegrams, which have been likened to extreme unction for the dying, were published in the Vatican newspaper on 12 May. They were the pope's most courageous public protest against German aggression. They were also the last. For the duration of the war, he maintained a public silence on the question of who was to blame for the war— much to the confusion of millions of Catholics and dismay of non-Catholics. In his behalf, it can be argued that if Pius had criticized any single belligerent, he might have ruined whatever chance remained for him to mediate the conflict. Moreover, he did not wish to do anything that might alienate from the church those Catholics who were fighting under the banner of nationalism or that might jeopardize the CONCORDATS negotiated with fascist Italy and NAZI GERMANY.

Mussolini was infuriated by the pope's telegrams to the Benelux sovereigns. Once again, he interfered with distribution of *L'Osservatore Romano*. In an ensuing tense meeting with the Italian ambassador, Pius raised his voice sharply: "Whatever may happen, we have absolutely nothing to be ashamed of, and we do not even fear deportation to a concentration camp. . . . We were not afraid of the revolvers pointed at us once before; we are even less so this second time." But the Vatican gave in. Henceforth, *L'Osservatore Romano* published only anodyne comments on the war. The Vatican felt it had no choice, for in a showdown Mussolini could have silenced the paper completely as well as cut off the Holy See from communication with the outside world. By yielding here, Pius hoped to preserve his freedom to intercede later for peace.

On 10 June Mussolini attacked France and Britain. *L'Osservatore Romano* published this news without comment. Some thirty Italian bishops, however, hastened to send the duce an effusive message of patriotic devotion, and the fascist press gave much publicity to their liturgical flag waving. In the wake of France's surrender to the Axis, the Vatican urged Britain also to make peace, but Prime Minister Churchill adamantly rejected such advice. Meanwhile, in line with Pius' legalistic conception of strict neutrality, the Vatican opened its doors in June 1940 to receive in asylum diplomatic representatives of those states that were now at war with Italy; and after the liberation of Rome in June 1944, the doors opened again to let out Allied diplomats and admit German and Japanese ones.

Fearful of aerial bombardment of the spiritual and administrative center of Roman Catholicism, Pius XII made great efforts after June 1940 to persuade the Allies to recognize Rome as an "open city," but with little success. After all, since Mussolini had demanded and obtained from Hitler the "privilege" in August 1940 of sending Italian bombers to join the Luftwaffe in raids on London, the British could hardly promise immunity to a city that was not just the center of the Catholic Church but also the capital of a country with which they were at war.

When Germany and Italy invaded the Soviet Union in June 1941, the pope's position was further complicated, for he was unwilling to make any public criticism of Hitler's Germany unless he also criticized Stalin's Russia; and as the latter was now the ally of the Western powers, he preferred to remain quiet. The entry of the United States into the war in December 1941 and President Roosevelt's dispatch of a "personal representative" to the pope added a new dimension to Vatican diplomacy. Pius was dismayed by Roosevelt's "unconditional surrender" policy and complacent assessments of Stalin's religious policy and war aims.

By 1941 and 1942, the influence of the Vatican in pursuing peace reached its low point. The persistent refusals of belligerent governments to answer the pope's appeals, made through private and diplomatic channels, led Pius to conclude that even less success would be gained through public denunciations. In many parts of German-conquered Europe, the church faced a veritable *KUL-*

TURKAMPF. Most horrendous of all was the fate of millions of Jews, who became the victims of the Nazi HOLOCAUST after 1941. In many countries numerous church officials acted in discreet ways to help the Jews. On some occasions in 1942–1943, the Vatican was able to persuade the Axis satellite states of Slovakia, Hungary, and Rumania to prevent deportation of Jews; but by 1944 the Nazis brutally countermanded these moves. In his lengthy Christmas radio message of 1942, Pius briefly mentioned "hundreds of thousands who, through no fault of their own, and solely because of their nation or race, have been condemned to death or progressive extinction." This was a reference to the Jews, but in the postwar era, Pius came to be criticized sharply for not speaking out more clearly and for not condemning Nazi Germany specifically.

Meanwhile, fascist Italy's humiliating military setbacks during the war finally led to the successful Allied invasion of Sicily on 10 July 1943. On the nineteenth, Allied planes carried out a massive bombardment of Rome's railroad yards. Pius at once visited the bombed-out San Lorenzo quarter. A few days later (24/25 July), King Victor Emmanuel III, with help from the army, arrested Mussolini in a coup. Marshal Pietro Badoglio became the head of a new post-fascist government. He announced Italy's unconditional surrender when the Allies landed at Salerno (8/9 September). As the king and Badoglio fled to the south, the Germans seized Rome. They also rescued Mussolini and installed him as their fascist puppet in northern Italy.

Though he risked being kidnapped, Pius chose not to leave VATICAN CITY throughout the German occupation of Rome, and he refused to recognize Mussolini's new regime. It became church policy to try to persuade both sides of the conflict not to engage in needless destruction. He provided sanctuary in Vatican buildings for several thousand Jews and antifascist politicians. Far less fortunate were 1,259 people whom the Germans rounded up in Jewish homes in central Rome on the sabbath, 16 October 1943. Pius instructed Msgr. Alois Hudal, the German rector of Santa Maria dell'Anima College in Rome, to complain directly to the German military commander, and the Vatican secretary of state called in the German ambassador. This led to release of 252 prisoners who were either entirely Aryan or of mixed marriages. The remaining 1,007 who were Jewish were hauled off to Auschwitz. More than 800 met immediate death.

Five months later, after Italian partisans ambushed thirty-two German soldiers in Rome, Hitler ordered, in reprisal, a massacre at Rome's Ardeatine Caves (24/25 March 1944) of 335 Italians—77 of them Jews. This time the Vatican could do nothing. But in June 1944, when Allied armies neared Rome, the German commander decided to withdraw his forces from the "open city" without a battle. On 5 June thousands of grateful Romans flocked to St. Peter's Square to acclaim Pius as their *defensor civitatis*. Meanwhile, Pius' fears of a communist takeover in Catholic Poland and elsewhere in Europe mounted rapidly as the inevitability of Hitler's defeat became clearer. The Allies seldom consulted the Vatican about major decisions for the postwar world. To counter the threat of

COMMUNISM, the church strengthened Catholic Action and encouraged new Catholic political parties and syndical organizations.

For further reference: Pierre Blet, Robert A. Graham, Angelo Martini, and Burkhart Schneider, eds., *Actes et documents du Saint Siège relatifs à la seconde guerre mondiale*, 11 vols. (Vatican City: Libreria Editrice Vaticana, 1965–1982); Owen Chadwick, *Britain and the Vatican during the Second World War* (Cambridge: Cambridge University Press, 1986); C. F. Delzell, "Pius XII, Italy, and the Outbreak of War," *Journal of Contemporary History* 2:4 (October 1967): 137–161; Ennio Di Nolfo, ed., *Vaticano e Stati Uniti 1939–1952: Dalle carte di Myron C. Taylor* (Milan: Franco Angeli, 1978); Anthony Rhodes, *The Vatican in the Age of the Dictators 1922–45* (London: Hodder and Stoughton, 1973).

Charles F. Delzell

WORMS, DIET OF, AND PAPACY. This was the conclave of ecclesiastics, princes, and secular officials of the Holy Roman Empire of the German nation, before which Martin Luther, on 6 May 1521, unsuccessfully defended his defiance of papal authority.

Immediately after Luther posted his 95 theses on the main door of his Wittenberg Cathedral, 31 October 1517, they were translated from Latin into German and achieved phenomenal circulation. Pope LEO X (1513–1521) bestirred himself to meet Luther's challenge head on. In November, he commissioned the Dominican scholar Sylvester Prierias to compose a rebuttal to the questions Luther had raised regarding papal authority and grants of indulgences. Within three days Prierias produced his "Dialogue concerning the Power of the POPE." On 3 February 1518, Leo commanded the vicar-general of the Augustinian Hermits, Gabriele della Volta, of Venice, to silence Luther, a monk of his order, to prevent him from disseminating false notions. Della Volta required Luther to attend a meeting of the German Observant Augustinians, set for April in Heidelberg, where he would either recant or submit a detailed explanation for his refusal and stance. Convinced that the Vatican was acting hastily, Prince Elector Frederick the Wise of Luther's home state of Saxony apparently persuaded the pope to exercise patience and hold off drastic measures.

In late May, members of the CURIA, at Leo's urgings, initiated a high-level review of Luther's teachings and publications, contesting their orthodoxy. The pope also directed the auditor of the Camerae Apostolicae to undertake an investigation of Luther's record and, if warranted, summon Luther to Rome. If this inquiry concluded that Luther's beliefs were not in keeping with Scripture or tradition, the German was to be compelled to appear in Rome to stand trial. The bishop's sentiments were incorporated in a letter sent to Cardinal De Veo Cajetan of Gaeta in early July. Appointed papal LEGATE to the Imperial Diet of the Holy Roman Empire, Cajetan forwarded this dispatch to the Diet and to Luther on 7 August. Luther was allowed 60 days, until 6 October, to arrive in Rome and submit to official judgment. Once again, Frederick intervened and used his prestige to persuade Leo that there was no need to question Luther in Rome. It would be more suitable to have Luther clarify his position by meeting with Cardinal Cajetan in Augsburg 12–13 October 1518. Emperor Maximilian I (1508–1519) concurred.

Although Leo X was preparing harsh steps against Luther, it was difficult, for the moment at least, to have them implemented. Since Prince Frederick was one of seven electors empowered to select the successor to the aged Maximilian, Leo refrained from any disciplinary or punitive action that might alienate the prince and have him cast his vote for a candidate not favored by the Vatican, such as Henry VIII, the English Tudor monarch, Francis I of France, or even Charles of Spain. It was a matter of priorities, and Leo unquestionably underestimated Luther and the forces rallied behind him.

The Augsburg confrontation between Luther and Cajetan resolved nothing. Based on Cajetan's report, Pope Leo issued the bull *Cum Postquam*, which had been drafted by the cardinal, dated 9 November 1518, and promulgated by him in Linz, Austria, 13 December 1518. The papal statement found Luther disobedient and subject to penalties. Appeals of the pope, the curia, and Cajetan to have Elector Frederick expel Luther from Saxony and deliver him to Rome were in vain. The elector explained that many theologians in Germany shared Luther's controversial views and respected them as biblically based. Luther deemed it fit to implore Pope Leo by personal letter for understanding. Attempts at mediation by the papal chamberlain, Karl von Miltitz, were unproductive. On 27 June 1519, Luther engaged the famed disputant John Eck in debate at Leipzig, widening the breach by rejecting papal INFALLIBILITY and even church COUNCILS.

On 15 June 1520, Leo issued the bull *Exsurge Domine*. It condemned Luther as a heretic and notified him he had 60 days to surrender. When the bull and a copy of the pertinent CANON LAW were delivered to Luther, he publicly burned them. In an attempt to break the deadlock, Leo, on 3 January 1521, formulated a sterner bull, *Decet Pontificem Romanum*, declaring that time had expired, as of 10 December 1520, and that Luther's lack of response had placed him beyond the pale. Leo ordered Emperor Charles V (1519–1558) to enforce the bull. Normal procedure would have the bull of EXCOMMUNICATION sent to the German bishops, who would, by the ringing of church bells and the throwing down of the tapers, have announced and forever sealed Luther's status of separation from the Roman church.

Facing an increasingly complicated and untenable dilemma, Prince Frederick insisted that Luther had not been granted a fair and impartial hearing. Having won the adherence of the youthful Charles, the elector brought Luther before a plenary session of the church and lay officials of the realm at the Diet of Worms, a city on the left bank of the Rhine River, in Hesse, western Germany, on 6 May 1521. Emperor Charles served as the presiding officer. As for Charles' attitude, he esteemed Catholicism to be the cohesive element that bound together the multiracial empire he headed and his Austrian and Spanish Hapsburg kingdoms. He did not wish to fall out of grace with the supreme pontiff and lose whatever possibility there may have been to annex northern Italy to the empire. Pope Leo X was thus assured that the ambitious ruler could be relied on to take a hard, unwavering line against the intransigent monk and nullify the considerable influence it was feared Elector Frederick would exert in favor of Luther.

Following several hours of intense exchanges between Luther and the dignitaries assembled at Worms. Charles indicated that the moment had arrived to close the proceedings by demanding of Luther a "yes or no" answer to the subjects of retraction and submission. With Luther's "Here I Stand Reply" out of the way, Emperor Charles presented the decree branding Luther a "convicted heretic." Luther was to be scorned and vilified as an outcast. None of his works, his defense included, were to be printed. The indictment had been written and handed to Charles by Cardinal Aleandro, acting under orders of Pope Leo. Accepted by the Diet, Luther was placed under the imperial ban even before the usual ceremonial formalities signifying excommunication had taken place. In fact, it was not until the fall of the year that they occurred.

The Edict of Worms proved impossible to execute. Before he might be seized, Luther was abducted by friendly princes and held as a "hostage" in Wartburg, Frederick's castle in Saxony, while Charles was dissuaded from pursuing the crisis any further because of the requirements imposed on his energies and resources by armed conflict with France and war against the Turks.

For further reference: James Atkinson, *The Trial of Luther* (London: Batsford, 1971); Ernest Gordon Rupp, *Luther at the Diet of Worms* (New York: Harper and Row, 1974); Fritz von Reuter, ed., *Luther in Worms, 1521–1971* (Worms: Stadarchy Worms, 1973).

Ronald S. Cunsolo

Z

ZACHARY (741–754). Zachary, or Zacharias, was the last of the Greek POPES. Born in Calabria of Greek background, he had worked closely as a deacon with GREGORY III (731–741). Educated and erudite, he had translated Gregory the Great's ''Dialogues'' into Greek and was personally admired for his compassionate nature, combined, however, with considerable political skill. As pope, he reversed Gregory III's hostile policy toward the Lombards, who had repeatedly been threatening Rome and in 742 met with their king Liutprand at Terni. There Zachary obtained the return of major towns and fortresses, other papal property, and the guarantee of a twenty-year truce. Then, a year later, when the Lombards attacked the Byzantine area of Ravenna, the pope mediated and gained an armistice.

Avoiding the open conflicts of his predecessors with the iconoclastic emperors in Constantinople, Zachary continued communication with the rulers while continuing to register his opposition to their ban on images. While the emperor remained a fanatical iconoclast, and the pontiff a firm defender of the orthodox position on images, they minimized these differences.

During his pontificate, Zachary's efforts with Boniface, the apostle of Germany, and with Carloman and Pepin III, the leaders of the Franks, were equally significant. Zachary gave Boniface, whom he had made his LEGATE, his full support, encouraging and guiding his program for the reform of the Frankish church. This was achieved by a series of synods in the Frankish church whose decisions were ultimately approved by the pope. As a result, the ties between that church and Rome were effectively strengthened, culminating in 747 with a firm expression of loyalty to Zachary at a full COUNCIL of the Frankish episcopate. In 750 Zachary issued the momentous ruling that the royal Frankish title should belong to whoever actually held power in the kingdom. This caused the deposition of the weak King Childeric III, the last of the Merovingian line, and the election in 751 of Pepin and his subsequent anointing as king by Boniface.

This transfer of the Crown to the Carolingian dynasty was of immense importance in future relations between the emperors and the papacy.

A capable, efficient, and energetic administrator, Zachary took an active role in the civil and military governance of the papal territories. He fostered a policy of land resettlement, the *domus cultae*, to encourage development of abandoned areas and, in part, to replace revenues lost through the confiscation of papal patrimonies in Sicily and Calabria by the Byzantine emperor Leo III in 730. Zachary restored the churches of Rome, such as Sta. Maria Antiqua, where a fresco painted of him remains. He also restored the papal residence to the Lateran. Zachary's feast day is celebrated on 15 March.

For further reference: L. Duchesne, ed., *Liber Pontificalis* (Paris: E. de Boccard, 1955); H. K. Mann, *The Lives of the Popes in the Early Middle Ages* (London: K. Paul, 1902–1932).

William Roberts

ZELANTI. The *Zelanti* were a faction within the Roman CURIA that took shape during the eighteenth century; their unifying principle was firm hostility to the encroachment of secular rulers upon the authority of the papacy or the freedom of the church. They usually formed the strongest single faction but were opposed by the *politicanti*, who stressed the need for accommodation with the secular power. After the French Revolution had attacked the church and the papacy, the *Zelanti* became bitterly hostile to revolution, to liberalism, and often to any change; their influence was largely responsible for preventing any reform of the administration in the PAPAL STATES and for the growth of popular discontent with papal rule that ultimately led to the downfall of the temporal power.

For further reference: Owen Chadwick. *The Popes and European Revolution* (New York: Oxford University Press, 1981); E. E. Y. Hales, *Revolution and Papacy* (Garden City, NY: Hanover House, 1960).

Alan J. Reinerman

ZEPHYRINUS (198/199–217). Little is known of the background of Zephyrinus except the unsubstantiated account in the *Liber Pontificalis* that he was a Roman, the son of Habundius. His bitter critic the unscrupulous Roman theologian HIPPOLYTUS, who would later (217–235) become ANTIPOPE, described him as uneducated, avaricious, and inexperienced in church affairs. Certainly, he relied on his efficient archdeacon Callistus, whom he had brought back from disgrace. Probably, Callistus arranged the system of ''titular,'' or parish, churches in Rome. Most likely Zephyrinus was the POPE Tertullian criticized for having initially recognized the Montanist movement, then rescinding his support at the instigation of a certain Praxeas.

During Zephyrinus' pontificate the most acrimonious debates were over dogmatic and doctrinal issues regarding the nature of Christ. The Adoptionist view that Jesus had been an ordinary man until his baptism was still widespread despite its condemnation by VICTOR I (189–198). Of even greater significance was the modalist theory, which practically eliminated the distinctions between the persons of the Trinity, taught by Sabellius, Praxeas, and Noetus. Hippolytus, in his tract against HERESY, the *Philosopheumena*, sharply rebuked Zephyrinus for not condemning and even for seeming to support the movement. But, in fact, in a credal statement published by Zephyrinus it is clear that he was not a modalist and sought to uphold the divinity of Christ and his distinction from the Father. He also denounced Hippolytus' theology as "ditheistic."

During Zephyrinus' reign the famous Origen, the greatest of contemporary Christian intellectuals, visited Rome. The tradition that Zephyrinus died a martyr is not substantiated, but it is very likely, as the *Liber Pontificalis* states, that he was buried "in his own cemetery near that of Callistus" on the Appian Way. His feast is 26 August.

For further reference: J. N. D. Kelly, *The Oxford Dictionary of Popes* (Oxford: Oxford University Press, 1986); M. Winter, *St. Peter and the Popes* (London: Helicon Press, 1960).

William Roberts

ZIONISM, ISRAEL, AND THE VATICAN. *1896–1917.* From its inception in 1896, the Catholic Church considered modern political Zionism (i.e., the return of the Jewish people to the land of Israel and the establishment of a Jewish state) as unacceptable on doctrinal and political grounds. The theological premises of this rejection were collective Jewish guilt for the Crucifixion and the consequent curse of eternal exile. Religious objections were articulated in the course of Theodor Herzl's audience with PIUS X (1903–1914) on 25 January 1904, during which the pontiff declared, "The Jews have not recognized our Lord, therefore we cannot recognize the Jewish people." At this time, the POPE also expressed concern regarding the prospect of Jewish control over Christian holy places. Opposition to Zionist aspirations continued, notwithstanding the sympathetic reception given to Nahum Sokolow, secretary-general of the World Zionist Organization, in his audience with BENEDICT XV (1914–1922) on 4 May 1917, at the conclusion of which the pope said, "I think we shall be good neighbors." The context of this statement was an assumption on the part of the pope that the topic of discussion was agricultural settlements for persecuted Jews outside the central area of Palestine where the holy places were located, which was to be an extraterritorial entity under the terms of the Sykes–Picot Agreement of 26 April 1916. The theme of internationalization of the holy places and subsequently of Jerusalem has since remained a constant of the Vatican position on Palestine and Israel.

1917–1948. The Balfour Declaration (2 November 1917), expressing British support for a Jewish national home in Palestine, and the British conquest of Jerusalem (9 December 1917) brought to the fore Vatican preoccupations of Jewish ascendancy and Protestant rule in the Holy Land. Thus, in his allocution of 10 March 1919, Benedict XV expressed concern that "infidels" were being granted a privileged position in Palestine and that Protestant sects were engaging in renewed proselytizing activities. In a clarification to the Belgian envoy to the Holy See, the secretary of state, Pietro Gasparri, specified, "The danger we most fear is the establishment of a Jewish state in Palestine." Accordingly, in the years 1920–1922, VATICAN DIPLOMACY strenuously opposed appointment by the League of Nations of Great Britain as sole mandatory power in the Holy Land, especially in view of the nomination of Sir Herbert Samuel, a Jew, as high commissioner for Palestine. In his second allocution on the subject (13 June 1921), Benedict XV outlined four points upon which the Vatican position was based until the end of the mandatory period: Jews were being granted a predominant position. Protestant conversionist propaganda was being spread among the Arab population, the holy places were being secularized and commercialized, and the international community should guarantee Catholic rights. Continued hostility to Zionism was expressed in a letter of 18 May 1943 from the secretary of state, Luigi Maglione, to Amleto Cicognani, APOSTOLIC DELEGATE in the United States, in which it was claimed that "the Catholics of the entire world . . . could not but feel wounded in their religious sentiment if Palestine were to be given over and entrusted in preponderance to the Jews." Nevertheless, Vatican diplomacy tacitly accepted the postwar partition of Palestine envisioned in UN Resolution 181 of 29 November 1947, because it provided for the internationalization of Jerusalem and Bethlehem.

1948–1993. The Vatican made no immediate comment regarding the proclamation of the state of Israel on 14 May 1948. On three separate occasions in 1948–1949, PIUS XII (1939–1958) called for the constitution of a *corpus separatum* for Jerusalem under international jurisdiction. As regards the Jewish state, the Holy See withheld formal diplomatic relations. Besides the status of the Holy City, five other factors contributed to Vatican–Israeli friction well into the 1950s (and beyond): damage caused by Israeli troops to Christian religious institutions; fears that the new state would fall into the Soviet orbit; the short-lived strategy of a Catholic–Islamic common front against COMMUNISM; concern that any rapprochement with Israel would negatively impact Christian minorities in Arab lands; finally, the return of Palestinian refugees, insisted upon for humanitarian as well as religious reasons, that is in order to assure and maintain a living Christian presence in the Holy Land. On 28 October 1965, the document of VATICAN II concerning non-Christians (*Nostra aetate*), in which the myth of Jewish decide was officially rejected, presumably removed the church's underlying doctrinal objections to Zionism, though it was not until 30 September 1987 that Vatican spokesmen explicitly excluded theological factors as an impediment to Vatican–Israeli relations. In the meantime, both PAUL VI (1963–1978) and JOHN PAUL II (1978–   ) had issued statements that acknowledged the sovereignty of the state of Israel and its right to peace and security (e.g., the apostolic letter *Redemptionis anno* of 20 April 1984). After the Six-Day War of 1967, previous Vatican insistence on the extraterritoriality of Jerusalem was modified to mean unspecified international guarantees for the parity of the three monotheistic faiths within the Holy City. On the other hand, starting with Paul VI's consistorial address of 21 December 1973, there has been an increasing emphasis in papal statements on the rights and aspirations of the Palestinian people from a political rather than essentially humanitarian perspective. Accordingly, following John Paul II's meeting with Yasser Arafat on 23 December 1988, a Vatican communique declared that Israelis and Palestinians have "an identical fundamental right to a homeland (patria)."

On 25 January 1991, the Vatican position on Israel was outlined by the papal press secretary, Joaquin Navarro-Valls, who explained that under international law the Holy See did, in fact, implicitly "recognize" the state of Israel but that full diplomatic relations had been delayed by unresolved "juridical difficulties" (the status of the occupied territories, the future of the Palestinians, the annexation of Jerusalem in 1980, the situation of the Catholic community in Israel). In the wake of the Gulf War and the ensuing regional peace talks, the Vatican and Israel established a bilateral permanent working commission (29 July 1992) to negotiate toward eventual full diplomatic ties. The negotiations resulted in the signing of a "Fundamental Agreement" in Jerusalem on 30 December 1993. Besides clearing the way for diplomatic normalization, the accord included a condemnation of anti-Semitism by the Vatican, a commitment by the Jewish state to "continuing respect for and protection of the character proper to Catholic sacred places," and a pledge by the Holy See to "remain extraneous" from territorial and border issues. However, the status of Jerusalem was not explicitly mentioned in the document, and, in clarifying statements, Vatican spokesmen repeated the call for an internationally guaranteed statute for the Holy City, an unresolved question that explains the eventual location of the papal nunciature in the Tel Aviv suburb of Jaffa rather than in the Israeli capital.

Conclusion. The foregoing survey indicates that the Vatican attitude toward Zionism and Israel has been conditioned both by internal doctrinal developments and by the force of external events and that, consequently, there has been an evolution in Vatican discourse from a preoccupation with fundamental theological issues to an emphasis on negotiable political and juridical questions.

For further reference: Francesco Margiotta Broglio, "L'accordo 'fondamentale' fra la Santa Sede e lo Stato d'Israele (30 dicembre 1993)," *Nuova Atnologia*, no. 2190 (April–June 1994): 151–170; Giovanni Caprile, "La Santa Sede e lo Stato d'Israele," *La Civiltà Cattolica, Anno 142*, vol. 1 (1991), pp. 352–360; Silvio Ferrari, *Vaticano e Israele dal secondo conflitto mondiale alla guerra del Golfo* (Florence: Sansoni Editore, 1991); Eugene J. Fisher, "The Holy See and the State of Israel: The Evolution of Attitudes and Policies," *Journal of Ecumenical Studies* 24 (1987): 191–211; Sergio I. Minerbi, *The Vatican and Zionism: Conflict in the Holy Land, 1895–1925* (New York and Oxford: Oxford University Press, 1990); Sergio I. Minerbi, "The Vatican and Israel," *Political Dictionary of the State of Israel. Supplement 1987–1993* (Jerusalem: Jerusalem Publishing House, 1993), pp. 412–414.

Andrew M. Canepa

ZOSIMUS (417–418). Zosimus Abramii's pontificate ran from 18 March 417 to his death on 26 December 418. He appears to have been a Greek by birth and possibly descended from Jews. Many church historians rank him as the first POPE venturing to "repudiate those political conceptions that threatened to circumscribe the extending influence of his office"; but he appears to have been heavy-handed in doing so.

Reportedly, Zosimus had an "Eastern disposition" and proved willing to temporize with, if not favor, Pelagianism, not hesitating to set aside decrees of his predecessor against the HERESY that was then being engaged by St. Augustine. There was also his contentious intervention in favor of Patroclus, bishop of Arles, who, despite his accession by usurpation, was encouraged by Zosimus to function virtually as a vicar of the pope in his dealings with the other bishops of southern Gaul. With respect to the Pelagian controversy, Zosimus permitted Pelagius and his chief associate to appeal to him directly, over the heads of the assembled African bishops, including St. Augustine. He deemed acceptable their verbal retractions of heretical beliefs charged against them. The African bishops were adamant, appealing to the emperor Honorius in Ravenna to intervene against the pope, whereupon Zosimus reversed himself, assuming an orthodox stance. St. Augustine, who had earlier articulated the objections of the African bishops to Zosimus' comportment, then spoke in his defense. He showed that Zosimus had never really approved the teachings of Pelagius and his colleague and that he had charitably accepted their professions of good faith and reversed himself when he saw through the deception.

For further reference: E. Caspar, *Geschichte des Papstums von den Anfängen bis zur Höhe der Weltherrschaft* (Tübingen: Verlag von J. C. B. Mohr); T. J. Jalland, *The Church and the Papacy* (London: Society for Promoting Christian Knowledge, 1944).

Henry Paolucci

Appendix A: Alphabetical List of Popes*

Adeodatus I, *see* Deusdedit

Adeodatus II (672–676)

Adrian I (772–795)

Adrian II (867–872)

Adrian III (884–885)

Adrian IV (1154–1159)

Adrian V (1276)

Adrian VI (1522–1523)

Agapitus I (535–536)

Agapitus II (946–955)

Agatho (678–681)

Alexander I (c. 109–c. 116)

Alexander II (1061–1073)

Alexander III (1159–1181)

Alexander IV (1254–1261)

Alexander VI (1492–1503)

Alexander VII (1655–1667)

Alexander VIII (1689–1691)

Anacletus (c. 79–c. 91)

Anastasius I (399–401)

Anastasias II (496–498)

Anastasias III (911–913)

Anastasias IV (1153–1154)

Anicetus (c. 155–c. 166)

Anterus (235–236)

Benedict I (575–579)

Benedict II (684–685)

Benedict III (855–858)

Benedict IV (900–903)

Benedict V (964)

Benedict VI (973–974)

Benedict VII (974–983)

Benedict VIII (1012–1024)

Benedict IX (1032–1044, 1045, 1047–1048)

Benedict XI (1303–1304)

Benedict XII (1334–1342)

Benedict XIII (1724–1730)

Benedict XIV (1740–1758)

Benedict XV (1914–1922)

Boniface I (418–422)

Boniface II (530–532)

Boniface III (607)

Boniface IV (608–615)

*Drawn from J. N. D. Kelly, *The Oxford Dictionary of Popes* (Oxford: Oxford University Press, 1986), pp. 1–4.

Boniface V (619–625)

Boniface VI (896)

Boniface VIII (1294–1303)

Boniface IX (1389–1404)

Caius, *see* Gaius

Callistus I (217–222)

Callistus II (1119–1124)

Callistus III (1455–1458)

Celestine I (422–432)

Celestine II (1143–1144)

Celestine III (1191–1198)

Celestine IV (1241)

Celestine V (1294)

Clement I (c. 91–c. 101)

Clement II (1046–1047)

Clement III (1187–1191)

Clement IV (1265–1268)

Clement V (1305–1314)

Clement VI (1342–1352)

Clement VII (1523–1534)

Clement VIII (1592–1605)

Clement IX (1667–1669)

Clement X (1670–1676)

Clement XI (1700–1721)

Clement XII (1730–1740)

Clement XIII (1758–1769)

Clement XIV (1769–1774)

Conon (686–687)

Constantine (708–715)

Cornelius (251–253)

Damasus I (366–384)

Damasus II (1048)

Deusdedit (later Adeodatus I) (615–618)

Dionysius (260–268)

Donus (676–678)

Eleutherius (or Eleutherus) (c. 174–189)

Eugene I (654–657)

Eugene II (824–827)

Eugene III (1145–1153)

Eugene IV (1431–1447)

Eusebius (310)

Eutychian (275–283)

Evaristus (c. 100–c. 109)

Fabian (236–250)

Felix (269–274)

Felix III (II) (483–492)

Felix IV (III) (526–530)

Formosus (891–896)

Gaius (or Caius) (283–296)

Gelasius I (492–496)

Gelasius II (1118–1119)

Gregory I (590–604)

Gregory II (715–731)

Gregory III (731–741)

Gregory IV (827–844)

Gregory V (996–999)

Gregory VI (1045–1046)

Gregory VII (1073–1085)

Gregory VIII (1187)

Gregory IX (1227–1241)

Gregory X (1271–1276)

Gregory XI (1370–1378)

Gregory XII (1406–1415)

Gregory XIII (1572–1585)

Gregory XIV (1590–1591)

Gregory XV (1621–1623)

Gregory XVI (1831–1846)

Hadrian, *see* Adrian

Hilarus (461–468)

Honorius I (625–638)

Honorius II (1124–1130)

Honorius III (1216–1227)

Honorius IV (1285–1287)

Hormisdas (514–523)

Hyginus (c. 138–c. 142)

Innocent I (401–417)

Innocent II (1130–1143)

Innocent III (1198–1216)

Innocent IV (1243–1254)

Innocent V (1276)

Innocent VI (1352–1362)

Innocent VII (1404–1406)

Innocent VIII (1484–1492)

Innocent IX (1591)

Innocent X (1644–1655)

Innocent XI (1676–1689)

Innocent XII (1691–1700)

Innocent XIII (1721–1724)

John I (523–526)

John II (533–535)

John III (561–574)

John IV (640–642)

John V (685–686)

John VI (701–705)

John VII (705–707)

John VIII (872–882)

John IX (898–900)

John X (914–928)

John XI (931–935/936)

John XII (955–964)

John XIII (965–972)

John XIV (983–984)

John XV (985–996)

John XVII (1003)

John XVIII (1003–1009)

John XIX (1024–1032)

[John XX: no such pope held office]

John XXI (1276–1277)

John XXII (1316–1334)

John XXIII (1958–1963)

John Paul I (1978)

John Paul II (1978–   )

Julius I (337–352)

Julius II (1503–1513)

Julius III (1550–1555)

Landus or Lando (913–914)

Leo I (440–461)

Leo II (682–683)

Leo III (795–816)

Leo IV (847–855)

Leo V (903)

Leo VI (928)

Leo VII (936–939)

Leo VIII (963–965)

Leo IX (1049–1054)

Leo X (1513–1521)

Leo XI (1605)

Leo XII (1823–1829)

Leo XIII (1878–1903)

Liberius (352–366)

Linus (c. 66–c. 78)

Lucius I (253–254)

Lucius II (1144–1145)

Lucius III (1181–1185)

Marcellinus (296–?304)

Marcellus I (306–308)

Marcellus II (1555)

Marcus or Mark (336)

Marinus I (882–884)

Marinus II (942–946)

Martin I (649–653)

Martin II, *see* Marinus I

Martin III, *see* Marinus II

Martin IV (1281–1285)

Martin V (1417–1431)

Miltiades (or Melchiades) (311–314)

Nicholas I (858–867)

Nicholas II (1058–1061)

Nicholas III (1277–1280)

Nicholas IV (1288–1292)

Nicholas V (1447–1455)

Paschal I (817–824)

Paschal II (1099–1118)

Paul I (757–767)

Paul II (1464–1471)

Paul III (1534–1549)

Paul IV (1555–1559)

Paul V (1605–1621)

Paul VI (1963–1978)

Pelagius I (556–561)

Pelagius II (579–590)

Peter the Apostle (d. c. 64)

Pius I (c. 142–c. 155)

Pius II (1458–1464)

Pius III (1503)

Pius IV (1559–1565)

Pius V (1566–1572)

Pius VI (1775–1799)

Pius VII (1800–1823)

Pius VIII (1829–1830)

Pius IX (1846–1878)

Pius X (1903–1914)

Pius XI (1922–1939)

Pius XII (1939–1958)

Pontian (230–235)

Romanus (897)

Sabinian (604–606)

Sergius I (687–701)

Sergius II (844–847)

Sergius III (904–911)

Sergius IV (1009–1012)

Severinus (640)

Silverius (536–537)

Silvester, see Sylvester

Simplicius (468–483)

Siricius (384–399)

Sisinnius (708)

Sixtus I (c. 116–c. 125)

Sixtus II (257–258)

Sixtus III (432–440)

Sixtus IV (1471–1484)

Sixtus V (1585–1590)

Soter (c. 166–c. 174)

Stephen I (254–257)

Stephen (II) (752)

Stephen II (III) (752–757)

Stephen III (IV) (768–772)

Stephen IV (V) (816–817)

Stephen V (VI) (885–891)

Stephen VI (VII) (896–897)

Stephen VII (VIII) (928–931)

Stephen VIII (IX) (939–942)

Stephen IX (X) (1057–1058)

Sylvester I (314–335)

Sylvester II (999–1003)

Sylvester III (1045)

Symmachus (498–514)

Telesphorus (c. 125–c. 136)

Theodore I (642–649)

Theodore II (897)

Urban I (222–230)

Urban II (1088–1099)

Urban III (1185–1187)

Urban IV (1261–1264)

Urban V (1362–1370)

Urban VI (1378–1389)

Urban VII (1590)

Urban VIII (1623–1644)

Valentine (827)

Victor I (189–198)

Victor II (1055–1057)

Victor III (1086–1087)

Vigilius (537–555)

Vitalian (657–672)

Xystus, see Sixtus

Zachary (741–754)

Zephyrinus (198/199–217)

Zosimus (417–418)

Appendix B: Alphabetical List of Antipopes

Parenthesis around number indicates that there was a pope by the same designation.

Albert (or Adalbert) (1101)

Alexander V (1409–1410)

Anacletus II (1130–1138)

Anastasius Bibliothecarius (855)

Benedict X (1058–1059)

Benedict (XIII) (1394–1417)

Benedict (XIV) (1425–?)

Boniface VII (974, 984–985)

Callistus III (1168–1178)

Celestine (II) (1124)

Christopher (903–904)

Clement (III) (1080, 1084–1100)

Clement (VII) (1378–1394)

Clement (VIII) (1423–1429)

Constantine II (767–768)

Dioscorus (530)

Eulalius (418–419)

Felix II (355–365)

Felix V (1439–1449)

Gregory (VI) (1012)

Gregory (VIII) (1118–1121)

Hippolytus (217–235)

Honorius (II) (1061–1064)

Innocent (III) (1179–1180)

John (844)

John XVI (997–998)

John (XXIII) (1410–1415)

Lawrence (498/499, 501–506)

Nicholas (V) (1328–1330)

Novatian (251–258)

Paschal (687)

Paschal III (1164–1168)

Philip (768)

Sylvester IV (1105–1111)

Theodore (687)

Theodoric (1100–1101)

Ursinus (366–367)

Victor IV (1138)

Victor IV (1159–1164)

Appendix C: Ecumenical Councils*

First Council of Nicaea (325)

First Council of Constantinople (381)

Council of Ephesus (431)

Council of Chalcedon (451)

Second Council of Constantinople (553)

Third Council of Constantinople (680–681)

Second Council of Nicaea (787)

Fourth Council of Constantinople (869–870)

First Lateran Council (1123)

Second Lateran Council (1139)

Third Lateran Council (1179)

Fourth Lateran Council (1215)

First Council of Lyons (1245)

Second Council of Lyons (1274)

Council of Vienne (1311–1312)

Council of Constance (1414–1418)

Council-of-Basal-Ferrara-Florence-Rome (1431–1445)

Fifth Lateran Council (1512–1517)

Council of Trent (1545–1547, 1551–1552, 1562–1563)

First Vatican Council (1869–1870)

Second Vatican Council (1962–1965)

*Drawn from Richard P. McBrien, ed., *The HarperCollins Encyclopedia of Catholicism* (San Francisco: Harper, 1995), pp. 452–454.

Index

Contributors

JOSEPH A. BIESINGER, Eastern Kentucky University

JOEL BLATT, University of Connecticut, Stamford

RAYMOND F. BULMAN, St. John's University

CHARLES BURNS, Archivist, Vatican Archives

JOSEPH J. CALIFANO, St. John's University

ANDREW M. CANEPA, San Francisco

ELISA A. CARRILLO, Marymount College

BERNARD J. CASSIDY, St. John's University

JOHN S. CONWAY, University of British Columbia

FRANCESCA COPPA, Muhlenburg College

FRANK J. COPPA, St. John's University

RONALD S. CUNSOLO, Nassau Community College

CHARLES F. DELZELL, Vanderbilt University

LORETTA DEVOY, St. John's University

ROY PALMER DOMENICO, University of Scranton

GERARD H. ETTLINGER, St. John's University

MARGERY A. GANZ, Spelman College

ALEXANDER GRAB, University of Maine

FRANK GRANDE, City College of the City University

WILLIAM D. GRIFFIN, St. John's University

CONRAD L. HARKINS, Franciscan Institute, St. Bonaventure University

JOHN C. HORGAN, Cedarburg, Wisconsin

WILLIAM V. HUDON, Bloomsburg University

RICHARD J. KEHOE, St. John's University

PETER C. KENT, University of New Brunswick

PATRICK McGUIRE, St. John's University

PATRICK J. McNAMARA, Washington, D.C.

THOMAS PATRICK MELADY, Washington, D.C.

NELSON H. MINNICH, Catholic University of America

CHRISTOPHER S. MYERS, Peter Lang Publishers

EMILIANA P. NOETHER, University of Connecticut, Storrs

DAVID M. O'CONNELL, Catholic University of America

GLENN W. OLSEN, University of Utah

JULIA L. ORTIZ-GRIFFIN, City University of New York

ANNE PAOLUCCI, City University of New York

HENRY PAOLUCCI, St. John's University

JOHN F. POLLARD, Anglia Polytechnic University, England

ALAN J. REINERMAN, Boston College

WILLIAM ROBERTS, Edward Williams College of Fairleigh Dickinson University

SALVATORE SALADINO, City University of New York

JOSÉ M. SANCHEZ, St. Louis University

TOM SCHEURING, Lamp Ministries, New York

WILLIAM C. SCHRADER, Tennessee Technological University

STEWART A. STEHLIN, New York University

JOHN J. TINGHINO, Columbia University Seminar on Modern Italy

STEVEN F. WHITE, Mount St. Mary's College

RICHARD J. WOLFF, Columbia University Seminar on Modern Italy

ELDA G. ZAPPI, City University of New York

JOHN K. ZEENDER, Catholic University of America

About the Editor

FRANK J. COPPA is a history professor at St. John's University. He has published and edited several books and articles including *Dictionary of Modern Italian History* (Greenwood, 1985) and *Modern Italian History*: *An Annotated Bibliography* (Greenwood, 1990).